REVISED
AND ENLARGED
EDITION

THE Billboard
BOOK OF
TOP 40
ALBUMS

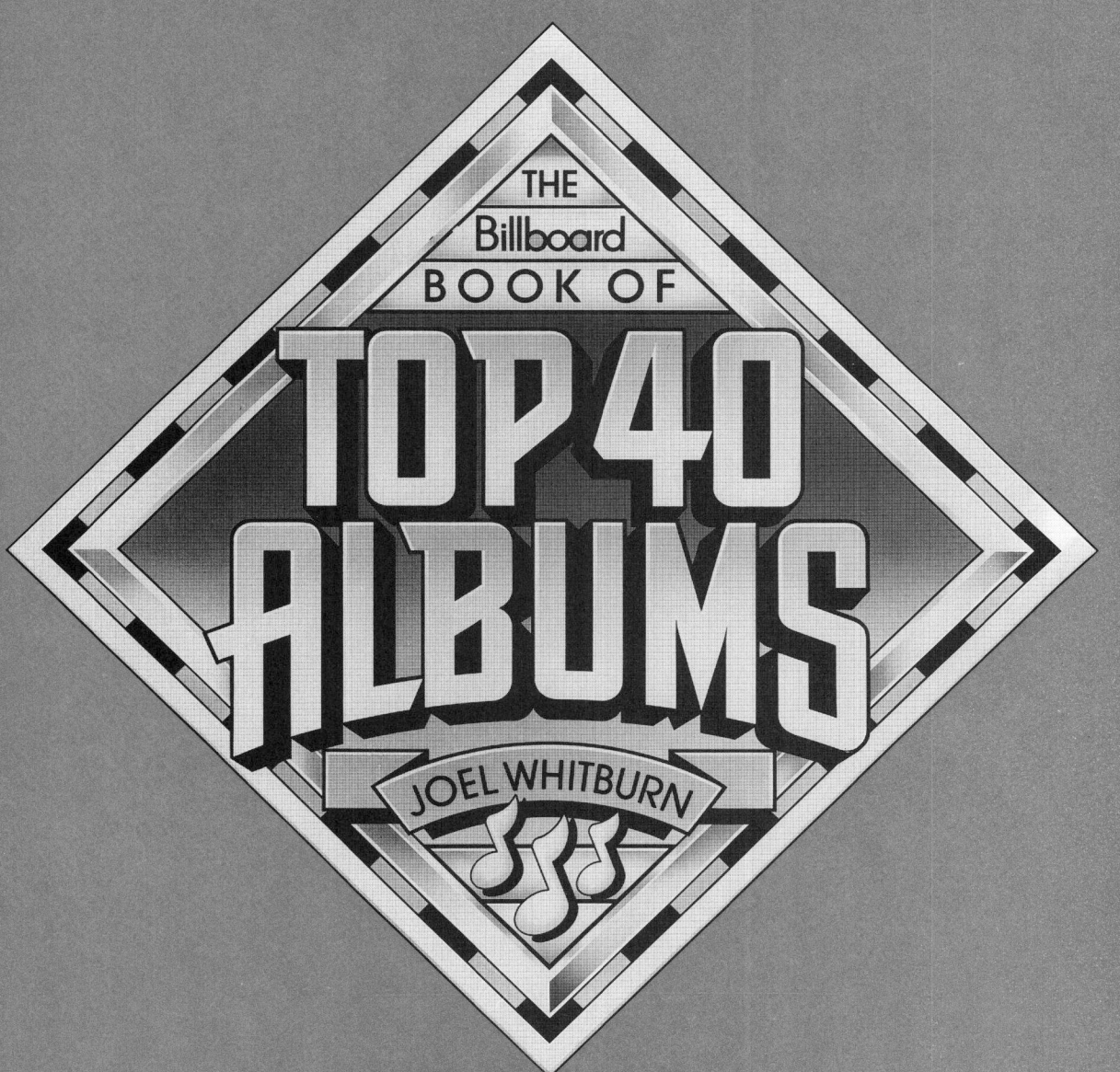

REVISED
AND ENLARGED
EDITION

THE
Billboard
BOOK OF
TOP 40
ALBUMS

JOEL WHITBURN

BILLBOARD BOOKS

An imprint of Watson-Guptill Publications/New York

Album covers selected from Joel Whitburn's personal collection
Photography by Malcolm Hjerstedt of Munroe Studios, Inc.
Photo captions by Dave DiMartino
Chart typesetting by TGA Communications, Inc.
Jacket design: Bob Fillie, Grafiti Graphics
Graphic production: Marybeth Tregarthen
Senior Editor: Tad Lathrop
Edited by John Istel

Revised and enlarged second edition
first published 1991 by Billboard Books, an imprint of
Watson-Guptill Publications, a division of BPI Communications,
Inc., 1515 Broadway, New York, NY 10036.

Library of Congress Cataloging-in-Publication Data
Whitburn, Joel.
    The Billboard book of top 40 albums / Joel Whitburn. —
Rev. and enlarged ed.
        p.   cm.
    ISBN 0-8230-7534-6
    1. Popular music—Discography.   I. Title. II. Title:
Billboard book of top forty albums.
ML156.4.P6W43   1991
016.78164'026'6—dc20   90-22777
                                                     CIP
                                                     MN

Manufactured in United States of America
First Printing, 1991
1 2 3 4 5 6 7 8 9 / 96 95 94 93 92 91

Dedicated to the vanishing art
of the vinyl record album cover—
its beauty and warmth graces
record collections everywhere

The author wishes to give thanks to
the staff of Record Research:

Bill Hathaway
Kim Whitburn
Fran Whitburn
Brent Olynick
Troy Kluess
Kim Gaarder
Joanne Wagner
Brian Niese
Joyce Riehl
Jeanne Olynick
Oscar Vidotto

A special note of thanks to my mother, Ruth Whitburn, for
her many years of diligent album research.

CONTENTS

AUTHOR'S NOTE

At this moment, somewhere in America, music lovers are filing into record shops and nominating the latest, hottest albums for the ongoing top 40 album race. With their purchasing dollars, the record buyers cast their ballots for their favorite artists. Every record sold is another vote edging an artist up *Billboard*'s Top Pop Albums chart.

All the titles within this book were one of the 40 best-selling albums in the country for at least one week. This is a select catalog considering the thousands of albums that contend for a spot on the top 200 albums chart.

Thirty-five years of pop album charts are represented within this book. Most of these albums were sold as vinyl LPs. A few recent albums make up the small percentage which were released only on cassette and compact disc. Vinyl is becoming a relic, replaced by the CD as the king of configurations. Although the convenience of CDs is hard to argue, I am sad to see the demise of the vinyl record album. The CD longboxes and the jewel box booklets don't have the same feel as those large glossy squares of cardboard which serve as vinyl album covers. Nostalgia not withstanding, vinyl's numbers are quickly diminishing.

However, the gradual extinction of a configuration nearly as old as the recording industry itself does not slow the top 40 race. In homage to the contenders that reign within the upper fifth of *Billboard*'s top 200, all titles are listed exactly as they appear on the album jackets, complete with unusual spelling, grammar and punctuation.

Enjoy this second edition of *The Billboard Book of Top 40 Albums*. And, as you read the impressive chart statistics for the albums in your collection, remember that you helped put them in the top 40.

JOEL WHITBURN

ABOUT THE AUTHOR

Joel Whitburn has stayed on top of the charts for over 30 years, categorizing and collecting his more than 40,000 albums and 60,000 singles. Whitburn's vast record library—the largest privately held collection in the world—completely fills an environmentally controlled underground vault adjacent to the Whitburn home in Menomonee Falls, Wisconsin. Included in the collection are all of the titles ever to appear on *Billboard*'s Top Pop Albums and Hot 100 charts, along with many of the records that made the other *Billboard* lists.

Researching *Billboard*'s charts gives Whitburn as much of a thrill today as it did when he first jotted down some record statistics on file cards over 20 years ago. Now armed with a vast computerized data base of chart information, Whitburn has firmly established himself as the single most reliable source for facts and figures on the music people listen to and love. His chart knowledge spans virtually every musical genre: from Rock 'n' Roll to Easy Listening, from Country to Rhythm & Blues.

Whitburn's firm, Record Research, has produced over 30 books to date, detailing the history and development of charted music from 1890 to the present. For each new volume, Joel and his team of researchers attempt to dissect and analyze *Billboard*'s charts in ever-greater depth and diversity, packing in more data and statistics. The result is a steady stream of detailed, highly accurate chart reference books that are widely acclaimed by collectors, disc jockeys, program directors, musicologists, artists and others active in the radio and music industries worldwide.

A SYNOPSIS OF THE BILLBOARD ALBUM CHARTS

DATE	POSITIONS	CHART TITLE
1/1/55	15	BEST-SELLING POPULAR ALBUMS (mostly biweekly charts with the exception of a 7-week gap and several 3-week gaps)
3/24/56	10-15-20-30	BEST-SELLING POPULAR ALBUMS (charts published weekly with size varying from a top 10 to a top 30)
6/2/56	15	BEST-SELLING POP ALBUMS
9/2/57	25	BEST-SELLING POP LP's
5/25/59	50	BEST-SELLING MONOPHONIC LP's
5/25/59	30	BEST-SELLING STEREOPHONIC LP's (separate Stereo and Mono charts published through 8/10/63)
1/4/60	40	MONO ACTION CHARTS (mono albums charted 39 weeks or less)
1/4/60	30	STEREO ACTION CHARTS (stereo albums charted 19 weeks or less—changed to 29 weeks or less on 5/30/60)
1/4/60	25	ESSENTIAL INVENTORY—MONO (mono albums charted 40 weeks or more)
1/4/60	20	ESSENTIAL INVENTORY—STEREO (stereo albums charted 20 weeks or more—changed to 30 weeks or more on 5/30/60)
1/9/61	25	ACTION ALBUMS—MONOPHONIC (mono albums charted 9 weeks or less)
1/9/61	15	ACTION ALBUMS—STEREOPHONIC (stereo albums charted 9 weeks or less)
1/9/61	—	Approximately 200 albums listed by category (no positions) and shown as essential inventory
4/3/61	150	TOP LP's—MONAURAL
4/3/61	50	TOP LP's—STEREO
8/17/63	150	TOP LP's (1 chart)
4/1/67	175	TOP LP's
5/13/67	200	TOP LP's
11/25/67	200	TOP LP's (3 pages)
2/15/69	200	TOP LP's (2 pages with A-Z artist listing)
2/19/72	200	TOP LP's & TAPES
10/20/84	200	TOP 200 ALBUMS
1/5/85	200	TOP POP ALBUMS

An album appearing on both the Mono and Stereo charts in the same week is tabulated as one weekly appearance.

The album's highest position is determined by the chart (Mono or Stereo) on which the album reached its highest position.

The Essential Inventory charts list albums that have already been charted for months on the Mono & Stereo charts and, therefore, were not researched for this book

THE TOP 40 ALBUMS

HOW TO USE THIS SECTION

This section lists, alphabetically by artist name, every album that hit the top 40 on *Billboard*'s pop album charts from January 8, 1955 through June 30, 1990. Each group or artist's charted hit record is listed in chronological order. A sequential number is shown in front of each record title to indicate the number of charted albums. If an album contains any singles that appeared in the top 10 of *Billboard*'s Hot 100 chart, each song title is listed in italics below the album title. The highest position each single reached in the top 10 is indicated in parentheses after the title.

Explanation of Headings and Symbols

DATE: Date album debuted in the top 40.

POS: Album's highest charted position (highlighted in bold type). The number in parentheses after No. 1 and No. 2 albums indicates total weeks album held that position.

WKS: Total weeks charted in the top 40.

LABEL & NO.: Original album label and number. Numeral in brackets following label number indicates the number of records in the album.

+   Indicates that the weeks-charted data is subject to change since the album was still accumulating weeks in the top 40 as of October 20, 1990.

•   RIAA certified gold album (500,000 units sold)
▲   RIAA certified platinum album (1,000,000 units sold)

The Record Industry Association of America (RIAA) began certifying gold albums in 1958 and platinum albums in 1976. Prior to these dates, there are some hits that most certainly would have qualified for these certifications. Also, some record labels have never requested RIAA certification for their hits, even though the records may have qualified for gold or platinum status.

Letter(s) in brackets after record titles indicate the following:

[C]	Comedy	[L]	Live Recording
[E]	Early Recording	[M]	Mini Album (10" or 12" EP)
[EP]	7" Extended Play Album	[N]	Novelty
[F]	Foreign Language	[OC]	Original Cast
[G]	Greatest Hits	[R]	Reissue of previously
[I]	Instrumental Recording		charted album

[T]	Talk/Spoken Word	[S]	Soundtrack
	Recording	[TV]	Television Soundtrack
[K]	Compilation	[X]	Christmas Recording

New Week-Counting Method

From January 4, 1960 through March 27, 1961, in conjunction with their regular Mono and Stereo Action charts, *Billboard* published Essential Inventory charts for both mono and stereo albums. Our use of the Essential Inventory charts has changed slightly since the last edition of *Top 40 Albums*. Previously, the Essential Inventory charts were used to calculate both top 40 weeks and total weeks charted, but they are now used to calculate total weeks charted only. Therefore, you will note a reduction in top 40 weeks for a few older albums.

New Alphabetical System

Throughout the years, due to a number of factors, it had become increasingly difficult to quickly locate an artist alphabetically in our books. In an effort to alleviate the problem in this volume, some major changes have been made. Each artist's last name is now shown first, in capital letters, followed by the first name, shown in upper and lower case (ABDUL, Paula). This change in itself will make it much easier to find an artist; however, we went even further and changed the method by which artists are alphabetized.

When looking up an artist alphabetically, the basic rule is to look at **all** upper case letters collectively, ignoring spaces and punctuation. Therefore, Godley & Creme precedes Go-Go's; Todd Rundgren precedes Run-D.M.C. Solo artists with common last names, such as WILSON, are grouped together as in the past, and alphabetized according to first name. A group name which begins with the same last name as a solo artist will follow the artist (JAMES, Bob precedes JAMES GANG, The). If a group's name is exactly the same as a solo artist's last name, then the group's name is shown first (SWEET precedes SWEET, Rachel). If a group's name begins with "The," and the second part of the group's name is the same as a solo artist's last name, the solo artist will be listed first (SYLVERS, Foster precedes SYLVERS, The).

Also, in the case of an artist like The Dave Clark Five, the main heading is shown simply as CLARK, Dave. The group's full name is shown just prior to the listing of their top 40 albums. This change was made to keep the artist headings short and easy to find.

DATE	POS	WKS	ARTIST—RECORD TITLE	LABEL & NO.

A

ABBA

Pop quartet formed in Stockholm, Sweden in 1970. Consisted of Frida Lyngstad and Agnetha Faltskog (vocals), Bjorn Ulvaeus (guitar) and Benny Andersson (keyboards). Benny and Bjorn recorded together in 1966. Bjorn and Agnetha married in 1971, divorced in 1978; Benny and Frida married in 1978, divorced in 1981. Disbanded in the early 1980s.

DATE	POS	WKS	ARTIST—RECORD TITLE	LABEL & NO.
2/26/77	**20**	9	● 1. Arrival *Dancing Queen* (1)	Atlantic 18207
3/25/78	**14**	17	▲ 2. The Album *Take A Chance On Me* (3)	Atlantic 19164
7/28/79	**19**	12	● 3. Voulez-Vous	Atlantic 16000
12/27/80	**17**	16	● 4. Super Trouper *The Winner Takes It All* (8)	Atlantic 16023
1/23/82	**29**	6	5. The Visitors	Atlantic 19332

ABBOTT, Gregory

Soul singer/songwriter from New York. At age eight, member of St. Patrick's Cathedral Choir. Psychology major at Boston University and Stanford; taught English at Berkeley.

DATE	POS	WKS	ARTIST—RECORD TITLE	LABEL & NO.
12/27/86	**22**	16	● 1. Shake You Down *Shake You Down* (1)	Columbia 40437

ABC

Electro-pop group from Sheffield, England. Formed as Vice Versa with Stephen Singleton and Mark White. Lead singer Martin Fry joined in 1980, group renamed ABC. Singleton left group in 1985.

DATE	POS	WKS	ARTIST—RECORD TITLE	LABEL & NO.
11/20/82	**24**	20	1. the Lexicon of Love	Mercury 4059
10/26/85	**30**	15	2. how to be a…Zillionaire! *Be Near Me* (9)	Mercury 824904

ABDUL, Paula

Los Angeles singer/choreographer born on 6/19/62 to Brazilian and French-Canadian parents. While still a teen, was the choreographer member of the Los Angeles Lakers cheerleaders. Choreographed Janet Jackson's *Control* LP videos and "The Tracy Ullman Show." In 1987, named "Choreographer of the Year" by MTV.

DATE	POS	WKS	ARTIST—RECORD TITLE	LABEL & NO.
1/28/89	**1**(10)	78	▲ 1. Forever Your Girl *Straight Up* (1)/*Forever Your Girl* (1)/*Cold Hearted* (1)/ *(It's Just) The Way That You Love Me* (3)/*Opposites Attract* (1)	Virgin 90943
6/2/90	**7**	16	▲ 2. Shut Up And Dance (The Dance Mixes) [K] remixes of Paula's hits	Virgin 91362

AC/DC

Hard-rock band formed in Sydney, Australia in 1974. Consisted of brothers Angus and Malcolm Young (guitars), Ron Belford "Bon" Scott (lead singer), Phil Rudd (drums) and Mark Evans (bass). Cliff Williams replaced Evans in 1977. Bon Scott died on 2/19/80 (age 33) from alcohol abuse and was replaced by Brian Johnson. Simon Wright replaced Rudd in 1985. Angus and Malcolm are the younger brothers of George Young of The Easybeats. Wright joined Dio in 1989, replaced by Chris Slade of The Firm.

DATE	POS	WKS	ARTIST—RECORD TITLE	LABEL & NO.
9/15/79	**17**	11	▲ 1. Highway To Hell	Atlantic 19244
8/23/80	**4**	45	▲ 2. Back In Black	Atlantic 16018
4/18/81	**3**	19	▲ 3. Dirty Deeds Done Dirt Cheap [R] recorded in 1976	Atlantic 16033

DATE	POS	WKS	ARTIST—RECORD TITLE	LABEL & NO.
12/12/81	**1**(3)	16	▲ 4. For Those About To Rock We Salute You	Atlantic 11111
9/10/83	**15**	11	● 5. Flick Of The Switch	Atlantic 80100
8/17/85	**32**	5	● 6. Fly On The Wall	Atlantic 81263
8/9/86	**33**	6	▲ 7. Who Made Who [S-K] soundtrack from the film *Maximum Overdrive*; includes three new songs	Atlantic 81650
3/5/88	**12**	12	▲ 8. Blow Up Your Video	Atlantic 81828
			ACE Pub-rock quintet from Sheffield, England led by vocalist Paul Carrack. Disbanded in 1977. Carrack joined Squeeze in 1981, then Mike + The Mechanics in 1985.	
4/5/75	**11**	11	1. Five-A-Side (an Ace album) *How Long* (3)	Anchor 2001
			ADAM & THE ANTS — see ANT, Adam	
			ADAMS, Bryan Rock singer/songwriter/guitarist born on 11/5/59 in Kingston, Ontario. Teamed with Jim Vallance in 1977 in songwriting partnership.	
4/2/83	**8**	24	▲ 1. Cuts Like A Knife *Straight From The Heart* (10)	A&M 4919
12/1/84	**1**(2)	66	▲ 2. Reckless *Run To You* (6)/*Heaven* (1)/*Summer Of '69* (5)	A&M 5013
4/18/87	**7**	22	▲ 3. Into The Fire *Heat Of The Night* (6)	A&M 3907
			ADDERLEY, "Cannonball" Born Julian Edwin Adderley on 9/15/28 in Tampa. Nickname derived from "cannibal" - a tribute to his love of eating. Alto saxophonist/leader of jazz combo featuring brother Nat Adderley (cornet) and Joe Zawinul (piano; left in 1971 to form Weather Report; replaced by George Duke). Died of a stroke on 8/8/75 (46) in Gary, Indiana.	
7/7/62	**30**	5	1. Nancy Wilson/Cannonball Adderley	Capitol 1657
4/13/63	**11**	11	**CANNONBALL ADDERLEY SEXTET:** 2. Jazz Workshop Revisited [I-L]	Riverside 444
3/25/67	**13**	9	**THE CANNONBALL ADDERLEY QUINTET:** 3. Mercy, Mercy, Mercy! [I-L]	Capitol 2663
			AEROSMITH Hard-rock band formed in Sunapee, New Hampshire in 1970. Consisted of Steven Tyler (lead singer; b: Steven Tallarico), Joe Perry and Brad Whitford (guitars), Tom Hamilton (bass) and Joey Kramer (drums). Perry left for own Joe Perry Project in 1979; replaced by Jimmy Crespo. Whitford left in 1981; replaced by Rick Dufay. Original band reunited in April of 1984.	
5/24/75	**11**	30	▲ 1. Toys In The Attic *Walk This Way* (10)	Columbia 33479
3/20/76	**21**	8	▲ 2. Aerosmith *Dream On* (6)	Columbia 32005
5/29/76	**3**	21	▲ 3. Rocks	Columbia 34165
1/7/78	**11**	8	▲ 4. Draw The Line	Columbia 34856
11/18/78	**13**	13	▲ 5. Live! Bootleg [L]	Columbia 35564 [2]
12/15/79	**14**	12	● 6. Night In The Ruts	Columbia 36050
10/2/82	**32**	6	● 7. Rock In A Hard Place	Columbia 38061
12/14/85	**36**	5	8. Done With Mirrors	Geffen 24091
10/3/87	**11**	52	▲ 9. Permanent Vacation *Angel* (3)	Geffen 24162

DATE	POS	WKS	ARTIST—RECORD TITLE	LABEL & NO.
9/30/89	5	53	▲ 10. Pump *Love In An Elevator* (5)/*Janie's Got A Gun* (4)/ *What It Takes* (9)	Geffen 24254
4/16/83	25	8	**AFTER THE FIRE** English band led by guitarist Andy Piercy. 1. ATF *Der Kommisar* (5)	Epic 38282
9/7/85	15	26	**a-ha** Trio formed in Oslo, Norway: Morten Harket (vocals), Pal Waaktaar (guitar, keyboards) and Mags Furuholem (keyboards). ● 1. Hunting High And Low *Take On Me* (1)	Warner 25300
			AIR FORCE — see BAKER, Ginger	
			AIR SUPPLY Melbourne, Australia duo: Russ Hitchcock (born on 6/15/49 in Melbourne) and Graham Russell (born on 6/1/50 in Nottingham, England). Russell recorded solo in 1988.	
9/6/80	22	19	▲ 1. Lost In Love *Lost In Love* (3)/*All Out Of Love* (2)/ *Every Woman In The World* (5)	Arista 4268
6/27/81	10	25	▲ 2. The One That You Love *The One That You Love* (1)/*Here I Am* (5)/*Sweet Dreams* (5)	Arista 9551
7/17/82	25	8	▲ 3. Now And Forever *Even The Nights Are Better* (5)	Arista 9587
9/3/83	7	26	▲ 4. Greatest Hits [G] *Making Love Out Of Nothing At All* (2)	Arista 8024
7/6/85	26	8	● 5. Air Supply	Arista 8283
			ALABAMA Country quartet from Fort Payne, Alabama: Randy Owen (vocals, guitar), Jeff Cook (keyboards, fiddle), Teddy Gentry (bass, vocals) and Mark Herndon (drums, vocals). Randy, Jeff and Teddy are cousins.	
5/2/81	16	42	▲ 1. Feels So Right	RCA 3930
3/20/82	14	20	▲ 2. Mountain Music	RCA 4229
3/26/83	10	15	▲ 3. The Closer You Get…	RCA 4663
2/18/84	21	17	▲ 4. Roll On	RCA 4939
3/16/85	28	5	▲ 5. 40 Hour Week	RCA 5339
3/8/86	24	15	▲ 6. Greatest Hits [G]	RCA 7170
2/15/86	39	3	**ALARM, The** Welsh rock quartet: Mike Peters (lead singer), Dave Sharp, Eddie MacDonald and Nigel Twist. Formed in 1977 by Peters and Twist as the Toilets. MacDonald and Sharp joined in 1978, and group changed their name to Seventeen (after a Sex Pistols' song). Renamed The Alarm in 1982. 1. Strength	I.R.S. 5666
11/29/75	37	2	**ALBERT, Morris** Brazilian singer/songwriter born Morris Albert Kaisermann. 1. Feelings *Feelings* (6)	RCA 1018
6/11/88	20	25	**AL B. SURE!** Black singer born Al Brown in Boston; raised in Mount Vernon, New York. ▲ 1. In Effect Mode *Nite And Day* (7)	Warner 25662

DATE	POS	WKS	ARTIST—RECORD TITLE	LABEL & NO.
			ALDRICH, Ronnie	
			British pianist/arranger.	
			RONNIE ALDRICH AND HIS TWO PIANOS:	
11/6/61	**20**	13	1. Melody And Percussion For Two Pianos [I]	London P. 4 44007
10/20/62	**36**	2	2. Ronnie Aldrich and his Two Pianos [I]	London P. 4 44018
			ALLAN, Davie/The Arrows	
			Davie began as a session guitarist for Mike Curb in Los Angeles.	
			DAVIE ALLAN AND THE ARROWS:	
12/3/66	**17**	13	1. The Wild Angels [S]	Tower 5043
			ALLEN, Dayton	
			Comedian on the Steve Allen TV show.	
12/19/60	**35**	1	1. Why Not! [C]	Grand Award 424
			ALLEN, Steve	
			Born on 12/26/21 in New York City. Comedian/actor/composer/author. In 1954, became the first host of TV's ''Tonight Show.'' Played title role in 1956 film *The Benny Goodman Story*. Hosted own variety and talk shows, 1956-80. Married to actress Jayne Meadows.	
5/14/55	**7**	10	1. Music For Tonight [I]	Coral 57004
			ALLMAN, Duane	
			Born Howard Duane Allman on 11/20/46. The Allman Brothers Band guitarist. Died on 10/29/71 in a motorcycle accident.	
1/20/73	**28**	6	● 1. An Anthology [K] features Duane's session work	Capricorn 0108 [2]
			ALLMAN, Gregg	
			Keyboardist/vocalist born on 12/8/47 in Nashville and raised in Daytona Beach, Florida. In 1965, Greg and brother Duane formed the Allman Joys which evolved into The Allman Brothers Band by 1969. Married briefly to Cher in 1975.	
12/8/73	**13**	17	● 1. Laid Back	Capricorn 0116
			THE GREGG ALLMAN BAND:	
5/2/87	**30**	6	2. I'm No Angel	Epic 40531
			ALLMAN BROTHERS BAND, The	
			Southern-rock band formed in Macon, Georgia in 1969. Consisted of brothers Duane (lead guitar) and Gregg Allman (keyboards), Dickey Betts (guitar), Berry Oakley (bass), and the drum duo of Butch Trucks and Jai Johnny Johanson (pronounced: J. Johnny Johnson). Duane and Gregg known earlier as Allman Joys and Hour Glass. Duane was the top session guitarist at Muscle Shoals studio; he was killed in a motorcycle crash on 10/29/71 (age 24). Oakley died in another cycle accident on 11/11/72 (age 24); he was replaced by Lamar Williams. Chuck Leavell (keyboards) added in 1972. Group split up in 1976. Gregg formed the Gregg Allman Band. Betts formed Great Southern. Leavell, Williams and Johanson formed the fusion-rock band Sea Level. Allman and Betts reunited with a new Allman Brothers lineup in 1978. Disbanded in 1981. Allman, Betts, Trucks and Johanson regrouped with Warren Haynes (guitar), Allen Woody (bass) and Johnny Neel (keyboards) in 1989.	
12/5/70	**38**	2	1. Idlewild South	Atco 342
7/31/71	**13**	11	● 2. At Fillmore East [L]	Capricorn 802 [2]
3/18/72	**4**	29	● 3. Eat A Peach [L] includes Duane's last three studio recordings	Capricorn 0102 [2]
4/7/73	**25**	6	● 4. Beginnings [R] reissue of album #1 above and LP *The Allman Brothers Band* (1970)	Atco 805 [2]
8/25/73	**1(5)**	24	● 5. Brothers And Sisters *Ramblin Man* (2)	Capricorn 0111

DATE	POS	WKS	ARTIST—RECORD TITLE	LABEL & NO.
9/27/75	5	8	● 6. Win, Lose Or Draw	Capricorn 0156
3/24/79	9	13	● 7. Enlightened Rogues	Capricorn 0218
9/6/80	27	6	8. Reach For The Sky	Arista 9535
			ALMEIDA, Laurindo	
			Born on 9/2/17 in Sao Paulo, Brazil. Guitarist/bandleader. **LAURINDO ALMEIDA AND THE BOSSA NOVA ALL STARS:**	
12/8/62	9	22	1. Viva Bossa Nova! [I]	Capitol 1759
			ALPERT, Herb/The Tijuana Brass	
			Herb was born on 3/31/35 in Los Angeles. Producer/composer/trumpeter/bandleader. Played trumpet since age eight. A&R for Keen Records, produced first Jan & Dean session, wrote "Wonderful World" hit for Sam Cooke. Formed A&M Records with Jerry Moss in 1962. Used studio musicians until early 1965, then formed own band. **HERB ALPERT & THE TIJUANA BRASS:**	
1/26/63	24	49	● 1. The Lonely Bull [I] *The Lonely Bull* (6)	A&M 101
6/12/65	1(8)	141	● 2. Whipped Cream & Other Delights * [I] *Taste Of Honey* (7)	A&M 110
11/6/65	1(6)	107	● 3. Going Places [I]	A&M 112
12/18/65	6	52	● 4. South Of The Border * [I]	A&M 108

3/5/66	17	13	● 5. Herb Alpert's Tijuana Brass, Volume 2 * [I]
			    *HERB ALPERT'S TIJUANA BRASS
			    Herb's 2nd album, recorded in 1963
				A&M 103

5/21/66	1(9)	59	● 6. What Now My Love [I]	A&M 4114
5/21/66	30	59	7. The Brass Are Comin' [I]	A&M 4228
12/17/66	2(6)	38	● 8. S.R.O. [I]	A&M 4119
6/10/67	1(1)	36	● 9. Sounds Like [I]	A&M 4124
12/30/67	4	18	● 10. Herb Alpert's Ninth [I]	A&M 4134
5/18/68	1(2)	28	● 11. The Beat Of The Brass [I] *This Guy's In Love With You* (1)	A&M 4146
7/19/69	28	7	● 12. Warm [I]	A&M 4190
			HERB ALPERT:	
10/20/79	6	19	▲ 13. Rise [I] *Rise* (1)	A&M 4790
8/9/80	28	4	14. Beyond [I]	A&M 3717
4/25/87	18	17	● 15. Keep Your Eye On Me *Diamonds* (5) featuring Janet Jackson	A&M 5125
			AMBROSIA	
			Los Angeles-based pop group: David Pack and Joe Puerta (lead singers), Burleigh Drummond and Christopher North. North left in 1977.	
7/26/75	22	8	1. Ambrosia	20th Century 434
11/4/78	19	9	2. Life Beyond L.A. *How Much I Feel* (3)	Warner 3135
5/31/80	25	7	3. One Eighty *Biggest Part Of Me* (3)	Warner 3368
			AMERICA	
			Trio formed in London in 1969. Consisted of Americans Dan Peek, Gerry Beckley and Englishman Dewey Bunnell. All played guitars. Met at U.S. Air Force base. Members of group Daze in 1970. Moved to the U.S. in February, 1972. Won the 1972 Best New Artist Grammy Award. Peek left in 1976.	
3/4/72	1(5)	22	▲ 1. America *A Horse With No Name* (1)/*I Need You* (9)	Warner 2576

DATE	POS	WKS	ARTIST—RECORD TITLE	LABEL & NO.
12/16/72	9	16	● 2. Homecoming *Ventura Highway* (8)	Warner 2655
12/1/73	28	5	3. Hat Trick	Warner 2728
8/24/74	3	17	● 4. Holiday *Tin Man* (4)/*Lonely People* (5)	Warner 2808
4/19/75	4	17	● 5. Hearts *Sister Golden Hair* (1)	Warner 2852
11/29/75	3	22	▲ 6. History/America's Greatest Hits [G]	Warner 2894
5/8/76	11	8	● 7. Hideaway	Warner 2932
3/26/77	21	4	8. Harbor	Warner 3017
			AMES, Ed One of The Ames Brothers. Played an Indian on the "Daniel Boone" TV series.	
3/18/67	4	19	● 1. My Cup Runneth Over *My Cup Runneth Over* (8)	RCA 3774
1/20/68	24	8	2. When The Snow Is On The Roses	RCA 3913
3/23/68	13	18	● 3. Who Will Answer? And Other Songs Of Our Time	RCA 3961
			AMES BROTHERS, The Vocal group from Malden, Massachusetts formed in the late 40s. Family name Urick. Consisted of Ed (b: 7/9/27), Gene (b: 2/13/25), Joe (b: 5/3/24) and Vic (b: 5/20/26, d: 1/23/78). Own TV series in 1955. Ed recorded solo and acted on Broadway and TV.	
12/2/57	16	4	1. There'll Always Be A Christmas [X]	RCA 1541
			ANDERSON, Bill Born James William Anderson III on 11/1/37 in Columbia, South Carolina. Country singer/songwriter/actor. Host of Nashville Network's TV game show "Fandango." Member of the Grand Ole Opry since 1961. Known as "Whispering Bill."	
7/27/63	36	5	1. Still *Still* (8)	Decca 74427
			ANDERSON, Ernestine Jazz singer born on 11/11/28 in Houston. Formerly with Eddie Heywood and Lionel Hampton.	
10/20/58	15	6	1. Hot Cargo!	Mercury 20354
			ANDERSON, Lynn Born on 9/26/47 in Grand Forks, North Dakota; raised in Sacramento. Country singer; daughter of Liz Anderson.	
2/13/71	19	12	▲ 1. Rose Garden *Rose Garden* (3)	Columbia 30411
			ANDERSON, BRUFORD, WAKEMAN, HOWE Vocalist Jon Anderson, drummer Bill Bruford, keyboardist Rick Wakeman and guitarist Steve Howe were members of the English progressive rock group Yes. Bruford was also a member of King Crimson. Howe was also with Asia.	
7/15/89	30	7	● 1. Anderson, Bruford, Wakeman, Howe	Arista 90126
			ANGELS, The Female pop trio from Orange, New Jersey. Formed as the Starlets with sisters Phyllis "Jiggs" & Barbara Allbut, and Linda Jansen (lead singer). Jansen was replaced by Peggy Santiglia in 1962. Disbanded in 1967.	
11/16/63	33	3	1. My Boyfriend's Back *My Boyfriend's Back* (1)	Smash 67039

DATE	POS	WKS	ARTIST—RECORD TITLE	LABEL & NO.
			ANIMALS, The	
			Formed in Newcastle, England in 1958 as the Alan Price Combo. Consisted of Eric Burdon (vocals), Alan Price (keyboards), Bryan "Chas" Chandler (bass), Hilton Valentine (guitar) and John Steel (drums). Price left in May of 1965, replaced by Dave Rowberry. Steel left in 1966, replaced by Barry Jenkins. Group disbanded in July, 1968. After a period with War, Burdon and the other originals reunited, 1983.	
10/3/64	7	15	1. The Animals *The House Of The Rising Sun* (1)	MGM 4264
3/12/66	6	51	● 2. The Best Of The Animals [G]	MGM 4324
9/24/66	20	12	3. Animalization *See See Rider* (10)	MGM 4384
1/14/67	33	3	4. Animalism	MGM 4414
			ANIMOTION	
			Techno-pop quintet led by Astrid Plane and Bill Wadhams. Four of five members replaced in 1988, including Plane and Wadhams. New vocalists are Paul Engemann (formerly of Device) and actress/dancer Cynthia Rhodes (appeared in the films *Staying Alive* and *Dirty Dancing*; married Richard Marx on 1/8/89).	
4/20/85	28	7	1. Animotion *Obsession* (6)	Mercury 822580
			ANKA, Paul	
			Born on 7/30/41 in Ottawa, Canada. Performer since age 12. Father financed first recording, "I Confess" (RPM 472), in 1956. Wrote "My Way" for Frank Sinatra, "She's A Lady" for Tom Jones. Also wrote theme for TV's "Tonight Show." Own variety show in 1973. Long-time popular entertainer in Las Vegas.	
7/4/60	4	54	1. Paul Anka Sings His Big 15 [G] *Diana* (1)/*You Are My Destiny* (7)/*Loney Boy* (1)/*Put Your Head On My Shoulder* (2)/*It's Time To Cry* (4)/*Puppy Love* (2)	ABC-Para. 323
12/5/60	23	3	2. Anka At The Copa [L]	ABC-Para. 353
9/28/74	9	14	● 3. Anka *(You're) Having My Baby* (1)/*One Man Woman/One Woman Man* (7)	United Art. 314
5/24/75	36	3	4. Feelings *I Don't Like To Sleep Alone* (8)	United Art. 367
1/17/76	22	9	● 5. Times Of Your Life [K] nine of 10 cuts from previous two United Artists albums *Times Of Your Life* (7)	United Art. 569
			ANNETTE	
			Born Annette Funicello on 10/22/42 in Utica, New York. Became a Mouseketeer in 1955. Backing group: The Afterbeats. Acted in several teen films in the early 60s. Co-starred with Frankie Avalon in the 1987 film *Back To The Beach*.	
3/21/60	21	9	1. Annette Sings Anka	Buena Vista 3302
9/26/60	38	3	2. Hawaiiannette	Buena Vista 3303
12/14/63	39	1	3. Annette's Beach Party [S] half of the songs are from the film *Beach Party*	Buena Vista 3316
			ANT, Adam	
			Born Stuart Goddard on 11/3/54 in London. Formed Adam & The Ants in 1976. Appeared in the films *World Gone Wild* and *Slam Dance* and the TV show "The Equalizer."	
12/11/82	16	16	● 1. Friend Or Foe	Epic 38370

DATE	POS	WKS	ARTIST—RECORD TITLE	LABEL & NO.
			ANTHONY, Ray	
			Born Raymond Antonini on 1/20/22 in Bentleyville, Pennsylvania; raised in Cleveland. Trumpeter/bandleader. Joined Al Donahue in 1939, then with Glenn Miller and Jimmy Dorsey from 1940-42. Led U.S. Army band. Own band in 1946. Own TV series in the 50s. Appeared in the film *Daddy Long Legs* with Fred Astaire in 1955. Wrote "Bunny Hop." Band disbanded in the mid-60s.	
3/19/55	**10**	6	1. Golden Horn　　　　　　　　　　　　　　　　　[I]	Capitol 563
6/23/56	**15**	1	2. Dream Dancing　　　　　　　　　　　　　　　[I]	Capitol 723
10/28/57	**11**	21	3. Young Ideas　　　　　　　　　　　　　　　　[I]	Capitol 866
5/19/58	**12**	10	4. The Dream Girl　　　　　　　　　　　　　　[I]	Capitol 969
8/11/62	**14**	13	5. Worried Mind　　　　　　　　　　　　　　　[I]	Capitol 1752
			ANTHRAX	
			New York hard-rock quintet: Joey Belladonna (vocals), Dan Spitz, Scott Ian, Frank Bello and Charlie Benante. Greg D'Angelo of White Lion was an early member.	
10/15/88	**30**	5	● 　1. State Of Euphoria	Island 91004
			APPICE, Carmine — see BECK, Jeff	
			APRIL WINE	
			Rock quintet from Montreal: Myles Goodwyn (lead singer, guitar), Brian Greenway (guitar), Steve Lang (bass), Gary Moffet (guitar) and Jerry Mercer (drums). Lang, Moffet and Mercer replaced by Daniel Barbe (keyboards), Jean Pellerin (bass) and Marty Simon (drums) in 1985.	
2/28/81	**26**	12	▲ 　1. The Nature Of The Beast	Capitol 12125
8/7/82	**37**	3	2. Power Play	Capitol 12218
			ARCADIA	
			English group features Duran Duran's Simon LeBon, Nick Rhodes and Roger Taylor. LeBon and Rhodes remain with Duran Duran.	
12/21/85	**23**	9	▲ 　1. So Red The Rose 　　　*Election Day* (6)	Capitol 12428
			ARGENT	
			British rock quartet. Consisted of ex-Zombies member Rod Argent (vocals, keyboards), Jim Rodford (bass, Argent's cousin), Robert Henrit (drums) and Russ Ballard (guitar, later a successful songwriter/producer). Rodford was a member of The Kinks by 1978. Ballard left in 1984, replaced by John Verity.	
9/2/72	**23**	7	1. All Together Now 　　　*Hold Your Head Up* (5)	Epic 31556
			ARMATRADING, Joan	
			Born on 12/9/50 in St. Kitts, West Indies. Vocalist/pianist/guitarist/composer. To Birmingham, England in 1958. First recorded for Cube in 1971.	
7/26/80	**28**	5	1. Me Myself I	A&M 4809
5/28/83	**32**	3	2. The Key	A&M 4912
			ARMSTRONG, Louis	
			Trumpeter/vocalist, born Daniel Louis Armstrong in New Orleans on 8/4/01 (not 7/4/1900, as Armstrong claimed). Nickname: Satchmo. Joined Joe "King" Oliver in Chicago in 1922. By 1929, had become the most widely known black musician in the world. Influenced dozens of singers and trumpet players, both black and white. Numerous appearances on radio, TV and in films. Died on 7/6/71 in New York. Inducted into the Rock and Roll Hall of Fame in 1990 as a forefather of rock music.	
10/1/55	**10**	2	1. Satch Plays Fats 　　　**LOUIS ARMSTRONG AND HIS ALL-STARS** 　　　a tribute to Fats Waller	Columbia 708

DATE	POS	WKS	ARTIST—RECORD TITLE	LABEL & NO.
12/15/56	**12**	2	2. Ella And Louis **ELLA FITZGERALD AND LOUIS ARMSTRONG** backing by the Oscar Peterson Trio, plus Buddy Rich	Verve 4003
5/23/64	**1**(6)	48	● 3. Hello, Dolly! *Hello, Dolly!* (1)	Kapp 3364

ARNOLD, Eddy

Born Richard Edward Arnold on 5/15/18 near Henderson, Tennessee. Became popular on Nashville's Grand Ole Opry as a singer with Pee Wee King (1940-43). Nicknamed "The Tennessee Plowboy" on all RCA recordings through 1954. Country music's most prolific recording artist fom 1945-55. Elected to the Country Music Hall Of Fame in 1966. CMA award: Entertainer of the Year - 1967.

DATE	POS	WKS	ARTIST—RECORD TITLE	LABEL & NO.
11/27/65	7	28	● 1. My World *Make The World Go Away* (6)	RCA 3466
5/21/66	26	5	2. I Want To Go With You	RCA 3507
3/11/67	36	2	3. Somebody Like Me	RCA 3715
6/24/67	34	2	● 4. The Best Of Eddy Arnold　　　　[G]	RCA 3565
11/25/67	34	5	5. Turn The World Around	RCA 3869

ARROWS, The — see ALLAN, Davie

ARTISTS UNITED AGAINST APARTHEID

Benefit group of 49 superstar artists formed to protest the South African apartheid government; proceeds went to political prisoners in South Africa. Arthur Baker and Miami Steven Van Zandt ("Little Steven") wrote and produced event.

DATE	POS	WKS	ARTIST—RECORD TITLE	LABEL & NO.
12/7/85	31	4	1. Sun City	Manhattan 53019

ASHFORD & SIMPSON

Husband-and-wife R&B vocal/songwriting duo: Nickolas Ashford (b: 5/4/42, Fairfield, South Carolina) and Valerie Simpson (b: 8/26/46, New York City). Team wrote for Chuck Jackson and Maxine Brown. Joined staff at Motown and wrote and produced for many of the label's top stars. Valerie recorded solo in 1972.

DATE	POS	WKS	ARTIST—RECORD TITLE	LABEL & NO.
9/23/78	20	12	● 1. Is It Still Good To Ya	Warner 3219
9/8/79	23	9	● 2. Stay Free	Warner 3357
9/13/80	38	2	3. A Musical Affair	Warner 3458
2/9/85	29	10	4. Solid	Capitol 12366

ASIA

English rock supergroup comprised of guitarist Steve Howe (Yes), drummer Carl Palmer (Emerson, Lake & Palmer), keyboardist Geoff Downes (Buggles, Yes) and vocalist/ bassist John Wetton (King Crimson, Uriah Heep, Roxy Music). Howe replaced by Mandy Meyer (Krokus) in 1985. Meyer replaced in 1990 by Oakland, California native Pat Thrall (Automatic Man, Pat Travers Band).

DATE	POS	WKS	ARTIST—RECORD TITLE	LABEL & NO.
4/3/82	**1**(9)	35	▲ 1. Asia *Heat Of The Moment* (4)	Geffen 2008
8/27/83	6	11	▲ 2. Alpha *Don't Cry* (10)	Geffen 4008

ASSOCIATION, The

Group formed in Los Angeles in 1965. Consisted of Terry Kirkman (plays 23 wind, reed and percussion instruments), Gary "Jules" Alexander (guitar), Brian Cole (bass), Jim Yester (guitar), Ted Bluechel, Jr. (drums) and Russ Giguere (percussion). Larry Ramos, Jr. joined in early 1968. Cole died on 8/2/73 of a heroin overdose.

DATE	POS	WKS	ARTIST—RECORD TITLE	LABEL & NO.
10/1/66	5	15	● 1. And Then…Along Comes The Association *Along Comes Mary* (7)/*Cherish* (1)	Valiant 5002

Dayton Allen, a comedian well known via Steve Allen's TV show, released a 1960 album that debuted at No. 35 and, by the next week, fell off the chart entirely. The appropriate LP title: *Why Not!*

America's success with their first hit single, 1972's "Horse With No Name," was so unexpected that after the trio had already released its eponymous debut album, Warner Bros. re-pressed the LP, this time including the Neil Young-inspired track. Of the group's first seven albums, only *Hat Trick*, their third, failed to be certified gold.

Ernestine Anderson's *Hot Cargo* peaked at No. 15 in 1958, when *Time* called her "the best new voice in the business." Since then, the vocalist—who first became a Buddhist and then restarted her career with jazz great Benny Carter in 1971—has recorded a series of critically praised albums for California jazz label Concord Records.

Paul Anka's well-known early hits such as "Diana," "Puppy Love," and "Lonely Boy" were all collected on the ABC-Paramount collection *Paul Anka Sings His Big 15*.

Ashford & Simpson's renown as writers has sometimes overshadowed the married duo's compelling recorded work—which with 1978's *Is It Still Good To Ya* first broke into the top 40. *Stay Free*, that album's follow-up, peaked at No. 23.

Badfinger's Apple debut of 1970, *Magic Christian Music*, was the first of several records by the group to be highly sought after by collectors. Follow-ups *No Dice* and *Straight Up* (pictured here), are similarly valued. In 1990, Rhino Records issued a best of Badfinger *Volume Two* set drawn from their post-Apple material; presumably *Volume One*, with the hits, will be forthcoming.

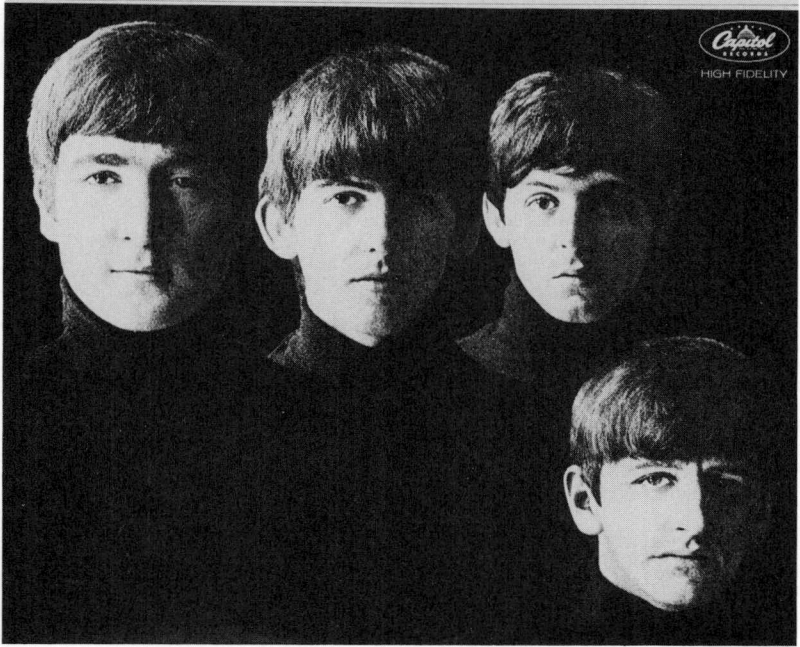

The **Beatles**' first album to reach the top 40 in the U.S., 1964's *Meet The Beatles!* stayed in the No. 1 slot for 11 weeks. Years later, its historic cover art was parodied by eccentric San Franciscan artists the Residents, among others.

The **Bee Gees** were 1990 recipients of the highest possible label honor: a multi-CD boxed set from PolyGram consisting of all their hits, from 1967's "New York Mining Disaster 1941" through their *Saturday Night Fever* era to their current Warner Bros. material.

Pat Benatar's swift rise to fame in the early 1980s, typified by 1982's *Get Nervous*, launched a legion of imitators and a host of critical articles regarding the role of "women in rock."

Tony Bennett's "I Left My Heart In San Francisco" was the title track of a 1962 Columbia album bearing the same name. That the song will live on forever was most recently affirmed by its ironic use in Steven Spielberg's 1990 film *Arachnophobia*.

George Benson's *Breezin'* of 1976, which stayed in the No. 1 slot for two weeks, officially began the jazz guitarist's singing career, though only one track, "This Masquerade," bore vocals. The Grammy-winning effort remains the best-selling jazz album of all time.

DATE	POS	WKS	ARTIST—RECORD TITLE	LABEL & NO.
3/4/67	**34**	3	2. Renaissance	Valiant 5004
8/5/67	**8**	25	● 3. Insight Out	Warner 1696
			Windy (1)/*Never My Love* (2)	
5/25/68	**23**	6	4. Birthday	Warner 1733
			Everything That Touches You (10)	
1/25/69	**4**	23	▲ 5. Greatest Hits [G]	Warner 1767
10/18/69	**32**	4	6. The Association	Warner 1800

ASTLEY, Rick

Pop singer/guitarist born on 2/6/66 in Warrington and raised in Manchester, England.

2/13/88	**10**	39	▲ 1. Whenever You Need Somebody	RCA 6822
			Never Gonna Give You Up (1)/*Together Forever* (1)/	
			It Would Take A Strong Man (10)	
2/4/89	**19**	10	● 2. Hold Me In Your Arms	RCA 8589
			She Wants To Dance With Me (6)	

ATKINS, Chet

Born on 6/20/24 in Luttrell, Tennessee. Revered guitarist, began recording for RCA in 1947. Moved to Nashville in 1950 and became prolific studio musician and producer. RCA's A&R manager in Nashville from 1960-68; RCA vice-president from 1968-82. Entered Country Music Hall of Fame in 1973 as the youngest inductee (age 49).

6/16/58	**21**	4	1. Chet Atkins At Home [I]	RCA 1544
2/22/60	**16**	12	2. Teensville [I]	RCA 2161
2/13/61	**7**	9	3. Chet Atkins' Workshop [I]	RCA 2232
4/28/62	**31**	4	4. Down Home [I]	RCA 2450
10/13/62	**33**	6	5. Caribbean Guitar [I]	RCA 2549

ATLANTA RHYTHM SECTION

Group formed of musicians from Studio One, Doraville, Georgia in 1971. Consisted of Rodney Justo (vocals), Barry Bailey, Paul Goddard, J.R. Cobb (guitars), Dean Daughtry (keyboards) and Robert Nix (drums). Cobb, Daughtry and band manager Buddy Buie had been with the Classics IV, others had been with Roy Orbison. Justo left after first album, replaced by Ronnie Hammond.

3/12/77	**11**	14	● 1. A Rock And Roll Alternative	Polydor 6080
			So In To You (7)	
4/8/78	**7**	15	▲ 2. Champagne Jam	Polydor 6134
			Imaginary Lover (7)	
7/7/79	**26**	7	● 3. Underdog	Polydor 6200

ATLANTIC STARR

Originally an eight-man, one-woman soul band formed in 1976 in White Plains, New York. Lead singers: brothers Wayne & David Lewis, and Sharon Bryant. In 1984, reduced to a quintet; Barbara Weathers replaced Bryant. Porscha Martin replaced Weathers in 1989.

4/17/82	**18**	7	1. Brilliance	A&M 4883
2/22/86	**17**	14	● 2. As The Band Turns	A&M 5019
			Secret Lovers (3)	
5/16/87	**18**	15	● 3. All In The Name Of Love	Warner 25560
			Always (1)	

AURRA

Ohio soul band: ex-Slave members Steve Washington and Tom Lockett, Jr. (saxophones) with Philip Fields (keyboards) and vocalists Starleana Young and Curt Jones. Young and Jones later formed the duo Deja.

4/17/82	**38**	3	1. A Little Love	Salsoul 8551

DATE	POS	WKS	ARTIST—RECORD TITLE	LABEL & NO.
			AUSTIN, Patti	
			Born on 8/10/48 in New York City. Backup work in New York. Goddaughter of Quincy Jones. Made Harlem's Apollo Theatre debut at age four. In the 1988 film *Tucker*.	
1/29/83	**36**	11	1. Every Home Should Have One *Baby, Come To Me* (1) with James Ingram	Qwest 3591
			AUTOGRAPH	
			Los Angeles-based rock quintet led by vocalist Steve Plunkett.	
2/23/85	**29**	12	● 1. Sign in Please	RCA 8040
			AVALON, Frankie	
			Born Francis Avallone on 9/18/39 in Philadelphia. Teen idol managed by Bob Marcucci. Worked in bands in Atlantic City, New Jersey in 1953. Radio and TV with Paul Whiteman, mid-50s. Singer/trumpet player with Rocco & His Saints in 1957 which included Bobby Rydell. Co-starred in many films with Annette. Appeared in films *Disc Jockey Jamboree* (1957), *Guns Of The Timberland* (1960), *The Carpetbaggers* (1962) and *Back To The Beach* (1987).	
1/4/60	**9**	13	1. Swingin' On A Rainbow	Chancellor 5004
			AVERAGE WHiTE BAND	
			Vocal/instrumental group formed in Scotland in 1972. Consisted of Alan Gorrie (vocal, bass), Hamish Stuart (vocal, guitar), Onnie McIntyre (vocal, guitar), Malcolm Duncan (saxophone), Roger Ball (keyboards, saxophone) and Robbie McIntosh (drums). McIntosh died of drug poisoning on 9/23/74, replaced by Steve Ferrone.	
12/21/74	**1**(1)	17	● 1. AWB *Pick Up The Pieces* (1)	Atlantic 7308
5/17/75	**39**	2	2. Put It Where You Want It [R] reissue of 1973 album *Show Your Hand*	MCA 475
7/5/75	**4**	11	● 3. Cut The Cake *Cut The Cake* (10)	Atlantic 18140
7/31/76	**9**	10	▲ 4. Soul Searching	Atlantic 18179
2/5/77	**28**	5	● 5. Person To Person [L]	Atlantic 1002 [2]
8/20/77	**33**	5	6. Benny And Us **AVERAGE WHITE BAND & BEN E. KING**	Atlantic 19105
4/22/78	**28**	5	● 7. Warmer Communications	Atlantic 19162
5/5/79	**32**	3	8. Feel No Fret	Atlantic 19207
			AYERS, Roy	
			Born on 9/10/40 in Los Angeles. R&B-jazz vibraphone player. With Herbie Mann in the early 60s. Formed own group Ubiquity in 1970.	
4/15/78	**33**	3	1. Let's Do It	Polydor 6126

B

DATE	POS	WKS	ARTIST—RECORD TITLE	LABEL & NO.
			BABYFACE	
			Vocalist/instrumentalist Kenneth Edmonds, formerly with Manchild and The Deele, dubbed "Babyface" by Bootsy Collins. Brother of Kevon and Melvin Edmonds of After 7. With L.A. Reid (of The Deele), co-wrote Pebbles' "Girlfriend" and The Whispers' "Rock Steady"; they also did writing/production work for Paula Abdul, Bobby Brown, The Boys, The Jacksons, Midnight Star and Karyn White.	
9/23/89	**14**	41	▲ 1. Tender Lover *It's No Crime* (7)/*Whip Appeal* (6)	Solar 45288

DATE	POS	WKS	ARTIST—RECORD TITLE	LABEL & NO.
			BABYS, The	
			British rock quartet led by vocalist John Waite who formed Bad English in 1989 with Babys' members Ricky Phillips and Jonathan Caine (also a member of Journey).	
12/17/77	**34**	3	1. Broken Heart	Chrysalis 1150
3/10/79	**22**	10	2. Head First	Chrysalis 1195
			BACHARACH, Burt	
			Born on 5/12/28 in Kansas City. Conductor/arranger/composer. With lyricist Hal David wrote "Close To You," "What's New Pussycat" and most of Dionne Warwick's hits. His compositions for film won three Oscars (two for "Raindrops Keep Fallin' On My Head" and one for "Arthur's Theme"), four Grammys and one Emmy (for his 1971 TV special). Formerly married to actress Angie Dickinson. Now married to songwriter Carole Bayer Sager.	
6/26/71	**18**	12	● 1. Burt Bacharach	A&M 3501
			BACHMAN-TURNER OVERDRIVE	
			Hard-rock group formed in Vancouver, Canada in 1972. Brothers Randy (vocals, guitar), Tim (guitar) and Robbie Bachman (drums) with C. Fred Turner (vocals, bass). Originally known as Brave Belt. Randy had been in The Guess Who and recorded solo. Tim left in 1973, replaced by Blair Thornton. Randy left in 1977. Randy and Tim regrouped with C.F. Turner in 1984.	
3/9/74	**4**	35	● 1. Bachman-Turner Overdrive II	Mercury 696
9/14/74	**1**(1)	25	● 2. Not Fragile	Mercury 1004
			You Ain't Seen Nothing Yet (1)	
6/7/75	**5**	9	● 3. Four Wheel Drive	Mercury 1027
1/31/76	**23**	7	● 4. Head On	Mercury 1067
9/11/76	**19**	6	● 5. Best Of B.T.O. (So Far) [G]	Mercury 1101
			BAD COMPANY	
			British band: Paul Rodgers (vocals), Mick Ralphs (guitar), Simon Kirke (drums) and Boz Burrell (bass). Rodgers and Kirke from Free; Ralphs from Mott The Hoople; and Burrell from King Crimson. Disbanded in 1982. Rodgers was a member of the supergroup The Firm. Rodgers and Burrell reunited group with new vocalist Brian Howe in 1988.	
8/3/74	**1**(1)	15	● 1. Bad Company	Swan Song 8410
			Can't Get Enough (5)	
4/26/75	**3**	11	● 2. Straight Shooter	Swan Song 8413
			Feel Like Makin' Love (10)	
2/21/76	**5**	15	▲ 3. Run With The Pack	Swan Song 8415
4/2/77	**15**	8	● 4. Burnin' Sky	Swan Song 8500
3/31/79	**3**	24	▲ 5. Desolation Angels	Swan Song 8506
9/18/82	**26**	6	6. Rough Diamonds	Swan Song 90001
			BAD ENGLISH	
			Rock supergroup: John Waite (vocals), Ricky Phillips (bass), Jonathan Cain (keyboards), Neal Schon (guitar) and Deen Castronovo (drums). Waite, Phillips and Cain were members of The Babys. Cain and Schon were members of Journey.	
10/21/89	**21**	22	▲ 1. Bad English	Epic 45083
			When I See You Smile (1)/*Price Of Love* (5)	
			BADFINGER	
			British quartet originally known as The Iveys. Leader Pete Ham (b: 4/27/47) committed suicide on 4/23/75. Keyboardist Tom Evans left in 1977 and committed suicide in 1983. Yes keyboardist Tony Kaye was a member from 1978-82.	
12/5/70	**28**	5	1. No Dice	Apple 3367
			No Matter What (8)	

DATE	POS	WKS	ARTIST—RECORD TITLE	LABEL & NO.
2/19/72	**31**	3	2. Straight Up produced by Todd Rundgren and George Harrison *Day After Day* (4)	Apple 3387
			BAEZ, Joan	
			Folk song stylist born in New York City on 1/9/41. Became a political activist while attending Boston University in the late 50s.	
12/18/61	**13**	70	● 1. Joan Baez, Vol. 2	Vanguard 2097
4/14/62	**15**	45	● 2. Joan Baez *Joan's first album, recorded in 1960*	Vanguard 2077
11/3/62	**10**	70	● 3. Joan Baez In Concert [L]	Vanguard 2122
12/14/63	**7**	23	4. Joan Baez In Concert, Part 2 [L]	Vanguard 2123
12/5/64	**12**	28	5. Joan Baez/5	Vanguard 79160
11/13/65	**10**	9	6. Farewell, Angelina	Vanguard 79200
10/14/67	**38**	2	7. Joan	Vanguard 79240
2/15/69	**30**	5	● 8. Any Day Now *songs of Bob Dylan*	Vanguard 79306 [2]
7/26/69	**36**	2	9. David's Album *dedicated to her imprisoned husband, David Harris*	Vanguard 79308
10/2/71	**11**	10	● 10. Blessed Are *The Night They Drove Old Dixie Down* (3)	Vanguard 6570 [2]
6/14/75	**11**	17	● 11. Diamonds & Rust	A&M 4527
3/6/76	**34**	3	12. From Every Stage [L]	A&M 3704 [2]
			BAILEY, Philip	
			Born on 5/8/51 in Denver. Percussionist/co-lead vocalist with Earth, Wind & Fire since 1971.	
1/19/85	**22**	11	1. Chinese Wall *Easy Lover* (2) with Phil Collins	Columbia 39542
			BAKER, Anita	
			Soul singer born in Memphis on 12/20/57 and raised in Detroit. Female lead singer of Chapter 8 (1976-84).	
9/13/86	**11**	72	▲ 1. Rapture *Sweet Love* (8)	Elektra 60444
11/5/88	**1(4)**	28	▲ 2. Giving You The Best That I Got *Giving You The Best That I Got* (3)	Elektra 60827
			BAKER, Ginger	
			Born Peter Baker on 8/19/39 in Lewisham, England. Drummer for Cream and Blind Faith. His group featured Steve Winwood and Denny Laine (member of Moody Blues and Wings).	
6/6/70	**33**	3	1. Ginger Baker's Air Force [L] *recorded live at London's Royal Albert Hall*	Atco 703 [2]
			BALIN, Marty	
			Born on 1/30/43 in Cincinnati. Co-founder of Jefferson Airplane/Jefferson Starship/KBC.	
8/15/81	**35**	3	1. Balin *Hearts* (8)	EMI America 17054
			BALL, Kenny	
			Born on 5/22/30 in Ilford, England. Leader of English Dixieland jazz band formed in 1958. **KENNY BALL AND HIS JAZZMEN:**	
4/14/62	**13**	15	1. Midnight In Moscow [I] *Midnight In Moscow* (2)	Kapp 1276

DATE	POS	WKS	ARTIST—RECORD TITLE	LABEL & NO.
			BANANARAMA	
			Female trio from London: Sarah Dallin, Keren Woodward and Siobhan Fahey. Group name is combination of the children's show "The Banana Splits" with the Roxy Music song "Pyjamarama." Fahey married Dave Stewart (Eurythmics) on 8/1/87; left group in early 1988, replaced by Jacqui O'Sullivan.	
9/15/84	30	7	1. Bananarama	London 820036
			reissued (#820165) October, 1984 with new song "Wild Life"	
			Cruel Summer (9)	
8/23/86	15	11	● 2. True Confessions	London 828013
			Venus (1)	
			BAND, The	
			Formed in Woodstock, New York in 1967: Robbie Robertson (guitar), Levon Helm (drums), Rick Danko (bass), Richard Manuel and Garth Hudson (keyboards). All from Canada (except Helm from Arkansas) and all were with Ronnie Hawkins' Hawks. Recorded extensively with Bob Dylan. Disbanded on Thanksgiving Day in 1976. Manuel committed suicide on 3/4/86 (age 42). Also see Bob Dylan.	
10/19/68	30	7	1. Music From Big Pink	Capitol 2955
			Big Pink: The Band's communal home in Woodstock	
10/18/69	9	24	● 2. The Band	Capitol 132
9/5/70	5	14	● 3. Stage Fright	Capitol 425
10/16/71	21	5	4. Cahoots	Capitol 651
9/23/72	6	14	● 5. Rock Of Ages [L]	Capitol 11045 [2]
12/15/73	28	6	6. Moondog Matinee	Capitol 11214
1/3/76	26	5	7. Northern Lights-Southern Cross	Capitol 11440
5/20/78	16	8	8. The Last Waltz [S-L]	Warner 3146 [3]
			farewell concert at the San Francisco Winterland with guests Bob Dylan, Eric Clapton, Neil Diamond, Ringo Starr & others	
			BANGLES	
			Female rock quartet formed in Los Angeles in January, 1981. Consists of sisters Vicki (lead guitar) & Debbi Peterson (drums), Michael Steele (bass) and Susanna Hoffs (guitar). Originally named The Bangs. Steele was previously in The Runaways. Hoffs starred in the 1987 film *The Allnighter*. Disbanded in October, 1989.	
3/8/86	2(2)	46	▲ 1. Different Light	Columbia 40039
			Manic Monday (2)/*Walk Like An Egyptian* (1)	
12/24/88	15	24	▲ 2. Everything	Columbia 44056
			In Your Room (5)/*Eternal Flame* (1)	
			BAR-KAYS	
			R&B vocal/instrumental combo: Jimmy King (guitar), Ronnie Caldwell (organ), James Alexander (bass), Carl Cunningham (drums), Phalon Jones (saxophone) and Ben Cauley (trumpet). Formed by Al Jackson, drummer with Booker T & The MG's. The plane crash that killed Otis Redding (12/10/67) also claimed the lives of all the Bar-Kays except Alexander (not on the plane) & Cauley (survived the crash). Alexander re-formed the band. Appeared in the film *Wattstax*; much session work at Stax. Alexander's son Phalon began solo career in 1990.	
12/15/79	35	4	● 1. Injoy	Mercury 3781
			BASIA	
			Britain-based, female pop-jazz singer/composer Basia Trzetrzelewska (pronounced: Basha Tshetshelevska). Raised in Jaworzno, Poland. Former vocalist of the group Matt Bianco.	
11/12/88	36	3	▲ 1. Time And Tide	Epic 40767
3/10/90	20	15	● 2. London Warsaw New York	Epic 45472

DATE	POS	WKS	ARTIST—RECORD TITLE	LABEL & NO.
			BASIE, Count	
			Born William Basie on 8/21/04 in Red Bank, New Jersey; died on 4/26/84. Jazz pianist/organist/band leader. Learned music and piano from mother, organ from Fats Waller. First recorded with own band in 1937 for Decca. Appeared in many films and toured into the 70s.	
2/9/63	**5**	22	1. Sinatra-Basie **FRANK SINATRA/COUNT BASIE**	Reprise 1008
7/20/63	**19**	4	2. This Time By Basie! Hits of the 50's And 60's [I]	Reprise 6070
9/12/64	**13**	15	3. It Might As Well Be Swing **FRANK SINATRA/COUNT BASIE**	Reprise 1012
			BASIL, Toni	
			Los Angeles vocalist/dancer/choreographer/actress/video director born in 1950. Worked on the TV shows "Shindig" and "Hullabaloo." Choreographed the film *American Grafitti*. Appeared in the film *Easy Rider*.	
11/27/82	**22**	9	● 1. Word Of Mouth *Mickey* (1)	Chrysalis 1410
			BAXTER, Les	
			Born 3/14/22 in Mexia, Texas. Orchestra leader/arranger. Began as a conductor on radio shows in the 30s. Member of Mel Torme's vocal group, the Mel-Tones. Musical arranger for Capitol Records (Nat King Cole, Margaret Whiting and others), in the 50s. Composed over 100 film scores.	
1/28/56	**6**	2	1. Tamboo! [I] **LES BAXTER/HIS CHORUS AND ORCHESTRA**	Capitol 655
3/16/57	**21**	2	2. Skins! [I]	Capitol 774
			BAY CITY ROLLERS	
			Formed in 1967 in Edinburgh, Scotland as the Saxons. Original members: brothers Alan & Derek Longmuir, Les McKeoun (lead singer), Eric Faulkner and Stuart "Woody" Wood.	
12/13/75	**20**	9	● 1. Bay City Rollers *Saturday Night* (1)	Arista 4049
7/24/76	**31**	4	● 2. Rock N' Roll Love Letter *Money Honey* (9)	Arista 4071
10/9/76	**26**	7	● 3. Dedication	Arista 4093
7/30/77	**23**	7	● 4. It's A Game *You Made Me Believe In Magic* (10)	Arista 7004
			BEACH BOYS, The	
			Group formed in Hawthorne, California in 1961. Consisted of brothers Brian (keyboards, bass), Carl (guitar), and Dennis Wilson (drums); their cousin Mike Love (lead vocals, saxophone), and Al Jardine (guitar). Known in high school as Kenny & The Cadets, Carl & The Passions, then The Pendletones. First recorded for X/Candix in 1961. Jardine replaced by David Marks from March, 1962 to March, 1963. Brian quit touring with group in December of 1964, replaced briefly by Glen Campbell until Bruce Johnston (of Bruce & Terry) joined permanently in April, 1965. Daryl Dragon (Captain & Tennille) was a keyboardist in their stage band. Brian continued to write for and produce group, returned to stage in 1983. Dennis Wilson drowned on 12/28/83 (age 39). Lineup of Carl, Brian, Mike, Alan and Bruce continues to perform into the 1990s. Group was inducted into the Rock and Roll Hall of Fame in 1988.	
12/8/62	**32**	7	1. Surfin' Safari	Capitol 1808
5/18/63	**2(2)**	30	● 2. Surfin' U.S.A. *Surfin' U.S.A.* (3)	Capitol 1890
10/26/63	**7**	18	● 3. Surfer Girl *Surfer Girl* (7)	Capitol 1981
12/7/63	**4**	20	● 4. Little Deuce Coupe *Be True To Your School* (6)	Capitol 1998

DATE	POS	WKS	ARTIST—RECORD TITLE		LABEL & NO.
5/2/64	**13**	22	● 5. Shut Down, Volume 2 *Fun, Fun, Fun* (5) Volume 1 listed in Miscellaneous section: Cars		Capitol 2027
8/8/64	**4**	38	● 6. All Summer Long *I Get Around* (1)		Capitol 2110
11/21/64	**1**(4)	40	● 7. Beach Boys Concert	[L]	Capitol 2198
4/17/65	**4**	29	● 8. The Beach Boys Today! *When I Grow Up* (9)/*Dance, Dance, Dance* (8)		Capitol 2269
8/7/65	**2**(1)	17	● 9. Summer Days (And Summer Nights!!) *Help Me Rhonda* (1)/*California Girls* (3)		Capitol 2354
12/4/65	**6**	14	10. Beach Boys' Party! *Barbara Ann* (2)		Capitol 2398
6/11/66	**10**	21	11. Pet Sounds *Sloop John B* (3)/*Wouldn't It Be Nice* (8)		Capitol 2458
8/13/66	**8**	18	● 12. Best Of The Beach Boys	[G]	Capitol 2545
1/27/68	**24**	9	13. Wild Honey		Capitol 2859
10/2/71	**29**	7	14. Surf's Up		Brother 6453
3/10/73	**36**	3	15. Holland		Brother 2118
1/5/74	**25**	5	● 16. The Beach Boys In Concert	[L]	Brother 6484 [2]
8/3/74	**1**(1)	19	● 17. Endless Summer	[K]	Capitol 11307 [2]
5/17/75	**8**	13	● 18. Spirit Of America	[K]	Capitol 11384 [2]
8/9/75	**25**	5	19. Good Vibrations-Best Of The Beach Boys	[G]	Brother 2223
7/24/76	**8**	12	● 20. 15 Big Ones 15: age of band and number of tracks *Rock And Roll Music* (5)		Brother 2251
			BEASTIE BOYS		
			New York white rap trio formed in 1981, consisting of King Ad-Rock (Adam Horovitz - son of playwright Israel Horovitz), MCA (Adam Yauch) and Mike D (Michael Diamond). Horovitz starred in the film *Lost Angels* in 1988.		
12/20/86	**1**(7)	37	▲ 1. Licensed To Ill *(You Gotta) Fight For Your Right (To Party!)* (7)		Def Jam 40238
8/19/89	**14**	8	● 2. Paul's Boutique		Capitol 91743
			BEATLES, The		
			The world's #1 rock group was formed in Liverpool, England in the late 1950s. Known in early forms as The Quarrymen, Johnny & the Moondogs, The Rainbows, and the Silver Beatles. Named The Beatles in 1960. Originally consisted of John Lennon, Paul McCartney, George Harrison (guitars), Stu Sutcliffe (bass) and Pete Best (drums). Sutcliffe left in April, 1961 (died on 4/10/62); McCartney moved to bass. Best replaced by Ringo Starr in August, 1962. Group managed by Brian Epstein (died on 8/27/67) and produced by George Martin. First U.S. tour in February, 1964. Won the 1964 Best New Artist Grammy Award. Group starred in films *A Hard Day's Night* (1964), *Help* (1965) and *Magical Mystery Tour* (1967); voices of *Yellow Submarine* cartoon (1968). Own Apple label in 1968. Disbanded on 4/17/70. Inducted into the Rock and Roll Hall of Fame in 1988.		
2/8/64	**1**(11)	27	● 1. Meet The Beatles! *I Want To Hold Your Hand* (1)		Capitol 2047
2/15/64	**2**(9)	26	2. Introducing...The Beatles 1st U.S. album; released July, 1963 *Please Please Me* (3)/*Twist And Shout* (2)/ *Do You Want To Know A Secret* (2)/*Love Me Do** (1)/ *P.S. I Love You** (10) *only on first pressing		Vee-Jay 1062
4/25/64	**1**(5)	26	● 3. The Beatles' Second Album *She Loves You* (1)		Capitol 2080
6/20/64	**20**	9	4. The American Tour With Ed Rudy interviews with The Beatles	[T]	RadioPulsebeat 2

DATE	POS	WKS	ARTIST—RECORD TITLE	LABEL & NO.
7/18/64	**1**(14)	40	5. A Hard Day's Night [S] features eight vocals and four instrumentals *Can't Buy Me Love* (1)/*A Hard Day's Night* (1)	United Art. 6366
8/15/64	**2**(9)	28	● 6. Something New includes five tunes from *A Hard Day's Night* album	Capitol 2108
12/19/64	**7**	9	● 7. The Beatles' Story [T] narrative featuring bits of their hits	Capitol 2222 [2]
1/9/65	**1**(9)	38	● 8. Beatles '65 *I Feel Fine* (1)/*She's A Woman* (4)	Capitol 2228
7/10/65	**1**(6)	21	● 9. Beatles VI *Eight Days A Week* (1)	Capitol 2358
9/11/65	**1**(9)	33	● 10. Help! [S] features seven vocals and five instrumentals *Ticket To Ride* (1)/*Help!* (1)	Capitol 2386
1/8/66	**1**(6)	39	● 11. Rubber Soul	Capitol 2442
7/16/66	**1**(5)	15	● 12. "Yesterday"...And Today [G] originally featured the "butcher cover" *Yesterday* (1)/*We Can Work It Out* (1)/*Day Tripper* (5)/ *Nowhere Man* (3)	Capitol 2553
9/10/66	**1**(6)	24	● 13. Revolver *Yellow Submarine* (2)	Capitol 2576
6/24/67	**1**(15)	63	● 14. Sgt. Pepper's Lonely Hearts Club Band 1967 Grammy winner: Album of the Year; also see soundtrack of the same name	Capitol 2653
12/30/67	**1**(8)	30	● 15. Magical Mystery Tour [S-G] six tunes from the film and five singles hits *Penny Lane* (1)/*Strawberry Fields Forever* (8)/ *All You Need Is Love* (1)/*Hello Goodbye* (1)	Capitol 2835
12/14/68	**1**(9)	25	● 16. The Beatles [White Album]	Apple 101 [2]
2/15/69	**2**(2)	12	● 17. Yellow Submarine [S] side 1: The Beatles; side 2: instrumentals by George Martin	Apple 153
10/25/69	**1**(11)	32	● 18. Abbey Road *Come Together* (1)/*Something* (3)	Apple 383
3/21/70	**2**(4)	17	● 19. Hey Jude [G] *Paperback Writer* (1)/*Lady Madonna* (4)/*Hey Jude* (1)/ *The Ballad Of John And Yoko* (8)	Apple 385
6/6/70	**1**(4)	20	● 20. Let It Be [S] film features The Beatles during recording sessions *Get Back* (1)/*Let It Be* (1)/*The Long And Winding Road* (1)	Apple 34001
4/21/73	**3**	18	● 21. The Beatles/1962-1966 [G]	Apple 3403 [2]
4/21/73	**1**(1)	21	● 22. The Beatles/1967-1970 [G]	Apple 3404 [2]
6/26/76	**2**(2)	13	▲ 23. Rock 'N' Roll Music [K] *Got To Get You Into My Life* (7)	Capitol 11537 [2]
5/21/77	**2**(2)	8	▲ 24. The Beatles At The Hollywood Bowl [E-L] concert recordings of 8/23/64 and 8/30/65	Capitol 11638
11/19/77	**24**	6	● 25. Love Songs [K]	Capitol 11711 [2]
4/19/80	**21**	9	26. Rarities [K]	Capitol 12060
4/10/82	**19**	8	● 27. Reel Music [K] tunes from The Beatles' five films	Capitol 12199
			BEAU BRUMMELS, The	
			Formed in 1964 in San Francisco. Led by Sal Valentino (b: 9/8/42, San Francisco; vocals) and Ron Elliott (b: 10/21/43, Haddsburg, California; guitar).	
6/26/65	**24**	7	1. Introducing The Beau Brummels *Just A Little* (8)	Autumn 103

DATE	POS	WKS	ARTIST—RECORD TITLE		LABEL & NO.
			BECK, Jeff		
			Veteran guitarist (b: 6/24/44 in Surrey, England). With the Yardbirds, 1964-66. Rod Stewart was a member of the Jeff Beck Group from 1967-69. Member of supergroup The Honeydrippers.		
9/14/68	**15**	14	1. Truth		Epic 26413
8/2/69	**15**	8	2. Beck-Ola *		Epic 26478
			above two with Rod Stewart (vocals)		
6/3/72	**19**	9	● 3. Jeff Beck Group *		Epic 31331
			*JEFF BECK GROUP		
4/28/73	**12**	11	4. Jeff Beck, Tim Bogert, Carmine Appice		Epic 32140
			BECK, BOGERT, APPICE		
			Bogert (bass) and Appice (drums) were both formerly with Cactus and Vanilla Fudge		
4/26/75	**4**	11	▲ 5. Blow By Blow	[I]	Epic 33409
7/17/76	**16**	9	▲ 6. Wired	[I]	Epic 33849
4/9/77	**23**	6	7. Jeff Beck with The Jan Hammer Group Live	[I-L]	Epic 34433
7/19/80	**21**	8	8. There And Back	[I]	Epic 35684
8/17/85	**39**	2	9. Flash		Epic 39483
			BEE GEES		
			Trio of brothers from Manchester, England: Barry (b: 9/1/47) and twins Robin and Maurice Gibb (b: 12/22/49). First performed December, 1955. To Australia in 1958, performed as the Gibbs, later as BG's, finally the Bee Gees. First recorded for Leedon/Festival in 1963. Returned to England in February, 1967, with guitarist Vince Melouney and drummer Colin Peterson. Toured Europe and the U.S. in 1968. Melouney left in December, 1968; Robin left for solo career in 1969. When Peterson left in August of 1969, Barry and Maurice went solo. After eight months, brothers reunited. Composed soundtracks of *Saturday Night Fever* and *Staying Alive*; in film *Sgt. Pepper's Lonely Hearts Club Band*. Youngest brother Andy Gibb was a successful solo singer.		
9/16/67	**7**	18	1. Bee Gees' 1st		Atco 223
2/24/68	**12**	7	2. Horizontal		Atco 233
9/28/68	**17**	7	3. Idea		Atco 253
			I've Gotta Get A Message To You (8)/I Started A Joke (6)		
3/8/69	**20**	10	4. Odessa		Atco 702 [2]
8/2/69	**9**	16	● 5. Best Of Bee Gees	[G]	Atco 292
2/6/71	**32**	5	6. 2 Years On		Atco 353
			Lonely Days (3)		
10/2/71	**34**	6	7. Trafalgar		Atco 7003
			How Can You Mend A Broken Heart (1)		
12/16/72	**35**	3	8. To Whom It May Concern		Atco 7012
8/16/75	**14**	22	● 9. Main Course		RSO 4807
			Jive Talkin (1)/Nights On Broadway (7)		
10/2/76	**8**	27	▲ 10. Children Of The World		RSO 3003
			You Should Be Dancing (1)/Love So Right (3)		
6/4/77	**8**	31	▲ 11. Here At Last...Bee Gees...Live	[L]	RSO 3901 [2]
12/10/77	**1**(24)	54	▲ 12. Saturday Night Fever	[S]	RSO 4001 [2]
			six cuts by the Bee Gees/others by various artists; 1978 Grammy winner: Album of the Year; the #1 selling soundtrack album of all-time (25 million)		
			How Deep Is Your Love (1)/Stayin' Alive (1)/Night Fever (1)		
2/17/79	**1**(6)	26	▲ 13. Spirits Having Flown		RSO 3041
			Too Much Heaven (1)/Tragedy (1)/Love You Inside Out (1)		
11/17/79	**1**(1)	17	▲ 14. Bee Gees Greatest	[G]	RSO 4200 [2]
			RSO hits only		

DATE	POS	WKS	ARTIST—RECORD TITLE	LABEL & NO.
7/30/83	**6**	14	▲ 15. Staying Alive [S] side 1: Bee Gees; side 2: various artists	RSO 813269
			BELAFONTE, Harry	
			Born Harold George Belafonte, Jr. on 3/1/27 in Harlem. Actor in American Negro Theater, Drama Workshop, mid-40s. Started career as a "straight pop" singer. Recorded for Jubilee Records in 1949, shortly afterward began specializing in folk music. Rode the crest of the calypso craze to worldwide stardom. Starred in eight films from 1953-74. Replaced Danny Kaye in 1987 as UNICEF goodwill ambassador.	
1/28/56	**3**	6	1. "Mark Twain" And Other Folk Favorites	RCA 1022
2/25/56	**1**(6)	62	● 2. Belafonte	RCA 1150
6/16/56	**1**(31)	72	● 3. Calypso *Banana Boat* (5)	RCA 1248
3/30/57	**2**(2)	20	● 4. An Evening With Belafonte	RCA 1402
9/16/57	**3**	12	5. Belafonte Sings Of The Caribbean	RCA 1505
10/20/58	**16**	15	6. Belafonte Sings The Blues	RCA 1972
5/25/59	**18**	10	7. Love Is A Gentle Thing	RCA 1927
6/22/59	**13**	19	8. Porgy & Bess **LENA HORNE/HARRY BELAFONTE**	RCA 1507
11/16/59	**3**	86	● 9. Belafonte At Carnegie Hall [L]	RCA 6006 [2]
3/21/60	**34**	1	10. My Lord What A Mornin' spirituals	RCA 2022
12/26/60	**3**	10	● 11. Belafonte Returns To Carnegie Hall [L] with Odetta-Miriam Makeba-Chad Mitchell Trio	RCA 6007 [2]
9/11/61	**3**	40	● 12. Jump Up Calypso	RCA 2388
6/2/62	**8**	18	13. The Midnight Special	RCA 2449
10/27/62	**25**	13	14. The Many Moods Of Belafonte	RCA 2574
7/13/63	**30**	5	15. Streets I Have Walked	RCA 2695
4/25/64	**17**	10	16. Belafonte At The Greek Theatre [L]	RCA 6009 [2]
			BELL & JAMES	
			R&B duo of Leroy Bell and Casey James. Began as songwriting team for Bell's uncle, producer Thom Bell.	
4/7/79	**31**	4	1. Bell & James	A&M 4728
			BELL BIV DeVOE	
			Trio of New Edition members: Ricky Bell, Michael Bivins and Ronnie DeVoe.	
4/14/90	**5**	27 +	▲ 1. Poison *Poison* (3)	MCA 6387
			BENATAR, Pat	
			Born Patricia Andrzejewski in Lindenhurst, Long Island, New York in 1952. Married her producer/guitarist Neil Geraldo in 1982. In 1989, acted in the ABC afterschool TV special "Torn Between Two Fathers."	
1/26/80	**12**	15	▲ 1. In The Heat Of The Night	Chrysalis 1236
8/30/80	**2**(5)	38	▲ 2. Crimes Of Passion *Hit Me With Your Best Shot* (9)	Chrysalis 1275
7/25/81	**1**(1)	30	▲ 3. Precious Time	Chrysalis 1346
11/27/82	**4**	27	▲ 4. Get Nervous	Chrysalis 1396
10/22/83	**13**	16	▲ 5. Live From Earth [L] two of the 10 songs are new studio tracks *Love Is A Battlefield* (5)	Chrysalis 41444
12/1/84	**14**	15	▲ 6. Tropico *We Belong* (5)	Chrysalis 41471

DATE	POS	WKS	ARTIST—RECORD TITLE	LABEL & NO.
12/21/85	**26**	9	7. Seven The Hard Way ''Invincible (Theme From *Legend Of Billie Jean*)'' (10)	Chrysalis 41507
8/6/88	**28**	10	● 8. Wide Awake In Dreamland	Chrysalis 41628

BENNETT, Tony

Born Anthony Dominick Benedetto on 8/13/25 in Queens, New York. Jazz/ballad vocalist. Worked local clubs while in high school, sang in U.S. Army bands. Audition record of ''Boulevard Of Broken Dreams'' earned a Columbia contract in 1950.

DATE	POS	WKS	ARTIST—RECORD TITLE	LABEL & NO.
2/23/57	**14**	9	1. Tony	Columbia 938
8/25/62	**5**	83	● 2. I Left My Heart In San Francisco	Columbia 8669
12/8/62	**37**	2	3. Tony Bennett At Carnegie Hall [L]	Columbia 23 [2]
4/6/63	**5**	23	4. I Wanna Be Around	Columbia 8800
9/21/63	**24**	8	5. This Is All I Ask	Columbia 8856
3/21/64	**20**	8	6. The Many Moods Of Tony	Columbia 8941
10/2/65	**20**	18	● 7. Tony's Greatest Hits, Volume III [G]	Columbia 9173
5/14/66	**18**	12	8. The Movie Song Album	Columbia 9272

BENSON, George

Born on 3/22/43 in Pittsburgh. R&B-jazz guitarist. Played guitar from age eight. Played in Brother Jack McDuff's trio in 1963. House musician at CTI Records to early 70s. Influenced heavily by Wes Montgomery.

DATE	POS	WKS	ARTIST—RECORD TITLE	LABEL & NO.
5/22/76	**1**(2)	22	▲ 1. Breezin' *This Masquerade* (10)	Warner 2919
2/19/77	**9**	17	▲ 2. In Flight	Warner 2983
2/18/78	**5**	19	▲ 3. Weekend In L.A. [L] *On Broadway* (7)	Warner 3139 [2]
3/24/79	**7**	13	● 4. Livin' Inside Your Love	Warner 3277 [2]
8/9/80	**3**	20	▲ 5. Give Me The Night *Give Me The Night* (4)	Warner 3453
12/12/81	**14**	14	● 6. The George Benson Collection [G] *Turn Your Love Around* (5)	Warner 3577 [2]
7/2/83	**27**	11	● 7. In Your Eyes	Warner 23744

BENTON, Brook

Born Benjamin Franklin Peay on 9/19/31 in Camden, South Carolina. R&B singer/ songwriter. In the Camden Jubilee Singers. To New York in 1948, joined Bill Langford's Langfordaires. With Jerusalem Stars in 1951. First recorded under own name for Okeh in 1953. Wrote ''Looking Back,'' ''A Lover's Question,'' ''The Stroll,'' ''It's Just A Matter Of Time,'' ''Endlessly,'' ''Thank You Baby,'' and many other hits. Died on 4/9/88 (age 56) of complications from spinal meningitis.

DATE	POS	WKS	ARTIST—RECORD TITLE	LABEL & NO.
12/29/62	**40**	1	1. Singing The Blues - Lie To Me	Mercury 60740
3/28/70	**27**	4	2. Brook Benton Today *Rainy Night In Georgia* (4)	Cotillion 9018

BERGEN, Polly

Born on 7/14/31 in Knoxville, Tennessee. Real name: Nellie Burgin. Singer/actress in movies and TV.

DATE	POS	WKS	ARTIST—RECORD TITLE	LABEL & NO.
6/10/57	**10**	5	1. Bergen Sings Morgan Polly portrayed Helen Morgan in a TV film	Columbia 994
11/4/57	**20**	1	2. The Party's Over	Columbia 1031

DATE	POS	WKS	ARTIST—RECORD TITLE	LABEL & NO.
			BERLIN	
			Los Angeles electro-pop group. Went from a six-piece band to a trio in 1985 featuring Terri Nunn (vocals), John Crawford (bass) and Rob Brill (drums). Nunn left in 1987.	
3/19/83	30	11	● 1. Pleasure Victim	Geffen 2036
5/26/84	28	4	● 2. Love Life	Geffen 4025
			BERMAN, Shelley	
			Born on 2/3/26 in Chicago. Popular nightclub comedian/actor. Made TV debut on the "Jack Paar Show." In films *The Best Man*, *The Wheeler Dealer* and *Divorce American Style*.	
4/27/59	2(5)	46	1. Inside Shelley Berman [C]	Verve 15003
11/30/59	6	39	2. Outside Shelley Berman [C]	Verve 15007
7/25/60	4	24	3. The Edge Of Shelley Berman [C]	Verve 15013
12/25/61	25	3	4. A Personal Appearance [C]	Verve 15027
			BERNSTEIN, Leonard	
			Conductor/pianist/composer. Born on 8/25/18 in Lawrence, Massachusetts; died on 10/14/90 of emphysema-related heart attack. First classical international superstar from U.S. Conductor of numerous major orchestras worldwide. Composed music for *West Side Story*, the film *On The Waterfront* and others.	
12/12/60	13	7	1. Bernstein Plays Brubeck Plays Bernstein [I] side 1: New York Philharmonic with the Dave Brubeck Quartet conducted by Leonard Bernstein; side 2: Dave Brubeck Quartet	Columbia 8257
			BERRY, Chuck	
			Born Charles Edward Anderson Berry on 10/18/26 in San Jose, California. Grew up in St. Louis. Muddy Waters introduced Chuck to Leonard Chess (Chess Records) in Chicago. First recording, "Maybellene," was an instant success. Appeared in the film *Rock, Rock, Rock* in 1956, and several others. Inducted into the Rock and Roll Hall of Fame in 1986. Film documentary/concert tribute to Chuck, "Hail! Hail! Rock 'N' Roll," released in 1987. Regarded by many as rock's most influential artist.	
10/5/63	29	2	1. Chuck Berry On Stage [L] live audience dubbed in	Chess 1480
8/22/64	34	3	2. Chuck Berry's Greatest Hits [G] *Maybellene* (5)/*School Day* (3)/*Rock & Roll Music* (8)/ *Sweet Little Sixteen* (2)/*Johnny B. Goode* (8)	Chess 1485
8/5/72	8	20	● 3. The London Chuck Berry Sessions [L] side 1: studio; side 2: live *My Ding-A-Ling* (1)	Chess 60020
			BETTS, Dickey	
			Born on 12/12/43 near Sarasota, Florida. Lead guitarist of The Allman Brothers Band. Wrote "Ramblin' Man" and "Jessica." In the late 70s, formed Great Southern.	
9/28/74	19	7	1. Highway Call **RICHARD BETTS** side 1: vocals; side 2: instrumentals	Capricorn 0123
5/21/77	31	2	2. Dickey Betts & Great Southern	Arista 4123
			B-52'S, The	
			New-wave band from Athens, Georgia formed in 1977. Guitarist Keith Strickland with vocalists Kate Pierson, Fred Schneider, Cindy Wilson and her brother Ricky Wilson (drums; died of AIDS on 10/12/85). B-52 is a slang word for the bouffant hairstyle worn by Kate and Cindy.	
9/27/80	18	9	● 1. Wild Planet	Warner 3471
3/6/82	35	4	2. Mesopotamia [M]	Warner 3641

DATE	POS	WKS	ARTIST—RECORD TITLE	LABEL & NO.
6/4/83	**29**	6	3. Whammy!	Warner 23819
9/9/89	**4**	41	4. Cosmic Thing *Love Shack* (3)/*Roam* (3)	Reprise 25854
			BIG BROTHER AND THE HOLDING COMPANY	
			Formed in San Francisco in 1965. Janis Joplin joined as lead singer in 1966. Other members: Peter Albin (bass), James Gurley (guitar), Sam Andrew (guitar) and David Getz (drums). Sensation at the Monterey Pop Festival in 1967. Disbanded in 1972.	
9/14/68	**1**(8)	29	● 1. Cheap Thrills	Columbia 9700
			BIG COUNTRY	
			Rock quartet formed in Dunfermline, Scotland: Stuart Adamson (vocals, guitar), Bruce Watson (guitar), Tony Butler (bass) and Mark Brzezicki (drums).	
10/8/83	**18**	18	● 1. The Crossing	Mercury 812870
			BILK, Mr. Acker	
			Clarinetist/composer, born Bernard Stanley Bilk on 1/28/29 in Somerset, England.	
5/19/62	**3**	24	● 1. Stranger On The Shore [I] *Stranger On The Shore* (1)	Atco 129
			BISHOP, Elvin	
			Born on 10/21/42 in Tulsa, Oklahoma. Lead guitarist with The Paul Butterfield Blues Band (1965-68).	
4/24/76	**18**	8	1. Struttin' My Stuff *Fooled Around And Fell In Love* (3)	Capricorn 0165
10/8/77	**38**	2	2. Live! Raisin' Hell [L]	Capricorn 0185 [2]
			BISHOP, Stephen	
			Pop-rock singer/songwriter from San Diego. Wrote movie theme for *The China Syndrome*. Cameo role as the "Charming Guy With Guitar" in *National Lampoon's Animal House*.	
10/8/77	**34**	3	1. Careless	ABC 954
11/4/78	**35**	4	● 2. Bish	ABC 1082
			BLACK, Bill	
			Bill was born on 9/17/26 in Memphis; died of a brain tumor on 10/21/65. Bass guitarist. Session work in Memphis; backed Elvis Presley (with Scotty Moore, guitar; D.J. Fontana, drums) on most of his early records. Formed own band in 1959. Labeled as "The Untouchable Sound." **BILL BLACK'S COMBO:**	
11/14/60	**23**	6	1. Solid And Raunchy [I]	Hi 12003
3/17/62	**35**	3	2. Let's Twist Her [I]	Hi 12006
			BLACK, Clint	
			Houston native. Former construction worker. Signed to RCA in December 1987.	
5/19/90	**31**	8	▲ 1. Killin' Time	RCA 9668
			BLACK, Stanley	
			Born on 6/14/13 in London. Pianist/arranger/composer. Conducted BBC Dance Orchestra for nine years, beginning in 1944. Wrote many film scores. **STANLEY BLACK AND HIS ORCHESTRA:**	
3/10/62	**30**	2	1. Exotic Percussion [I]	London P. 4 44004
10/6/62	**33**	2	2. Spain [I]	London P. 4 44016

DATE	POS	WKS	ARTIST—RECORD TITLE	LABEL & NO.
			BLACKBYRDS, The	
			Soul group founded in 1973 by jazz studies professor Donald Byrd while teaching at Howard University in Washington, D.C.	
3/8/75	30	7	1. Flying Start	Fantasy 9472
			Walking In Rhythm (6)	
4/3/76	16	9	● 2. City Life	Fantasy 9490
1/29/77	34	4	● 3. Unfinished Business	Fantasy 9518
			BLACKMORE, Ritchie — see RAINBOW	
			BLACK SABBATH	
			Heavy-metal group formed as blues band, Earth, in Birmingham, England in 1968. Changed name to Black Sabbath in late 1969. Original lineup included: Tony Iommi, John "Ozzie" Osbourne, William Ward and Terry "Geezer" Butler. Vocalist Osbourne formed the Blizzard of Ozz in 1979, replaced by Ronnie James Dio (Rainbow). Ian Gillan replaced Dio in 1983. Fluctuating lineup since then. 1987 personnel included: Iommi, Eric Singer, Dave Spitz, Bob Daisley, Geoff Nicholls, Tony Martin (vocals) and Bev Bevan (formerly with Move and ELO). In 1990, reduced to a quartet of Iommi, Martin, Cozy Powell (ex-drummer of Emerson, Lake & Powell) and Neil Murray (bass).	
11/28/70	23	10	▲ 1. Black Sabbath	Warner 1871
2/20/71	12	34	▲ 2. Paranoid	Warner 1887
9/11/71	8	17	▲ 3. Master Of Reality	Warner 2562
11/4/72	13	13	▲ 4. Black Sabbath, Vol. 4	Warner 2602
2/9/74	11	11	▲ 5. Sabbath Bloody Sabbath	Warner 2695
9/13/75	28	4	6. Sabotage	Warner 2822
6/21/80	28	9	▲ 7. Heaven And Hell	Warner 3372
12/5/81	29	8	● 8. Mob Rules	Warner 3605
2/19/83	37	4	9. Live Evil [L]	Warner 23742 [2]
11/5/83	39	2	10. Born Again	Warner 23978
			BLAND, Bobby	
			Born Robert Calvin Bland on 1/27/30 in Rosemark, Tennessee. Nicknamed "Blue." Sang in gospel group The Miniatures in Memphis, late 40s. Member of the Beale Streeters which included Johnny Ace, B.B. King, Rosco Gordon, Earl Forest and Willie Nix in 1949. Driver and valet for B.B. King; appeared in the Johnny Ace Revue, early 50s. First recorded in 1952, for the Modern label. Frequent tours with B.B. King into the 80s.	
8/3/63	11	7	1. Call On Me/That's The Way Love Is	Duke 77
			BLASTERS, The	
			Los Angeles rockabilly group led by brothers Phil (lead singer, guitar) and Dave (lead guitar) Alvin. Dave was also a member of The Knitters.	
5/1/82	36	4	1. The Blasters	Slash 3680
			BLIND FAITH	
			Short-lived British supergroup: Eric Clapton, Steve Winwood, Ginger Baker and Rick Grech. Group formed and disbanded in 1969.	
8/23/69	1(2)	20	● 1. Blind Faith	Atco 304
			BLONDIE	
			New York City techno-pop sextet formed in 1975. Consisted of Debbie Harry (lead singer), Chris Stein, Frank Infante, Jimmy Destri, Gary Valentine and Clem Burke. Stein and Harry were married. Harry had been in the folk-rock group Wind In The Willows. Did solo work from 1980; appeared in several films. Disbanded in 1983.	
3/17/79	6	16	▲ 1. Parallel Lines	Chrysalis 1192
			Heart Of Glass (1)	

DATE	POS	WKS	ARTIST—RECORD TITLE	LABEL & NO.
10/27/79	**17**	19	▲ 2. Eat To The Beat	Chrysalis 1225
12/13/80	**7**	23	▲ 3. Autoamerican *The Tide Is High* (1)/*Rapture* (1)	Chrysalis 1290
11/21/81	**30**	11	● 4. The Best Of Blondie [G] *Call Me* (1)	Chrysalis 1337
6/26/82	**33**	4	5. The Hunter	Chrysalis 1384
			BLOODROCK	
			Rock group from Fort Worth, Texas; Jim Rutledge, lead vocals.	
1/23/71	**21**	8	● 1. Bloodrock 2	Capitol 491
4/17/71	**27**	8	2. Bloodrock 3	Capitol 765
			BLOODSTONE	
			Soul group from Kansas City, Missouri. Formed as the Sinceres; consisted of Charles McCormick, Willis Draffen, Charles Love, Henry Williams and Roger Durham (d: 1973).	
6/30/73	**30**	7	1. Natural High *Natural High* (10)	London 620
			BLOOD, SWEAT & TEARS	
			Pop-jazz group formed by Al Kooper in 1968. Nucleus consisted of Kooper (keyboards), Steve Katz (guitar), Bobby Colomby (drums) and Jim Fielder (bass). Kooper replaced by lead singer David Clayton-Thomas in 1969. Clayton-Thomas replaced by Jerry Fisher in 1972. Katz left in 1973. Clayton-Thomas rejoined in 1974. Colomby later worked as a television music reporter and an executive with Epic, Capitol, EMI and CBS.	
2/1/69	**1**(7)	66	▲ 1. Blood, Sweat & Tears 1969 Grammy winner: Album of the Year *You've Made Me So Very Happy* (2)/*Spinning Wheel* (2)/ *And When I Die* (2)	Columbia 9720
7/18/70	**1**(2)	19	● 2. Blood, Sweat & Tears 3	Columbia 30090
7/17/71	**10**	11	● 3. B, S & T; 4	Columbia 30590
3/25/72	**19**	6	▲ 4. Blood, Sweat & Tears Greatest Hits [G]	Columbia 31170
11/25/72	**32**	7	5. New Blood	Columbia 31780
			BLOOMFIELD, Mike	
			Born on 7/28/44 in Chicago; died on 2/15/81. Blues guitarist. With The Paul Butterfield Blues Band, and Electric Flag. Later with semi-supergroup KGB.	
10/5/68	**12**	10	● 1. Super Session **MIKE BLOOMFIELD/AL KOOPER/STEVE STILLS**	Columbia 9701
2/15/69	**18**	10	2. The Live Adventures Of Mike Bloomfield And Al Kooper [L]	Columbia 6 [2]
			BLOW MONKEYS, The	
			British quartet fronted by Dr. Robert (Robert Howard). Includes: Mick Anker, Neville Henry and Tony Kiley.	
7/19/86	**35**	5	1. Animal Magic	RCA 8065
			BLUE CHEER	
			San Francisco hard-rock group led by Dickie Peterson (vocals, bass).	
3/30/68	**11**	11	1. Vincebus Eruptum	Philips 264
			BLUE OYSTER CULT	
			New York hard-rock quintet led by Donald "Buck Dharma" Roeser (lead guitar) and Eric Bloom (lead vocal).	
4/5/75	**22**	4	● 1. On Your Feet Or On Your Knees [L]	Columbia 33371 [2]
9/25/76	**29**	9	▲ 2. Agents Of Fortune	Columbia 34164
8/16/80	**34**	3	3. Cultosaurus Erectus	Columbia 36550

DATE	POS	WKS	ARTIST—RECORD TITLE	LABEL & NO.
8/1/81	**24**	11	● 4. Fire Of Unknown Origin	Columbia 37389
6/12/82	**29**	5	5. Extraterrestrial Live [L]	Columbia 37946 [2]

BLUES BROTHERS

Jake (John Belushi; b: 1/24/49, Chicago) and Elwood Blues (Dan Aykroyd; b: 7/1/52, Ottawa, Ontario); originally created for TV's "Saturday Night Live." Belushi died of a drug overdose on 3/5/82 (age 33).

DATE	POS	WKS	ARTIST—RECORD TITLE	LABEL & NO.
1/6/79	**1**(1)	16	▲ 1. Briefcase Full Of Blues	Atlantic 19217
7/5/80	**13**	12	● 2. The Blues Brothers [S] with Aretha Franklin, James Brown and Ray Charles	Atlantic 16017

BLUES MAGOOS

Bronx, New York psychedelic rock quintet led by Peppy Castro. Originally known as the Bloos Magoos. Castro later became lead singer of Balance.

DATE	POS	WKS	ARTIST—RECORD TITLE	LABEL & NO.
2/18/67	**21**	5	1. Psychedelic Lollipop *(We Ain't Got) Nothin' Yet* (5)	Mercury 61096

BOFILL, Angela

Vocalist born in West Bronx, New York in 1954. Formed group the Puerto Rican Supremes at Hunter College High School; attended Manhattan School Of Music. Toured and recorded with Ricardo Morrero. Performed with Dizzy Gillespie and Cannonball Adderley. Featured vocalist for the Dance Theater of Harlem at age 22.

DATE	POS	WKS	ARTIST—RECORD TITLE	LABEL & NO.
12/22/79	**34**	8	1. Angel of the Night	GRP 5501
4/2/83	**40**	3	2. Too Tough	Arista 9616

BOGERT, Tim — see BECK, Jeff

BOHN, Rudi

German conductor of polkas.
RUDI BOHN AND HIS BAND:

DATE	POS	WKS	ARTIST—RECORD TITLE	LABEL & NO.
10/16/61	**38**	2	1. Percussive Oompah [I]	London P. 4 44009

BOLTON, Michael

Born Michael Bolotin from New Haven, Connecticut. Lead singer of Blackjack in the late 70s. Began recording as Michael Bolton in 1983.

DATE	POS	WKS	ARTIST—RECORD TITLE	LABEL & NO.
12/23/89	**3**	44 +	▲ 1. Soul Provider *How Am I Supposed To Live Without You* (1)/*How Can We Be Lovers* (3)/*When I'm Back On My Feet Again* (7)	Columbia 45012

BONDS, Gary U.S.

Singer/songwriter, born Gary Anderson on 6/6/39 in Jacksonville, Florida. To Norfolk, Virginia in the mid-50s. Signed to Legrand by Frank Guida. Wrote "Friend Don't Take Her," hit for Johnny Paycheck in 1972.

DATE	POS	WKS	ARTIST—RECORD TITLE	LABEL & NO.
8/21/61	**6**	11	1. Dance 'til Quarter To Three **U.S. BONDS** *New Orleans* (6)/*Quarter To Three* (1)/*School Is Out* (5)	Legrand 3001
5/16/81	**27**	7	2. Dedication	EMI America 17051

BONHAM

British hard-rock quartet led by drummer Jason Bonham - the son of Led Zeppelin's drummer, the late John Bonham. Includes vocalist Daniel MacMaster, guitarist Ian Hatton and keyboardist John Smithson.

DATE	POS	WKS	ARTIST—RECORD TITLE	LABEL & NO.
12/16/89	**38**	6	● 1. The Disregard Of Timekeeping	WTG 45009

BON JOVI

New Jersey hard-rock quintet consisting of Jon Bon Jovi (actual spelling: Bongiovi; lead vocals), Richie Sambora (guitar), Dave Bryan (keyboards), Alec John Such (bass) and Tico Torres (drums).

DATE	POS	WKS	ARTIST—RECORD TITLE	LABEL & NO.
6/8/85	**37**	5	▲ 1. 7800° Fahrenheit title refers to the temperature of an exploding volcano	Mercury 824509

DATE	POS	WKS	ARTIST—RECORD TITLE	LABEL & NO.
9/20/86	**1**(8)	60	▲　2. Slippery When Wet 　　*You Give Love A Bad Name* (1)/*Livin' On A Prayer* (1)/ 　　*Wanted Dead Or Alive* (7)	Mercury 830264
10/8/88	**1**(4)	52	▲　3. New Jersey 　　*Bad Medicine* (1)/*Born To Be My Baby* (3)/ 　　*I'll Be There For You* (1)/*Lay Your Hands On Me* (7)/ 　　*Living In Sin* (9)	Mercury 836345
			BONOFF, Karla	
			Singer/songwriter; born on 12/27/52 in Los Angeles.	
10/13/79	**31**	8	1. Restless Nights	Columbia 35799
			BOOGIE DOWN PRODUCTIONS	
			Brooklyn-based rap outfit led by Blastmaster KRS One (Kris Parker). Co-founder/DJ Scott "La Rock" Sterling was fatally shot on 8/25/87 (age 24) in a scuffle at a men's shelter in the Bronx. Rapper Derrick "D-Nice" Jones later recorded solo.	
8/5/89	**36**	4	●　　1. Ghetto Music: The Blueprint Of Hip Hop	Jive 1187
			BOOKER T. & THE MG'S	
			Band formed by session men from Stax Records, Memphis, in 1962. Consisted of Booker T. Jones (b: 11/12/44, Memphis), keyboards; Steve Cropper (b: 10/21/42, Ozark Mountains, Missouri), guitar; Donald "Duck" Dunn (b: 11/24/41, Memphis), bass; and Al Jackson, Jr. (b: 11/27/34, Memphis; murdered in 1975), drums. MG stands for Memphis Group. Jones produced Willie Nelson's *Stardust* album. Cropper and Dunn joined the Blues Brothers. Group disbanded in 1968 and reorganized for a short time in 1973.	
1/12/63	**33**	2	1. Green Onions　　　　　　　　　　　　[I] 　　*Green Onions* (3)	Stax 701
9/16/67	**35**	4	2. Hip Hug-Her　　　　　　　　　　　　[I]	Stax 717
			BOONE, Debby	
			Born Deborah Anne Boone on 9/22/56 in Hackensack, New Jersey. Third daughter of Pat and Shirley Boone and granddaughter of Red Foley. Worked with the Boone Family from 1969, sang with sisters in the Boones' gospel quartet. Went solo in 1977. Popular Contemporary Christian artist. Married Gabriel Ferrer, the son of Rosemary Clooney and Jose Ferrer, in 1982. Won the 1977 Best New Artist Grammy Award.	
11/12/77	**6**	10	▲　　1. You Light Up My Life 　　*You Light Up My Life* (1)	Warner 3118
			BOONE, Pat	
			Born Charles Eugene Boone on 6/1/34 in Jacksonville, Florida. To Nashville in the early 50s, attended Lipscomb College. Direct descendant of Daniel Boone. Won Ted Mack's Amateur Hour, Arthur Godfrey's Talent Scouts, in 1954. First recorded for Republic Records in 1954. Married Red Foley's daughter, Shirley, in 1954. Appeared in 15 films. Toured with wife and daughters Cherry, Linda Lee, Deborah Ann and Laura Gene in the mid-60s. Trademark: white buck shoes.	
10/27/56	**14**	4	1. Howdy!	Dot 3030
6/24/57	**13**	7	2. A Closer Walk with Thee　　　　　　[EP] 　　7″ EP (four sacred songs)	Dot 1056
7/8/57	**19**	3	3. "Pat"	Dot 3050
9/2/57	**5**	5	4. Four By Pat　　　　　　　　　　　　[EP] 　　7″ EP (four songs)	Dot 1057
10/7/57	**20**	2	5. Pat Boone 　　*Pat's first album* 　　*Ain't That A Shame* (1)/*At My Front Door* (7)/*I'll Be Home* (4)	Dot 3012

DATE	POS	WKS	ARTIST—RECORD TITLE	LABEL & NO.
10/21/57	**3**	36	● 6. Pat's Great Hits [G] *I Almost Lost My Mind* (1)/*Friendly Persuasion* (5)/ *Don't Forbid Me* (1)/*Why Baby Why* (5)/ *Love Letters In The Sand* (1)/*Remember You're Mine* (6)/ *Chains Of Love* (10)	Dot 3071
12/23/57	**12**	13	7. April Love [S] *April Love* (1)	Dot 9000
12/23/57	**21**	4	8. Hymns We Love	Dot 3068
7/28/58	**2**(1)	32	9. Star Dust	Dot 3118
11/24/58	**13**	2	10. Yes Indeed!	Dot 3121
7/20/59	**17**	9	11. Tenderly	Dot 3180
5/23/60	**26**	3	12. Moonglow	Dot 3270
8/7/61	**29**	6	13. Moody River *Moody River* (1)	Dot 3384
1/13/62	**39**	1	14. White Christmas [X]	Dot 3222

BOOTSY'S RUBBER BAND

Bootsy is William Collins, born on 10/26/51 in Cincinnati. Member of James Brown's JB's from 1969-71. Joined Funkadelic/Parliament in 1972.

DATE	POS	WKS	ARTIST—RECORD TITLE	LABEL & NO.
3/5/77	**16**	12	● 1. Ahh…The Name Is Bootsy, Baby!	Warner 2972
3/11/78	**16**	10	● 2. Bootsy? Player Of The Year	Warner 3093

BOSTON

Rock group from Boston, spearheaded by Tom Scholz (guitars and keyboards) and Brad Delp (lead vocals). Originally a quintet, group also included Barry Goudreau (guitar), Fran Sheehan (bass) and Sib Hashian (drums). After a long absence from the charts, Boston returned in 1986 as basically a duo: Scholz and Delp.

DATE	POS	WKS	ARTIST—RECORD TITLE	LABEL & NO.
10/16/76	**3**	49	▲ 1. Boston *More Than A Feeling* (5)	Epic 34188
9/2/78	**1**(2)	13	▲ 2. Don't Look Back *Don't Look Back* (4)	Epic 35050
10/18/86	**1**(4)	29	▲ 3. Third Stage *Amanda* (1)/*We're Ready* (9)	MCA 6188

BOSTON POPS ORCHESTRA

Conductor Arthur Fiedler was born in Boston on 12/17/1894; died on 7/10/79. Fiedler joined the Boston Pops Orchestra around 1915 as a viola player. Began his long reign as conductor in 1930, where he remained until his death.

DATE	POS	WKS	ARTIST—RECORD TITLE	LABEL & NO.
2/2/59	**9**	16	1. Offenbach: Gaite Parisienne; Khachaturian: Gayne Ballet Suite [I]	RCA 2267
9/15/62	**29**	4	2. Pops Roundup [I]	RCA 2595
3/23/63	**36**	2	3. Our Man In Boston [I]	RCA 2599
4/13/63	**5**	18	4. "Jalousie" And Other Favorites In The Latin Flavor [I]	RCA 2661
6/22/63	**29**	7	5. Star Dust [I]	RCA 2670
11/7/64	**18**	12	6. "Pops" Goes The Trumpet [I] **AL HIRT/BOSTON POPS/ARTHUR FIEDLER**	RCA 2729

BOSTON SYMPHONY Orchestra

DATE	POS	WKS	ARTIST—RECORD TITLE	LABEL & NO.
5/18/63	**17**	7	1. Ravel: Bolero/Pavan For A Dead Princess/ La Valse [I] *Charles Munch, conductor*	RCA 2664

DATE	POS	WKS	ARTIST—RECORD TITLE	LABEL & NO.
			BOWIE, David	
			Born David Robert Jones on 1/8/47 in London. First recorded as David Jones & the King Bees, Lower Third, Manish Boys in 1963. Brought highly theatrical values to rock through work with Lindsay Kemp Mime Troupe. Periods of reclusiveness heightened his appeal. Films include *The Man Who Fell To Earth*, 1976; *Labyrinth*, 1986; and *Absolute Beginners*, 1986. In Broadway play *The Elephant Man*, 1980. Formed the group Tin Machine in 1988.	
3/3/73	**16**	10	1. Space Oddity [R] first rock album, recorded in 1968	RCA 4813
5/26/73	**17**	8	● 2. Aladdin Sane	RCA 4852
11/24/73	**23**	9	3. Bowie Pin Ups David's versions of his favorite pop hits from '64-'67	RCA 0291
6/22/74	**5**	10	● 4. Diamond Dogs	RCA 0576
11/9/74	**8**	8	● 5. David Live [L] recorded at the Tower Theatre, Philadelphia	RCA 0771 [2]
3/29/75	**9**	17	● 6. Young Americans *Fame* (1)	RCA 0998
2/14/76	**3**	13	● 7. Station To Station *Golden Years* (10)	RCA 1327
6/26/76	**10**	8	▲ 8. Changesonebowie [G]	RCA 1732
2/5/77	**11**	7	9. Low	RCA 2030
11/26/77	**35**	3	10. "Heroes"	RCA 2522
6/23/79	**20**	8	11. Lodger	RCA 3254
10/18/80	**12**	12	12. Scary Monsters	RCA 3647
5/7/83	**4**	35	▲ 13. Let's Dance *Let's Dance* (1)/*China Girl* (10)	EMI America 17093
10/20/84	**11**	11	▲ 14. Tonight *Blue Jean* (8)	EMI America 17138
5/30/87	**34**	4	● 15. Never Let Me Down features Peter Frampton (lead guitar)	EMI America 17267
5/19/90	**39**	4	● 16. Changesbowie [G] David's greatest hits from 1969-90	Ryko 20171
			BOYS, The	
			Quartet of brothers, ages 9-14 in 1988, from Northridge, California: Khiry (lead), Hakeem, Tajh and Bilal Samad. All are members of performing gymnastic troupes.	
2/4/89	**33**	7	▲ 1. Messages From The Boys	Motown 6260
			BRAM TCHAIKOVSKY	
			Rock quartet led by Bram (real name Peter Bramall).	
8/11/79	**36**	4	1. Strange Man, Changed Man	Polydor 6211
			BRANIGAN, Laura	
			Born on 7/3/57 in Brewster, New York. Pop singer. Has done some acting work. Acted in the 1984 film *Mugsy's Girl*.	
11/27/82	**34**	9	● 1. Branigan *Gloria* (2)	Atlantic 19289
5/14/83	**29**	5	● 2. Branigan 2 *Solitaire* (7)	Atlantic 80052
6/9/84	**23**	19	● 3. Self Control *Self Control* (4)	Atlantic 80147
			BRASS CONSTRUCTION	
			Nine-man, multi-ethnic disco ensemble. Formed as Dynamic Soul by vocalist Randy Muller in 1968. Randy also produced the band Skyy.	
3/20/76	**10**	13	▲ 1. Brass Construction	United Art. 545

DATE	POS	WKS	ARTIST—RECORD TITLE		LABEL & NO.
12/4/76	26	9	● 2. Brass Construction II		United Art. 677
			BREAD		
			Formed in Los Angeles in 1969. Consisted of leader David Gates (vocals, guitar, keyboards), James Griffin (guitar), Robb Royer (guitar) and Jim Gordon (drums). Originally called Pleasure Faire. Griffin and Royer co-wrote award-winning "For All We Know" with Fred Karlin in 1969. Mike Botts replaced Gordon after first album. Royer replaced by Larry Knechtel in 1971. Disbanded in 1973, reunited briefly in 1976. All songs written, produced and arranged by David Gates.		
8/22/70	12	8	● 1. On The Waters *Make It With You* (1)		Elektra 74076
4/10/71	21	10	● 2. Manna *If* (4)		Elektra 74086
2/12/72	3	20	● 3. Baby I'm-A Want You *Baby I'm-A Want You* (3)/*Everything I Own* (5)		Elektra 75015
12/2/72	18	16	● 4. Guitar Man		Elektra 75047
4/7/73	2(1)	23	● 5. The Best Of Bread	[G]	Elektra 75056
7/6/74	32	3	● 6. The Best Of Bread, Volume Two	[G]	Elektra 1005
2/5/77	26	6	● 7. Lost Without Your Love *Lost Without Your Love* (9)		Elektra 1094
			BREATHE		
			Band from suburban London: David Glasper (vocals), Ian "Spike" Spice, Marcus Lillington and Michael Delahunty (who left in 1988).		
12/3/88	34	8	● 1. All That Jazz *Hands To Heaven* (2)/*How Can I Fall?* (3)/*Don't Tell Me Lies* (10)		A&M 5163
			BREWER & SHIPLEY		
			Folk-rock duo formed in Los Angeles: Mike Brewer and Tom Shipley.		
4/24/71	34	3	1. Tarkio *One Toke Over The Line* (10)		Kama Sutra 2024
			BRICK		
			Disco/jazz group formed in Atlanta in 1972. Consisted of Jimmy Brown (vocals), Ray Ransom, Donald Nevins, Reggie Hargis and Eddie Irons. Session work in the early 70s.		
12/25/76	19	8	1. Good High *Dazz* (3)		Bang 408
10/8/77	15	9	2. Brick		Bang 409
			BRICKELL, Edie		
			Vocalist Brickell (pronounced Bree-kell) joined the Dallas-based band in 1985. Varying personnel since then. Brickell was born in Oak Cliff, Texas; her father, Eddie, is a pro bowler. Bohemians' lineup: Brad Houser, Kenny Withrow and John Bush. **EDIE BRICKELL & NEW BOHEMIANS:**		
12/3/88	4	28	▲ 1. Shooting Rubberbands At The Stars *What I Am* (7)		Geffen 24192
			BRIDGES, Alicia		
			Atlanta-based disco singer/songwriter; originally from Lawndale, North Carolina.		
12/16/78	33	7	1. Alicia Bridges *I Love The Nightlife* (5)		Polydor 6158
			BRITNY FOX		
			Philadelphia heavy-metal quartet - "Dizzy" Dean Davidson, vocals.		
10/8/88	39	2	● 1. Britny Fox		Columbia 44140

DATE	POS	WKS	ARTIST—RECORD TITLE	LABEL & NO.
			BRONSKI BEAT	
			British techno-pop trio: Jimmy Somerville (vocals), Steve Bronski and Larry Steinbachek (synthesizers).	
3/2/85	**36**	3	1. The Age Of Consent	MCA 5538
			BROTHERS FOUR, The	
			Folk-pop quartet: Dick Foley, Bob Flick, John Paine and Mike Kirkland. Formed while fraternity brothers at the University of Washington.	
4/18/60	**11**	19	1. The Brothers Four	Columbia 1402
			Greenfields (2)	
2/13/61	**4**	7	2. B.M.O.C. (Best Music On/Off Campus)	Columbia 1578
			BROTHERS JOHNSON, The	
			Los Angeles R&B-funk duo of brothers George (b: 5/17/53) and Louis Johnson (b: 4/13/55). Played since age seven. Own band, the Johnson Three + 1, with brother Tommy and cousin Alex Weir. With Billy Preston's band to 1975. Also see Quincy Jones.	
4/17/76	**9**	24	▲ 1. Look Out For #1	A&M 4567
			I'll Be Good To You (3)	
5/28/77	**13**	26	▲ 2. Right On Time	A&M 4644
			Strawberry Letter 23 (5)	
8/19/78	**7**	10	▲ 3. Blam!!	A&M 4714
3/15/80	**5**	16	▲ 4. Light Up The Night	A&M 3716
			Stomp! (7)	
			BROWN, Arthur	
			Arthur was born on 6/24/44 in Whitby, England. Band included Carl Palmer of Emerson, Lake & Palmer.	
10/12/68	**7**	10	1. The Crazy World Of Arthur Brown	Track 8198
			Fire (2)	
			BROWN, Bobby	
			Born on 2/5/69 in Boston. Former member of the teen R&B-pop group New Edition. Had a bit part in the film *Ghostbusters II*.	
8/13/88	**1**(6)	69	▲ 1. Don't Be Cruel	MCA 42185
			Don't Be Cruel (8)/*My Prerogative* (1)/*Roni* (3)/ *Every Little Step* (3)/*Rock Wit'cha* (7)	
12/16/89	**9**	17	▲ 2. Dance!...Ya Know It! [K]	MCA 6342
			previously unreleased, re-edited versions of Bobby's hits	
			BROWN, Chuck	
			Washington, D.C.-based, nine-member group.	
			CHUCK BROWN & THE SOUL SEARCHERS:	
3/10/79	**31**	5	● 1. Bustin' Loose	Source 3076
			BROWN, James	
			Born on 5/3/28 in Macon, Georgia. Raised in Augusta. Formed own vocal group, the Famous Flames. Cut a demo record of own composition "Please Please Please" in November of 1955 at radio station WIBB in Macon. Signed to King/Federal Records in January, 1956 and re-recorded the song. Cameo appearances in films *The Blues Brothers* and *Rocky IV*. One of the originators of "Soul" music, variously labelled on Polydor as "Soul I," "The Creator," "The Godfather Of Soul," "The Hit Man" and "Minister of New New Super Heavy Funk." His backing group, The JB's, featured various personnel, including: Nat Kendrick, Bootsy Collins, Maceo Parker and Fred Wesley. Inducted into the Rock and Roll Hall of Fame in 1986. On 12/15/88, received a six-year prison sentence for leading police in an interstate car chase.	
7/6/63	**2**(2)	33	1. Live At The Apollo [L]	King 826
			recorded at the Apollo Theater, New York City, 10/24/62	

DATE	POS	WKS	ARTIST—RECORD TITLE	LABEL & NO.
3/28/64	**10**	13	2. Pure Dynamite! Live At The Royal [L] recorded at the Royal Theater, Baltimore, Maryland	King 883
12/4/65	**26**	8	3. Papa's Got A Brand New Bag Papa's Got A Brand New Bag (8)	King 938
2/26/66	**36**	4	4. I Got You (I Feel Good) I Got You (I Feel Good) (3)	King 946
10/28/67	**35**	2	5. Cold Sweat Cold Sweat (7)	King 1020
4/13/68	**17**	6	6. I Can't Stand Myself (When You Touch Me)	King 1030
12/14/68	**32**	7	7. Live At The Apollo, Volume II [L]	King 1022 [2]
9/13/69	**26**	7	8. It's A Mother	King 1063
9/27/69	**40**	1	9. James Brown plays & directs The Popcorn [I]	King 1055
10/24/70	**29**	6	10. Sex Machine [L]	King 1115 [2]
9/18/71	**22**	7	11. Hot Pants	Polydor 4054
1/29/72	**39**	2	12. Revolution Of The Mind - Live At The Apollo, Volume III [L]	Polydor 3003 [2]
4/7/73	**31**	5	13. Black Caesar [S]	Polydor 6014
3/30/74	**34**	8	● 14. The Payback	Polydor 3007 [2]
9/7/74	**35**	2	15. Hell	Polydor 9001 [2]

BROWN, Les

Born on 3/14/12 in Reinerton, Pennsylvania. Clarinetist/bandleader; worked as an arranger for Jimmy Dorsey, Larry Clinton and other bands before his own orchestra took off. In the 1950s, Brown's band was featured on Steve Allen's TV show. Worked on Bob Hope's programs and overseas tours for over two decades.

LES BROWN AND HIS BAND OF RENOWN:

DATE	POS	WKS	ARTIST—RECORD TITLE	LABEL & NO.
2/19/55	**15**	2	1. Concert At The Palladium [I-L] recorded at the Hollywood Palladium, September 1953	Coral CX-1 [2]

BROWN, Peter

Soul vocalist/keyboardist/producer, born on 7/11/53 in Blue Island, Illinois. Attended the Art Institute of Chicago.

DATE	POS	WKS	ARTIST—RECORD TITLE	LABEL & NO.
4/1/78	**11**	19	1. A Fantasy Love Affair Dance With Me (8)	Drive 104

BROWNE, Jackson

Born on 10/9/48 in Heidelberg, Germany. Vocalist/guitarist/pianist/composer. To Los Angeles in 1951. With Tim Buckley and Nico in 1967 in New York City. Returned to Los Angeles, concentrated on songwriting. His songs were recorded by Linda Ronstadt, Tom Rush, Joe Cocker, The Byrds, Johnny Rivers, Bonnie Raitt, and many others. Worked with the Eagles; produced Warren Zevon's first album. Wife Phyllis committed suicide on 3/25/76. Activist against nuclear power.

DATE	POS	WKS	ARTIST—RECORD TITLE	LABEL & NO.
11/2/74	**14**	12	▲ 1. Late For The Sky	Asylum 1017
11/27/76	**5**	18	▲ 2. The Pretender	Asylum 1079
1/7/78	**3**	25	▲ 3. Running On Empty	Asylum 113
7/19/80	**1(1)**	21	▲ 4. Hold Out	Asylum 511
8/27/83	**8**	12	● 5. Lawyers In Love	Asylum 60268
3/22/86	**23**	9	● 6. Lives In The Balance	Asylum 60457

BROWNE, Tom

Jazz-funk trumpeter first played classical music at the High School of Music and Art in New York City. With Weldon Ervine in 1975, Sonny Fortune and Fatback Band in 1976.

DATE	POS	WKS	ARTIST—RECORD TITLE	LABEL & NO.
9/20/80	**18**	9	● 1. Love Approach [I]	GRP 5008
3/21/81	**37**	2	2. Magic	GRP 5503

DATE	POS	WKS	ARTIST—RECORD TITLE	LABEL & NO.
			BRUBECK, Dave	
			Born David Warren on 12/6/20 in Concord, California. Leader of jazz quartet consisting of Brubeck (piano), Paul Desmond (alto sax), Joe Morello (drums) and Eugene Wright (bass). One of America's all-time most popular jazz groups on college campuses.	
			DAVE BRUBECK QUARTET:	
2/5/55	8	6	1. Dave Brubeck At Storyville: 1954 [I-L]	Columbia 590
3/19/55	5	22	2. Brubeck Time [I]	Columbia 622
11/12/55	7	3	3. Jazz: Red Hot And Cool [I-L]	Columbia 699
7/8/57	18	1	4. Jazz Impressions of the U.S.A. [I]	Columbia 984
9/30/57	24	1	5. Jazz Goes To Junior College [I-L]	Columbia 1034
11/28/60	2(1)	86	● 6. Time Out Featuring "Take Five" [I]	Columbia 8192
12/12/60	13	7	7. Bernstein Plays Brubeck Plays Bernstein [I]	Columbia 8257
			side 1: New York Philharmonic with the Dave Brubeck Quartet conducted by Leonard Bernstein; side 2: Dave Brubeck Quartet	
1/27/62	8	31	8. Time Further Out [I]	Columbia 8490
7/7/62	24	9	9. Countdown - Time In Outer Space [I]	Columbia 8575
3/23/63	14	10	10. Bossa Nova U.S.A. [I]	Columbia 8798
8/3/63	37	2	11. The Dave Brubeck Quartet At Carnegie Hall [I-L]	Columbia 826 [2]
			BRYSON, Peabo	
			Born Robert Peabo Bryson on 4/13/51 in Greenville, South Carolina. R&B singer/ producer. First solo recording for Bang in 1970.	
2/10/79	35	4	● 1. Crosswinds	Capitol 11875
2/27/82	40	2	2. I Am Love	Capitol 12179
			PEABO BRYSON/ROBERTA FLACK:	
9/10/83	25	14	● 3. Born To Love	Capitol 12284
			B.T. EXPRESS	
			Brooklyn, New York disco septet. B.T. stands for Brothers Trucking.	
12/14/74	5	18	● 1. Do It ('Til You're Satisfied)	Roadshow 5117
			Do It ('Til You're Satisfied) (2)/Express (4)	
8/23/75	19	8	2. Non-Stop	Roadshow 41001
			BUCKINGHAM, Lindsey	
			Born on 10/3/47 in Palo Alto, California. Guitarist/vocalist. Lindsey, along with Stevie Nicks, joined Fleetwood Mac in 1975. Lindsey left Fleetwood Mac in 1987.	
11/28/81	32	6	1. Law And Order	Asylum 561
			Trouble (9)	
			BUCKNER & GARCIA	
			Atlanta-based duo: Jerry Buckner and Gary Garcia.	
5/8/82	24	5	● 1. Pac-Man Fever [N]	Columbia 37941
			album inspired by popular video games	
			Pac-Man Fever (9)	
			BUFFETT, Jimmy	
			Born on 12/25/46 in Mobile, Alabama. Has BS degree in history and journalism from the University of Southern Mississippi. After working in New Orleans, moved to Nashville in 1969. Settled in Key West in 1971.	
3/29/75	25	4	1. A1A	Dunhill 50183
			A1A: beach access road off U.S. 1 in Florida	
3/26/77	12	19	▲ 2. Changes In Latitudes, Changes In Attitudes	ABC 990
			Margaritaville (8)	
4/15/78	10	9	▲ 3. Son Of A Son Of A Sailor	ABC 1046

DATE	POS	WKS	ARTIST—RECORD TITLE	LABEL & NO.
9/22/79	**14**	11	● 4. Volcano	MCA 5102
3/14/81	**30**	4	5. Coconut Telegraph	MCA 5169
1/30/82	**31**	6	6. Somewhere Over China	MCA 5285
			BULLETBOYS	
			Los Angeles hard-rock quartet: Marq Torien (vocals), Mick Sweda, Lonnie Vencent and Jimmy D-Anda.	
2/4/89	**34**	5	● 1. BulletBoys	Warner 25782
			BURDON, Eric	
			Born on 5/11/41 in Newcastle-On-Tyne, England. Lead singer of The Animals.	
			ERIC BURDON AND WAR:	
7/11/70	**18**	13	1. Eric Burdon Declares "War"	MGM 4663
			Spill The Wine (3)	
			BUSH, Kate	
			Born on 7/30/58 in Bexley, Kent, England. Signed to EMI while still in high school.	
11/9/85	**30**	6	1. Hounds Of Love	EMI America 17171
			BUSHKIN, Joe	
			Born on 11/7/16 in New York City. Pianist/composer.	
5/26/56	**14**	1	1. Midnight Rhapsody [I]	Capitol 711
			BUTLER, Jerry	
			Born on 12/8/39 in Sunflower, Mississippi. Older brother of Billy Butler. Sang in the Northern Jubilee Gospel Singers, with Curtis Mayfield. Later with the Quails. In 1957, Butler and Mayfield joined the Roosters with Sam Gooden and brothers Arthur & Richard Brooks. Changed name to The Impressions in 1957. Left for solo career in autumn of 1958. Teamed again with writer Mayfield for a string of hits from 1960-66.	
5/10/69	**29**	6	1. The Ice Man Cometh	Mercury 61198
			Only The Strong Survive (4)	
			BUTTERFIELD, Billy — see CONNIFF, Ray	
			BYRD, Charlie	
			Born on 9/16/25 in Chuckatuch, Virginia. Jazz and classical guitar virtuoso.	
			STAN GETZ/CHARLIE BYRD:	
10/13/62	**1**(1)	44	1. Jazz Samba [I]	Verve 8432
			BYRD, Donald	
			Trumpeter/flugelhorn player, born on 12/9/32 in Detroit. Founded The Blackbyrds in 1973 while teaching jazz at Howard University in Washington, D.C.	
7/14/73	**36**	2	1. Black Byrd	Blue Note 047
5/11/74	**33**	3	2. Street Lady [I]	Blue Note 140

DATE	POS	WKS	ARTIST—RECORD TITLE	LABEL & NO.
			BYRDS, The	
			Folk-rock group formed in Los Angeles in 1964. Consisted of James "Roger" McGuinn, (12-string guitar), David Crosby (guitar), Gene Clark (percussion), Chris Hillman (bass) and Mike Clarke (drums). McGuinn, who changed his name to Roger in 1968, had been with Bobby Darin and The Chad Mitchell Trio. Clark had been with The New Christy Minstrels. All except Clarke had folk music background. Professional debut in March of 1965. First recorded as the Beefeaters for Elektra in 1965. Also recorded as the Jet Set. Clark left after "Eight Miles High." Crosby left in 1968 to form Crosby, Stills & Nash. Re-formed in 1968 with McGuinn, Hillman, Kevin Kelly (drums) and Gram Parsons (guitar). Hillman and Parsons left that same year to form the Flying Burrito Brothers. McGuinn again re-formed with Clarence White (guitar), John York (bass) and Gene Parsons (drums). Reunions with original members in 1973 and 1979. Gram Parsons died on 9/19/73 (age 26) of a heroin overdose. McGuinn, Clark and Hillman later recorded as a trio. In 1986, Hillman formed popular country group, The Desert Rose Band.	
7/17/65	**6**	4	1. Mr. Tambourine Man *Mr. Tambourine Man* (1)	Columbia 9172
2/12/66	**17**	10	2. Turn! Turn! Turn! *Turn! Turn! Turn!* (1)	Columbia 9254
9/17/66	**24**	8	3. Fifth Dimension	Columbia 9349
4/22/67	**24**	5	4. Younger Than Yesterday	Columbia 9442
9/16/67	**6**	15	▲ 5. The Byrds' Greatest Hits [G]	Columbia 9516
1/10/70	**36**	3	6. Ballad Of Easy Rider	Columbia 9942
11/28/70	**40**	2	7. The Byrds (Untitled)	Columbia 30127 [2]
4/14/73	**20**	7	8. Byrds reunion of original five Byrds	Asylum 5058

C

DATE	POS	WKS	ARTIST—RECORD TITLE	LABEL & NO.
			CAFFERTY, John/Beaver Brown Band	
			Rock sextet from Rhode Island. Wrote and recorded the music for the soundtrack of *Eddie And The Cruisers*. Band, led by singer/guitarist Cafferty, includes Bob Cotoia, Gary Gramolini, Kenny Jo Silva, Pat Lupo and Michael Antunes.	
			EDDIE AND THE CRUISERS:	
8/25/84	**9**	24	▲ 1. Eddie And The Cruisers [S] *On The Dark Side* (7)	Scotti Br. 38929
			JOHN CAFFERTY AND THE BEAVER BROWN BAND:	
7/6/85	**40**	3	2. Tough All Over	Scotti Br. 39405
			CALDWELL, Bobby	
			Vocalist/composer/multi-instrumentalist, born on 8/15/51 in New York City. Wrote tracks for "New Mickey Mouse Club" TV show and commercials. Drummer with Johnny Winter's band in the early 1970s.	
2/17/79	**21**	10	1. Bobby Caldwell *What You Won't Do For Love* (9)	Clouds 8804
			CAMEO	
			New York City soul-funk group, formed in 1974 as The New York City Players by Larry "Mr. B" Blackmon (drums) and Gregory "Straps" Johnson (keyboards). Vocals by Wayne Cooper and Tomi "Tee" Jenkins. Lineup since 1985: Blackmon, Jenkins and Nathan Leftenant.	
7/12/80	**25**	10	● 1. Cameosis	Choc. City 2011
4/24/82	**23**	6	● 2. Alligator Woman	Choc. City 2021
4/7/84	**27**	9	● 3. She's Strange	Atl. Art. 814984

DATE	POS	WKS	ARTIST—RECORD TITLE	LABEL & NO.
10/11/86	**8**	31	▲ 4. Word Up! *Word Up* (6)	Atl. Art. 830265

CAMPBELL, Glen

Born on 4/22/36 in Billstown, Arkansas. Vocalist/guitarist/composer. With his uncle Dick Bills' band, 1954-58. To Los Angeles; recorded with The Champs in 1960; became prolific studio musician; with The Beach Boys, 1965. Own TV show, "The Glen Campbell Goodtime Hour," 1968-72. In films *True Grit*, *Norwood* and *Strange Homecoming*.

DATE	POS	WKS	ARTIST—RECORD TITLE	LABEL & NO.
4/27/68	**15**	35	● 1. By The Time I Get To Phoenix *1968 Grammy winner: Album of the Year*	Capitol 2851
6/8/68	**26**	4	● 2. Hey, Little One	Capitol 2878
8/10/68	**5**	40	● 3. Gentle On My Mind	Capitol 2809
9/14/68	**24**	5	4. A New Place In The Sun	Capitol 2907
11/9/68	**11**	13	● 5. Bobbie Gentry & Glen Campbell	Capitol 2928
11/30/68	**1**(5)	29	● 6. Wichita Lineman *Wichita Lineman* (3)	Capitol 103
4/12/69	**2**(1)	18	● 7. Galveston *Galveston* (4)	Capitol 210
9/27/69	**13**	14	● 8. Glen Campbell - "Live" [L]	Capitol 0268 [2]
2/14/70	**12**	11	● 9. Try A Little Kindness	Capitol 389
6/20/70	**38**	3	10. Oh Happy Day *inspirational songs*	Capitol 443
10/31/70	**27**	5	11. The Glen Campbell Goodtime Album *It's Only Make Believe* (10)	Capitol 493
5/29/71	**39**	1	● 12. Glen Campbell's Greatest Hits [G]	Capitol 752
9/6/75	**17**	13	● 13. Rhinestone Cowboy *Rhinestone Cowboy* (1)	Capitol 11430
4/16/77	**22**	7	● 14. Southern Nights *Southern Nights* (1)	Capitol 11601

CANNED HEAT

Blues-rock band formed in Los Angeles in 1966. Consisted of Bob "The Bear" Hite (vocals, harmonica), Alan "Blind Owl" Wilson (guitar, harmonica, vocals), Henry Vestine (guitar), Larry Taylor (bass) and Frank Cook (drums). Cook replaced by Fito de la Parra in 1968. Vestine replaced by Harvey Mandel in 1969. Wilson died of a drug overdose on 9/3/70 (age 27). Hite died of a drug-related heart attack on 4/6/81 (age 36).

DATE	POS	WKS	ARTIST—RECORD TITLE	LABEL & NO.
9/7/68	**16**	14	1. Boogie With Canned Heat	Liberty 7541
12/28/68	**18**	9	2. Living The Blues [L] *second LP in set recorded live*	Liberty 27200 [2]
8/30/69	**37**	2	3. Hallelujah	Liberty 7618

CANO, Eddie

Latin-jazz pianist/bandleader. Played with Latin bandleader Miguilito Valdez in the late 1940s. Died of a heart attack in Los Angeles on 1/30/88 (age 60).

DATE	POS	WKS	ARTIST—RECORD TITLE	LABEL & NO.
9/1/62	**31**	3	1. Eddie Cano At P.J.'s [I]	Reprise 6030

CAPTAIN & TENNILLE

The Captain: Daryl Dragon (b: 8/27/42, Los Angeles); and Toni Tennille (b: 5/8/43, Montgomery, Alabama). Husband and wife. Dragon is the son of notable conductor Carmen Dragon. Keyboardist with The Beach Boys, nicknamed the "Captain" by Mike Love. Duo had own TV show on ABC from 1976-77.

DATE	POS	WKS	ARTIST—RECORD TITLE	LABEL & NO.
6/21/75	**2**(1)	14	● 1. Love Will Keep Us Together *Love Will Keep Us Together* (1)/*The Way I Want To Touch You* (4)	A&M 3405
3/27/76	**9**	16	▲ 2. Song Of Joy *Lonely Night* (3)/*Shop Around* (4)/*Muskrat Love* (4)	A&M 4570

Black Sabbath is the closest thing to an institution heavy metal has ever had. Such albums as *Sabbath Bloody Sabbath* introduced lead vocalist Ozzy Osbourne to the world; upon his departure, singer Ronnie James Dio stepped in, followed by former Deep Purple vocalist Ian Gillan.

Booker T. & The MG's were one of many 60s outfits to pay tribute to the Beatles. Their *McLemore Avenue* album of 1970 was an instrumental version of *Abbey Road*, with a nearly identical cover featuring the group crossing the street directly across from the Stax "Soulsville U.S.A." marquee. However, it never matched the chart success of their classic LP, *Green Onions*.

Bread, led by Tulsa, Oklahoma's David Gates, scored seven top 40 albums during their career, starting with *On The Waters* in 1970. The only holdout was their first album, *Bread*, which peaked at No. 127 in 1969, despite the presence of "It Don't Matter To Me."

Jackson Browne's first official album, released in 1972, came several years after the singer/songwriter's work had already appeared on albums by such artists as the Nitty Gritty Dirt Band—of which Browne was once a member—and former Velvet Underground singer Nico. His only No. 1 album, *Hold Out*, held onto the top spot for one week in 1980.

Jerry Butler, better known as the "Ice Man" to soul fans, left the Impressions in 1958 and later recorded a series of duet albums with such partners as Betty Everett, Gene Chandler and Thelma Houston.

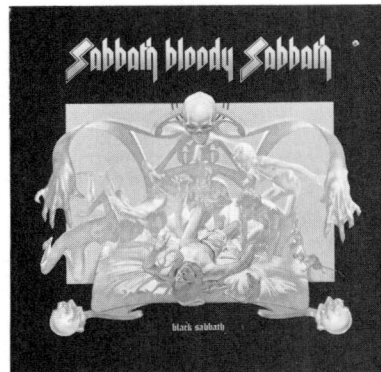

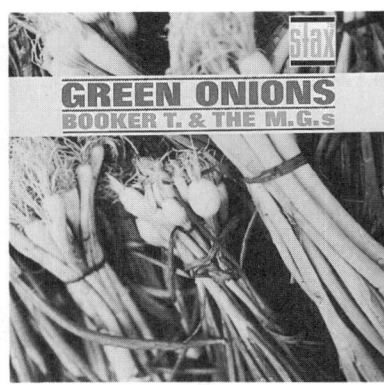

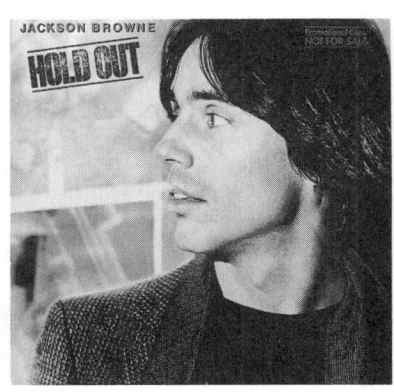

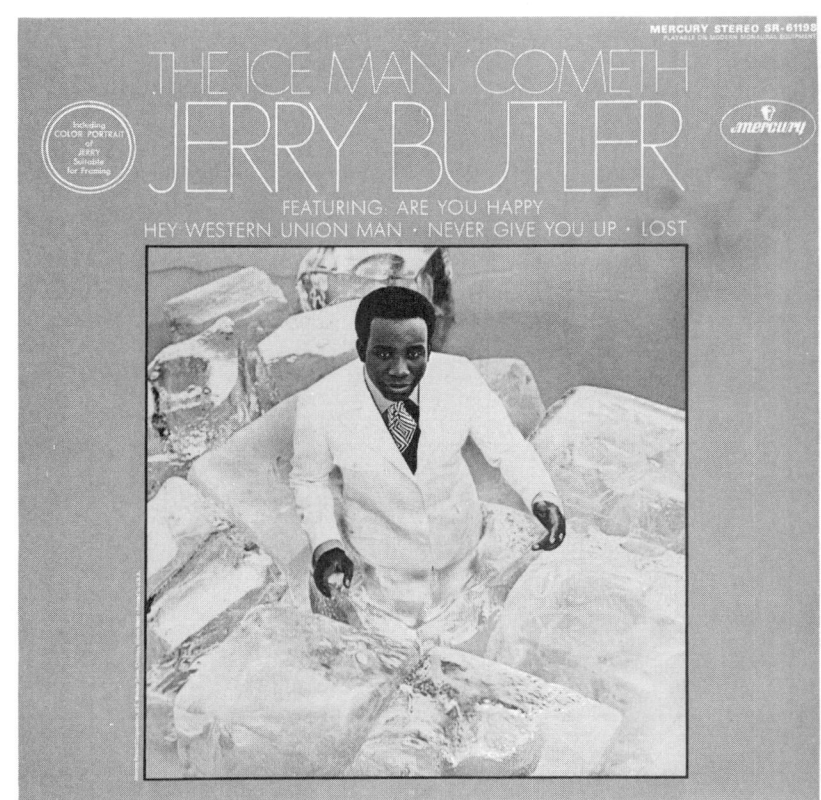

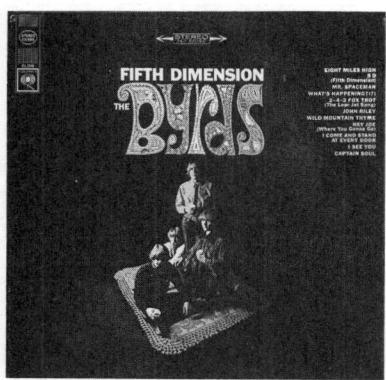

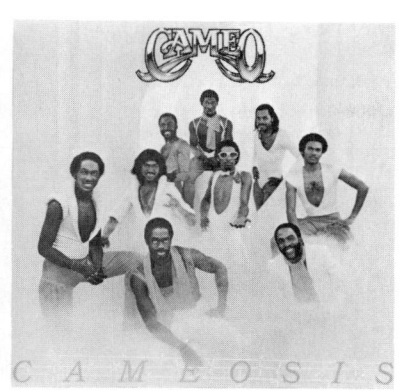

The **Byrds**, with such efforts as *Fifth Dimension*, became among the most influential groups to have ever performed rock 'n' roll. Artists that left the famed 60s band to have booming recording careers of their own include leader Roger McGuinn, Gene Clark, David Crosby, Chris Hillman, Clarence White and Gram Parsons.

Cameo, the long-lived and influential soul/funk group, hit its commercial stride with 1986's "Word Up" single—and, with leader Larry Blackmon at the helm as always, continues to be at funk's forefront. *Cameosis* was their first top 40 album.

The Captain & Tennille, known to their friends as Daryl Dragon and Toni Tennille, steered their ship to the No. 2 position in 1975 via their *Love Will Keep Us Together* debut album. The 1976 follow-up, *Song Of Joy*, didn't do as well, peaking at No. 9—and only 1979's single "Do That To Me One More Time" would reach the No. 1 spot again.

The **Carpenters**' string of top 10 records in the 70s—beginning with *Close To You*—has yet to be forgotten; witness the recent issue of a boxed CD collection of their work in the U.K. and a much-publicized 1989 TV film about their lives.

Johnny Cash's long career may have peaked in terms of chart performance between July 1969 and February 1970—between those nine months, eight Cash albums made the Top 200, beginning with his famed No. 1 album *Johnny Cash At San Quentin* through *Hello, I'm Johnny Cash*, which hit No. 6.

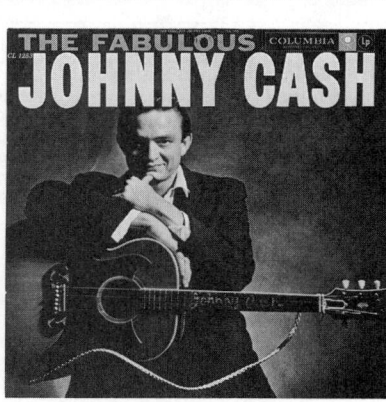

DATE	POS	WKS	ARTIST—RECORD TITLE	LABEL & NO.
4/23/77	**18**	7	● 3. Come In From The Rain	A&M 4700
1/5/80	**23**	9	● 4. Make Your Move	Casablanca 7188
			Do That To Me One More Time (1)	
			CARLIN, George	
			Comedian, actor. Born on 5/12/37 in New York City. In films *Bill & Ted's Excellent Adventure, Outrageous Fortune, Car Wash* and *Americathon*.	
3/18/72	**13**	16	● 1. FM & AM [C]	Little David 7214
10/28/72	**22**	10	● 2. Class Clown [C]	Little David 1004
12/1/73	**35**	5	● 3. Occupation: Foole [C]	Little David 1005
1/4/75	**19**	7	● 4. Toledo Window Box [C]	Little David 3003
12/27/75	**34**	3	5. An Evening With Wally Londo Featuring Bill	
			Slaszo [C]	Little David 1008
			CARLISLE, Belinda	
			Born on 8/17/58 in Hollywood. Lead singer of the Go-Go's, 1978-84. Married to Morgan Mason, son of late actor James Mason.	
7/5/86	**13**	16	● 1. Belinda	I.R.S. 5741
			Mad About You (3)	
11/7/87	**13**	35	▲ 2. Heaven On Earth	MCA 42080
			Heaven Is A Place On Earth (1)/*I Get Weak* (2)/	
			Circle In The Sand (7)	
12/9/89	**37**	2	● 3. Runaway Horses	MCA 6339
			CARLOS, Walter	
			Born in 1939 in Pawtucket, Rhode Island. Classical musician who performs on the Moog Synthesizer.	
3/1/69	**10**	17	● 1. Switched-On Bach [I]	Columbia 7194
			CARLTON, Carl	
			Soul singer, born in 1952 in Detroit. Singing since age nine. First recorded for Lando Records in 1964.	
10/3/81	**34**	3	1. Carl Carlton	20th Century 628
			CARMEN, Eric	
			Born on 8/11/49 in Cleveland. Classical training at Cleveland Institute of Music from early years to mid-teens. Lead singer of the Raspberries from 1970-74.	
2/21/76	**21**	8	● 1. Eric Carmen	Arista 4057
			All By Myself (2)	
			CARNES, Kim	
			Vocalist/pianist/composer. Born on 7/20/45 in Los Angeles. Member of The New Christy Minstrels with husband/co-writer Dave Ellingson and Kenny Rogers, late 1960s. Wrote and performed commercials.	
5/9/81	**1**(4)	23	▲ 1. Mistaken Identity	EMI America 17052
			Bette Davis Eyes (1)	
			CARPENTERS	
			Richard Carpenter (b: 10/15/46) and sister Karen (b: 3/2/50; d: 2/4/83 of heart failure due to anorexia). From New Haven, Connecticut. Richard played piano from age nine. To Downey, California in 1963. Karen played drums in group with Richard and bass player Wes Jacobs in 1965. The trio recorded for RCA in 1966. After a period with the band Spectrum, the Carpenters recorded as a duo for A&M in 1969. Won the 1970 Best New Artist Grammy Award. Hosts of the TV variety show "Make Your Own Kind Of Music" in 1971. 1988 TV movie "The Karen Carpenter Movie" was based on Karen's life.	
9/26/70	**2**(1)	53	● 1. Close To You	A&M 4271
			Close To You (1)/*We've Only Just Begun* (2)	

DATE	POS	WKS	ARTIST—RECORD TITLE	LABEL & NO.
6/5/71	**2**(2)	39	● 2. Carpenters *For All We Know* (3)/*Rainy Days And Mondays* (2)/*Superstar* (2)	A&M 3502
7/8/72	**4**	19	● 3. A Song For You *Hurting Each Other* (2)/*Goodbye To Love* (7)	A&M 3511
6/9/73	**2**(1)	19	● 4. Now & Then side 2: medley of 60s hits with D.J. Tony Peluso *Sing* (3)/*Yesterday Once More* (2)	A&M 3519
12/8/73	**1**(1)	17	● 5. The Singles 1969-1973 [G] *Top Of The World* (1)	A&M 3601
6/28/75	**13**	11	● 6. Horizon *Please Mr. Postman* (1)/*Only Yesterday* (4)	A&M 4530
7/31/76	**33**	5	● 7. A Kind Of Hush	A&M 4581
			CARR, Vikki	
			Born Florencia Martinez Cardona on 7/19/41 in El Paso, Texas. A regular on the Ray Anthony musical variety TV show in 1962.	
12/2/67	**12**	16	1. It Must Be Him *It Must Be Him* (3)	Liberty 7533
6/7/69	**29**	7	2. For Once In My Life [L]	Liberty 7604
			CARROLL, David	
			Born Nook Schrier on 10/15/13 in Chicago. Arranger/conductor since 1951 for many top Mercury artists. **DAVID CARROLL AND HIS ORCHESTRA:**	
6/1/59	**21**	6	1. Let's Dance	Mercury 60001
1/11/60	**6**	30	2. Let's Dance Again	Mercury 60152
			CARS, The	
			Rock group formed in Boston in 1976. Consisted of Ric Ocasek (lead vocals, guitar), Elliot Easton (guitar), Greg Hawkes (keyboards), Benjamin Orr (bass, vocals) and David Robinson (drums; formerly with the Modern Lovers). Ocasek, Orr and Hawkes had been in trio in the early 70s. Group named by Robinson, got start at the Rat Club in Boston. All songs written by Ocasek. Disbanded in 1988.	
9/23/78	**18**	37	▲ 1. The Cars	Elektra 135
7/7/79	**3**	21	▲ 2. Candy-O	Elektra 507
9/6/80	**5**	11	▲ 3. Panorama	Elektra 514
11/28/81	**9**	24	▲ 4. Shake It Up *Shake It Up* (4)	Elektra 567
4/7/84	**3**	48	▲ 5. Heartbeat City *You Might Think* (7)/*Drive* (3)	Elektra 60296
11/23/85	**12**	16	▲ 6. The Cars Greatest Hits [G] *Tonight She Comes* (7)	Elektra 60464
9/26/87	**26**	8	● 7. Door To Door	Elektra 60747
			CASH, Johnny	
			Born on 2/26/32 in Kingsland, Arkansas. To Dyess, Arkansas at age three. Brother Roy led the Dixie Rhythm Ramblers band in late 40s. In U.S. Air Force, 1950-54. Formed trio with Luther Perkins (guitar) and Marshall Grant (bass) in 1955. First recorded for Sun in 1955. On Louisiana Hayride and Grand Ole Opry in 1957. Own TV show for ABC from 1969-71. Worked with June Carter from 1961, married her in March of 1968. Daughter Rosanne Cash and stepdaughter Carlene Carter currently enjoying successful singing careers. Elected to the Country Music Hall Of Fame in 1980.	
12/8/58	**19**	9	1. The Fabulous Johnny Cash	Columbia 1253
9/14/63	**26**	9	● 2. Ring Of Fire (The Best Of Johnny Cash) [K]	Columbia 8853
7/20/68	**13**	39	▲ 3. Johnny Cash At Folsom Prison [L]	Columbia 9639

DATE	POS	WKS	ARTIST—RECORD TITLE	LABEL & NO.
7/12/69	**1(4)**	35	▲ 4. Johnny Cash At San Quentin [L] *A Boy Named Sue* (2)	Columbia 9827
2/21/70	**6**	17	● 5. Hello, I'm Johnny Cash	Columbia 9943
			CASH, Rosanne	
			Born on 5/24/55 in Memphis, daughter of Johnny Cash and Vivian Liberto. Raised by her mother in California, then moved to Nashville after high school graduation. Worked in the Johnny Cash Road Show. Married Rodney Crowell in 1979.	
6/6/81	**26**	9	● 1. Seven Year Ache	Columbia 36965
			CASSIDY, David	
			Son of actor Jack Cassidy and actress Evelyn Ward, born on 4/12/50 in New York City. Played Keith and was lead singer for TV's "The Partridge Family." Married for a time to actress Kay Lenz. Recording comeback in fall of 1990.	
2/19/72	**15**	8	● 1. Cherish *Cherish* (9)	Bell 6070
			CASSIDY, Shaun	
			Born on 9/27/59 in Los Angeles. Son of actor Jack Cassidy and actress Shirley Jones. Played Joe Hardy on TV's "The Hardy Boys." Shaun and David Cassidy are half-brothers. Cast member of TV's soap series "General Hospital" in 1987.	
7/9/77	**3**	26	▲ 1. Shaun Cassidy *Da Doo Ron Ron* (1)/*That's Rock 'N' Roll* (3)	Warner 3067
12/3/77	**6**	11	▲ 2. Born Late *Hey Deanie* (7)	Warner 3126
9/2/78	**33**	4	▲ 3. Under Wraps	Warner 3222
			CASTOR, Jimmy	
			R&B singer/saxophonist/composer/arranger. Born on 6/2/43 in New York City. Formed the Jimmy Castor Bunch in 1972, with Gerry Thomas (keyboards), Doug Gibson (bass), Harry Jensen (guitar), Lenny Fridie, Jr. (congas) and Bobby Manigault (drums). **THE JIMMY CASTOR BUNCH:**	
6/24/72	**27**	6	1. It's Just Begun *Troglodyte* (6)	RCA 4640
			CAVALLARO, Carmen	
			Born on 5/6/13 in New York City. Classically trained pianist who played in the 1930s with Al Kavelin, Rudy Vallee and Abe Lyman.	
5/26/56	**1(1)**	99	1. The Eddy Duchin Story [S-I] biographical film about the popular pianist/orchestra leader	Decca 8289
			CETERA, Peter	
			Born on 9/13/44 in Chicago. Lead singer and bass guitarist of Chicago for their first 17 albums.	
7/26/86	**23**	25	● 1. Solitude/Solitaire *Glory Of Love* (1)/*The Next Time I Fall* (1) with Amy Grant	Warner 25474
			CHACKSFIELD, Frank	
			Born on 5/9/14 in Sussex, England. Orchestra leader. **FRANK CHACKSFIELD AND HIS ORCHESTRA:**	
1/9/61	**36**	1	1. Ebb Tide	Richmond 30078
			CHAD & JEREMY	
			Folk-rock duo formed in the early 60s: Chad Stuart (b: 12/10/43, England) and Jeremy Clyde (b: 3/22/44, England). Broke up in 1967. Re-formed briefly in 1982.	
1/23/65	**22**	11	1. Yesterday's Gone *A Summer Song* (7)	World Art. 2002

DATE	POS	WKS	ARTIST—RECORD TITLE	LABEL & NO.
8/21/65	37	3	2. Before And After	Columbia 9174
			CHAKIRIS, George	
			Portrayed Bernardo in the film *West Side Story*.	
9/15/62	28	4	1. George Chakiris	Capitol 1750
			CHAMBERLAIN, Richard	
			Born on 3/31/35 in Los Angeles. Leading film, theater and television actor. Played lead role in TV's "Dr. Kildare," 1961-66.	
2/16/63	5	24	1. Richard Chamberlain Sings	MGM 4088
			Theme From Dr. Kildare (10)	
			CHAMBERS BROTHERS, The	
			Four Mississippi-born brothers: George (bass), Willie (guitar), Lester (harmonica) and Joe (guitar). Formed as a gospel group in Los Angeles in 1954. Drummer Brian Keenan added in 1965.	
9/14/68	4	17	● 1. The Time Has Come	Columbia 9522
11/23/68	16	6	2. A New Time-A New Day	Columbia 9671
			CHANGE	
			European/American studio group formed by Italian producer Jacques Fred Petrus. Led by Paolo Granolio (guitar) and David Romani (bass). Luther Vandross sang on several songs from group's first two albums. Later group, based in New York, included lead vocals by James Robinson and Deborah "Crab" Cooper. One-time band member Rick Gallway married Sharon Bryant, former lead singer of Atlantic Starr.	
6/21/80	29	7	● 1. The Glow Of Love	RFC 3438
			CHANTAY'S	
			Teenage surf-rock quintet from Santa Ana, California: Bob Spickard (lead guitar), Brian Carman (rhythm guitar), Rob Marshall (piano), Warren Waters (bass) and Bob Welsh (drums). First recorded for Downey in 1962. Disbanded in 1966.	
6/22/63	26	4	1. Pipeline [I]	Dot 25516
			Pipeline (4)	
			CHAPIN, Harry	
			Folk-rock balladeer. Born on 12/7/42 in New York City. Died in an auto accident on 7/16/81.	
10/26/74	4	17	● 1. Verities & Balderdash	Elektra 1012
			Cat's In The Cradle (1)	
			CHAPMAN, Tracy	
			Boston-based singer/songwriter born in Cleveland. Graduated from Tufts University in 1986 with an anthropology degree. Won the 1988 Best New Artist Grammy Award.	
6/4/88	1(1)	46	▲ 1. Tracy Chapman	Elektra 60774
			Fast Car (6)	
10/28/89	9	14	▲ 2. Crossroads	Elektra 60888
			CHARLENE	
			Born Charlene D'Angelo on 6/1/50 in Hollywood.	
6/5/82	36	3	1. I've Never Been To Me	Motown 6009
			I've Never Been To Me (3)	

DATE	POS	WKS	ARTIST—RECORD TITLE	LABEL & NO.
			CHARLES, Ray	
			Born Ray Charles Robinson on 9/23/30 in Albany, Georgia. To Greenville, Florida while still an infant. Partially blind at age five, completely blind at seven (glaucoma). Studied classical piano and clarinet at State School for Deaf and Blind Children, St. Augustine, Florida, 1937-45. With local Florida bands, moved to Seattle in 1948. Formed the McSon Trio (also known as the Maxim Trio and the Maxine Trio) with G.D. McGhee (guitar) and Milton Garred (bass). First recordings were very much in the King Cole Trio style. Formed own band in 1954. Inducted into the Rock and Roll Hall of Fame in 1986. Extremely popular performer with many TV and film appearances.	
2/15/60	**17**	37	1. The Genius Of Ray Charles *	Atlantic 1312
7/18/60	**13**	18	2. Ray Charles In Person * [L] recorded on 5/28/59 at Herndon Stadium, Atlanta, Georgia	Atlantic 8039
10/10/60	**9**	13	3. The Genius Hits The Road *Georgia On My Mind* (1)	ABC-Para. 335
3/6/61	**11**	16	4. Dedicated To You	ABC-Para. 355
3/27/61	**4**	29	5. Genius + Soul = Jazz featuring top jazz artists including Count Basie's band *One Mint Julep* (8)	Impulse! 2
1/20/62	**11**	24	6. Do The Twist! * [K]	Atlantic 8054
5/12/62	**1(14)**	59	● 7. Modern Sounds In Country And Western Music *I Can Stop Loving You* (1)/*You Don't Know Me* (2)	ABC-Para. 410
6/23/62	**20**	4	8. What'd I Say * [K] *What'd I Say* (6)	Atlantic 8029
9/1/62	**5**	23	● 9. Ray Charles' Greatest Hits [G] *Hit The Road Jack* (1)/*Unchain My Heart* (9)	ABC-Para. 415
9/1/62	**14**	9	10. The Ray Charles Story * [K] *all Atlantic albums recorded 1952-1959	Atlantic 900 [2]
11/10/62	**2(2)**	38	● 11. Modern Sounds In Country And Western Music (Volume Two) *You Are My Sunshine* (7)/*Take These Chains From My Heart* (8)	ABC-Para. 435
9/14/63	**2(2)**	21	12. Ingredients In A Recipe For Soul *Busted* (4)	ABC-Para. 465
4/4/64	**9**	11	13. Sweet & Sour Tears	ABC-Para. 480
9/26/64	**36**	5	14. Have A Smile With Me	ABC-Para. 495
4/30/66	**15**	20	15. Crying Time *Crying Time* (6)	ABC-Para. 544
			CHARLES, Ray/Singers	
			Ray was born on 9/13/18 in Chicago. Arranger and conductor for many TV shows including the "Perry Como Show," "Glen Campbell Goodtime Hour" and "Sha-Na-Na." **THE RAY CHARLES SINGERS:**	
5/30/64	**11**	15	1. Something Special For Young Lovers *Love Me With All Your Heart* (3)	Command 866
			CHARLESTON CITY ALL-STARS	
			Conducted by Enoch Light.	
9/2/57	**16**	14	1. The Roaring 20's, Volume 2 [I]	Grand Award 340
9/2/57	**17**	2	2. The Roaring 20's, Volume 3 [I]	Grand Award 353
			CHASE	
			Jazz-rock band organized by trumpeter Bill Chase (formerly with Woody Herman and Stan Kenton). Bill Chase and three other members were killed in a plane crash on 8/9/74.	
7/3/71	**22**	10	1. Chase	Epic 30472

DATE	POS	WKS	ARTIST—RECORD TITLE	LABEL & NO.
			CHEAP TRICK	
			Rock quartet from Rockford, Illinois consisting of Rick Nielsen (guitar), Bun E. Carlos (real name: Brad Carlson; drums), Robin Zander (vocals) and Tom Petersson (bass; replaced by Jon Brant in 1980. Founded by Nielsen and Petersson, former members of Nazz. Petersson returned in 1988 (replaced Brant).	
3/3/79	**4**	30	▲ 1. Cheap Trick At Budokan [L] *I Want You To Want Me* (7)	Epic 35795
10/6/79	**6**	10	▲ 2. Dream Police	Epic 35773
7/19/80	**39**	2	3. Found All The Parts [M] *10" mini LP; recorded 1976-1979*	Epic 36453
11/22/80	**24**	7	● 4. All Shook Up	Epic 36498
6/19/82	**39**	10	5. One On One	Epic 38021
10/5/85	**35**	4	6. Standing On The Edge	Epic 39592
5/21/88	**16**	28	▲ 7. Lap Of Luxury *The Flame* (1)/*Don't Be Cruel* (4)	Epic 40922
			CHECKER, Chubby	
			Born Ernest Evans on 10/3/41 in Philadelphia. Did impersonations of famous singers. First recorded for Parkway in 1959. Cover version of Hank Ballard's "The Twist" started worldwide dance craze.	
10/31/60	**3**	42	1. Twist With Chubby Checker *The Twist* (1)	Parkway 7001
12/4/61	**11**	16	2. Let's Twist Again *Let's Twist Again* (8)	Parkway 7004
12/18/61	**2**(6)	36	3. Your Twist Party [K] features songs from above three albums and "It's Pony Time" album	Parkway 7007
12/25/61	**7**	11	4. Bobby Rydell/Chubby Checker	Cameo 1013
1/20/62	**8**	22	5. For Twisters Only	Parkway 7002
4/14/62	**17**	17	6. For Teen Twisters Only *The Fly* (7)/*Slow Twistin'* (3)	Parkway 7009
7/21/62	**29**	3	7. Don't Knock The Twist [S] six cuts by Chubby, who also stars in the film	Parkway 7011
11/10/62	**23**	8	8. All The Hits (For Your Dancin' Party) *Limbo Rock* (2)	Parkway 7014
12/29/62	**11**	19	9. Limbo Party	Parkway 7020
2/9/63	**27**	8	10. Chubby Checker's Biggest Hits [G] *Popeye The Hitchhiker* (10)	Parkway 7022
			CHEECH & CHONG	
			Comedians Richard "Cheech" Marin (b: Watts, California) and Thomas Chong (b: 5/24/40, Edmonton, Alberta, Canada). Starred in movies since 1980. Chong was the guitarist of Bobby Taylor's Vancouvers.	
1/29/72	**28**	10	● 1. Cheech And Chong [C]	Ode 77010
7/15/72	**2**(1)	20	● 2. Big Bambu [C]	Ode 77014
9/8/73	**2**(1)	29	● 3. Los Cochinos [C]	Ode 77019
10/26/74	**5**	9	● 4. Cheech & Chong's Wedding Album [C] *Earache My Eye Featuring Alice Bowie* (9)	Ode 77025
7/10/76	**25**	6	5. Sleeping Beauty [C]	Ode 77040

DATE	POS	WKS	ARTIST—RECORD TITLE	LABEL & NO.
			CHER	
			Born Cherilyn LaPierre on 5/20/46 in El Centro, California. Worked as backup singer for Phil Spector. Recorded with Sonny Bono as ''Caesar & Cleo'' in 1963. Recorded as ''Bonnie Jo Mason'' and ''Cherilyn'' in 1964. Married Bono in 1963, divorced in 1974. Married for a short time to Gregg Allman. Own TV series with Bono from 1971-77. Acclaimed film actress (won Best Actress Oscar in 1987 for *Moonstruck*).	
10/16/65	**16**	10	1. All I Really Want To Do	Imperial 12292
6/18/66	**26**	7	2. The Sonny Side Of Cher *Bang Bang* (9)	Imperial 12301
10/30/71	**16**	11	3. Gypsys, Tramps & Thieves *Gypsys, Tramps & Thieves* (1)/*The Way of Love* (7)	Kapp 3649
10/27/73	**28**	4	● 4. Half-Breed *Half-Breed* (1)	MCA 2104
4/14/79	**25**	6	● 5. Take Me Home *Take Me Home* (8)	Casablanca 7133
3/19/88	**32**	12	● 6. Cher *I Found Someone* (10)	Geffen 24164
8/26/89	**10**	31	▲ 7. Heart Of Stone *After All* (6) with Peter Cetera/*If I Could Turn Back Time* (3)/ *Just Like Jesse James* (8)	Geffen 24239
			CHERRELLE	
			Born Cheryl Norton in Los Angeles. Soul vocalist/drummer. Cousin of vocalist Pebbles. Moved to Detroit in 1979. Discovered by Michael Henderson.	
4/12/86	**36**	1	1. High Priority accompanied by The Secrets: Jimmy ''Jam'' Harris, Terry Lewis and Monte Moir (all ex-members of Time)	Tabu 40094
			CHERRY, Don	
			Born on 1/11/24 in Wichita Falls, Texas. Studied voice after service in mid-40s. Vocalist with Jan Garber band in late 40s. Accomplished professional golfer.	
9/22/56	**15**	7	1. Swingin' For Two with Ray Conniff & His Orchestra	Columbia 893
			CHERRY, Neneh	
			London-based singer born on 8/10/64 in Stockholm, of Swedish and West African parentage; raised in New York City. Stepdaughter of jazz trumpeter Don Cherry.	
9/16/89	**40**	1	1. Raw Like Sushi *Buffalo Stance* (3)/*Kisses On The Wind* (8)	Virgin 91252
			CHIC	
			Disco group formed in New York City by producers Bernard Edwards (bass) and Nile Rodgers (guitar). Vocalists: Norma Jean Wright (replaced by Alfa Anderson) and Luci Martin; drums: Tony Thompson. Wright began solo career in 1978; recorded as Norma Jean. Edwards recorded with the studio group Roundtree in 1978. Rodgers joined The Honeydrippers in 1984. Thompson joined the Power Station in 1985 and Edwards became their producer.	
2/4/78	**27**	9	● 1. Chic *Dance, Dance, Dance* (6)	Atlantic 19153
12/9/78	**4**	22	▲ 2. C'est Chic *Le Freak* (1)/*I Want Your Love* (7)	Atlantic 19209
8/25/79	**5**	11	▲ 3. Risque *Good Times* (1)	Atlantic 16003
8/23/80	**30**	3	4. Real People	Atlantic 16016

DATE	POS	WKS	ARTIST—RECORD TITLE	LABEL & NO.
			CHICAGO	
			Jazz-oriented rock group formed in Chicago in 1967. Consisted of Robert Lamm (keyboards), James Pankow (trombone), Lee Loughnane (trumpet), Terry Kath (guitar; d: 1/23/78 playing Russian roulette [age 31]), Walt Parazaider (reeds), Peter Cetera (bass) and Danny Seraphine (drums). Originally called The Big Thing, later Chicago Transit Authority. To Los Angeles in late 60s. Following death, Kath replaced by Donnie Dacus (left in 1979). Bill Champlin (keyboards) joined in 1982. Cetera left in 1985, replaced by Jason Scheff.	
5/31/69	**17**	42	▲ 1. Chicago Transit Authority *Does Anybody Really Know What Time It Is?* (7)/*Beginnings* (7)	Columbia 8 [2]
2/21/70	**4**	53	● 2. Chicago II *Make Me Smile* (9)/*25 Or 6 To 4* (4)	Columbia 24 [2]
1/30/71	**2**(2)	22	▲ 3. Chicago III	Columbia 30110 [2]
11/20/71	**3**	19	▲ 4. Chicago At Carnegie Hall　　　　　　　[L] four-album boxed set	Columbia 30865 [4]
7/29/72	**1**(9)	20	▲ 5. Chicago V *Saturday In The Park* (3)	Columbia 31102
7/21/73	**1**(5)	27	▲ 6. Chicago VI *Feelin' Stronger Every Day* (10)/*Just You 'N' Me* (4)	Columbia 32400
4/6/74	**1**(1)	35	▲ 7. Chicago VII *(I've Been) Searchin' So Long* (9)/*Call On Me* (6)	Columbia 32810 [2]
4/12/75	**1**(2)	15	▲ 8. Chicago VIII *Old Days* (5)	Columbia 33100
11/29/75	**1**(5)	22	▲ 9. Chicago IX - Chicago's Greatest Hits　　[G]	Columbia 33900
7/4/76	**3**	30	▲ 10. Chicago X *If You Leave Me Now* (1)	Columbia 34200
10/1/77	**6**	10	▲ 11. Chicago XI *Baby, What A Big Surprise* (4)	Columbia 34860
10/21/78	**12**	11	▲ 12. Hot Streets	Columbia 35512
9/8/79	**21**	5	● 13. Chicago 13	Columbia 36105
7/17/82	**9**	18	▲ 14. Chicago 16 *Hard To Say I'm Sorry* (1)	Full Moon 23689
6/16/84	**4**	44	▲ 15. Chicago 17 *Hard Habit To Break* (3)/*You're The Inspiration* (3)	Full Moon 25060
2/21/87	**35**	4	● 16. Chicago 18 *Will You Still Love Me?* (3)	Warner 25509
1/7/89	**37**	4	▲ 17. 19 *I Don't Wanna Live Without Your Love* (3)/*Look Away* (1)/ *You're Not Alone* (10)	Reprise 25714
1/20/90	**37**	5	● 18. Greatest Hits 1982-1989　　　　　　[G] *What Kind Of Man Would I Be?* (5)	Reprise 26080
			CHI-LITES, The	
			R&B vocal group from Chicago. Consisted of Eugene Record (lead vocals), Robert "Squirrel" Lester (tenor), Marshall Thompson (baritone) and Creadel "Red" Jones (bass). First recorded as the Hi-Lites on Daran in 1963. Record went solo in 1976.	
9/25/71	**12**	14	1. (For God's Sake) Give More Power To The People *Have You Seen Her* (3)	Brunswick 754170
5/13/72	**5**	16	2. A Lonely Man *Oh Girl* (1)	Brunswick 754179

DATE	POS	WKS	ARTIST—RECORD TITLE	LABEL & NO.
			CHIPMUNKS, The	
			Characters created by Ross Bagdasarian ("David Seville"). Named Alvin, Simon and Theodore after Liberty executives Alvin Bennett, Simon Waronker and Theodore Keep. Bagdasarian died on 1/16/72 (age 52); his son resurrected the act in 1980.	
12/7/59	4	28	1. Let's All Sing With The Chipmunks * [N] *The Chipmunk Song* (1)/*Alvin's Harmonica* (3)	Liberty 3132
6/20/60	31	5	2. Sing Again With The Chipmunks * [N] ***DAVID SEVILLE AND THE CHIPMUNKS**	Liberty 3159
9/19/64	14	11	3. The Chipmunks Sing The Beatles Hits [N]	Liberty 7388
8/23/80	34	6	● 4. Chipmunk Punk [N] 'group' resurrected by Seville's son	Excelsior 6008
			CHRISTY, June	
			Born Shirley Luster on 11/20/25 in Springfield, Illinois. Jazz singer. Achieved national fame with the Stan Kenton band. Orchestra conducted by Pete Rugolo. Died on 6/21/90 of kidney failure.	
9/29/56	14	4	1. The Misty Miss Christy	Capitol 725
7/22/57	16	4	2. June - Fair and Warmer!	Capitol 833
			CINDERELLA	
			Pennsylvania-based, heavy-metal band consisting of Tom Keifer (lead singer, guitar, piano), Jeff LaBar (guitar), Eric Brittingham (bass) and Fred Coury (drums).	
8/23/86	3	49	▲ 1. Night Songs	Mercury 830076
7/30/88	10	32	▲ 2. Long Cold Winter	Mercury 834612
			CLAPTON, Eric	
			Prolific rock-blues guitarist/vocalist; born on 3/30/45 in Ripley, England. With The Roosters in 1963, The Yardbirds, 1963-65, and John Mayall's Bluesbreakers, 1965-66. Formed Cream with Jack Bruce and Ginger Baker in 1966. Formed Blind Faith in 1968; worked with John Lennon's Plastic Ono Band, and Delaney & Bonnie. Formed Derek and The Dominos in 1970, featuring Bobby Whitlock, Jim Gordon and Carl Radle (died on 5/30/80). After two years of reclusion (1971-72), Clapton performed his comeback concert at London's Rainbow Theatre in January, 1973. Began actively recording and touring again in 1974.	
8/8/70	13	10	1. Eric Clapton	Atco 329
11/28/70	16	19	● 2. Layla * with Duane Allman *Layla* (10)	Atco 704 [2]
4/22/72	6	22	● 3. History Of Eric Clapton [K] recordings with groups listed in above artist notes	Atco 803 [2]
2/17/73	20	9	● 4. Derek & The Dominos In Concert * [L] ***DEREK AND THE DOMINOS**	RSO 8800 [2]
10/6/73	18	6	5. Eric Clapton's Rainbow Concert [L] Clapton's comeback concert at London's Rainbow Theatre with Pete Townshend, Steve Winwood, Ron Wood and Jim Capaldi	RSO 877
7/27/74	1(4)	14	● 6. 461 Ocean Boulevard address where recorded in Miami, Florida *I Shot The Sheriff* (1)	RSO 4801
4/26/75	21	5	7. There's One In Every Crowd	RSO 4806
9/13/75	20	7	8. E.C. Was Here [L]	RSO 4809
10/16/76	15	12	9. No Reason To Cry	RSO 3004
12/24/77	2(5)	30	▲ 10. Slowhand *Lay Down Sally* (3)	RSO 3030
12/2/78	8	17	▲ 11. Backless *Promises* (9)	RSO 3039

DATE	POS	WKS	ARTIST—RECORD TITLE	LABEL & NO.
5/10/80	**2**(6)	19	● 12. Just One Night [L] *recorded live at the Budokan Theatre, Japan*	RSO 4202 [2]
3/21/81	**7**	13	● 13. Another Ticket *I Can't Stand It* (10)	RSO 3095
2/26/83	**16**	10	14. Money And Cigarettes	Duck 23773
4/13/85	**34**	7	● 15. Behind the Sun	Duck 25166
2/21/87	**37**	5	● 16. August	Duck 25476
5/14/88	**34**	3	● 17. Crossroads [K] *contains 73 digitally mastered tracks of Clapton's 25-year career*	Poly. 835261 [6]
12/2/89	**16**	26	▲ 18. Journeyman	Duck 26074

CLARK, Dave

Leader of own rock group formed in Tottenham, England in 1960. Consisted of Clark (drums), Mike Smith (lead vocals, keyboards), Lenny Davidson (guitar), Dennis Payton (sax) and Rick Huxley (bass). First recorded for Ember/Pye in 1962. On the Ed Sullivan Show in March of 1964. Group appeared in the film *Having A Wild Weekend* in 1965. Disbanded in 1973. Clark had been a stuntman in films; formed group to raise money for his soccer team, the Tottenham Hotspurs. Clark wrote the London stage musical *Time*.

DATE	POS	WKS	ARTIST—RECORD TITLE	LABEL & NO.
			THE DAVE CLARK FIVE:	
4/25/64	**3**	25	● 1. Glad All Over *Glad All Over* (6)/*Bits And Pieces* (4)	Epic 26093
7/4/64	**5**	13	2. The Dave Clark Five Return! *Can't You See That She's Mine* (4)	Epic 26104
9/5/64	**11**	9	3. American Tour *Because* (3)	Epic 26117
1/16/65	**6**	13	4. Coast To Coast	Epic 26128
5/15/65	**24**	6	5. Weekend In London	Epic 26139

9/18/65	**15**	11	6. Having A Wild Weekend [S]
			     the Dave Clark Five star in the film
			     Catch Us If You Can (4)
				Epic 26162

1/22/66	**32**	6	7. I Like It Like That *I Like It Like That* (7)	Epic 26178
4/2/66	**9**	20	● 8. The Dave Clark Five's Greatest Hits [G] *Over And Over* (1)	Epic 26185

CLARK, Dick — see VARIOUS - Radio/TV Celebrity Compilations

CLARK, Petula

Born on 11/15/32 in Epsom, England. On radio at age nine; own show "Pet's Parlour" at age 11. TV series in England in 1950. First U.S. record release for Coral in 1951. Appeared in over 20 British films, 1944-57; revived her film career in late 60s, starring in *Finian's Rainbow* and *Goodbye Mr. Chips*.

DATE	POS	WKS	ARTIST—RECORD TITLE	LABEL & NO.
3/20/65	**21**	16	1. Downtown *Downtown* (1)	Warner 1590
9/23/67	**27**	10	2. These Are My Songs *This Is My Song* (3)/*Don't Sleep In The Subway* (5)	Warner 1698
5/24/69	**37**	3	3. Portrait Of Petula	Warner 1789

CLARKE, Stanley

Born on 6/30/51 in Philadelphia. Bassist/violinist/cellist. With Chick Corea in Return To Forever. Much session work, solo debut in 1974. Member of Animal Logic in 1989.

DATE	POS	WKS	ARTIST—RECORD TITLE	LABEL & NO.
11/29/75	**34**	3	1. Journey To Love [I]	Nemperor 433
10/23/76	**34**	4	2. School Days [I]	Nemperor 439

DATE	POS	WKS	ARTIST—RECORD TITLE	LABEL & NO.
6/6/81	33	8	**STANLEY CLARKE/GEORGE DUKE:** 3. The Clarke/Duke Project	Epic 36918
			CLASH, The	
			Eclectic new-wave rock group formed in London in 1976. Consisted of Joe Strummer (vocals, lyricist), Mick Jones (guitar), Paul Simonon (bass) and Topper Headon (drums). Headon left in May, 1983; replaced by Peter Howard. Jones left band in 1984 to form Big Audio Dynamite. Political activists, they wrote songs protesting racism and oppression. Strummer disbanded The Clash in early 1986. Strummer appeared in the 1987 film *Straight To Hell*.	
3/8/80	27	9	1. London Calling	Epic 36328 [2]
2/21/81	24	5	2. Sandinista!	Epic 37037 [3]
6/26/82	7	39	▲ 3. Combat Rock *Rock The Casbah* (8)	Epic 37689
			CLAY, Andrew Dice	
			Comedian from Brooklyn. Appeared in the films *Pretty In Pink*, *Casual Sex*, *The Adventures of Ford Fairlane* and TV's "Crime Story."	
6/2/90	39	2	1. The Day The Laughter Died [C]	Def Amer. 24287 [2]
			CLIBURN, Van	
			Born Harvey Cliburn, Jr. on 7/12/34 in Shreveport, Louisiana. Classical pianist.	
8/4/58	1(7)	76	▲ 1. Tchaikovsky: Piano Concerto No. 1 [I] Kiril Kondrashin, conductor	RCA 2252
7/13/59	10	37	2. Rachmaninoff: Piano Concerto No. 3 [I-L] Carnegie Hall performance of 5/19/58	RCA 2355
3/24/62	25	7	3. Brahms: Piano Concerto No. 2 [I] Fritz Reiner conducts the Chicago Symphony Orchestra	RCA 2581
			CLIFFORD, Linda	
			Black vocalist from Brooklyn. Former Miss New York State. With Jericho Jazz Singers; had own trio in 1967.	
7/1/78	22	5	1. If My Friends Could See Me Now	Curtom 5021
4/21/79	26	8	2. Let Me Be Your Woman	RSO 3902 [2]
			CLIMAX BLUES BAND	
			Blues-rock band formed in Stafford, England. Nucleus consisted of Colin Cooper (sax, vocals), Peter Haycock (guitar, vocals), Derek Holt (bass) and John Cuffley (drums).	
10/5/74	37	2	1. Sense Of Direction	Sire 7501
6/11/77	27	6	2. Gold Plated *Couldn't Get It Right* (3)	Sire 7523
			CLINTON, George	
			Born on 7/22/40 in Plainfield, Ohio. Lead singer of The Parliaments. Became leader/ producer of Funkadelic and Parliament. Headed "A Parliafunkadelicament Thang," a corporation of nearly 40 musicians that recorded as Parliament and Funkadelic plus various offshoot bands: Bootsy's Rubber Band, The Brides Of Funkenstein, Horny Horns, Parlet and the P. Funk All Stars. Appeared in the film *House Party*.	
4/30/83	40	1	1. Computer Games	Capitol 12246
			CLOONEY, Rosemary — see HI-LO'S, The	
			CLUB NOUVEAU	
			Sacramento-based dance/disco group formed and fronted by Jay King (producer/owner of King Jay Records; produced the Timex Social Club).	
2/28/87	6	16	▲ 1. Life, Love & Pain *Lean On Me* (1)	Warner 25531

DATE	POS	WKS	ARTIST—RECORD TITLE	LABEL & NO.
			COBHAM, Billy	
			Born on 5/16/44 in Panama; raised in New York City. Jazz-rock drummer. Formerly with Miles Davis and John McLaughlin.	
1/12/74	**26**	9	1. Spectrum [I]	Atlantic 7268
5/25/74	**23**	6	2. Crosswinds [I]	Atlantic 7300
1/25/75	**36**	1	3. Total Eclipse [I]	Atlantic 18121
			COCKER, Joe	
			Born John Robert Cocker on 5/20/44 in Sheffield, England. Own skiffle band, the Cavaliers, late 50s, later reorganized as Vance Arnold & The Avengers. Assembled the Grease Band in the mid-60s. First U.S. tour, Woodstock Festival, in August of 1969. Successful tour with 43-piece revue, Mad Dogs & Englishmen, in 1970. Notable spastic stage antics were based on Ray Charles' movements at the piano.	
7/19/69	**35**	3	● 1. With A Little Help From My Friends with Jimmy Page and Stevie Winwood	A&M 4182
11/29/69	**11**	26	● 2. Joe Cocker! with Leon Russell and The Grease Band	A&M 4224
9/5/70	**2(1)**	16	● 3. Mad Dogs & Englishmen [S-L] title refers to Cocker's 1970 concert tour with an entourage of 43 including Leon Russell and Chris Stainton *The Letter* (7)	A&M 6002 [2]
12/30/72	**30**	7	4. Joe Cocker	A&M 4368
9/21/74	**11**	10	5. I Can Stand A Little Rain *You Are So Beautiful* (5)	A&M 3633
			COFFEY, Dennis	
			Detroit native Coffey was a session guitarist for The Temptations, The Jackson 5 and others. Coffey later formed C.J. & Co. **DENNIS COFFEY AND THE DETROIT GUITAR BAND:**	
1/8/72	**36**	4	1. Evolution [I] *Scorpio* (6)	Sussex 7004
			COLD BLOOD	
			Bay-area rock group led by Lydia Pense.	
3/7/70	**23**	6	1. Cold Blood	San Francisco 200
			COLE, Natalie	
			Born on 2/6/50 in Los Angeles. Daughter of Nat "King" Cole. Professional debut at age 11. Married for a time to her producer, Marvin Yancey, Jr. Later married Andre Fischer, former drummer of Rufus and producer for Brenda Russell, Michael Franks and Andre Crouch. Natalie won the 1975 Best New Artist Grammy Award.	
11/1/75	**18**	8	● 1. Inseparable *This Will Be* (6)	Capitol 11429
6/5/76	**13**	11	● 2. Natalie	Capitol 11517
3/12/77	**8**	13	▲ 3. Unpredictable *I've Got Love On My Mind* (5)	Capitol 11600
1/28/78	**16**	17	▲ 4. Thankful *Our Love* (10)	Capitol 11708
8/5/78	**31**	7	● 5. Natalie...Live! [L]	Capitol 11709 [2]

DATE	POS	WKS	ARTIST—RECORD TITLE	LABEL & NO.
			COLE, Nat "King"	
			Born Nathaniel Adams Coles on 3/17/17 in Montgomery, Alabama. Died of lung cancer on 2/15/65 in Santa Monica, California. Raised in Chicago. Own band, the Royal Dukes, at age 17. First recorded in 1936 in band led by brother Eddie. Toured with "Shuffle Along" musical revue, resided in Los Angeles. Formed King Cole Trio in 1939: Nat (piano), Oscar Moore (guitar; later joined brother's group, Johnny Moore's Three Blazers) and Wesley Prince (bass; replaced several years later by Johnny Miller). Long series of top-selling records led to his solo career in 1950. In films *St. Louis Blues*, *Cat Ballou*, and many other film and TV appearances. Stopped performing in 1964 due to ill health. Daughter Natalie is also a recording star.	
4/28/56	**16**	2	1. Ballads Of The Day *Darling Je Vous Aime Beaucoup* (7)/*A Blossom Fell* (2)	Capitol 680
3/9/57	**13**	2	2. After Midnight with the King Cole Trio	Capitol 782
4/6/57	**1**(8)	55	● 3. Love Is The Thing	Capitol 824
9/23/57	**18**	3	4. This Is Nat "King" Cole	Capitol 870
12/16/57	**18**	6	5. Just One Of Those Things	Capitol 903
5/5/58	**18**	3	6. St. Louis Blues　　　　　　　　　　　　[S] Nat portrayed W.C. Handy in the film about Handy's life	Capitol 993
9/22/58	**12**	5	7. Cole Español　　　　　　　　　　　　[F]	Capitol 1031
12/1/58	**17**	2	8. The Very Thought Of You	Capitol 1084
4/18/60	**33**	2	9. Tell Me All About Yourself	Capitol 1331
10/24/60	**4**	11	10. Wild Is Love	Capitol 1392
5/12/62	**27**	9	11. Nat King Cole sings/George Shearing plays	Capitol 1675
9/29/62	**3**	53	● 12. Ramblin' Rose *Ramblin' Rose* (2)	Capitol 1793
1/5/63	**24**	10	13. Dear Lonely Hearts	Capitol 1838
7/20/63	**14**	9	14. Those Lazy-Hazy-Crazy Days Of Summer *Those Lazy-Hazy-Crazy Days Of Summer* (6)	Capitol 1932
8/22/64	**18**	4	15. I Don't Want To Be Hurt Anymore	Capitol 2118
3/6/65	**4**	25	16. L-O-V-E	Capitol 2195
5/8/65	**30**	11	● 17. Unforgettable　　　　　　　　　　[R] reissue of his 1953 10" album	Capitol 357
			COLLINS, Judy	
			Contemporary folk singer born on 5/1/39 in Seattle; raised in Denver.	
7/13/68	**5**	19	● 1. Wildflowers *Both Sides Now* (8)	Elektra 74012
2/1/69	**29**	11	● 2. Who Knows Where The Time Goes	Elektra 74033
10/11/69	**29**	3	3. Recollections　　　　　　　　　　　[K] recordings from 1963-1965	Elektra 74055
12/12/70	**17**	16	● 4. Whales & Nightingales	Elektra 75010
7/1/72	**37**	3	● 5. Colors Of The Day/The Best Of Judy Collins　[G]	Elektra 75030
3/24/73	**27**	4	6. True Stories And Other Dreams	Elektra 75053
5/3/75	**17**	17	● 7. Judith	Elektra 1032
9/25/76	**25**	4	8. Bread & Roses	Elektra 1076
			COLLINS, Phil	
			Born on 1/30/51 in London. Vocalist/drummer/composer. Stage actor as a young child; played the Artful Dodger in the London production of *Oliver*. With group Flaming Youth. Joined Genesis in 1970, became lead singer in 1975. Also with jazz-rock group Brand X. First solo album, 1981. Starred in 1988 film *Buster*.	
4/4/81	**7**	26	▲ 1. Face Value	Atlantic 16029

DATE	POS	WKS	ARTIST—RECORD TITLE	LABEL & NO.
12/4/82	**8**	21	▲ 2. Hello, I Must Be Going! *You Can't Hurry Love* (10)	Atlantic 80035
3/9/85	**1**(7)	70	▲ 3. No Jacket Required 1985 Grammy winner: Album of the Year *One More Night* (1)/*Sussudio* (1)/*Don't Lose My Number* (4)/ *Take Me Home* (7)	Atlantic 81240
12/9/89	**1**(1)	46+	▲ 4. ...But Seriously *Another Day In Paradise* (1)/*I Wish It Would Rain Down* (3)/ *Do You Remember?* (4)/*Something Happened On The Way To Heaven* (4)	Atlantic 82050
			COLLINS, William — see BOOTSY'S RUBBER BAND	
			COLTER, Jessi — see JENNINGS, Waylon or NELSON, Willie	
			COMMAND ALL-STARS — see LIGHT, Enoch	
			COMMODORES	
			Formed in Tuskegee, Alabama in 1970. Consisted of Lionel Richie (vocals, saxophone), William King (trumpet), Thomas McClary (guitar), Milan Williams (keyboards), Ronald LaPread (bass) and Walter "Clyde" Orange (drums). First recorded for Motown in 1972. In film *Thank God It's Friday*. Richie began solo work in 1981.	
7/5/75	**26**	5	1. Caught In The Act	Motown 820
11/29/75	**29**	9	2. Movin' On *Sweet Love* (5)	Motown 848
8/7/76	**12**	25	3. Hot On The Tracks *Just To Be Close To You* (7)	Motown 867
4/16/77	**3**	31	4. Commodores *Easy* (4)/*Brick House* (5)	Motown 884
11/12/77	**3**	16	5. Commodores Live! [L]	Motown 894 [2]
6/3/78	**3**	23	▲ 6. Natural High *Three Times A Lady* (1)	Motown 902
12/23/78	**23**	6	7. Commodores' Greatest Hits [G]	Motown 912
8/18/79	**3**	30	8. Midnight Magic *Sail On* (4)/*Still* (1)	Motown 926
6/28/80	**7**	15	▲ 9. Heroes	Motown 939
7/11/81	**13**	19	▲ 10. In The Pocket *Lady (You Bring Me Up)* (8)/*Oh No* (4)	Motown 955
1/15/83	**37**	4	11. All The Great Hits [G]	Motown 6028
3/23/85	**12**	15	● 12. Nightshift *Nightshift* (3)	Motown 6124
			COMO, Perry	
			Born Pierino Como on 5/18/12 in Canonsburg, Pennsylvania. Owned barbershop in hometown. With Freddy Carlone band in 1933; with Ted Weems, 1936-1942. In the films *Something For The Boys*, *Doll Face*, *If I'm Lucky* and *Words And Music*, 1944-48. Own "Supper Club" radio series to late 1940s. Television shows (15 minutes) from 1948-55. Host of hourly TV shows from 1955-63.	
10/15/55	**7**	15	1. So Smooth	RCA 1085
9/2/57	**8**	10	2. We Get Letters	RCA 1463
12/16/57	**8**	5	● 3. Merry Christmas Music [X]	RCA 1243
12/16/57	**11**	9	4. Dream Along With Me	RCA Camden 403
6/23/58	**18**	2	5. Saturday Night With Mr. C.	RCA 1004

DATE	POS	WKS	ARTIST—RECORD TITLE	LABEL & NO.
9/1/58	**24**	2	6. Como's Golden Records [G] *Hot Diggity* (1)/*Round And Round* (1)/*Catch A Falling Star* (1)/ *Magic Moments* (4)	RCA 1007
12/15/58	**9**	4	7. Merry Christmas Music [X-R]	RCA 1243
1/5/59	**16**	7	8. When You Come To The End Of The Day	RCA 1885
11/2/59	**17**	3	9. Como Swings	RCA 2010
1/4/60	**22**	1	● 10. Season's Greetings [X]	RCA 2066
12/31/60	**27**	1	11. Season's Greetings [X-R]	RCA 2066
1/13/62	**33**	1	12. Season's Greetings [X-R]	RCA 2066
12/8/62	**32**	3	13. By Request	RCA 2567
2/6/71	**22**	12	14. It's Impossible *It's Impossible* (10)	RCA 4473
7/7/73	**34**	4	● 15. And I Love You So	RCA 0100

CON FUNK SHUN

Soul band formed as Project Soul in Vallejo, California in 1968 by high school classmates Mike Cooper (lead vocals, guitar) and Louis McCall (drums). Moved to Memphis in 1972, changed name to Con Funk Shun. Cooper went solo in 1986.

DATE	POS	WKS	ARTIST—RECORD TITLE	LABEL & NO.
8/5/78	**32**	7	● 1. Loveshine	Mercury 3725
5/10/80	**30**	5	● 2. Spirit Of Love	Mercury 3806

CONNIFF, Ray

Born on 11/6/16 in Attleboro, Massachusetts. Trombonist/arranger with Bunny Berigan, Bob Crosby, Harry James, Vaughn Monroe and Artie Shaw bands; later conductor/ arranger for Columbia's leading singers in the 50s and 60s. Ray's non-instrumental albums feature The Ray Charles Singers.

DATE	POS	WKS	ARTIST—RECORD TITLE	LABEL & NO.
			RAY CONNIFF AND HIS ORCHESTRA:	
3/23/57	**11**	7	1. 'S Wonderful! [I]	Columbia 925
12/23/57	**10**	31	● 2. 'S Marvelous [I]	Columbia 1074
6/23/58	**9**	43	3. 'S Awful Nice [I]	Columbia 1137
9/29/58	**9**	39	● 4. Concert In Rhythm [I]	Columbia 1163
7/6/59	**29**	5	5. Hollywood In Rhythm [I]	Columbia 1310
12/14/59	**8**	32	6. Conniff Meets Butterfield [I]	Columbia 1346
			RAY CONNIFF & BILLY BUTTERFIELD (trumpeter)	
1/4/60	**14**	1	● 7. Christmas With Conniff [X]	Columbia 1390
2/15/60	**8**	32	8. It's The Talk Of The Town	Columbia 1334
3/7/60	**13**	16	9. Concert In Rhythm - Volume II [I]	Columbia 1415
8/15/60	**6**	13	10. Young At Heart	Columbia 1489
10/10/60	**4**	28	11. Say It With Music (A Touch Of Latin) [I]	Columbia 1490
12/31/60	**15**	1	12. Christmas With Conniff [X-R]	Columbia 1390
2/13/61	**4**	27	● 13. Memories Are Made Of This [I]	Columbia 1574
3/27/61	**10**	3	14. Broadway In Rhythm [I]	Columbia 1252
9/18/61	**14**	21	15. Somebody Loves Me	Columbia 1642
1/6/62	**16**	3	16. Christmas With Conniff [X-R]	Columbia 1390
2/17/62	**5**	23	● 17. So Much In Love	Columbia 1720
5/12/62	**6**	18	18. 'S Continental [I]	Columbia 1776
10/27/62	**28**	5	19. Rhapsody In Rhythm [I]	Columbia 1878
12/22/62	**32**	2	▲ 20. We Wish You A Merry Christmas [X]	Columbia 1892
3/9/63	**20**	8	21. The Happy Beat [I]	Columbia 8749
11/14/64	**23**	11	22. Invisible Tears	Columbia 9064

DATE	POS	WKS	ARTIST—RECORD TITLE	LABEL & NO.
7/10/65	34	6	23. Music From Mary Poppins, The Sound Of Music, My Fair Lady, & Other Great Movie Themes	Columbia 9166
7/30/66	3	41	▲ 24. Somewhere My Love *Somewhere My Love* (9)	Columbia 9319
7/8/67	30	6	25. This Is My Song	Columbia 9476
1/6/68	39	2	26. Hawaiian Album	Columbia 9547
3/30/68	25	13	● 27. It Must Be Him	Columbia 9595
7/27/68	22	9	● 28. Honey	Columbia 9661

CONNORS, Norman

Born on 3/1/48 in Philadelphia. Jazz drummer with Archie Shepp, John Coltrane, Pharoah Sanders and others. Own group on Buddah in 1972. Featured vocalists Michael Henderson, Jean Carn and Phyllis Hyman. Formed disco group Aquarian Dream.

DATE	POS	WKS	ARTIST—RECORD TITLE	LABEL & NO.
10/9/76	39	1	● 1. You Are My Starship	Buddah 5655

COOKE, Sam

Son of a Baptist minister. Born on 1/22/35 in Chicago; died from a gunshot wound on 12/11/64 (age 29) in Los Angeles. Sang in choir from age six. His nephew is singer R.B. Greaves. Sam joined gospel group, the Highway Q.C.'s. Lead singer of the Soul Stirrers from 1950-56. First recorded secular songs in 1956 as "Dale Cook" on Specialty. String of hits on Keen label led to contract with RCA. Shot by female motel manager under mysterious circumstances. Inducted into the Rock and Roll Hall of Fame in 1986. Revered as the definitive soul singer.

DATE	POS	WKS	ARTIST—RECORD TITLE	LABEL & NO.
3/10/58	16	2	1. Sam Cooke *You Send Me* (1)	Keen 2001
11/3/62	22	7	2. The Best Of Sam Cooke [G] *Chain Gang* (2)	RCA 2625
7/4/64	34	3	3. Ain't That Good News *Another Saturday Night* (10)	RCA 2899
2/20/65	29	5	4. Sam Cooke At The Copa [L]	RCA 2970

COOLIDGE, Rita

Born on 5/1/44 in Nashville. Had her own group, R.C. and the Moonpies, at Florida State University. Moved to Los Angeles in the late 60s. Did backup work for Delaney & Bonnie, Leon Russell, Joe Cocker and Eric Clapton. With Kris Kristofferson from 1971, married to him from 1973-80. Known as "The Delta Lady," for whom Leon Russell wrote the song of the same name.

DATE	POS	WKS	ARTIST—RECORD TITLE	LABEL & NO.
10/13/73	26	6	● 1. Full Moon **KRIS KRISTOFFERSON & RITA COOLIDGE**	A&M 4403
7/9/77	6	21	▲ 2. Anytime…Anywhere *(Your Love Has Lifted Me) Higher And Higher* (2)/ *We're All Alone* (7)	A&M 4616
7/15/78	32	5	● 3. Love Me Again	A&M 4699

COOPER, Alice

Born Vincent Furnier on 2/4/48 in Detroit. Formed rock group in Phoenix in 1965; changed name to Alice Cooper in 1966. To Los Angeles in 1968, then to Detroit in 1969. Alice is known primarily for his bizarre stage antics. Appeared in the 1987 film *Prince Of Darkness*.

DATE	POS	WKS	ARTIST—RECORD TITLE	LABEL & NO.
4/3/71	35	6	● 1. Love It To Death	Warner 1883
12/18/71	21	16	▲ 2. Killer	Warner 2567
7/15/72	2(3)	15	● 3. School's Out *School's Out* (7)	Warner 2623
3/24/73	1(1)	23	▲ 4. Billion Dollar Babies	Warner 2685
12/15/73	10	10	● 5. Muscle Of Love	Warner 2748
9/28/74	8	10	▲ 6. Alice Cooper's Greatest Hits [G]	Warner 2803

DATE	POS	WKS	ARTIST—RECORD TITLE		LABEL & NO.
3/29/75	**5**	17	▲ 7. Welcome To My Nightmare		Atlantic 18130
8/21/76	**27**	7	● 8. Alice Cooper Goes To Hell		Warner 2896
9/16/89	**20**	22	▲ 9. Trash		Epic 45137
			Poison (7)		
			CORNELIUS BROTHERS & SISTER ROSE		
			Family group from Dania, Florida. Consisted of Edward, Carter and Rose. Billie Jo was added in 1973. All 15 Cornelius children play instruments or sing. Carter currently lives in Florida as Gideon Israel, the leader of a Muslim religious sect.		
9/30/72	**29**	6	1. Cornelius Brothers & Sister Rose		United Art. 5568
			Treat Her Like A Lady (3)/*Too Late To Turn Back Now* (2)		
			COSBY, Bill		
			Born on 7/12/38 in Philadelphia. Top comedian who has appeared in nightclubs, on film and on TV. His first seven comedy albums were all million sellers. Played Alexander Scott on TV series "I Spy." Star of the highly rated NBC-TV series "The Cosby Show."		
2/6/65	**32**	5	▲ 1. I Started Out As A Child	[C]	Warner 1567
10/23/65	**19**	55	● 2. Why Is There Air?	[C]	Warner 1606
6/18/66	**7**	54	▲ 3. Wonderfulness	[C]	Warner 1634
7/9/66	**21**	34	▲ 4. Bill Cosby Is A Very Funny Fellow, Right!	[C]	Warner 1518
5/20/67	**2**(1)	28	● 5. Revenge	[C]	Warner 1691
9/9/67	**18**	12	6. Bill Cosby Sings/Silver Throat		Warner 1709
			Little Ole Man (4)		
4/13/68	**7**	23	● 7. To Russell, My Brother, Whom I Slept With	[C]	Warner 1734
11/16/68	**16**	11	● 8. 200 M.P.H.	[C]	Warner 1757
3/8/69	**37**	3	9. It's True! It's True!	[C]	Warner 1770
7/5/86	**26**	4	● 10. Those Of You With Or Without Children, You'll Understand	[C]	Geffen 24104
			COSTELLO, Elvis		
			Born Declan McManus in Liverpool, England on 8/25/55. Changed name to Elvis Costello in 1976. Formed backing band The Attractions in 1977. Appeared in the 1987 film *Straight To Hell*. Married Cait O'Riordan, former bassist with The Pogues.		
3/4/78	**32**	5	● 1. My Aim Is True		Columbia 35037
5/6/78	**30**	4	2. This Year's Model		Columbia 35331
2/3/79	**10**	11	● 3. Armed Forces		Columbia 35709
3/22/80	**11**	8	4. Get Happy!!		Columbia 36347
10/25/80	**28**	3	5. Taking Liberties	[K]	Columbia 36839
			previously released and unreleased tracks		
2/21/81	**28**	4	6. Trust		Columbia 37051
8/28/82	**30**	7	7. Imperial Bedroom		Columbia 38157
8/20/83	**24**	12	8. Punch The Clock		Columbia 38897
7/21/84	**35**	3	9. Goodbye Cruel World		Columbia 39429
4/5/86	**39**	3	10. The Costello Show (Featuring Elvis Costello) - King Of America		Columbia 40173
3/18/89	**32**	11	● 11. Spike		Warner 25848
			COUGAR, John — see MELLENCAMP		

DATE	POS	WKS	ARTIST—RECORD TITLE	LABEL & NO.
			COUNTRY JOE AND THE FISH	
			Country Joe (Joseph McDonald, b: 1/1/42, El Monte, California) And The Fish were San Francisco's leading political rock band of the 60s.	
9/23/67	39	3	1. Electric Music For The Mind And Body	Vanguard 79244
7/27/68	23	7	2. Together	Vanguard 79277
			COWARD, Noel	
			Born on 12/16/1899 in Teddington, England; died on 3/26/73. Enormously popular and enduring actor/playwright/personality in England. Knighted by Queen Elizabeth II in 1970.	
1/28/56	14	2	1. Noel Coward At Las Vegas [L]	Columbia 5063
			COWBOY JUNKIES	
			Canadian country-punk quartet: vocalist Margo Timmins with brothers Michael and Peter Timmins, and Alan Anton.	
3/11/89	26	9	● 1. The Trinity Session	RCA 8568
			COWSILLS, The	
			Family pop group from Newport, Rhode Island. Consisted of five brothers (Bill, Bob, Paul, Barry and John) with their little sister (Susan) and mother (Barbara, d: 1/31/85 [age 56]). Bob, Paul, John and Susan reunited for touring in 1990.	
12/9/67	31	7	1. The Cowsills	MGM 4498
			The Rain, The Park & Other Things (2)	
5/17/69	16	10	2. The Cowsills In Concert [L]	MGM 4619
			Hair (2)	
			CRANE, Les	
			TV talk-show host from San Francisco.	
12/25/71	32	4	1. Desiderata	Warner 2570
			Les talks, accompanied by a musical background *Desiderata* (8)	
			CRAWFORD, Johnny	
			Born on 3/26/46 in Los Angeles. One of the original Mouseketeers. Played Chuck Connor's son (Mark McCain) in the TV series "The Rifleman," 1958-63.	
9/22/62	40	1	1. A Young Man's Fancy	Del-Fi 1223
			Cindy's Birthday (8)	
			CRAY, Robert	
			Born on 8/1/53 in Columbus, Georgia. Blues guitarist/vocalist. Played bass with fictional band, Otis Day & The Knights, in the film *Animal House*. Band formed in 1974 as backing tour band for Albert Collins. 1988 lineup: Richard Cousins, Peter Boe and David Olson.	
			THE ROBERT CRAY BAND:	
1/31/87	13	26	▲ 1. Strong Persuader	Mercury 830568
9/10/88	32	7	● 2. Don't Be Afraid Of The Dark	Mercury 834923
			CRAZY OTTO	
			German pianist Fritz Schulz-Reichel.	
4/16/55	1(2)	20	1. Crazy Otto [I]	Decca 8113
			CREAM	
			British supergroup: Eric Clapton (guitar), Ginger Baker (drums) and Jack Bruce (bass).	
12/23/67	4	50	● 1. Disraeli Gears	Atco 232
			Sunshine Of Your Love (5)	
7/20/68	1(4)	30	● 2. Wheels Of Fire [L]	Atco 700 [2]
			record 1: studio; record 2: Live At The Fillmore	
			White Room (6)	

Harry Chapin popularized the so-called "story song" with such singles as "Taxi" and "Cat's In The Cradle." The latter track, which reached the No. 1 slot, helped make 1974's *Verities & Balderdash* Chapin's only top 40 album.

Cheap Trick may be the best argument that the original is still the greatest: When original bassist Tom Petersson rejoined the Chicago quartet in 1988 after a six-year sabbatical, the group went on to have its biggest hit ever, the No. 1 single, "The Flame."

Chubby Checker knows you *can* go home again, at least as far as hit records go. His 1960 version of "The Twist," which appeared on his first top 40 LP *Twist With Chubby Checker*, was his first No. 1 single; 28 years later, a new version recorded with comic rappers the Fat Boys reached a brand new audience and peaked at No. 16.

The **Clash**, one of the most respected British bands to emerge from the late 70s "punk" movement, scored their best-selling album late in their career, with 1982's *Combat Rock*. Ironically, the album's hit "Rock the Casbah" was one of the few Clash songs said to be penned by drummer Topper Headon.

Joe Cocker's near-legendary status has been assured by his Woodstock appearance and his well-publicized Mad Dogs & Englishmen tour. The resulting 1970 soundtrack set was issued on CD in the 80s by both A&M and the Mobile Fidelity audiophile label.

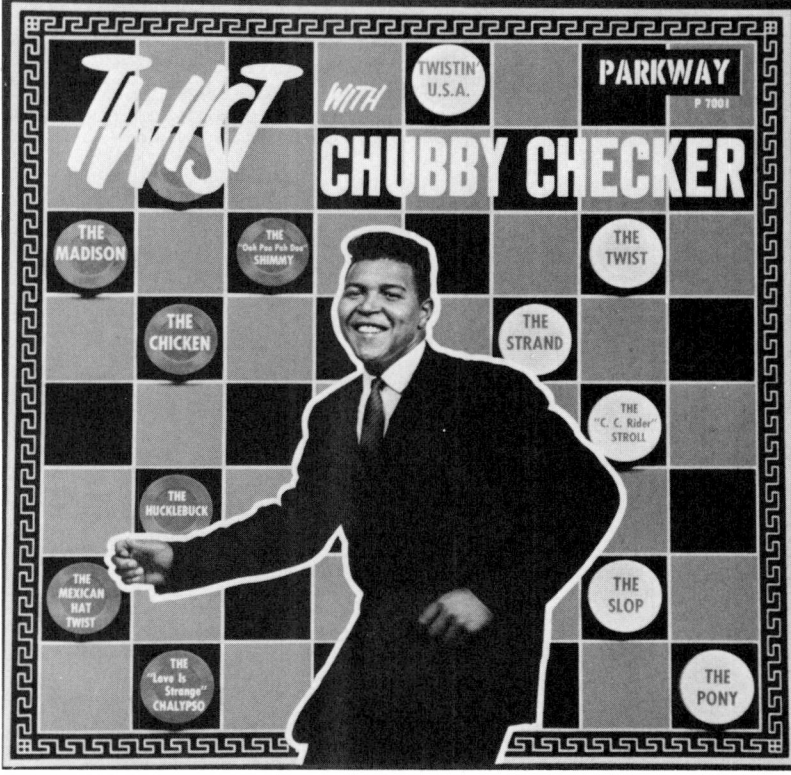

The **Commodores** are best known for launching the career of Lionel Richie, who went solo in the early 80s and left his old group struggling without him. Proof: 1983's *Commodores 13*, their first album without him, only reached No. 103 on the charts, though its 1981 platinum predecessor *In the Pocket* hit No. 13.

Ray Conniff's arranging and conducting for Columbia Records in the late 50s and early 60s resulted in 28 of his albums reaching the top 40 of the Top Pop Albums charts. *Rhapsody In Rhythm* was one of his five LPs that made it in 1962. His last appearance on the chart altogether came with 1973's *Harmony*, which peaked at No. 194.

Phil Collins' solo works, coupled with his triumphs with Genesis and side project Brand X, have made him one of the most recognizable pop artists of the past few decades. 1982's *Hello, I Must Be Going!*, his second solo album, was his first to achieve platinum certification.

Alice Cooper was on a hot streak between 1971-1976, when every album between *Love It To Death* and *Alice Cooper Goes To Hell*, including 1975's *Welcome To My Nightmare*, was gold-certified by the RIAA. A well-received new album, *Trash*, and the CD reissue of his first two efforts made 1989 a hot year for the Arizona musician.

Elvis Costello's emergence in 1977 with *My Aim Is True* was the first glimmering that the bespectacled U.K. singer was an artist to reckon with. *This Year's Model* was his slightly less successful follow-up. Since then, albums by the prolific Costello—born Declan McManus—have been a consistent presence in the charts.

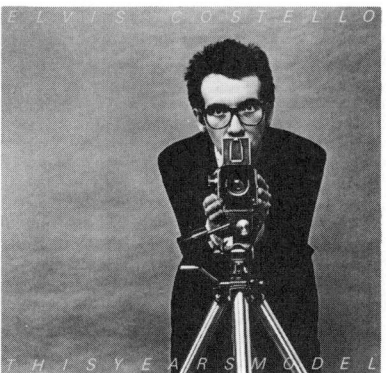

DATE	POS	WKS	ARTIST—RECORD TITLE	LABEL & NO.
8/31/68	**39**	1	● 3. Fresh Cream	Atco 206
3/15/69	**2**(2)	20	● 4. Goodbye	Atco 7001
7/26/69	**3**	20	● 5. Best Of Cream [G]	Atco 291
5/9/70	**15**	9	● 6. Live Cream [L]	Atco 328
4/15/72	**27**	5	● 7. Live Cream - Volume II [L]	Atco 7005
			CREEDENCE CLEARWATER REVIVAL	
			Rock group formed while members attended high school at El Cerrito, California. Consisted of John Fogerty (vocals, guitar), brother Tom Fogerty (guitar), Stu Cook (keyboards, bass) and Doug Clifford (drums). First recorded as the Blue Velvets for the Orchestra label in 1959. Recorded as the Golliwogs for Fantasy in 1964. Tom Fogerty left for a solo career in 1971 and group disbanded in October, 1972. Tom Fogerty died on 9/6/90 (age 48) of respiratory failure.	
3/1/69	**7**	37	● 1. Bayou Country *Proud Mary* (2)	Fantasy 8387
9/20/69	**1**(4)	23	● 2. Green River *Bad Moon Rising* (2)/*Green River* (2)	Fantasy 8393
12/20/69	**3**	24	● 3. Willy and the Poorboys *Down On The Corner* (3)	Fantasy 8397
7/25/70	**1**(9)	26	● 4. Cosmo's Factory *Travelin' Band* (2)/*Up Around The Bend* (4)/ *Lookin' Out My Back Door* (2)	Fantasy 8402
12/26/70	**5**	22	● 5. Pendulum *Have You Ever Seen The Rain* (8)	Fantasy 8410
5/6/72	**12**	12	● 6. Mardi Gras *Sweet Hitch-Hiker* (6)	Fantasy 9404
1/6/73	**15**	6	● 7. Creedence Gold [G]	Fantasy 9418
			CRICKETS, The — see HOLLY, Buddy	
			Born on 1/10/43 in Philadelphia; killed in plane crash on 9/20/73 in Natchitoches, Louisiana. Vocalist/guitarist/composer. Recorded with wife Ingrid for Capitol in 1968. Lead guitarist on his hits, Maury Muehleisen, was killed in the same crash.	
9/9/72	**1**(5)	42	● 1. You Don't Mess Around With Jim *You Don't Mess Around With Jim* (8)/*Time In A Bottle* (1)	ABC 756
7/21/73	**7**	26	● 2. Life And Times *Bad, Bad Leroy Brown* (1)	ABC 769
12/22/73	**2**(2)	26	● 3. I Got A Name *I Got A Name* (10)/*I'll Have To Say I Love You In A Song* (9)	ABC 797
10/12/74	**2**(2)	15	● 4. Photographs & Memories/His Greatest Hits [G]	ABC 835
			CROSBY, Bing	
			One of the most popular entertainers of the 20th century's first 50 years. Harry Lillis Crosby was born on 5/2/01 (or 04) in Tacoma, Washington. He and singing partner Al Rinker were hired in 1926 by Paul Whiteman; with Harry Barris they became the Rhythm Boys and gained an increasing following. The trio split from Whiteman in 1930, and Bing sang briefly with Gus Arnheim's band. It was his early-1931 smash with Arnheim, "I Surrender, Dear," which earned Bing a CBS radio contract and launched an unsurpassed solo career. Over the next three decades the resonant Crosby baritone and breezy persona sold more than 300 million records and was featured in over 50 movies (won Academy Award for *Going My Way*, 1944). Crosby died of a heart attack on 10/14/77 on a golf course near Madrid, Spain.	
12/22/56	**21**	1	1. A Christmas Sing With Bing Around The World [X] from the CBS Radio Program; features various choirs	Decca 8419

DATE	POS	WKS	ARTIST—RECORD TITLE	LABEL & NO.
12/2/57	**1**(1)	7	● 2. Merry Christmas [X] first charted in 1945; the #1 Christmas album of all-time; includes classic single "White Christmas"	Decca 8128
3/31/58	**13**	2	3. Shillelaghs and Shamrocks	Decca 8207
12/15/58	**2**(1)	4	4. Merry Christmas [X-R]	Decca 8128
12/28/59	**17**	2	5. Merry Christmas [X-R]	Decca 8128
12/19/60	**9**	3	6. Merry Christmas [X-R]	Decca 8128
1/6/62	**22**	3	7. Merry Christmas [X-R]	Decca 8128

CROSBY, David

Born David Van Cortland on 8/14/41 in Los Angeles. Vocalist/guitarist with The Byrds from 1964-68. Frequent troubles with the law due to drug charges.

DATE	POS	WKS	ARTIST—RECORD TITLE	LABEL & NO.
3/20/71	**12**	10	● 1. If I Could Only Remember My Name with West Coast guests Jerry Garcia, Grace Slick and Joni Mitchell	Atlantic 7203

DAVID CROSBY/GRAHAM NASH:

DATE	POS	WKS	ARTIST—RECORD TITLE	LABEL & NO.
4/29/72	**4**	14	● 2. Graham Nash/David Crosby	Atlantic 7220
10/25/75	**6**	12	● 3. Wind On The Water	ABC 902
8/21/76	**26**	6	● 4. Whistling Down The Wire	ABC 956

CROSBY, STILLS & NASH

Trio from Laurel Canyon, California, formed in 1968. Consisted of David Crosby (b: 8/14/41, Los Angeles; guitar), Stephen Stills (b: 1/3/45, Dallas; guitar, keyboards, bass) and Graham Nash (b: 1942, Lancashire, England; guitar). Crosby had been in the Byrds, Stills had been in Buffalo Springfield, and Nash was with The Hollies. Won the 1969 Best New Artist Grammy Award. Neil Young (b: 11/12/45, Toronto; guitar) joined group in the summer of 1969, left in 1974. Reunion in 1988.

DATE	POS	WKS	ARTIST—RECORD TITLE	LABEL & NO.
7/5/69	**6**	40	● 1. Crosby, Stills & Nash	Atlantic 8229
4/4/70	**1**(1)	38	● 2. Deja Vu *	Atlantic 7200
4/24/71	**1**(1)	26	● 3. 4 Way Street * [L]	Atlantic 902 [2]
9/14/74	**1**(1)	12	● 4. So Far * [G]	Atlantic 18100
7/16/77	**2**(4)	20	▲ 5. CSN *Just A Song Before I Go* (7)	Atlantic 19104
7/31/82	**8**	30	▲ 6. Daylight Again *Wasted On The Way* (9)	Atlantic 19360
12/10/88	**16**	11	▲ 7. American Dream * ***CROSBY, STILLS, NASH & YOUNG**	Atlantic 81888

CROSS, Christopher

Born Christopher Geppert on 5/3/51 in San Antonio, Texas. Formed own group with Rob Meurer (keyboards), Andy Salmon (bass) and Tommy Taylor (drums) in 1973. Won the 1980 Best New Artist Grammy Award.

DATE	POS	WKS	ARTIST—RECORD TITLE	LABEL & NO.
3/29/80	**6**	81	▲ 1. Christopher Cross 1980 Grammy winner: Album of the Year *Ride Like The Wind* (2)/*Sailing* (1)	Warner 3383
2/26/83	**11**	11	● 2. Another Page *Think Of Laura* (9)	Warner 23757

CROWDED HOUSE

New Zealand/Australian trio founded by former Split Enz members Neil Finn (vocals, guitar, piano) and Paul Hester (drums) with Nick Seymour (bass).

DATE	POS	WKS	ARTIST—RECORD TITLE	LABEL & NO.
3/21/87	**12**	24	● 1. Crowded House *Don't Dream It's Over* (2)/*Something So Strong* (7)	Capitol 12485
8/13/88	**40**	2	2. Temple of Low Men	Capitol 48763

DATE	POS	WKS	ARTIST—RECORD TITLE		LABEL & NO.
			CRUSADERS, The		
			Instrumental jazz-oriented group formed in Houston, as the Swingsters, in the early 50s. To California in the early 60s, name changed to Jazz Crusaders. Became The Crusaders in 1971. Included Joe Sample (keyboards), Wilton Felder (reeds), Nesbert "Stix" Hooper (drums) and Wayne Henderson (trombone). Henderson left in 1975.		
12/21/74	**31**	3	● 1. Southern Comfort [I]		Blue Thumb 9002 [2]
9/13/75	**26**	5	2. Chain Reaction [I]		Blue Thumb 6022
7/10/76	**38**	3	3. Those Southern Knights [I]		Blue Thumb 6024
8/12/78	**34**	8	● 4. Images [I]		Blue Thumb 6030
6/23/79	**18**	17	● 5. Street Life [I]		MCA 3094
			with guest vocalist Randy Crawford on "Street Life"		
8/2/80	**29**	4	6. Rhapsody And Blues [I]		MCA 5124
			with guest vocalist Bill Withers on "Soul Shadows"		
			CULT, The		
			British rock quartet led by Ian Astbury (vocals). Reduced to a trio of Astbury, guitarist Billy Duffy and bassist Jamie Stewart by 1989; drummer Matt Sorum joined Guns N' Roses in 1990. Stewart left in 1990.		
5/16/87	**38**	4	● 1. Electric		Sire 25555
5/6/89	**10**	20	▲ 2. Sonic Temple		Sire 25871
			CULTURE CLUB		
			Formed in London in 1981. Consisted of George "Boy George" O'Dowd (b: 6/14/61; vocals), Roy Hay (guitar, keyboards), Michael Craig (bass) and Jon Moss (drums). Designer Sue Clowes originated distinctive costuming for the group. Won the 1983 Best New Artist Grammy Award. Boy George went solo in 1987.		
2/12/83	**14**	38	▲ 1. Kissing To Be Clever		Epic 38398
			Do You Really Want To Hurt Me (2)/ Time (Clock Of My Heart) (2)/I'll Tumble 4 Ya (9)		
11/12/83	**2(6)**	38	▲ 2. Colour By Numbers		Epic 39107
			Church Of The Poison Mind (10)/Karma Chameleon (1)/ Miss Me Blind (5)		
11/24/84	**26**	9	▲ 3. Waking Up With The House On Fire		Virgin 39881
5/10/86	**32**	6	4. From Luxury To Heartache		Virgin 40345
			CUMMINGS, Burton		
			Born on 12/31/47 in Winnipeg, Canada. Lead singer of The Guess Who.		
12/18/76	**30**	7	1. Burton Cummings		Portrait 34261
			Stand Tall (10)		
			CURE, The		
			British techno-rock quintet led by Robert Smith (vocals, guitar, keyboards) and Laurence Tolhurst (keyboards). Producer Phil Thornalley was an early member; he joined Johnny Hates Jazz as lead singer in 1989.		
7/4/87	**35**	8	▲ 1. Kiss Me, Kiss Me, Kiss Me		Elektra 60737 [2]
5/27/89	**12**	26	▲ 2. Disintegration		Elektra 60855
			Love Song (2)		
			CUTTING CREW		
			British rock group led by singer Nick Van Eede, with Kevin Scott MacMichael (guitar; from Canada), Colin Farley (bass) and Martin Beedle (drums).		
4/18/87	**16**	10	● 1. Broadcast		Virgin 90573
			(I Just) Died In Your Arms (1)/I've Been In Love Before (9)		

DATE	POS	WKS	ARTIST—RECORD TITLE	LABEL & NO.
			# D	
			DALTREY, Roger	
			Born on 3/1/44 in London, England. Formed the band, the Detours, that later became The Who. Roger was The Who's lead singer and starred in the films *Tommy*, *Lisztomania* and *McVicar*.	
8/30/75	**28**	5	1. Ride A Rock Horse	MCA 2147
8/30/80	**22**	6	2. McVicar [S]	Polydor 6284
			Daltrey stars in the film; soundtrack features all members of The Who	
			DAMN YANKEES	
			Superstar rock group: guitarist Ted Nugent (Amboy Dukes), bassist/vocalist Jack Blades (Night Ranger), guitarist/vocalist Tommy Shaw (Styx) and drummer Michael Cartellone.	
5/12/90	**30**	7	● 1. Damn Yankees	Warner 26159
			DAMONE, Vic	
			Born Vito Farinola on 6/12/28 in Brooklyn. Vic is among the most popular of postwar ballad singers; he also appeared in several movies and hosted a TV series (1956-57).	
10/13/56	**14**	8	1. That Towering Feeling!	Columbia 900
			DANA, Bill	
			Born Bill Szathmary on 10/5/24 of Hungarian descent. Raised in Quincy, Massachusetts. Developed his famous 'Jose Jimenez' character while working as a comedy writer for the Steve Allen Show.	
8/1/60	**15**	21	1. My Name…Jose Jimenez [C]	Signature 1013
8/21/61	**5**	19	2. Jose Jimenez - The Astronaut (The First Man In Space) [C]	Kapp 1238
4/7/62	**32**	2	3. Jose Jimenez In Orbit/Bill Dana On Earth [C]	Kapp 1257
11/17/62	**16**	5	4. Jose Jimenez Talks To Teenagers Of All Ages [C]	Kapp 1304
3/16/63	**30**	3	5. Jose Jimenez - Our Secret Weapon [C]	Kapp 1320
			DANA, Vic	
			Born on 8/26/42 in Buffalo, New York. Moved to California as a teen.	
5/1/65	**13**	11	1. Red Roses For A Blue Lady	Dolton 8034
			Red Roses For A Blue Lady (10)	
			DANGERFIELD, Rodney	
			Born Jack Roy in 1921 in New York. Owner of Dangerfields, a club in New York City. Comedian and star of the films *Caddyshack*, *Easy Money* and *Back To School*. Featured in many "Miller Lite" beer commercials.	
12/24/83	**36**	3	1. Rappin' Rodney [C]	RCA 4869
			DANIELS, Charlie	
			Formed own band in Nashville in 1971. Consisted of Daniels (b: 10/28/36, Wilmington, North Carolina; vocals, guitar, fiddle), Tom Crain (guitar), Joe "Taz" DiGregorio (keyboards), Charles Hayward (bass) and James W. Marshall (drums). Daniels led the Jaguars from 1958-67. Went solo in 1968 and worked as a session musician in Nashville. Played on Bob Dylan's *Nashville Skyline* hit album. In the film *Urban Cowboy*.	
			THE CHARLIE DANIELS BAND:	
3/15/75	**38**	2	● 1. Fire On The Mountain	Kama Sutra 2603
6/19/76	**35**	3	● 2. Saddle Tramp	Epic 34150

DATE	POS	WKS	ARTIST—RECORD TITLE	LABEL & NO.
6/30/79	5	17	▲ 3. Million Mile Reflections *The Devil Went Down To Georgia* (3)	Epic 35751
8/16/80	11	9	▲ 4. Full Moon	Epic 36571
4/24/82	26	6	● 5. Windows	Epic 37694
			D'ARBY, Terence Trent	
			England-based, soul-pop singer, born on 3/15/62 in New York City. Last name originally spelled Darby. Was a member of U.S. Army boxing team.	
3/5/88	4	32	▲ 1. Introducing The Hardline According To Terence Trent D'Arby *Wishing Well* (1)/*Sign Your Name* (4)	Columbia 40964
			DARIN, Bobby	
			Vocalist/pianist/guitarist/drummer, born Walden Robert Cassotto on 5/14/36 in the Bronx. Died of heart failure on 12/20/73 (age 37) in Los Angeles. First recorded in 1956 with The Jaybirds (Decca). First appeared on TV in March, 1956 on the Tommy Dorsey Show. Won the 1959 Best New Artist Grammy Award. Married to actress Sandra Dee, 1960-67. Nominated for an Oscar for his performance in the film *Captain Newman, MD*, 1963. Formed own record company, Direction, in 1968. Inducted into the Rock and Roll Hall of Fame in 1990.	
10/5/59	7	39	1. That's All *Mack The Knife* (1)/*Beyond The Sea* (6)	Atco 104
3/7/60	6	38	2. This Is Darin	Atco 115
10/17/60	9	12	3. Darin At The Copa [L]	Atco 122
6/26/61	18	20	4. The Bobby Darin Story [G] *Splish Splash* (3)/*Queen Of The Hop* (9)/*Dream Lover* (2)	Atco 131
			DAVID & DAVID	
			Los Angeles duo: David Baerwald and David Ricketts.	
12/6/86	39	2	1. Boomtown	A&M 5134
			DAVIDSON, John	
			Born on 12/13/41 in Pittsburgh. Singer/actor. Co-host of TV's "That's Incredible" and host of the new "Hollywood Squares."	
11/19/66	19	10	1. The Time Of My Life!	Columbia 9380
			DAVIS, Mac	
			Born on 1/21/42 in Lubbock, Texas. Vocalist/guitarist/composer. Worked as a regional rep for Vee-Jay and Liberty Records. Wrote "In The Ghetto," "Don't Cry Daddy," hits for Elvis Presley. Host of his own musical variety TV series from 1974-76. Appearances in several films, including *North Dallas Forty* in 1979.	
9/30/72	11	13	▲ 1. Baby Don't Get Hooked On Me *Baby Don't Get Hooked On Me* (1)	Columbia 31770
8/10/74	13	15	● 2. Stop And Smell The Roses *Stop And Smell The Roses* (9)	Columbia 32582
3/8/75	21	5	● 3. All The Love In The World	Columbia 32927
			DAVIS, Miles	
			Born on 5/26/26 in Alton, Illinois. Innovative jazz trumpeter who influenced the jazz fusion movement. Began career in 1944 with Billy Eckstine's orchestra. Formed own quintet in 1955. Members of band included Herbie Hancock and Wayne Shorter. Received 23 Grammy nominations. Married to actress Cicely Tyson from 1981-88.	
6/27/70	35	4	● 1. Bitches Brew [I]	Columbia 26 [2]

DATE	POS	WKS	ARTIST—RECORD TITLE	LABEL & NO.
			DAVIS, Sammy, Jr.	
			Born on 12/8/25 in New York City. Died of throat cancer on 5/15/90. Vocalist/dancer/actor. With father and uncle in dance act, the Will Mastin Trio, from the early 40s. First recorded for Decca in 1954. Lost his left eye and had his nose smashed in an auto accident in Las Vegas on 11/19/54; returned to performing in January of 1955. Frequent appearances on TV, Broadway and in films.	
5/14/55	**1**(6)	27	1. Starring Sammy Davis, Jr.	Decca 8118
10/15/55	**5**	9	2. Just For Lovers	Decca 8170
11/17/62	**14**	9	3. What Kind Of Fool Am I and Other Show-Stoppers	Reprise 6051
5/23/64	**26**	6	4. The Shelter Of Your Arms	Reprise 6114
3/15/69	**24**	8	5. I've Gotta Be Me	Reprise 6324
6/17/72	**11**	8	6. Sammy Davis Jr. Now *The Candy Man* (1)	MGM 4832
			DAWN	
			Vocal trio formed in New York City: Tony Orlando (b: 4/3/44, New York City), Telma Hopkins (b: 10/28/48, Louisville) and Joyce Vincent (b: 12/14/46, Detroit). Orlando had recorded solo from 1961-63; Hopkins and Vincent had been backup singers. Orlando was manager for April-Blackwood Music at the time of their first hit. Own TV show from 1974-76. Hopkins in TV series "Bosom Buddies," "Gimme A Break" and "Family Matters." All of their hits produced by Hank Medress (The Tokens) and Dave Appell.	
1/30/71	**35**	3	1. Candida *Candida* (3)/*Knock Three Times* (1)	Bell 6052
5/26/73	**30**	5	● 2. Tuneweaving *Tie A Yellow Ribbon Round The Ole Oak Tree* (1)	Bell 1112
			TONY ORLANDO & DAWN:	
1/11/75	**16**	8	3. Prime Time	Bell 1317
5/31/75	**20**	4	4. He Don't Love You (Like I Love You) *He Don't Love You (Like I Love You)* (1)	Elektra 1034
8/2/75	**16**	6	● 5. Greatest Hits [G]	Arista 4045
			DAY, Doris	
			Born Doris Kappelhoff on 4/3/22 in Cincinnati. Doris sang briefly with Bob Crosby in 1940 and shortly thereafter became a major star with the Les Brown band ("Sentimental Journey"). Her great solo recording success was soon transcended by Hollywood as Doris became the #1 box office star of the late 50s and early 60s; her 1968-73 TV series was also popular.	
2/5/55	**15**	2	1. Young At Heart [S] 10" album; six songs by Doris, two by Frank Sinatra	Columbia 6339
6/25/55	**1**(17)	28	2. Love Me Or Leave Me [S] Doris portrayed singer Ruth Etting in the film	Columbia 710
2/9/57	**11**	6	3. Day By Day	Columbia 942
5/30/60	**26**	7	4. Listen To Day	Columbia DD1
			DAY, Morris	
			Leader of Minneapolis funk group, The Time (formerly Prince's backing band). Born in Springfield, Illinois; raised in Minneapolis. Acted in the films *Purple Rain* and *The Adventures Of Ford Fairlane*.	
11/16/85	**37**	3	1. Color Of Success	Warner 25320
			DAYNE, Taylor	
			Real name: Leslie Wonderman. Female singer from Long Island.	
2/20/88	**21**	34	▲ 1. Tell It To My Heart *Tell It To My Heart* (7)/*Prove Your Love* (7)/ *I'll Always Love You* (3)/*Don't Rush Me* (2)	Arista 8529

DATE	POS	WKS	ARTIST—RECORD TITLE	LABEL & NO.
1/6/90	**25**	36	▲ 2. Can't Fight Fate *With Every Beat Of My Heart (5)/Love Will Lead You Back (1)/* *I'll Be Your Shelter (4)*	Arista 8581
			DAZZ BAND	
			Cleveland ultrafunk band, formerly Kinsman Dazz. "Dazz" means "danceable jazz."	
5/29/82	**14**	11	● 1. Keep It Live *Let It Whip (5)*	Motown 6004
			DEAD OR ALIVE	
			British disco outfit formed by lead singer Pete Burns.	
8/17/85	**31**	6	1. Youthquake	Epic 40119
			DEAN, Jimmy	
			Born Seth Ward on 8/10/28 in Plainview, Texas. Vocalist/piano/guitar/ composer. With Tennessee Haymakers in Washington, D.C. in 1948. Own Texas Wildcats in 1952. Recorded for Four Star in 1952. Own CBS-TV series, 1957-58; ABC-TV series, 1963-66.	
12/11/61	**23**	11	1. Big Bad John And Other Fabulous Songs And Tales *Big Bad John (1)*	Columbia 8535
			DEAUVILLE, Ronnie	
			Made a miraculous recovery from tuberculosis.	
12/9/57	**13**	2	1. Smoke Dreams	Era 20002
			DeBARGE	
			Family group from Grand Rapids, Michigan. Consisted of lead vocalist Eldra (keyboards), Mark (trumpet, saxophone), James (keyboards), Randy (bass) and Bunny DeBarge (vocals). Brothers Bobby and Tommy were in Switch. James was briefly married to Janet Jackson in 1984.	
5/28/83	**24**	7	● 1. All This Love	Gordy 6012
2/4/84	**36**	5	● 2. In A Special Way	Gordy 6061
4/20/85	**19**	24	● 3. Rhythm Of The Night *Rhythm Of The Night (3)/Who's Holding Donna Now (6)*	Gordy 6123
			DeBARGE, El	
			Eldra DeBarge (b: 6/4/61), lead singer of family group DeBarge.	
6/21/86	**24**	11	● 1. El DeBarge *Who's Johnny (3)*	Gordy 6181
			DeBURGH, Chris	
			British pop-rock singer, born Christopher John Davidson on 10/15/48 in Argentina.	
5/30/87	**25**	8	● 1. Into The Light *The Lady In Red (3)*	A&M 5121
			DEE, Joey	
			Born Joseph DiNicola on 6/11/40 in Passaic, New Jersey. In September, 1960, Joey & The Starlighters became the house band at the Peppermint Lounge, New York City. After 1964, group included three members who later formed The Young Rascals, plus guitarist Jimi Hendrix. In films *Hey, Let's* *Twist* and *Two Tickets To Paris*. **JOEY DEE & THE STARLITERS:**	
12/25/61	**2(6)**	36	1. Doin' The Twist At The Peppermint Lounge [L] *Peppermint Twist-Part 1 (1)/Shout (6)*	Roulette 25166
3/10/62	**18**	13	2. Hey, Let's Twist! [S] with Jo-Ann Campbell, Teddy Randazzo and Kay Armen; filmed at New York's Peppermint Lounge	Roulette 25168

DATE	POS	WKS	ARTIST—RECORD TITLE	LABEL & NO.
			DEE, Kiki	
			Born Pauline Matthews on 3/6/47 in Yorkshire, England.	
			THE KIKI DEE BAND:	
12/7/74	28	4	1. I've Got The Music In Me	Rocket 458
			DEE, Lenny	
			Organist; raised in Illinois and Florida.	
7/9/55	11	6	1. Dee-lightful! [I]	Decca 8114
			DEEP PURPLE	
			British hard-rock band: Ritchie Blackmore (guitar), Rod Evans (vocals), Jon Lord (keyboards), Ian Paice (drums) and Nicky Simper (bass). Evans and Simper left in 1969, replaced by Ian Gillan and Roger Glover. Gillan and Glover left in late 1973. New members included David Coverdale and Tommy Bolin (ex-James Gang; d: 1976). Blackmore left to form Rainbow (which Glover later joined). Coverdale, Lord and Paice formed Whitesnake. Blackmore, Gillan, Lord and Paice reunited in 1984. Gillan left in 1989 to form Garth Rockett & The Moonshiners. Former Rainbow vocalist Joe Lynn Turner joined in 1990.	
10/12/68	24	10	1. Shades Of Deep Purple *Hush* (4)	Tetragramm. 102
9/4/71	32	3	2. Fireball	Warner 2564
5/6/72	7	30	▲ 3. Machine Head *Smoke On The Water* (4)	Warner 2607
2/10/73	15	14	● 4. Who Do We Think We Are!	Warner 2678
5/12/73	6	23	▲ 5. Made In Japan [L]	Warner 2701 [2]
3/23/74	9	12	● 6. Burn new members: David Coverdale (replaces Gillan), Glenn Hughes (replaces Glover)	Warner 2766
12/14/74	20	6	● 7. Stormbringer	Warner 2832
12/8/84	17	18	▲ 8. Perfect Strangers reunion of Blackmore/Gillan/Glover/Lord/Paice	Mercury 824003
2/14/87	34	4	9. The House Of Blue Light	Mercury 831318
			DEF LEPPARD	
			Heavy-metal quintet formed in Sheffield, England in 1977: Joe Elliott (lead singer), Pete Willis & Steve Clark (lead guitars), Rick Savage (bass) and Rick Allen (drums; lost his left arm in an auto accident on New Year's Eve in 1984). Phil Collen replaced Pete Willis in late 1982.	
10/3/81	38	3	▲ 1. High 'n' Dry	Mercury 4021
2/12/83	2(2)	58	▲ 2. Pyromania	Mercury 810308
8/22/87	1(6)	96	▲ 3. Hysteria *Hysteria* (10)/*Pour Some Sugar On Me* (2)/*Love Bites* (1)/ *Armageddon It* (3)	Mercury 830675
			DELANEY & BONNIE	
			Delaney Bramlett (b: 7/1/39, Acton, Illinois) & wife Bonnie Lynn Bramlett (b: 11/8/44, Pontotoc County, Mississippi) & Friends - backing artists who included at various times Leon Russell, Rita Coolidge, Dave Mason, Eric Clapton, Duane Allman and many others. Friends Bobby Whitlock, Carl Radle and Jim Gordon later became Eric Clapton's Dominos. Delaney & Bonnie dissolved their marriage and group in 1972.	
4/25/70	29	6	1. Delaney & Bonnie & Friends On Tour with Eric Clapton [L]	Atco 326

DATE	POS	WKS	ARTIST—RECORD TITLE		LABEL & NO.
			DE LA SOUL		
			Psychedelic rap trio from Amityville, Long Island, New York: Posdnous (Kelvin Mercer), Trugoy the Dove (David Jolicoeur) and P.A. Pasemaster Mase (Vincent Mason, Jr.).		
5/20/89	**24**	10	● 1. 3 Feet High And Rising		Tommy B. 1019
			DELLS, The		
			R&B vocal group formed at Thornton Township High School in Harvey, Illinois: Johnny Funches (lead), Marvin Junior (tenor), Verne Allison (tenor), Mickey McGill (baritone) and Chuck Barksdale (bass). First recorded as the El-Rays for Chess in 1953. Group remained intact into the 80s, with exception of Funches, who was replaced by Johnny Carter (ex-Flamingos) in 1960.		
8/10/68	**29**	5	1. There Is *Stay In My Corner* (10)		Cadet 804
			DENNY, Martin		
			Born on 4/10/11 in New York City. Composer/arranger/pianist. Originated the "Exotic Sounds of Martin Denny" in Hawaii, featuring Julius Wechter (Baja Marimba Band) on vibes and marimba.		
5/4/59	**1**(5)	46	1. Exotica * *Quiet Village* (4)	[I]	Liberty 7034
9/14/59	**8**	31	2. Quiet Village * ***THE EXOTIC SOUNDS OF MARTIN DENNY**	[I]	Liberty 7122
10/6/62	**6**	21	3. A Taste Of Honey	[I]	Liberty 7237
			DENVER, John		
			Born John Henry Deutschendorf on 12/31/43 in Roswell, New Mexico. To Los Angeles in 1964. With the Chad Mitchell Trio from 1965-68. Wrote "Leaving On A Jet Plane." Starred in the film *Oh, God* in 1978.		
6/19/71	**15**	31	● 1. Poems, Prayers & Promises *Take Me Home, Country Roads* (2)		RCA 4499
11/11/72	**4**	27	● 2. Rocky Mountain High *Rocky Mountain High* (9)		RCA 4731
6/30/73	**16**	13	● 3. Farewell Andromeda		RCA 0101
7/6/74	**1**(1)	37	● 4. Back Home Again *Annie's Song* (1)/*Back Home Again* (5)		RCA 0548
3/8/75	**2**(2)	19	● 5. An Evening With John Denver *Thank God I'm A Country Boy* (1)	[L]	RCA 0764 [2]
10/4/75	**1**(2)	22	● 6. Windsong *I'm Sorry* (1)/*Calypso* (2)		RCA 1183
12/6/75	**14**	6	● 7. Rocky Mountain Christmas	[X]	RCA 1201
9/4/76	**7**	14	▲ 8. Spirit		RCA 1694
3/5/77	**1**(3)	7	● 9. John Denver's Greatest Hits *Sunshine On My Shoulders* (1)	[G]	RCA 0374
3/5/77	**6**	7	▲ 10. John Denver's Greatest Hits, Volume 2	[G]	RCA 2195
2/10/79	**25**	6	● 11. John Denver		RCA 3075
12/22/79	**26**	4	▲ 12. A Christmas Together **JOHN DENVER & THE MUPPETS**	[X]	RCA 3451
4/19/80	**39**	2	13. Autograph		RCA 3449
9/5/81	**32**	4	● 14. Some Days Are Diamonds		RCA 4055
5/22/82	**39**	2	● 15. Seasons Of The Heart		RCA 4256

DATE	POS	WKS	ARTIST—RECORD TITLE	LABEL & NO.
			DEODATO	
			Born Eumir Deodato Almeida on 6/21/42 in Rio de Janeiro, Brazil. Keyboardist/composer/producer/arranger. Kool & The Gang's producer from 1979-82.	
2/24/73	**3**	13	1. Prelude [I]	CTI 6021
			Also Sprach Zarathustra (2001) (2)	
9/8/73	**19**	10	2. Deodato 2 [I]	CTI 6029
			DEPECHE MODE	
			All-synthesized band formed in Basildon, England consisting of David Gahan (vocals), Martin Gore, Vince Clarke and Andy Fletcher. Clarke left in 1982 (formed Yaz, then Erasure), replaced by Alan Wilder. Group name is French for "fast fashion."	
11/14/87	**35**	3	● 1. Music For The Masses	Sire 25614
4/14/90	**7**	28 +	▲ 2. Violator	Sire 26081
			Enjoy The Silence (8)	
			DEREK AND THE DOMINOS — see CLAPTON, Eric	
			DERRINGER, Rick	
			Born Richard Zehringer on 8/5/47 in Celina, Ohio. Lead singer/guitarist of The McCoys. Performed on and produced sessions for both Edgar & Johnny Winter's bands.	
1/5/74	**25**	8	1. All American Boy	Blue Sky 32481
			DESMOND, Johnny — see MILLER, Glenn	
			DEVO	
			Robotic rock group formed in Akron, Ohio, consisting of brothers Mark and Bob Mothersbaugh, brothers Jerry and Bob Casale, and Alan Myers. David Kendrick replaced Myers by 1988. Mark and Jerry met while both were art students at Kent State.	
10/11/80	**22**	16	▲ 1. Freedom Of Choice	Warner 3435
10/17/81	**23**	6	2. New Traditionalists	Warner 3595
			DEXYS MIDNIGHT RUNNERS	
			Kevin Rowland (b: 8/17/53, Wolverhampton, England), leader of eight-piece Birmingham, England band.	
			KEVIN ROWLAND & DEXYS MIDNIGHT RUNNERS:	
3/19/83	**14**	12	1. Too-Rye-Ay	Mercury 4069
			Come On Eileen (1)	
			DeYOUNG, Dennis	
			Born on 2/18/47 in Chicago. Lead singer/keyboardist of Styx.	
11/10/84	**29**	4	1. Desert Moon	A&M 5006
			Desert Moon (10)	
			DIAMOND, Neil	
			Born on 1/24/41 in Brooklyn. Vocalist/guitarist/prolific composer. With Roadrunners folk group, 1954-56. Worked as song-plugger/staff writer in New York City. Wrote for The Monkees TV show. First recorded for Duel in 1961. Wrote score for film *Jonathan Livingston Seagull*; starred in and composed the music for *The Jazz Singer*.	
1/17/70	**30**	6	● 1. Touching You Touching Me	Uni 73071
			Holly Holy (6)	
8/29/70	**10**	19	● 2. Neil Diamond/Gold [L]	Uni 73084
			recorded at the Troubadour in Hollywood	
11/21/70	**13**	14	● 3. Tap Root Manuscript	Uni 73092
			Cracklin' Rosie (1)	

DATE	POS	WKS	ARTIST—RECORD TITLE		LABEL & NO.
11/20/71	**11**	13	● 4. Stones *I Am...I Said* (4)		Uni 93106
7/22/72	**5**	24	● 5. Moods *Song Sung Blue* (1)		Uni 93136
12/23/72	**5**	19	● 6. Hot August Night recorded 8/24/72 at the Greek Theatre, Los Angeles	[L]	MCA 8000 [2]
3/10/73	**36**	4	7. Double Gold	[K]	Bang 227 [2]
9/29/73	**35**	4	● 8. Rainbow reissue of cuts from Uni albums	[K]	MCA 2103
11/17/73	**2(1)**	16	▲ 9. Jonathan Livingston Seagull	[S]	Columbia 32550
6/29/74	**29**	7	● 10. Neil Diamond/His 12 Greatest Hits	[G]	MCA 2106
11/9/74	**3**	19	▲ 11. Serenade *Longfellow Serenade* (5)		Columbia 32919
7/4/76	**4**	16	▲ 12. Beautiful Noise		Columbia 33965
3/5/77	**8**	9	▲ 13. Love At The Greek recorded August, 1976 at the Greek Theatre	[L]	Columbia 34404 [2]
12/10/77	**6**	14	▲ 14. I'm Glad You're Here With Me Tonight		Columbia 34990
12/16/78	**4**	12	▲ 15. You Don't Bring Me Flowers *You Don't Bring Me Flowers* (1) with Barbra Streisand		Columbia 35625
1/19/80	**10**	10	▲ 16. September Morn		Columbia 36121
11/29/80	**3**	32	▲ 17. The Jazz Singer film is a remake of Al Jolson's 1927 classic *Love On The Rocks* (2)/*Hello Again* (6)/*America* (8)	[S]	Capitol 12120
12/5/81	**17**	11	▲ 18. On The Way To The Sky		Columbia 37628
10/23/82	**9**	19	▲ 19. Heartlight *Heartlight* (5)		Columbia 38359
9/1/84	**35**	5	● 20. Primitive		Columbia 39199
5/31/86	**20**	11	● 21. Headed For The Future		Columbia 40368
			DIGITAL UNDERGROUND Seven-member, rap-funk crew based in Northern California. Formed by Shock-G (keyboards, vocals) and Chopmaster J (samples, percussion). Features vocalists Humpty Hump and Money B.		
4/21/90	**24**	18	● 1. Sex Packets		Tommy Boy 1026
			DINO Singer/songwriter/producer, born in Encino, California. Raised in Hawaii and Connecticut. Former DJ/music director at KCEP in Las Vegas.		
8/26/89	**34**	6	● 1. 24/7 *I Like It* (7)		4th & B'way 4011
			DIO Ronnie James Dio, former lead singer of Black Sabbath and Rainbow. Born Ronald Padavona on 7/10/49 in Portsmouth, New Hampshire; raised in Cortland, New York.		
7/28/84	**23**	10	▲ 1. The Last In Line		Warner 25100
9/14/85	**29**	10	● 2. Sacred Heart		Warner 25292
			DION Born Dion DiMucci on 7/18/39 in the Bronx. Formed Dion & The Timberlanes in 1957, then Dion & The Belmonts in 1958. Belmonts included: Angelo D'Aleo, Freddie Milano and Carlo Mastrangelo. Group named for Belmont Ave. in the Bronx. Dion went solo in 1960. Brief reunion with the Belmonts in 1967 and 1972, periodically since then. He currently records contemporary Christian songs. Inducted into the Rock and Roll Hall of Fame in 1989.		
12/4/61	**11**	21	1. Runaround Sue *Runaround Sue* (1)/*The Wanderer* (2)		Laurie 2009

DATE	POS	WKS	ARTIST—RECORD TITLE	LABEL & NO.
7/28/62	**12**	12	2. Lovers Who Wander *Lovers Who Wander* (3)/*Little Diane* (8)	Laurie 2012
2/23/63	**29**	3	3. Dion Sings His Greatest Hits [G] two cuts: Dion; 10 cuts: Dion & The Belmonts *A Teenager In Love* (5)/*Where Or When* (3)	Laurie 2013
4/6/63	**20**	6	4. Ruby Baby *Ruby Baby* (2)	Columbia 8810
			DIRE STRAITS Rock group formed in London by Mark Knopfler (lead vocals, lead guitar, songwriter, producer) and his brother David Knopfler (guitar), with John Illsley (bass) and Pick Withers (drums). David left in late 1979, replaced by Hal Lindes (who left in 1985). Added keyboardist Alan Clark in 1982. Terry Williams replaced drummer Pick Withers in 1983. Guitarist Guy Fletcher added in 1984. Mark and Guy formed The Notting Hillbillies in 1990.	
2/3/79	**2**(1)	21	▲ 1. Dire Straits *Sultans Of Swing* (4)	Warner 3266
7/7/79	**11**	8	● 2. Communique	Warner 3330
11/22/80	**19**	17	● 3. Making Movies	Warner 3480
10/16/82	**19**	8	● 4. Love Over Gold	Warner 23728
6/15/85	**1**(9)	55	▲ 5. Brothers In Arms *Money For Nothing* (1)/*Walk Of Life* (7)	Warner 25264
			DIRKSEN, Senator Everett McKinley U.S. senator from Illinois, 1950-69. Born in Pekin, Illinois in 1896; died on 9/7/69 (age 73).	
1/28/67	**16**	8	1. Gallant Men [T] features patriotic stories and recitations to a musical background	Capitol 2643
			DISCO TEX & HIS SEX-O-LETTES Disco studio group assembled by producer Bob Crewe. Featuring lead voice Sir Monti Rock III (real name: Joseph Montanez, Jr.), owner of a chain of hairdressing salons.	
8/23/75	**36**	3	1. Disco Tex & His Sex-O-Lettes *Get Dancin'* (10)	Chelsea 505
			D.J. JAZZY JEFF & THE FRESH PRINCE Philadelphia rap duo: D.J. Jeff Townes with rapper Will Smith.	
6/18/88	**4**	23	▲ 1. He's The D.J., I'm The Rapper	Jive 1091 [2]
12/2/89	**39**	7	● 2. And In This Corner...	Jive 1188
			D.O.C., The Pronounced "dock." 21-year-old Dallas rapper Tray Curry.	
9/2/89	**20**	10	● 1. No One Can Do It Better	Ruthless 91275
			DR. BUZZARD'S ORIGINAL "SAVANNAH" BAND New York City Thirties-styled disco group formed by brothers Stony Browder and August Darnell (real name: Thomas August Darnell Browder) with Cory Daye, lead singer. Darnell left in 1980 to form Kid Creole & The Coconuts.	
10/9/76	**22**	18	● 1. Dr. Buzzard's Original Savannah Band	RCA 1504
3/11/78	**36**	3	2. Dr. Buzzard's Original Savannah Band Meets King Penett	RCA 2402
			DR. JOHN Born Malcolm "Mac" Rebennack on 11/21/40 in New Orleans. Pioneer "swamp rock"-styled instrumentalist.	
6/9/73	**24**	9	1. In The Right Place *Right Place Wrong Time* (9)	Atco 7018

DATE	POS	WKS	ARTIST—RECORD TITLE	LABEL & NO.
			DOKKEN	
			Los Angeles-based, hard-rock band: Don Dokken (lead vocals), George Lynch (guitar), Jeff Pilson (bass) and Mick Brown (drums). Disbanded in 1988. Don Dokken assembled new self-named band in 1990 with John Norum (guitar), Billy White (guitar), Peter Baltes (bass) and Mikkey Dee (drums).	
2/1/86	**32**	5	▲ 1. Under Lock And Key	Elektra 60458
12/5/87	**13**	15	▲ 2. Back For The Attack	Elektra 60735
12/17/88	**33**	4	● 3. Beast From The East [L]	Elek. 60823 [2]
			recorded live in Japan in April of 1988	
			DOLBY, Thomas	
			Born Thomas Morgan Dolby Robertson of British parentage on 10/14/58 in Cairo, Egypt. Master of computer-generated music and self-directed videos. Keyboardist of Bruce Woolley & The Camera Club, and the Lene Lovich band (1979-80). Began solo career in 1981. Film *Howard The Duck* featured Dolby's music under moniker "Dolby's Cube." Married to actress Kathleen Beller (Kirby Colby on TV's "Dynasty").	
3/12/83	**20**	11	1. Blinded By Science [M]	Harvest 15007
			She Blinded Me With Science (5)	
4/23/83	**13**	13	2. The Golden Age Of Wireless	Capitol 12271
4/14/84	**35**	3	3. The Flat Earth	Capitol 12309
			DOMINGO, Placido	
			Born on 1/21/41 in Madrid, Spain. One of the world's leading operatic tenors. Emigrated to Mexico in 1950. Debuted at the New York Metropolitan Opera in 1968.	
12/26/81	**18**	8	▲ 1. Perhaps Love	CBS 37243
			with John Denver on the title cut	
			DOMINO, Fats	
			Born Antoine Domino on 2/26/28 in New Orleans. Classic New Orleans R&B piano-playing vocalist; heavily influenced by Fats Waller and Albert Ammons. Joined the Dave Bartholomew Band, mid-40s. Signed to Imperial record label in 1949. His first recording "The Fat Man" reportedly was a million-seller. Heard on many sessions cut by other R&B artists, including Lloyd Price and Joe Turner. In films *Shake, Rattle And Roll*, *Jamboree*, *The Big Beat* and *The Girl Can't Help It*. Teamed with co-writer Dave Bartholomew on majority of his hits. Lives in New Orleans with wife Rosemary and eight children. Frequently appears in Las Vegas. Inducted into the Rock and Roll Hall of Fame in 1986. One of the most popular and influential R&B stars.	
11/10/56	**18**	6	1. Fats Domino - Rock And Rollin'	Imperial 9009
			I'm In Love Again (3)	
2/23/57	**19**	2	2. This Is Fats Domino!	Imperial 9028
			Blueberry Hill (2)/*Blue Monday* (5)	
3/23/57	**17**	4	3. Rock And Rollin' With Fats Domino	Imperial 9004
			Fats' first album	
			Ain't That A Shame (10)	
			DONOVAN	
			Born Donovan Phillip Leitch on 2/10/46 near Glasgow, Scotland. Singer/songwriter/guitarist. To London at age 10. Worked Newport Folk Festival in 1965. Wrote score for film *If It's Tuesday This Must Be Belgium*. In films *The Pied Piper Of Hamlin* (1972) and *Brother Sun, Sister Moon* (1973). In retirement from 1974-81.	
10/30/65	**30**	4	1. Catch The Wind	Hickory 123
10/15/66	**11**	12	2. Sunshine Superman	Epic 26217
			Sunshine Superman (1)	
3/11/67	**14**	8	3. Mellow Yellow	Epic 26239
			Mellow Yellow (2)	

DATE	POS	WKS	ARTIST—RECORD TITLE	LABEL & NO.
1/27/68	**19**	7	● 4. A Gift From A Flower To A Garden deluxe box set of previous two albums	Epic 171 [2]
8/10/68	**18**	14	5. Donovan In Concert [L]	Epic 26386
11/16/68	**20**	9	6. The Hurdy Gurdy Man *Hurdy Gurdy Man* (5)	Epic 26420
3/1/69	**4**	33	● 7. Donovan's Greatest Hits [G]	Epic 26439

10/11/69	**23**	6	8. Barabajagal
			        with The Jeff Beck Group on two cuts
			        Atlantis (7)
				Epic 26481

7/25/70	**16**	6	9. Open Road	Epic 30125
5/5/73	**25**	8	10. Cosmic Wheels	Epic 32156
			DOOBIE BROTHERS, The	
			Rock/R&B-styled group formed in San Jose, California in 1970: Pat Simmons (vocals, guitar), Tom Johnston (lead vocals, guitar, keyboards), John Hartman (percussion) and Dave Shogren (bass). First recorded for Warner in 1971. Shogren replaced by Tiran Porter (bass). Mike Hossack (percussion), added in 1972 (later replaced by Keith Knudsen). Jeff "Skunk" Baxter (slide guitar), formerly with Steely Dan, added in 1974. Michael McDonald (lead vocals, keyboards), added in 1975. Johnston left, 1978. Baxter, Hartman replaced by Cornelius Bumpus (keyboards, saxophone), John McFee (guitar) and Chet McCracken (drums) in 1979. Tom Johnston wrote majority of hits from 1972-75; Michael McDonald from 1976-83. Disbanded in 1983. Re-formed in early 1988 with Johnston, Simmons, Hartman, Porter, Hossack, and Bobby LaKind (percussion).	
10/28/72	**21**	9	▲ 1. Toulouse Street	Warner 2634
4/28/73	**7**	33	▲ 2. The Captain And Me *Long Train Runnin'* (8)	Warner 2694
3/23/74	**4**	30	▲ 3. What Were Once Vices Are Now Habits *Black Water* (1)	Warner 2750
5/24/75	**4**	13	● 4. Stampede	Warner 2835
4/24/76	**8**	10	▲ 5. Takin' It To The Streets	Warner 2899
11/27/76	**5**	14	▲ 6. Best Of The Doobies [G]	Warner 2978
9/24/77	**10**	8	● 7. Livin' On The Fault Line	Warner 3045
1/6/79	**1**(5)	30	▲ 8. Minute By Minute *What A Fool Believes* (1)	Warner 3193
10/11/80	**3**	18	▲ 9. One Step Closer	Warner 3452
12/5/81	**39**	3	● 10. Best Of The Doobies, Volume II [G]	Warner 3612
6/17/89	**17**	11	● 11. Cycles *The Doctor* (9)	Capitol 90371
			DOORS, The	
			Rock group formed in Los Angeles in 1965. Consisted of Jim Morrison (b: 12/8/43, Melbourne, Florida; d: 7/3/71, Paris, France; lead singer), Ray Manzarek (keyboards), Robby Krieger (guitar) and John Densmore (drums). Controversial onstage performances by Morrison caused several arrests and cancellations. Morrison left group on 12/12/70. In film *A Feast Of Friends*. Group disbanded in 1973.	
6/24/67	**2**(2)	53	▲ 1. The Doors *Light My Fire* (1)	Elektra 74007
11/11/67	**3**	23	● 2. Strange Days	Elektra 74014
8/17/68	**1**(4)	14	▲ 3. Waiting For The Sun *Hello, I Love You* (1)	Elektra 74024
8/9/69	**6**	2	▲ 4. The Soft Parade *Touch Me* (3)	Elektra 75005
3/14/70	**4**	12	● 5. Morrison Hotel/Hard Rock Cafe	Elektra 75007
8/15/70	**8**	12	● 6. Absolutely Live [L]	Elektra 9002 [2]

DATE	POS	WKS	ARTIST—RECORD TITLE	LABEL & NO.
12/26/70	25	7	▲ 7. 13 [G]	Elektra 74079
5/15/71	9	22	▲ 8. L.A. Woman	Elektra 75011
11/27/71	31	5	9. Other Voices	Elektra 75017
11/15/80	17	17	▲ 10. The Doors Greatest Hits [G]	Elektra 515
11/19/83	23	9	● 11. Alive, She Cried [E-L] recorded 1968-1970	Elektra 60269
			DORATI, Antal	
			Hungarian-born composer/conductor. Principal conductor of BBC Symphony from 1962-66 and of Stockholm Philharmonic from 1966-74; music director of Washington National Symphony from 1970-77; principal conductor of Britain's Royal Philharmonic from 1975-78; music director of Detroit Symphony from 1977-81.	
3/16/59	3	46	● 1. Tchaikovsky: 1812 Festival Overture/Capriccio Italien [I] with the Minneapolis Symphony Orchestra	Mercury 50054
7/3/61	20	8	2. Beethoven: Wellington's Victory/Leonore Overture No. 3/Prometheus Overture [I] with the London Symphony Orchestra	Mercury 9000
			DORSEY, Jimmy	
			Jimmy was born on 2/29/04 in Shenandoah, Pennsylvania. Died of cancer on 6/12/57. Great alto sax and clarinet soloist/bandleader beginning in 1935.	
10/7/57	19	4	1. The Fabulous Jimmy Dorsey eight of 12 cuts were recorded after Jimmy's death *So Rare* (2)	Fraternity 1008
			DORSEY, Tommy	
			Tommy was born on 11/19/05 in Mahanoy Plane, Pennsylvania; choked to death on 11/26/56. Great trombonist and bandleader beginning in 1935. Tommy and brother Jimmy recorded together as the Dorsey Brothers Orchestra from 1928-35, reunited, 1953-56. Hosted musical variety TV show from 1954-56. Warren Covington fronted band after Tommy's death. **TOMMY DORSEY AND HIS ORCHESTRA FEATURING JIMMY DORSEY:**	
5/19/58	15	6	1. The Fabulous Dorseys In Hi-Fi [I]	Columbia 1190
			THE TOMMY DORSEY ORCHESTRA:	
6/1/59	38	1	2. Tea For Two Cha Chas [I] band led by Warren Covington	Decca 8842
			DOUBLE	
			German pop quartet led by Kurt Maloo and Felix Haug. Both were in jazz trio Ping Pong.	
9/13/86	30	6	1. Blue	A&M 5133
			DOUGLAS, Carl	
			Born in Jamaica, West Indies. Studied engineering in the U.S. and in England.	
1/25/75	37	2	1. Kung Fu Fighting And Other Great Love Songs *Kung Fu Fighting* (1)	20th Century 464
			DOVE, Ronnie	
			Born on 9/7/40 in Herndon, Virginia; raised in Baltimore. Sang in rock vocal group while in high school. Served in U.S. Coast Guard. Worked clubs in Baltimore.	
6/4/66	35	6	1. The Best Of Ronnie Dove [G]	Diamond 5005
			DRAGON, Carmen	
			Carmen conducted the Capitol Symphony Orchestra. Died on 3/28/84 (age 69). Father of Daryl Dragon (of Captain & Tennille). Also see Pennario, Leonard.	
4/28/62	36	3	1. Nightfall [I] classical melodies	Capitol 8575

DATE	POS	WKS	ARTIST—RECORD TITLE	LABEL & NO.
			DRAMATICS, The	
			Soul group from Detroit. First recorded for Wingate as the Dynamics, 1966. Members in 1971: Ron Banks (lead singer), William Howard, Larry Demps, Willie Ford and Elbert Wilkins. Howard and Wilkins replaced by L.J. Reynolds and Lenny Mayes in 1973. Reynolds, formerly of Chocolate Syrup, began solo career in 1981.	
3/4/72	**20**	11	1. Whatcha See Is Whatcha Get	Volt 6018
			Whatcha See Is Whatcha Get (9)/*In The Rain* (5)	
5/17/75	**31**	3	2. The Dramatic Jackpot	ABC 867
			DREAM ACADEMY, The	
			English trio: Nick Laird-Clowes (guitar, vocals), Gilbert Gabriel (keyboards) and Kate St. John (vocals, oboe, saxophone).	
2/8/86	**20**	9	1. The Dream Academy	Warner 25265
			Life In A Northern Town (7)	
			DRIFTERS, The	
			Vocal group formed to showcase lead singer Clyde McPhatter on Atlantic in 1953. Included Gerhart and Andrew Thrasher, Bill Pinkney and McPhatter (who went solo in 1955). Group continued with various lead singers until 1958. In 1958, manager George Treadwell disbanded the group and brought in The Five Crowns and renamed them The Drifters. The majority of The Drifters' pop hits were sung by three different lead singers: Ben E. King (1959-60), Rudy Lewis (1961-63) and Johnny Moore (1957; 1963-66.) Rudy died of a heart attack in summer of 1964. Many personnel changes throughout career and several groups have used the name in later years. Inducted into the Rock and Roll Hall of Fame in 1988.	
11/7/64	**40**	2	1. Under The Boardwalk	Atlantic 8099
			On Broadway (9)/*Under The Boardwalk* (4)	
			DUCHIN, Eddy — see CAVALLARO, Carmen	
			DUKE, George	
			Born on 1/12/46 in San Rafael, California. Top jazz-rock keyboardist. Played with Jean-Luc Ponty, the Mothers of Invention, and Cannonball Adderley's band.	
12/3/77	**25**	9	● 1. Reach For It	Epic 34883
7/8/78	**39**	1	2. Don't Let Go	Epic 35366
			STANLEY CLARKE/GEORGE DUKE:	
6/6/81	**33**	8	3. The Clarke/Duke Project	Epic 36918
			DUKES OF DIXIELAND	
			New Orleans dixieland jazz combo led by Assunto brothers: Fred (trombone; d: 4/21/66) and Frank (trumpet; d: 2/25/74).	
9/9/57	**6**	26	1. Marching Along With The Dukes Of Dixieland, Vol. 3 [I]	Audio Fidel. 1851
12/11/61	**10**	21	2. The Best Of The Dukes Of Dixieland [G-I]	Audio Fidel. 1956
			DURAN DURAN	
			Romantic-styled band formed in Birmingham, England in 1980. Consisted of Simon LeBon (b: 10/27/58; vocals), Andy Taylor (b: 2/16/61; guitar), Nick Rhodes (b: 6/8/62; keyboards), John Taylor (b: 6/20/60; bass) and Roger Taylor (b: 4/26/60; drums). None of the Taylors are related. Group named after a villain in the Jane Fonda film *Barbarella*. In 1984, Andy and Roger left group. In 1985, Andy and John recorded with supergroup The Power Station; Simon, Nick and Roger recorded as Arcadia. Duran Duran reduced to a trio in 1986 of Simon, Nick and John. Changed spelling of name to Duranduran in 1988. Expanded to a quintet in 1990 with the addition of Warren Cuccurullo (ex-guitarist of Missing Persons) and Sterling Campbell.	
1/29/83	**6**	21	▲ 1. Rio	Harvest 12211
			Hungry Like The Wolf (3)	

Creedence Clearwater Revival's enormous musical role in the late 60s and early 70s was reflected in the sales of all their albums, each of which—from their 1968 debut to 1972's *Mardi Gras*—has been gold-certified. Of those, only the first, which featured "Suzie Q.," failed to reach the top 40. *Green River* was their first No. 1 LP.

Culture Club's star rose and fell comparatively quickly in the early 80s, apparently due to the personal problems of the group's flamboyant vocalist Boy George—who told Americans on a TV broadcast, "You sure know a good drag queen when you see one." 1983's *Colour By Numbers* contained the group's "Karma Chameleon" and "Miss Me Blind" singles.

Martin Denny's exotic sounds of the late 50s and early 60s made his albums big sellers. Most notable were *Exotica*, *Quiet Village* and *A Taste Of Honey*, all of which cracked the top 10 between 1959-62.

John Denver's career took off enormously beginning with 1971's *Poems, Prayers, And Promises*, which contained the hit "Take Me Home, Country Roads." His 1973 greatest hits collection was the first of his three No. 1 LPs.

Devo, one of the first bands to emerge from the late 70s new wave "Akron scene," won accolades for their many pioneering videos—not to mention their zany style of dress, which surfaced on occasion via upside-down flowerpot hats.

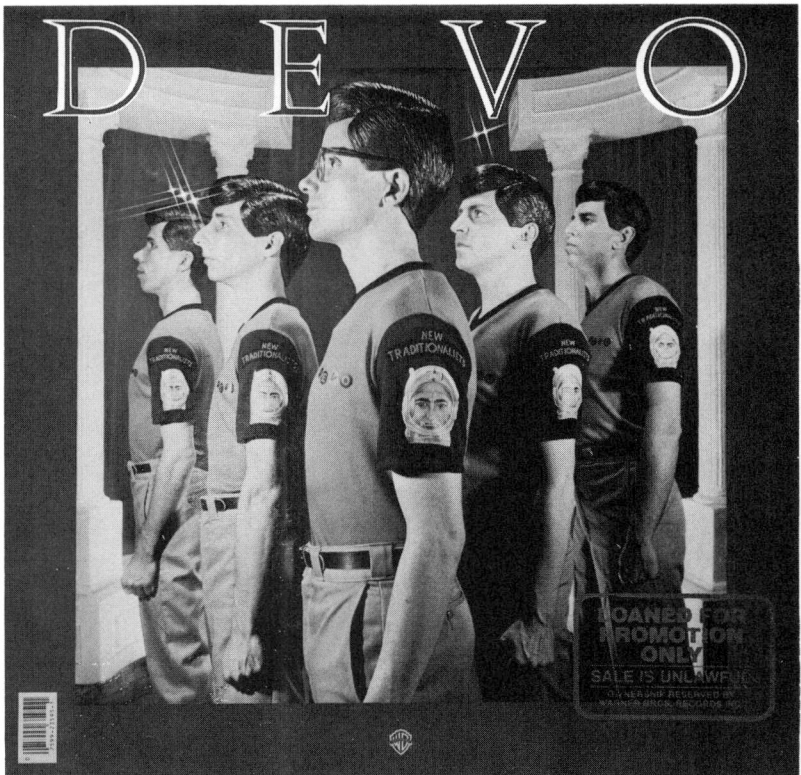

Fats Domino's influence in the world of rock 'n' roll may be undeniable, yet the well-known artist's albums managed to reach the top 40 regions only three times, beginning with *This Is Fats Domino!* in 1956.

The **Doobie Brothers** became icons of the 70s after joining forces with former Steely Dan backing vocalist Michael McDonald and scoring with such hits as "What A Fool Believes." At the close of the 80s, a Doobies reunion album without McDonald sold more than McDonald's own solo effort.

Duran Duran—who took their name from a character in the 60s film *Barbarella*, starring Jane Fonda—became the first of many teen idols to draw their fan base from MTV. *Seven And The Ragged Tiger* contained the group's hit single, "The Reflex."

The **Eagles**' streak of No. 1 albums from 1975 through 1979—*Hotel California* was the third—helped solidify them as one of the supergroups of the 70s. Fans were jubilant in 1990 when rumors were rife that the group—whose members included Don Henley and Glenn Frey—might reunite.

Duane Eddy's "twangy" guitar sound was integral not only to his late 50s, early 60s success but also to the titles of such albums as his *Have "Twangy" Guitar-Will Travel, The "Twangs" The Thang* and *$1,000,000.00 Worth Of Twang.*

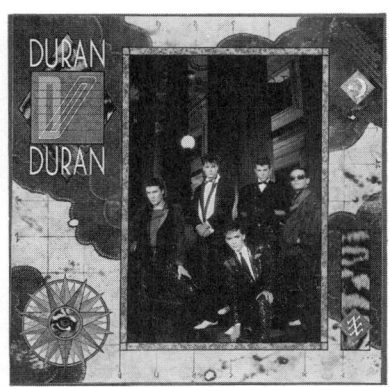

DATE	POS	WKS	ARTIST—RECORD TITLE	LABEL & NO.
7/2/83	**10**	14	▲ 2. Duran Duran [R] *their first album, released in 1981* *Is There Something I Should Know (4)*	Capitol 12158
12/10/83	**8**	41	▲ 3. Seven And The Ragged Tiger *Union Of The Snake (3)/New Moon On Monday (10)/* *The Reflex (1)*	Capitol 12310
12/8/84	**4**	15	▲ 4. Arena [L] *The Wild Boys (2)*	Capitol 12374
12/20/86	**12**	14	▲ 5. Notorious *Notorious (2)*	Capitol 12540
11/12/88	**24**	14	**DURANDURAN:** ● 6. Big Thing *I Don't Want Your Love (4)*	Capitol 90958
			DURANTE, Jimmy Born on 2/10/1893 in New York City; died on 1/29/80. Much-beloved comedian who started on vaudeville and became star of many Broadway shows and movies as well as his own TV show (1954-56).	
10/26/63	**30**	4	1. September Song *serious singing by the great comedian*	Warner 1506
			DYLAN, Bob Born Robert Allen Zimmerman on 5/24/41 in Duluth, Minnesota. Singer/songwriter/guitarist/harmonica player. Took stage name from poet Dylan Thomas. To New York City in December, 1960. Worked Greenwich Village folk clubs. Signed to Columbia Records in October, 1961. Innovator of folk-rock style, 1965. Motorcycle crash on 7/29/66 led to short retirement. Films *Don't Look Back* (1965), *Eat The Document* (1969) and *Pat Garrett And Billy The Kid* (1973). Made film *Renaldo And Clara* (1978). Newly found Christian faith reflected in his recordings of 1979. Co-starred with Fiona in the 1987 film *Hearts Of Fire*. Inducted into the Rock and Roll Hall of Fame in 1988. Member of the 1988 supergroup Traveling Wilburys.	
9/28/63	**22**	14	● 1. The Freewheelin' Bob Dylan	Columbia 8786
3/28/64	**20**	5	2. The Times They Are A-Changin'	Columbia 8905
5/15/65	**6**	32	● 3. Bringing It All Back Home	Columbia 9128
10/9/65	**3**	24	● 4. Highway 61 Revisited *Like A Rolling Stone (2)*	Columbia 9189
8/6/66	**9**	15	● 5. Blonde On Blonde *Rainy Day Women #12 & 35 (2)*	Columbia 841 [2]
5/20/67	**10**	21	▲ 6. Bob Dylan's Greatest Hits [G] *Positively 4th Street (7)*	Columbia 9463
2/10/68	**2(4)**	21	● 7. John Wesley Harding	Columbia 9604
5/3/69	**3**	31	▲ 8. Nashville Skyline *Lay Lady Lay (7)*	Columbia 9825
7/11/70	**4**	12	● 9. Self Portrait	Columbia 30050 [2]
11/14/70	**7**	12	● 10. New Morning	Columbia 30290
12/11/71	**14**	17	▲ 11. Bob Dylan's Greatest Hits, Vol. II [G]	Columbia 31120 [2]
9/1/73	**16**	14	12. Pat Garrett & Billy The Kid [S] *Dylan appeared as Alias in the film; three vocals by Dylan*	Columbia 32460
1/5/74	**17**	7	● 13. Dylan [K] *outtake recordings from 1969-70*	Columbia 32747
2/9/74	**1(4)**	12	● 14. Planet Waves *with The Band*	Asylum 1003
7/20/74	**3**	10	● 15. Before The Flood [L] *Bob Dylan/The Band concert tour*	Asylum 201 [2]
2/8/75	**1(2)**	14	▲ 16. Blood On The Tracks	Columbia 33235
8/2/75	**7**	9	17. The Basement Tapes [E] *recorded at Big Pink in Woodstock with The Band in 1967*	Columbia 33682 [2]

DATE	POS	WKS	ARTIST—RECORD TITLE	LABEL & NO.
1/24/76	**1**(5)	17	▲ 18. Desire	Columbia 33893
10/9/76	**17**	5	● 19. Hard Rain [L]	Columbia 34349
			recorded during his tour, the "Rolling Thunder Revue"	
7/15/78	**11**	8	● 20. Street-Legal	Columbia 35453
5/19/79	**13**	7	21. Bob Dylan At Budokan [L]	Columbia 36067 [2]
			recorded in Japan on 3/1/78	
9/15/79	**3**	13	▲ 22. Slow Train Coming	Columbia 36120
7/19/80	**24**	5	23. Saved	Columbia 36553
9/19/81	**33**	3	24. Shot Of Love	Columbia 37496
11/26/83	**20**	10	● 25. Infidels	Columbia 38819
6/29/85	**33**	6	26. Empire Burlesque	Columbia 40110
1/11/86	**33**	2	● 27. Biograph [K]	Columbia 38830 [5]
			consists of a 53-song collection from 1962-81 (18 songs previously unreleased)	
2/25/89	**37**	3	● 28. Dylan & The Dead [L]	Columbia 45056
			BOB DYLAN & GRATEFUL DEAD recordings from six concert dates in July of 1987	
10/14/89	**30**	6	29. Oh Mercy	Columbia 45281

E

EAGLES

Formed in Los Angeles in 1971. Consisted of Glenn Frey (vocals, guitar), Bernie Leadon (guitar), Randy Meisner (bass) and Don Henley (drums). Meisner had founded Poco; Leadon had been in the Flying Burrito Brothers; and Frey and Henley were with Linda Ronstadt. Debut album recorded in England in 1972. Don Felder (guitar) added in 1975. Leadon replaced by Joe Walsh in 1975; and Meisner replaced by Timothy B. Schmit in 1977. Frey and Henley were the only members to play on all albums. Disbanded in 1982.

DATE	POS	WKS	ARTIST—RECORD TITLE	LABEL & NO.
7/22/72	**22**	7	● 1. Eagles	Asylum 5054
			Witchy Woman (9)	
4/27/74	**17**	24	● 2. On The Border	Asylum 1004
			Best Of My Love (1)	
6/28/75	**1**(5)	43	● 3. One Of These Nights	Asylum 1039
			One Of These Nights (1)/*Lyin' Eyes* (2)/*Take It To The Limit* (4)	
3/6/76	**1**(5)	57	▲ 4. Eagles/Their Greatest Hits 1971-1975 [G]	Asylum 1052
12/25/76	**1**(8)	32	▲ 5. Hotel California	Asylum 1084
			New Kid In Town (1)/*Hotel California* (1)	
10/20/79	**1**(9)	36	▲ 6. The Long Run	Asylum 508
			Heartache Tonight (1)/*The Long Run* (8)/*I Can't Tell You Why* (8)	
11/29/80	**6**	16	▲ 7. Eagles Live [L]	Asylum 705 [2]

EARTH, WIND & FIRE

R&B group formed in Los Angeles in 1969, by Chicago-bred Maurice White (b: 12/19/41, Memphis; lead vocals, percussion, kalimba, songwriter, producer). Co-lead singer Philip Bailey joined in 1972. White had been a session drummer for Chess Records and with the Ramsey Lewis Trio, 1966-69. Group generally contained 8-10 members, with frequent personnel shuffling. In films *Sgt. Pepper's Lonely Hearts Club Band* and *That's The Way Of The World*. Group members Philip Bailey, Wade Flemons, Ronnie Laws and Maurice White had solo hits.

DATE	POS	WKS	ARTIST—RECORD TITLE	LABEL & NO.
7/14/73	**27**	10	● 1. Head To The Sky	Columbia 32194
4/13/74	**15**	18	▲ 2. Open Our Eyes	Columbia 32712

DATE	POS	WKS	ARTIST—RECORD TITLE	LABEL & NO.
3/22/75	**1**(3)	29	▲ 3. That's The Way Of The World [S] group portrayed a rock band in the film *Shining Star* (1)	Columbia 33280
12/13/75	**1**(3)	21	▲ 4. Gratitude [L] contains some studio cuts *Sing A Song* (5)	Columbia 33694 [2]
10/16/76	**2**(2)	18	▲ 5. Spirit	Columbia 34241
12/10/77	**3**	18	▲ 6. All 'N All	Columbia 34905
12/2/78	**6**	18	▲ 7. The Best Of Earth, Wind & Fire, Vol. I [G] *Got To Get You Into My Life* (9)/*September* (8)	ARC 35647
6/23/79	**3**	20	▲ 8. I Am *Boogie Wonderland* (6)/*After The Love Has Gone* (2)	ARC 35730
11/22/80	**10**	12	● 9. Faces	ARC 36795 [2]
11/14/81	**5**	18	▲ 10. Raise! *Let's Groove* (3)	ARC 37548
3/12/83	**12**	12	● 11. Powerlight	Columbia 38367
1/7/84	**40**	2	12. Electric Universe	Columbia 38980
12/5/87	**33**	6	● 13. Touch The World	Columbia 40596
			EASTON, Sheena	
			Born on 4/27/59 in Glasgow, Scotland. Vocalist/actress. Portrayed singer in the 1980 BBC-TV documentary "The Big Time." Won the 1981 Best New Artist Grammy Award. Portrayed Sonny Crockett's girlfriend/wife in five episodes of TV's "Miami Vice."	
5/2/81	**24**	8	● 1. Sheena Easton *Morning Train (Nine To Five)* (1)	EMI America 17049
10/1/83	**33**	9	2. Best Kept Secret *Telefone (Long Distance Love Affair)* (9)	EMI America 17101
11/24/84	**15**	22	● 3. A Private Heaven *Strut* (7)/*Sugar Walls* (9)	EMI America 17132
12/14/85	**40**	2	4. Do You	EMI America 17173
			EDDY, Duane	
			Born on 4/26/38 in Corning, New York. Began playing guitar at age five. At age 13, moved to Tucson, then to Coolidge, Arizona. To Phoenix in 1955, and then began long association with producer/songwriter Lee Hazlewood. Eddy's backing band, The Rebels, included three top sessionmen, Larry Knechtel on piano and Jim Horn and Steve Douglas on sax. Films *Because They're Young*, *A Thunder Of Drums*, *The Wild Westerners*, *The Savage Seven* and *Kona Coast*. Married to Jessi Colter, 1962-68. Duane originated the "twangy" guitar sound and is the all-time #1 rock and roll instrumentalist. Currently resides in the Nashville area.	
1/19/59	**5**	42	1. Have 'Twangy' Guitar-Will Travel [I] *Rebel-'Rouser* (6)	Jamie 3000
8/17/59	**24**	13	2. Especially For You... [I]	Jamie 3006
1/25/60	**18**	13	3. The "Twangs" The "Thang" [I]	Jamie 3009
12/26/60	**11**	9	4. $1,000,000.00 Worth Of Twang [I-G] *Forty Miles Of Bad Road* (9)/*Because They're Young* (4)	Jamie 3014
			EDWARDS, Vincent	
			Born Vincento Eduardo Zoine on 7/9/28 in New York City. Stage, film and TV actor. Best known as the star of the TV series "Ben Casey."	
7/21/62	**5**	11	1. Vincent Edwards Sings	Decca 4311
			ELECTRIC FLAG	
			Chicago blues band formed by Mike Bloomfield and Buddy Miles.	
5/11/68	**31**	5	1. A Long Time Comin'	Columbia 9597

DATE	POS	WKS	ARTIST—RECORD TITLE	LABEL & NO.
			ELECTRIC LIGHT ORCHESTRA	
			Group formed in Birmingham, England in 1971, by Roy Wood, Bev Bevans and Jeff Lynne of The Move. Wood left after their first album, leaving Lynne as the group's leader. Much personnel shuffling from then on. From a group size of eight in 1971, the 1986 ELO consisted of three members: Lynne (vocals, guitar, keyboards), Bevan (drums) and Richard Tandy (keyboards). Lynne is a member of the 1988 supergroup Traveling Wilburys.	
11/9/74	16	17	● 1. Eldorado *Can't Get It Out Of My Head* (9)	United Art. 339
11/8/75	8	14	● 2. Face The Music *Evil Woman* (10)	United Art. 546
7/17/76	32	5	● 3. Ole ELO [K]	United Art. 630
11/13/76	5	44	▲ 4. A New World Record *Telephone Line* (7)	United Art. 679
11/26/77	4	21	▲ 5. Out Of The Blue	Jet 823 [2]
6/23/79	5	17	▲ 6. Discovery *Shine A Little Love* (8)/*Don't Bring Me Down* (4)	Jet 35769
12/15/79	30	8	▲ 7. ELO's Greatest Hits [G]	Jet 36310

8/9/80	4	15	▲ 8. Xanadu [S]
			    side 1: Olivia Newton-John; side 2: ELO
			    Xanadu (8) with Olivia Newton-John
				MCA 6100

8/22/81	16	12	● 9. Time *Hold On Tight* (10)	Jet 37371
8/20/83	36	1	10. Secret Messages	Jet 38490
			ELFMAN, Danny	
			Lead singer of Oingo Boingo from Los Angeles. Scored the films *Beetlejuice*, *Batman* and *Dick Tracy*.	

9/2/89	30	4	1. Batman Original Motion Picture Score [S-I]
			    Elfman-composed music performed by the Sinfonia of London
			    Orchestra; songs from and songs inspired by the film *Batman*
				Warner 25977

			ELGART, Larry	
			Larry was born on 3/20/22 in New London, Connecticut. Alto saxman in brother Les's band and his own band. **LARRY ELGART AND HIS MANHATTAN SWING ORCHESTRA:**	
7/3/82	24	15	▲ 1. Hooked On Swing [I]	RCA 4343
			ELGART, Les	
			Les was born on 8/3/18 in New Haven, Connecticut. Trumpeter and bandleader since 1945. **LES ELGART AND HIS ORCHESTRA:**	
11/3/56	13	7	1. The Elgart Touch [I]	Columbia 875
8/19/57	14	7	2. For Dancers Also [I]	Columbia 1008
			ELLIMAN, Yvonne	
			Born on 12/29/51 in Honolulu. Portrayed Mary Magdalene on the concept LP and in the rock opera and film of *Jesus Christ Superstar*. Joined with Eric Clapton during his 1974 comeback tour.	
4/29/78	40	2	1. Night Flight *If I Can't Have You* (1)	RSO 3031
			ELLINGTON, Duke	
			Born Edward Kennedy Ellington on 4/29/1899 in Washington, D.C. One of jazz music's leading bandleader/composer/arrangers. Died on 5/24/74.	
6/24/57	14	1	1. Ellington At Newport [I-L] recorded at the Newport Jazz Festival on 7/7/56	Columbia 934

DATE	POS	WKS	ARTIST—RECORD TITLE	LABEL & NO.
			EMERSON, LAKE & PALMER	
			English classical-oriented rock trio formed in 1969. Consisted of Keith Emerson (with The Nice; keyboards), Greg Lake (King Crimson; vocals, bass, guitars) and Carl Palmer (Atomic Rooster, Crazy World of Arthur Brown; drums). Group split up in 1979, with Palmer joining supergroup Asia. Emerson and Lake re-grouped in 1986 with new drummer Cozy Powell. Palmer returned in 1987, replacing Powell who joined Black Sabbath in 1990.	
2/27/71	**18**	18	● 1. Emerson, Lake & Palmer	Cotillion 9040
7/10/71	**9**	11	● 2. Tarkus	Cotillion 9900
1/29/72	**10**	12	● 3. Pictures At An Exhibition [L]	Cotillion 66666
			based on Mussorgsky's classical composition	
8/5/72	**5**	20	● 4. Trilogy	Cotillion 9903
12/29/73	**11**	16	● 5. Brain Salad Surgery	Manticore 66669
9/14/74	**4**	11	● 6. Welcome back, my friends, to the show that never ends - Ladies and Gentlemen [L]	Manticore 200 [3]
4/16/77	**12**	10	● 7. Works, Volume 1	Atlantic 7000 [2]
1/7/78	**37**	3	● 8. Works, Volume 2	Atlantic 19147
			above two albums feature mostly solo material	
6/28/86	**23**	12	9. Emerson, Lake & Powell	Polydor 829297
			EMOTIONS, The	
			Black female trio from Chicago, consisting of sisters Wanda (lead), Sheila and Jeanette Hutchinson. First worked as child gospel group called the Heavenly Sunbeams. Left gospel, became The Emotions in 1968. Jeanette replaced by cousin Theresa Davis in 1970, and later by sister Pamela. Jeanette returned to group in 1978.	
7/2/77	**7**	21	▲ 1. Rejoice	Columbia 34762
			Best Of My Love (1)	
9/9/78	**40**	3	● 2. Sunbeam	Columbia 35385
			ENGLAND DAN & JOHN FORD COLEY	
			Pop duo from Austin, Texas: Dan Seals (b: 2/8/50) and Coley (b: 10/13/51). Dan (brother of Jim Seals of Seals & Crofts) is currently a hot country artist.	
9/25/76	**17**	12	● 1. Nights Are Forever	Big Tree 89517
			I'd Really Love To See You Tonight (2)/ *Nights Are Forever Without You* (10)	
			ENGLISH BEAT	
			English "ska" (reggae/R&B) sextet led by Dave Wakeling and Ranking Roger (Roger Charley). Disbanded in 1983. Wakeling and Roger formed General Public. Roger recorded solo in 1988.	
4/9/83	**39**	3	1. Special Beat Service	I.R.S. 70032
			EN VOGUE	
			Black female vocal quartet from the San Francisco Bay area. Formed by the production team of Denzil Foster and Thomas McElroy. Consists of Dawn Robinson, Terry Ellis, Cindy Herron and Maxine Jones.	
5/26/90	**21**	19	● 1. Born To Sing	Atlantic 82084
			Hold On (2)	
			ENYA	
			Born Eithne Ni Bhraonain in Donegal, Ireland. From 1980-82, she was a member of her siblings' folk-rock group Clannad.	
3/11/89	**25**	13	● 1. Watermark	Geffen 24233
			EPPS, Preston	
			Bongo player from Oakland. Discovered by Original Sound owner, Art Laboe.	
8/15/60	**35**	1	1. Bongo Bongo Bongo [I]	Original Snd. 5002

DATE	POS	WKS	ARTIST—RECORD TITLE	LABEL & NO.
			ERIC B. & RAKIM	
			Rap duo: DJ Eric Barrier (from Elmhurst, New York) and rapper William Griffin, Jr. (from Long Island, New York).	
8/20/88	22	7	● 1. Follow The Leader	Uni 3
			ESCAPE CLUB, The	
			London-based rock quartet formed in 1983: Trevor Steel (vocals), John Holliday (guitar), Johnnie Christo (bass) and Milan Zekavica (drums).	
10/29/88	27	14	● 1. Wild Wild West *Wild, Wild West* (1)	Atlantic 81871
			ESSEX, David	
			Born David Cook on 7/23/47 in London, England. Portrayed Christ in the London production of *Godspell*. Star of British films since 1970.	
3/9/74	32	3	1. Rock On *Rock On* (5)	Columbia 32560
			ESTEFAN, Gloria/Miami Sound Machine	
			Latin American flavored pop music band based in Miami, led by singer Gloria Estefan with her husband, percussionist Emilio Estefan, Jr. Band formed in 1975. Gloria came to Miami from Cuba in 1960 at 16 months of age. Emilio emigrated in 1965. On March 20, 1990, both were involved in a serious bus accident in which Gloria suffered a broken vertebra.	
			MIAMI SOUND MACHINE:	
3/1/86	21	34	▲ 1. Primitive Love	Epic 40131
			GLORIA ESTEFAN and MIAMI SOUND MACHINE:	
7/4/87	6	48	▲ 2. Let It Loose *Rhythm Is Gonna Get You* (5)/*Can't Stay Away From You* (6)/ *Anything For You* (1)/*1-2-3* (3)	Epic 40769
			GLORIA ESTEFAN:	
8/5/89	8	41	▲ 3. Cuts Both Ways cassette and CD versions contain Spanish versions of two tracks *Don't Wanna Lose You* (1)/*Here We Are* (6)	Epic 45217
			ETHERIDGE, Melissa	
			Singer/guitarist born and raised in Leavenworth, Kansas. Studied guitar at Boston's Berklee College of Music. Discovered in Long Beach, California by Island Records' founder Chris Blackwell.	
3/25/89	22	14	● 1. Melissa Etheridge	Island 90875
10/14/89	22	10	● 2. Brave And Crazy	Island 91285
			EUROPE	
			Swedish rock quintet: Joey Tempest (vocals), Kee Marcello (guitar), John Leven (bass), Mic Michaeli (keyboards) and Ian Haugland (drums).	
2/7/87	8	42	▲ 1. The Final Countdown *The Final Countdown* (8)/*Carrie* (3)	Epic 40241
9/3/88	19	11	▲ 2. Out Of This World	Epic 44185
			EURYTHMICS	
			Synthesizer/pop duo: Annie Lennox (b: 12/25/54, Aberdeen, Scotland; vocals, keyboards, flute, composer) and David Stewart (b: 9/9/52, England; keyboards, guitar, synthesizer, composer). Both had been in the Tourists from 1977-80. First album recorded in Cologne, Germany, with drummer Clem Burke, formerly of Blondie. Stewart married Siobhan Fahey of Bananarama on 8/1/87. Lennox appeared in TV film *The Room*.	
7/16/83	15	17	● 1. Sweet Dreams (Are Made Of This) *Sweet Dreams (Are Made Of This)* (1)	RCA 4681
2/11/84	7	23	▲ 2. Touch *Here Comes The Rain Again* (4)	RCA 4917

DATE	POS	WKS	ARTIST—RECORD TITLE	LABEL & NO.
6/1/85	**9**	24	▲ 3. Be Yourself Tonight *Would I Lie To You?* (5)	RCA 5429
8/16/86	**12**	15	● 4. Revenge	RCA 5847
11/18/89	**34**	9	5. We Too Are One	Arista 8606
			EVERLY BROTHERS, The	
			Donald (real name: Isaac Donald) was born on 2/1/37 in Brownie, Kentucky; Philip on 1/19/39 in Chicago. Vocal duo/guitarists/songwriters. Parents were folk and country singers. Don (beginning at age eight) and Phil (age six) sang with parents through high school. Invited to Nashville by Chet Atkins and first recorded there for Columbia in 1955. Signed to Archie Bleyer's Cadence Records in 1957. Phil married for a time to the daughter of Archie and Janet (Chordettes) Bleyer. Duo split up in July of 1973 and reunited in September of 1983. Inducted into the Rock and Roll Hall of Fame in 1986. The #1 duo of the rock era.	
2/10/58	**16**	3	1. The Everly Brothers *Bye Bye Love* (2)/*Wake Up Little Susie* (1)	Cadence 3003
5/23/60	**9**	10	2. It's Everly Time! *So Sad (To Watch Good Love Go Bad)* (7)	Warner 1381
8/22/60	**23**	8	3. The Fabulous Style Of The Everly Brothers [K] *('Til) I Kissed You* (4)/*Let It Be Me* (7)/ *When Will I Be Loved* (8)	Cadence 3040
12/5/60	**9**	9	4. A Date With The Everly Brothers *Cathy's Clown* (1)	Warner 1395
9/15/62	**35**	3	5. The Golden Hits Of The Everly Brothers [G] *Ebony Eyes* (8)/*Walk Right Back* (7)/*Crying In The Rain* (6)/ *That's Old Fashioned* (9)	Warner 1471
10/27/84	**38**	3	6. EB 84	Mercury 822431
			EXILE	
			Band formed in Lexington, Kentucky in 1963 as The Exiles; J.P. Pennington, lead singer. Toured with Dick Clark in 1965. Changed name to Exile in 1973. Pennington left band in early 1989, replaced by Paul Martin. Currently a hot country band.	
9/23/78	**14**	8	● 1. Mixed Emotions *Kiss You All Over* (1)	Warner 3205
			EXPOSE	
			Miami-based dance/disco trio: Ann Curless, Jeanette Jurado and Gioia Carmen.	
3/21/87	**16**	52	▲ 1. Exposure *Come Go With Me* (5)/*Point Of No Return* (5)/ *Let Me Be The One* (7)/*Seasons Change* (1)	Arista 8441
7/22/89	**33**	6	● 2. What You Don't Know *What You Don't Know* (8)/*When I Looked At Him* (10)/ *Tell Me Why* (9)	Arista 8532
			F	
			FABIAN	
			Born Fabian Forte on 2/6/43 in Philadelphia. Discovered at age 14 (because of his good looks and intriguing name) by a chance meeting with Bob Marcucci, owner of Chancellor Records. Began acting career in 1959 with *Hound Dog Man*.	
5/18/59	**5**	18	1. Hold That Tiger! *Turn Me Loose* (9)	Chancellor 5003

DATE	POS	WKS	ARTIST—RECORD TITLE	LABEL & NO.
12/28/59	**3**	19	2. Fabulous Fabian	Chancellor 5005
			FABRIC, Bent	
			Born Bent Fabricius-Bjerre on 12/7/42 in Copenhagen. Head of Metronome Records in Denmark. Composer/pianist/TV personality/A&R man.	
			BENT FABRIC & HIS PIANO:	
11/24/62	**13**	22	1. Alley Cat [I]	Atco 148
			Alley Cat (7)	
			FABULOUS THUNDERBIRDS, The	
			Austin, Texas rock and roll group: Kim Wilson (lead singer), Jimmie Vaughan (guitar; brother of Stevie Ray Vaughan), Preston Hubbard (bass) and Fran Christina (drums). Vaughan appeared in the 1989 film *Great Balls Of Fire*.	
4/26/86	**13**	25	▲ 1. Tuff Enuff	CBS Assoc. 40304
			FACES	
			Rod Stewart (joined by Ron Wood of the Jeff Beck Group) replaced Steve Marriott (formed Humble Pie) as leader of the revamped British group Small Faces in 1969. Other members: Ian McLagen, Kenny Jones and Ronnie Lane. Lane left in 1973, replaced by ex-Free bassist Tetsu Yamauchi. Group disbanded in late 1975. Wood joined The Rolling Stones in 1976 and Jones replaced the late Keith Moon of The Who in 1978.	
4/3/71	**29**	5	1. Long Player	Warner 1892
1/1/72	**6**	14	● 2. A Nod Is As Good As A Wink…To A Blind Horse	Warner 2574
5/12/73	**21**	7	3. Ooh La La	Warner 2665
			FAGEN, Donald	
			Born on 1/10/48 in Passaic, New Jersey. Worked as backup with Jay & The Americans. Fagen and Walter Becker founded Steely Dan.	
11/6/82	**11**	10	● 1. The Nightfly	Warner 23696
			FAITH, Percy	
			Born on 4/7/08 in Toronto, Canada; died on 2/9/76. Orchestra leader. Moved to the United States in 1940. Joined Columbia Records in 1950 as conductor/arranger for their leading singers (Tony Bennett, Doris Day, Rosemary Clooney, Johnny Mathis and others).	
7/28/56	**18**	2	1. Passport To Romance [I]	Columbia 880
4/29/57	**8**	2	2. My Fair Lady [I]	Columbia 895
5/25/59	**17**	14	3. Porgy And Bess [I]	Columbia 8105
1/11/60	**7**	17	● 4. Bouquet [I]	Columbia 8124
11/28/60	**7**	8	5. Jealousy [I]	Columbia 8292
1/9/61	**6**	10	6. Camelot [I]	Columbia 8370
11/6/61	**38**	1	7. Mucho Gusto! More Music Of Mexico [I]	Columbia 8439
4/14/62	**26**	5	8. Bouquet Of Love [I]	Columbia 8481
6/29/63	**12**	13	● 9. Themes for Young Lovers [I]	Columbia 8823
			FAITHFULL, Marianne	
			English songstress; born on 12/29/46 in Hampstead, London. Discovered by Rolling Stones' manager, Andrew Loog Oldham. Involved in a long, tumultuous relationship with Mick Jagger. Acted in several stage and screen productions. Married to American playwright Giorgio Dellaterza.	
8/14/65	**12**	15	1. Marianne Faithfull	London 423
			FALCO	
			Falco (Johann Holzel) was born on 2/19/57 in Vienna, Austria.	
3/15/86	**3**	18	● 1. Falco 3	A&M 5105
			Rock Me Amadeus (1)	

DATE	POS	WKS	ARTIST—RECORD TITLE	LABEL & NO.
			FARRELL, Eileen	
			Born on 2/13/20 in Willimantic, Connecticut. Operatic soprano. Major debut came with the San Francisco Opera in 1956. Metropolitan Opera debut in February, 1960.	
1/9/61	**15**	7	1. I've Got A Right To Sing The Blues	Columbia 1465
			FASTWAY	
			British rock group led by Motorhead's Fast Eddie Clarke (guitar) with David King (vocals), Jerry Shirley (drums) and Charlie McCracken (bass; joined in 1984).	
8/13/83	**31**	6	1. Fastway	Columbia 38662
			FAT BOYS	
			Brooklyn-born rap trio: Darren "The Human Beat Box" Robinson, Mark "Prince Markie Dee" Morales and Damon "Kool Rock-ski" Wimbley. Combined weight of over 750 pounds. Appeared in the 1987 film *Disorderlies*.	
7/11/87	**8**	21	▲ 1. Crushin'	Tin Pan A. 831948
7/30/88	**33**	5	● 2. Coming Back Hard Again	Tin Pan 835809
			FELICIANO, Jose	
			Born on 9/8/45 in Puerto Rico; raised in New York City. Blind since birth. Virtuoso acoustic guitarist. Won the 1968 Best New Artist Grammy Award.	
8/17/68	**2**(3)	26	● 1. Feliciano!	RCA 3957
			Light My Fire (3)	
1/11/69	**24**	4	2. Souled	RCA 4045
8/2/69	**16**	13	● 3. Feliciano/10 To 23	RCA 4185
			featuring a recording by Jose at age 10	
1/3/70	**29**	4	● 4. Alive Alive-O! [L]	RCA 6021 [2]
			in concert at the London Palladium	
			FENDER, Freddy	
			Born Baldemar Huerta on 6/4/37 in San Benito, Texas. Mexican-American singer/guitarist. First recorded in Spanish under his real name for Falcon in 1956. In the film *The Milagro Beanfield War*.	
6/7/75	**20**	11	● 1. Before The Next Teardrop Falls	ABC/Dot 2020
			Before The Next Teardrop Falls (1)/ *Wasted Days And Wasted Nights* (8)	
			FERGUSON, Maynard	
			Jazz trumpeter, born on 5/4/28 in Verdun, Quebec, Canada. Moved to the United States in 1949. Played for Charlie Barnet and then Stan Kenton's Band (1950-56).	
5/21/77	**22**	7	● 1. Conquistador [I]	Columbia 34457
			FERRANTE & TEICHER	
			Piano duo: Arthur Ferrante (b: 9/7/21, New York City) and Louis Teicher (b: 8/24/24, Wilkes-Barre, Pennsylvania). Met as children while attending the Juilliard School of Music in New York.	
12/11/61	**10**	27	1. West Side Story & Other Motion Picture & Broadway Hits [I]	United Art. 6166
			Tonight (8)	
12/25/61	**23**	7	2. Love Themes [I]	United Art. 8514
3/24/62	**30**	2	3. Golden Piano Hits [I]	United Art. 8505
			Exodus (2)	
3/31/62	**11**	25	4. Tonight [I]	United Art. 6171
7/13/63	**23**	8	5. Love Themes From Cleopatra [I]	United Art. 6290
1/2/65	**35**	6	6. The People's Choice [I]	United Art. 6385

DATE	POS	WKS	ARTIST—RECORD TITLE	LABEL & NO.
			FIELDS, Richard "Dimples"	
			R&B vocalist; owner of the Cold Duck Music Lounge in San Francisco.	
8/29/81	**33**	4	1. Dimples	Boardwalk 33232
			FIELDS, W.C.	
			Born on 2/20/1879 in Philadelphia; died on 12/25/46. Classic comedian of American film.	
2/8/69	**30**	11	1. The Original Voice Tracks From His Greatest Movies [C]	Decca 79164
			5TH DIMENSION, The	
			Los Angeles-based group formed in 1966: Marilyn McCoo, Florence LaRue, Billy Davis, Jr., Lamont McLemore and Ron Townson. McLemore and McCoo had been in the Hi-Fi's; Townson and Davis had been with groups in St. Louis. First called the Versatiles. Davis and McCoo were married in 1969 and recorded as a duo from 1976.	
7/8/67	**8**	11	● 1. Up, Up And Away *Up-Up And Away* (7)	Soul City 92000
9/28/68	**21**	8	2. Stoned Soul Picnic *Stoned Soul Picnic* (3)	Soul City 92002
5/31/69	**2(2)**	30	● 3. The Age Of Aquarius *Aquarius/Let The Sunshine In* (1)/*Wedding Bell Blues* (1)	Soul City 92005
5/23/70	**5**	18	● 4. The 5th Dimension/Greatest Hits [G]	Soul City 33900
5/23/70	**20**	16	● 5. Portrait *One Less Bell To Answer* (2)	Bell 6045
3/27/71	**17**	8	● 6. Love's Lines, Angles And Rhymes	Bell 6060
11/13/71	**32**	4	● 7. The 5th Dimension/Live!! [L]	Bell 9000 [2]
10/14/72	**14**	10	● 8. Greatest Hits On Earth [G] greatest hits from both Soul City and Bell labels	Bell 1106
			50 GUITARS OF TOMMY GARRETT, The	
			A Tommy "Snuff" Garrett production. Tommy was born in 1939 in Dallas. A&R man/ producer for Liberty, 1958-66. Guitar solos by Tommy Tedesco.	
1/20/62	**36**	1	1. 50 Guitars Go South Of The Border [I]	Liberty 14005
			FINE YOUNG CANNIBALS	
			Pop trio from Birmingham, England: Roland Gift (vocals) and English Beat members David Steele (bass) and Andy Cox (guitar). Group appeared in the film *Tin Men*; Gift was in the film *Scandal*.	
3/18/89	**1(7)**	40	▲ 1. The Raw & The Cooked *She Drives Me Crazy* (1)/*Good Thing* (1)	I.R.S. 6273
			FIREBALLS, The — see GILMER, Jimmy	
			FIREFALL	
			Mellow rock group formed in Boulder, Colorado. Original lineup: Rick Roberts (lead singer), Larry Burnett (guitar), Jack Bartley (lead guitar), Mark Andes (bass; formerly with Spirit and Jo Jo Gunne) and Mike Clarke (drums). David Muse (keyboards) joined in 1977. Andes joined Heart in 1980.	
7/4/76	**28**	14	● 1. Firefall *You Are The Woman* (9)	Atlantic 18174
9/3/77	**27**	5	● 2. Luna Sea	Atlantic 19101
12/2/78	**27**	7	▲ 3. Elan	Atlantic 19183
			FIRM, The	
			British supergroup: Jimmy Page (Led Zeppelin; guitar), Paul Rodgers (Bad Company; vocals), Chris Slade (Manfred Mann; drums) and Tony Franklin (keyboards; joined Blue Murder in 1989. Slade joined AC/DC in 1990.	
3/9/85	**17**	16	● 1. The Firm	Atlantic 81239

DATE	POS	WKS	ARTIST—RECORD TITLE	LABEL & NO.
3/1/86	**22**	7	2. Mean Business	Atlantic 81628
			FIRST EDITION, The — see ROGERS, Kenny	
			FISHER, Eddie	
			Born Edwin Jack Fisher on 8/10/28 in Philadelphia. Radio work while still in high school; at Copacabana night club in New York at age 17. With Buddy Morrow and Charlie Ventura in 1946. On Eddie Cantor radio show in 1949. Armed Forces Special Services, 1952-53. Married Debbie Reynolds in 1955. Other marriages to Elizabeth Taylor and Connie Stevens. Daughter with Debbie is actress Carrie Fisher. Daughter with Connie is singer Tricia Leigh Fisher. Own "Coke Time" 15-minute TV series, 1953-57. In films *All About Eve* (1950), *Bundle Of Joy* (1956) and *Butterfield 8* (1960). Eddie was the #1 idol of bobbysoxers during the early 1950s.	
4/30/55	**8**	10	1. I Love You	RCA 1097
			FITZGERALD, Ella	
			The most honored jazz singer of all time. Ella Fitzgerald was born on 4/25/18 in Newport News, Virginia. Discovered after winning the Harlem Amateur Hour in 1934, she was hired by Chick Webb and in 1938 created a popular sensation with "A-Tisket, A-Tasket." Following Chick's death in 1939, Ella took over the band for three years. Winner of the *Down Beat* poll as top female vocalist more than 20 times, she remains among the undisputed royalty of 20th century popular music.	
9/17/55	**7**	10	1. Songs from Pete Kelly's Blues **PEGGY LEE & ELLA FITZGERALD**	Decca 8166
7/28/56	**15**	1	2. Ella Fitzgerald sings the Cole Porter Song Book	Verve 4001 [2]
12/15/56	**12**	2	3. Ella And Louis **ELLA FITZGERALD AND LOUIS ARMSTRONG** backing by the Oscar Peterson Trio, plus Buddy Rich	Verve 4003
3/16/57	**11**	4	4. Ella Fitzgerald sings the Rodgers and Hart Song Book albums 2 & 4 above arranged and conducted by Buddy Bregman	Verve 4002 [2]
9/12/60	**11**	20	5. Mack The Knife - Ella In Berlin [L]	Verve 4041
1/6/62	**35**	1	6. Ella In Hollywood [L]	Verve 4052
			FIXX, The	
			London-based techno-pop group: Cy Curnin (lead singer, piano), Jamie West-Oram (guitars), Rupert Greenall (keyboards), Adam Woods (drums) and Dan K. Brown (bass).	
11/26/83	**8**	28	▲ 1. Reach The Beach *One Thing Leads To Another* (4)	MCA 39001
9/15/84	**19**	10	● 2. Phantoms	MCA 5507
7/5/86	**30**	8	3. Walkabout	MCA 5705
			FLACK, Roberta	
			Born on 2/10/39 in Asheville, North Carolina; raised in Arlington, Virginia. Played piano from an early age. Music scholarship to Howard University at age 15; classmate of Donny Hathaway. Discovered by jazz musician Les McCann. Signed to Atlantic in 1969.	
10/17/70	**33**	13	● 1. Chapter Two	Atlantic 1569
12/11/71	**18**	21	● 2. Quiet Fire	Atlantic 1594
3/25/72	**1**(5)	26	● 3. First Take *The First Time Ever I Saw Your Face* (1)	Atlantic 8230
9/1/73	**3**	14	● 4. Killing Me Softly *Killing Me Softly With His Song* (1)	Atlantic 7271
4/19/75	**24**	5	5. Feel Like Makin' Love *Feel Like Makin' Love* (1)	Atlantic 18131
2/18/78	**8**	17	● 6. Blue Lights In The Basement *The Closer I Get To You* (2)	Atlantic 19149

DATE	POS	WKS	ARTIST—RECORD TITLE	LABEL & NO.
4/26/80	**3**	10	● 7. Roberta Flack & Donny Hathaway *Where Is The Love* (5)	Atlantic 7216
4/26/80	**25**	10	● 8. Roberta Flack Featuring Donny Hathaway **PEABO BRYSON/ROBERTA FLACK:**	Atlantic 16013
9/10/83	**25**	14	● 9. Born To Love	Capitol 12284

FLASH
English rock quartet led by Peter Banks (guitar) and Colin Carter (vocals).

8/26/72	**33**	5	1. Flash	Capitol 11040

FLEETWOOD MAC
Formed as a British blues band in 1967 by ex-John Mayall's Bluesbreakers Peter Green (guitar), Mick Fleetwood (drums) and John McVie (bass), along with guitarist Jeremy Spencer. Many lineup changes followed as group headed toward rock super-stardom. Green and Spencer left in 1970. Christine McVie (keyboards) joined in August, 1970. Bob Welch (guitar) joined in April, 1971, stayed thru 1974. Group relocated to California in 1974, whereupon Lindsey Buckingham (guitar) and Stevie Nicks (vocals) joined in January, 1975. Buckingham left in summer of 1987. Guitarists/vocalists Billy Burnette (son of Dorsey Burnette) and Rick Vito joined in July of 1987. Christine McVie and Nicks left at the end of 1990.

11/16/74	**34**	2	1. Heroes Are Hard To Find	Reprise 2196
8/23/75	**1**(1)	68	▲ 2. Fleetwood Mac *Americans Stevie Nicks & Lindsey Buckingham join group*	Reprise 2225
2/26/77	**1**(31)	60	▲ 3. Rumours *1977 Grammy winner: Album of the Year* *Go Your Own Way* (10)/*Dreams* (1)/*Don't Stop* (3)/ *You Make Loving Fun* (9)	Warner 3010
11/3/79	**4**	22	▲ 4. Tusk *Tusk* (8)/*Sara* (7)	Warner 3350 [2]
1/10/81	**14**	8	● 5. Fleetwood Mac Live [L]	Warner 3500 [2]
7/24/82	**1**(5)	21	▲ 6. Mirage *Hold Me* (4)	Warner 23607
5/9/87	**7**	44	▲ 7. Tango In The Night *Big Love* (5)/*Little Lies* (4)	Warner 25471
12/24/88	**14**	12	▲ 8. Greatest Hits [G]	Warner 25801
5/5/90	**18**	9	● 9. Behind The Mask	Warner 26111

FLOATERS, The
Detroit soul group: Charles Clarke (lead), Larry Cunningham, Paul & Ralph Mitchell and Jonathan "Mighty Midget" Murray (joined in 1978).

7/23/77	**10**	13	▲ 1. Floaters *Float On* (2)	ABC 1030

FLOCK OF SEAGULLS, A
British techno-rock group led by vocalist Mike Score. Quartet until 1988 when three Philadelphia natives joined the group.

7/3/82	**10**	25	● 1. A Flock Of Seagulls *I Ran (So Far Away)* (9)	Jive 66000
6/4/83	**16**	11	2. Listen	Jive 8013

FOCUS
Dutch progressive rock quartet led by guitar virtuoso Jon Akkerman and flutist Thijs van Leer.

3/3/73	**8**	21	● 1. Moving Waves [I] *Hocus Pocus* (9)	Sire 7401
6/9/73	**35**	4	● 2. Focus 3 [I]	Sire 3901 [2]

DATE	POS	WKS	ARTIST—RECORD TITLE	LABEL & NO.
			FOGELBERG, Dan	
			Born on 8/13/51 in Peoria, Illinois. Vocalist/composer. Worked as a folk singer in Los Angeles. With Van Morrison in the early 70s. Session work in Nashville.	
1/18/75	**17**	11	▲ 1. Souvenirs Joe Walsh, producer and guitarist	Full Moon 33137
10/18/75	**23**	6	● 2. Captured Angel	Full Moon 33499
6/18/77	**13**	12	▲ 3. Nether Lands	Full Moon 34185
9/23/78	**8**	13	▲ 4. Twin Sons Of Different Mothers **DAN FOGELBERG & TIM WEISBERG**	Full Moon 35339
12/15/79	**3**	27	▲ 5. Phoenix *Longer* (2)	Full Moon 35634
9/19/81	**6**	31	▲ 6. The Innocent Age *Same Old Lang Syne* (9)/*Hard To Say* (7)/ *Leader Of The Band* (9)	Full Moon 37393 [2]
11/20/82	**15**	12	▲ 7. Dan Fogelberg/Greatest Hits [G]	Full Moon 38308
2/25/84	**15**	10	● 8. Windows and Walls	Full Moon 39004
5/25/85	**30**	5	9. High Country Snows	Full Moon 39616
			FOGERTY, John	
			Born on 5/28/45 in Berkeley, California; multi-instrumentalist. With his brother Tom in the Blue Velvets in 1959. Group became the Golliwogs and recorded for Fantasy in 1964. Re-named Creedence Clearwater Revival in 1967. Wrote "Proud Mary," "Have You Ever Seen The Rain," "Bad Moon Rising," "Lookin' Out My Back Door" and many others. Went solo in 1972 and recorded as The Blue Ridge Rangers.	
2/2/85	**1**(1)	28	▲ 1. Centerfield *The Old Man Down The Road* (10)	Warner 25203
10/18/86	**26**	6	● 2. Eye Of The Zombie	Warner 25449
			FOGHAT	
			British rock quartet: Lonesome Dave Peverett (vocals, guitar; formerly with Savoy Brown), Rod Price (guitar), Tony Stevens (bass) and Roger Earl (drums). Settled in New York City in 1975, many bass player changes since. Price replaced by Erik Cartwright in 1981.	
3/16/74	**34**	3	● 1. Energized	Bearsville 6950
11/30/74	**40**	2	● 2. Rock And Roll Outlaws	Bearsville 6956
3/6/76	**23**	7	▲ 3. Fool For The City	Bearsville 6959
12/11/76	**36**	2	● 4. Night Shift	Bearsville 6962
9/24/77	**11**	9	▲ 5. Foghat Live [L]	Bearsville 6971
6/10/78	**25**	7	● 6. Stone Blue	Bearsville 6977
10/20/79	**35**	3	7. Boogie Motel	Bearsville 6990
			FONDA, Jane — see AEROBICS section	
			FONTAINE, Frank	
			Born on 4/19/20 in Cambridge, Massachusetts. Comedian/singer/actor. Played "Crazy Guggenheim" on the Jackie Gleason TV show.	
2/23/63	**1**(5)	28	* 1. Songs I Sing On The Jackie Gleason Show	ABC-Para. 442
			FORBERT, Steve	
			Born in 1955 in Meridian, Mississippi. Moved to New York City in 1976.	
2/2/80	**20**	6	1. Jackrabbit Slim	Nemperor 36191

DATE	POS	WKS	ARTIST—RECORD TITLE	LABEL & NO.
			FORD, Lita	
			Born in London. Lead guitarist of Los Angeles-based female rock group The Runaways, at age 15, in 1975.	
4/23/88	**29**	23	▲ 1. Lita	RCA 6397
			Close My Eyes Forever (8)	
			FORD, "Tennessee" Ernie	
			Born Ernest Jennings Ford on 2/13/19 in Bristol, Tennessee. Began career as a DJ. Host of musical variety TV shows, 1955-65. America's favorite hymn singer.	
4/28/56	**12**	3	1. This Lusty Land!	Capitol 700
1/5/57	**2(3)**	138	● 2. Hymns	Capitol 756
5/6/57	**5**	39	● 3. Spirituals	Capitol 818
6/9/58	**5**	49	● 4. Nearer The Cross	Capitol 1005
12/22/58	**4**	3	● 5. The Star Carol [X]	Capitol 1071
12/28/59	**7**	2	6. The Star Carol [X-R]	Capitol 1071
5/2/60	**23**	14	7. Sing A Hymn With Me	Capitol 1332
			includes a hymn book	
12/31/60	**28**	1	8. The Star Carol [X-R]	Capitol 1071
			FOREIGNER	
			British/American rock group formed in New York City, 1976. Consisted of Mick Jones (guitar), Lou Gramm (vocals), Ian McDonald (guitar, keyboards), Ed Gagliardi (bass), Al Greenwood (keyboards) and Dennis Elliott (drums). Most of material written by Jones (formerly with Spooky Tooth) and Gramm. Re-formed in 1980 with Jones, Gramm, Elliott and Rick Wills (bass). Gramm, Gagliardi and Greenwood are from New York.	
5/7/77	**4**	43	▲ 1. Foreigner	Atlantic 18215
			Feels Like The First Time (4)/*Cold As Ice* (6)	
7/8/78	**3**	37	▲ 2. Double Vision	Atlantic 19999
			Hot Blooded (3)/*Double Vision* (2)	
9/29/79	**5**	22	▲ 3. Head Games	Atlantic 29999
7/25/81	**1(10)**	52	▲ 4. 4	Atlantic 16999
			Urgent (4)/*Waiting For A Girl Like You* (2)	
12/25/82	**10**	12	● 5. Foreigner Records [G]	Atlantic 80999
1/5/85	**4**	24	▲ 6. Agent Provocateur	Atlantic 81999
			I Want To Know What Love Is (1)	
1/9/88	**15**	14	▲ 7. Inside Information	Atlantic 81808
			Say You Will (6)/*I Don't Want To Live Without You* (5)	
			FOUNTAIN, Pete	
			Born on 7/3/30 in New Orleans. Clarinetist. With Al Hirt, 1956-57. Performed on Lawrence Welk's weekly TV show, 1957-59. Own club in New Orleans, The French Quarter Inn.	
2/22/60	**8**	31	1. Pete Fountain's New Orleans [I]	Coral 57282
5/9/60	**31**	4	2. Pete Fountain Day [I-L]	Coral 57313
8/4/62	**30**	4	3. Music From Dixie [I]	Coral 57401
			FOUR FRESHMEN, The	
			Jazz-styled vocal and instrumental group formed in 1948 while at Arthur Jordan Conservatory of Music in Indianapolis. Consisted of brothers Ross and Don Barbour, their cousin Bob Flanigan and Ken Errair.	
2/25/56	**6**	33	1. Four Freshmen and 5 Trombones	Capitol 683
10/13/56	**11**	8	2. Freshmen Favorites [G]	Capitol 743
3/2/57	**9**	7	3. 4 Freshmen and 5 Trumpets	Capitol 763
11/18/57	**25**	1	4. Four Freshmen and Five Saxes	Capitol 844

DATE	POS	WKS	ARTIST—RECORD TITLE	LABEL & NO.
9/29/58	**17**	1	5. The Four Freshmen In Person [L]	Capitol 1008
11/3/58	**11**	6	6. Voices In Love	Capitol 1074
1/11/60	**40**	1	7. The Four Freshmen and Five Guitars	Capitol 1255

FOUR LADS, The

Vocal group from Toronto, Canada: Bernie Toorish (lead tenor), Jimmie Arnold (second tenor), Frankie Busseri (baritone) and Connie Codarini (bass). Sang in choir at St. Michael's Cathedral in Toronto. Worked local hotels and clubs. Worked Le Ruban Bleu in New York City. Signed as backup singers by Columbia in 1950. Backed Johnnie Ray on his #1 hit "Cry."

DATE	POS	WKS	ARTIST—RECORD TITLE	LABEL & NO.
10/6/56	**14**	2	1. On The Sunny Side	Columbia 912

FOUR PREPS, The

Vocal group formed while at Hollywood High School: Bruce Belland, Glen Larson, Ed Cobb and Marvin Ingraham. Belland was later in duo with Dave Somerville of the Diamonds.

DATE	POS	WKS	ARTIST—RECORD TITLE	LABEL & NO.
9/4/61	**8**	13	1. The Four Preps On Campus [L]	Capitol 1566
5/12/62	**40**	1	2. Campus Encore [L]	Capitol 1647

4 SEASONS, The

Vocal group formed in Newark, New Jersey. In 1955, lead singer Frankie Valli (Francis Castelluccio) formed the Variatones with the brothers Nick and Tommy DeVito, and Hank Majewski. Changed name to The Four Lovers in 1956. Bob Gaudio (of The Royal Teens) joined as keyboardist and songwriter in 1959, replacing Nick DeVito. Nick Massi replaced Majewski, and their 1961 lineup was set: Valli, Gaudio, Massi and Tommy DeVito. Group had been doing session work for their producer Bob Crewe and took their new name from a New Jersey bowling alley, The Four Seasons. In 1965, Nick Massi was replaced by the group's arranger Charlie Callelo and then by Joe Long. In 1971, Tommy DeVito retired, and Gaudio left (as a performer) the following year. Numerous personnel changes from then on. Inducted into the Rock and Roll Hall of Fame in 1990. Also recorded as The Wonder Who?

DATE	POS	WKS		ARTIST—RECORD TITLE	LABEL & NO.
11/3/62	**6**	20		1. Sherry & 11 others *Sherry (1)/Big Girls Don't Cry (1)*	Vee-Jay 1053
10/5/63	**15**	11		2. Golden Hits of the 4 Seasons [G]	Vee-Jay 1065
4/4/64	**6**	10		3. Dawn (Go Away) and 11 other great songs *Dawn (Go Away) (3)*	Philips 124
8/15/64	**7**	13		4. Rag Doll *Ronnie (6)/Rag Doll (1)/Save It For Me (10)*	Philips 146
1/15/66	**10**	22	●	5. The 4 Seasons' Gold Vault of Hits [G] *Let's Hang On! (3)*	Philips 196
1/7/67	**22**	10	●	6. 2nd Vault Of Golden Hits [G] nine of 12 cuts are Vee-Jay hits *I've Got You Under My Skin (9)*	Philips 221
7/22/67	**8**	2		7. Big Girls Don't Cry and Twelve others *Walk Like A Man (1)*	Vee-Jay 1056
7/22/67	**37**	2		8. New Gold Hits *Tell It To The Rain (10)/C'mon Marianne (9)*	Philips 243
3/1/69	**37**	2	●	9. Edizione D'Oro (The 4 Seasons Gold Edition-29 Gold Hits) [G]	Philips 6501 [2]
1/24/76	**38**	2		10. Who Loves You *Who Loves You (3)/December, 1963 (Oh, What A Night) (1)*	Warner 2900

DATE	POS	WKS	ARTIST—RECORD TITLE	LABEL & NO.

FOUR TOPS

Native Detroit group formed in 1954 as the Four Aims. Consisted of Levi Stubbs (lead singer), Renaldo "Obie" Benson, Lawrence Payton and Abdul "Duke" Fakir. First recorded for Chess in 1956, then Red Top and Columbia, before signing with Motown in 1963. Group has had no personnel changes since its formation. Stubbs is the voice of Audrey II (the voracious vegetation) in the 1986 film *Little Shop of Horrors*. Group inducted into the Rock and Roll Hall of Fame in 1990.

DATE	POS	WKS	ARTIST—RECORD TITLE	LABEL & NO.
1/8/66	**20**	8	1. Four Tops Second Album *I Can't Help Myself* (1)/*It's The Same Old Song* (5)	Motown 634
10/29/66	**32**	5	2. 4 Tops On Top	Motown 647
1/28/67	**17**	18	3. Four Tops Live! [L]	Motown 654
8/19/67	**11**	14	4. Four Tops Reach Out *Reach Out I'll Be There* (1)/ *Standing In The Shadows Of Love* (6)/*Bernadette* (4)	Motown 660
10/7/67	**4**	37	5. The Four Tops Greatest Hits [G]	Motown 662
6/27/70	**21**	14	6. Still Waters Run Deep	Motown 704
12/30/72	**33**	3	7. Keeper Of The Castle *Keeper Of The Castle* (10)/ *Ain't No Woman (Like The One I've Got)* (4)	Dunhill 50129
10/31/81	**37**	4	8. Tonight!	Casablanca 7258

FOX, Samantha

British; born in 1966. Rose to stardom as a topless model for the U.K. "Daily Sun" newspaper.

DATE	POS	WKS	ARTIST—RECORD TITLE	LABEL & NO.
1/31/87	**24**	11	● 1. Touch Me *Touch Me (I Want Your Body)* (4)	Jive 1012
2/11/89	**37**	4	● 2. I Wanna Have Some Fun *I Wanna Have Some Fun* (8)	Jive 1150

FOXY

Miami-based Latino dance band. Four of five members came to Florida with the Cuban emigres of 1959. Lead vocalist/guitarist Ish Ledesma later founded and produced Company B.

DATE	POS	WKS	ARTIST—RECORD TITLE	LABEL & NO.
8/26/78	**12**	12	1. Get Off *Get Off* (9)	Dash 30005
4/28/79	**29**	6	2. Hot Numbers	Dash 30010

FRAMPTON, Peter

Born on 4/22/50 in Beckenham, England. Vocalist/guitarist/composer. Joined British band The Herd at age 16, before forming Humble Pie in 1969, which he left in 1971 to form Frampton's Camel.

DATE	POS	WKS	ARTIST—RECORD TITLE	LABEL & NO.
5/10/75	**32**	3	● 1. Frampton	A&M 4512
2/14/76	**1**(10)	55	▲ 2. Frampton Comes Alive! [L] *Show Me The Way* (6)/*Do You Feel Like We Do* (10)	A&M 3703 [2]
6/25/77	**2**(4)	15	▲ 3. I'm In You *I'm In You* (2)	A&M 4704
6/30/79	**19**	7	● 4. Where I Should Be	A&M 3710

FRANCHI, Sergio

Italian tenor.

DATE	POS	WKS	ARTIST—RECORD TITLE	LABEL & NO.
12/8/62	**17**	9	1. Sergio Franchi	RCA 2640

DATE	POS	WKS	ARTIST—RECORD TITLE	LABEL & NO.
			FRANCIS, Connie	
			Born Concetta Rosa Maria Franconero on 12/12/38 in Newark, New Jersey. First recorded for MGM in 1955. Films: *Where The Boys Are, Follow The Boys, Looking For Love* and *When The Boys Meet The Girls*, 1961-65. Connie stopped performing after she was raped on 11/8/74, for which she was awarded $3,000,000 in damages. Began comeback with a performance on "Dick Clark's Live Wednesday" TV show in 1978.	
2/8/60	**4**	48	1. Italian Favorites [F] *Mama* (8)	MGM 3791
2/22/60	**17**	25	2. Connie's Greatest Hits [G] *Who's Sorry Now* (4)/*My Happiness* (2)/ *Lipstick On Your Collar* (5)/*Frankie* (9)	MGM 3793
12/12/60	**9**	11	3. More Italian Favorites [F]	MGM 3871
9/25/61	**39**	1	4. More Greatest Hits [G] *Among My Souvenirs* (7)/*Everybody's Somebody's Fool* (1)/ *My Heart Has A Mind Of Its Own* (1)/*Many Tears Ago* (7)/ *Where The Boys Are* (4)	MGM 3942
11/6/61	**11**	23	5. Never On Sunday and other title songs from motion pictures	MGM 3965
10/27/62	**22**	2	6. Country Music Connie Style	MGM 4079
			FRANKE & THE KNOCKOUTS	
			Soft-rock quintet led by Franke Previte of New Brunswick, New Jersey.	
5/23/81	**31**	5	1. Franke & The Knockouts *Sweetheart* (10)	Millennium 7755
			FRANKIE GOES TO HOLLYWOOD	
			Rock quintet from Liverpool, England; vocals by Holly Johnson and Paul Rutherford.	
12/8/84	**33**	14	1. Welcome To The Pleasuredome *Relax* (10)	Island 90232 [2]
			FRANKLIN, Aretha	
			Born on 3/25/42 in Memphis; raised in Buffalo and Detroit. Daughter of Rev. Cecil L. Franklin, pastor of New Bethel Church in Detroit. First recorded for JVB/Battle in 1956. Signed to Columbia Records in 1960 by John Hammond, then dramatic turn in style and success after signing with Atlantic and working with producer Jerry Wexler. Appeared in the 1980 film *The Blues Brothers*. In 1987, became the first woman to be inducted into the Rock and Roll Hall of Fame. The all-time Queen of Soul Music.	
4/29/67	**2**(3)	28	● 1. I Never Loved A Man The Way I Love You *I Never Loved A Man (The Way I Love You)* (9)/*Respect* (1)	Atlantic 8139
9/2/67	**5**	19	2. Aretha Arrives *Baby I Love You* (4)	Atlantic 8150
2/24/68	**2**(2)	33	● 3. Aretha: Lady Soul *A Natural Woman* (8)/*Chain of Fools* (2)/ *(Sweet Sweet Baby) Since You've Been Gone* (5)	Atlantic 8176
7/20/68	**3**	20	● 4. Aretha Now *Think* (7)/*I Say A Little Prayer* (10)	Atlantic 8186
12/7/68	**13**	9	5. Aretha In Paris [L] recorded at the Olympia Theatre in Paris, France on 5/7/68	Atlantic 8207
2/22/69	**15**	12	6. Aretha Franklin: Soul '69	Atlantic 8212
7/26/69	**18**	11	7. Aretha's Gold [G] *The House That Jack Built* (6)	Atlantic 8227
2/21/70	**17**	13	8. This Girl's In Love With You	Atlantic 8248
9/26/70	**25**	8	9. Spirit In The Dark	Atlantic 8265
6/12/71	**7**	18	● 10. Aretha Live At Fillmore West [L]	Atlantic 7205

DATE	POS	WKS	ARTIST—RECORD TITLE	LABEL & NO.
10/9/71	**19**	10	11. Aretha's Greatest Hits [G] *Bridge Over Troubled Water* (6)/*Spanish Harlem* (2)	Atlantic 8295
2/26/72	**11**	17	● 12. Young, Gifted & Black *Rock Steady* (9)/*Day Dreaming* (5)	Atlantic 7213
7/1/72	**7**	11	● 13. Amazing Grace [L] with James Cleveland & The Southern California Community Choir	Atlantic 906 [2]
8/11/73	**30**	7	14. Hey Now Hey (The Other Side Of The Sky)	Atlantic 7265
3/30/74	**14**	11	15. Let Me In Your Life *Until You Come Back To Me (That's What I'm Gonna Do)* (3)	Atlantic 7292
7/4/76	**18**	11	● 16. Sparkle [S]	Atlantic 18176
9/26/81	**36**	3	17. Love All The Hurt Away	Arista 9552
9/4/82	**23**	9	● 18. Jump To It	Arista 9602
8/20/83	**36**	3	19. Get It Right	Arista 8019
8/10/85	**13**	35	● 20. Who's Zoomin' Who? *Freeway Of Love* (3)/*Who's Zoomin' Who* (7)	Arista 8286
12/13/86	**32**	8	● 21. Aretha *I Knew You Were Waiting (For Me)* (1) with George Michael	Arista 8442

FREBERG, Stan

Born on 8/7/26 in Pasadena, California. Began career doing impersonations on Cliffie Stone's radio show in 1943. Did cartoon voices for the major film studios. His first in a long string of brilliant satirical recordings was ''John And Marsha'' in 1951. Launched highly successful advertising career in early 60s; winner of 21 Clio awards.

DATE	POS	WKS	ARTIST—RECORD TITLE	LABEL & NO.
7/24/61	**34**	3	1. Stan Freberg Presents The United States Of America [C] with Jesse White and Paul Frees; musical score by Billy May	Capitol 1573

FREDDIE & THE DREAMERS

Freddie Garrity was born on 11/14/40 in Manchester, England. Formed The Dreamers in 1961, consisting of Garrity (lead singer), Derek Quinn (lead guitar), Roy Crewsdon (guitar), Peter Birrell (bass) and Bernie Dwyer (drums).

DATE	POS	WKS	ARTIST—RECORD TITLE	LABEL & NO.
5/22/65	**19**	7	1. Freddie & The Dreamers	Mercury 61017

FREE

British band formed in 1968: Paul Rodgers (vocals), Paul Kossoff (guitar), Simon Kirke (drums) and Andy Fraser (bass). Kossoff left to form Back Street Crawler, but died of drug-induced heart failure in 1976. Rodgers and Kirke formed Bad Company in 1974. Rodgers joined supergroup The Firm in mid-80s.

DATE	POS	WKS	ARTIST—RECORD TITLE	LABEL & NO.
9/26/70	**17**	11	1. Fire And Water *All Right Now* (4)	A&M 4268

FREHLEY, Ace

Born on 4/27/51 in the Bronx. Kiss lead guitarist until 1983. Currently leads his band Frehley's Comet.

DATE	POS	WKS	ARTIST—RECORD TITLE	LABEL & NO.
11/25/78	**26**	10	▲ 1. Ace Frehley	Casablanca 7121

FREY, Glenn

Born on 11/6/48 in Detroit. Singer/songwriter/guitarist. Founding member of the Eagles. Appeared in episodes of TV's ''Miami Vice'' and ''Wiseguy.''

DATE	POS	WKS	ARTIST—RECORD TITLE	LABEL & NO.
7/24/82	**32**	11	● 1. No Fun Aloud	Asylum 60129
8/25/84	**22**	14	● 2. The Allnighter	MCA 5501
10/8/88	**36**	7	3. Soul Searchin'	MCA 6239

DATE	POS	WKS	ARTIST—RECORD TITLE	LABEL & NO.
			FRIENDS OF DISTINCTION, The	
			Los Angeles-based soul-MOR group. Original lineup: Floyd Butler (b: 6/5/41, San Diego), Harry Elston (b: 11/4/38, Dallas), Jessica Cleaves (b: 12/10/48, Los Angeles) and Barbara Jean Love (b: 7/24/41, Los Angeles). Butler and Elston were in the Hi-Fi's with LaMonte McLemore and Marilyn McCoo (later with The 5th Dimension).	
7/5/69	**35**	3	1. Grazin'	RCA 4149
			Grazing In The Grass (3)	
			FRIJID PINK	
			Rock group formed in Detroit: Kelly Green (lead singer), Gary Thompson (guitar), Tom Beaudry (bass) and Rich Stevens (drums).	
3/7/70	**11**	12	1. Frijid Pink	Parrot 71033
			House Of The Rising Sun (7)	
			FRYE, David	
			Comedian/impressionist.	
1/10/70	**19**	8	1. I Am The President　　　　　　　　[C]	Elektra 75006
			FUNKADELIC	
			Funk aggregation formed in 1968, consisting of The Parliaments plus a backing band. While recording for Westbound, group also recorded for Invictus as Parliament in 1971. Formed corporation "A Parliafunkadelicament Thang" through which they recorded under both names. By 1974, leader/producer George Clinton reorganized the Parliament/Funkadelic corporation to include varying membership.	
10/7/78	**16**	9	▲　1. One Nation Under A Groove	Warner 3209
10/20/79	**18**	6	●　2. Uncle Jam Wants You	Warner 3371

G

DATE	POS	WKS	ARTIST—RECORD TITLE	LABEL & NO.
			GABRIEL, Peter	
			Born on 2/13/50 in London. Lead singer of Genesis from 1966-75.	
4/30/77	**38**	2	1. Peter Gabriel	Atco 147
7/5/80	**22**	14	2. Peter Gabriel	Mercury 3848
10/16/82	**28**	12	●　3. Peter Gabriel (Security)	Geffen 2011
6/14/86	**2**(3)	30	▲　4. So	Geffen 24088
			Sledgehammer (1)/*Big Time* (8)	
			GAP BAND, The	
			Soul trio from Tulsa, Oklahoma consisting of brothers Charles, Ronnie and Robert Wilson. Named for three streets in Tulsa: Greenwood, Archer and Pine. Cousins of Bootsy Collins. Charles is part of the Eurythmics' backing band.	
2/14/81	**16**	17	▲　1. The Gap Band III	Mercury 4003
6/26/82	**14**	17	▲　2. Gap Band IV	Total Exp. 3001
9/24/83	**28**	7	●　3. Gap Band V - Jammin'	Total Exp. 3004
			GARCIA, Jerry	
			Founder and lead guitarist of the Grateful Dead. Born on 8/1/42 in San Francisco. Prior to forming the Grateful Dead, played banjo in Mother McCree's Uptown Jug Champions.	
2/12/72	**35**	3	1. Garcia	Warner 2582

DATE	POS	WKS	ARTIST—RECORD TITLE	LABEL & NO.
			GARDNER, Dave	
			Comedian "Brother Dave"; born on 6/11/26 in Jackson, Tennessee.	
6/20/60	5	28	1. Rejoice, Dear Hearts! [C]	RCA 2083
8/29/60	5	19	2. Kick Thy Own Self [C]	RCA 2239
9/18/61	15	10	3. Ain't That Weird? [C]	RCA 2335
5/18/63	28	5	4. It Don't Make No Difference [C]	Capitol 1867
			GARFUNKEL, Art	
			Born on 10/13/42 in Queens, New York. Appeared in films *Catch 22*, *Carnal Knowledge* and *Bad Timing*. Has masters degree in mathematics from Columbia University. Half of Simon & Garfunkel duo.	
10/6/73	5	13	● 1. Angel Clare *All I Know* (9)	Columbia 31474
11/1/75	7	15	▲ 2. Breakaway *My Little Town* (9) with Paul Simon	Columbia 33700
2/11/78	19	9	● 3. Watermark	Columbia 34975
			GARLAND, Judy	
			Born Frances Gumm on 6/10/22 in Grand Rapids, Michigan. Star of MGM film musicals from 1935-54. Hosted own TV variety series, 1963-64. Died on 1/22/69.	
10/29/55	5	7	1. Miss Show Business	Capitol 676
11/10/56	17	5	2. Judy	Capitol 734
6/17/57	17	3	3. Alone	Capitol 835
8/7/61	1(13)	73	● 4. Judy At Carnegie Hall [L] 1961 Grammy winner: Album of the Year	Capitol 1569 [2]
9/8/62	33	5	5. The Garland Touch	Capitol 1710
			GARNER, Erroll	
			Jazz pianist/composer born on 6/15/21 in Pittsburgh; died on 1/2/77. No formal training on piano; could not read music. Composer of "Misty," later a hit for Johnny Mathis and others.	
11/25/57	16	2	1. Other Voices [I] featuring the jukebox hit *Misty*	Columbia 1014
3/10/58	12	7	2. Concert By The Sea [I-L] recorded in 1956 in Carmel, California	Columbia 883
6/26/61	35	2	3. Dreamstreet [I]	ABC-Para. 365
			GARRETT, Leif	
			Born on 11/8/61 in Hollywood, California. Began film career in 1969; appeared in all three *Walking Tall* films.	
2/4/78	37	3	● 1. Leif Garrett	Atlantic 19152
1/20/79	34	5	● 2. Feel The Need *I Was Made For Dancin'* (10)	Scotti Br. 7100
			GARRETT, Tommy — see 50 GUITARS, The	
			GARY, John	
			Born in Watertown, New York on 11/29/32. Singer on Don McNeill's radio program, "Breakfast Club," for two years.	
11/30/63	19	27	1. Catch A Rising Star	RCA 2745
3/7/64	16	10	2. Encore	RCA 2804
3/20/65	17	8	3. A Little Bit Of Heaven	RCA 2994
8/14/65	11	13	4. The Nearness Of You	RCA 3349
12/4/65	21	7	5. Your All-Time Favorite Songs	RCA 3411

Eurythmics' Dave Stewart and Annie Lennox had released records prior to their group's early 80s formation under the name the Tourists. Yet with such albums as 1986's *Revenge*, and its single "Missionary Man," the duo found international success far surpassing that of their earlier band.

The **Everly Brothers** reached a whole new audience in the late 80s when popular oldies label Rhino Records reissued many of their classic albums. *A Date With The Everly Brothers* (1960) contained their last No. 1 hit, "Cathy's Clown."

Over **Fleetwood Mac**'s 20-year existence the shifting personnel has resulted in solo albums by group members including Peter Green, Jeremy Spencer, Danny Kirwan, Bob Welch, Christine McVie, Mick Fleetwood, Stevie Nicks and Lindsey Buckingham. *Heroes Are Hard To Find*, the last album to feature Welch, preceded 1975's multi-platinum *Fleetwood Mac*.

The **Four Tops** may be synonomous with the Motown label, but upon leaving it in 1972, they further managed to rack up high-charting albums for the Dunhill and Casablanca labels. In the early 90s, they continued to record for Arista.

Connie Francis, known to her parents as Constance Franconero, knew how to please them, ethnically speaking: Her two highest charting albums were *Italian Favorites* and *More Italian Favorites*, both issued in 1960.

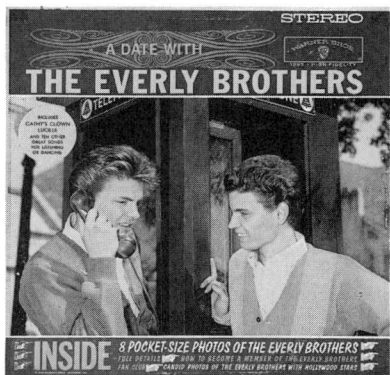

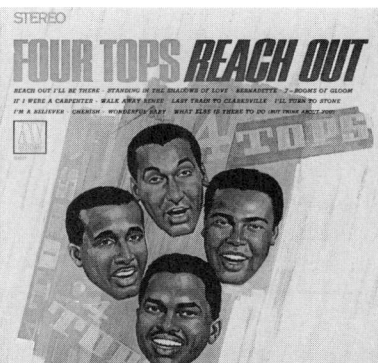

Aretha Franklin, known as the "Queen of Soul" since the mid-60s, might well have been called the "Queen of Duets" by the late 80s: by then she'd recorded with a diverse group, including James Brown, Whitney Houston, Mavis Staples, Peter Wolf, George Michael, the Eurythmics and Larry Graham. This album, *Jump To It*, was her 18th top 40 LP.

Marvin Gaye's distinguished career, tragically cut short in 1984 when his father shot him fatally, was capped for many by his classic album, *What's Going On*, which peaked at No. 6 in 1971 and contained the hit title track as well as "Mercy Mercy Me" and "Inner City Blues."

Debbie Gibson seemed but one in a wave of teen stars that included Tiffany and Tracie Spencer in the late 80s. However, her constant flow of hits—the bulk self-penned—has garnered her considerably more respect than has been accorded her contemporaries. Her first top 40 LP, *Out Of The Blue*, contained four top 10 singles.

Lesley Gore's mid-60s hits in which she portrayed the tragic teen heroine, typified by "It's My Party" and "She's A Fool," sometimes overshadowed the early feminist message of such tracks as the startlingly prescient "You Don't Own Me." *I'll Cry If I Want To* was Gore's sole LP to reach the top 40.

Grand Funk railroaded to stardom on the heels of such early hard-rocking efforts as 1969's *On Time* and 1970's *Grand Funk* and *Closer To Home*, as well as highly energetic performances at various pop festivals of the time. Never critical favorites, the band sometimes raised eyebrows among the disbelievers by choosing producers such as Frank Zappa and Todd Rundgren.

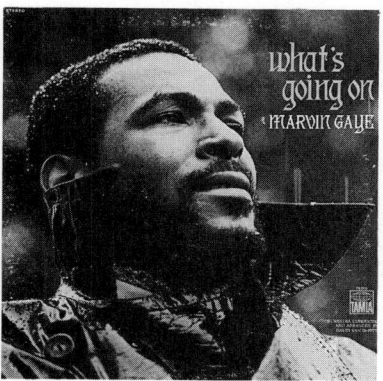

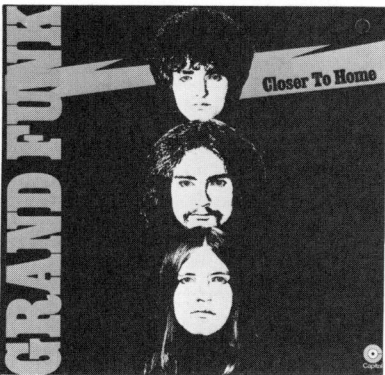

DATE	POS	WKS	ARTIST—RECORD TITLE	LABEL & NO.
			GAYE, Marvin	
			Born Marvin Pentz Gay, Jr. on 4/2/39 in Washington, D.C. Sang in his father's Apostolic church. In vocal groups the Rainbows and Marquees. Joined Harvey Fuqua in the re-formed Moonglows. To Detroit in 1960. Session work as a drummer at Motown; married to Berry Gordy's sister Anna, 1961-75. First recorded under own name for Tamla in 1961. In seclusion for several months following the death of Tammi Terrell, 1970. Problems with drugs and the IRS led to his moving to Europe for three years. Fatally shot by his father after a quarrel on 4/1/84 in Los Angeles. Inducted into the Rock and Roll Hall of Fame in 1987.	
6/28/69	**33**	4	1. M.P.G. *Too Busy Thinking About My Baby* (4)/ *That's The Way Love Is* (7)	Tamla 292
6/26/71	**6**	27	2. What's Going On *What's Going On* (2)/*Mercy Mercy Me* (4)/ *Inner City Blues* (9)	Tamla 310
1/13/73	**14**	11	3. Trouble Man [S] *Marvin sings on 3 of the 13 cuts (others are instrumentals)* *Trouble Man* (7)	Tamla 322
9/15/73	**2**(1)	18	4. Let's Get It On *Let's Get It On* (1)	Tamla 329
12/8/73	**26**	5	5. Diana & Marvin **DIANA ROSS & MARVIN GAYE**	Motown 803
7/27/74	**8**	13	6. Marvin Gaye Live! [L]	Tamla 333
4/10/76	**4**	15	7. I Want You	Tamla 342
4/16/77	**3**	19	8. Marvin Gaye Live At The London Palladium [L] *Got To Give It Up* (1)	Tamla 352 [2]
1/20/79	**26**	7	9. Here, My Dear	Tamla 364 [2]
2/28/81	**32**	4	10. In Our Lifetime	Tamla 374
11/20/82	**7**	13	▲ 11. Midnight Love *Sexual Healing* (3)	Columbia 38197
			GAYLE, Crystal	
			Born Brenda Gail Webb on 1/9/51 in Paintsville, Kentucky; raised in Wabash, Indiana. Youngest sister of Loretta Lynn. First country artist to tour China (1979).	
10/22/77	**12**	10	▲ 1. We Must Believe In Magic *Don't It Make My Brown Eyes Blue* (2)	United Art. 771
11/24/79	**36**	4	● 2. Miss The Mississippi	Columbia 36203
			GAYNOR, Gloria	
			Born on 9/7/49 in Newark, New Jersey. Disco singer. With the Soul Satisfiers group in 1971.	
2/22/75	**25**	5	1. Never Can Say Goodbye *Never Can Say Goodbye* (9)	MGM 4982
2/3/79	**4**	15	▲ 2. Love Tracks *I Will Survive* (1)	Polydor 6184
			GEILS, J.	
			Leader of own rock band formed in Boston in 1967. Consisted of Jerome Geils (guitar), Peter "Wolf" Blankfield (vocals), "Magic Dick" Salwitz (harmonica), Seth Justman (keyboards), Danny Klein (bass) and Stephen Jo Bladd (drums). First recorded for Atlantic in 1969. Wolf left for a solo career in the fall of 1983. **THE J. GEILS BAND:**	
5/19/73	**10**	14	● 1. Bloodshot	Atlantic 7260
11/23/74	**26**	4	2. Nightmares...and other tales from the vinyl jungle	Atlantic 18107
10/25/75	**36**	2	3. Hotline	Atlantic 18147
6/26/76	**40**	1	4. Live - Blow Your Face Out [L]	Atlantic 507 [2]

DATE	POS	WKS	ARTIST—RECORD TITLE	LABEL & NO.
3/8/80	**18**	17	● 5. Love Stinks	EMI America 17016
11/21/81	**1**(4)	29	▲ 6. Freeze-Frame	EMI America 17062
			Centerfold (1)/*Freeze-Frame* (4)	
12/18/82	**23**	10	● 7. Showtime! [L]	EMI America 17087

GENERAL PUBLIC

Fronted by former English Beat vocalists Dave Wakeling and Ranking Roger (Roger Charley). Disbanded in March of 1987. Roger recorded solo in 1988.

DATE	POS	WKS	ARTIST—RECORD TITLE	LABEL & NO.
1/19/85	**26**	11	1. ...All The Rage	I.R.S. 70046

GENESIS

Rock group formed in England in 1967. Consisted of Peter Gabriel (lead vocals), Anthony Phillips (guitar), Tony Banks (keyboards), Michael Rutherford (guitar, bass) and John Mayhew (drums). Phillips and Mayhew left after second album, replaced by Steve Hackett (guitar) and Phil Collins (drums). Gabriel left in June, 1975, with Collins replacing him as new lead singer. Hackett went solo in 1977, leaving group as a trio: Collins, Rutherford and Banks. Rutherford also in own group, Mike + The Mechanics, formed in 1985. Hackett later formed group GTR.

DATE	POS	WKS	ARTIST—RECORD TITLE	LABEL & NO.
5/1/76	**31**	6	● 1. A Trick Of The Tail	Atco 129
2/19/77	**26**	8	● 2. Wind & Wuthering	Atco 144
4/29/78	**14**	8	▲ 3. And Then There Were Three...	Atlantic 19173
			from here on, group consists of Banks, Collins & Rutherford	
5/3/80	**11**	21	▲ 4. Duke	Atlantic 16014
10/24/81	**7**	29	▲ 5. Abacab	Atlantic 19313
7/10/82	**10**	11	● 6. Three Sides Live [L]	Atlantic 2000 [2]
			side four: studio cuts from '79-'81	
11/5/83	**9**	27	▲ 7. Genesis	Atlantic 80116
			That's All (6)	
6/28/86	**3**	61	▲ 8. Invisible Touch	Atlantic 81641
			Invisible Touch (1)/*Throwing It All Away* (4)/ *Land Of Confusion* (4)/*Tonight, Tonight, Tonight* (3)/ *In Too Deep* (3)	

GENTRY, Bobbie

Born Roberta Streeter on 7/27/44 in Chickasaw County, Mississippi; raised in Greenwood, Mississippi. Singer/songwriter. Won the 1967 Best New Artist Grammy Award. Married singer Jim Stafford in 1978.

DATE	POS	WKS	ARTIST—RECORD TITLE	LABEL & NO.
9/23/67	**1**(2)	18	● 1. Ode To Billie Joe	Capitol 2830
			Ode To Billie Joe (1)	
11/9/68	**11**	13	● 2. Bobbie Gentry & Glen Campbell	Capitol 2928

GEORGIA SATELLITES

Rock quartet formed in Atlanta in 1980, led by dual guitarists/vocalists Dan Baird and Rick Richards with bassist Rich Price and drummer Mauro Magellan.

DATE	POS	WKS	ARTIST—RECORD TITLE	LABEL & NO.
12/20/86	**5**	20	▲ 1. Georgia Satellites	Elektra 60496
			Keep Your Hands To Yourself (2)	

GERRY AND THE PACEMAKERS

Pop-rock group formed in Liverpool, England in 1959: Gerry Marsden (b: 9/24/42; vocals, guitar), Leslie Maguire (piano), Les Chadwick (bass) and Freddie Marsden (drums). The Marsden brothers had been in skiffle bands; Gerry had own rock band Mars-Bars in 1958. Signed in 1962 by The Beatles' manager Brian Epstein.

DATE	POS	WKS	ARTIST—RECORD TITLE	LABEL & NO.
8/15/64	**29**	5	1. Don't Let The Sun Catch You Crying	Laurie 2024
			Don't Let The Sun Catch You Crying (4)/ *How Do You Do It?* (9)	

DATE	POS	WKS	ARTIST—RECORD TITLE	LABEL & NO.
4/3/65	**13**	12	2. Ferry Cross The Mersey [S] nine of 12 songs by Gerry & The Pacemakers (they star in the film which was set in Liverpool) *Ferry Cross The Mersey* (6)	United Art. 6387
			GETZ, Stan Born on 2/2/27 in Philadelphia. Jazz tenor saxophonist. Played with Stan Kenton (1944-45), Jimmy Dorsey (1945-46), Benny Goodman (1946) and most importantly Woody Herman (1947-49).	
10/13/62	**1**(1)	44	1. Jazz Samba [I] **STAN GETZ/CHARLIE BYRD (guitar)**	Verve 8432
1/5/63	**13**	20	2. Big Band Bossa Nova [I] with the Gary McFarland Orchestra	Verve 8494
6/20/64	**2**(2)	50	● 3. Getz/Gilberto **STAN GETZ/JOAO GILBERTO** 1964 Grammy winner: Album of the Year; Gilberto, Brazilian singer/guitarist *The Girl From Ipanema* (5) vocal by Gilberto's wife Astrud	Verve 8545
2/13/65	**24**	17	4. Getz Au Go Go [L] **THE NEW STAN GETZ QUARTET FEATURING ASTRUD GILBERTO**	Verve 8600
			GIBB, Andy Born Andrew Roy Gibb on 3/5/58 in Manchester, England. Moved to Australia when six months old, then back to England at age nine. Youngest brother of Barry, Robin and Maurice Gibb - The Bee Gees. Hosted TV's "Solid Gold" from 1981-82. Died on 3/10/88 (age 30) of an inflammatory heart virus in Oxford, England.	
8/27/77	**19**	18	▲ 1. Flowing Rivers *I Just Want To Be Your Everything* (1)/ *(Love Is) Thicker Than Water* (1)	RSO 3019
6/24/78	**7**	15	▲ 2. Shadow Dancing *Shadow Dancing* (1)/*An Everlasting Love* (5)/ *(Our Love) Don't Throw It All Away* (9)	RSO 3034
3/8/80	**21**	7	● 3. After Dark *Desire* (4)	RSO 3069
			GIBSON, Debbie Singer/songwriter/pianist from Long Island. Signed with Atlantic in 1987 at age 16.	
12/19/87	**7**	45	▲ 1. Out Of The Blue *Only In My Dreams* (4)/*Shake Your Love* (4)/*Out Of The Blue* (3)/ *Foolish Beat* (1)	Atlantic 81780
2/18/89	**1**(5)	25	▲ 2. Electric Youth *Lost In Your Eyes* (1)	Atlantic 81932
			GILBERTO, Joao — see GETZ, Stan	
			GILDER, Nick Born on 11/7/51 in London, England. Moved to Vancouver, Canada at age 10. Founding member of the rock band Sweeney Todd.	
11/11/78	**33**	5	1. City Nights *Hot Child In The City* (1)	Chrysalis 1202
			GILL, Johnny Washington, D.C. singer discovered by Stacy Lattisaw. Sang in family group, Wings Of Faith, from age five. Recorded solo at age 16 in 1983. Joined New Edition in 1988.	
5/12/90	**8**	24 +	▲ 1. Johnny Gill *Rub You The Right Way* (3)	Motown 6283

DATE	POS	WKS	ARTIST—RECORD TITLE	LABEL & NO.
			GILMER, Jimmy/The Fireballs	
			Rock and roll band formed while high schoolers in Raton, New Mexico: George Tomsco (lead guitar), Dan Trammell (rhythm guitar), Eric Budd (drums), Stan Lark (bass) and Chuck Tharp (vocalist). Tharp quit group in 1960 and was replaced by Jimmy Gilmer (lead vocals, piano). Gilmer was introduced to The Fireballs by their record producer Norman Petty at his famed Clovis, New Mexico studio.	
			JIMMY GILMER & THE FIREBALLS:	
11/30/63	**26**	5	1. Sugar Shack	Dot 25545
			Sugar Shack (1)	
			GILMOUR, David	
			Born on 3/6/47 in Cambridge, England. Guitarist/vocalist with Pink Floyd.	
8/5/78	**29**	6	1. David Gilmour	Columbia 35388
4/21/84	**32**	10	2. About Face	Columbia 39296
			GIUFFRIA	
			California-based rock quintet led by Gregg Giuffria (keyboardist with Angel) and David Glen Eisley (vocals).	
1/26/85	**26**	7	1. Giuffria	MCA 5524
			GLASER, Tompall — see JENNINGS, Waylon or NELSON, Willie	
			GLASS TIGER	
			Canadian rock quintet: Alan Frew (vocals), Sam Reid (keyboards), Al Connelly (guitar), Wayne Parker (bass) and Michael Hanson (drums).	
10/4/86	**27**	28	● 1. The Thin Red Line	Manhattan 53032
			Don't Forget Me (When I'm Gone) (2)/*Someday* (7)	
			GLEASON, Jackie	
			Born Herbert John Gleason on 2/26/16 in Brooklyn; died on 6/24/87. Star of stage and screen before enormous popularity on TV's "The Honeymooners" (1955-56) and his own CBS-TV variety series. Although famous as a TV comedian, Jackie's albums feature dreamy mood music by studio orchestras featuring the trumpets of Bobby Hackett and Pee Wee Erwin.	
3/5/55	**5**	16	1. Music To Remember Her [I]	Capitol 570
6/25/55	**1**(2)	23	2. Lonesome Echo [I]	Capitol 627
11/12/55	**2**(2)	11	3. Romantic Jazz [I]	Capitol 568
1/28/56	**7**	7	4. Music For Lovers Only/Music To Make You Misty [R-I]	Capitol 475 [2]
			reissue of albums from 1953 & 1954	
2/25/56	**8**	5	5. Music To Change Her Mind [I]	Capitol 632
6/9/56	**10**	10	6. Night Winds [I]	Capitol 717
12/8/56	**16**	3	7. Merry Christmas [X-I]	Capitol 758
8/26/57	**13**	2	● 8. Music For The Love Hours [I]	Capitol 816
9/9/57	**16**	10	9. Velvet Brass [I]	Capitol 859
12/9/57	**14**	4	10. Jackie Gleason presents "Oooo!" [I]	Capitol 905
			GODLEY & CREME	
			Kevin Godley (b: 10/7/45, Manchester, England) and Lol Creme (b: 9/19/47, Manchester, England) formed duo after leaving British group 10cc.	
9/28/85	**37**	3	1. The History Mix Volume 1	Polydor 825981

DATE	POS	WKS	ARTIST—RECORD TITLE	LABEL & NO.
			GO-GO'S	
			Female rock group formed in 1978 in Los Angeles, consisting of Belinda Carlisle (vocals), Jane Wiedlin (guitar), Charlotte Caffey (guitar), Kathy Valentine (bass) and Gina Schock (drums). Disbanded in 1984. Brief reunion tour in 1990 included all but Caffey.	
9/26/81	1(6)	38	▲ 1. Beauty And The Beat *We Got The Beat* (2)	I.R.S. 70021
8/21/82	8	10	● 2. Vacation *Vacation* (8)	I.R.S. 70031
4/21/84	18	18	3. Talk Show	I.R.S. 70041
			GOLD, Marty	
			MARTY GOLD AND HIS ORCHESTRA:	
4/27/63	10	11	1. Soundpower! [I]	RCA 2620
			GOLDEN EARRING	
			Rock band from The Netherlands: Barry Hay (vocals), George Kooymans (guitars, vocals), Cesar Zuiderwijk (drums) and Rinus Gerritsen (bass, keyboards).	
6/15/74	12	13	● 1. Moontan	Track 396
2/26/83	24	12	2. Cut *Twilight Zone* (10)	21 Records 9004
			GOLDSBORO, Bobby	
			Born on 1/18/41 in Marianna, Florida. Singer/songwriter/guitarist. To Dothan, Alabama in 1956. Toured with Roy Orbison, 1962-64.	
5/4/68	5	22	● 1. Honey *Honey* (1)	United Art. 6642
			GOODMAN, Benny	
			Born on 5/30/09 in Chicago. Nicknamed "King of Swing." Clarinetist/big band leader since the 30s. Fletcher Henderson arranged many of his early 30s hits. Died on 6/13/86.	
3/19/55	7	16	1. B.G. In Hi-Fi [I]	Capitol 565

3/24/56	4	10	2. The Benny Goodman Story [S-I]
			    although Goodman is portrayed by Steve Allen in the film,
			    Benny and his musicians play the music
				Decca 8252/3 [2]

			GORE, Lesley	
			Born on 5/2/46 in New York City; raised in Tenafly, New Jersey. Discovered by Quincy Jones while singing at a hotel in Manhattan. In films *Girls On The Beach*, *Ski Party* and *The T.A.M.I. Show*.	
7/27/63	24	7	1. I'll Cry If I Want To *It's My Party* (1)/*Judy's Turn To Cry* (5)	Mercury 60805
			GORME, Eydie	
			Born on 8/16/31 in New York City. Vocalist with the big bands of Tommy Tucker and Tex Beneke in the late 40s. Featured on Steve Allen's Tonight Show from 1953. Married Steve Lawrence on 12/29/57. Recorded as the duo Parker & Penny in 1979.	
5/6/57	14	10	1. Eydie Gorme	ABC-Para. 150
10/28/57	19	4	2. Eydie Swings The Blues	ABC-Para. 192
3/31/58	19	4	3. Eydie Gorme Vamps The Roaring 20's	ABC-Para. 218
11/3/58	20	1	4. Eydie In Love...	ABC-Para. 246
4/27/63	22	9	5. Blame It On The Bossa Nova *Blame It On The Bossa Nova* (7)	Columbia 8812
6/4/66	22	9	6. Don't Go To Strangers	Columbia 9276

DATE	POS	WKS	ARTIST—RECORD TITLE	LABEL & NO.
			GOULD, Morton	
			Born on 12/10/13 in Long Island, New York. Composer of semi-classical music; co-wrote two Broadway musicals. Conductor/arranger on NBC radio for years.	
			MORTON GOULD AND HIS ORCHESTRA:	
11/9/59	5	33	1. Tchaikovsky: 1812 Overture/ Ravel: Bolero [I]	RCA 2345
7/18/60	3	25	2. Grofe: Grand Canyon Suite/ Beethoven: Wellington's Victory [I]	RCA 2433
			GOULET, Robert	
			Born on 11/26/33 in Lawrence, Massachusetts. Began concert career in Edmonton, Canada. Launched career as Sir Lancelot in the hit Broadway musical *Camelot*. Won the 1962 Best New Artist Grammy Award.	
11/10/62	20	14	1. Two Of Us	Columbia 8626
1/12/63	9	27	2. Sincerely Yours…	Columbia 8731
5/4/63	11	14	3. The Wonderful World Of Love	Columbia 8793
11/9/63	16	10	4. Robert Goulet In Person [L]	Columbia 8888
			recorded live at the Chicago Opera House	
6/27/64	31	7	5. Manhattan Tower/The Man Who Loves Manhattan	Columbia 2450
			composed and conducted by Gordon Jenkins	
1/23/65	5	18	● 6. My Love Forgive Me	Columbia 9096
10/9/65	31	5	7. Summer Sounds	Columbia 9180
1/29/66	33	4	8. Robert Goulet On Broadway	Columbia 9218
			GQ	
			Bronx, New York soul group: Emmanuel Rahiem LeBlanc (lead singer), Keith Crier, Herb Lane and Paul Service. Group became a trio with the departure of Service, 1980.	
4/21/79	13	19	▲ 1. Disco Nights	Arista 4225
			GRAHAM, Larry	
			Born on 8/14/46 in Beaumont, Texas. To Oakland at the age of two. Bass player with Sly & The Family Stone from 1966-72. Formed Graham Central Station in 1973.	
8/2/80	26	9	● 1. One In A Million You	Warner 3447
			One In A Million You (9)	
			GRAHAM CENTRAL STATION	
			Soul/dance group from Oakland, formed in 1973 by Larry Graham. Originally known as Hot Chocolate. Consisted of Graham (lead), Hershall Kennedy, Robert Sam, Willie Sparks, Patrice Banks, and David Vega. Graham went solo in 1980.	
8/30/75	22	6	● 1. Ain't No 'Bout-A-Doubt It	Warner 2876
			GRAMM, Lou	
			Born on 5/2/50 in Rochester, New York. Lead singer of Foreigner. Member of Black Sheep, 1970-75.	
3/28/87	27	7	1. Ready Or Not	Atlantic 81728
			Midnight Blue (5)	

DATE	POS	WKS	ARTIST—RECORD TITLE		LABEL & NO.
2/7/70	11	15	● 2. Grand Funk		Capitol 406
7/11/70	6	24	● 3. Closer To Home		Capitol 471
12/5/70	5	25	● 4. Live Album	[L]	Capitol 633 [2]
5/1/71	6	21	● 5. Survival		Capitol 764
12/4/71	5	15	● 6. E Pluribus Funk		Capitol 853
5/20/72	17	9	● 7. Mark, Don & Mel 1969-71	[K]	Capitol 11042 [2]
10/21/72	7	13	● 8. Phoenix		Capitol 11099
8/18/73	2(2)	17	● 9. We're An American Band * *We're An American Band* (1)		Capitol 11207
4/6/74	5	21	● 10. Shinin' On * *The Loco-Motion* (1)		Capitol 11278

1/4/75	10	10	● 11. All The Girls In The World Beware!!! *
			       GRAND FUNK
			       Some Kind Of Wonderful (3)/*Bad Time* (4)
					Capitol 11356

9/27/75	21	5	12. Caught In The Act	[L]	Capitol 11445 [2]
			GRANT, Amy		
			Born on 11/25/60 in Augusta, Georgia. The first lady of contemporary Christian music. Married to singer/songwriter Gary Chapman.		
8/24/85	35	4	▲ 1. Unguarded		A&M 5060
			GRANT, Earl		
			Organist/pianist/vocalist born in Oklahoma City in 1931. First recorded for Decca in 1957. In the films *Tender Is The Night*, *Imitation Of Life* and *Tokyo Night*. Died in an automobile accident on 6/10/70 (age 39).		
8/28/61	7	32	● 1. Ebb Tide	[I]	Decca 74165
7/14/62	17	13	2. Beyond The Reef	[I]	Decca 74231
			GRANT, Eddy		
			Born Edmond Montague Grant on 3/5/48 in Plaisance, Guyana. Moved to London in 1960. Formed group The Equals in London, 1967. Moved to Barbados in 1982.		
5/21/83	10	15	● 1. Killer On The Rampage *Electric Avenue* (2)		Portrait 38554
			GRANT, Gogi — see SOUNDTRACK "Helen Morgan Story"		
			GRASS ROOTS, The		
			Rock group formed in San Francisco in 1964 by drummer Joel Larson and lead singer Bill Fulton. Originally called The Bedouins. New group recruited in 1967 by pop producer Lou Adler and songwriters Steve Barri and P.F. Sloan (known as the Fantastic Baggies). Consisted of Rob Grill (lead singer, bass), Warren Entner and Creed Bratton (guitars), and Rick Coonce (drums). New lineup in 1971 included Entner, Grill, Reed Kailing, Joel Larson and Virgil Webber.		
1/25/69	25	6	● 1. Golden Grass *Midnight Confessions* (5)	[G]	Dunhill 50047
12/20/69	36	6	2. Leaving It All Behind		Dunhill 50067

DATE	POS	WKS	ARTIST—RECORD TITLE	LABEL & NO.
			GRATEFUL DEAD	
			Psychedelic rock band formed in San Francisco in 1966. Consisted of Jerry Garcia, lead guitar; Bob Weir, rhythm guitar; Ron "Pigpen" McKernan, organ, harmonica; Phil Lesh, bass; and Bill Kreutzmann, drums. Mickey Hart (2nd drummer) and Tom Constanten (keyboards) added in 1968. Constanten left in 1970, Hart in 1971. Keith Godchaux (piano) and his wife Donna (vocals) joined in 1972. Pigpen died of a liver ailment on 3/8/73. Hart returned in 1975. Brent Mydland (keyboards) added in 1979, replacing Keith and Donna Godchaux. Mydland was a member of Silver. Keith Godchaux died in a motorcycle accident in 1980. Mydland died on 7/26/90 (age 37) of a drug overdose. Tubes keyboardist Vince Welnick replaced Mydland.	
7/11/70	27	10	▲ 1. Workingman's Dead	Warner 1869
12/26/70	30	6	▲ 2. American Beauty	Warner 1893
10/16/71	25	6	3. Grateful Dead [L]	Warner 1935 [2]
1/6/73	24	8	● 4. Europe '72 [L]	Warner 2668 [3]
11/17/73	18	6	5. Wake Of The Flood	Grateful Dead 01
7/20/74	16	9	6. Grateful Dead From The Mars Hotel	Grateful Dead 102
9/20/75	12	9	7. Blues For Allah	Grateful Dead 494
9/10/77	28	4	● 8. Terrapin Station	Arista 7001
5/24/80	23	8	9. Go To Heaven	Arista 9508
10/3/81	29	3	10. Dead Set [L] recorded live in New York City and San Francisco in 1980	Arista 8606 [2]
8/1/87	6	17	▲ 11. In The Dark *Touch Of Grey* (9)	Arista 8452
2/25/89	37	3	12. Dylan & The Dead [L] **BOB DYLAN & GRATEFUL DEAD** recordings from six concert dates in July of 1987	Columbia 45056
11/25/89	27	3	● 13. Built To Last	Arista 8575
			GRAY, Glen	
			Alto saxophonist/bandleader. Led the Casa Loma Orchestra swing band. Organized in 1927; named for a Toronto nightclub. Gray died on 8/23/63. **GLEN GRAY AND THE CASA LOMA ORCHESTRA:**	
2/23/57	18	9	1. Casa Loma In Hi-Fi! [I]	Capitol 747
6/29/59	28	2	2. Sounds Of The Great Bands! [I]	Capitol 1022
			GREAN, Charles Randolph	
			Charles is a former artist & repertoire director at RCA and Dot Records. Married singer Betty Johnson. **THE CHARLES RANDOLPH GREAN SOUNDE:**	
8/16/69	23	5	1. Quentin's Theme [I] title cut is from TV's "Dark Shadows"	Ranwood 8055
			GREAT WHITE	
			Los Angeles heavy-metal quintet, led by vocalist Jack Russell and guitarist Mark Kendall. Current lineup includes Michael Lardie (keyboards), Audie Desbrow (drums) and Tony Montana (bass).	
9/12/87	23	18	▲ 1. Once Bitten	Capitol 12565
5/13/89	9	26	▲ 2. Twice Shy *Once Bitten Twice Shy* (5)	Capitol 90640
			GREELEY, George	
			Guest pianist with the Warner Bros. Orchestra.	
6/19/61	29	5	1. The Best Of The Popular Piano Concertos [I-K]	Warner 1410

DATE	POS	WKS	ARTIST—RECORD TITLE	LABEL & NO.

GREEN, Al

Born on 4/13/46 in Forest City, Arkansas. Singer/songwriter. With gospel group the Greene Brothers. To Grand Rapids, Michigan in 1959. First recorded for Fargo in 1960. In group The Creations from 1964-67. Sang with his brother Robert and Lee Virgins in the group Soul Mates from 1967-68. Went solo in 1969. Wrote most of his songs. Returned to gospel music in 1980.

DATE	POS	WKS	ARTIST—RECORD TITLE	LABEL & NO.
2/26/72	**8**	20	● 1. Let's Stay Together *Let's Stay Together* (1)	Hi 32070
11/4/72	**4**	26	● 2. I'm Still In Love With You *Look What You Done For Me* (4)/ *I'm Still In Love With You* (3)	Hi 32074
2/3/73	**19**	11	3. Green Is Blues [E] *Al's first album on the Hi label*	Hi 32055
5/26/73	**10**	20	● 4. Call Me *You Ought To Be With Me* (3)/*Call Me (Come Back Home)* (10)/ *Here I Am (Come And Take Me)* (10)	Hi 32077
1/19/74	**24**	8	● 5. Livin' For You	Hi 32082
12/7/74	**15**	16	● 6. Al Green Explores Your Mind *Sha-La-La (Make Me Happy)* (7)	Hi 32087
3/22/75	**17**	8	7. Al Green/Greatest Hits [G]	Hi 32089
10/11/75	**28**	6	8. Al Green Is Love	Hi 32092

GREENBAUM, Norman

Born on 11/20/42 in Malden, Massachusetts. Moved to the West Coast in 1965 and formed the psychedelic jug band Dr. West's Medicine Show & Junk Band.

DATE	POS	WKS	ARTIST—RECORD TITLE	LABEL & NO.
4/18/70	**23**	5	1. Spirit In The Sky *Spirit In The Sky* (3)	Reprise 6365

GREENE, Lorne

Born on 2/12/14 in Ottawa, Canada; died on 9/11/87 of cardiac arrest. Chief newscaster for CBC radio, 1940-43. Studied acting, appeared in films *The Silver Challice* and *Tight Spot*; starred in TV series "Bonanza" and "Battlestar Galactica."

DATE	POS	WKS	ARTIST—RECORD TITLE	LABEL & NO.
1/16/65	**35**	4	1. Welcome To The Ponderosa *Ringo* (1)	RCA 2843

GREGORY, Dick

Black comedian and civil rights activist.

DATE	POS	WKS	ARTIST—RECORD TITLE	LABEL & NO.
7/24/61	**23**	5	1. In Living Black & White [C]	Colpix 417

GROSS, Henry

Rock singer from Brooklyn. Original lead guitarist of Sha-Na-Na.

DATE	POS	WKS	ARTIST—RECORD TITLE	LABEL & NO.
4/12/75	**26**	3	1. Plug Me Into Something	A&M 4502

GTR

British hard-rock quintet featuring superstar guitarists Steve Hackett (Genesis) and Steve Howe (Yes & Asia), and vocalist Max Bacon.

DATE	POS	WKS	ARTIST—RECORD TITLE	LABEL & NO.
5/31/86	**11**	17	● 1. GTR	Arista 8400

GUARALDI, Vince

Born on 7/17/32 in San Francisco; died of a heart attack on 2/6/76. Pianist and leader of own jazz trio. Formerly with Woody Herman and Cal Tjader. Wrote the music for the "Charlie Brown" TV specials.

VINCE GUARALDI TRIO:

DATE	POS	WKS	ARTIST—RECORD TITLE	LABEL & NO.
4/13/63	**24**	7	1. Jazz Impressions of Black Orpheus [I] *features Vince's interpretations of four songs from the film Black Orpheus*	Fantasy 3337

DATE	POS	WKS	ARTIST—RECORD TITLE	LABEL & NO.
			GUESS WHO, The	
			Rock group formed in Winnipeg, Canada in 1963. Consisted of Allan "Chad Allan" Kobel (guitar, vocals), Randy Bachman (lead guitar), Garry Peterson (drums), Bob Ashley (piano) and Jim Kale (bass). Recorded as The Reflections, and Chad Allan & The Expressions. Ashley replaced by new lead singer Burton Cummings in 1966. Allan left shortly thereafter. Bachman left in July, 1970, to form Bachman-Turner Overdrive. Replaced by Kurt Winter and Greg Leskiw. Leskiw and Kale left in 1972, replaced by Don McDougall and Bill Wallace. Domenic Troiano replaced both Winter and McDougall in 1974. Group disbanded in 1975; several reformations since then.	
3/7/70	9	23	● 1. American Woman *No Time* (5)/*American Woman* (1)	RCA 4266
11/28/70	14	11	● 2. Share The Land *Share The Land* (10)	RCA 4359
4/24/71	12	23	● 3. The Best of The Guess Who [G]	RCA 1004
10/14/72	39	1	4. Live At The Paramount (Seattle) [L]	RCA 4779
			GUNS N' ROSES	
			Los Angeles-based, hard-rock quintet: lead singer W. Axl Rose (Bill Bailey) with bassist Duff "Rose" McKagan, guitarists Izzy Stradlin and Slash (Saul Hudson), and drummer Steven Adler. Axl Rose married Erin Everly (daughter of Don) on 4/27/90, divorced three weeks later. Adler left in 1990, replaced by former Cult drummer Matt Sorum.	
1/30/88	1(5)	78	▲ 1. Appetite For Destruction *Sweet Child O' Mine* (1)/*Welcome To The Jungle* (7)/ *Paradise City* (5)	Geffen 24148
12/24/88	2(1)	33	▲ 2. G N' R Lies side A: reissue of their 1986 four-song EP, "Live Like A Suicide"; side B: four tracks recorded in 1988 *Patience* (4)	Geffen 24198
			GUTHRIE. Arlo	
			Born on 7/10/47 in Coney Island, New York. Son of legendary folk singer Woody Guthrie.	
1/27/68	17	23	▲ 1. Alice's Restaurant side 1 is the 18-minute tale "Alice's Restaurant Massacree"	Reprise 6267
11/28/70	33	3	2. Washington County	Reprise 6411
			GUY	
			New York City black trio formed and fronted by Teddy Riley. Includes brothers Aaron and Albert Damion Hall. By age 20, in 1988, Riley (ex-member of R&B group Kids At Work) was a renowned producer.	
4/8/89	27	13	▲ 1. Guy	Uptown 42176
			# H	
			HAGAR, Sammy	
			Born on 10/13/47 in Monterey, California. Rock singer/songwriter/guitarist. Lead singer of Montrose (1973-75). Replaced David Lee Roth as lead singer of Van Halen in 1985.	
2/20/82	28	14	● 1. Standing Hampton	Geffen 2006
1/29/83	17	14	● 2. Three Lock Box	Geffen 2021
11/3/84	32	9	▲ 3. VOA	Geffen 24043
7/25/87	14	11	4. Sammy Hagar as a result of an MTV contest, album title changed to "I Never Said Goodbye," however, none were pressed with the new title	Geffen 24144

DATE	POS	WKS	ARTIST—RECORD TITLE	LABEL & NO.
			HAGGARD, Merle	
			Born on 4/6/37 in Bakersfield, California. Country singer/songwriter/guitarist. Served nearly three years in San Quentin prison on a burglary charge, 1957-60. Signed to Capitol Records in 1965 and then formed backing band, The Strangers. Merle's had 38 #1 singles on the country charts.	
			MERLE HAGGARD/WILLIE NELSON:	
8/20/83	**37**	1	▲ 1. Poncho & Lefty	Epic 37958
			HAIRCUT ONE HUNDRED	
			British pop-rock sextet founded by vocalist Nick Heyward. Disbanded in 1983.	
7/10/82	**31**	7	1. Pelican West	Arista 6600
			HALEY, Bill	
			Born William John Clifton Haley, Jr. on 7/6/25 in Highland Park, Michigan. Began career as a singer with a New England country band, the Down Homers. Formed the Four Aces of Western Swing in 1948. In 1949 formed the Saddlemen, who recorded on various labels before signing with the Essex label (as Bill Haley & The Comets) in 1952; signed with Decca in 1954. The original Comets band who backed Haley on "Rock Around The Clock" were: Danny Cedrone (lead guitar), Joey D'Ambrose (sax), Billy Williamson (steel guitar), Johnny Grande (piano), Marshall Lytle (bass) and Dick Richards (drums). Comets lineup on subsequent recordings included Williamson, Grande, Rudy Pompilli (sax), Al Rex (bass), Ralph Jones (drums) and Frannie Beecher (lead guitar). Bill died of a heart attack in Harlingen, Texas on 2/9/81. Inducted into the Rock and Roll Hall of Fame in 1987.	
			BILL HALEY AND HIS COMETS:	
1/28/56	**12**	4	1. Rock Around The Clock [G] *Shake, Rattle And Roll* (7) 1954/*Rock Around The Clock* (1)/ *Burn That Candle* (9)	Decca 8225
10/13/56	**18**	5	2. Rock 'n Roll Stage Show	Decca 8345
			HALL, Daryl	
			Born Daryl Franklin Hohl on 10/11/48 in Philadelphia. Half of Hall & Oates duo.	
9/20/86	**29**	6	1. Three Hearts in the Happy Ending Machine *Dreamtime* (5)	RCA 7196
			HALL, Daryl/John Oates	
			Daryl Hall (see previous entry) & John Oates (b: 4/7/49 in New York City) met while students at Temple University in 1967. Hall sang backup for many top soul groups before teaming up with Oates in 1972. Duo's sophisticated "blue-eyed soul" style has earned them the #2 ranking (behind the Everly Brothers) as the all-time top duo of the rock era.	
5/22/76	**17**	11	● 1. Daryl Hall & John Oates *Sara Smile* (4)	RCA 1144
9/18/76	**13**	35	● 2. Bigger Than Both Of Us *Rich Girl* (1)	RCA 1467
10/30/76	**33**	4	● 3. Abandoned Luncheonette *She's Gone* (7)	Atlantic 7269
9/24/77	**30**	5	● 4. Beauty On A Back Street	RCA 2300
10/7/78	**27**	6	● 5. Along The Red Ledge	RCA 2804
11/24/79	**33**	6	6. X-Static	RCA 3494
8/30/80	**17**	35	▲ 7. Voices *Kiss On My List* (1)/*You Make My Dreams* (5)	RCA 3646
9/26/81	**5**	32	▲ 8. Private Eyes *Private Eyes* (1)/*I Can't Go For That* (1)/ *Did It In A Minute* (9)	RCA 4028
11/6/82	**3**	46	▲ 9. H2O *Maneater* (1)/*One On One* (7)/*Family Man* (6)	RCA 4383
11/19/83	**7**	28	▲ 10. Rock 'N Soul, Part 1 [G] *Say It Isn't So* (2)/*Adult Education* (8)	RCA 4858

DATE	POS	WKS	ARTIST—RECORD TITLE		LABEL & NO.
10/27/84	**5**	31	▲ 11. Big Bam Boom *Out Of Touch* (1)/*Method Of Modern Love* (5)		RCA 5309
10/5/85	**21**	8	● 12. Live At The Apollo with David Ruffin & Eddie Kendrick recorded at the re-opening of New York's Apollo Theater; side 1 features guest vocalists Ruffin and Kendrick	[L]	RCA 7035
5/28/88	**24**	7	▲ 13. ooh yeah! *Everything Your Heart Desires* (3)		Arista 8539
			HAMMER, Jan — see BECK, Jeff and TV SOUNDTRACK "Miami Vice"		
			HANCOCK, Herbie		
			Born on 4/12/40 in Chicago. Jazz electronic keyboardist. Pianist with the Miles Davis band, 1963-68. Won an Oscar in 1987 for his *Round Midnight* film score. Also scored the 1988 film *Colors*.		
2/16/74	**13**	21	▲ 1. Head Hunters	[I]	Columbia 32731
10/12/74	**13**	9	2. Thrust	[I]	Columbia 32965
11/8/75	**21**	4	3. Man-Child	[I]	Columbia 33812
4/21/79	**38**	3	4. Feets Don't Fail Me Now		Columbia 35764
			HARMONICATS		
			Harmonica trio formed in 1944: Jerry Murad, Al Fiore and Don Les. **JERRY MURAD'S "FABULOUS" HARMONICATS:**		
3/20/61	**17**	1	1. Cherry Pink And Apple Blossom White	[I]	Columbia 8356
			HARNELL, Joe		
			Born on 8/2/24 in the Bronx. Conductor/arranger for Frank Sinatra, Peggy Lee and others. Musical director for many TV shows, including the Mike Douglas Show. **JOE HARNELL HIS PIANO AND ORCHESTRA:**		
1/26/63	**3**	27	1. Fly Me To The Moon and the Bossa Nova Pops	[I]	Kapp 3318
			HARRIS, Eddie		
			Born on 10/20/36 in Chicago. Jazz tenor saxophonist.		
6/19/61	**2**(1)	22	1. Exodus To Jazz	[I]	Vee-Jay 3016
9/7/68	**36**	1	2. The Electrifying Eddie Harris	[I]	Atlantic 1495
			LES McCANN & EDDIE HARRIS:		
1/31/70	**29**	5	3. Swiss Movement recorded live at The Montreux Jazz Festival, Switzerland	[I-L]	Atlantic 1537
			HARRIS, Emmylou		
			Born on 4/2/47 in Birmingham, Alabama. Contemporary country vocalist. Sang backup with Gram Parsons until his death in 1973. Own band from 1975.		
2/7/76	**25**	8	● 1. Elite Hotel		Reprise 2236
2/5/77	**21**	8	● 2. Luxury Liner		Warner 3115
2/25/78	**29**	5	● 3. Quarter Moon In A Ten Cent Town		Warner 3141
6/7/80	**26**	11	● 4. Roses In The Snow		Warner 3422
2/28/81	**22**	9	● 5. Evangeline		Warner 3508
			DOLLY PARTON, LINDA RONSTADT, EMMYLOU HARRIS:		
3/28/87	**6**	14	▲ 6. Trio		Warner 25491

DATE	POS	WKS	ARTIST—RECORD TITLE	LABEL & NO.
			HARRIS, Major	
			Born on 2/9/47 in Richmond, Virginia. Soul singer; sang with The Jarmels, Teenagers, and Impacts in the early 60s. With The Delfonics from 1971-74.	Atlantic 18119
6/28/75	**28**	3	1. My Way *Love Won't Let Me Wait (5)*	
			HARRIS, Richard	
			Born on 10/1/30 in Limerick, Ireland. Began prolific acting career in 1958. Portrayed King Arthur in the film version of *Camelot*.	
6/1/68	**4**	16	1. A Tramp Shining *MacArthur Park (2)*	Dunhill 50032
12/14/68	**27**	6	2. The Yard Went On Forever...	Dunhill 50042
11/10/73	**25**	9	3. Jonathan Livingston Seagull [T] narration from the book; music composed by Terry James	Dunhill 50160
1/25/75	**29**	5	4. The Prophet by Kahlil Gibran [T] Harris recites Gibran's classic work	Atlantic 18120
			HARRIS, Rolf	
			Born in Perth, Australia on 3/30/30. Played piano from age nine. Moved to England in the mid-50s. Developed his unique "wobble board sound" out of a sheet of masonite. Had own BBC-TV series from 1970.	
8/17/63	**29**	4	1. Tie Me Kangaroo Down, Sport & Sun Arise [N] *Tie Me Kangaroo Down, Sport (3)*	Epic 26053
			HARRIS, Sam	
			Winner of TV's "Star Search" male vocalist category in 1984.	
11/17/84	**35**	3	● 1. Sam Harris	Motown 6103
			HARRISON, George	
			Born on 2/25/43 in Liverpool, England. Formed his first group, the Rebels, at age 13. Joined John Lennon and Paul McCartney in The Quarrymen in 1958; group later evolved into The Beatles, with Harrison as lead guitarist. Organized the Bangladesh benefit concerts at Madison Square Garden in 1971. Member of the 1988 supergroup Traveling Wilburys.	
12/19/70	**1(7)**	22	● 1. All Things Must Pass *My Sweet Lord (1)/What Is Life (10)*	Apple 639 [3]
1/8/72	**2(6)**	23	● 2. The Concert For Bangla Desh [L] 1972 Grammy winner: Album of the Year; Madison Square Garden benefit concert on 8/1/71 - with guests Bob Dylan, Eric Clapton and Ringo Starr	Apple 3385 [3]
6/16/73	**1(5)**	15	● 3. Living In The Material World *Give Me Love (Give Me Peace On Earth) (1)*	Apple 3410
1/4/75	**4**	9	● 4. Dark Horse	Apple 3418
10/11/75	**8**	7	● 5. Extra Texture (Read All About It)	Apple 3420
12/11/76	**31**	3	● 6. The Best of George Harrison [G] side 1: hits while with The Beatles; side 2: solo hits	Capitol 11578
12/18/76	**11**	8	● 7. Thirty-Three & 1/3 33 1/3: record playing speed and George's age	Dark Horse 3005
3/17/79	**14**	9	● 8. George Harrison	Dark Horse 3255
6/20/81	**11**	7	9. Somewhere In England *All Those Years Ago (2)*	Dark Horse 3492
11/28/87	**8**	23	▲ 10. Cloud Nine co-producer: Jeff Lynne (Electric Light Orchestra) *Got My Mind Set On You (1)*	Dark Horse 25643

DATE	POS	WKS	ARTIST—RECORD TITLE	LABEL & NO.
			HARRY, Debbie	
			Born on 7/1/45 in New York City. Lead singer of Blondie. In films *Roadie*, *Videodrome* and *Hairspray*. Appeared in episodes of TV's "Wiseguy."	
9/5/81	25	4	● 1. KooKoo	Chrysalis 1347
			HART, Corey	
			Born in Montreal; raised in Spain and Mexico. Singer/songwriter/keyboardist.	
9/1/84	31	6	● 1. First Offense	EMI America 17117
			Sunglasses At Night (7)	
8/3/85	20	15	● 2. Boy In The Box	EMI America 17161
			Never Surrender (3)	
			HART, Freddie	
			Born Fred Segrest on 12/21/26 in Lochapoka, Alabama. Country singer/songwriter/guitarist.	
11/27/71	37	4	● 1. Easy Loving	Capitol 838
			HATHAWAY, Donny	
			Born on 10/1/45 in Chicago; raised in St. Louis. Committed suicide by jumping from the 15th floor of New York City's Essex House hotel on 1/13/79. R&B singer/songwriter/keyboardist/producer/arranger. Gospel singer since age three. Attended Washington, D.C.'s Howard University on a fine arts scholarship; classmate of Roberta Flack. Wife Eulalah was a classical singer; daughter Lalah Hathaway began solo recording career in 1990.	
3/25/72	18	23	● 1. Donny Hathaway Live [L]	Atco 386
5/20/72	3	21	● 2. Roberta Flack & Donny Hathaway	Atlantic 7216
			Where Is The Love (5)	
4/26/80	25	10	● 3. Roberta Flack Featuring Donny Hathaway	Atlantic 16013
			HAVENS, Richie	
			Born on 1/21/41 in Brooklyn. Black folk singer/guitarist.	
5/15/71	29	7	1. Alarm Clock	Stormy F. 6005
			Here Comes The Sun	
			HAWKINS, Edwin	
			Formed gospel group with Betty Watson in Oakland in 1967 as the Northern California State Youth Choir, later The Edwin Hawkins' Singers. Member Dorothy Morrison went on to a solo career.	
			THE EDWIN HAWKINS' SINGERS:	
5/17/69	15	8	1. Let Us Go Into The House Of The Lord	Pavilion 10001
			Oh Happy Day (4)	
			HAYES, Isaac	
			Born on 8/20/42 in Covington, Tennessee. Soul singer/songwriter/keyboardist/producer/actor. Session musician for Otis Redding and other artists on the Stax label. Teamed with songwriter David Porter to compose "Soul Man," "Hold On! I'm A Comin'fs6u" and many others. Composed film score for *Shaft*, *Tough Guys* and *Truck Turner*.	
8/2/69	8	36	● 1. Hot Buttered Soul	Enterprise 1001
5/2/70	8	28	2. The Isaac Hayes Movement	Enterprise 1010
12/5/70	11	20	3. To Be Continued	Enterprise 1014
8/28/71	1(1)	30	4. Shaft [S-I]	Enterprise 5002 [2]
			three of 15 tracks feature vocals	
			Theme From Shaft (1)	
12/18/71	10	15	5. Black Moses	Enterprise 5003 [2]
6/2/73	14	11	● 6. Live At The Sahara Tahoe [L]	Enterprise 5005 [2]
11/17/73	16	14	● 7. Joy	Enterprise 5007
7/5/75	18	9	● 8. Chocolate Chip	HBS 874

DATE	POS	WKS	ARTIST—RECORD TITLE		LABEL & NO.
1/19/80	39	1	● 9. Don't Let Go		Polydor 6224
			HAYWARD, Justin		
			Justin was born on 10/14/46 in Swindon, England. John Lodge was born on 7/20/45 in Birmingham, England. Justin (lead singer, lead guitar) and John (vocals, bass) joined The Moody Blues in the summer of 1966.		
4/19/75	16	8	1. Blue Jays		Threshold 14
			JUSTIN HAYWARD/JOHN LODGE		
			album title also refers to the name of their duo		
5/7/77	37	3	2. Songwriter		Deram 18073
			HAZLEWOOD, Lee — see SINATRA, Nancy		
			HEALEY, Jeff		
			Leader of Toronto-based, blues-rock trio formed in late 1985. Vocalist/guitarist Healey, blind since age one, has played guitar since age three. Appeared in the 1989 film *Road House*. Trio includes Tom Stephen (drums) and Joe Rockman (bass).		
			THE JEFF HEALEY BAND:		
9/2/89	22	8	● 1. See The Light		Arista 8553
			Angel Eyes (5)		
6/23/90	27	12	2. Hell To Pay		Arista 8632
			HEART		
			Rock band formed in Seattle in 1973. Originally known as The Army, then White Heart, shortened to Heart in 1974. Group features Ann Wilson (lead singer) and her sister Nancy (guitar, keyboards). Band moved to Vancouver, Canada in 1975 when their manager Mike Fisher was drafted, and signed with new Mushroom label. When amnesty was declared, group returned to Seattle and signed with the CBS Portrait label in 1976. In addition to the Wilson sisters, the lineup since 1982 includes guitarist Howard Leese, bassist Mark Andes (ex-Spirit, Jo Jo Gunne and Firefall member) and drummer Denny Carmassi.		
8/7/76	7	21	▲ 1. Dreamboat Annie		Mushroom 5005
			Magic Man (9)		
6/4/77	9	22	▲ 2. Little Queen		Portrait 34799
4/29/78	17	7	▲ 3. Magazine		Mushroom 5008
			recorded in 1976 but not released until 1978 because of a legal fight		
10/14/78	17	22	▲ 4. Dog & Butterfly		Portrait 35555
3/8/80	5	13	● 5. Bebe Le Strange		Epic 36371
12/6/80	13	12	● 6. Greatest Hits/Live [G-L]		Epic 36888 [2]
			six of 18 tracks are live		
			Tell It Like It Is (8)		
6/19/82	25	4	7. Private Audition		Epic 38049
10/15/83	39	2	8. Passionworks		Epic 38800
7/27/85	1(1)	58	▲ 9. Heart		Capitol 12410
			What About Love? (10)/*Never* (4)/*These Dreams* (1)/ *Nothin' At All* (10)		
6/13/87	2(3)	36	▲ 10. Bad Animals		Capitol 12546
			Alone (1)/*Who Will You Run To* (7)		
4/28/90	3	22	▲ 11. Brigade		Capitol 91820
			All I Wanna Do Is Make Love To You (2)		
			HEATH, Ted		
			Born Edward Heath on 3/30/1900 in London, England; died on 11/18/69. Trombonist/ leader of own band since 1945.		
			TED HEATH AND HIS MUSIC:		
10/16/61	28	8	1. Big Band Percussion [I]		London P. 4 44002
9/15/62	36	2	2. Big Band Bash [I]		London P. 4 44017

DATE	POS	WKS	ARTIST—RECORD TITLE	LABEL & NO.
			HEATWAVE	
			Multinational, interracial group formed in Germany by Johnnie and Keith Wilder of Dayton, Ohio. Johnnie became a paraplegic due to car accident in 1979.	
9/17/77	**11**	12	▲ 1. Too Hot To Handle	Epic 34761
			Boogie Nights (2)	
5/6/78	**10**	12	▲ 2. Central Heating	Epic 35260
			The Groove Line (7)	
6/9/79	**38**	3	● 3. Hot Property	Epic 35970
			HEAVY D. & THE BOYZ	
			Rap quartet from Mt. Vernon, New York: leader Heavy D. (Dwight Meyers), G. Whiz (Glen Parrish), Trouble T-Roy (Troy Dixon) and DJ Eddie F (Edward Ferrell). Dixon died on 7/15/90 (age 22) from a fall in a freak stage accident in Indianapolis.	
7/22/89	**19**	14	▲ 1. Big Tyme	Uptown 42302
			HEFTI, Neal	
			Born on 10/29/22 in Hastings, Nebraska. Trumpeter; most famous as arranger for Woody Herman (1944-46), Harry James and Count Basie, then as composer of TV themes.	
			NEAL HEFTI AND HIS ORCHESTRA:	
2/5/55	**8**	2	1. Music Of Rudolf Friml [I]	"X" 3021
			10" album	
			HEINDORF, Ray/Matty Matlock	
			Ray Heindorf conducting the Warner Bros. Orchestra and Matty Matlock and his Jazz Band. Also see Jack Webb.	
9/3/55	**9**	6	1. Pete Kelly's Blues [I]	Columbia 690
			HENDERSON, Michael	
			Born in 1951 in Yazoo City, Mississippi. Soul singer/bass player. To Detroit in the early 60s. Worked as session musician. Toured with Stevie Wonder, Aretha Franklin and Miles Davis. Also see Norman Connors.	
9/23/78	**38**	2	● 1. In The Night-Time	Buddah 5712
10/11/80	**35**	5	2. Wide Receiver	Buddah 6001
			HENDRIX, Jimi	
			Born on 11/27/42 in Seattle. Died of a drug overdose in London on 9/18/70. Legendary psychedelic-blues guitarist. Began career as a studio guitarist. In 1965 formed own band, Jimmy James & The Blue Flames. Created The Jimi Hendrix Experience in 1966 with Noel Redding on bass and Mitch Mitchell on drums. Formed new group in 1969, Band of Gypsys, with Buddy Miles on drums and Billy Cox on bass.	
9/16/67	**5**	77	▲ 1. Are You Experienced? *	Reprise 6261
2/17/68	**3**	13	▲ 2. Axis: Bold As Love *	Reprise 6281
11/2/68	**1**(2)	17	▲ 3. Electric Ladyland *	Reprise 6307 [2]
8/9/69	**6**	17	▲ 4. Smash Hits * [G]	Reprise 2025
			***THE JIMI HENDRIX EXPERIENCE**	
5/2/70	**5**	23	● 5. Band Of Gypsys [L]	Capitol 472
			with Buddy Miles (drums) and Billy Cox (bass); recorded New Year's Eve in 1969 at New York's Fillmore East	
9/26/70	**16**	8	● 6. Monterey International Pop Festival [S-L]	Reprise 2029
			OTIS REDDING/THE JIMI HENDRIX EXPERIENCE recorded June, 1967 and featured in the film *Monterey Pop*	
3/6/71	**3**	17	● 7. The Cry Of Love	Reprise 2034
			Jimi's last self-authorized album	
10/16/71	**15**	9	● 8. Rainbow Bridge [S]	Reprise 2040
			recordings from 1968-1970	

DATE	POS	WKS	ARTIST—RECORD TITLE	LABEL & NO.
3/11/72	12	9	● 9. Hendrix In The West [K-L]	Reprise 2049
3/29/75	5	9	● 10. Crash Landing [K]	Reprise 2204

HENLEY, Don

Born on 7/22/47 in Gilmer, Texas. Singer/songwriter/drummer. Own band, Shiloh, in the early 70s. Worked with Glenn Frey in Linda Ronstadt's backup band, then the two formed the Eagles with Randy Meisner and Bernie Leadon. Went solo in 1982.

DATE	POS	WKS	ARTIST—RECORD TITLE	LABEL & NO.
9/25/82	24	20	● 1. I Can't Stand Still *Dirty Laundry (3)*	Asylum 60048
12/22/84	13	30	▲ 2. Building The Perfect Beast *The Boys Of Summer (5)/All She Wants To Do Is Dance (9)*	Geffen 24026
7/29/89	8	58	▲ 3. The End Of The Innocence *The End Of The Innocence (8)*	Geffen 24217

HERMAN, Woody

Born Woodrow Charles Herman on 5/16/13 in Milwaukee. Saxophonist/clarinetist in dance bands beginning in 1929. Formed own band in 1936. Band dubbed The Herman Herd in 1944. One of the most innovative and contemporary of all big-band leaders. Died on 10/29/87 of cardiac arrest.
WOODY HERMAN AND HIS ORCHESTRA:

DATE	POS	WKS	ARTIST—RECORD TITLE	LABEL & NO.
2/19/55	11	2	1. The 3 Herds [K-I] *recordings from 1945-1954*	Columbia 592

HERMAN'S HERMITS

Formed in Manchester, England in 1964. Named after a cartoon character in TV's "The Bullwinkle Show." Consisted of Peter "Herman" Noone (b: 11/5/47; vocals), Derek Leckenby and Keith Hopwood (guitars), Karl Green (bass) and Barry Whitman (drums). First called The Heartbeats. Noone left in 1972 for a solo career.

DATE	POS	WKS	ARTIST—RECORD TITLE	LABEL & NO.
3/27/65	2(4)	26	● 1. Introducing Herman's Hermits *Mrs. Brown You've Got A Lovely Daughter (1)*	MGM 4282
6/26/65	2(6)	24	● 2. Herman's Hermits On Tour *Can't You Hear My Heartbeat (2)/Silhouettes (5)/ I'm Henry VIII, I Am (1)*	MGM 4295
11/27/65	5	27	● 3. The Best Of Herman's Hermits [G] *Wonderful World (4)/Just A Little Bit Better (7)*	MGM 4315
4/30/66	14	7	4. Hold On! [S] group stars in film *A Must To Avoid (8)/Leaning On The Lamp Post (9)*	MGM 4342
1/7/67	20	7	● 5. The Best Of Herman's Hermits, Volume 2 [G] *Listen People (3)/Dandy (5)*	MGM 4416
3/25/67	13	13	● 6. There's A Kind Of Hush All Over The World *There's A Kind Of Hush (4)*	MGM 4438

HEYWOOD, Eddie

Born on 12/4/15 in Atlanta; died on 1/2/89. Black jazz pianist/composer/arranger. Played professionally by age 14. Own band in New York City in 1941. Worked with Billie Holiday. To the West Coast in 1947, with own trio. Active into the 70s.

DATE	POS	WKS	ARTIST—RECORD TITLE	LABEL & NO.
5/25/59	16	4	1. Canadian Sunset [I] title song written by Eddie, not the same version as with Hugo Winterhalter in 1956	RCA 1529

HIBBLER, Al

Born on 8/16/15 in Little Rock, Arkansas. Blind since birth, studied voice at Little Rock's Conservatory for the Blind. First recorded with Jay McShann for Decca in 1942. With Duke Ellington, 1943-51. Also recorded with Harry Carney, Tab Smith, Mercer Ellington and Billy Strayhorn.

DATE	POS	WKS	ARTIST—RECORD TITLE	LABEL & NO.
8/4/56	20	2	1. Starring Al Hibbler	Decca 8328

DATE	POS	WKS	ARTIST—RECORD TITLE	LABEL & NO.
			HIGGINS, Bertie	
			Singer/songwriter, born in 1946 in Tarpon Springs, Florida. First recorded for ABC in 1964. Worked as a drummer with the Roemans from 1964-66.	
6/12/82	38	3	1. Just Another Day In Paradise	Kat Family 37901
			Key Largo (8)	
			HIGH INERGY	
			Female soul group from Pasadena, California: Barbara Mitchell, Linda Howard, Michelle Rumph and Vernessa Mitchell (Vernessa left in 1978; group continued as a trio).	
12/10/77	28	7	1. Turnin' On	Gordy 978
			HILL, Dan	
			Born on 6/3/54 in Toronto, Canada. Author/singer/songwriter.	
2/11/78	21	8	● 1. Longer Fuse	20th Century 547
			Sometimes When We Touch (3)	
			HI-LO'S, The	
			Vocal quartet formed in 1953: Gene Puerling, Clark Burroughs, Bob Morse and Bob Strasen. Numerous appearances on Rosemary Clooney's television show.	
4/13/57	13	3	1. Suddenly It's The Hi-Lo's	Columbia 952
7/22/57	14	7	2. Ring Around Rosie	Columbia 1006
			ROSEMARY CLOONEY AND THE HI-LO'S	
10/14/57	19	4	3. Now Hear This	Columbia 1023
			HIRT, Al	
			Born Alois Maxwell Hirt on 11/7/22 in New Orleans. Trumpet virtuoso. Toured with Jimmy and Tommy Dorsey, Ray McKinley and Horace Heidt. Formed own Dixieland combo (with clarinetist Pete Fountain) in the late 50s.	
8/14/61	21	11	1. The Greatest Horn In The World [I]	RCA 2366
3/10/62	24	5	2. Horn A-Plenty [I]	RCA 2446
12/28/63	3	66	● 3. Honey In The Horn	RCA 2733
			Anita Kerr Singers do background vocals on some tracks	
			Java (4)	
6/6/64	6	38	● 4. Cotton Candy [I]	RCA 2917
9/19/64	9	20	● 5. Sugar Lips	RCA 2965
11/7/64	18	12	6. "Pops" Goes The Trumpet [I]	RCA 2729
			AL HIRT/BOSTON POPS/ARTHUR FIEDLER	
2/13/65	13	26	● 7. The Best Of Al Hirt [G-I]	RCA 3309
4/17/65	28	10	8. That Honey Horn Sound	RCA 3337
4/23/66	39	3	9. They're Playing Our Song [I]	RCA 3492
			HO, Don	
			Don was born on 8/13/30 in Oahu, Hawaii. Nightclub singer/actor.	
			DON HO AND THE ALIIS:	
3/4/67	15	8	1. Tiny Bubbles	Reprise 6232
			HOLLIDAY, Jennifer	
			Born on 10/19/60 in Houston. 1982 Tony award-winner for best actress in a musical in Broadway's *Dreamgirls*. Also in Broadway's *Your Arm's Too Short To Box With God* (1978) and *Sing, Mahalia Sing* (1985).	
11/5/83	31	5	1. Feel My Soul	Geffen 4014

DATE	POS	WKS	ARTIST—RECORD TITLE	LABEL & NO.
			HOLLIES, The	
			Formed in Manchester, England in 1962. Consisted of Allan Clarke (lead vocals), Graham Nash and Tony Hicks (guitars), Eric Haydock (bass) and Don Rathbone (drums). Clarke and Nash had worked as duo, the Guytones, added other members, became the Fourtones, Deltas, then The Hollies. First recorded for Parlophone in 1963. Rathbone left in 1963, replaced by Bobby Elliott. Haydock left in 1966, replaced by Bernie Calvert (first heard on song "Bus Stop"). Nash left in December, 1968, replaced by Terry Sylvester, formerly in the Swinging Blue Jeans. Regrouped in 1983 with Clarke, Nash, Hicks and Elliott.	
7/1/67	11	12	1. The Hollies' Greatest Hits [G]	Imperial 12350
4/11/70	32	4	2. He Ain't Heavy, He's My Brother	Epic 26538
			He Ain't Heavy, He's My Brother (7)	
8/26/72	21	5	3. Distant Light	Epic 30958
			Long Cool Woman (In A Black Dress) (2)	
8/10/74	28	2	4. Hollies	Epic 32574
			The Air That I Breathe (6)	
			HOLLY, Buddy/The Crickets	
			Born Charles Hardin Holley on 9/7/36 in Lubbock, Texas. Began recording western and bop demos with Bob Montgomery in 1954. Signed to Decca label in January, 1956 and recorded in Nashville as Buddy Holly & The Three Tunes (Sonny Curtis, lead guitar; Don Guess, bass; and Jerry Allison, drums). In February of 1957, Buddy assembled his backing group, The Crickets (Allison; Niki Sullivan, rhythm guitar; and Joel B. Mauldin, bass) for recordings at Norman Petty's studio in Clovis, New Mexico. Signed to Brunswick and Coral labels (subsidiaries of Decca Records). Because of contract arrangements, all Brunswick records were released as The Crickets and all Coral records were released as Buddy Holly. Holly split from The Crickets in autumn, 1958. Buddy, Ritchie Valens and the Big Bopper were killed in a plane crash near Mason City, Iowa on 2/3/59 (age 22). Holly was inducted into the Rock and Roll Hall of Fame in 1986.	
4/27/59	11	24	● 1. The Buddy Holly Story [G]	Coral 57279
			includes four songs with The Crickets	
			That'll Be The Day (1)/*Peggy Sue* (3)/*Oh, Boy!* (10)	
4/20/63	40	1	2. Reminiscing [K]	Coral 57426
			instrumental backing by The Fireballs dubbed in (1962)	
			HOLLYRIDGE STRINGS, The	
			Arranged and conducted by Stu Phillips.	
7/25/64	15	9	1. The Beatles Song Book [I]	Capitol 2116
			HOLLYWOOD BOWL SYMPHONY ORCHESTRA	
			— see PENNARIO, Leonard	
			HOLLYWOOD STUDIO ORCHESTRA, The	
3/27/61	23	1	1. Exodus [I]	United Art. 6123
			this is not the original soundtrack album	
			HOLMES, Rupert	
			Born on 2/24/47 in Cheshire, England. Moved to New York at age six. Wrote and arranged for The Drifters, Platters and Gene Pitney. Arranged/produced for Barbra Streisand. Wrote the Broadway musical *Drood*.	
1/5/80	33	12	● 1. Partners In Crime	Infinity 9020
			Escape (The Pina Colada Song) (1)/*Him* (6)	
			HONEYDRIPPERS, The	
			A rock superstar gathering: Robert Plant, Jimmy Page, Jeff Beck and Nile Rodgers.	
11/3/84	4	18	▲ 1. Volume One [M]	Es Paranza 90220
			Sea Of Love (3)	

DATE	POS	WKS	ARTIST—RECORD TITLE	LABEL & NO.
			HOOTERS	
			Philadelphia rock quintet led by Rob Hyman and Eric Bazilian (arrangers/musicians/ backing vocalists on Cyndi Lauper's platinum album "She's So Unusual"). Hooter: nickname of their keyboard-harmonica.	
9/28/85	12	30	● 1. Nervous Night	Columbia 39912
8/22/87	27	5	● 2. One Way Home	Columbia 40659
			HOPKIN, Mary	
			Born on 5/3/50 in Pontardawe, Wales. Discovered by the model Twiggy.	
4/12/69	28	7	1. Post Card produced by Paul McCartney *Those Were The Days* (2)	Apple 3351
			HOPKINS, Nicky	
			Born on 2/24/44 in London. Session pianist for The Rolling Stones, The Who, The Kinks and others.	
2/19/72	33	3	1. Jamming With Edward! [I] jam session with Ry Cooder, Mick Jagger, Bill Wyman and Charlie Watts	Rolling S. 39100
			HORNE, Lena	
			Born on 6/30/17 in Brooklyn. Broadway and movie musical star, long married to bandleader Lennie Hayton. Her career reached a new peak in the early 80s with her one-woman Broadway show.	
9/16/57	24	2	1. Lena Horne at the Waldorf Astoria [L]	RCA 1028
11/17/58	20	1	2. Give The Lady What She Wants	RCA 1879
			LENA HORNE/HARRY BELAFONTE:	
6/22/59	13	19	3. Porgy & Bess	RCA 1507
			HORNSBY, Bruce	
			Singer/songwriter/pianist. Leader of piano-based, jazz-influenced pop quintet The Range. Raised in Williamsburg, Virginia and moved to Los Angeles in 1980. Formerly the pianist of Sheena Easton's band. Won the 1986 Best New Artist Grammy Award. The Range includes George Marinelli, Jr., Peter Harris, Joe Puerta and John Molo. **BRUCE HORNSBY AND THE RANGE:**	
10/25/86	3	42	▲ 1. The Way It Is originally released on RCA 8058 (with different cover) *The Way It Is* (1)/*Mandolin Rain* (4)	RCA 5904
5/28/88	5	19	▲ 2. scenes from the southside *The Valley Road* (5)	RCA 6686
			HOROWITZ, Vladimir	
			Classical pianist born Vladimir Gorowicz on 10/3/03 in the U.S.S.R. In 1925, left the U.S.S.R. Changed his name in 1926. Moved to the U.S. in 1928. Married for 56 years (until his death) to Wanda, the daughter of famed conductor Arturo Toscanini. His last public performance was in 1987. Died of a heart attack on 11/5/89 (age 86).	
11/17/62	14	11	1. Vladimir Horowitz (Chopin, Schumann, Rachmaninoff, Liszt) [I]	Columbia 6371
8/28/65	22	8	2. Horowitz at Carnegie Hall - An Historic Return [I-L]	Columbia 728 [2]
			HORTON, Johnny	
			Country singer, born on 4/3/29 in Tyler, Texas. Married to Billie Jean Jones, widow of country music superstar Hank Williams. Killed in an auto accident on 11/5/60.	
2/27/61	8	14	▲ 1. Johnny Horton's Greatest Hits [G] *The Battle Of New Orleans* (1)/*Sink The Bismarck* (3)/ *North To Alaska* (4)	Columbia 8396

DATE	POS	WKS	ARTIST—RECORD TITLE	LABEL & NO.
			HOT CHOCOLATE	
			Interracial rock-soul group formed in England by lead singer Errol Brown in 1970.	
2/17/79	**31**	4	1. Every 1's A Winner	Infinity 9002
			Every 1's A Winner (6)	
			HOT TUNA	
			Formed by Jefferson Airplane members Jorma Kaukonen and Jack Casady.	
8/15/70	**30**	5	1. Hot Tuna [L]	RCA 4353
			HOUSTON, Thelma	
			Soul singer/actress from Leland, Mississippi. In films *Norman...Is That You?*, *Death Scream* and *The Seventh Dwarf*.	
2/26/77	**11**	16	1. Any Way You Like It	Tamla 345
			Don't Leave Me This Way (1)	
			HOUSTON, Whitney	
			Born on 8/9/63 in New Jersey. Daughter of Cissy Houston and cousin of Dionne Warwick. Began career as a fashion model, then worked as a backing vocalist.	
6/15/85	**1(14)**	78	▲ 1. Whitney Houston	Arista 8212
			You Give Good Love (3)/*Saving All My Love For You* (1)/ *How Will I Know* (1)/*Greatest Love Of All* (1)	
6/27/87	**1(11)**	51	▲ 2. Whitney	Arista 8405
			I Wanna Dance With Somebody (Who Loves Me) (1)/*Didn't We Almost Have It All* (1)/*So Emotional* (1)/*Where Do Broken Hearts Go* (1)/*Love Will Save The Day* (9)	
			HUDSON and LANDRY	
			Los Angeles DJs Bob Hudson and Ron Landry. Split up in 1976.	
6/12/71	**30**	4	1. Hanging In There [C]	Dore 324
1/1/72	**33**	4	2. Losing Their Heads [C]	Dore 326
			HUES CORPORATION, The	
			Black vocal trio formed in Los Angeles in 1969: St. Clair Lee, Fleming Williams and H. Ann Kelley. Williams replaced by Tommy Brown after "Rock The Boat."	
7/20/74	**20**	7	1. Freedom For The Stallion	RCA 0323
			Rock The Boat (1)	
			HUGO & LUIGI	
			Producers, songwriters and label executives Hugo Peretti and Luigi Creatore. Hugo died on 5/1/86 (age 68).	
5/11/63	**14**	8	1. The Cascading Voices of the Hugo & Luigi Chorus	RCA 2641
			HUMAN LEAGUE, The	
			Electro-pop band from Sheffield, England, featuring lead singer/synthesizer player Philip Oakey, with vocalists Joanne Catherall and Susanne Sulley.	
4/3/82	**3**	20	● 1. Dare	A&M 4892
			Don't You Want Me (1)	
7/16/83	**22**	8	2. Fascination! [M]	A&M 12501
			(Keep Feeling) Fascination (8)	
11/1/86	**24**	12	3. Crash	A&M 5129
			Human (1)	

DATE	POS	WKS	ARTIST—RECORD TITLE	LABEL & NO.
			HUMBLE PIE	
			Hard-rock band formed in late 1968 in Essex, England. Consisted of Peter Frampton (guitar, vocals), Steve Marriott (vocals, guitar), Greg Ridley (bass) and Jerry Shirley (drums). Frampton left, 1971, replaced by Clem Clempson. Disbanded in 1975.	
11/13/71	21	8	● 1. Performance-Rockin' The Fillmore [L]	A&M 3506 [2]
4/1/72	6	14	● 2. Smokin'	A&M 4342
11/18/72	37	4	3. Lost And Found [E-R] re-issue of their first two albums "Town And Country" and "As Safe As Yesterday Is"	A&M 3513 [2]
4/14/73	13	7	4. Eat It side 4 recorded live in Glasgow, Scotland	A&M 3701 [2]
			HUMPERDINCK, Engelbert	
			Born Arnold George Dorsey on 5/2/36 in Madras, India. To Leicester, England in 1947. First recorded for Decca in 1958. Met Tom Jones' manager, Gordon Mills, in 1965, who suggested his name change to Engelbert Humperdinck (a famous German opera composer). Starred in his own musical variety TV series in 1970.	
7/1/67	7	31	● 1. Release Me *Release Me* (4)	Parrot 71012
1/6/68	10	11	● 2. The Last Waltz	Parrot 71015
9/21/68	12	19	● 3. A Man Without Love	Parrot 71022
4/5/69	12	11	● 4. Engelbert	Parrot 71026
1/3/70	5	19	● 5. Engelbert Humperdinck	Parrot 71030
7/18/70	19	8	● 6. We Made It Happen	Parrot 71038
2/27/71	22	8	● 7. Sweetheart	Parrot 71043
9/18/71	25	5	● 8. Another Time, Another Place	Parrot 71048
12/25/76	17	8	▲ 9. After The Lovin' *After The Lovin'* (8)	Epic 34381
			HUMPHREY, Bobbi	
			Born on 4/25/50 in Dallas. Jazz Flutist. Studied at Southern Methodist and Texas Southern University. First recorded for Blue Note in 1971.	
2/22/75	30	4	1. Satin Doll	Blue Note 344
			HUNTER, Ian	
			Born on 6/3/46 in Shrewsbury, England. Singer/guitarist; leader of "Mott The Hoople," 1969-74.	
6/2/79	35	6	1. You're Never Alone With A Schizophrenic	Chrysalis 1214
			HYMAN, Dick	
			Born on 3/8/27 in New York City. Piano playing composer/conductor/arranger who toured Europe with Benny Goodman in 1950. Staff pianist at WMCA and WNBC-New York from 1951-57. Musical director of the Arthur Godfrey Show from 1958-62.	
11/25/57	21	2	1. 60 Great All Time Songs, Vol. 3 [I] groups of medleys played by Dick on the piano	MGM 3537
6/21/69	30	8	2. Moog - The Electric Eclectics of Dick Hyman [I] synthesized songs on the moog	Command 938

The **Grass Roots**, who recorded many hits for Dunhill in the 60s, claimed their famous name first—so another 60s group with the same name, led by rock legend Arthur Lee, gave themselves the even hipper moniker of Love.

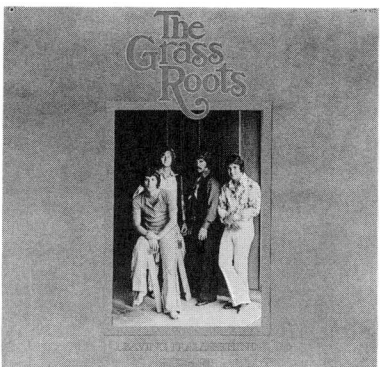
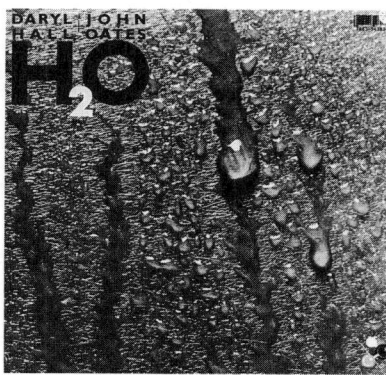

Hall & Oates' highest-charting album ever, 1982's H_2O, climbed to No. 3 and contained the No. 1 hit "Maneater," as well as "One On One" and "Family Man." The album was third in a lengthy streak of platinum albums for the blue-eyed soul duo.

Heart, led by Seattle-based sisters Ann and Nancy Wilson, beat their way to the top in 1976 with *Dreamboat Annie*. After personnel changes and a label switch to Capitol, the siblings pumped life back into their group's flagging career with 1985's *Heart*.

Herman's Hermits racked up 11 top 10 singles in the mid-60s, starred in pop films such as *Hold On!* and *Mrs. Brown, You've Got A Lovely Daughter*, and years later spawned a new wave inspired band called the Tremblers. Both bands featured lead singer Peter "Herman" Noone—who would later go on to host a nostalgia show on the VH-1 music video network.

The Hollies, who took their name from 50s hero Buddy Holly, recorded a reunion album in the 80s. They initially formed in the hottest music town of the 90s—Manchester, England. *The Hollies' Greatest Hits* LP on Imperial was their first top 40 album.

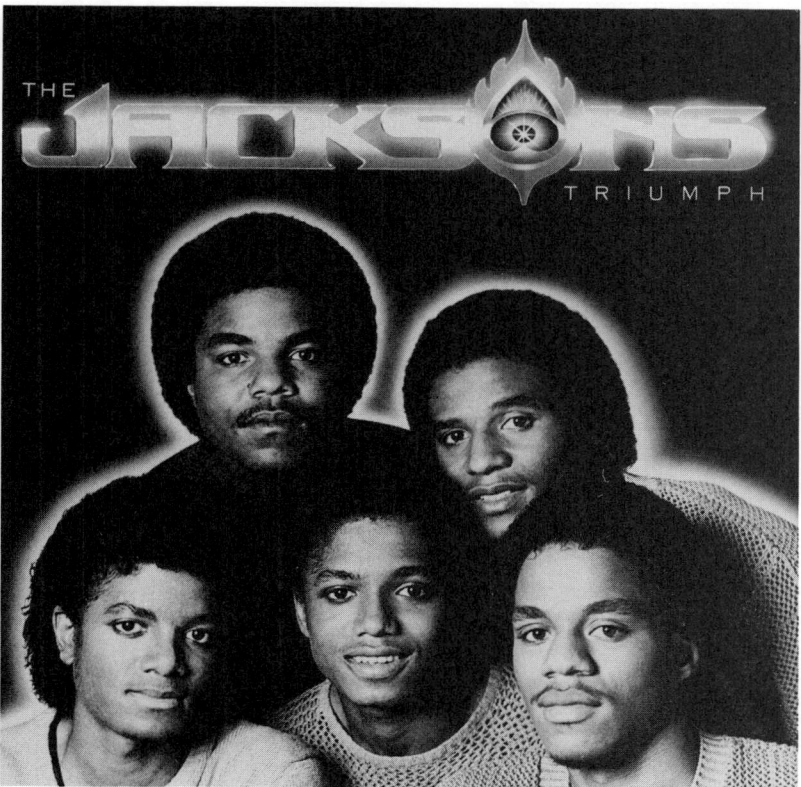

Whitney Houston's debut album, *Whitney Houston*, bore three No. 1 singles—including "Saving All My Love For You," "How Will I Know" and "Greatest Love Of All." Her next LP, *Whitney*, did even better—four of its singles hit the top of the charts.

Billy Idol, former lead vocalist with Brit punkers Generation X, went on to solo fame in the U.S. with such efforts as *Whiplash Smile*. He was reportedly headed for a very major role in the Oliver Stone film about the Doors, but an unfortunate motorcycle accident resulted in his being recast in a less prominent role.

The **Jacksons**, first called the Jackson 5, initially included brothers Michael, Jermaine, Marlon, Jackie, Tito, and later, Randy. Musical family members not in the band, but also hitmakers in their own right, include sisters Janet, LaToya and Rebbie. 1980's *Triumph* included the hit "Can You Feel It."

Jethro Tull's first lead guitarist Mick Abrahams left the band after the group's first album, 1969's *This Was*, to form the equally unlikely-named Blodwyn Pig. Since then, Tull leader Ian Anderson's constant guitar foil has been Martin Barre, and high regard for albums such as 1971's *Aqualung* has continued unabated.

Elton John took his name from two British musicians he'd once played with—saxophonist Elton Dean and Long John Baldry—and, starting with "Your Song," he has become one of the biggest recording artists of all time. 1975's *Rock Of The Westies* was John's last No. 1 record.

DATE	POS	WKS	ARTIST—RECORD TITLE	LABEL & NO.

▮

IAN, Janis

Born Janis Eddy Fink on 4/7/51, New York City. Singer/songwriter/pianist/guitarist.

DATE	POS	WKS	ARTIST—RECORD TITLE	LABEL & NO.
8/19/67	**29**	4	1. Janis Ian	Verve Folk. 3017
			Society's Child	
6/21/75	**1**(1)	24	▲ 2. Between The Lines	Columbia 33394
			At Seventeen (3)	
1/31/76	**12**	10	3. Aftertones	Columbia 33919

ICE CUBE

Oshea Jackson - former lyricist of the Los Angeles rap group N.W.A.

DATE	POS	WKS	ARTIST—RECORD TITLE	LABEL & NO.
6/16/90	**19**	12	● 1. AmeriKKKa's Most Wanted	Priority 57120

ICE-T

Los Angeles-based rapper Tracy Morrow. In films *Breakin'* and *Breakin' II*. Formed own record label, Rhyme Syndicate, in 1988.

DATE	POS	WKS	ARTIST—RECORD TITLE	LABEL & NO.
10/22/88	**35**	5	● 1. Power	Sire 25765
			ICE-T THE ICEBERG:	
11/4/89	**37**	3	● 2. Freedom Of Speech…Just Watch What You Say	Sire 26028

ICICLE WORKS

Liverpool rock trio: Ian McNabb, Chris Layhe and Chris Sharrock.

DATE	POS	WKS	ARTIST—RECORD TITLE	LABEL & NO.
6/30/84	**40**	2	1. Icicle Works	Arista 8202

IDOL, Billy

Born Willem Wolfe Broad on 11/30/55 in London. Leader of the London punk band Generation X from 1977-81. Suffered serious leg injuries from a motorcycle crash on 2/6/90.

DATE	POS	WKS	ARTIST—RECORD TITLE	LABEL & NO.
2/25/84	**6**	38	▲ 1. Rebel Yell	Chrysalis 41450
			Eyes Without A Face (4)	
11/8/86	**6**	21	▲ 2. Whiplash Smile	Chrysalis 41514
			To Be A Lover (6)	
10/17/87	**10**	18	▲ 3. Vital Idol [K]	Chrysalis 41620
			remix versions of eight of Billy's hits	
			Mony Mony 'Live' (1)	
5/26/90	**11**	19	● 4. Charmed Life	Chrysalis 21735
			Cradle Of Love (2)	

IGLESIAS, Julio

Born on 9/23/43 in Madrid, Spain. Spanish singer, immensely popular worldwide. Soccer goalie for the pro Real Madrid team until temporary paralysis from car crash.

DATE	POS	WKS	ARTIST—RECORD TITLE	LABEL & NO.
4/30/83	**32**	9	▲ 1. Julio [F]	Columbia 38640
9/8/84	**5**	21	▲ 2. 1100 Bel Air Place	Columbia 39157
			To All The Girls I've Loved Before (5) with Willie Nelson	

DATE	POS	WKS	ARTIST—RECORD TITLE	LABEL & NO.
			IMPRESSIONS, The	
			Soul group formed in Chicago in 1957, originally known as The Roosters. Consisted of Jerry Butler, Curtis Mayfield, Sam Gooden and brothers Arthur and Richard Brooks. Butler left for a solo career in 1958, replaced by Fred Cash. The Brooks brothers left in 1962, leaving Mayfield as the trio's leader. Mayfield left in 1970 for a solo career, replaced by Leroy Hutson. In 1973, Hutson was replaced by Reggie Torian and Ralph Johnson (Johnson joined Mystique in 1976). Group did film soundtrack for *Three The Hard Way*, 1974. Butler, Mayfield, Gooden and Cash reunited for a tour in 1983.	
9/12/64	8	21	1. Keep On Pushing *Keep On Pushing* (10)/*Amen* (7)	ABC-Para. 493
4/17/65	23	9	2. People Get Ready	ABC-Para. 505
5/4/68	35	5	3. We're A Winner	ABC 635
			INDIGO GIRLS	
			Duo of singers/guitarists Amy Ray and Emily Saliers from Decatur, Georgia.	
7/29/89	22	11	● 1. Indigo Girls	Epic 45044
			INFORMATION SOCIETY	
			Pop-funk-dance outfit formed in Minneapolis in 1985: songwriter Paul Robb, vocalist Kurt Valaquen, keyboardist Amanda Kramer and bassist James Cassidy.	
10/8/88	25	9	● 1. Information Society *What's On Your Mind (Pure Energy)* (3)/*Walking Away* (9)	Tommy Boy 25691
			INGRAM, Luther	
			Born on 11/30/44 in Jackson, Tennessee. Soul singer/songwriter. Sang in gospel group with his brothers. First recorded for Smash in 1965. In the film *Wattstax*.	
12/9/72	39	3	1. If Loving You Is Wrong I Don't Want To Be Right *(If Loving You Is Wrong) I Don't Want To Be Right* (3)	Koko 2202
			INSTANT FUNK	
			Large funk ensemble formed in Philadelphia in 1977. Led by singer/percussionist James Carmichael. Former backup band for Bunny Sigler.	
3/10/79	12	13	● 1. Instant Funk	Salsoul 8513
			INXS	
			Rock sextet formed in Sydney, Australia as The Farris Brothers. Members since group's formation in 1977: Michael Hutchence (lead singer), Kirk Pengilly (guitar), Garry Beers (bass), and brothers Tim (guitar), Andy (keyboards, guitar) and Jon (drums) Farriss. Hutchence starred in the 1987 film *Dogs In Space* and co-founded the 1989 band Max Q.	
2/22/86	11	16	▲ 1. Listen Like Thieves *What You Need* (5)	Atlantic 81277
11/21/87	3	66	▲ 2. Kick *Need You Tonight* (1)/*Devil Inside* (2)/*New Sensation* (3)/ *Never Tear Us Apart* (7)	Atlantic 81796
			IRISH ROVERS, The	
			Irish-born folk quintet. Group formed in Alberta, Canada in 1964.	
5/25/68	24	11	1. The Unicorn *The Unicorn* (7)	Decca 74951

DATE	POS	WKS	ARTIST—RECORD TITLE	LABEL & NO.
			IRON BUTTERFLY	
			San Diego heavy-metal rock band. Consisted of Doug Ingle (lead vocals, keyboards), Erik Braunn (lead guitar), Lee Dorman (bass) and Ron Bushy (drums). Braunn left in late 1969, replaced by Mike Pinera and Larry Reinhardt.	
9/7/68	4	87	● 1. In-A-Gadda-Da-Vida _side 2 is a 17-minute version of the album title_	Atco 250
2/22/69	3	19	● 2. Ball	Atco 280
5/23/70	20	6	3. Iron Butterfly Live [L] _side 2 is a 19-minute version of "In-A-Gadda-Da-Vida"_	Atco 318
9/19/70	16	7	4. Metamorphosis	Atco 339
			IRON MAIDEN	
			Heavy-metal quintet from London. 1981 lineup: Paul Di'anno (lead vocals), Clive Burr, Dave Murray, Steve Harris and Adrian Smith. Burr and Di'anno left in 1982, replaced by Bruce Dickinson (lead vocals) and Nicko McBrain.	
5/22/82	33	5	▲ 1. The Number Of The Beast _features new lead singer Bruce Dickinson_	Harvest 12202
6/18/83	14	14	▲ 2. Piece Of Mind	Capitol 12274
10/6/84	21	7	● 3. Powerslave	Capitol 12321
11/23/85	19	10	4. Live After Death [L]	Capitol 12441 [2]
10/18/86	11	18	● 5. Somewhere In Time	Capitol 12524
5/7/88	12	11	● 6. Seventh Son Of A Seventh Son	Capitol 90258
			ISLEY BROTHERS, The	
			R&B trio of brothers from Cincinnati. Formed in early 50s as a gospel group. Consisted of O'Kelly, Ronald and Rudolph Isley. Moved to New York in 1957 and first recorded for Teenage Records. Trio added their younger brothers Ernie (guitar, drums) and Marvin Isley (bass, percussion) and cousin Chris Jasper (keyboards), from 1973-84. Formed own label T-Neck in 1969. Ernie, Marvin and Chris began recording as the trio Isley, Jasper, Isley in 1984. O'Kelly died of a heart attack on 3/31/86 (age 48).	
5/17/69	22	7	1. It's Our Thing _It's Your Thing_ (2)	T-Neck 3001
9/9/72	29	8	2. Brother, Brother, Brother	T-Neck 3009
9/22/73	8	13	● 3. 3 + 3 _That Lady_ (6)	T-Neck 32453
10/5/74	14	9	● 4. Live It Up	T-Neck 33070
6/21/75	1(1)	21	● 5. The Heat Is On _Fight The Power_ (4)	T-Neck 33536
6/5/76	9	14	● 6. Harvest For The World	T-Neck 33809
4/23/77	6	14	▲ 7. Go For Your Guns	T-Neck 34432
4/22/78	4	14	▲ 8. Showdown	T-Neck 34930
6/23/79	14	7	● 9. Winner Takes All	T-Neck 36077 [2]
4/19/80	8	13	▲ 10. Go All The Way	T-Neck 36305
4/11/81	28	5	● 11. Grand Slam	T-Neck 37080
6/18/83	19	9	● 12. Between The Sheets	T-Neck 38674
			IT'S A BEAUTIFUL DAY	
			San Francisco group led by electric violinist/vocalist David LaFlamme.	
7/18/70	28	5	1. Marrying Maiden	Columbia 1058

DATE	POS	WKS	ARTIST—RECORD TITLE	LABEL & NO.
			IVES, Burl	
			Born on 6/14/09 in Huntington Township, Illinois. Actor/author/singer. Played semi-pro football. Began Broadway career in the late 30s. Worked in "This Is The Army" service show during World War II. Own CBS network radio show "The Wayfaring Stranger" in 1944. Appeared in many films, including *Our Man In Havana*, *East Of Eden*, *Smokey*, *Cat On A Hot Tin Roof* and *The Big Country*. Worked on TV series "The Bold Ones" in the early 70s.	
3/31/62	35	5	1. The Versatile Burl Ives! *A Little Bitty Tear* (9)	Decca 4152
6/30/62	24	4	2. It's Just My Funny Way Of Laughin' *Funny Way Of Laughin'* (10)	Decca 4279
			# J	
			JACKSON, Freddie	
			Soul singer/songwriter; raised in Harlem. Backup singer for Melba Moore, Evelyn King and others. Member of Mystic Merlin.	
7/13/85	10	36	▲ 1. Rock Me Tonight	Capitol 12404
11/22/86	23	26	▲ 2. Just Like The First Time	Capitol 12495
			JACKSON, Janet	
			Born on 5/16/66 in Gary, Indiana. Sister of The Jacksons (youngest of nine children). Debuted at age seven at the MGM Grand in Las Vegas with her brothers. At age 10, she played Penny Gordon Woods in the TV series "Good Times" (1977-79); in the cast of "Diff'rent Strokes" (1981-82) and later "Fame." Married briefly in 1984 to James DeBarge.	
3/29/86	1(2)	77	▲ 1. Control *What Have You Done For Me Lately* (4)/*Nasty* (3)/ *When I Think Of You* (1)/*Control* (5)/*Let's Wait Awhile* (2)	A&M 5106
10/7/89	1(4)	55+	▲ 2. Janet Jackson's Rhythm Nation 1814 "1814" refers to year Francis Scott Key wrote national anthem *Miss You Much* (1)/*Rhythm Nation* (2)/*Escapade* (1)/*Alright* (4)/ *Come Back To Me* (2)	A&M 3920
			JACKSON, Jermaine	
			Born on 12/11/54 in Gary, Indiana. Fourth oldest of the Jackson family. Vocalist/ bassist of The Jackson 5 until group left Motown in 1976. Married Hazel Joy Gordy, daughter of Berry Gordy, Jr., on 12/15/73. Re-joined The Jacksons in 1984 for their "Victory" album and tour.	
9/23/72	27	8	1. Jermaine *Daddy's Home* (9)	Motown 752
5/3/80	6	17	● 2. Let's Get Serious *Let's Get Serious* (9)	Motown 928
5/26/84	19	16	● 3. Jermaine Jackson	Arista 8203
			JACKSON, Joe	
			Born on 8/11/55 in Burton-on-Trent, England. Singer/songwriter/pianist, featuring an ever-changing music style. Moved to New York City in 1982.	
6/2/79	20	11	● 1. Look Sharp!	A&M 4743
11/10/79	22	8	2. I'm The Man	A&M 4794
9/18/82	4	30	● 3. Night And Day *Steppin' Out* (6)	A&M 4906
4/21/84	20	16	4. Body and Soul	A&M 5000
5/3/86	34	8	5. Big World [L] three-sided album from a special live concert set; includes an eight-page booklet with lyrics in six different languages	A&M 6021 [2]

DATE	POS	WKS	ARTIST—RECORD TITLE	LABEL & NO.
			JACKSON, Michael	
			Born on 8/29/58 in Gary, Indiana; seventh of nine children. Became lead singer of his brothers' group, The Jackson 5 (later known as The Jacksons), at age five. His 1982 *Thriller* album, with sales of over 40 million copies, is the best-selling album in history. Internationally recognized as one of the most popular stars of the 80s.	
2/26/72	**14**	12	1. Got To Be There *Got To Be There* (4)/*Rockin' Robin* (2)	Motown 747
9/23/72	**5**	15	2. Ben *Ben* (1)	Motown 755
9/8/79	**3**	52	▲ 3. Off The Wall *Don't Stop 'Til You Get Enough* (1)/*Rock With You* (1)/ *Off The Wall* (10)/*She's Out Of My Life* (10)	Epic 35745
12/25/82	**1**(37)	91	▲ 4. Thriller the best-selling album in history; produced by Quincy Jones; 1983 Grammy winner: Album of the Year *The Girl Is Mine* (2)/*Billie Jean* (1)/*Beat It* (1)/ *Wanna Be Startin' Somethin'* (5)/*Human Nature* (7)/ *P.Y.T. (Pretty Young Thing)* (10)/*Thriller* (4)	Epic 38112
9/26/87	**1**(6)	54	▲ 5. Bad *I Just Can't Stop Loving You* (1)/*Bad* (1)/ *The Way You Make Me Feel* (1)/*Man In The Mirror* (1)/ *Dirty Diana* (1)/*Smooth Criminal* (7)	Epic 40600
			JACKSON, Millie	
			Born on 7/15/44 in Thompson, Georgia. Soul singer/songwriter. To Newark, New Jersey in 1958. Worked as a model in New York City. Professional singing debut at Club Zanzibar in Hoboken, New Jersey, in 1964. First recorded for MGM in 1970.	
12/7/74	**21**	12	● 1. Caught Up	Spring 6703
12/17/77	**34**	7	● 2. Feelin' Bitchy	Spring 6715
			JACKSON 5/JACKSONS, The	
			Quintet of brothers formed and managed by their father beginning in 1966 in Gary, Indiana. Consisted of Sigmund ''Jackie'' (b: 5/4/51), Toriano ''Tito'' (b: 10/15/53), Jermaine (b: 12/11/54), Marlon (b: 3/12/57) and lead singer Michael (b: 8/29/58). First recorded for Steeltown in 1968. Known as The Jackson 5 from 1968-75. Jermaine replaced by Randy (b: 10/29/61) in 1976. Jermaine re-joined the group for 1984's highly publicized *Victory* album and tour. Michael has also recorded solo since 1971. Marlon left for a solo career in 1987. Their sisters Rebbie, La Toya and Janet backed the group; each had a string of solo hits. Quartet lineup since 1989: Jackie, Tito, Jermaine and Randy Jackson. **THE JACKSON 5:**	
1/31/70	**5**	21	1. Diana Ross Presents The Jackson 5 *I Want You Back* (1)	Motown 700
6/6/70	**4**	21	2. ABC *ABC* (1)/*The Love You Save* (1)	Motown 709
9/26/70	**4**	23	3. Third Album *I'll Be There* (1)/*Mama's Pearl* (2)	Motown 718
5/8/71	**11**	14	4. Maybe Tomorrow *Never Can Say Goodbye* (2)	Motown 735
10/16/71	**16**	11	5. Goin' Back To Indiana [TV] TV special with guests Bill Cosby and Tom Smothers	Motown 742
1/8/72	**12**	15	6. Jackson 5 Greatest Hits [G] *Sugar Daddy* (10)	Motown 741
6/17/72	**7**	17	7. Lookin' Through The Windows	Motown 750
11/2/74	**16**	7	8. Dancing Machine	Motown 780
8/2/75	**36**	3	9. Moving Violation	Motown 829

DATE	POS	WKS	ARTIST—RECORD TITLE	LABEL & NO.
			THE JACKSONS:	
1/29/77	**36**	3	● 10. The Jacksons	Epic 34229
			Enjoy Yourself (6)	
3/10/79	**11**	15	▲ 11. Destiny	Epic 35552
			Shake Your Body (Down To The Ground) (7)	
10/18/80	**10**	18	▲ 12. Triumph	Epic 36424
12/12/81	**30**	8	13. Jacksons Live [L]	Epic 37545 [2]
7/21/84	**4**	15	▲ 14. Victory	Epic 38946
			State Of Shock (3)	
			JAGGER, Mick	
			Born Michael Phillip Jagger on 7/26/43 in Dartford, England. Lead singer of The Rolling Stones.	
3/16/85	**13**	12	▲ 1. She's The Boss	Columbia 39940
			Just Another Night	
			JAMAL, Ahmad	
			Born Fritz Jones on 7/2/30 in Pittsburgh. Jazz pianist/leader. With George Hudson. Formed own trio, the Three Strings with Ray Crawford (guitar) and Eddie Calhoun (bass). Recorded for Okeh in 1951.	
9/22/58	**3**	52	1. But Not For Me/Ahmad Jamal at the Pershing [I-L]	Argo 628
11/17/58	**11**	16	2. Ahmad Jamal, Volume IV [I-L]	Argo 636
2/1/60	**32**	7	3. Jamal At The Penthouse [I]	Argo 646
			JAMES, Bob	
			Jazz fusion keyboardist. Born on 12/25/39 in Marshall, Missouri. Discovered by Quincy Jones in 1962. Was Sarah Vaughan's musical director for four years. In 1973, became arranger of CTI records. In 1976, appointed director of progressive A&R at CBS Records. Formed own label, Tappan Zee, in 1977. Wrote/performed theme for the TV show "Taxi."	
5/7/77	**38**	2	1. BJ4 [I]	CTI 7074
2/24/79	**37**	2	● 2. Touchdown [I]	Tappan Zee 35594
			BOB JAMES AND EARL KLUGH:	
12/1/79	**23**	13	● 3. One On One [I]	Tappan Zee 36241
			JAMES, Harry	
			Born on 3/15/16 in Albany, Georgia; died on 7/5/83. Star trumpet player and bandleader. Achieved fame playing with Benny Goodman in the late 30s. His own band was very popular during the 40s.	
11/12/55	**10**	2	1. Harry James in Hi-Fi	Capitol 654
			featuring vocals by Helen Forrest	
			JAMES, Rick	
			"Punk funk" singer/songwriter/guitarist. Born James Johnson on 2/1/52 in Buffalo. In Mynah Birds band with Neil Young in the late 60s. To London; formed the band Main Line. Returned to the U.S. and formed Stone City Band; produced Teena Marie, Mary Jane Girls, Eddie Murphy and others.	
7/22/78	**13**	16	● 1. Come Get It!	Gordy 981
2/17/79	**16**	16	2. Bustin' Out Of L Seven	Gordy 984
12/1/79	**34**	3	3. Fire It Up	Gordy 990
5/30/81	**3**	27	▲ 4. Street Songs	Gordy 1002
6/12/82	**13**	10	● 5. Throwin' Down	Gordy 6005
9/10/83	**16**	12	● 6. Cold Blooded	Gordy 6043

DATE	POS	WKS	ARTIST—RECORD TITLE	LABEL & NO.
			JAMES, Tommy	
			Born Thomas Jackson on 4/29/47 in Dayton, Ohio. To Niles, Michigan at age 11. Formed pop group The Shondells at age 12. Recorded "Hanky Panky" on the Snap label in 1963. Tommy relocated to Pittsburgh in 1965 after a DJ there popularized "Hanky Panky." Original master was sold to Roulette, whereupon Tommy recruited Pittsburgh group The Raconteurs to become the official Shondells. Consisted of Mike Vale (bass), Pete Lucia (drums), Eddie Gray (guitar) and Ronnie Rosman (organ). Began recording as a solo artist in 1970.	
			TOMMY JAMES AND THE SHONDELLS:	
2/8/69	**8**	14	1. Crimson & Clover	Roulette 42023
			Crimson & Clover (1)/*Crystal Blue Persuasion* (2)	
12/27/69	**21**	10	2. The Best Of Tommy James & The Shondells [G]	Roulette 42040
			JAMES GANG, The	
			Cleveland hard-rock band. Lineup in 1969 consisted of Joe Walsh (guitar, keyboards, vocals), Jim Fox (drums) and Tom Kriss (bass). Kriss replaced by Dale Peters in 1970. Walsh left in late 1971, replaced by Dominic Troiano and Roy Kenner. Troiano left in 1973, replaced by Tommy Bolin. Group disbanded in 1976.	
8/29/70	**20**	12	● 1. James Gang Rides Again	ABC 711
5/8/71	**27**	16	● 2. Thirds	ABC 721
9/25/71	**24**	5	● 3. James Gang Live In Concert [L]	ABC 733
			JAN & DEAN	
			Jan Berry (b: 4/3/41) and Dean Torrence (b: 3/10/40) formed group called the Barons while attending high school in Los Angeles. Jan & Dean and Barons member Arnie Ginsburg recorded "Jennie Lee" in Jan's garage. Dean left for a six-month Army Reserve stint, whereupon Jan signed with Doris Day's label, Arwin, and the record was released as by Jan & Arnie. Upon Dean's return from the service, Arnie joined the Navy, and Jan & Dean signed with Herb Alpert's Dore label. Jan was critically injured in an auto accident on 4/19/66. Duo made a comeback in 1978, after their biographical film *Dead Man's Curve* aired on TV.	
9/21/63	**32**	4	1. Surf City And Other Swingin' Cities	Liberty 7314
			Surf City (1)	
2/22/64	**22**	2	2. Drag City	Liberty 7339
			Drag City (10)	
1/16/65	**40**	1	3. The Little Old Lady From Pasadena	Liberty 7377
			The Little Old Lady (From Pasadena) (3)	
5/8/65	**33**	3	4. Command Performance/Live In Person [L]	Liberty 7403
			JANKOWSKI, Horst	
			Born on 1/30/36 in Berlin, Germany. Jazz pianist.	
7/24/65	**18**	12	1. The Genius Of Jankowski! [I]	Mercury 60993
			A Walk In The Black Forest	
			JARREAU, Al	
			Born on 3/12/40 in Milwaukee. Soul-jazz vocalist. Has won four Grammys. Has masters degree in psychology from the University of Iowa. Worked clubs in San Francisco with George Duke.	
8/2/80	**27**	5	● 1. This Time	Warner 3434
8/29/81	**9**	20	▲ 2. Breakin' Away	Warner 3576
4/23/83	**13**	12	● 3. Jarreau	Warner 23801

DATE	POS	WKS	ARTIST—RECORD TITLE	LABEL & NO.
			JAY & THE AMERICANS	
			Group formed in late 1959 by New York University students as the Harbor-Lites: John "Jay" Traynor (formerly with the Mystics), Sandy Yaguda, Kenny Vance (later a Hollywood musical director) and Howie Kane. Guitarist Marty Sanders joined during production of their first album in 1961. Traynor left after their first hit and was replaced by lead singer Jay Black (real name: David Blatt; b: 11/2/38) in 1962.	
1/15/66	**21**	5	1. Jay & The Americans Greatest Hits! [G]	United Art. 6453
			JEFFERSON AIRPLANE/STARSHIP	
			Formed as Jefferson Airplane in San Francisco, 1965. Consisted of Marty Balin and Signe Anderson (vocals), Paul Kantner (vocals, guitar), Jorma Kaukonen (guitar), Jack Casady (bass) and Skip Spence (drums). Grace Slick and Spencer Dryden joined in 1966, replacing Anderson and Spence. Slick had been in the Great Society. Spence then formed Moby Grape. Dryden replaced by Joey Covington in 1970. Casady and Kaukonen left by 1974 to go full-time with Hot Tuna. Balin left in 1971, rejoined in 1975, by which time group was renamed Jefferson Starship and consisted of Slick, Kantner, Papa John Creach (violin), David Freiberg (bass), Craig Chaquico (pronounced Chuck-ee-so; guitar), Pete Sears (bass) and John Barbata (drums). Slick left group from June, 1978 to January, 1981 due to personal problems. In 1979, singer Mickey Thomas joined (replaced Balin), along with Aynsley Dunbar who replaced Barbata. Don Baldwin (formerly with Snail) replaced Dunbar in 1982. Kantner left in 1984, and, due to legal difficulties, band's name was shortened to Starship, whose lineup included Slick, Thomas, Sears, Chaquico and Baldwin. Slick left in early 1988. In 1989, the original 1966 lineup, Balin, Slick, Kantner, Kaukonen and Casady, reunited as Jefferson Airplane with Kenny Aronoff (formerly with John Cougar Mellencamp) replacing Dryden. Continuing as Starship were Thomas, Chaquico, Baldwin, Brett Bloomfield (bass) and Mark Morgan (keyboards).	
			JEFFERSON AIRPLANE:	
1/7/67	**17**	9	1. After Bathing At Baxter's	RCA 1511
5/6/67	**3**	29	● 2. Surrealistic Pillow	RCA 3766
			Somebody To Love (5)/*White Rabbit* (8)	
9/21/68	**6**	12	● 3. Crown Of Creation	RCA 4058
3/8/69	**17**	8	4. Bless Its Pointed Little Head [L]	RCA 4133
11/29/69	**13**	13	● 5. Volunteers	RCA 4238
12/12/70	**12**	14	● 6. The Worst Of Jefferson Airplane [G]	RCA 4459
9/18/71	**11**	11	● 7. Bark	Grunt 1001
9/9/72	**20**	9	● 8. Long John Silver	Grunt 1007
			JEFFERSON STARSHIP:	
11/23/74	**11**	10	● 9. Dragon Fly	Grunt 0717
7/26/75	**1**(4)	32	● 10. Red Octopus	Grunt 0999
			Miracles (3)	
7/24/76	**3**	16	▲ 11. Spitfire	Grunt 1557
2/19/77	**37**	3	● 12. Flight Log (1966-1976) [K]	Grunt 1255 [2]
			anthology of Airplane, Starship, Hot Tuna, Slick and Kantner solo releases	
3/18/78	**5**	23	▲ 13. Earth	Grunt 2515
			Count On Me (8)	
2/24/79	**20**	5	● 14. Gold [G]	Grunt 3247
12/8/79	**10**	17	● 15. Freedom At Point Zero	Grunt 3452
5/9/81	**26**	16	● 16. Modern Times	Grunt 3848
11/13/82	**26**	11	17. Winds Of Change	Grunt 4372
7/7/84	**28**	8	● 18. Nuclear Furniture	Grunt 4921
			STARSHIP:	
10/26/85	**7**	33	● 19. Knee Deep In The Hoopla	Grunt 5488
			We Built This City (1)/*Sara* (1)	

DATE	POS	WKS	ARTIST—RECORD TITLE		LABEL & NO.
8/1/87	**12**	9	● 20. No Protection *It's Not Over ('Til It's Over)* (9)/ *Nothing's Gonna Stop Us Now* (1)		Grunt 6413
			JENKINS, Gordon		
			Born on 5/12/10 in Webster Groves, Missouri; died on 5/1/84. Pianist/arranger in the early 1930s with Isham Jones, Benny Goodman and others. Musical director and conductor for Decca Records beginning in 1945.		
11/24/56	**13**	4	1. Gordon Jenkins complete Manhattan Tower a musical narrative originally composed by Jenkins in 1945		Capitol 766
			JENNINGS, Waylon		
			Born on 6/15/37 in Littlefield, Texas. While working as a DJ in Lubbock, Texas, Waylon befriended Buddy Holly. Holly produced Waylon's first record "Jole Blon" in 1958. Waylon then joined with Buddy's backing band as bass guitarist on the fateful "Winter Dance Party" tour in 1959. Established himself in the mid-70s as a leader of the "outlaw" movement in country music. Married to Jessi Colter since 1969. In the films *Nashville Rebel*, *MacKintosh And T.J.* and *Urban Cowboy*.		
2/14/76	**10**	14	▲ 1. The Outlaws **WAYLON JENNINGS/WILLIE NELSON/JESSI COLTER/TOMPALL GLASER**		RCA 1321
8/21/76	**34**	2	● 2. Are You Ready For The Country		RCA 1816
5/28/77	**15**	12	▲ 3. Ol' Waylon		RCA 2317
2/18/78	**12**	9	▲ 4. Waylon & Willie **WAYLON JENNINGS & WILLIE NELSON**		RCA 2686
6/23/79	**28**	4	▲ 5. Greatest Hits	[G]	RCA 3378
7/5/80	**36**	3	● 6. Music Man		RCA 3602
4/24/82	**39**	2	7. Black On Black		RCA 4247
			JETHRO TULL		
			Progressive rock group formed in 1968 in Blackpool, England. Consisted of Ian Anderson (b: 8/10/47, Edinburgh, Scotland; lead singer, flutist), Mick Abrahams (guitar), Glenn Cornick (bass) and Clive Bunker (drums). Named band after 18th century agriculturist Jethro Tull. Abrahams replaced by Martin Barre in 1968. Added keyboardist John Evans in 1970. Cornick replaced by Jeffrey Hammond-Hammond in 1971. Bunker left in late 1971 and was replaced by Barriemore Barlow, who in turn was replaced by John Glascock (died in 1979). Ian has revamped his lineup several times since then. 1989 lineup included Anderson, Barre, bassist David Pegg and drummer Doane Perry.		
10/25/69	**20**	9	● 1. Stand Up		Reprise 6360
5/16/70	**11**	17	● 2. Benefit		Reprise 6400
5/15/71	**7**	32	▲ 3. Aqualung		Reprise 2035
5/20/72	**1**(2)	20	● 4. Thick As A Brick		Reprise 2072
11/18/72	**3**	21	● 5. Living In The Past primarily features unreleased material (1968-1971); side 3 recorded live in Carnegie Hall	[K]	Chrysalis 2106 [2]
7/28/73	**1**(1)	14	● 6. A Passion Play		Chrysalis 1040
11/2/74	**2**(3)	23	● 7. War Child		Chrysalis 1067
10/4/75	**7**	8	● 8. Minstrel In The Gallery		Chrysalis 1082
1/31/76	**13**	9	▲ 9. M.U. - The Best Of Jethro Tull	[G]	Chrysalis 1078
6/5/76	**14**	7	10. Too Old To Rock 'N' Roll: Too Young To Die!		Chrysalis 1111
3/12/77	**8**	14	● 11. Songs From The Wood		Chrysalis 1132
5/6/78	**19**	8	● 12. Heavy Horses		Chrysalis 1175
10/28/78	**21**	8	● 13. Jethro Tull Live - Bursting Out	[L]	Chrysalis 1201 [2]
10/13/79	**22**	5	● 14. Stormwatch		Chrysalis 1238

DATE	POS	WKS	ARTIST—RECORD TITLE	LABEL & NO.
10/4/80	**30**	4	15. "A"	Chrysalis 1301
5/22/82	**19**	7	16. The Broadsword And The Beast	Chrysalis 1380
12/5/87	**32**	8	● 17. Crest Of A Knave	Chrysalis 41590

JETS, The

Minneapolis-based family band consisting of eight brothers and sisters: Leroy, Eddie, Eugene, Haini, Rudy, Kathi, Elizabeth and Moana Wolfgramm. Their parents are from the South Pacific country of Tonga. All members play at least two instruments. Eugene left group and formed duo Boys Club in 1988.

DATE	POS	WKS	ARTIST—RECORD TITLE	LABEL & NO.
5/17/86	**21**	25	▲ 1. The Jets *Crush On You* (3)/*You Got It All* (3)	MCA 5667
6/11/88	**35**	6	● 2. Magic *Cross My Broken Heart* (7)/*Rocket 2 U* (6)/*Make It Real* (4)	MCA 42085

JETT, Joan

Born on 9/22/60 in Philadelphia. Played guitar with the Los Angeles female rock band The Runaways, 1975-78. Formed her backing band The Blackhearts in 1980. Starred in the 1987 film *Light Of Day* as the leader of a rock band called The Barbusters.

JOAN JETT & THE BLACKHEARTS:

DATE	POS	WKS	ARTIST—RECORD TITLE	LABEL & NO.
2/6/82	**2**(3)	20	▲ 1. I Love Rock-n-Roll *I Love Rock 'N Roll* (1)/*Crimson And Clover* (7)	Boardwalk 33243
7/23/83	**20**	10	● 2. Album	Blackheart 5437
9/10/88	**19**	18	▲ 3. Up Your Alley *I Hate Myself For Loving You* (8)	Blackheart 44146

JOAN JETT:

DATE	POS	WKS	ARTIST—RECORD TITLE	LABEL & NO.
2/24/90	**36**	3	4. The Hit List *Joan's cover versions of rock classics of the last three decades*	Blackheart 45473

JIMENEZ, Jose — see DANA, Bill

JIVE BUNNY AND THE MASTERMIXERS

British dance outfit: composer/mixer John Pickles, DJ Les Hemstock and mixers Andy Pickles and Ian Morgan.

DATE	POS	WKS	ARTIST—RECORD TITLE	LABEL & NO.
1/27/90	**26**	6	● 1. The Album	Atco/Music Fan. 91322

JOBIM, Antonio Carlos

Brazilian guitarist/pianist/vocalist.

DATE	POS	WKS	ARTIST—RECORD TITLE	LABEL & NO.
5/13/67	**19**	6	1. Francis Albert Sinatra & Antonio Carlos Jobim	Reprise 1021

JOEL, Billy

Born William Martin Joel on 5/9/49 in Long Island, New York. Formed his first band The Echoes in 1964, which later became The Lost Souls. Member of Long Island group The Hassles in the late 60s. Later formed rock duo, Attila, with The Hassles' drummer Jon Small. Signed solo to Columbia Records in 1973. Involved in a serious motorcycle accident on Long Island in 1982. Married supermodel Christie Brinkley in 1985. Toured and recorded in Russia in 1987. Joel composed all of his hits.

DATE	POS	WKS	ARTIST—RECORD TITLE	LABEL & NO.
3/23/74	**27**	7	▲ 1. Piano Man	Columbia 32544
12/21/74	**35**	2	● 2. Streetlife Serenade	Columbia 33146
11/12/77	**2**(6)	70	▲ 3. The Stranger *Just The Way You Are* (3)	Columbia 34987
11/4/78	**1**(8)	34	▲ 4. 52nd Street *1979 Grammy winner: Album of the Year* *My Life* (3)	Columbia 35609
3/22/80	**1**(6)	35	▲ 5. Glass Houses *You May Be Right* (7)/*It's Still Rock And Roll To Me* (1)	Columbia 36384

DATE	POS	WKS	ARTIST—RECORD TITLE	LABEL & NO.
10/3/81	8	10	▲ 6. Songs In The Attic [L] 1980 concert tour recordings of pre-*Stranger* songs	Columbia 37461
10/16/82	7	23	▲ 7. The Nylon Curtain	Columbia 38200
8/20/83	4	62	▲ 8. An Innocent Man *Tell Her About It* (1)/*Uptown Girl* (3)/*An Innocent Man* (10)	Columbia 38837
7/27/85	6	26	▲ 9. Greatest Hits, Volume I & Volume II [G] *You're Only Human (Second Wind)* (9)	Columbia 40121 [2]
8/23/86	7	29	▲ 10. The Bridge *Modern Woman* (10)/*A Matter Of Trust* (10)	Columbia 40402
11/21/87	38	3	● 11. Kohu,ept [L] 16 hits recorded live in the Soviet Union in 1987; translation of Russian title: "In Concert"	Columbia 40996 [2]
11/11/89	1(1)	28	▲ 12. Storm Front *We Didn't Start The Fire* (1)/*I Go To Extremes* (6)	Columbia 44366

JOHN, Elton

Born Reginald Kenneth Dwight on 3/25/47 in Pinner, Middlesex, England. Formed his first group Bluesology in 1966. Group backed visiting U.S. soul artists and later became Long John Baldry's backing band. Took the name of Elton John from the first names of Bluesology members Elton Dean and John Baldry. Teamed up with lyricist Bernie Taupin beginning in 1969. Formed Rocket Records in 1973. Played the Pinball Wizard in the film version of *Tommy*.

DATE	POS	WKS	ARTIST—RECORD TITLE	LABEL & NO.
10/31/70	4	28	● 1. Elton John *Your Song* (8)	Uni 73090
1/23/71	5	20	● 2. Tumbleweed Connection	Uni 73096
4/17/71	36	4	● 3. "Friends" [S]	Paramount 6004
5/29/71	11	12	4. 11-17-70 [L] title is date of a live New York radio concert broadcast	Uni 93105
12/4/71	8	25	● 5. Madman Across The Water	Uni 93120
6/24/72	1(5)	25	● 6. Honky Chateau *Rocket Man* (6)/*Honky Cat* (8)	Uni 93135
2/17/73	1(2)	27	● 7. Don't Shoot Me I'm Only The Piano Player *Crocodile Rock* (1)/*Daniel* (2)	MCA 2100
10/20/73	1(8)	43	● 8. Goodbye Yellow Brick Road *Goodbye Yellow Brick Road* (2)/*Bennie And The Jets* (1)	MCA 10003 [2]
7/6/74	1(4)	20	● 9. Caribou *Don't Let The Sun Go Down On Me* (2)/*The Bitch Is Back* (4)	MCA 2116
11/30/74	1(10)	20	● 10. Elton John - Greatest Hits [G]	MCA 2128
2/8/75	6	8	11. Empty Sky [E-R] Elton's first album originally released in 1969	MCA 2130
6/7/75	1(7)	24	● 12. Captain Fantastic And The Brown Dirt Cowboy *Someone Saved My Life Tonight* (4)	MCA 2142
11/8/75	1(3)	9	● 13. Rock Of The Westies *Island Girl* (1)	MCA 2163
5/22/76	4	8	● 14. Here And There [L] side 1: live in London; side 2: live in New York (both 1974)	MCA 2197
11/13/76	3	12	▲ 15. Blue Moves [2] *Sorry Seems To Be The Hardest Word* (6)	MCA/Rocket 11004
10/29/77	21	8	▲ 16. Elton John's Greatest Hits, Volume II [G] *Lucy In The Sky With Diamonds* (1)/*Philadelphia Freedom* (1)/ *Don't Go Breaking My Heart* (1) with Kiki Dee	MCA 3027
11/18/78	15	7	▲ 17. A Single Man	MCA 3065
11/10/79	35	4	18. Victim Of Love	MCA 5104
6/7/80	13	9	● 19. 21 At 33 *Little Jeannie* (3)	MCA 5121

DATE	POS	WKS	ARTIST—RECORD TITLE	LABEL & NO.
6/13/81	**21**	5	20. The Fox	Geffen 2002
5/15/82	**17**	8	● 21. Jump Up!	Geffen 2013
6/25/83	**25**	13	● 22. Too Low For Zero *I Guess That's Why They Call It The Blues* (4)	Geffen 4006
7/28/84	**20**	14	● 23. Breaking Hearts *Sad Songs (Say So Much)* (5)	Geffen 24031
1/9/88	**24**	8	● 24. Live In Australia [L] recorded live, on 12/14/86, in Sydney, Australia with the Melbourne Symphony Orchestra *Candle In The Wind* (6)	MCA 8022 [2]
7/9/88	**16**	19	● 25. Reg Strikes Back *I Don't Wanna Go On With You Like That* (2)	MCA 6240
9/23/89	**23**	11	▲ 26. Sleeping With The Past	MCA 6321

JOHNNY AND THE HURRICANES

Rock and roll instrumental band formed as the Orbits in Toledo, Ohio in 1958. Consisted of leader John Pocisk "Paris" (saxophone), Paul Tesluk (organ), Dave Yorko (guitar), Lionel "Butch" Mattice (bass) and Tony Kaye (drums; replaced in late 1959 by Bo Savich). First recorded for Twirl in 1959. Paris had own Attila label from 1965-70.

DATE	POS	WKS	ARTIST—RECORD TITLE	LABEL & NO.
4/18/60	**34**	3	1. Stormsville [I]	Warwick 2010

JOHNSON, Don

Born on 12/15/49 in Flatt Creek, Missouri. Actor/singer. Played Sonny Crockett on TV's "Miami Vice."

DATE	POS	WKS	ARTIST—RECORD TITLE	LABEL & NO.
9/20/86	**17**	11	● 1. Heartbeat *Heartbeat* (5)	Epic 40366

JOLI, France

French-Canadian singer from Montreal. Age 16 in 1979.

DATE	POS	WKS	ARTIST—RECORD TITLE	LABEL & NO.
10/13/79	**26**	6	1. France Joli	Prelude 12170

JOLSON, Al

Born Asa Yoelson in St. Petersburg, Russia on 3/26/1886; died on 10/23/50. Raised in Washington, D.C. and after performing with a minstrel show troupe and in vaudeville, he first electrified Broadway in 1911 with his dramatic vocal style, extraordinary stage presence and personal rapport with audiences. For most of the next 20 years, Jolson was the king of the American musical. Appeared in 1927's *The Jazz Singer*, which ushered in the age of sound motion pictures; but by the 30s his career was in decline. The hit 1946 film *The Jolson Story*, with Al's newly recorded vocals, brought about an incredible comeback.

DATE	POS	WKS	ARTIST—RECORD TITLE	LABEL & NO.
6/22/63	**40**	1	1. The Best Of Jolson [G] Al's recordings for the soundtracks *The Jolson Story* and *Jolson Sings Again*	Decca 169 [2]

JONES, Grace

Model/film actress/singer, born on 5/19/52 in Spanishtown, Jamaica. Moved to Syracuse, New York in 1964. Appeared in the films *Conan The Destroyer*, *A View To A Kill* and *Vamp*.

DATE	POS	WKS	ARTIST—RECORD TITLE	LABEL & NO.
7/11/81	**32**	4	1. Nightclubbing	Island 9624

JONES, Howard

Born on 2/23/55 in Southampton, England. Pop singer/songwriter/synthesizer wizard.

DATE	POS	WKS	ARTIST—RECORD TITLE	LABEL & NO.
5/4/85	**10**	21	▲ 1. Dream Into Action *Things Can Only Get Better* (5)	Elektra 60390
6/14/86	**34**	6	2. Action Replay [M] six tracks; includes three remixes and two previously unreleased songs *No One Is To Blame* (4)	Elektra 60466

DATE	POS	WKS	ARTIST—RECORD TITLE	LABEL & NO.
			JONES, Jack	
			Born on 1/14/38 in Los Angeles. Son of actor/singer Allan Jones, who had the #8 pop hit "The Donkey Serenade" the year Jack was born.	
2/8/64	**18**	24	1. Wives And Lovers	Kapp 3352
2/6/65	**11**	11	2. Dear Heart	Kapp 3415
7/3/65	**29**	6	3. My Kind Of Town	Kapp 3433
9/3/66	**9**	15	4. The Impossible Dream	Kapp 3486
4/29/67	**23**	6	5. Lady	Kapp 3511
			JONES, Jonah	
			Born Robert Jones on 12/31/08 in Louisville, Kentucky. Jazz trumpet player.	
3/10/58	**7**	17	1. Muted Jazz [I]	Capitol 839
			THE JONAH JONES QUARTET:	
4/28/58	**7**	19	2. Swingin' On Broadway [I]	Capitol 963
9/8/58	**14**	5	3. Jumpin' With Jonah [I]	Capitol 1039
			JONES, Quincy	
			Born Quincy Delight Jones, Jr. on 3/14/33 in Chicago. Raised in Seattle. Composer/producer/conductor/arranger. Began as a jazz trumpeter with Lionel Hampton, 1950-53. Music director for Mercury Records in 1961, then vice president in 1964. Wrote scores for many films, 1965-73. Scored TV series "Roots" in 1977. Arranger and producer for hundreds of successful singers and orchestras. Produced Michael Jackson's mega albums *Off The Wall*, *Thriller* and *Bad*. Established own label, Qwest in 1981. Line producer for the film *The Color Purple*. Winner of 19 Grammy Awards. Won prestigious NARAS Trustees Award in 1989. Married for 12 years to actress Peggy Lipton (TV's "Twin Peaks" and "Mod Squad").	
6/22/74	**6**	22	● 1. Body Heat	A&M 3617
9/6/75	**16**	11	2. Mellow Madness this album introduces The Brothers Johnson	A&M 4526
3/5/77	**21**	6	● 3. Roots [TV]	A&M 4626
7/1/78	**15**	9	▲ 4. Sounds...And Stuff Like That!!	A&M 4685
4/18/81	**10**	26	▲ 5. The Dude featuring James Ingram's vocals on "Just Once" and "One Hundred Ways"	A&M 3721
12/23/89	**9**	22	▲ 6. Back On The Block vocals and instrumentation by many of the pop and jazz artists Quincy has worked with, among them: Ray Charles, Miles Davis, Ella Fitzgerald, Dizzy Gillespie, Ice-T, Chaka Khan and Sarah Vaughan	Qwest 26020
			JONES, Rickie Lee	
			Born on 11/8/54 in Chicago. Pop-jazz-styled singer/songwriter. Moved to Los Angeles in 1977. Won the 1979 Best New Artist Grammy Award.	
4/28/79	**3**	24	▲ 1. Rickie Lee Jones *Chuck E.'s In Love* (4)	Warner 3296
8/8/81	**5**	15	● 2. Pirates	Warner 3432
7/30/83	**39**	2	3. Girl At Her Volcano [M] 10″ album; two of the seven tracks are live performances	Warner 23805
11/18/89	**39**	2	4. Flying Cowboys	Geffen 24246
			JONES, Tom	
			Born Thomas Jones Woodward on 6/7/40 in Pontypridd, South Wales. Worked local clubs as Tommy Scott; formed own trio The Senators in 1963. Began solo career in London in 1964. Won the 1965 Best New Artist Grammy Award. Host of own TV musical variety series from 1969-71.	
2/8/69	**5**	25	● 1. Help Yourself	Parrot 71025

DATE	POS	WKS	ARTIST—RECORD TITLE	LABEL & NO.
4/19/69	**14**	13	● 2. The Tom Jones Fever Zone	Parrot 71019
4/26/69	**13**	21	● 3. Tom Jones Live! [L] *originally recorded and released in 1967*	Parrot 71014
6/21/69	**4**	26	● 4. This Is Tom Jones	Parrot 71028
11/15/69	**3**	26	● 5. Tom Jones Live In Las Vegas [L]	Parrot 71031
5/16/70	**6**	13	● 6. Tom *Without Love (There Is Nothing)* (5)	Parrot 71037
12/5/70	**23**	3	● 7. I (Who Have Nothing)	Parrot 71039
5/29/71	**17**	9	● 8. She's A Lady *She's A Lady* (2)	Parrot 71046
			JOPLIN, Janis	
			Born on 1/19/43 in Port Arthur, Texas. White blues-rock singer. Nicknamed Pearl. To San Francisco in 1966, joined Big Brother & The Holding Company. Left band to go solo in 1968. Died of a heroin overdose in Hollywood on 10/4/70. The Bette Midler film *The Rose* was inspired by Joplin's life.	
10/18/69	**5**	16	● 1. I Got Dem Ol' Kozmic Blues Again Mama!	Columbia 9913
2/6/71	**1**(9)	23	▲ 2. Pearl *Me And Bobby McGee* (1)	Columbia 30322
5/20/72	**4**	16	● 3. Joplin In Concert [L] *side 1: with Big Brother & The Holding Co.* *side 2: with Full Tilt Boogie Band*	Columbia 31160 [2]
8/18/73	**37**	2	▲ 4. Janis Joplin's Greatest Hits [G]	Columbia 32168
			JOURNEY	
			Rock group formed in San Francisco in 1973. Consisted of Neal Schon, George Tickner (guitars), Gregg Rolie (keyboards, vocals), Ross Valory (bass) and Aynsley Dunbar (drums). Schon and Rolie had been in Santana. Tickner left in 1975. Steve Perry (lead vocals) added in 1978. Dunbar was replaced by Steve Smith in 1979. Jonathan Cain (ex-keyboardist of The Babys) added in 1981, replacing Rolie. In 1986 group pared down to a three-man core: Perry, Schon and Cain. The latter two hooked up with Bad English in 1989.	
3/25/78	**21**	13	▲ 1. Infinity	Columbia 34912
4/28/79	**20**	22	▲ 2. Evolution	Columbia 35797
3/22/80	**8**	17	▲ 3. Departure	Columbia 36339
2/21/81	**9**	12	▲ 4. Captured [L]	Columbia 37016 [2]
8/8/81	**1**(1)	58	▲ 5. Escape *Who's Crying Now* (4)/*Don't Stop Believin'* (9)/ *Open Arms* (2)	Columbia 37408
2/19/83	**2**(9)	42	▲ 6. Frontiers *Separate Ways (Worlds Apart)* (8)	Columbia 38504
5/10/86	**4**	29	▲ 7. Raised On Radio *Be Good To Yourself* (9)	Columbia 39936
12/17/88	**10**	16	▲ 8. Greatest Hits [G]	Columbia 44493
			JUDAS PRIEST	
			Heavy-metal group formed in Birmingham, England in 1973. Consists of vocalist Rob Halford, guitarists K.K. Downing and Glenn Tipton, bassist Ian Hill and drummer Dave Holland.	
7/5/80	**34**	3	▲ 1. British Steel	Columbia 36443
5/23/81	**39**	2	● 2. Point Of Entry	Columbia 37052
8/7/82	**17**	22	▲ 3. Screaming For Vengeance	Columbia 38160
2/11/84	**18**	12	▲ 4. Defenders Of The Faith	Columbia 39219
4/19/86	**17**	11	▲ 5. Turbo	Columbia 40158
7/4/87	**38**	3	6. Priest...Live! [L]	Columbia 40794 [2]

DATE	POS	WKS	ARTIST—RECORD TITLE	LABEL & NO.
6/18/88	**31**	6	● 7. Ram It Down	Columbia 44244

K

KAEMPFERT, Bert

Born on 10/16/23 in Hamburg, Germany. Multi-instrumentalist/bandleader/ producer/composer/arranger for Polydor Records in Germany. Produced the first Beatles recording session. Died on 6/21/80 in Zug, Switzerland.
BERT KAEMPFERT AND HIS ORCHESTRA:

DATE	POS	WKS	ARTIST—RECORD TITLE	LABEL & NO.
12/31/60	**1**(5)	28	● 1. Wonderland By Night [I] *Wonderland By Night* (1)	Decca 74101
10/6/62	**14**	12	2. That Happy Feeling [I]	Decca 74305
2/27/65	**5**	27	● 3. Blue Midnight [I]	Decca 74569
10/9/65	**27**	10	4. The Magic Music Of Far Away Places [I]	Decca 74616
9/3/66	**39**	2	5. Strangers In The Night [I]	Decca 74795
12/17/66	**30**	6	● 6. Bert Kaempfert's Greatest Hits [G-I]	Decca 74810

KAJAGOOGOO

English pop-synthesizer quintet led by Limahl (Chris Hamill).

DATE	POS	WKS	ARTIST—RECORD TITLE	LABEL & NO.
7/9/83	**38**	2	1. White Feathers *Too Shy* (5)	EMI America 17094

KANE, Big Daddy

Antonio M. Hardy from Brooklyn, New York. Rap lyricist for Cold Chillin' Records. Wrote songs for Roxanne Shante and Biz Markie. Toured as Shante's DJ in 1985.

DATE	POS	WKS	ARTIST—RECORD TITLE	LABEL & NO.
10/14/89	**33**	4	● 1. It's A Big Daddy Thing	Cold Chill. 25941

KANSAS

Progressive rock group formed in Topeka in 1970. Consisted of Steve Walsh (lead vocals, keyboards), Kerry Livgren (guitar, keyboards), Phil Ehart (drums), Robby Steinhardt (violin), Rich Williams (guitar) and Dave Hope (bass). Walsh left in 1981 and was replaced by John Elefante. Re-formed lineup in 1986: Walsh, Ehart, Williams, Steve Morse (guitarist from Dixie Dregs) and Billy Greer (bass).

DATE	POS	WKS	ARTIST—RECORD TITLE	LABEL & NO.
12/11/76	**5**	26	▲ 1. Leftoverture *Carry On Wayward Son*	Kirshner 34224
10/29/77	**4**	33	▲ 2. Point Of Know Return *Dust In The Wind* (6)	Kirshner 34929
12/9/78	**32**	6	▲ 3. Two For The Show [L]	Kirshner 35660 [2]
6/16/79	**10**	9	● 4. Monolith	Kirshner 36008
10/11/80	**26**	8	● 5. Audio-Visions	Kirshner 36588
6/26/82	**16**	6	6. Vinyl Confessions	Kirshner 38002
1/10/87	**35**	5	7. Power featuring new guitarist Steve Morse (from Dixie Dregs)	MCA 5838

KANTNER, Paul

Born on 3/12/42 in San Francisco. Original member of the rock group Jefferson Airplane, later known as Jefferson Starship.
PAUL KANTNER/JEFFERSON STARSHIP:

DATE	POS	WKS	ARTIST—RECORD TITLE	LABEL & NO.
12/26/70	**20**	11	● 1. Blows Against The Empire with Grace Slick, Jerry Garcia, David Crosby and Graham Nash	RCA 4448

DATE	POS	WKS	ARTIST—RECORD TITLE	LABEL & NO.
			KAOMA	
			Paris-based, multinational outfit of singers, musicians and dancers. Fronted by keyboardist/arranger Jean-Claude Bonaventure.	
3/31/90	40	2	● 1. World Beat	Epic 46010
			KATRINA AND THE WAVES	
			British-based, pop-rock quartet fronted by Kansas-born Katrina Leskanich, with American Vince de la Cruz (bass) and Britons Alex Cooper (drums) and Kimberley Rew (guitar, former member of the Soft Boys with Robyn Hitchcock).	
5/25/85	25	9	1. Katrina And The Waves *Walking On Sunshine (9)*	Capitol 12400
			KAYE, Sammy	
			Born on 3/13/10 in Rocky River, Ohio; died on 6/2/87 (cancer). Durable leader of popular "sweet" dance band with the slogan "Swing and Sway with Sammy Kaye." Also played clarinet and alto sax.	
8/4/56	20	1	1. My Fair Lady (For Dancing) [I]	Columbia 885
			SAMMY KAYE AND HIS SWINGING AND SWAYING STRINGS:	
11/17/56	19	1	2. What Makes Sammy Swing and Sway [I]	Columbia 891
			KC AND THE SUNSHINE BAND	
			Disco-R&B band formed in Florida in 1973 by lead singer/keyboardist Harry "KC" Casey (b: 1/31/51, Hialeah, Florida) and bassist Richard Finch (b: 1/25/54, Indianapolis). Integrated band contained from 7 to 11 members. Casey and Finch wrote, arranged and produced all of their hits.	
9/6/75	4	22	1. KC And The Sunshine Band *Get Down Tonight (1)/That's The Way (I Like It) (1)*	TK 603
10/23/76	13	26	2. Part 3 *(Shake, Shake, Shake) Shake Your Booty (1)/* *I'm Your Boogie Man (1)/Keep It Comin' Love (2)*	TK 605
9/9/78	36	5	3. Who Do Ya (Love)	TK 607
			KENDRICKS, Eddie	
			Born on 12/17/39 in Union Springs, Alabama; raised in Birmingham. Joined R&B group the Primes in Detroit in the late 50s. Group later evolved into The Temptations; Eddie sang lead from 1960-71. Eddie later dropped letter "s" from his last name.	
9/29/73	18	8	1. Eddie Kendricks *Keep On Truckin' (1)*	Tamla 327
4/6/74	30	4	2. Boogie Down! *Boogie Down (2)*	Tamla 330
4/17/76	38	2	3. He's A Friend	Tamla 343
			KENNEDY, John Fitzgerald	
			Tributes to President Kennedy who was assassinated on 11/22/63 (age 46).	
1/11/64	8	8	1. The Presidential Years 1960-1963 [T] narrated by David Teig	20th Century 3127
1/25/64	5	8	2. That Was The Week That Was [T] the BBC telecast tribute to Kennedy on 11/23/63	Decca 9116
2/1/64	18	4	● 3. A Memorial Album [T] narrated by Ed Brown; a broadcast by WMCA, New York on 11/22/63	Premier 2099
2/22/64	29	4	4. Four Days That Shocked The World [T] Nov. 22-25, 1963 (complete story narrated by Reid Collins)	Colpix 2500

DATE	POS	WKS	ARTIST—RECORD TITLE	LABEL & NO.
			KENNY G	
			Kenny Gorelick; fusion saxophonist from Seattle. With Barry White's Love Unlimited Orchestra at age 17. Worked with Jeff Lorber.	
5/9/87	6	41	▲ 1. Duotones *Songbird* (4)	Arista 8427
10/29/88	8	27	▲ 2. Silhouette [I]	Arista 8457
12/23/89	16	21	▲ 3. Live [L] recorded August 26-27, 1989 in Seattle	Arista 8613 [2]
			KENTON, Stan	
			Born on 2/19/12 in Wichita, Kansas; died in Los Angeles on 8/25/79. Progressive jazz bandleader/pianist/composer. Organized his first jazz band in 1941. Third person named to the Jazz Hall of Fame.	
9/8/56	13	2	1. Kenton in Hi-Fi [I]	Capitol 724
9/15/56	17	4	2. Cuban Fire! [I]	Capitol 731
11/20/61	16	7	3. Kenton's West Side Story [I]	Capitol 1609
			KESNER, Dick	
			Violin player. A regular on TV's "The Lawrence Welk Show" (1955-59).	
			DICK KESNER & HIS STRADIVARIUS VIOLIN:	
1/12/59	22	2	1. Lawrence Welk Presents Dick Kesner [I]	Brunswick 54044
			KHAN, Chaka	
			Born Yvette Marie Stevens on 3/23/53 in Great Lakes, Illinois. Became lead singer of Rufus in 1972. Recorded solo and with Rufus since 1978. Sister of vocalists Taka Boom and Mark Stevens (Jamaica Boys).	
11/18/78	12	8	● 1. Chaka	Warner 3245
5/16/81	17	9	● 2. What Cha' Gonna Do For Me	Warner 3526
11/3/84	14	16	▲ 3. I Feel For You *I Feel For You* (3)	Warner 25162
			KIHN, Greg	
			Greg is a rock singer/songwriter/guitarist from Baltimore. Formed band in Berkeley, California, in 1975.	
			GREG KIHN BAND:	
8/1/81	32	5	1. Rockihnroll	Beserkley 10069
5/15/82	33	4	2. Kihntinued	Beserkley 60101
3/19/83	15	12	3. Kihnspiracy *Jeopardy* (2)	Beserkley 60224
			KIM, Andy	
			Born Andrew Joachim on 12/5/46 in Montreal, Canada. His parents were from Lebanon. Pop singer/songwriter. Teamed with Jeff Barry to write "Sugar, Sugar."	
10/26/74	21	6	1. Andy Kim *Rock Me Gently* (1)	Capitol 11318
			KING, B.B.	
			Born Riley B. King on 9/16/25 in Itta Bena, Mississippi. Moved to Memphis in 1946. Own radio show on WDIA-Memphis from 1949-50, where he was dubbed "The Beale Street Blues Boy," later shortened to "Blues Boy," then simply "B.B." First recorded for Bullet in 1949. Inducted into the Rock and Roll Hall of Fame in 1987. Appeared in the 1987 film *Amazon Women On The Moon*. The most famous blues singer/guitarist in the world today.	
4/4/70	38	3	1. Completely Well *The Thrill Is Gone*	BluesWay 6037
11/7/70	26	6	2. Indianola Mississippi Seeds	ABC 713
3/13/71	25	7	3. Live In Cook County Jail [L]	ABC 723

DATE	POS	WKS	ARTIST—RECORD TITLE	LABEL & NO.
			KING, Ben E.	
			Born Benjamin Earl Nelson on 9/23/38 in Henderson, North Carolina. To New York in 1947. Worked with The Moonglows for six months while still in high school. Joined the Five Crowns in 1957, who became the new Drifters in 1959. Wrote lyrics to "There Goes My Baby," his first lead performance with The Drifters. Went solo in May of 1960.	
6/28/75	39	1	1. Supernatural *Supernatural Thing (5)*	Atlantic 18132
			AVERAGE WHITE BAND & BEN E. KING:	
8/20/77	33	5	2. Benny And Us	Atlantic 19105
			KING, Carole	
			Born Carole Klein on 2/9/42 in Brooklyn. Singer/songwriter/pianist. Married lyricist Gerry Goffin in 1958, team wrote four #1 hits: "Will You Love Me Tomorrow," "Go Away Little Girl," "Take Good Care Of My Baby" and "The Loco-Motion." Divorced Goffin in 1968, first solo album in 1970. One of the most successful female songwriters of the rock era. She and Goffin were inducted as songwriting team into the Rock and Roll Hall of Fame in 1990.	
4/24/71	1(15)	68	● 1. Tapestry 1971 Grammy winner: Album of the Year *It's Too Late (1)*	Ode 77009
12/18/71	1(3)	20	● 2. Music *Sweet Seasons (9)*	Ode 77013
11/11/72	2(5)	20	● 3. Rhymes & Reasons	Ode 77016
6/30/73	6	15	● 4. Fantasy	Ode 77018
10/5/74	1(1)	13	● 5. Wrap Around Joy *Jazzman (2)/Nightingale (9)*	Ode 77024
3/29/75	20	4	6. Really Rosie [TV] from the original animated TV soundtrack	Ode 77027
2/7/76	3	14	● 7. Thoroughbred	Ode 77034
8/13/77	17	7	● 8. Simple Things	Capitol 11667
			KING, Evelyn	
			Born on 6/29/60 in the Bronx. To Philadelphia in 1970. Employed as a cleaning woman at Sigma Studios when discovered.	
7/22/78	14	13	● 1. Smooth Talk *Shame (9)*	RCA 2466
5/12/79	35	3	● 2. Music Box	RCA 3033
8/15/81	28	6	3. I'm In Love	RCA 3962
10/9/82	27	7	● 4. Get Loose	RCA 4337
			KING CRIMSON	
			English progressive rock group formed in 1969 by the eccentric Robert Fripp. Group featured an ever-changing lineup of top British artists.	
2/28/70	28	6	● 1. In The Court Of The Crimson King - An Observation By King Crimson	Atlantic 8245
9/19/70	31	5	2. In The Wake Of Poseidon Greg Lake, lead singer on above 2 albums	Atlantic 8266
			KINGDOM COME	
			Hard-rock quintet formed and fronted by vocalist Lenny Wolf. In 1984, Wolf formed and fronted rock band Stone Fury.	
3/26/88	12	12	● 1. Kingdom Come	Polydor 835368
			KING FAMILY	
			Featuring songs by the entire cast of their 1965 variety TV series.	
7/31/65	34	4	1. The King Family Show!	Warner 1601

Jack Jones's first two hits—1963's "Wives And Lovers" and 1964's "Dear Heart"—drew their inspiration from the films of Hollywood and established him solidly as an album artist. His biggest seller: 1966's *The Impossible Dream* on Kapp, which peaked at No. 9 and spent over a year on the charts.

Quincy Jones' reputation as a musical renaissance man has been well known among musicians for years, yet such albums as *The Dude*—released on A&M in 1981 to enormous popular favor and featuring vocalist James Ingram—first helped cement that reputation among the general public.

Kansas, a late 70s, early 80s progressive rock group hailing from Topeka, brought the progressive sounds popularized by King Crimson, Emerson, Lake & Palmer and Yes directly to the heart of the U.S. pop scene. Despite earlier hit singles like "Carry On Wayward Son" and "Dust In The Wind," later works such as 1980's *Audio-Visions* found the group working strictly in the album-rock mode.

John F. Kennedy is credited for many accomplishments, as ex-Presidents should be. Yet few remember that the charismatic leader was featured on no less than 10 albums between 1963-65, all of which made the Top Pop Albums chart and two of which actually reached the top 10.

The **Knack** burst onto the pop scene vividly with the single "My Sharona" from the album *Get The Knack* in 1979. Two years later they broke up amid criticism that they had "sold out." Bandleader Doug Fieger was no stranger to the industry: He'd already been a key member of Sky, who'd released two albums on RCA in 1970-71.

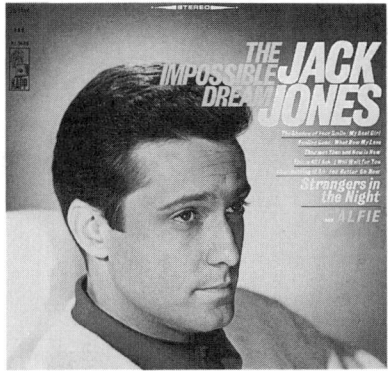

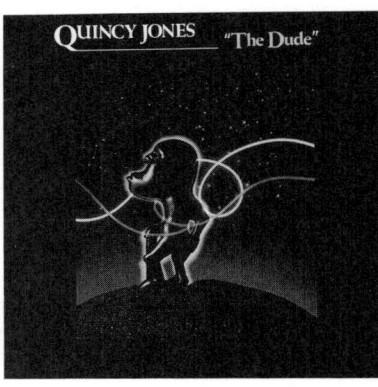

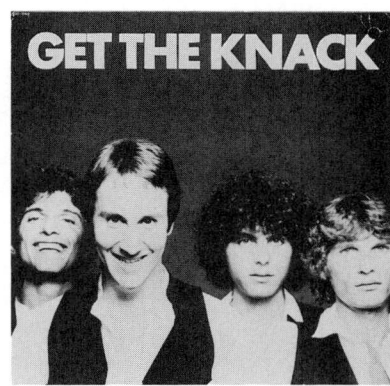

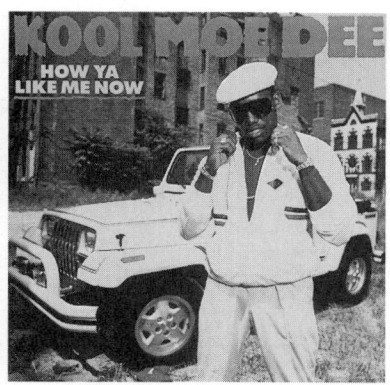

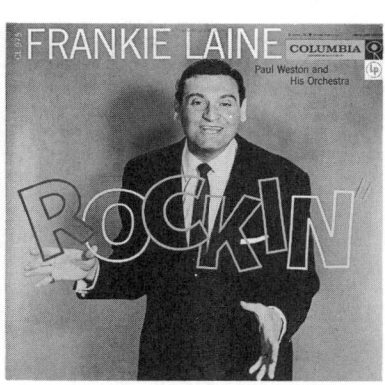

Kool & The Gang, perennials on the Top Pop Albums chart, first charted back in 1971 with their *Live At The Sex Machine* album on De-Lite. It took the group a full eight years to finally reach the top 10 with their now-classic *Celebrate!*, featuring "Celebration," the aerobic anthem of the 80s.

Kool Moe Dee first rose to chart prominence with his singles "How Ya Like Me Now" from the album of the same name and "Wild Wild West" in 1987-88. Born Mohandas Dewese, the Harlem rapper was formerly with the Treacherous Three.

Patti LaBelle's recording career has taken her through a full four decades; yet it wasn't until her 1986 MCA debut, *Winner In You*, that the distinguished singer finally held the No. 1 position on the album charts.

Frankie Laine might have been a notable figure for his many mid-50s hits, but for the Baby Boom Generation, he may be best remembered for singing the theme from "Rawhide," issued on his 1961 Columbia album, *Hell Bent For Leather!*. *Rockin'* was his first top 40 LP, released four years earlier in 1957.

Cyndi Lauper's 1983 breakthough debut album *She's So Unusual*, bearing both her "Girls Just Want To Have Fun" and "Time After Time" hits, actually followed her group debut with little-known Polydor group Blue Angel in 1980. *True Colors*, Lauper's 1986 follow-up, bore the title-track hit as well as "Change Of Heart."

DATE	POS	WKS	ARTIST—RECORD TITLE	LABEL & NO.
			KINGSMEN, The	
			Rock band formed in Portland, Oregon in 1957. Consisted of Jack Ely (lead singer, guitar), Lynn Easton (drums), Mike Mitchell (guitar), Bob Nordby (bass) and Don Gallucci (keyboards). After release of "Louie Louie" (featuring lead vocal by Ely), Easton took over leadership of band and replaced Ely as lead singer. One of America's premier 60s garage bands.	
2/22/64	**20**	28	1. The Kingsmen In Person [L] *Louie, Louie* (2)	Wand 657
10/17/64	**15**	9	2. The Kingsmen, Volume II [L]	Wand 659
4/10/65	**22**	7	3. The Kingsmen, Volume 3 [L] *The Jolly Green Giant* (4)	Wand 662
			KINGSTON TRIO, The	
			Folk trio formed in San Francisco in 1957. Consisted of Dave Guard (banjo), Bob Shane and Nick Reynolds (guitars). Big break came at San Francisco's Purple Onion, where they stayed for eight months. Guard left in 1961 to form the Whiskeyhill Singers, John Stewart replaced him. Disbanded in 1968, Shane formed New Kingston Trio. The originators of the folk music craze of the 60s.	
11/3/58	**1**(1)	114	● 1. The Kingston Trio *Tom Dooley* (1)	Capitol 996
2/16/59	**2**(4)	47	● 2. From The Hungry i [L] the Hungry i is a nightclub in San Francisco	Capitol 1107
6/22/59	**1**(15)	43	● 3. The Kingston Trio At Large	Capitol 1199
11/9/59	**1**(8)	40	● 4. Here We Go Again!	Capitol 1258
4/25/60	**1**(12)	42	● 5. Sold Out	Capitol 1352
8/15/60	**1**(10)	27	● 6. String Along	Capitol 1407
9/5/60	**15**	13	7. Stereo Concert [L] concert in Liberty Hall, El Paso, Texas	Capitol 1183
12/5/60	**11**	4	8. The Last Month Of The Year [X]	Capitol 1446
2/27/61	**2**(1)	30	9. Make Way!	Capitol 1474
7/17/61	**3**	20	10. Goin' Places	Capitol 1564
10/16/61	**3**	24	11. Close-Up John Stewart replaces Dave Guard from here on	Capitol 1642
3/17/62	**3**	26	12. College Concert [L] concert on the campus of UCLA	Capitol 1658
6/23/62	**7**	48	● 13. The Best Of The Kingston Trio [G]	Capitol 1705
8/25/62	**7**	18	14. Something Special with orchestral and chorus background	Capitol 1747
1/5/63	**16**	23	15. New Frontier	Capitol 1809
4/6/63	**4**	23	16. The Kingston Trio #16 *Reverend Mr. Black* (8)	Capitol 1871
8/31/63	**7**	13	17. Sunny Side!	Capitol 1935
2/22/64	**18**	7	18. Time To Think	Capitol 2011
6/27/64	**22**	5	19. Back In Town [L] recorded at San Francisco's "Hungry i"	Capitol 2081
			KINKS, The	
			Rock group formed in London in 1963 by Ray Davies (lead singer, guitar) and his brother Dave Davies (lead guitar, vocals). Original lineup also included Peter Quaife (bass) and Mike Avory (drums). Numerous personnel changes during the 70s. 1987 lineup consisted of Ray & Dave Davies, Ian Gibbons (keyboards, left by 1989), Bob Henrit (drums) and Jim Rodford (bass, formerly with Argent). Group inducted into the Rock and Roll Hall of Fame in 1990.	
2/20/65	**29**	5	1. You Really Got Me *You Really Got Me* (7)	Reprise 6143

DATE	POS	WKS	ARTIST—RECORD TITLE	LABEL & NO.
5/1/65	**13**	11	2. Kinks-Size *All Day And All Of The Night* (7)/ *Tired Of Waiting For You* (6)	Reprise 6158
9/17/66	**9**	15	● 3. The Kinks Greatest Hits! [G]	Reprise 6217
1/9/71	**35**	3	4. Lola Versus Powerman and The Moneygoround, Part One *Lola* (9)	Reprise 6423
3/19/77	**21**	8	5. Sleepwalker	Arista 4106
7/15/78	**40**	1	6. Misfits	Arista 4167
8/4/79	**11**	10	● 7. Low Budget	Arista 4240
7/5/80	**14**	14	● 8. One For The Road [L]	Arista 8401 [2]
9/26/81	**15**	9	● 9. Give The People What They Want	Arista 9567
6/25/83	**12**	12	10. State of Confusion *Come Dancing* (6)	Arista 8018

KISS

Hard-rock band formed in New York City in 1973. Consisted of Gene Simmons (bass), Paul Stanley (guitar), Ace Frehley (lead guitar) and Peter Criss (drums). Noted for elaborate makeup and highly theatrical stage shows. Criss replaced by Eric Carr in 1981. Frehley replaced by Vinnie Vincent in 1982. Group appeared without makeup for the first time in 1983 on album cover "Lick It Up." Mark St. John replaced Vincent in 1984. Bruce Kulick replaced St. John in 1985.

DATE	POS	WKS	ARTIST—RECORD TITLE	LABEL & NO.
6/7/75	**32**	3	● 1. Dressed To Kill	Casablanca 7016
11/1/75	**9**	17	● 2. Alive! [L]	Casablanca 7020 [2]
4/10/76	**11**	14	▲ 3. Destroyer *Beth* (7)	Casablanca 7025
9/18/76	**36**	3	4. The Originals [R] reissue of their first three albums	Casablanca 7032 [3]
11/20/76	**11**	26	▲ 5. Rock And Roll Over	Casablanca 7037
7/9/77	**4**	4	▲ 6. Love Gun	Casablanca 7057
11/26/77	**7**	14	▲ 7. Alive II [L]	Casablanca 7076 [2]
6/10/78	**22**	5	▲ 8. Double Platinum [G] during October, 1978, each member of Kiss issued a solo album - all but Peter Criss' made the Top 40	Casablanca 7100 [2]
6/23/79	**9**	11	▲ 9. Dynasty	Casablanca 7152
7/12/80	**35**	4	● 10. Kiss Unmasked	Casablanca 7225
10/29/83	**24**	7	● 11. Lick It Up group shown unmasked for the first time	Mercury 814297
10/20/84	**19**	17	▲ 12. Animalize	Mercury 822495
10/12/85	**20**	16	● 13. Asylum	Mercury 826099
10/17/87	**18**	17	▲ 14. Crazy Nights	Mercury 832626
12/10/88	**21**	11	▲ 15. Smashes, Thrashes & Hits [G]	Mercury 836427
11/11/89	**29**	5	● 16. Hot In The Shade *Forever* (8)	Mercury 838913

KLAATU

Canadian rock trio: Terry Draper, Dee Long and John Woloschuck. Anonymous first release had people speculating that they might be The Beatles.

DATE	POS	WKS	ARTIST—RECORD TITLE	LABEL & NO.
4/30/77	**32**	3	1. Klaatu	Capitol 11542

DATE	POS	WKS	ARTIST—RECORD TITLE	LABEL & NO.
			KLUGH, Earl	
			Born on 9/16/53 in Detroit. Jazz acoustic guitarist/pianist. Taught guitar from age 15. Worked Baker's Keyboard Lounge. Toured with Chick Corea's Return To Forever and George Benson. First solo recording for Blue Note in 1976.	
12/1/79	**23**	13	● 1. One On One [I]	Tappan Zee 36241
			BOB JAMES AND EARL KLUGH	
6/11/83	**38**	3	2. Low Ride [I]	Capitol 12253
			KLYMAXX	
			Black female band founded by drummer/producer Bernadette Cooper in Los Angeles in 1979. Lead vocals by Lorena Porter Shelby and Joyce "Fenderella" Irby. Pared down to a trio of Shelby, Cheryl Cooley (guitar) and Robbin Grider (keyboards) in 1990.	
12/14/85	**18**	15	● 1. Meeting In The Ladies Room	Constell. 5529
			I Miss You (5)	
			KNACK, The	
			Rock group formed in Los Angeles in 1978. Consisted of Doug Fieger (lead singer, guitar), Berton Averre (guitar), Bruce Gary (drums) and Prescott Niles (bass). Disbanded in 1982. Reunited in 1990.	
7/14/79	**1**(5)	22	▲ 1. Get The Knack	Capitol 11948
			My Sharona (1)	
3/8/80	**15**	9	● 2. But The Little Girls Understand	Capitol 12045
			KNIGHT, Gladys/Pips	
			Leader R&B family group The Pips, from Atlanta. Formed in 1952 when Gladys was eight years old. Consisted of Gladys (b: 5/28/44, Atlanta), her brother Merald "Bubba" Knight and sister Brenda, and cousins William and Eleanor Guest. Named "Pips" for their manager, cousin James "Pip" Woods. First recorded for Brunswick in 1958. Brenda and Eleanor replaced by cousins Edward Patten and Langston George in 1959. Langston left group in 1962 and group has remained a quartet with the same members ever since. Due to legal problems, Gladys could not record with the Pips from 1977-80. Gladys was a cast member of the 1985 TV series "Charlie & Co."	
			GLADYS KNIGHT & THE PIPS:	
8/7/71	**35**	2	1. If I Were Your Woman	Soul 731
			If I Were Your Woman (9)	
3/31/73	**9**	10	2. Neither One Of Us	Soul 737
			Neither One Of Us (Wants To Be The First To Say Goodbye) (2)	
11/10/73	**9**	33	● 3. Imagination	Buddah 5141
			Midnight Train To Georgia (1)/	
			I've Got To Use My Imagination (4)/	
			Best Thing That Ever Happened To Me (3)	
7/13/74	**35**	3	● 4. Claudine [S]	Buddah 5602
			On And On (5)	
12/7/74	**17**	13	● 5. I Feel A Song	Buddah 5612
11/22/75	**24**	4	● 6. 2nd Anniversary	Buddah 5639
			title refers to their signing with Buddah Records	
3/20/76	**36**	4	7. The Best Of Gladys Knight & The Pips [G]	Buddah 5653
6/18/83	**34**	6	● 8. Visions	Columbia 38205
3/5/88	**39**	3	● 9. All Our Love	MCA 42004

DATE	POS	WKS	ARTIST—RECORD TITLE	LABEL & NO.
			KOOL & THE GANG	
			R&B group formed in Jersey City, New Jersey in 1964 by bass player Robert "Kool" Bell as the Jazziacs. Session work in New York City, 1964-68. First recorded for De-Lite in 1969. Added lead singer James "J.T." Taylor in 1979. Current lineup consists of brothers Robert and Ronald Bell (sax, keyboards), George Brown (drums), Curtis "Fitz" Williams (keyboards) and Charles Smith (guitar). Taylor left in 1988; replaced by lead singers Gary Brown, Odeen Mays and former Dazz Band lead vocalist Skip Martin.	
2/23/74	33	4	● 1. Wild And Peaceful *Jungle Boogie (4)/Hollywood Swinging (6)*	De-Lite 2013
10/20/79	13	28	▲ 2. Ladies' Night *Ladies Night (8)/Too Hot (5)*	De-Lite 9513
11/22/80	10	24	▲ 3. Celebrate! *Celebration (1)*	De-Lite 9518
10/24/81	12	30	▲ 4. Something Special *Get Down On It (10)*	De-Lite 8502
10/23/82	29	12	● 5. As One	De-Lite 8505
1/21/84	29	11	● 6. In The Heart *Joanna (2)*	De-Lite 8508
2/16/85	13	51	▲ 7. Emergency *Misled (10)/Fresh (9)/Cherish (2)*	De-Lite 822943
12/20/86	25	9	● 8. Forever *Victory (10)/Stone Love (10)*	Mercury 830398
			KOOL MOE DEE	
			Rapper from Harlem. Real name: Mohandas DeWese. Formerly with the Treacherous Three.	
5/7/88	35	4	▲ 1. How Ya Like Me Now	Jive 1079
7/1/89	25	8	● 2. Knowledge Is King	Jive 1182
			KOOPER, Al	
			Born on 2/5/44 in Brooklyn. Top session keyboardist/guitarist/vocalist. Founded Blood, Sweat & Tears in 1968, left in 1969. A member of The Royal Teens in 1959. Founded The Blues Project in 1967.	
10/5/68	12	10	● 1. Super Session **MIKE BLOOMFIELD/AL KOOPER/STEVE STILLS**	Columbia 9701
2/15/69	18	10	2. The Live Adventures Of Mike Bloomfield And Al Kooper [L]	Columbia 6 [2]
			KOSTELANETZ, Andre	
			Born on 12/23/01 in St. Petersburg, Russia; died on 1/13/80. Conductor/arranger on radio and records from the 30s to the 70s. **ANDRE KOSTELANETZ AND HIS ORCHESTRA:**	
10/1/55	4	11	1. Meet Andre Kostelanetz [K-I]	Columbia KZ 1
			KRAFTWERK	
			German all-electronic duo: Ralf Hutter and Florian Schneider.	
3/8/75	5	11	1. Autobahn [I] side 1 is a 22 1/2-minute recording of "Autobahn"	Vertigo 2003
			KRISTOFFERSON, Kris	
			Born on 6/22/36 in Brownsville, Texas. Singer/songwriter/actor. Married to Rita Coolidge from 1973-80. Wrote "Me And Bobby McGee," "For The Good Times" and "Help Me Make It Through The Night." Has starred in many films since 1972.	
8/21/71	21	14	● 1. The Silver Tongued Devil And I	Monument 30679
9/22/73	31	4	● 2. Jesus Was A Capricorn	Monument 31909
			KRIS KRISTOFFERSON & RITA COOLIDGE:	
10/13/73	26	6	● 3. Full Moon	A&M 4403

DATE	POS	WKS	ARTIST—RECORD TITLE	LABEL & NO.
			KROKUS	
			Heavy-metal band formed in Zurich, Switzerland. Led by Marc Storace (vocals) and Fernando Von Arb (guitar).	
6/11/83	**25**	8	● 1. Headhunter	Arista 9623
9/29/84	**31**	6	● 2. The Blitz	Arista 8243

L

DATE	POS	WKS	ARTIST—RECORD TITLE	LABEL & NO.
			LaBELLE	
			Vocal trio from Philadelphia consisting of Patti LaBelle, Sara Dash and Nona Hendryx. Formed as The Blue Belles in 1960 (included Cindy Birdsong who joined The Supremes in 1967). Shortened name to LaBelle in 1971. Disbanded in 1977.	
2/15/75	**7**	11	● 1. Nightbirds *Lady Marmalade* (1)	Epic 33075
			LaBELLE, Patti	
			Born Patricia Holt on 5/24/44 in Philadelphia. Began singing career as leader of the Ordettes which evolved into The Blue Belles, and later LaBelle.	
3/3/84	**40**	2	● 1. I'm In Love Again	Phil. Int. 38539
5/24/86	**1**(1)	19	▲ 2. Winner In You *On My Own* (1) with Michael McDonald	MCA 5737
			LAINE, Frankie	
			Born Frank Paul LoVecchio on 3/30/13 in Chicago. To Los Angeles in the early 40s. First recorded for Exclusive in 1945. With Johnny Moore's Three Blazers. Signed to Mercury label in 1947. Dynamic style found favor with black and white audiences.	
4/20/57	**13**	12	1. Rockin'	Columbia 975
6/17/67	**16**	9	2. I'll Take Care Of Your Cares	ABC 604
			LAKESIDE	
			Funk aggregation from Dayton, Ohio.	
1/10/81	**16**	12	● 1. Fantastic Voyage	Solar 3720
			LANIN, Lester	
			Born on 8/26/11. Leader of society-styled dance bands. First five albums below contain medleys of 25-50 songs with a party atmosphere background. **LESTER LANIN AND HIS ORCHESTRA:**	
6/24/57	**7**	10	1. Dance To The Music Of Lester Lanin [I]	Epic 3340
11/11/57	**18**	2	2. Lester Lanin And His Orchestra [I]	Epic 3242
2/3/58	**17**	2	3. Lester Lanin At The Tiffany Ball [I]	Epic 3410
6/9/58	**19**	3	4. Lester Lanin Goes To College [I]	Epic 3474
11/17/58	**12**	4	5. Have Band, Will Travel [I]	Epic 3520
2/10/62	**37**	1	6. Twistin' in High Society! [I]	Epic 3825
			LANZA, Mario	
			Born Alfredo Cocozza on 1/31/21 in Philadelphia. Mario Lanza became the most spectacularly popular operatic tenor since Caruso, his voice featured in seven movies (though no theatrical operas) before his death on 10/7/59 (age 38).	
4/28/56	**9**	6	1. Serenade [S]	RCA 1996
3/17/58	**7**	8	2. Seven Hills Of Rome [S] side 1: soundtrack; side 2: various Lanza recordings	RCA 2211

DATE	POS	WKS	ARTIST—RECORD TITLE	LABEL & NO.
11/2/59	5	30	3. For The First Time　　　　　　　　　　[S]	RCA 2338
			Mario sings and stars in the above three films	
12/14/59	4	4	4. Lanza Sings Christmas Carols　　　　　[X]	RCA 2333
5/16/60	4	32	5. Mario Lanza Sings Caruso Favorites　　[F]	RCA 2393
			recorded in Rome, June, 1959	

LARSON, Nicolette

Born on 7/17/52 in Helena, Montana; raised in Kansas City. To San Francisco, 1974. Session vocalist with Neil Young, Linda Ronstadt, Van Halen and many others.

DATE	POS	WKS	ARTIST—RECORD TITLE	LABEL & NO.
1/20/79	15	12	● 1. Nicolette	Warner 3243
			Lotta Love (8)	

LAST POETS, The

Black protest poetry set to music.

DATE	POS	WKS	ARTIST—RECORD TITLE	LABEL & NO.
8/29/70	29	7	1. The Last Poets	Douglas 3

LAUPER, Cyndi

Born on 6/20/53 in Queens, New York. Recorded an album for Polydor Records in 1980 with the group Blue Angel. Won the 1984 Best New Artist Grammy Award. In the 1988 film *Vibes*.

DATE	POS	WKS	ARTIST—RECORD TITLE	LABEL & NO.
2/11/84	4	62	▲ 1. She's So Unusual	Portrait 38930
			Girls Just Want To Have Fun (2)/*Time After Time* (1)/	
			She Bop (3)/*All Through The Night* (5)	
10/11/86	4	23	▲ 2. True Colors	Portrait 40313
			True Colors (1)/*Change Of Heart* (3)	
6/24/89	37	4	3. A Night To Remember	Epic 44318
			I Drove All Night (6)	

LAWRENCE, Steve

Born Sam Leibowitz on 7/8/35 in Brooklyn. Regular performer on the Steve Allen "Tonight Show" for five years. First recorded for King Records in 1953. Married to singer Eydie Gorme since 12/29/57. Recorded as the duo Parker & Penny in 1979.

DATE	POS	WKS	ARTIST—RECORD TITLE	LABEL & NO.
6/2/58	19	2	1. Here's Steve Lawrence	Coral 57204
3/2/63	27	7	2. Winners!	Columbia 8753
			Go Away Little Girl (1)	

LAWS, Ronnie

Born on 10/3/50 in Houston. R&B-jazz saxophonist. Brother of Hubert, Eloise and Debra Laws. With Earth, Wind & Fire from 1972-73.

DATE	POS	WKS	ARTIST—RECORD TITLE	LABEL & NO.
6/18/77	37	2	● 1. Friends And Strangers　　　　　　　[I]	Blue Note 730
3/8/80	24	6	2. Every Generation	United Art. 1001

LED ZEPPELIN

British heavy-metal rock supergroup formed in October, 1968. Consisted of Robert Plant (lead singer), Jimmy Page (lead guitar), John Paul Jones (bass, keyboards) and John Bonham (drums). First known as the New Yardbirds. Page had been in the Yardbirds, 1966-68. U.S. tour in 1973 broke many box-office records. Formed own Swan Song label in 1974. Plant seriously injured in an auto accident in Greece on 8/4/75. In concert film *The Song Remains The Same* in 1976. Bonham died on 9/25/80 (age 33) of asphyxiation. Group disbanded in December, 1980. Their most famous recording, "Stairway To Heaven" (on album *Led Zeppelin IV*), was never released as a single.

DATE	POS	WKS	ARTIST—RECORD TITLE	LABEL & NO.
2/22/69	10	50	● 1. Led Zeppelin	Atlantic 8216
11/15/69	1(7)	29	● 2. Led Zeppelin II	Atlantic 8236
			Whole Lotta Love (4)	
10/24/70	1(4)	19	● 3. Led Zeppelin III	Atlantic 7201
11/27/71	2(4)	24	● 4. Led Zeppelin IV (untitled)	Atlantic 7208

DATE	POS	WKS	ARTIST—RECORD TITLE	LABEL & NO.
4/21/73	**1**(2)	39	● 5. Houses Of The Holy	Atlantic 7255
3/15/75	**1**(6)	15	● 6. Physical Graffiti	Swan Song 200 [2]
4/24/76	**1**(2)	13	▲ 7. Presence	Swan Song 8416
11/6/76	**2**(3)	12	▲ 8. The Soundtrack From The Film *The Song Remains The Same* [S-L] soundtrack recorded live at Madison Square Garden	Swan Song 201 [2]
9/8/79	**1**(7)	28	▲ 9. In Through The Out Door six versions of cover released depicting same bar scene photographed at six different angles	Swan Song 16002
12/18/82	**6**	9	▲ 10. Coda [K] previously unreleased recordings from 1969-1978	Swan Song 90051

LEE, Brenda

Born Brenda Mae Tarpley on 12/11/44 in Lithonia, Georgia. Professional singer since age six. Signed to Decca Records in 1956. Became known as "Little Miss Dynamite." Successful country singer since 1971.

DATE	POS	WKS	ARTIST—RECORD TITLE	LABEL & NO.
8/22/60	**5**	20	1. Brenda Lee *Sweet Nothin's* (4)/*I'm Sorry* (1)/ *That's All You Gotta Do* (6)	Decca 74039
11/21/60	**4**	9	2. This Is.....Brenda *I Want To Be Wanted* (1)	Decca 74082
4/10/61	**24**	11	3. Emotions *Emotions* (7)	Decca 74104
9/11/61	**17**	10	4. All The Way *Dum Dum* (4)	Decca 74176
4/21/62	**29**	3	5. Sincerely	Decca 74216
11/17/62	**20**	4	6. Brenda, That's All *You Can Depend On Me* (6)/*Fool #1* (3)	Decca 74326
3/23/63	**25**	8	7. All Alone Am I *All Alone Am I* (3)	Decca 74370
1/25/64	**39**	1	8. Let Me Sing *Break It To Me Gently* (4)/*Losing You* (6)	Decca 74439
11/13/65	**36**	2	9. Too Many Rivers	Decca 74684

LEE, Peggy

Born Norma Jean Egstrom on 5/26/20 in Jamestown, North Dakota. Jazz singer with Jack Wardlow band (1936-40), Will Osborne (1940-41) and Benny Goodman (1941-43). Went solo in March of 1943. In films *Mister Music* (1950), *The Jazz Singer* (1953) and *Pete Kelly's Blues* (1955). Co-wrote many songs with husband Dave Barbour.

DATE	POS	WKS	ARTIST—RECORD TITLE	LABEL & NO.
9/17/55	**7**	10	1. Songs from Pete Kelly's Blues **PEGGY LEE AND ELLA FITZGERALD**	Decca 8166
9/23/57	**20**	1	2. The Man I Love orchestra conducted by Frank Sinatra	Capitol 864
7/14/58	**15**	2	3. Jump For Joy	Capitol 979
12/8/58	**16**	1	4. Things Are Swingin'	Capitol 1049
4/11/60	**11**	34	5. Latin ala Lee!	Capitol 1290
2/9/63	**40**	1	6. Sugar 'N' Spice	Capitol 1772
5/4/63	**18**	9	7. I'm A Woman	Capitol 1857

LeGRAND, Michel

Pianist/composer/conductor/arranger. Born on 2/24/32 in Paris, France. Scored over 50 motion pictures.
MICHEL LeGRAND AND HIS ORCHESTRA:

DATE	POS	WKS	ARTIST—RECORD TITLE	LABEL & NO.
5/28/55	**5**	16	1. Holiday In Rome [I]	Columbia 647
9/17/55	**13**	2	2. Vienna Holiday [I]	Columbia 706

DATE	POS	WKS	ARTIST—RECORD TITLE	LABEL & NO.
6/30/56	**9**	4	3. Castles In Spain [I]	Columbia 888
			LEHRER, Tom	
			Born on 4/9/28 in New York City. Satirist (in song) who performed on the TV show "That Was The Week That Was." Alumnus of Harvard, where he also taught mathematics.	
12/11/65	**18**	19	1. That Was The Year That Was [C]	Reprise 6179
			LENNON, John	
			Born on 10/9/40 in Liverpool, England. Founding member of The Beatles. Married Cynthia Powell on 8/23/62, had son Julian. Divorced Powell on 11/8/68. Met Yoko Ono (b: 2/18/34 in Japan) in 1966 and married her on 3/20/69. Formed Plastic Ono Band in 1969. To New York City in 1971. Fought deportation from the U.S., 1972-76, until he was granted a permanent visa. Lennon was shot to death on 12/8/80 in New York City.	
1/24/70	**10**	13	● 1. The Plastic Ono Band - Live Peace In Toronto 1969 [L] 9/13/69 concert featuring Eric Clapton on guitar	Apple 3362
12/26/70	**6**	12	● 2. John Lennon/Plastic Ono Band Plastic Ono Band: John's backing musicians; also see Yoko Ono/Plastic Ono Band	Apple 3372
10/2/71	**1**(1)	17	● 3. Imagine *Imagine* (3)	Apple 3379
11/24/73	**9**	11	● 4. Mind Games	Apple 3414
10/19/74	**1**(1)	11	● 5. Walls And Bridges *Whatever Gets You Thru The Night* (1)/*#9 Dream* (9)	Apple 3416
3/15/75	**6**	9	6. Rock 'N' Roll	Apple 3419
11/15/75	**12**	6	7. Shaved Fish [G] *Instant Karma* (3) 1970	Apple 3421
12/6/80	**1**(8)	27	▲ 8. Double Fantasy seven songs by John, seven by Yoko; 1981 Grammy winner: Album of the Year *(Just Like) Starting Over* (1)/*Woman* (2)/ *Watching The Wheels* (10)	Geffen 2001
12/11/82	**33**	8	9. The John Lennon Collection [G]	Geffen 2023
2/11/84	**11**	10	● 10. Milk and Honey six songs by John and six by Yoko; recorded in 1980 *Nobody Told Me* (5)	Polydor 817160
11/5/88	**31**	5	● 11. Imagine: John Lennon [S] from the film documentary of Lennon's life	Cap. 90803 [2]
			LENNON, Julian	
			Born John Charles Julian Lennon on 4/8/63. First child to be born to any of The Beatles.	
11/24/84	**17**	28	● 1. Valotte *Valotte* (9)/*Too Late For Goodbyes* (5) title refers to the French studio where album was recorded	Atlantic 80184
4/19/86	**32**	5	● 2. The Secret Value of DayDreaming	Atlantic 81640
			LETTERMEN, The	
			Harmonic vocal group formed in Los Angeles in 1960. Consisted of Tony Butala (b: 11/20/40), Jim Pike (b: 11/6/38) and Bob Engemann (b: 2/19/36). First recorded for Warner Bros. Engemann replaced by Gary Pike (Jim's brother), 1968.	
3/10/62	**6**	25	1. A Song For Young Love *When I Fall In Love* (7)	Capitol 1669
7/21/62	**30**	2	2. Once Upon A Time	Capitol 1711
3/14/64	**31**	3	3. A Lettermen Kind Of Love	Capitol 2013
4/17/65	**27**	5	4. Portrait Of My Love	Capitol 2270

DATE	POS	WKS	ARTIST—RECORD TITLE	LABEL & NO.
9/18/65	**13**	10	5. The Hit Sounds Of The Lettermen	Capitol 2359
11/19/66	**17**	11	● 6. The Best Of The Lettermen [G]	Capitol 2554
8/5/67	**31**	4	7. Spring!	Capitol 2711
1/27/68	**10**	16	● 8. The Lettermen!!!...and "Live!" [L]	Capitol 2758
			Goin' Out Of My Head/Can't Take My Eyes Off You (7)	
4/20/68	**13**	14	● 9. Goin' Out Of My Head	Capitol 2865
9/20/69	**17**	11	● 10. Hurt So Bad	Capitol 269
			LEVEL 42	
			Pop-soul-jazz foursome from Manchester, England: Mark King (lead vocals), Mike Lindup, and brothers Phil and Boon Gould. The brothers left the band in October, 1987; replaced by Alan Murphy (guitar) and Gary Husband (drums).	
5/10/86	**18**	13	1. World Machine	Polydor 827487
			Something About You (7)	
6/20/87	**23**	10	2. Running In The Family	Polydor 831593
			LEVERT	
			Soul trio from Ohio: Gerald & Sean Levert (sons of the O'Jays' Eddie Levert), and Marc Gordon.	
10/3/87	**32**	7	● 1. The Big Throwdown	Atlantic 81773
			Casanova (5)	
			LEWIS, Gary	
			Leader of pop-rock group The Playboys, formed in Los Angeles in 1964. Consisted of Gary (vocals, drums), Al Ramsey, John West (guitars), David Walker (keyboards) and David Costell (bass). Lewis (b: 7/31/46) is the son of comedian Jerry Lewis. Group worked regularly at Disneyland in 1964. Lewis inducted into the Army on New Year's Day in 1967, resumed career after discharge in 1968.	
			GARY LEWIS AND THE PLAYBOYS:	
5/8/65	**26**	5	1. This Diamond Ring	Liberty 7408
			This Diamond Ring (1)	
10/30/65	**18**	5	2. A Session With Gary Lewis And The Playboys	Liberty 7419
			Count Me In (2)/Save Your Heart For Me (2)	
11/19/66	**10**	13	● 3. Golden Greats [G]	Liberty 7468
			LEWIS, Huey	
			Born Hugh Cregg III on 7/5/50 in New York City. Joined the country-rock band Clover in the late 70s. Formed his six-man pop-rock band The News in San Francisco in 1980: Huey (lead singer), Chris Hayes (lead guitar), Mario Cipollina (bass; brother of Quicksilver Messenger Service guitarist John Cipollina), Bill Gibson (drums), Sean Hopper (keyboards) and Johnny Colla (sax, guitar).	
			HUEY LEWIS AND THE NEWS:	
4/10/82	**13**	14	● 1. Picture This	Chrysalis 1340
			Do You Believe In Love (7)	
11/5/83	**1**(1)	71	▲ 2. Sports	Chrysalis 41412
			Heart And Soul (8)/I Want A New Drug (6)/ The Heart Of Rock & Roll (6)/If This Is It (6)	
9/20/86	**1**(1)	41	▲ 3. Fore!	Chrysalis 41534
			Stuck With You (1)/Hip To Be Square (3)/Jacob's Ladder (1) I Know What I Like (9)/Doing It All For My Baby (6)	
8/20/88	**11**	12	▲ 4. Small World	Chrysalis 41622
			Perfect World (3)	
			LEWIS, Jerry	
			Born Joseph Levitch on 3/16/25 in Newark, New Jersey. Formed comedy team with Dean Martin in 1946 at Atlantic City. Film debut in 1949 in *My Friend Irma*. National chairman in campaign against muscular dystrophy.	
12/22/56	**3**	19	1. Jerry Lewis Just Sings	Decca 8410
			Rock-A-Bye Your Baby With A Dixie Melody (10)	

DATE	POS	WKS	ARTIST—RECORD TITLE	LABEL & NO.
			LEWIS, Jerry Lee	
			Born on 9/29/35 in Ferriday, Louisiana. Played piano since age nine, professionally since age 15. First recorded for Sun in 1956. Appeared in the film *Disc Jockey Jamboree* in 1957. Career waned in 1958 after marriage to 13-year-old cousin, Myra Gale Brown, daughter of his bass player. Made comeback in country music beginning in 1968. Nicknamed "The Killer," Lewis has been surrounded by personal tragedies in the past two decades, survived several serious illnesses in the past six years. Cousin to country singer Mickey Gilley and TV evangelist Jimmy Swaggart. Inducted into the Rock and Roll Hall of Fame in 1986. Jerry's early career documented in the 1989 film *Great Balls Of Fire* starring Dennis Quaid.	
5/19/73	**37**	3	1. The Session recorded in London with Peter Frampton, Rory Gallagher, Albert & Alvin Lee and others	Mercury 803 [2]
			LEWIS, Ramsey	
			Ramsey formed the Gentlemen Of Swing, a jazz-oriented trio, in 1956 in Chicago. Consisted of Ramsey (b: 5/27/35, Chicago; piano), Eldee Young (bass) and Isaac "Red" Holt (drums). All had been in The Clefs in the early 50s. First recorded for Chess/Argo in 1956. Disbanded in 1965; Young and Holt then formed the Young-Holt Trio. Lewis re-formed his trio with Cleveland Eaton (bass) and Maurice White (later with Earth, Wind & Fire; drums). Reunited with Young and Holt in 1983.	
			THE RAMSEY LEWIS TRIO:	
9/11/65	**2**(1)	33	1. The In Crowd [I-L] *The 'In' Crowd* (5)	Argo 757
3/12/66	**15**	15	2. Hang On Ramsey! [I-L] above albums are by the original trio	Cadet 761
			RAMSEY LEWIS:	
10/8/66	**16**	13	3. Wade In The Water [I]	Cadet 774
2/8/75	**12**	14	● 4. Sun Goddess with Earth, Wind & Fire on two of six cuts	Columbia 33194
			LIGHT, Enoch	
			Enoch was born on 8/18/07 in Canton, Ohio. Died in New York City on 7/31/78. Conductor of own orchestra, The Light Brigade, since 1935. President of Grand Award label and managing director for Command Records, for whom he produced a long string of hit stereo percussion albums in the 60s. Enoch's studio musicians variously billed as Terry Snyder And The All-Stars (Terry died on 3/15/63 [age 47]), and The Command All-Stars. Also see Charleston City All-Stars, Los Admiradores, and Tony Mottola.	
6/15/59	**38**	2	1. I Want To Be Happy Cha Cha's * [I]	Grand Award 388
1/25/60	**1**(13)	105	● 2. Persuasive Percussion ** [I]	Command 800
1/25/60	**2**(5)	68	3. Provocative Percussion *** [I]	Command 806
8/22/60	**3**	36	4. Persuasive Percussion, Volume 2 ** [I]	Command 808
9/19/60	**4**	31	5. Provocative Percussion, Volume 2 * [I]	Command 810
5/1/61	**3**	15	6. Persuasive Percussion, Volume 3 *** [I]	Command 817
10/9/61	**1**(7)	57	7. Stereo 35/MM **** [I] 35/MM: magnetic film used in recording process	Command 826
2/17/62	**8**	22	8. Stereo 35/MM, Volume Two **** [I]	Command 831
3/3/62	**34**	5	9. Persuasive Percussion, Volume 4 *** [I]	Command 830
4/21/62	**27**	12	10. Great Themes From Hit Films **** [I]	Command 835
12/22/62	**8**	29	11. Big Band Bossa Nova [I]	Command 844
			*ENOCH LIGHT AND THE LIGHT BRIGADE ****TERRY SNYDER AND THE ALL STARS** *****THE COMMAND ALL-STARS** ******ENOCH LIGHT AND HIS ORCHESTRA**	

DATE	POS	WKS	ARTIST—RECORD TITLE	LABEL & NO.
			LIGHTFOOT, Gordon	
			Born on 11/17/38 in Orillia, Ontario, Canada. Folk-pop-country singer/songwriter/ guitarist. Worked on "Country Hoedown," CBC-TV series. Teamed with Jim Whalen as the Two Tones in the mid-60s. Wrote hit "Early Mornin' Rain" for Peter, Paul and Mary. First recorded for Chateau in 1965.	
1/30/71	**12**	12	● 1. Sit Down Young Stranger *If You Could Read My Mind* (5)	Reprise 6392
7/3/71	**38**	3	2. Summer Side Of Life	Reprise 2037
3/16/74	**1**(2)	23	▲ 3. Sundown *Sundown* (1)/*Carefree Highway* (10)	Reprise 2177
3/15/75	**10**	9	4. Cold On The Shoulder	Reprise 2206
1/3/76	**34**	4	▲ 5. Gord's Gold [G] first record features re-recordings of his 60s songs	Reprise 2237 [2]
7/17/76	**12**	26	▲ 6. Summertime Dream *Wreck Of The Edmund Fitzgerald* (2)	Reprise 2246
2/11/78	**22**	7	● 7. Endless Wire	Warner 3149
			LIMELITERS, The	
			Folk trio formed in Hollywood in 1959. Consisted of Glen Yarbrough (tenor), Lou Gottlieb (bass) and Alex Hassilev (baritone). Yarbrough went solo in 1963.	
2/27/61	**5**	42	1. Tonight: In Person [L] recorded at the Ash Grove, Hollywood, California	RCA 2272
10/2/61	**40**	2	2. The Limeliters	Elektra 7180
10/9/61	**8**	22	3. The Slightly Fabulous Limeliters [L]	RCA 2393
2/17/62	**14**	21	4. Sing Out!	RCA 2445
6/16/62	**25**	11	5. Through Children's Eyes [L] featuring 70 children from Berkeley, California	RCA 2512
10/13/62	**21**	6	6. Folk Matinee	RCA 2547
3/9/63	**37**	2	7. Our Men In San Francisco [L]	RCA 2609
			LINDSAY, Mark	
			Born on 3/9/42 in Cambridge, Idaho. Lead singer of Paul Revere & The Raiders.	
3/28/70	**36**	4	1. Arizona *Arizona* (10)	Columbia 9986
			LIPPS, INC.	
			Funk project from Minneapolis formed by producer/songwriter/ multi-instrumentalist Steven Greenberg. Vocals by Miss Black Minnesota U.S.A. of 1976, Cynthia Johnson.	
5/3/80	**5**	13	● 1. Mouth To Mouth *Funkytown* (1)	Casablanca 7197
			LISA LISA AND CULT JAM	
			Harlem R&B-rap trio: Lisa Velez, Mike Hughes and Alex "Spanador" Moseley.	
5/16/87	**7**	29	▲ 1. Spanish Fly all songs written, arranged and produced by Full Force *Head To Toe* (1)/*Lost In Emotion* (1)	Columbia 40477
			LITTLE, Rich	
			Born on 11/26/38 in Ottawa, Canada. Comedian/impressionist. Made first U.S. television appearance on "The Judy Garland Show" in 1964.	
2/27/82	**29**	6	1. The First Family Rides Again [C] with Melanie Chartoff, Michael Richards, Shelley Hack, Jenilee Harrison, Earle Doud (producer) and Vaughn Meader	Boardwalk 33248

DATE	POS	WKS	ARTIST—RECORD TITLE	LABEL & NO.
			LITTLE FEAT	
			Los Angeles rock band formed in 1969, fronted by guitarist Paul Barrere and vocalist Lowell George with Bill Payne, Richie Hayward, Kenny Gradney and Sam Clayton. George died on 6/29/79 (age 34) of drug-related heart failure. Reunited briefly in 1985. Re-grouped in 1988 with Craig Fuller (formerly with Pure Prairie League) as lead singer; Fred Tackett also added to lineup.	
11/16/74	36	2	● 1. Feats Don't Fail Me Now	Warner 2784
12/6/75	36	3	2. The Last Record Album	Warner 2884
6/4/77	34	4	● 3. Time Loves A Hero	Warner 3015
3/25/78	18	11	▲ 4. Waiting For Columbus [L]	Warner 3140 [2]
12/15/79	29	7	5. Down On The Farm	Warner 3345
9/19/81	39	2	6. Hoy-Hoy! [K]	Warner 3538 [2]
10/1/88	36	4	● 7. Let It Roll	Warner 25750
			LITTLE RICHARD	
			Born Richard Wayne Penniman on 12/5/32 in Macon, Georgia. R&B/rock and roll singer/pianist. Talent contest win led to first recordings for RCA-Victor in 1951. Worked with the Tempo Toppers, 1953-55. Earned degree in theology in 1961 and was ordained a minister. Left R&B for gospel music, 1959-62 and again in mid-70s. The key figure in the transition from R&B to rock and roll. Appeared in three early rock and roll films: *Don't Knock The Rock*, *The Girl Can't Help It* and *Mister Rock 'n' Roll* and the comedy film *Down & Out In Beverly Hills* in 1986. Inducted into the Rock and Roll Hall of Fame in 1986.	
8/5/57	13	5	1. Here's Little Richard [G]	Specialty 2100
			Long Tall Sally (6)/*Jenny, Jenny* (10)	
			LITTLE RIVER BAND	
			Pop-rock group formed in Australia in 1975. Consisted of Glenn Shorrock (lead singer), Rick Formosa, Beeb Birtles and Graham Goble (guitars), Roger McLachlan (bass) and Derek Pellicci (drums). Formosa, McLachlan, replaced by David Briggs (guitar) and George McArdle (bass) after first album. Shorrock replaced by John Farnham in 1983. Numerous personnel changes since 1985. Shorrock replaced Farnham in 1987. 1988 lineup includes: Shorrock, Goble and Pellicci. Band named after a resort town 30 miles outside Melbourne.	
8/26/78	16	12	▲ 1. Sleeper Catcher	Harvest 11783
			Reminiscing (3)/*Lady* (10)	
8/18/79	10	15	▲ 2. First Under The Wire	Capitol 11954
			Lonesome Loser (6)/*Cool Change* (10)	
10/3/81	21	9	● 3. Time Exposure	Capitol 12163
			The Night Owls (6)/*Take It Easy On Me* (10)	
1/8/83	33	12	● 4. Little River Band/Greatest Hits [G]	Capitol 12247
			LIVING COLOUR	
			Black rock quartet from New York City; London-born, Brooklyn-raised lead guitarist/ songwriter Vernon Reid, vocalist Corey Glover (appeared in the film *Platoon*), bassist Muzz Skillings and drummer William Calhoun.	
2/4/89	6	39	▲ 1. Vivid	Epic 44099
			LIVING STRINGS	
			European orchestra.	
2/27/61	26	1	1. Living Strings Play All The Music From Camelot [I]	RCA Camden 657
			L.L. COOL J	
			Real name: James Todd Smith. Rap artist from Queens, New York. Stage name is abbreviation for Ladies Love Cool James.	
6/27/87	3	23	▲ 1. Bigger And Deffer	Def Jam 40793
7/8/89	6	14	▲ 2. Walking With A Panther	Def Jam 45172
			LP features 16 tracks, 18 on the CD and 20 on the cassette	

DATE	POS	WKS	ARTIST—RECORD TITLE	LABEL & NO.
			LOBO	
			Born Roland Kent Lavoie on 7/31/43 in Tallahassee, Florida. Pop singer/songwriter/ guitarist. Played with the Legends in Tampa in 1961. This group included Jim Stafford, Gerald Chambers, Gram Parsons and Jon Corneal. Own publishing company, Boo Publishing, since 1974.	
12/16/72	37	7	1. Of A Simple Man *I'd Love You To Want Me* (2)/ *Don't Expect Me To Be Your Friend* (8)	Big Tree 2013
			LODGE, John — see HAYWARD, Justin	
			LOFGREN, Nils	
			Born in 1952 in Chicago; raised in Maryland. Pop-rock singer/guitarist/ pianist. Leader of Grin (1969-1974). Member of Bruce Springsteen's E Street Band, 1984-85.	
5/22/76	32	3	1. Cry Tough	A&M 4573
4/23/77	36	2	2. I Came To Dance	A&M 4628
			LOGGINS, Kenny	
			Born on 1/7/47 in Everett, Washington. Pop-rock singer/songwriter/guitarist. Signed as a solo artist with Columbia in 1971 where he met and recorded with Jim Messina from 1972-76. Also see Soundtracks *Footloose* and *Top Gun.*	
6/11/77	27	7	▲ 1. Celebrate Me Home	Columbia 34655
8/5/78	7	17	▲ 2. Nightwatch *Whenever I Call You 'Friend'* (5)	Columbia 35387
10/27/79	16	24	▲ 3. Keep The Fire	Columbia 36172
10/11/80	11	11	● 4. Kenny Loggins Alive [L]	Columbia 36738 [2]
9/25/82	13	9	● 5. High Adventure	Columbia 38127
			LOGGINS & MESSINA	
			Duo of Kenneth Clarke Loggins (b: 1/7/47, Everett, Washington) and James Messina (b: 12/5/47, Maywood, California). Loggins was raised in Alhambra, California and played guitar from age 13. Worked with Second Helping and Gator Creek and recorded in the late 60s. Wrote "House On Pooh Corner" hit for the Dirt Band. Messina was raised in Harlingen, Texas and played in bands from age 13. Worked as a recording engineer and producer from 1965. Worked with Buffalo Springfield and Poco. Duo formed in 1970.	
12/30/72	16	13	▲ 1. Loggins And Messina *Your Mama Don't Dance* (4)	Columbia 31748
11/24/73	10	17	▲ 2. Full Sail	Columbia 32540
5/25/74	5	16	● 3. On Stage [L]	Columbia 32848 [2]
11/23/74	8	12	● 4. Mother Lode	Columbia 33175
9/20/75	21	8	5. So Fine featuring popular 50s tunes	Columbia 33810
2/7/76	16	9	● 6. Native Sons	Columbia 33578
			LOMBARDO, Guy	
			Born on 6/19/02 in London, Ontario, Canada; died on 11/5/77. Leader of the #1 dance band of the 30s and 40s. Familiar yet today for his classic theme "Auld Lang Syne," which he traditionally played to climax his annual New Year's Eve broadcasts. **GUY LOMBARDO AND HIS ROYAL CANADIANS:**	
1/19/57	18	2	1. Your Guy Lombardo Medley [I] medley of 40 tunes	Capitol 739
7/28/58	12	4	2. Berlin By Lombardo [I] medley of 40 Irving Berlin songs	Capitol 1019

DATE	POS	WKS	ARTIST—RECORD TITLE	LABEL & NO.
			LONDON, Julie	
			Born on 9/26/26 in Santa Rosa, California. Singer/actress. Played Dixie McCall on the TV series "Emergency." Married to Jack Webb, 1945-53.	
1/28/56	**2**(2)	14	1. Julie Is Her Name *Cry Me A River* (9)	Liberty 3006
8/11/56	**16**	8	2. Lonely Girl	Liberty 3012
12/15/56	**18**	6	3. Calendar Girl	Liberty 9002
7/22/57	**15**	4	4. About The Blues	Liberty 3043
			LONG, Loretta — see CHILDRENS section	
			LONGET, Claudine	
			Born on 1/29/42 in France. Singer/actress. Formerly married to Andy Williams.	
6/3/67	**11**	22	● 1. Claudine	A&M 4121
11/25/67	**33**	6	2. The Look Of Love	A&M 4129
6/1/68	**29**	5	3. Love Is Blue	A&M 4142
			LOPEZ, Trini	
			Born Trinidad Lopez III on 5/15/37 in Dallas. Pop-folk singer/guitarist. Discovered by Don Costa while performing at PJ's nightclub in Los Angeles. Portrayed Pedro Jiminez in film *The Dirty Dozen*.	
8/3/63	**2**(6)	48	● 1. Trini Lopez At PJ'S [L] *If I Had A Hammer* (3)	Reprise 6093
12/21/63	**11**	8	2. More Trini Lopez At PJ'S [L]	Reprise 6103
7/11/64	**32**	2	3. On The Move [L]	Reprise 6112
9/19/64	**18**	11	4. The Latin Album [F]	Reprise 6125
11/28/64	**30**	7	5. Live At Basin St. East [L]	Reprise 6134
2/27/65	**18**	9	6. The Folk Album	Reprise 6147
7/24/65	**32**	3	7. The Love Album	Reprise 6165
			LOS ADMIRADORES	
			Percussion group produced by Enoch Light.	
8/29/60	**2**(1)	34	1. Bongos Bongos Bongos [I]	Command 809
10/24/60	**3**	16	2. Bongos/Flutes/Guitars [I]	Command 812
			LOS INDIOS TABAJARAS	
			Brazilian Indian brothers: Natalicio and Antenor Lima.	
11/30/63	**7**	11	1. Maria Elena [I] *Maria Elena* (6)	RCA 2822
			LOS LOBOS	
			Rock quintet based in Los Angeles. Includes: David Hidalgo (lead vocals), Cesar Rosas, Conrad Lozano, Louie Perez and Steve Berlin.	
8/8/87	**1**(2)	19	▲ 1. La Bamba [S] film based on the life of Ritchie Valens; eight cuts by Los Lobos, plus four by other artists *La Bamba* (1)	Slash 25605
			LOVE AND ROCKETS	
			British trio: Daniel Ash (guitar, vocals), Kevin Haskins (drums) and David J. (bass). All were members of Bauhaus, 1979-83. Band name taken from the title of an underground comic book.	
6/10/89	**14**	17	● 1. Love And Rockets *So Alive* (3)	Begr. B. 9715

Gary Lewis and his group the Playboys scored several top 10 hits in the mid-60s but were typically scorned by hippies of the era as being too blatantly commercial. Only later did it become evident that counterculture icons Al Kooper and Leon Russell had played an integral part of the group's recording career.

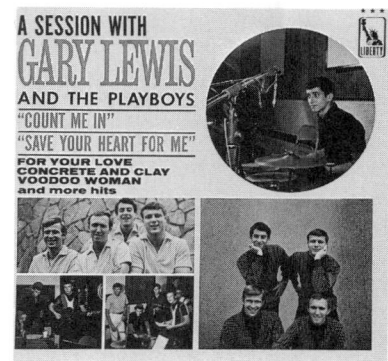

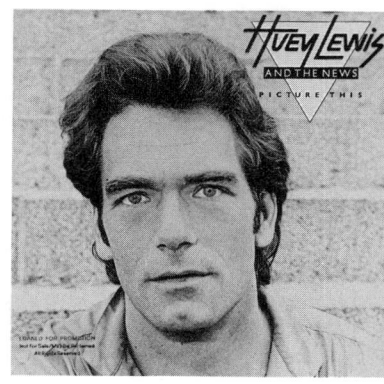

Huey Lewis and the News had a No. 1 album in 1983 with the hit-filled *Sports*. Lewis became a major pop figure in the 80s, but his antics years earlier with the San Francisco band Clover—who'd recorded pre-Lewis for Fantasy in the 60s and with Lewis for Mercury in the 70s—still intrigue record collectors and rock historians alike.

Jerry Lewis's ties to the music community might be viewed now as a function of his ties with partner Dean Martin and son Gary, but his recordings for Capitol in the early 50s, reissued on CD in 1990, proved he was no stranger to the recording studio.

The **Limeliters** scored two top 10 albums in 1961 with *Tonight: In Person* and *The Slightly Fabulous Limeliters*, and their *Sing Out!* reached No. 14 in 1962. Key group figure Glenn Yarbrough would later hit solo in 1965 with his single "Baby The Rain Must Fall."

Loggins and Messina's high profile in the 70s took a curious turn in the 80s: After a split, Loggins became known as the "soundtrack king" for his work on such films as *Caddyshack* and *Top Gun*, while Messina, after laying low for a time, re-formed his previous band Poco in 1989 and surprised many with a high-charting reunion album.

Julie London's influence has been of remarkable duration: her famous 1955 hit "Cry Me A River" was covered on a 1983 Mercury album, *Show People*, by U.K. singer Mari Wilson, bearing an album design much in keeping with London's own late 50s classics on Liberty such as *Calendar Girl*.

Loverboy, a Vancouver quintet formed in the late 70s, dominated the airwaves of the early 80s with such hits as "Turn Me Loose," "Working For The Weekend" and "Hot Girls In Love." Lead singer Mike Reno would go on to score a top 10 hit in 1984 with "Almost Paradise . . . Love Theme from *Footloose*," accompanied by Heart vocalist Ann Wilson.

Trini Lopez may now only be remembered for his mid-60s hits "If I Had A Hammer" and "Lemon Tree," but during that era, Lopez's accomplishments as an album artist were evidenced by his 14 LPs that reached the Top Pop Albums chart between 1963-67—including this one, which made it to No. 11 in 1963.

Gloria Lynne's work on the small Everest label reached its peak in 1963, when *Gloria, Marty & Strings*, an album arranged and conducted by Marty Paich, reached No. 27 on the charts.

Lynyrd Skynyrd's first album—*Pronounced leh-nerd skin-nerd*, issued in 1973—was one of MCA's first signings to the Sounds Of The South label. The group's famed track "Free Bird" later became one of the most widely-played songs in the history of album radio.

DATE	POS	WKS	ARTIST—RECORD TITLE	LABEL & NO.
			LOVERBOY	
			Rock quintet formed in Vancouver, Canada in 1978: Mike Reno (lead singer), Paul Dean (lead guitar), Scott Smith (bass), Matt Frenette (drums) and Doug Johnson (keyboards, left by 1989).	
3/28/81	**13**	17	▲ 1. Loverboy	Columbia 36762
12/5/81	**7**	51	▲ 2. Get Lucky	Columbia 37638
7/2/83	**7**	22	▲ 3. Keep It Up	Columbia 38703
9/21/85	**13**	22	▲ 4. Lovin' Every Minute Of It	Columbia 39953
			Lovin' Every Minute Of It (9)/*This Could Be The Night* (10)	
			LOVE UNLIMITED	
			Female soul trio from San Pedro, California: sisters Glodean & Linda James, and Diane Taylor. Barry White, who married Glodean on 7/4/74, was their manager and producer. Glodean recorded duets with Barry in 1981.	
12/8/73	**3**	17	● 1. Under The Influence Of...	20th Century 414
			LOVE UNLIMITED ORCHESTRA	
			Studio orchestra conducted and arranged by Barry White.	
2/23/74	**8**	11	● 1. Rhapsody In White [I]	20th Century 433
			Love's Theme (1); first appeared on Love Unlimited's album *Under The Influence Of...*	
12/28/74	**28**	2	● 2. White Gold [I]	20th Century 458
			LOVIN' SPOONFUL, The	
			Jug-band rock group formed in New York City in 1965. Consisted of John Sebastian (lead vocals, songwriter, guitarist, harmonica), Zal Yanovsky (lead guitar), Steve Boone (bass) and Joe Butler (drums). Sebastian had been with the Even Dozen Jug Band; did session work at Elektra. Yanovsky and Sebastian were members of the Mugwumps with Cass Elliott and Denny Doherty (later with The Mamas & The Papas). Yanovsky replaced by Jerry Yester (keyboards) in 1967. Disbanded in 1968.	
5/7/66	**10**	11	1. Daydream	Kama Sutra 8051
			You Didn't Have To Be So Nice (10)/*Daydream* (2)	
7/16/66	**32**	7	2. Do You Believe In Magic	Kama Sutra 8050
			Do You Believe In Magic (9)/ *Did You Ever Have To Make Up Your Mind* (2)	
1/21/67	**14**	8	3. Hums Of The Lovin' Spoonful	Kama Sutra 8054
			Summer In The City (1)/*Rain On The Roof* (10)/ *Nashville Cats* (8)	
3/25/67	**3**	26	● 4. The Best Of The Lovin' Spoonful [G]	Kama Sutra 8056
			LOWE, Nick	
			Born on 3/25/49 in Woodbridge, Suffolk, England. With Brinsley Schwarz (1970-75) and Rockpile. Married to Carlene Carter. Produced albums for Elvis Costello and Graham Parker and The Rumour.	
9/8/79	**31**	7	1. Labour Of Lust	Columbia 36087
			L.T.D.	
			Ten-man, R&B-funk band from Greensboro, North Carolina; Jeffrey Osborne, lead singer. Osborne left in 1980, replaced by Leslie Wilson and Andre Ray. L.T.D. means Love, Togetherness and Devotion.	
9/10/77	**21**	14	● 1. Something To Love	A&M 4646
			(Every Time I Turn Around) Back In Love Again (4)	
7/22/78	**18**	11	▲ 2. Togetherness	A&M 4705
8/4/79	**29**	5	● 3. Devotion	A&M 4771
9/20/80	**28**	8	4. Shine On	A&M 4819

DATE	POS	WKS	ARTIST—RECORD TITLE	LABEL & NO.
			## LUBOFF, Norman	
			Born on 5/14/17 in Chicago; died of cancer on 9/22/87. Composer/conductor; formed own choral group.	
			THE NORMAN LUBOFF CHOIR:	
10/15/55	**15**	3	1. Songs Of The West	Columbia 657
7/14/56	**19**	2	2. Songs Of The South	Columbia 860
5/27/57	**19**	4	3. Calypso Holiday	Columbia 1000
1/13/58	**22**	1	4. Songs Of Christmas [X]	Columbia 926
			## LULU	
			Born Marie Lawrie on 11/3/48 near Glasgow, Scotland. Married to Maurice Gibb (Bee Gees) from 1969-73.	
12/2/67	**24**	10	1. To Sir With Love	Epic 26339
			To Sir With Love (1); also see soundtrack of same title	
			## LYMAN, Arthur	
			Born on the island of Kauai, Hawaii in 1934. Plays vibraphone, guitar, piano and drums. Formerly with the Martin Denny Trio.	
5/12/58	**6**	62	1. Taboo [I]	HiFi 806
7/24/61	**10**	18	2. Yellow Bird [I]	HiFi 1004
			Yellow Bird (4)	
4/6/63	**36**	1	3. I Wish You Love [I]	HiFi 1009
			## LYMON, Frankie — see TEENAGERS	
			## LYNN, Cheryl	
			Born on 3/11/57 in Los Angeles. Soul singer. Discovered on TV's "Gong Show." Cousin of D'La Vance.	
1/27/79	**23**	6	● 1. Cheryl Lynn	Columbia 35486
			## LYNNE, Gloria	
			Born on 11/23/31 in New York City. Jazz-styled vocalist.	
3/16/63	**39**	4	1. Gloria Lynne at the Las Vegas Thunderbird [L]	Everest 5208
			with the Herman Foster Trio	
4/18/64	**27**	10	2. Gloria, Marty & Strings	Everest 5220
			arranged and conducted by Marty Paich	
			## LYNYRD SKYNYRD	
			Southern-rock band formed while members were in high school in Jacksonville, Florida in 1965. Named after their gym teacher Leonard Skinner. Band nucleus consisted of Ronnie Van Zant (b: 1/15/49; lead singer), Gary Rossington (guitar) and Allen Collins (guitar). Plane crash on 10/20/77 in Gillsburg, Mississippi killed Van Zandt and members Steve and Cassie Gaines. Gary and Allen formed the Rossington Collins Band in 1980; split in 1982. Collins (paralyzed in a car accident in 1986) died of pneumonia on 1/23/90 (age 37).	
5/25/74	**12**	19	▲ 1. Second Helping	MCA/Sounds 413
			Sweet Home Alabama (8)	
2/15/75	**27**	4	▲ 2. Lynyrd Skynyrd (pronounced leh-nerd skin-nerd)	MCA/Sounds 363
4/19/75	**9**	10	▲ 3. Nuthin' Fancy	MCA 2137
3/13/76	**20**	5	● 4. Gimme Back My Bullets	MCA 2170
10/16/76	**9**	15	▲ 5. One More From The Road [L]	MCA 6001 [2]
11/19/77	**5**	15	▲ 6. Street Survivors	MCA 3029
			album released three days before the plane crash	
9/30/78	**15**	7	▲ 7. Skynyrd's First And...Last [E]	MCA 3047
			recordings from 1970-1972	
1/5/80	**12**	11	▲ 8. Gold & Platinum [G]	

DATE	POS	WKS	ARTIST—RECORD TITLE	LABEL & NO.

M

MABLEY, Moms

Born Loretta Mary Aiken on 3/19/1894 in Brevard, North Carolina; died on 5/23/75. Bawdy comedienne/actress. In the films *Boarding House Blues*, *Emperor Jones* and *Amazing Grace*.

DATE	POS	WKS	ARTIST—RECORD TITLE		LABEL & NO.
5/29/61	16	11	1. Moms Mabley At The "UN"	[C]	Chess 1452
12/11/61	39	1	2. Moms Mabley at The Playboy Club	[C]	Chess 1460
4/28/62	28	6	3. Moms Mabley At Geneva Conference	[C]	Chess 1463
9/29/62	27	4	4. Moms Mabley Breaks It Up	[C]	Chess 1472
3/2/63	19	5	5. Young Men, Si - Old Men, No	[C]	Chess 1477

MacDONALD, Jeanette, & Nelson Eddy

Top movie duo of the 30s. Jeanette was born on 6/18/01 in Philadelphia; died on 1/14/65. Nelson was born on 6/29/01 in Providence, Rhode Island; died on 3/6/67.

DATE	POS	WKS	ARTIST—RECORD TITLE	LABEL & NO.
5/25/59	40	1	● 1. Favorites In Hi-Fi	RCA 1738

MacGREGOR, Mary

Born on 5/6/48 in St. Paul, Minnesota. Pop singer.

DATE	POS	WKS	ARTIST—RECORD TITLE	LABEL & NO.
2/19/77	17	7	1. Torn Between Two Lovers *Torn Between Two Lovers* (1)	Ariola Am. 50015

MADONNA

Born Madonna Louise Ciccone on 8/16/58 in Bay City, Michigan. To New York in the late 70s; performed with the Pearl Lange and Alvin Ailey dance troupes. Starred in the films *Desperately Seeking Susan*, *Shanghai Surprise*, *Who's That Girl?*, *Bloodhounds Of Broadway* and *Dick Tracy*. Appeared in Broadway's *Speed-The-Plow*. Married to actor Sean Penn from 1985-89.

DATE	POS	WKS	ARTIST—RECORD TITLE		LABEL & NO.
2/18/84	8	36	▲ 1. Madonna *Borderline* (10)/*Lucky Star* (4)		Sire 23867
12/8/84	1(3)	52	▲ 2. Like A Virgin *Like A Virgin* (1)/*Material Girl* (2)/*Angel* (5)/ *Dress You Up* (5)		Sire 25157
7/19/86	1(5)	52	▲ 3. True Blue *Live To Tell* (1)/*Papa Don't Preach* (1)/*True Blue* (3)/ *Open Your Heart* (1)/*La Isla Bonita* (4)		Sire 25442
8/22/87	7	13	▲ 4. Who's That Girl four of nine cuts are by Madonna *Who's That Girl* (1)/*Causing A Commotion* (2)	[S]	Sire 25611
12/12/87	14	12	▲ 5. You Can Dance features seven extended remixes of Madonna's dance hits	[K]	Sire 25535
4/8/89	1(6)	31	▲ 6. Like A Prayer *Like A Prayer* (1)/*Express Yourself* (2)/*Cherish* (2)/ *Keep It Together* (8)		Sire 25844
6/16/90	2(3)	16	▲ 7. I'm Breathless *Vogue* (1)/*Hanky Panky* (10) songs from and songs inspired by the film *Dick Tracy*	[S]	Sire/Warner 26209

MAHARIS, George

Born on 9/1/33 in New York City. Played Buz Murdock on TV's "Route 66."

DATE	POS	WKS	ARTIST—RECORD TITLE	LABEL & NO.
7/14/62	10	8	1. George Maharis Sings!	Epic 26001
9/15/62	32	3	2. Portrait In Music	Epic 26021

DATE	POS	WKS	ARTIST—RECORD TITLE	LABEL & NO.
			MAHAVISHNU ORCHESTRA — see McLAUGHLIN, John	
			MALMSTEEN, Yngwie J.	
			Swedish; former lead guitarist of Alcatrazz. Backed by his band Rising Force: Anders Johansson, Joe Lynn Turner (vocals) and Jens Johansson.	
			YNGWIE J. MALMSTEEN'S RISING FORCE:	
5/14/88	**40**	2	1. Odyssey	Polydor 835451
			MALO	
			Latin-rock band formed by Jorge Santana (brother of Carlos).	
3/18/72	**14**	14	1. Malo	Warner 2584
			MAMAS & THE PAPAS, The	
			Quartet formed in New York City in 1963. Consisted of John Phillips (b: 8/30/35, Paris Island, South Carolina); Holly Michelle Gilliam Phillips (b: 6/4/45, Long Beach, California); Dennis Doherty (b: 11/29/41, Halifax, Nova Scotia, Canada) and Cass Elliot. Phillips had been in the Journeymen, married Michelle Gilliam in 1962. Elliot had been in the Mugwumps with Doherty and future Lovin' Spoonful member Zal Yanovsky. Group moved to Los Angeles in 1964. Disbanded in 1968, reunited briefly in 1971. Michelle Phillips in films *Dillinger* and *Valentino*. Formed new group in 1982: John and daughter, actress MacKenzie Phillips, Dennis Doherty and Spanky McFarlane of Spanky & Our Gang. Michelle later married actor Dennis Hopper.	
4/23/66	**1**(1)	34	● 1. If You Can Believe Your Eyes And Ears *California Dreamin'* (4)/*Monday, Monday* (1)	Dunhill 50006
10/8/66	**4**	32	● 2. The Mamas & The Papas *I Saw Her Again* (5)/*Words Of Love* (5)	Dunhill 50010
3/25/67	**2**(7)	25	● 3. The Mamas & The Papas Deliver *Dedicated To The One I Love* (2)/*Creeque Alley* (5)	Dunhill 50014
11/25/67	**5**	18	● 4. Farewell To The First Golden Era [G]	Dunhill 50025
6/22/68	**15**	11	5. The Papas & The Mamas	Dunhill 50031
			MANASSAS — see STILLS, Stephen	
			MANCHESTER, Melissa	
			Born on 2/15/51 in the Bronx. Vocalist/pianist/composer. Studied with Paul Simon at University School of the Arts in the early 70s. Former backup singer for Bette Midler.	
7/19/75	**12**	11	● 1. Melissa *Midnight Blue* (6)	Arista 4031
2/28/76	**24**	8	2. Better Days & Happy Endings	Arista 4067
3/17/79	**33**	3	3. Don't Cry Out Loud *Don't Cry Out Loud* (10)	Arista 4186
8/28/82	**19**	8	4. Hey Ricky *You Should Hear How She Talks About You* (5)	Arista 9574
			MANCINI, Henry	
			Born on 4/16/24 in Cleveland. Leading film and TV composer/arranger/conductor. Staff composer for Universal Pictures, 1952-58. Won more Oscars (4) and Grammys (20) than any other pop artist.	
2/9/59	**1**(10)	47	● 1. The Music From Peter Gunn 1958 Grammy winner: Album of the Year	[TV-I] RCA 1956
6/29/59	**7**	28	2. More Music From Peter Gunn	[TV-I] RCA 2040
3/28/60	**2**(1)	35	3. Music From Mr. Lucky	[TV-I] RCA 2198
5/8/61	**28**	10	4. Mr. Lucky Goes Latin [I]	RCA 2360
10/9/61	**1**(12)	69	● 5. Breakfast At Tiffany's [S-I]	RCA 2362
3/10/62	**28**	7	6. Combo! [I] recorded June, 1960	RCA 2258

DATE	POS	WKS	ARTIST—RECORD TITLE		LABEL & NO.
6/30/62	37	1	7. Experiment In Terror	[S-I]	RCA 2442
7/28/62	4	35	8. Hatari!	[S-I]	RCA 2559
2/23/63	12	23	9. Our Man In Hollywood		RCA 2604
7/6/63	5	11	10. Uniquely Mancini	[I]	RCA 2692
2/1/64	6	18	11. Charade	[S-I]	RCA 2755
4/25/64	8	41	● 12. The Pink Panther	[S-I]	RCA 2795
8/15/64	15	7	13. The Concert Sound of Henry Mancini medleys of 30 tunes - with a 70-piece orchestra	[I]	RCA 2897
2/20/65	11	11	14. Dear Heart And Other Songs About Love		RCA 2990
6/7/69	5	19	● 15. A Warm Shade Of Ivory *Love Theme From Romeo & Juliet* (1)	[I]	RCA 4140
3/6/71	26	4	16. Mancini plays the Theme From Love Story		RCA 4466

MANDRILL

Brooklyn Latin jazz-rock septet formed in 1968 by Wilson brothers: Louis "Sweet Lou," Richard "Dr. Ric" and Carlos "Mad Dog".

DATE	POS	WKS	ARTIST—RECORD TITLE		LABEL & NO.
5/12/73	28	8	1. Composite Truth		Polydor 5043

MANFRED MANN

Rock group formed in England in 1964: Manfred Mann (real name: Michael Lubowitz; keyboards), Paul Jones (vocals), Mike Hugg (drums), Michael Vickers (guitar) and Tom McGuiness (bass). Manfred Mann formed his new Earth Band in 1971, featuring Mick Rogers (vocals), Colin Pattenden (bass) and Chris Slade (drums). Mick replaced by Chris Thompson (vocals, guitar) in 1976. Thompson also recorded with own group Night in 1979.

DATE	POS	WKS	ARTIST—RECORD TITLE		LABEL & NO.
1/23/65	35	4	1. the Manfred Mann album *Do Wah Diddy Diddy* (1)		Ascot 16015
			MANFRED MANN'S EARTH BAND:		
1/22/77	10	11	● 2. The Roaring Silence *Blinded By The Light* (1)		Warner 2965
3/24/84	40	2	3. Somewhere In Afrika		Arista 8194

MANGIONE, Chuck

Born on 11/29/40 in Rochester, New York. Flugelhorn/bandleader/composer. Recorded with older brother Gaspare ("Gap") as the Jazz Brothers for Riverside in 1960. To New York City in 1965; played with Maynard Ferguson, Kai Winding, and Art Blakey's Jazz Messengers.

DATE	POS	WKS	ARTIST—RECORD TITLE		LABEL & NO.
2/18/78	2(2)	28	▲ 1. Feels So Good *Feels So Good* (4)	[I]	A&M 4658
9/30/78	14	10	● 2. Children of Sanchez	[S-I]	A&M 6700 [2]
7/28/79	27	6	3. An Evening Of Magic - Chuck Mangione Live At The Hollywood Bowl	[I-L]	A&M 6701 [2]
3/1/80	8	11	● 4. Fun and Games	[I]	A&M 3715

MANHATTANS, The

Soul vocal group from Jersey City, New Jersey. Consisted of George "Smitty" Smith (d: 1970, spinal meningitis; lead vocals), Winfred "Blue" Lovett (bass), Edward "Sonny" Bivins and Kenneth "Wally" Kelly (tenors) and Richard Taylor (baritone). Smith replaced by Gerald Alston in 1971. First recorded for Piney in 1962. Taylor (aka Abdul Rashid Talhah) left in 1976; died 12/7/87 (age 47) following a lengthy illness. Alston began solo career in 1988.

DATE	POS	WKS	ARTIST—RECORD TITLE		LABEL & NO.
6/19/76	16	12	● 1. The Manhattans *Kiss And Say Goodbye* (1)		Columbia 33820
6/7/80	24	10	● 2. After Midnight *Shining Star* (5)		Columbia 36411

DATE	POS	WKS	ARTIST—RECORD TITLE	LABEL & NO.
			MANHATTAN TRANSFER, The	
			Versatile vocal harmony quartet formed in New York City in 1972: Tim Hauser, Alan Paul, Janis Siegel and Cheryl Bentyne (replaced by Laurel Masse in 1979).	
6/28/75	33	4	● 1. The Manhattan Transfer	Atlantic 18133
7/4/81	22	13	2. Mecca For Moderns	Atlantic 16036
			Boy From New York City (7)	
			MANILOW, Barry	
			Born Barry Alan Pincus on 6/17/49 in Brooklyn. Vocalist/pianist/composer. Studied at New York's Juilliard School of Music. On the WCBS-TV series "Callback." Worked at New York's Continental Baths bathhouse in New York in 1972 as Bette Midler's accompanist; later produced her first two albums. Wrote and sang jingles for Dr. Pepper, Pepsi and McDonalds ("You Deserve A Break Today").	
1/11/75	9	11	▲ 1. Barry Manilow II	Arista 4016
			Mandy (1)	
10/4/75	28	6	● 2. Barry Manilow I	Arista 4007
			above two albums previously released on the Bell label	
			Could It Be Magic (6)	
11/29/75	5	15	▲ 3. Tryin' To Get The Feeling	Arista 4060
			I Write The Songs (1)/*Tryin' To Get The Feeling Again* (10)	
8/21/76	6	27	▲ 4. This One's For You	Arista 4090
			Weekend In New England (10)/*Looks Like We Made It* (1)	
5/28/77	1(1)	26	▲ 5. Barry Manilow/Live [L]	Arista 8500 [2]
3/4/78	3	28	▲ 6. Even Now	Arista 4164
			Can't Smile Without You (3)/*Copacabana (At The Copa)* (8)/	
			Somewhere In The Night (9)	
12/2/78	7	16	▲ 7. Greatest Hits [G]	Arista 8601 [2]
10/20/79	9	15	▲ 8. One Voice	Arista 9505
			Ships (9)	
12/20/80	15	9	▲ 9. Barry	Arista 9537
			I Made It Through The Rain (10)	
10/24/81	14	11	● 10. If I Should Love Again	Arista 9573
1/8/83	32	6	● 11. Here Comes The Night	Arista 9610
12/17/83	30	7	● 12. Barry Manilow/Greatest Hits, Vol. II [G]	Arista 8102
1/5/85	28	6	● 13. 2:00 AM Paradise Cafe	Arista 8254
			with jazz greats Sarah Vaughan, Gerry Mulligan and Mel Torme	
			MANN, Herbie	
			Born Herbert Jay Solomon on 4/16/30 in Brooklyn. Saxophonist/flutist/reeds. First recorded with Mat Mathews Quintet for Brunswick in 1953. First recorded as a solo for Bethlehem in 1954.	
11/3/62	30	11	1. Herbie Mann at the Village Gate [I-L]	Atlantic 1380
6/21/69	20	17	2. Memphis Underground [I]	Atlantic 1522
			with Roy Ayers (vibes) and Larry Coryell (guitar)	
6/7/75	27	3	3. Discotheque [I]	Atlantic 1670
			MANN, Manfred — see MANFRED	
			MANNA, Charlie	
			Comedian from New York.	
9/11/61	27	1	1. Manna Overboard!! [C]	Decca 4159

DATE	POS	WKS	ARTIST—RECORD TITLE		LABEL & NO.
			MANNHEIM STEAMROLLER		
			Classical-rock group from Omaha, Nebraska. Best known for their Fresh Aire albums. Under the direction of composer/producer/drummer Chip Davis, who founded American Gramophone Records in 1974. Gained recognition through performance on a series of "Old Home Bread" TV commercials. Davis wrote C.W. McCall's "Convoy." Group's personnel fluctuated; named after Europe's mid-18th century Mannheim School.		
12/17/88	36	4	▲ 1. A Fresh Aire Christmas [X-I]		American G. 1988
			MANTOVANI		
			Born Annunzio Paolo Mantovani on 11/15/05 in Venice, Italy; died on 3/29/80. Played classical violin in England before forming his own orchestra in the early 30s. Achieved international fame 20 years later with his 40-piece orchestra and distinctive "cascading strings" sound.		
			MANTOVANI AND HIS ORCHESTRA:		
2/19/55	13	2	1. The Music Of Rudolf Friml [I]		London 1150
3/19/55	14	2	2. Waltz Time [I]		London 1094
			Charmaine (10) 1951)		
7/9/55	8	8	● 3. Song Hits From Theatreland [I]		London 1219
5/26/56	12	7	4. Waltzes Of Irving Berlin [I]		London 1452
5/27/57	1(1)	113	● 5. Film Encores [I]		London 1700
12/9/57	4	6	● 6. Christmas Carols [X-I]		London 913
3/24/58	22	1	7. Mantovani Plays Tangos [I]		London 768
			above two released in 1953		
5/19/58	5	56	● 8. Gems Forever... [I]		London 3032
11/24/58	7	24	● 9. Strauss Waltzes [I]		London 685
			first released in 1953		
12/22/58	3	3	10. Christmas Carols [X-R]		London 913
2/16/59	13	44	11. Continental Encores [I]		London 3095
6/1/59	6	11	12. Mantovani Stereo Showcase [K-I]		London SS1
6/22/59	14	15	13. Film Encores, Vol. 2 [I]		London 3117
12/21/59	16	3	14. Christmas Carols [X-R]		London 913
1/4/60	8	18	15. All-American Showcase [K-I]		London 3122 [2]
			one side each: Sigmund Romberg, Victor Herbert, Irving Berlin, Rudolf Friml		
3/28/60	11	30	16. The American Scene [I]		London 3136
			side 1 features the music of Stephen Foster		
7/25/60	21	18	17. Songs To Remember [I]		London 3149
12/5/60	2(5)	44	● 18. Mantovani plays music from Exodus and other great themes [I]		London 3231
12/19/60	8	3	19. Christmas Carols [X-R]		London 913
2/20/61	22	1	20. Operetta Memories [I]		London 3181
6/26/61	8	15	21. Italia Mia [I]		London 3239
8/21/61	29	5	22. Themes From Broadway [I]		London 3250
1/6/62	36	2	23. Christmas Carols [X-R]		London 913
6/16/62	8	19	24. American Waltzes [I]		London 248
11/3/62	24	8	25. Moon River and other great film themes [I]		London 249
6/1/63	10	13	26. Latin Rendezvous [I]		London 295
12/19/64	37	3	27. The Incomparable Mantovani [I]		London 392
5/1/65	26	8	28. The Mantovani Sound - Big Hits From Broadway And Hollywood [I]		London 419
4/16/66	23	8	29. Mantovani Magic [I]		London 448
11/26/66	27	7	30. Mr. Music...Mantovani [I]		London 474

DATE	POS	WKS	ARTIST—RECORD TITLE	LABEL & NO.
			MARIE, Teena	
			White funk singer/composer/keyboardist/guitarist/producer/actress, born Mary Christine Brockert in Santa Monica in 1957; raised in Venice, California.	
11/22/80	38	3	1. Irons In The Fire	Gordy 997
7/18/81	23	9	● 2. It Must Be Magic	Gordy 1004
3/2/85	31	9	● 3. Starchild	Epic 39528
			Lovergirl (4)	
			MARKETTS, The	
			Hollywood, California instrumental surf quintet.	
3/14/64	37	2	1. Out Of Limits! [I]	Warner 1537
			Out Of Limits (3)	
			MARLEY, Bob	
			Singer/guitarist born on 2/6/45 in Rhoden Hall, Jamaica. Died of brain cancer on 5/11/81. Bob and his Jamaican band The Wailers are considered the masters of reggae. Band included Peter Tosh and Bunny Wailer. Wrote Eric Clapton's hit "I Shot The Sheriff."	
			BOB MARLEY & THE WAILERS:	
5/15/76	8	14	1. Rastaman Vibration	Island 9383
7/9/77	20	11	2. Exodus	Island 9498
			MARLEY, Ziggy	
			Leader of Kingston, Jamaica family reggae group The Melody Makers. Children of the late reggae master Bob Marley: David ("Ziggy"), Stephen, Cedella and Sharon.	
			ZIGGY MARLEY AND THE MELODY MAKERS:	
5/14/88	23	16	● 1. Conscious Party	Virgin 90878
8/26/89	26	8	2. One Bright Day	Virgin 91256
			MARSHALL TUCKER BAND, The	
			Southern-rock band formed in South Carolina in 1971: Doug Gray (lead singer), brothers Toy (lead guitarist) and Tommy Caldwell (bass; d: 4/28/80; replaced by Franklin Wilkie.) George McCorkle (rhythm guitar), Paul Riddle (drums) and Jerry Eubanks (sax, flute).	
10/6/73	29	8	● 1. The Marshall Tucker Band	Capricorn 0112
3/30/74	37	3	● 2. A New Life	Capricorn 0124
10/11/75	15	8	● 3. Searchin' For A Rainbow	Capricorn 0161
7/24/76	32	5	4. Long Hard Ride	Capricorn 0170
4/2/77	23	15	▲ 5. Carolina Dreams	Capricorn 0180
6/3/78	22	5	● 6. Together Forever	Capricorn 0205
6/2/79	30	3	7. Running Like The Wind	Warner 3317
4/5/80	32	5	8. Tenth	Warner 3410
			MARTIKA	
			Nineteen-year-old, Los Angeles-based, Cuban-American singer/writer/actress/dancer born Martika Marrero. Starred in TV program "Kids, Incorporated." Appeared in the 1982 film musical *Annie*.	
7/22/89	15	12	● 1. Martika	Columbia 44290
			Toy Soldiers (1)	
			MARTIN, Dean	
			Born Dino Crocetti on 6/7/17 in Steubenville, Ohio. Vocalist/actor. To California in 1937, worked local clubs. Teamed with comedian Jerry Lewis in Atlantic City in 1946. First film, *My Friend Irma* in 1949. Team broke up after 16th film *Hollywood Or Bust* in 1956. Appeared in many films since then; own TV series from 1965-74.	
8/22/64	2(4)	32	● 1. Everybody Loves Somebody	Reprise 6130
			Everybody Loves Somebody (1)	

DATE	POS	WKS	ARTIST—RECORD TITLE	LABEL & NO.
10/10/64	**15**	9	● 2. Dream With Dean	Reprise 6123
11/28/64	**9**	15	● 3. The Door Is Still Open To My Heart	Reprise 6140
			The Door Is Still Open To My Heart (6)	
3/13/65	**13**	9	● 4. Dean Martin Hits Again	Reprise 6146
10/2/65	**12**	16	* 5. (Remember Me) I'm The One Who Loves You	Reprise 6170
12/4/65	**11**	17	● 6. Houston	Reprise 6181
			I Will (10)	
5/14/66	**40**	2	● 7. Somewhere There's A Someone	Reprise 6201
1/21/67	**34**	3	8. The Dean Martin TV Show	Reprise 6233
9/16/67	**20**	16	● 9. Welcome To My World	Reprise 6250
7/13/68	**26**	12	● 10. Dean Martin's Greatest Hits! Vol. 1 [G]	Reprise 6301
2/8/69	**14**	9	● 11. Gentle On My Mind	Reprise 6330

MARTIN, Steve

Popular TV and film comedian. Born in Waco, Texas in 1945; raised in California. Comedy writer for the "Smothers Brothers Comedy Hour" TV show and others.

DATE	POS	WKS	ARTIST—RECORD TITLE	LABEL & NO.
10/15/77	**10**	12	▲ 1. Let's Get Small [C]	Warner 3090
11/11/78	**2**(6)	18	▲ 2. A Wild And Crazy Guy [C]	Warner 3238
10/20/79	**25**	5	● 3. Comedy Is Not Pretty! [C]	Warner 3392

MARTINO, Al

Born Alfred Cini on 10/7/27 in Philadelphia. Encouraged by success of boyhood friend, Mario Lanza. Winner on Arthur Godfrey's "Talent Scouts" in 1952. Portrayed singer Johnny Fontane in the 1972 film *The Godfather*.

DATE	POS	WKS	ARTIST—RECORD TITLE	LABEL & NO.
6/29/63	**7**	13	1. I Love You Because	Capitol 1914
			I Love You Because (3)	
10/26/63	**9**	21	2. Painted, Tainted Rose	Capitol 1975
2/29/64	**13**	10	3. Living A Lie	Capitol 2040
8/15/64	**31**	6	4. I Love You More And More Every Day/ Tears And Roses	Capitol 2107
			I Love You More And More Every Day (9)	
2/12/66	**19**	8	5. My Cherie	Capitol 2362
3/12/66	**8**	26	● 6. Spanish Eyes	Capitol 2435
8/12/67	**23**	4	7. Daddy's Little Girl	Capitol 2733

MARX, Richard

Chicago-bred, pop-rock singer/songwriter. Professional jingle singer since age five. Backing singer for Lionel Richie. Co-wrote Kenny Rogers' hit "What About Me." On 1/8/89, married Cynthia Rhodes, lead singer of Animotion.

DATE	POS	WKS	ARTIST—RECORD TITLE	LABEL & NO.
8/15/87	**8**	63	▲ 1. Richard Marx	EMI-Manhattan 53049
			Don't Mean Nothing (3)/*Should've Known Better* (3)/ *Endless Summer Nights* (2)/*Hold On To The Nights* (1)	
5/27/89	**1**(1)	48	▲ 2. Repeat Offender	EMI 90380
			Satisfied (1)/*Right Here Waiting* (1)/*Angelia* (4)	

MARY JANE GIRLS

Female "funk & roll" quartet: Joanne McDuffie, Candice Ghant, Kim Wuletick and Yvette Marine. Formed and produced by Rick James.

DATE	POS	WKS	ARTIST—RECORD TITLE	LABEL & NO.
5/25/85	**18**	11	1. Only Four You	Gordy 6092
			In My House (7)	

DATE	POS	WKS	ARTIST—RECORD TITLE	LABEL & NO.
			MASEKELA, Hugh	
			Born Hugh Ramapolo Masekela on 4/4/39 in Wilbank, South Africa. Trumpeter/ bandleader/arranger. Played trumpet since age 14. To England in 1959; New York City in 1960. Married to Miriam Makeba from 1964-66. Formed own band in 1964.	
7/20/68	17	10	1. The Promise of a Future *Grazing In The Grass* (1)	Uni 73028
			MASON, Dave	
			Born on 5/10/46 in Worcester, England. Vocalist/composer/guitarist. Original member of Traffic.	
7/11/70	22	2	● 1. Alone Together with guests Leon Russell, Jim Capaldi, Rita Coolidge and Delaney & Bonnie	Blue Thumb 19
11/30/74	25	4	● 2. Dave Mason	Columbia 33096
11/1/75	27	6	3. Split Coconut with guests The Manhattan Transfer, David Crosby and Graham Nash	Columbia 33698
5/28/77	37	2	● 4. Let It Flow	Columbia 34680
			MATHIS, Johnny	
			Born on 9/30/35 in San Francisco. Studied opera from age 13. Track scholarship at the San Francisco State College. Invited to Olympic try-outs, chose singing career instead. Discovered by George Avakian of Columbia Records. Initially recorded as jazz-styled singer. Columbia A&R executive Mitch Miller switched him to singing pop ballads. To New York City in 1956.	
9/9/57	4	26	1. Wonderful Wonderful the title song is not included on the album	Columbia 1028
12/23/57	2(4)	50	● 2. Warm	Columbia 1078
4/7/58	10	12	3. Good Night, Dear Lord	Columbia 1119
4/14/58	1(3)	178	▲ 4. Johnny's Greatest Hits [G] *It's Not For Me To Say* (5)/*Chances Are* (1)/ *The Twelfth Of Never* (9)	Columbia 1133
9/8/58	6	16	● 5. Swing Softly	Columbia 1165
12/15/58	3	4	▲ 6. Merry Christmas [X]	Columbia 1195
2/9/59	4	74	● 7. Open Fire, Two Guitars	Columbia 1270
7/27/59	2(2)	39	● 8. More Johnny's Greatest Hits [G]	Columbia 1344
9/21/59	1(5)	40	▲ 9. Heavenly	Columbia 1351
12/28/59	10	2	10. Merry Christmas [X-R]	Columbia 1195
1/18/60	2(1)	39	● 11. Faithfully	Columbia 8219
8/29/60	4	21	12. Johnny's Mood	Columbia 8326
10/3/60	6	13	13. The Rhythms And Ballads Of Broadway	Columbia 803 [2]
12/31/60	10	2	14. Merry Christmas [X-R]	Columbia 8021
7/17/61	38	1	15. I'll Buy You A Star	Columbia 8423
9/4/61	2(7)	28	16. Portrait Of Johnny [G]	Columbia 8444
1/6/62	31	2	17. Merry Christmas [X-R]	Columbia 8021
3/24/62	14	12	18. Live It Up!	Columbia 8511
11/3/62	12	14	19. Rapture	Columbia 8715
12/22/62	12	2	20. Merry Christmas [X-R]	Columbia 8021
4/27/63	6	17	21. Johnny's Newest Hits [G] *Gina* (6)/*What Will Mary Say* (9)	Columbia 8816
9/21/63	20	9	22. Johnny	Columbia 8844
1/25/64	23	7	23. Romantically	Columbia 8898
2/29/64	13	16	24. Tender Is The Night	Mercury 60890

DATE	POS	WKS	ARTIST—RECORD TITLE	LABEL & NO.
6/27/64	**35**	4	25. I'll Search My Heart and Other Great Hits [K]	Columbia 8943
12/26/64	**40**	1	26. This Is Love	Mercury 60942
5/14/66	**9**	16	27. The Shadow Of Your Smile	Mercury 61073
6/8/68	**26**	6	28. Love Is Blue	Columbia 9637
5/9/70	**38**	2	29. Raindrops Keep Fallin' On My Head	Columbia 1005
4/22/78	**9**	11	▲ 30. You Light Up My Life	Columbia 35259
			Too Much, Too Little, Too Late (1) with Deniece Williams	
			JOHNNY MATHIS & DENIECE WILLIAMS:	
7/29/78	**19**	8	● 31. That's What Friends Are For	Columbia 35435
			MATLOCK, Matty — see HEINDORF, Ray, and WEBB, Jack	
			MAURIAT, Paul	
			French conductor/arranger; born in 1925.	
2/10/68	**1**(5)	25	● 1. Blooming Hits [I]	Philips 248
			Love Is Blue (1)	
			MAXWELL, Robert	
			Born on 4/19/21 in New York City. Jazz harpist/composer. With NBC Symphony under Toscanini at age 17. Also recorded as Mickey Mozart.	
			ROBERT MAXWELL HIS HARP AND ORCHESTRA:	
5/23/64	**17**	12	1. Shangri-La [I]	Decca 74421
			MAY, Billy	
			Born on 1/10/16 in Pittsburgh. Arranger/conductor/sideman for many of the big bands.	
			BILLY MAY AND HIS ORCHESTRA:	
3/5/55	**7**	6	1. Sorta-May [I]	Capitol 562
			MAYALL, John	
			Born on 11/29/43 in Manchester, England. Bluesman John Mayall & his Bluesbreakers band spawned many of Britain's leading rock musicians.	
11/8/69	**32**	2	● 1. The Turning Point [L]	Polydor 4004
			featuring Jon Mark and Johnny Almond	
4/11/70	**33**	4	2. Empty Rooms	Polydor 4010
10/31/70	**22**	5	3. USA Union	Polydor 4022
			featuring Harvey Mandel and other American artists	
			MAYFIELD, Curtis	
			Born on 6/3/42 in Chicago. Soul singer/songwriter/producer. With Jerry Butler in the gospel group Northern Jubilee Singers. Joined The Impressions in 1957. Wrote most of the hits for The Impressions, Jerry Butler and himself. Own labels: Windy C, Mayfield and Curtom. Went solo in 1970. Scored *Superfly*, *Claudine*, *A Piece Of The Action* and *Short Eyes* film soundtracks. Appeared in *Short Eyes*. Paralyzed from the neck down when a stage lighting tower fell on him prior to a concert on 8/13/90.	
10/24/70	**19**	18	● 1. Curtis	Curtom 8005
6/12/71	**21**	11	2. Curtis/Live! [L]	Curtom 8008 [2]
12/11/71	**40**	1	3. Roots	Curtom 8009
9/16/72	**1**(4)	30	● 4. Superfly [S]	Curtom 8014
			Freddie's Dead (4)/*Superfly* (8)	
6/23/73	**16**	10	● 5. Back To The World	Curtom 8015
7/6/74	**39**	1	6. Sweet Exorcist	Curtom 8601

DATE	POS	WKS	ARTIST—RECORD TITLE	LABEL & NO.
			MAZE FEATURING FRANKIE BEVERLY	
			Soul group formed in Philadelphia as the Butlers (later, Raw Soul); moved to San Francisco in 1972. Nucleus consisted of Frankie Beverly (vocals), Wayne Thomas, Sam Porter, Robin Duhe, Roame Lowry and McKinley Williams.	
3/4/78	**27**	5	● 1. Golden Time Of Day	Capitol 11710
5/12/79	**33**	3	● 2. Inspiration	Capitol 11912
9/13/80	**31**	4	● 3. Joy And Pain	Capitol 12087
8/8/81	**34**	4	● 4. Live In New Orleans [L]	Capitol 12156 [2]
			side 4 contains new studio recordings	
6/4/83	**25**	5	5. We Are One	Capitol 12262
10/7/89	**37**	3	● 6. Silky Soul	Warner 25802
			McCALL, C.W.	
			Born William Fries on 11/15/28 in Audubon, Iowa. The character "C.W. McCall" was created for the Metz Bread Company. Fries was their advertising man. Elected mayor of Ouray, Colorado in the early 80s.	
1/10/76	**12**	8	● 1. Black Bear Road	MGM 5008
			Convoy (1)	
			McCALLUM, David	
			Born on 9/19/33 in Glasgow, Scotland. Son of a concert violinist. Portrayed secret agent Illya Kuryakin on TV's "The Man From U.N.C.L.E."	
4/16/66	**27**	8	1. Music - A Part Of Me [I]	Capitol 2432
			David conducts a studio orchestra	
			McCANN, Les	
			Born on 9/23/35 in Lexington, Kentucky. Jazz keyboardist/vocalist. First recorded with Leroy Vinnegar (bass) and Ron Jefferson (drums), as Les McCann Ltd, for Pacific Jazz in 1959.	
			LES McCANN & EDDIE HARRIS:	
1/31/70	**29**	5	1. Swiss Movement [I-L]	Atlantic 1537
			recorded live at the Montreux Jazz Festival, Switzerland	
			McCARTNEY, Paul	
			Born James Paul McCartney on 6/18/42 in Liverpool, England. Writer of over 50 top 10 singles. Founding member/bass guitarist of The Beatles. Married Linda Eastman on 3/12/69. First solo album in 1970. Formed group Wings in 1971 with wife Linda (keyboards, backing vocals), Denny Laine (ex-Moody Blues; guitar) and Denny Seiwell (drums). Henry McCullough (guitar) joined in 1972. Seiwell and McCullough left in 1973. In 1975, Joe English (drums) and ex-Thunderclap Newman guitarist James McCulloch (d: 9/27/79 [age 26] of heart failure) joined; both left in 1977. Wings officially disbanded in April of 1981.	
5/9/70	**1**(3)	20	● 1. McCartney	Apple 3363
			recorded at home by Paul as a one-man band	
			PAUL & LINDA McCARTNEY:	
6/5/71	**2**(2)	28	● 2. RAM	Apple 3375
			Uncle Albert/Admiral Halsey (1)	
			WINGS:	
12/25/71	**10**	10	● 3. Wild Life	Apple 3386
5/19/73	**1**(3)	16	● 4. Red Rose Speedway	Apple 3409
			My Love (1)	
12/22/73	**1**(4)	40	● 5. Band On The Run	Apple 3415
			Helen Wheels (10)/*Jet* (7)/*Band On The Run* (1)	
6/14/75	**1**(1)	17	● 6. Venus And Mars	Capitol 11419
			Listen To What The Man Said (1)	
4/10/76	**1**(7)	27	▲ 7. Wings At The Speed Of Sound	Capitol 11525
			Silly Love Songs (1)/*Let 'Em In* (3)	

DATE	POS	WKS	ARTIST—RECORD TITLE		LABEL & NO.
12/25/76	**1**(1)	18	▲ 8. Wings Over America thirty tracks from their 1976 U.S. tour *Maybe I'm Amazed* (10)	[L]	Capitol 11593 [3]
4/15/78	**2**(6)	16	▲ 9. London Town *With A Little Luck* (1)		Capitol 11777
1/6/79	**29**	5	▲ 10. Wings Greatest *Another Day* (5) 1971/*Hi, Hi, Hi* (10) 1973/ *Live And Let Die* (2) 1973/*Junior's Farm* (3) 1975	[G]	Capitol 11905
7/7/79	**8**	11	▲ 11. Back To The Egg		Columbia 36057
6/14/80	**3**	12	**PAUL McCARTNEY:** ● 12. McCartney II recorded solely by Paul at his home *Coming Up* (1)		Columbia 36511
5/15/82	**1**(3)	18	▲ 13. Tug Of War *Ebony And Ivory* (1) with Stevie Wonder/*Take It Away* (10)		Columbia 37462
11/26/83	**15**	12	▲ 14. Pipes Of Peace above two produced by George Martin *Say Say Say* (1) with Michael Jackson		Columbia 39149
11/10/84	**21**	10	● 15. Give my regards to Broad Street thirteen of 16 cuts are re-recordings of Beatles/McCartney hits *No More Lonely Nights* (6)	[S]	Columbia 39613
9/27/86	**30**	5	16. Press To Play		Capitol 12475
7/1/89	**21**	6	● 17. Flowers In The Dirt		Capitol 91653
			McCLINTON, Delbert		
			Born on 11/4/40 in Lubbock, Texas. Played harmonica on Bruce Channel's hit "Hey Baby." Leader of the Ron-Dels.		
2/21/81	**34**	4	1. The Jealous Kind *Giving It Up For Your Love* (8)		Capitol 12115
			McCOO, Marilyn, & Billy Davis, Jr.		
			Marilyn (b: 9/30/43) and husband Billy (b: 6/26/39) were members of The Fifth Dimension. Marilyn co-hosted TV's "Solid Gold" from 1981-84.		
12/18/76	**30**	7	● 1. I Hope We Get To Love In Time *You Don't Have To Be A Star (To Be In My Show)* (1)		ABC 952
			McCOY, Van		
			Pianist/producer/songwriter/singer born on 1/6/44 in Washington, D.C.; died on 7/6/79 of a heart attack. Formed own Rock'N label in 1960. Produced The Shirelles, Gladys Knight, The Stylistics and Brenda & The Tabulations. Own MAXX label, mid-60s.		
6/14/75	**12**	9	**VAN McCOY & THE SOUL CITY SYMPHONY:** 1. Disco Baby *The Hustle* (1)		Avco 69006
			McCRAE, George		
			Born on 10/19/44 in West Palm Beach, Florida. Duets with wife Gwen McCrae; became her manager.		
9/7/74	**38**	2	1. Rock Your Baby *Rock Your Baby* (1)		TK 501
			McDONALD, Country Joe — see COUNTRY JOE		
			McDONALD, Michael		
			Vocalist/keyboardist from St. Louis, Missouri. Formerly with Steely Dan and The Doobie Brothers. Married to singer Amy Holland.		
9/11/82	**6**	11	● 1. If That's What It Takes *I Keep Forgettin'* (4)		Warner 23703

DATE	POS	WKS	ARTIST—RECORD TITLE	LABEL & NO.
			McFADDEN & WHITEHEAD	
			R&B duo of Gene McFadden and John Whitehead from Philadelphia. Wrote songs for many Philadelphia soul acts; defined "The Sound Of Philadelphia."	Phil. Int. 35800
6/9/79	**23**	8	● 1. McFadden & Whitehead *Ain't No Stoppin' Us Now*	
			McFERRIN, Bobby	
			Unaccompanied, jazz-styled improvisational vocalist born in New York City. Winner of five "Best Male Jazz Vocalist" Grammy Awards. Sang 1987 "Cosby Show" theme and "Levi's 501 Blues" jingle. Father was a baritone with the New York Metropolitan Opera.	EMI-Man. 48059
9/3/88	**5**	16	▲ 1. Simple Pleasures *Don't Worry Be Happy* (1)	
			MC5	
			Detroit hard-rock quintet - Rob Tyner, lead singer.	Elektra 74042
5/10/69	**30**	3	1. Kick Out The Jams [L]	
			McGRATH, Bob — see CHILDRENS section	
			McGRIFF, Jimmy	
			Born on 4/3/36 in Philadelphia. Jazz-R&B organist/multi-instrumentalist. Toured with Don Gardner and Arthur Prysock.	Sue 1012
12/29/62	**22**	14	1. I've Got A Woman [I]	
			McGUINN, CLARK & HILLMAN	
			Roger McGuinn (b: 7/13/42; vocals, guitar), Gene Clark (b: 11/17/44; guitar) and Chris Hillman (b: 6/4/42; bass). All are former members of The Byrds.	Capitol 11910
4/28/79	**39**	2	1. McGuinn, Clark & Hillman	
			McGUIRE, Barry	
			Born on 10/15/37 in Oklahoma City. Member of The New Christy Minstrels.	Dunhill 50003
11/27/65	**37**	3	1. Eve Of Destruction *Eve Of Destruction* (1)	
			McGUIRE SISTERS, The	
			Sisters Christine (b: 7/30/29), Dorothy (b: 2/13/30) and Phyllis (b: 2/14/31) from Middletown, Ohio. Replaced the Chordettes on the Arthur Godfrey Show in 1953. Phyllis went solo in 1964. Reunited in 1986.	Coral 56123
3/5/55	**11**	6	1. By Request… [M] 10" album of eight songs *Sincerely* (1)	
			M.C. HAMMER	
			Born Stanley Kirk Burrell on 3/30/63 in Oakland. Rapper/producer/founder/leader of The Posse, an eight-member group of dancers, DJs and singers. Burrell was an Oakland A's batboy in the 1970s; his nickname "The Little Hammer" stemmed from his resemblance to Hank "The Hammer" Aaron. Oaktown's 3-5-7 and Ace Juice are members of The Posse.	
5/6/89	**30**	23	▲ 1. Let's Get It Started	Capitol 909245
3/17/90	**1**(19) +	32 +	▲ 2. Please Hammer Don't Hurt 'Em *U Can't Touch This* (8)	Capitol 92857
			McKENZIE, Bob & Doug	
			Canadian comedians Rick Moranis and Dave Thomas of "SCTV." Both featured in the film *Strange Brew*. Moranis later starred in *Ghostbusters*, *Spaceballs*, *Honey, I Shrunk The Kids* and many others.	Mercury 4034
2/6/82	**8**	13	● 1. Great White North [C]	
			McKINLEY, Ray — see MILLER, Glenn	

DATE	POS	WKS	ARTIST—RECORD TITLE	LABEL & NO.
			McLAUGHLIN, John	
			Born on 1/4/42 in Yorkshire, England. Jazz-fusion guitar virtuoso. Formed his Mahavishnu Orchestra in 1971 with Billy Cobham, Jan Hammer, Rick Laird and Jerry Goodman. Original group disbanded in 1973.	
			MAHAVISHNU ORCHESTRA:	
3/10/73	**15**	11	1. Birds Of Fire [I]	Columbia 31996
			CARLOS SANTANA/MAHAVISHNU JOHN McLAUGHLIN:	
7/21/73	**14**	7	● 2. Love Devotion Surrender [I]	Columbia 32034
			McLEAN, Don	
			Born on 10/2/45 in New Rochelle, New York. Singer/songwriter/poet. The hit "Killing Me Softly With His Song" was written about Don.	
12/11/71	**1**(7)	26	● 1. American Pie	United Art. 5535
			American Pie (1)	
2/3/73	**23**	7	2. Don McLean	United Art. 5651
3/21/81	**28**	6	3. Chain Lightning	Millennium 7756
			Crying (5)	
			McVIE, Christine	
			Born Christine Perfect on 7/12/43 in Birmingham, England. Vocalist with Fleetwood Mac since 1970. Married to Fleetwood Mac bassist John McVie until 1976. Quit touring with group after 1990.	
3/3/84	**26**	7	1. Christine McVie	Warner 25059
			Got A Hold On Me (10)	
			MEADER, Vaughn	
			President John F. Kennedy impersonator; produced by Bob Booker and Earle Doud.	
12/8/62	**1**(12)	26	● 1. The First Family [C]	Cadence 3060
			1962 Grammy winner: Album of the Year	
6/1/63	**4**	11	2. The First Family, volume two [C]	Cadence 3065
			above albums feature Naomi Brossart as Jackie Kennedy	
			MEAT LOAF	
			Born Marvin Lee Aday on 9/27/47 in Dallas. Sang lead vocals on Ted Nugent's 1976 Free-For-All LP. Played Eddie in the film The Rocky Horror Picture Show. Appeared in films Americathon (1979), Roadie (1980) and The Squeeze (1987).	
5/13/78	**14**	28	▲ 1. Bat Out Of Hell	Cleve. I. 34974
			MECO	
			Disco producer Meco Monardo; born on 11/29/39 in Johnsonburg, Pennsylvania.	
9/10/77	**13**	9	▲ 1. Star Wars And Other Galactic Funk [I]	Millennium 8001
			Star Wars Theme/Cantina Band (1)	
			MEGADETH	
			Heavy-metal group formed in Southern California by Dave Mustaine (former guitarist of Metallica) and Dave Ellefson (bass).	
2/13/88	**28**	6	● 1. so far, so good...so what!	Capitol 48148
			MELACHRINO, George	
			Born on 5/1/09 in London of Greek parentage; died on 6/18/65. Multi-instrumentalist. First to use masses of strings to produce sentimental mood music.	
			GEORGE MELACHRINO AND HIS ORCHESTRA:	
1/8/55	**10**	2	1. Christmas in High Fidelity [X-I]	RCA 1045
5/25/59	**30**	1	2. Under Western Skies [I]	RCA 1676

DATE	POS	WKS	ARTIST—RECORD TITLE	LABEL & NO.
			MELANIE	
			Born Melanie Safka on 2/3/47 in Queens, New York. Neighborhood Records formed by Melanie and her husband/producer Peter Schekeryk.	
6/13/70	**17**	11	● 1. Candles In The Rain	Buddah 5060
			Lay Down (Candles In The Rain) (6)	
9/26/70	**33**	4	2. Leftover Wine [L]	Buddah 5066
12/11/71	**15**	14	● 3. Gather Me	Neighbor. 47001
			Brand New Key (1)	
			MELLENCAMP, John Cougar	
			Born on 10/7/51 in Seymour, Indiana. Rock singer/songwriter/producer. Worked outside of music until 1975. First recorded for MCA in 1976.	
			JOHN COUGAR:	
5/16/81	**37**	3	1. Nothin' Matters And What If It Did	Riva 7403
5/29/82	**1**(9)	41	▲ 2. American Fool	Riva 7501
			Hurts So Good (2)/Jack & Diane (1)	
			JOHN COUGAR MELLENCAMP:	
11/12/83	**9**	36	▲ 3. Uh-Huh	Riva 7504
			Crumblin' Down (9)/Pink Houses (8)	
9/21/85	**2**(3)	48	▲ 4. Scarecrow	Riva 824865
			Lonely Ol' Night (6)/Small Town (6)/	
			R.O.C.K. In The U.S.A. (2)	
9/19/87	**6**	37	▲ 5. The Lonesome Jubilee	Mercury 832465
			Paper In Fire (9)/Cherry Bomb (8)	
6/3/89	**7**	15	▲ 6. Big Daddy	Mercury 838220
			MELVIN, Harold	
			Leader of Philadelphia soul group The Blue Notes, formed in 1954: Harold Melvin, Bernard Williams, Jesse Gillis, Jr., Franklin Peaker and Roosevelt Brodie. First recorded for Josie in 1956. Numerous personnel changes until 1970, when Teddy Pendergrass joined as drummer and lead singer. Pendergrass went solo in 1976, replaced by David Ebo.	
			HAROLD MELVIN & THE BLUE NOTES:	
5/3/75	**26**	12	● 1. To Be True	Phil. Int. 33148
12/27/75	**9**	12	● 2. Wake Up Everybody	Phil. Int. 33808
			MEN AT WORK	
			Melbourne, Australia rock quintet formed in 1979. Colin Hay (lead singer, guitar), Ron Strykert (lead guitar), Greg Ham (sax, keyboards), Jerry Speiser (drums) and John Rees (bass). Won the 1982 Best New Artist Grammy Award. Speiser and Rees left in 1984. Hay went solo as Colin James Hay in 1987.	
8/28/82	**1**(15)	48	▲ 1. Business As Usual	Columbia 37978
			Who Can It Be Now? (1)/Down Under (1)	
5/7/83	**3**	23	▲ 2. Cargo	Columbia 38660
			Overkill (3)/It's A Mistake (6)	
			MENDES, Sergio	
			Born on 2/11/41 in Niteroi, Brazil. Pianist/leader of Latin-styled group originating from Brazil. Member Lani Hall (vocals) married Herb Alpert.	
			SERGIO MENDES & BRASIL '66:	
10/15/66	**7**	30	● 1. Sergio Mendes & Brasil '66	A&M 4116
5/20/67	**24**	6	● 2. Equinox	A&M 4122
4/6/68	**5**	33	● 3. Look Around	A&M 4137
			The Look Of Love (4)	
12/21/68	**3**	16	● 4. Fool On The Hill	A&M 4160
			The Fool On The Hill (6)	
9/27/69	**33**	2	5. Crystal Illusions	A&M 4197

DATE	POS	WKS	ARTIST—RECORD TITLE	LABEL & NO.

6/11/83	27	10	**SERGIO MENDES:**
			   6. Sergio Mendes
			   Never Gonna Let You Go (4)
				A&M 4937

8/20/83	13	14	## MEN WITHOUT HATS Nucleus of techno-rock band from Montreal, Canada consists of Ivan Doroschuk (singer/songwriter) with his brother Stefan (guitar). Fluctuating personnel included their brother Colin (1983-84). ● 1. Rhythm Of Youth *The Safety Dance* (3)	Backstreet 39002

7/12/69	38	3	## MERCY, The
			Florida group led by Jack Sigler, Jr.
			   1. The Mercy & Love (Can Make You Happy)
			   Love (Can Make You Happy) (2)
				Sundi 803

4/12/86 9/26/87 9/24/88	29 28 6	7 8 34	## METALLICA Speed-metal quartet formed by Lars Ulrich (drums) and James Hetfield (vocals) in Los Angeles in 1981. Early rhythm guitarist Dave Mustaine (now the leader of Megadeth) was replaced by Kirk Hammett in 1982. Bassist Cliff Burton was killed in a bus crash in Sweden on 9/27/86 (age 24); replaced by Jason Newsted. ▲ 1. Master Of Puppets ▲ 2. The $5.98 E.P.: Garage Days Re-Revisited [M] ▲ 3. ...And Justice For All	Elektra 60439 Elektra 60757 Elektra 60812 [2]

3/9/74
1/10/76
	4
	39
		14
		2
			## MFSB
			Large racially-mixed studio band formed by producers Kenny Gamble and Leon Huff. Also recorded as The James Boys, and Family. Name means ''Mothers, Fathers, Sisters, Brothers.''
			● 1. Love Is The Message [I]
			   TSOP (The Sound Of Philadelphia) (1)
			   2. Philadelphia Freedom [I]
				Phil. Int. 32707
				Phil. Int. 33845

			## MIAMI SOUND MACHINE — see ESTEFAN, Gloria	

11/28/87	1(12)	69	## MICHAEL, George
			Born Georgios Kyriacos Panayiotou on 6/26/63 in Bushey, England. Lead singer/ songwriter of Wham!
			▲ 1. Faith
			   1988 Grammy winner: Album of the Year
			   I Want Your Sex (2)/*Faith* (1)/*Father Figure* (1)/
			   One More Try (1)/*Monkey* (1)/*Kissing A Fool* (5)
				Columbia 40867

9/11/71	16	12	## MICHAELS, Lee
			Born on 11/24/45 in Los Angeles. Rock organist/vocalist.
			   1. ''5th''
			   Do You Know What I Mean (6)
				A&M 4302

3/17/90	35	6	## MICHEL'LE Michel'le (pronounced: Mee-shell-LAY) Toussant is an 18-year-old black singer from Los Angeles. Former backing singer of the World Class Wreckin Cru. ● 1. Michel'le *No More Lies* (7)	Ruthless 91282

DATE	POS	WKS	ARTIST—RECORD TITLE	LABEL & NO.
			MIDLER, Bette	
			Born on 12/1/45 in Paterson, New Jersey. Vocalist/actress. Raised in Hawaii. In the Broadway show *Fiddler On The Roof* for three years. Won the 1973 Best New Artist Grammy Award. Nominated for an Oscar in *The Rose* (1979). Roles in films *Down And Out In Beverly Hills*, *Ruthless People*, *Outrageous Fortune*, *Beaches* and *Stella*.	
1/13/73	**9**	23	▲ 1. The Divine Miss M *Boogie Woogie Bugle Boy* (8)	Atlantic 7238
12/22/73	**6**	11	● 2. Bette Midler accompanied by Barry Manilow (piano) on above two	Atlantic 7270
2/7/76	**27**	6	3. Songs For The New Depression	Atlantic 18155
1/12/80	**12**	23	▲ 4. The Rose [S-L] *The Rose* (3)	Atlantic 16010
12/13/80	**34**	4	5. Divine Madness [S-L] film captures a live concert at Pasadena Civic Auditorium	Atlantic 16022
2/25/89	**2**(3)	33	▲ 6. Beaches [S] *Wind Beneath My Wings* (1)	Atlantic 81933
			MIDNIGHT OIL	
			Australian quintet: Peter Garrett (lead vocals), Peter Gifford, Martin Rotsey, James Moginie and Rob Hirst (replaced by bassist Bones Hillman in 1987). Garrett was a candidate in the 1984 Australian Senate race.	
4/30/88	**21**	26	▲ 1. Diesel And Dust	Columbia 40967
3/24/90	**21**	14	● 2. Blue Sky Mining	Columbia 45398
			MIDNIGHT STAR	
			R&B-funk group formed in 1976 at Kentucky State University. Lead vocals by Belinda Lipscomb. Until 1988, band led by brothers Reginald (trumpet) and Vincent (trombone) Calloway. Reginal and Vincent produced many artists in the mid-1980s; formed own duo Calloway in 1988.	
9/17/83	**27**	30	▲ 1. No Parking On The Dance Floor	Solar 60241
1/19/85	**32**	7	● 2. Planetary Invasion	Solar 60384
			MIDNIGHT STRING QUARTET	
			Snuff Garrett, producer.	
2/11/67	**17**	12	1. Rhapsodies For Young Lovers [I]	Viva 6001
			MIKE + THE MECHANICS	
			Rock quintet consisting of bassist Mike Rutherford (Genesis), vocalists Paul Carrack (Ace, Squeeze) and Paul Young (Sad Cafe), drummer Peter Van Hooke (Van Morrison) and keyboardist Adrian Lee.	
2/8/86	**26**	21	● 1. Mike + The Mechanics *Silent Running* (6)/*All I Need Is A Miracle* (5)	Atlantic 81287
2/25/89	**13**	13	● 2. Living Years *The Living Years* (1)	Atlantic 81923
			MILES, Buddy	
			Born George Miles on 9/5/46 in Omaha. R&B vocalist/drummer. Prominent session musician. Worked as sideman in the Dick Clark Revue, 1963-64. With Wilson Pickett, 1965-66. In Michael Bloomfield's Electric Flag, 1967. In Jimi Hendrix's Band Of Gypsys, 1969-70. In 1987, was the voice of The California Raisins, the clamation TV ad characters.	
8/29/70	**35**	5	1. Them Changes	Mercury 61280
7/29/72	**8**	14	▲ 2. Carlos Santana & Buddy Miles! Live! [L]	Columbia 31308

DATE	POS	WKS	ARTIST—RECORD TITLE	LABEL & NO.
			MILLER, Glenn	
			Born on 3/1/04 in Clarinda, Iowa. Leader of most popular big band of all-time. Played trombone for Ben Pollack, Red Nichols, Benny Goodman and the Dorsey Brothers, became de facto leader of Ray Noble's 1935 American band, and did arrangements for Glen Gray and others before starting his own band in 1937. Glenn disappeared on a plane flight from England to France on 12/15/44 (age 40).	
			GLENN MILLER & HIS ORCHESTRA:	
9/16/57	**16**	6	1. Marvelous Miller Moods [E]	RCA 1494
			Glenn Miller Army Air Force Band with Johnny Desmond (vocals); from radio broadcasts during 1943-44	
12/9/57	**17**	4	2. The New Glenn Miller Orchestra In Hi Fi	RCA 1522
			directed by Ray McKinley (leader of the band after Glenn's death)	
2/24/58	**19**	3	3. The Glenn Miller Carnegie Hall Concert [E-L]	RCA 1506
			recorded on 10/06/39	
			MILLER, Mitch	
			Born on 7/4/11 in Rochester, New York. Producer/conductor/arranger. Oboe soloist with the CBS Symphony from 1936-47. A&R executive for both Columbia and Mercury Records. Best known for his sing-along albums and TV show (1961-64).	
			MITCH MILLER AND THE GANG:	
7/14/58	**1(8)**	128	● 1. Sing Along With Mitch	Columbia 1160
11/10/58	**4**	117	● 2. More Sing Along With Mitch	Columbia 1243
12/29/58	**1(2)**	5	● 3. Christmas Sing-Along With Mitch [X]	Columbia 1205
3/23/59	**4**	71	● 4. Still More! Sing Along With Mitch	Columbia 1283
6/15/59	**11**	31	● 5. Folk Songs Sing Along With Mitch	Columbia 1316
8/31/59	**7**	66	● 6. Party Sing Along With Mitch	Columbia 1331
12/14/59	**8**	4	● 7. Christmas Sing-Along With Mitch [X-R]	Columbia 1205
1/4/60	**10**	30	8. Fireside Sing Along With Mitch	Columbia 1389
4/4/60	**8**	40	● 9. Saturday Night Sing Along With Mitch	Columbia 1414
6/27/60	**5**	32	● 10. Sentimental Sing Along With Mitch	Columbia 1457
10/10/60	**40**	1	11. March Along With Mitch [I]	Columbia 1475
			MITCH MILLER AND THE BRASS, PICCOLOS AND DRUMS	
10/31/60	**5**	25	● 12. Memories Sing Along With Mitch	Columbia 8342
12/19/60	**6**	3	● 13. Christmas Sing-Along With Mitch [X-R]	Columbia 8027
3/6/61	**9**	8	14. Mitch's Greatest Hits [G]	Columbia 8344
			The Yellow Rose Of Texas (1) 1955/ *Song For A Summer Night* (8) 1956	
3/13/61	**5**	23	● 15. Happy Times! Sing Along With Mitch	Columbia 8368
6/12/61	**3**	40	16. TV Sing Along With Mitch	Columbia 8428
10/2/61	**6**	23	17. Your Request Sing Along With Mitch	Columbia 8471
12/4/61	**1(1)**	13	● 18. Holiday Sing Along With Mitch [X]	Columbia 8501
12/11/61	**9**	7	● 19. Christmas Sing-Along With Mitch [X-R]	Columbia 8027
3/10/62	**21**	7	20. Rhythm Sing Along With Mitch	Columbia 8527
7/21/62	**27**	5	21. Family Sing Along With Mitch	Columbia 8573
12/29/62	**33**	1	● 22. Holiday Sing Along With Mitch [X-R]	Columbia 8501
12/29/62	**37**	1	● 23. Christmas Sing-Along With Mitch [X-R]	Columbia 8027
			MILLER, Mrs.	
			Mrs. Elva Miller. Tone-deaf singer from Claremont, California.	
6/4/66	**15**	10	1. Mrs. Miller's Greatest Hits	Capitol 2494
			featuring the novel operatic voice of housewife Mrs. Miller	

DATE	POS	WKS	ARTIST—RECORD TITLE	LABEL & NO.
			MILLER, Roger	
			Country vocalist/humorist/guitarist/composer. Born on 1/2/36 in Fort Worth, Texas; raised in Erick, Oklahoma. To Nashville in the mid-50s, began songwriting career. With Faron Young as writer/drummer in 1962. Won six Grammys in 1965. Own TV show in 1966. Songwriter of 1985's Tony Award-winning Broadway musical *Big River*.	
12/12/64	37	2	● 1. Roger And Out [N] *Dang Me* (7)/*Chug-A-Lug* (9)	Smash 67049
3/13/65	4	29	● 2. The Return Of Roger Miller *King Of The Road* (4)	Smash 67061
8/7/65	13	9	3. The 3rd Time Around *Engine Engine #9* (7)	Smash 67068
12/11/65	6	21	● 4. Golden Hits [G] *England Swings* (8)	Smash 67073
			MILLER, Steve	
			Born on 10/5/43 in Milwaukee; raised in Dallas. Blues-rock singer/songwriter/guitarist. While at the University of Wisconsin-Madison, Steve led the blues-rock band the Ardells, later known as the Fabulous Night Trains, featuring Boz Scaggs. To San Francisco in 1966; formed the Steve Miller Band, which featured a fluctuating lineup. **STEVE MILLER BAND:**	
11/16/68	24	8	1. Sailor Boz Scaggs was a band member on above album	Capitol 2984
7/5/69	22	8	2. Brave New World	Capitol 184
12/27/69	38	5	3. Your Saving Grace	Capitol 331
8/15/70	23	7	4. Number 5	Capitol 436
11/3/73	2(1)	20	▲ 5. The Joker *The Joker* (1)	Capitol 11235
6/12/76	3	48	▲ 6. Fly Like An Eagle *Rock'n Me* (1)/*Fly Like An Eagle* (2)	Capitol 11497
5/28/77	2(2)	27	▲ 7. Book Of Dreams *Jet Airliner* (8)	Capitol 11630
12/23/78	18	9	▲ 8. Greatest Hits 1974-78 [G]	Capitol 11872
11/21/81	26	5	● 9. Circle Of Love	Capitol 12121
7/10/82	3	18	▲ 10. Abracadabra *Abracadabra* (1)	Capitol 12216
			MILLI VANILLI	
			U.K.-based Euro-pop duo: Rob Pilatus (from Germany) and Fabrice Morvan (from France). Milli Vanilli is Turkish for positive energy. Pilatus and Morvan met in 1985 in Los Angeles. They were stripped of their 1989 Best New Artist Grammy Award when it was revealed that they did not sing a note on their debut album, *Girl You Know It's True*	
4/1/89	1(8)	61	▲ 1. Girl You Know It's True *Girl You Know It's True* (2)/*Baby Don't Forget My Number* (1)/ *Girl I'm Gonna Miss You* (1)/*Blame It On The Rain* (1)/ *All Or Nothing* (4)	Arista 8592
6/23/90	32	5	● 2. The Remix Album [K] five of nine tracks are remixes of hits from the above album	Arista 8622
			MILLS, Frank	
			Pianist/composer/producer/arranger.	
4/14/79	21	5	● 1. Music Box Dancer [I] *Music Box Dancer* (3)	Polydor 6192

DATE	POS	WKS	ARTIST—RECORD TITLE	LABEL & NO.
			MILLS, Stephanie	
			Born in 1957 in Brooklyn. In 1967, appeared for four weeks at the Apollo Theater with The Isley Brothers. At age 15, won starring role of Dorothy in the hit Broadway musical *The Wiz*. Briefly married to Jeffrey Daniels of Shalamar in 1980.	
8/18/79	**22**	9	● 1. Whatcha Gonna Do…With My Lovin'?	20th Century 583
5/10/80	**16**	22	● 2. Sweet Sensation	20th Century 603
			Never Knew Love Like This Before (6)	
6/6/81	**30**	5	● 3. Stephanie	20th Century 700
8/15/87	**30**	9	● 4. If I Were Your Woman	MCA 5996
			MILLS BROTHERS, The	
			Smooth R&B-pop family vocal group from Piqua, Ohio. Consisted of brothers John, Jr. (b: 1911; d: 1936), Herbert (b: 1912; d: 4/12/89 [age 77]), Harry (b: 1913; d: 6/28/82 [age 68]) and Donald (b: 1915). Originally featured unusual vocal style of imitating instruments. Achieved national fame via radio broadcasts and appearances in films. Father, John, Sr., joined group in 1936, replacing John, Jr.; remained in group until 1956 (d: 12/8/67). Group continued as a trio until 1982. Donald and his son John III continued singing as a duo.	
4/13/68	**21**	10	1. Fortuosity	Dot 25809
			MILSAP, Ronnie	
			Born on 1/16/46 in Robbinsville, North Carolina. Country singer/pianist/guitarist. Blind since birth; multi-instrumentalist by age 12. With J.J. Cale band, own band from 1965.	
2/14/81	**36**	4	▲ 1. Greatest Hits [G]	RCA 3772
10/3/81	**31**	3	● 2. There's No Gettin' Over Me	RCA 4060
			(There's) No Gettin' Over Me (5)	
6/11/83	**36**	3	3. Keyed Up	RCA 4670
			MINNELLI, Liza	
			Born on 3/12/46 in Los Angeles. Singer and Broadway/film actress. Daughter of Judy Garland and film director Vincente Minnelli. Starred in many films (*Arthur*, among them) and in Broadway productions. Won the 1972 Best Actress Oscar for *Cabaret*. Winner of three Tony Awards. Married to Peter Allen from 1967-73.	
10/21/72	**19**	11	1. Liza With A "Z" [TV-L]	Columbia 31762
5/5/73	**38**	2	2. Liza Minnelli The Singer	Columbia 32149
			MIRACLES, The	
			R&B group formed at Northern High School in Detroit in 1955. Consisted of William "Smokey" Robinson (lead), Emerson and Bobby Rogers (tenors), Ronnie White (baritone) and Warren "Pete" Moore (bass). Emerson Rogers left in 1956 for U.S. Army, replaced by Claudette Rogers Robinson, Smokey's wife. First recorded for End in 1958. Claudette retired in 1964. Smokey wrote many hit songs for the group and other Motown artists. Smokey went solo in 1972, replaced by William Griffin.	
5/29/65	**21**	14	1. Greatest Hits From The Beginning [G]	Tamla 254 [2]
			Shop Around (2) 1961	
			SMOKEY ROBINSON & THE MIRACLES:	
1/1/66	**8**	19	2. Going To A Go-Go	Tamla 267
11/11/67	**28**	7	3. Make It Happen	Tamla 276
			The Tears Of A Clown (1) 1970	
3/2/68	**7**	11	4. Greatest Hits, Vol. 2 [G]	Tamla 280
			I Second That Emotion (4)	
8/16/69	**25**	8	5. Time Out for Smokey Robinson & The Miracles	Tamla 295
			Baby, Baby Don't Cry (8)	

DATE	POS	WKS	ARTIST—RECORD TITLE	LABEL & NO.
1/3/76	**33**	10	**THE MIRACLES:** 6. City Of Angels *Love Machine* (1)	Tamla 339
11/13/82	**17**	26	**MISSING PERSONS** Rock quintet formed in Los Angeles in 1980. Dale Bozzio (lead singer; former Playboy bunny from Boston), husband Terry Bozzio, Warren Cuccurullo (joined Duran Duran in 1990), Patrick O'Hearn and Chuck Wild. ● 1. Spring Session M title is an anagram of group's name	Capitol 12228
11/2/85	**1(1)**	34	**MR. MISTER** Los Angeles-based, pop-rock quartet: Richard Page (vocals), Steve George, Pat Mastelotto and Steve Farris (left in 1989; replaced by Buzz Feiten, ex-guitarist of Paul Butterfield Blues Band, Stevie Wonder's band, and the Larsen-Feiten Band). ▲ 1. Welcome To The Real World *Broken Wings* (1)/*Kyrie* (1)/*Is It Love* (8)	RCA 8045
6/2/62	**39**	1	**MITCHELL, Chad** Leader of folk-pop trio which included Mike Kobluk and Joe Frazier. Formed while sophomores at Gonzaga University in Spokane, Washington. **THE CHAD MITCHELL TRIO:** 1. Mighty Day On Campus [L] Jim McGuinn (Byrds) played guitar on above album	Kapp 3262
12/21/63	**39**	1	2. Singin' Our Mind	Mercury 60838
4/11/64	**29**	4	3. Reflecting	Mercury 60891
6/21/69	**31**	6	**MITCHELL, Joni** Born Roberta Joan Anderson on 11/7/43 in McLeod, Alberta, Canada. Singer/songwriter/ guitarist/pianist. Moved to New York in 1966. Wrote the hits ''Both Sides Now'' and ''Woodstock.'' Married to producer/bassist Larry Klein. 1. Clouds	Reprise 6341
4/25/70	**27**	9	▲ 2. Ladies Of The Canyon	Reprise 6376
7/10/71	**15**	12	▲ 3. Blue	Reprise 2038
12/30/72	**11**	12	● 4. For The Roses	Asylum 5057
2/9/74	**2(4)**	31	● 5. Court And Spark *Help Me* (7)	Asylum 1001
12/21/74	**2(1)**	14	● 6. Miles Of Aisles [L] with Tom Scott & The L.A. Express	Asylum 202
12/13/75	**4**	10	● 7. The Hissing Of Summer Lawns	Asylum 1051
12/18/76	**13**	8	● 8. Hejira	Asylum 1087
1/14/78	**25**	4	● 9. Don Juan's Reckless Daughter	Asylum 701 [2]
7/14/79	**17**	9	10. Mingus music composed by Charles Mingus (d: 1/5/79 [age 56])	Asylum 505
10/18/80	**38**	3	11. Shadows And Light [L] with guests Pat Metheny, Michael Brecker and Jaco Pastorius	Asylum 704 [2]
12/4/82	**25**	5	12. Wild Things Run Fast	Geffen 2019
7/29/67	**24**	7	**MOBY GRAPE** Rock group from San Francisco. Original lineup: Bob Mosley, Jerry Miller, Don Stevenson, Peter Lewis and Alexander Spence (ex-drummer of Jefferson Airplane). 1. Moby Grape ten of 13 cuts released simultaneously on 45s	Columbia 9498

5/18/68	**20**	6	2. Wow
			    includes bonus LP titled *Grape Jam* (jam sessions with
			    Al Kooper and Mike Bloomfield)
				Columbia 9613 [2]

Moms Mabley, whose real name was Loretta Mary Aiken, was introduced to most Americans via the late 60s CBS comedy show starring the Smothers Brothers. Yet many of her albums for Chess, released earlier in the decade, hit the Top 40 regularly—most notably, *Moms Mabley At The "UN,"* which peaked at No. 16 in 1961.

Madonna maintained her track record as one of the premiere recording artists of all time in 1990: her controversial "Tie Me Up" became her 20th top 10 single, and fans watched her play Breathless Mahoney in the film *Dick Tracy.*

Barry Manilow's hot streak during the 70s occasionally made him the target of some harsh criticisms from music writers; the same writers, however, were quick to praise 1984's *2:00 AM Paradise Cafe*, which featured Manilow alongside jazz greats such as Sarah Vaughan and Gerry Mulligan.

Stephanie Mills, the petite songstress who first garnered attention starring as Dorothy in the Broadway version of the *The Wiz*, scored her first gold album in 1980 with *Never Knew Love Like This Before* on 20th Century.

Smokey Robinson & The Miracles released four albums as "The Miracles" before singer Robinson's name was given front billing. It made a difference: Album No. 5, *Going To A Go-Go*, was the group's first top 10 album. *Time Out For...* was the last LP to hit the top 40 before Robinson went solo.

Joni Mitchell started her career with strong folk music roots on such efforts as 1969's *Clouds*. By the mid-70s the Canadian singer increasingly incorporated jazz into her music, and high-charting efforts like *Court And Spark*, *Mingus* and *Shadows And Light* featured jazz artists such as Wayne Shorter, Jaco Pastorious, Pat Metheny and Tom Scott, among others.

Molly Hatchet enjoyed prosperity in the late 70s as part of the Southern rock contingent with such albums as *Flirtin' With Disaster* and *Beatin' The Odds*. The Jacksonville, Florida-based group lost its lead singer, Danny Joe Brown, after its second album, but Brown—who temporarily attempted a solo career—eventually returned to the fold.

The **Moody Blues** typified one of the noticeable trends of the 70s: Each of the group's members—Justin Hayward, John Lodge, Mike Pinder, Ray Thomas and Graeme Edge—released a seemingly limitless flow of solo projects. 1983's *The Present* featured the band with keyboardist Patrick Moraz—himself a prolific artist who'd recorded with Yes and Refugee, among other groups.

Mott The Hoople, named after an obscure book, featured both Ian Hunter and Mick Ralphs. The British group's career had flagged in the early 70s after their *Brain Capers* album but was given a boost by David Bowie, who produced 1972's *All The Young Dudes*. Their next effort, *Mott*, became their first top 40 LP.

Ricky Nelson officially became "Rick" with a 1961 album appropriately dubbed *Rick Is 21*. Ironically, his only No. 1 LP was his earlier, 1957 effort, *Ricky*. The late artist's last charting album was 1981's *Playing To Win*, on Capitol. Nine years later, the singer's two sons formed a group called Nelson and recorded a debut album on the DGC label.

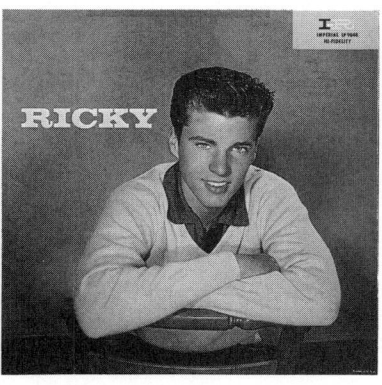

DATE	POS	WKS	ARTIST—RECORD TITLE	LABEL & NO.
			MODUGNO, Domenico	
			Born on 1/9/28 in Polignano a Mare, Italy. Singer/actor.	
9/15/58	8	6	1. Nel Blu Dipinto Di Blu (Volare) and other Italian favorites [F] *Nel Blu Dipinto Di Blu* (1)	Decca 8808
			MOLLY HATCHET	
			Southern hard-rock sextet from Jacksonville, Florida. Original lineup: Danny Joe Brown (lead singer), Bruce Crump, Bonner Thomas, Duane Roland, Dave Hlubek and Steve Holland. John Farrar replaced Brown in 1980; Brown returned and replaced Farrar in 1983.	
10/6/79	19	18	▲ 1. Flirtin' With Disaster	Epic 36110
10/4/80	25	6	● 2. Beatin' The Odds	Epic 36572
12/26/81	36	4	3. Take No Prisoners Jimmy Farrar, lead singer on above two	Epic 37480
			MONEY, Eddie	
			Born Edward Mahoney on 3/2/49 in New York City. Rock singer discovered and subsequently managed by West Coast promoter Bill Graham. Formerly an officer with the New York Police Department.	
4/22/78	37	2	▲ 1. Eddie Money	Columbia 34909
2/3/79	17	10	● 2. Life For The Taking	Columbia 35598
9/6/80	35	5	3. Playing For Keeps	Columbia 36514
8/21/82	20	13	▲ 4. No Control	Columbia 37960
10/18/86	20	21	▲ 5. Can't Hold Back *Take Me Home Tonight* (4)/*Walk On Water* (9)	Columbia 40096
			MONKEES, The	
			Formed in Los Angeles in 1965. Chosen from over 400 applicants for new Columbia TV series. Consisted of Davy Jones (b: 12/30/45, Manchester, England; vocals), Michael Nesmith (b: 12/30/42, Houston; guitar, vocals), Peter Tork (b: 2/13/44, Washington, D.C.; bass, vocals) and Micky Dolenz (b: 3/8/45, Tarzana, California; drums, vocals). Dolenz had appeared in TV series "Circus Boy," using the name Mickey Braddock in 1956. Jones had been a race-horse jockey, and appeared in London musicals *Oliver* and *Pickwick*. Tork had been in the Phoenix Singers; Nesmith had done session work for Stax/Volt. TV show dropped after 58 episodes, 1966-68. Tork left in 1968. Group disbanded in 1969; re-formed (less Nesmith) in 1986.	
10/15/66	1(13)	49	● 1. The Monkees *Last Train To Clarksville* (1)	Colgems 101
2/11/67	1(18)	45	● 2. More Of The Monkees *I'm A Believer* (1)	Colgems 102
6/17/67	1(1)	41	● 3. Headquarters	Colgems 103
11/25/67	1(5)	19	● 4. Pisces, Aquarius, Capricorn & Jones Ltd. *Pleasant Valley Sunday* (3)	Colgems 104
5/18/68	3	15	● 5. The Birds, The Bees & The Monkees *Daydream Believer* (1)/*Valleri* (3)	Colgems 109
3/22/69	32	5	6. Instant Replay	Colgems 113
8/16/86	21	12	▲ 7. Then & Now...The Best Of The Monkees [G] includes three new songs by Micky Dolenz and Peter Tork	Arista 8432
			MONTE, Lou	
			Born on 4/2/17 in Lyndhurst, New Jersey. Vocalist/guitarist.	
1/5/63	9	18	1. Pepino The Italian Mouse & Other Italian Fun Songs [N] *Pepino The Italian Mouse* (5)	Reprise 6058

DATE	POS	WKS	ARTIST—RECORD TITLE	LABEL & NO.
			MONTENEGRO, Hugo	
			Born in 1925; raised in New York City; died on 2/6/81. Conductor/composer.	
4/13/68	9	17	**HUGO MONTENEGRO AND HIS ORCHESTRA:** ● 1. Music From "A Fistful Of Dollars" & "For A Few Dollars More" & "The Good, The Bad And The Ugly" *The Good, The Bad And The Ugly* (2)	[I] RCA 3927
			MONTEZ, Chris	
			Born Christopher Montanez on 1/17/43 in Los Angeles. Protege of Ritchie Valens.	
9/3/66	33	4	1. The More I See You/Call Me	A&M 4115
			MONTGOMERY, Wes	
			Born John Leslie Montgomery on 3/6/25 in Indianapolis; died on 6/15/68. Jazz guitarist. Brother Monk plays bass, brother Buddy plays piano.	
11/11/67	13	23	● 1. A Day In The Life [I]	A&M 3001
8/31/68	38	1	2. Down Here On The Ground [I]	A&M 3006
			MOODY BLUES, The	
			Formed in Birmingham, England in 1964. Consisted of Denny Laine (guitar, vocals), Ray Thomas (flute, vocals), Mike Pinder (keyboards, vocals), Clint Warwick (bass) and Graeme Edge (drums). Laine and Warwick left in the summer of 1966, replaced by Justin Hayward (lead vocals, lead guitar) and John Lodge (vocals, bass). Laine joined Wings in 1971. Patrick Moraz (former Yes keyboardist) replaced Pinder, 1978.	
9/28/68	3	23	▲ 1. Days Of Future Passed with The London Festival Orchestra *Nights In White Satin* (2) 1972	Deram 18012
10/12/68	23	11	● 2. In Search Of The Lost Chord	Deram 18017
6/7/69	20	13	● 3. On The Threshold Of A Dream	Deram 18025
1/31/70	14	12	● 4. To Our Children's Children's Children	Threshold 1
9/19/70	3	17	● 5. A Question Of Balance	Threshold 3
8/21/71	2(3)	21	● 6. Every Good Boy Deserves Favour	Threshold 5
11/25/72	1(5)	23	● 7. Seventh Sojourn	Threshold 7
12/7/74	11	9	● 8. This Is The Moody Blues [G]	Threshold 12/13 [2]
7/2/77	26	5	9. Caught Live + 5 [L] first three sides recorded live at the Royal Albert Hall in '69; side 4: previously unreleased studio recordings	London 690/1 [2]
7/8/78	13	9	▲ 10. Octave	London 708
6/20/81	1(3)	23	▲ 11. Long Distance Voyager Patrick Moraz replaces Mike Pinder on keyboards	Threshold 2901
9/24/83	26	6	12. The Present	Threshold 2902
5/17/86	9	22	● 13. The Other Side Of Life *Your Wildest Dreams* (9)	Threshold 829179
7/9/88	38	5	14. Sur la mer	Polydor 835756
			MOORE, Bob	
			Born on 11/30/32 in Nashville. Top session bass player. Led the band on Roy Orbison's sessions for Monument Records. Also worked as sideman for Elvis Presley, Brenda Lee, Pat Boone and others.	
11/20/61	33	2	**BOB MOORE AND HIS ORCHESTRA:** 1. Mexico and Other Great Hits! [I] *Mexico* (7)	Monument 4005

DATE	POS	WKS	ARTIST—RECORD TITLE	LABEL & NO.
			MOORE, Dorothy	
			Born in Jackson, Mississippi in 1946. Lead singer of The Poppies.	
6/26/76	**29**	7	1. Misty Blue *Misty Blue (3)*	Malaco 6351
			MORGAN, Jane	
			Born Jane Currier in Boston; raised in Florida. Popular singer in France before achieving U.S. fame via TV and nightclub entertaining.	
12/9/57	**13**	3	1. Fascination with the violins of The Troubadors *Fascination (7)*	Kapp 1066
			MORGAN, Lee	
			Born on 7/10/38 in Philadelphia; fatally shot on 2/19/72. Jazz trumpeter.	
12/26/64	**25**	7	1. The Sidewinder [I]	Blue Note 84157
			MORMON TABERNACLE CHOIR, The	
			Three hundred and seventy-five-voice choir directed by Richard P. Condie (died on 12/22/85).	
10/19/59	**1**(1)	38	● 1. The Lord's Prayer features Eugene Ormandy conducting The Philharmonic Orchestra	Columbia 6068
12/28/59	**5**	2	2. The Spirit Of Christmas [X]	Columbia 6100
			MORRISON, Van	
			Born George Ivan on 8/31/45 in Belfast, Ireland. Blue-eyed soul singer/songwriter. Leader of Them. Wrote the classic hit "Gloria."	
5/30/70	**29**	3	▲ 1. Moondance	Warner 1835
12/26/70	**32**	5	2. His Band And The Street Choir *Domino (9)*	Warner 1884
11/13/71	**27**	6	● 3. Tupelo Honey	Warner 1950
9/2/72	**15**	12	4. Saint Dominic's Preview	Warner 2633
8/25/73	**27**	6	5. Hard Nose The Highway	Warner 2712
11/18/78	**28**	5	6. Wavelength	Warner 3212
			MOTELS, The	
			Los Angeles-based quintet led by vocalist Martha Davis. Formed in Berkeley. To Los Angeles in the early 70s. Re-formed in 1978, signed to Capitol in 1979. Disbanded in 1987.	
5/29/82	**16**	15	● 1. All Four One *Only The Lonely (9)*	Capitol 12177
10/22/83	**22**	8	● 2. Little Robbers *Suddenly Last Summer (9)*	Capitol 12288
9/21/85	**36**	2	3. Shock	Capitol 12378
			MOTHERS OF INVENTION, The — see ZAPPA, Frank	
			MOTLEY CRUE	
			Los Angeles-based, heavy-metal band: "Vince Neil" Wharton (lead vocals), Mick Mars (real name: Bob Deal; guitar), Nikki Sixx (Frank Ferranno; bass) and Tommy Lee Bass (drums; married to actress Heather Locklear).	
12/3/83	**17**	28	▲ 1. Shout At The Devil	Elektra 60289
7/20/85	**6**	18	▲ 2. Theatre Of Pain	Elektra 60418
6/13/87	**2**(1)	26	▲ 3. Girls, Girls, Girls	Elektra 60725
9/23/89	**1**(2)	55	▲ 4. Dr. Feelgood *Dr. Feelgood (6)/Without You (8)*	Elektra 60829

DATE	POS	WKS	ARTIST—RECORD TITLE	LABEL & NO.
			MOTTOLA, Tony	
			Born on 4/18/18 in Kearney, New Jersey. Latin-style guitarist. Produced by Enoch Light. **TONY MOTTOLA AND HIS ORCHESTRA:**	
4/14/62	26	10	1. Roman Guitar [I]	Command 816
			MOTT THE HOOPLE	
			British glitter-rock group led by vocalist Ian Hunter. Group name taken from a Willard Manus novel. Various personnel, including guitarist Mick Ralphs (left in 1973 to form Bad Company). Hunter left in 1976; members Pete ''Overend'' Watts, Morgan Fisher and Dale ''Buffin'' Griffin formed the British Lions.	
10/13/73	35	4	1. Mott	Columbia 32425
5/18/74	28	7	2. The Hoople	Columbia 32871
1/4/75	23	4	3. Mott The Hoople Live [L]	Columbia 33282
			MOUNTAIN	
			New York power-rock group led by Leslie West (b: Leslie Weinstein, 10/22/45, New York City) and Felix Pappalardi (b: 1939, the Bronx; fatally shot on 4/17/83 [age 44] in New York City). Also see West, Bruce & Laing.	
4/11/70	17	21	● 1. Mountain Climbing!	Windfall 4501
2/13/71	16	7	● 2. Nantucket Sleighride	Windfall 5500
1/22/72	35	4	3. Flowers Of Evil	Windfall 5501
			MTUME	
			Progressive funk band led by James Mtume (pronounced Em-too-may). Mtume had been a percussionist with Miles Davis in the early 70s.	
6/18/83	26	7	1. Juicy Fruit	Epic 38588
			MULDAUR, Maria	
			Born Maria D'Amato on 9/12/43 in New York City. Member of Jim Kweskin's Jug Band with former husband Geoff Muldaur (divorced, 1972).	
3/16/74	3	21	● 1. Maria Muldaur *Midnight At The Oasis* (6)	Reprise 2148
12/7/74	23	6	2. Waitress In The Donut Shop	Reprise 2194
			MULLIGAN, Gerry	
			Born on 4/6/27 in New York City. West Coast-based jazz baritone saxophonist. Teamed with trumpeter Chet Baker in 1951. **GERRY MULLIGAN'S JAZZ COMBO:**	
5/25/59	39	2	1. I Want To Live! [S-I] with Shelly Manne (drums) and Art Farmer (trumpet)	United Art. 5006
			MUNCH, Charles — see BOSTON SYMPHONY ORCHESTRA	
			MUPPETS — see CHILDRENS section	
			MURAD, Jerry — see HARMONICATS	
			MURPHEY, Michael	
			Born in Dallas, Texas. Progressive country singer/songwriter. Toured as Travis Lewis of The Lewis & Clarke Expedition in 1967. Worked as a staff writer for Screen Gems. Lived in Austin from 1971-74; Colorado from 1974-79. Based in Taos, New Mexico since 1979.	
5/3/75	18	13	● 1. Blue Sky-Night Thunder *Wildfire* (3)	Epic 33290

DATE	POS	WKS	ARTIST—RECORD TITLE	LABEL & NO.
			MURPHY, Eddie	
			Born on 4/3/61 in Hempstead, New York. Comedian/actor. Former cast member of TV's "Saturday Night Live." Starred in the films *Beverly Hills Cop (I & II)*, *Trading Places*, *48 Hours*, *The Golden Child* and *Coming To America*.	
1/14/84	35	3	▲ 1. Eddie Murphy: Comedian [C]	Columbia 39005
12/7/85	26	10	2. How Could It Be	Columbia 39952
			Party All The Time (2)	
			MURPHY, Walter	
			Born in 1952 in New York City. Studied classical and jazz piano at Manhattan School of Music. Former arranger for Doc Severinsen and "The Tonight Show" orchestra.	
			THE WALTER MURPHY BAND:	
10/2/76	15	6	● 1. A Fifth Of Beethoven	Private S. 2015
			A Fifth Of Beethoven (1)	
			MURRAY, Anne	
			Born Morna Anne Murray on 6/20/45 in Springhill, Nova Scotia. With CBC-TV show "Sing Along Jubilee." First recorded for ARC in 1969. Regular on Glen Campbell's "Goodtime Hour" TV series. Currently resides in Toronto.	
6/2/73	39	2	1. Danny's Song	Capitol 11172
			Danny's Song (7)	
7/13/74	24	6	2. Love Song	Capitol 11266
			You Won't See Me (8)	
10/19/74	32	2	● 3. Country [K]	Capitol 11324
10/14/78	12	8	▲ 4. Let's Keep It That Way	Capitol 11743
			You Needed Me (1)	
3/10/79	23	6	▲ 5. New Kind Of Feeling	Capitol 11849
12/8/79	24	9	● 6. I'll Always Love You	Capitol 12012
11/1/80	16	17	▲ 7. Anne Murray's Greatest Hits [G]	Capitol 12110
			MURRAY THE "K" — see VARIOUS - Radio/TV Celebrity Compilations	
			MUSICAL YOUTH	
			Five schoolboys (ages 11 to 16 in 1983) from Birmingham, England: Dennis Seaton (lead), with brothers Kelvin (guitar) & Michael Grant (keyboards), and Patrick (bass) & Junior Waite (drums).	
2/5/83	23	8	1. The Youth Of Today	MCA 5389
			Pass The Dutchie (10)	
			MYLES, Alannah	
			Rock singer born in Toronto and raised in Buckhorn, Canada.	
2/17/90	5	19	▲ 1. Alannah Myles	Atlantic 81956
			Black Velvet (1)	
			# N	
			NABORS, Jim	
			Born on 6/12/32 in Sylacauga, Alabama. Gomer Pyle on TV's "Andy Griffith Show" (1963-64) and "Gomer Pyle-U.S.M.C." (1964-69). Own TV variety series "The Jim Nabors Hour" (1969-71).	
12/3/66	24	7	● 1. Jim Nabors Sings Love Me With All Your Heart	Columbia 9358
7/4/70	34	3	2. The Jim Nabors Hour	Columbia 1020

DATE	POS	WKS	ARTIST—RECORD TITLE	LABEL & NO.
			NAKED EYES	
			English duo: Pete Byrne (vocals) and Rob Fisher (keyboards, synthesizer). Split in 1984. Fisher later in duo Climie Fisher.	
6/4/83	32	4	1. Naked Eyes *Always Something There To Remind Me* (8)	EMI America 17089
			NASH, Graham	
			Born on 2/2/42 in Blackpool, England. Co-founding member of The Hollies. Formed Crosby, Stills & Nash in 1970.	
6/19/71	15	11	● 1. Songs For Beginners	Atlantic 7204
4/29/72	4	14	● 2. Graham Nash/David Crosby *	Atlantic 7220
2/23/74	34	3	3. Wild Tales	Atlantic 7288
10/25/75	6	12	● 4. Wind On The Water *	ABC 902
8/21/76	26	6	● 5. Whistling Down The Wire * *DAVID CROSBY/GRAHAM NASH	ABC 956
			NASH, Johnny	
			Born on 8/19/40 in Houston. Vocalist/guitarist/actor. Appeared on local TV from age 13. With Arthur Godfrey's TV/radio show from 1956-63. In the film *Take A Giant Step* in 1959. Own JoDa label in 1965. Began recording in Jamaica in the late 60s.	
11/18/72	23	8	1. I Can See Clearly Now *I Can See Clearly Now* (1)	Epic 31607
			NAZARETH	
			Hard-rock group formed in Scotland in 1969: Dan McCafferty (lead singer), Manny Charlton (lead guitar), Pete Agnew (bass) and Darrell Sweet (drums). Billy Rankin (lead guitar) and John Locke (keyboards) added in 1981.	
2/14/76	17	9	● 1. Hair Of The Dog *Love Hurts* (8)	A&M 4511
5/8/76	24	7	2. Close Enough For Rock 'N' Roll	A&M 4562
			NEKTAR	
			English art-rock quartet based in Germany - Roye Albrighton, lead singer.	
10/26/74	19	6	1. Remember The Future	Passport 98002
4/12/75	32	3	2. Down To Earth	Passport 98005
			NELSON, Ricky	
			Born Eric Hilliard Nelson on 5/8/40 in Teaneck, New Jersey. Died on 12/31/85 in a plane crash in DeKalb, Texas. Son of bandleader Ozzie Nelson and vocalist Harriet Hilliard. Rick and brother David appeared on Nelson's radio show from March, 1949, later on TV, 1952-66. Formed own Stone Canyon Band in 1969. Films *Rio Bravo*, *Wackiest Ship In The Army* and *Love And Kisses*. Married the sister of actor Mark Harmon. Their daughter Tracy is a film/TV actress. Their twin sons began recording as Nelson in 1990. Ricky is one of the first teen idols of the rock era. Inducted into the Rock and Roll Hall of Fame in 1987.	
11/11/57	1(2)	33	1. Ricky *Be-Bop Baby* (3)	Imperial 9048
7/28/58	7	9	2. Ricky Nelson *Poor Little Fool* (1)	Imperial 9050
2/2/59	14	19	3. Ricky Sings Again *Believe What You Say* (4)/*Lonesome Town* (7)/ *Never Be Anyone Else But You* (6)/*It's Late* (9)	Imperial 9061
10/5/59	22	24	4. Songs By Ricky *Just A Little Too Much* (9)/*Sweeter Than You* (9)	Imperial 9082
8/29/60	18	11	5. More Songs By Ricky	Imperial 9122
6/26/61	8	17	6. Rick Is 21 *Travelin' Man* (1)/*Hello Mary Lou* (9)	Imperial 9152

DATE	POS	WKS	ARTIST—RECORD TITLE	LABEL & NO.
6/2/62	**27**	6	7. Album Seven By Rick	Imperial 9167
6/22/63	**20**	5	8. For Your Sweet Love	Decca 74419
1/18/64	**14**	12	9. Rick Nelson sings "For You" *For You* (6)	Decca 74479
1/20/73	**32**	5	**RICK NELSON AND THE STONE CANYON BAND:** 10. Garden Party *Garden Party* (6)	Decca 75391

NELSON, Sandy

Born Sander Nelson on 12/1/38 in Santa Monica, California. Rock 'n' roll drummer. Became prominent studio musician. Heard on "Alley Oop," "To Know Him Is To Love Him," "A Thousand Stars" and many others. Lost portion of right leg in a motorcycle accident in 1963. Returned to performing in 1964.

2/3/62	**6**	21	1. Let There Be Drums [I] *Let There Be Drums* (7)	Imperial 9159
5/26/62	**29**	3	2. Drums Are My Beat! [I]	Imperial 9168

NELSON, Willie

Born on 4/30/33 in Ft. Worth, Texas; raised in Abbott, Texas. Prolific country singer/songwriter. Moved to Nashville in 1960. Played bass for Ray Price. Moved back to Texas in 1970. Pioneered "outlaw" country movement. Appeared in several films including *The Electric Horseman* (1979) and *Honeysuckle Rose* (1980). Also see Various Artists.

11/15/75	**28**	4	▲ 1. Red Headed Stranger	Columbia 33482
2/14/76	**10**	14	▲ 2. The Outlaws **WAYLON JENNINGS/WILLIE NELSON/JESSI COLTER/TOMPALL GLASER**	RCA 1321
2/18/78	**12**	9	▲ 3. Waylon & Willie **WAYLON JENNINGS & WILLIE NELSON**	RCA 2686
6/17/78	**30**	3	▲ 4. Stardust an album of pop standards from 1926-55 (produced by Booker T. Jones)	Columbia 35305
1/13/79	**32**	4	▲ 5. Willie and Family Live [L] recorded at Harrah's, Lake Tahoe, Nevada	Columbia 35642 [2]
7/7/79	**25**	5	● 6. One For The Road **WILLIE NELSON AND LEON RUSSELL**	Columbia 36064 [2]
9/13/80	**11**	13	▲ 7. Honeysuckle Rose [S-L]	Columbia 36752 [2]
3/21/81	**31**	6	▲ 8. Somewhere Over The Rainbow	Columbia 36883
10/3/81	**27**	6	▲ 9. Willie Nelson's Greatest Hits (& Some That Will Be) [G]	Columbia 37542 [2]
3/27/82	**2**(4)	28	▲ 10. Always On My Mind *Always On My Mind* (5)	Columbia 37951
5/21/83	**39**	1	11. Tougher Than Leather	Columbia 38248
8/20/83	**37**	1	**MERLE HAGGARD/WILLIE NELSON:** ▲ 12. Poncho & Lefty	Epic 37958

NENA

Gabriele "Nena" Kerner with four-member backup group from West Germany.

3/31/84	**27**	6	1. 99 Luftballons *99 Luftballons* (2)	Epic 39294

NERO, Peter

Born on 5/22/34 in Brooklyn. Pop-jazz-classical pianist. Won the 1961 Best New Artist Grammy Award.

8/7/61	**34**	5	1. Piano Forte [I]	RCA 2334
10/2/61	**32**	3	2. New Piano In Town [I]	RCA 2383

DATE	POS	WKS	ARTIST—RECORD TITLE	LABEL & NO.
4/14/62	**22**	9	3. Young And Warm And Wonderful [I]	RCA 2484
8/11/62	**16**	12	4. For The Nero-Minded [I]	RCA 2536
3/30/63	**40**	1	5. The Colorful Peter Nero [I]	RCA 2618
4/13/63	**5**	18	6. Hail The Conquering Nero	RCA 2638
11/16/63	**31**	3	7. Peter Nero In Person [I-L]	RCA 2710
6/27/64	**38**	2	8. Reflections [I]	RCA 2853
12/25/71	**23**	10	● 9. Summer of '42 [I]	Columbia 31105

NEVIL, Robbie

Pop singer/songwriter/guitarist from Los Angeles.

1/31/87	**37**	3	1. Robbie Nevil *C'est La Vie* (2)/*Wot's It To Ya* (10)	Manhattan 53006

NEW BIRTH, The

R&B vocal group portion of New Birth, Inc. Original group consisted of vocalists Londee Loren, Bobby Downs, Melvin Wilson, Leslie Wilson, Ann Bogan and soloist Alan Frye, with instrumental backing by The Nite-Liters. Melvin, Leslie and Ann recorded as Love, Peace & Happiness in 1972.

5/26/73	**31**	4	1. Birth Day	RCA 4797

NEW CHRISTY MINSTRELS, The

Folk/balladeer troupe named after the Christy Minstrels (formed in 1842 by Edwin "Pop" Christy). Group founded and led by Randy Sparks; Barry McGuire, member.

10/27/62	**19**	8	1. The New Christy Minstrels	Columbia 8672
3/2/63	**30**	4	2. The New Christy Minstrels In Person [L]	Columbia 8741
6/29/63	**20**	7	3. Tall Tales! Legends & Nonsense	Columbia 8817
9/14/63	**15**	23	● 4. Ramblin' featuring Green, Green	Columbia 8855
5/16/64	**9**	20	5. Today [S] featuring songs from the film *Advance To The Rear*	Columbia 8959
7/31/65	**22**	8	6. Chim Chim Cher-ee	Columbia 9169

NEW EDITION

Boston R&B teen vocal quintet (ages 13 to 15 in 1983): Ralph Tresvant, Ronald DeVoe, Michael Bivins, Ricky Bell and Bobby Brown. Formed in 1982 by future New Kids On The Block and Perfect Gentlemen producer, Maurice Starr. Brown left for solo career in 1986; replaced by solo singer Johnny Gill in 1988. Bell, Bivins and DeVoe recorded as Bell Biv DeVoe in 1990.

11/17/84	**6**	29	▲ 1. New Edition *Cool It Now* (4)	MCA 5515
1/11/86	**32**	15	▲ 2. All For Love	MCA 5679
7/23/88	**12**	37	▲ 3. Heart Break *If It Isn't Love* (7)	MCA 42207

NEWHART, Bob

Born on 9/5/29 in Oak Park, Illinois. Bob starred in two very successful TV situation comedies, "The Bob Newhart Show" (1972-78) and "Newhart" (1982-90).

5/16/60	**1**(14)	67	● 1. The Button-Down Mind Of Bob Newhart [C] *1960 Grammy winner: Album of the Year*	Warner 1379
11/14/60	**1**(1)	31	● 2. The Button-Down Mind Strikes Back! [C]	Warner 1393
11/6/61	**10**	11	3. Behind The Button-Down Mind Of Bob Newhart [C]	Warner 1417
10/27/62	**28**	3	4. The Button-Down Mind On TV [C] *Bob hosted a comedy variety show from 1961-62*	Warner 1467

DATE	POS	WKS	ARTIST—RECORD TITLE	LABEL & NO.
			NEW KIDS ON THE BLOCK	
			Boston teen quintet: Joe McIntyre (b: 12/31/72, lead singer), Donny Wahlberg (b: 8/17/69), Danny Wood (b: 5/14/69), and brothers Jordan (b: 5/17/70) and Jon Knight (b: 11/29/68). Formed in the summer of 1984 by producer Maurice Starr who later produced Perfect Gentlemen.	
2/11/89	**1**(2)	71	▲ 1. Hangin' Tough *Please Don't Go Girl* (10)/*You Got It (The Right Stuff)* (3)/ *I'll Be Loving You (Forever)* (1)/*Hangin' Tough* (1)/ *Cover Girl* (2)	Columbia 40985
10/14/89	**25**	18	▲ 2. New Kids On The Block　　　　　　　　　　　　[E] their first album, originally released in 1987 *Didn't I Blow Your Mind* (8)	Columbia 40475
10/21/89	**9**	14	▲ 3. Merry, Merry Christmas　　　　　　　　　　　[X] *This One's For The Children* (7)	Columbia 45280
6/23/90	**1**(1)	18 +	▲ 4. Step By Step *Step By Step* (1)/*Tonight* (7) all of above produced by Maurice Starr	Columbia 45129
			NEWMAN, Randy	
			Born on 11/28/43 in New Orleans. Singer/composer/pianist. Nephew of composers Alfred, Emil and Lionel Newman. Scored the films *Ragtime* and *The Natural*.	
11/30/74	**36**	2	1. Good Old Boys background vocals by the Eagles' Glen Frey and Don Henley	Reprise 2193
11/19/77	**9**	18	● 2. Little Criminals guest appearances by members of the Eagles *Short People* (2)	Warner 3079
			NEW ORDER	
			Techno-dance group from Manchester, England, formerly known as Joy Division. Lineup since 1986: Bernard Sumner, Stephen Morris, Peter Hook and Gillian Gilbert.	
10/17/87	**36**	4	● 1. Substance　　　　　　　　　　　　　　　　　[G]	Qwest 25621 [2]
2/25/89	**32**	6	● 2. Technique	Qwest 25845
			NEW RIDERS OF THE PURPLE SAGE	
			San Francisco country-rock band formed in 1969 by Jerry Garcia as an offshoot of the Grateful Dead. Garcia left after first album in 1971.	
10/30/71	**39**	2	1. New Riders Of The Purple Sage	Columbia 30888
6/17/72	**33**	6	2. Powerglide	Columbia 31284
			NEW SEEKERS, The	
			British-Australian group formed by former Seekers' member Keith Potger after disbandment of The Seekers in 1969. Consisted of Eve Graham, Lyn Paul, Peter Doyle, Marty Kristian and Paul Layton.	
1/29/72	**37**	2	1. We'd Like To Teach The World To Sing *I'd Like To Teach The World To Sing (In Perfect Harmony)* (7)	Elektra 74115
			NEWTON, Juice	
			Born Judy Kay Newton on 2/18/52 in Virginia Beach, Virginia. Pop-country singer.	
4/25/81	**22**	34	▲ 1. Juice *Angel Of The Morning* (4)/*Queen Of Hearts* (2)/ *The Sweetest Thing (I've Ever Known)* (7)	Capitol 12136
6/5/82	**20**	8	● 2. Quiet Lies *Love's Been A Little Bit Hard On Me* (7)	Capitol 12210

DATE	POS	WKS	ARTIST—RECORD TITLE	LABEL & NO.
			NEWTON, Wayne	
			Born on 4/3/42 in Roanoke, Virginia. Singer/multi-instrumentalist. Top Las Vegas entertainer. First big break came in 1962 on TV's "The Jackie Gleason Show." Bobby Darin saw Wayne, signed him up and produced his first charted single. Appeared in the film *The Adventures Of Ford Fairlane*.	
6/5/65	**17**	8	1. Red Roses For A Blue Lady	Capitol 2335
8/19/72	**34**	5	2. Daddy Don't You Walk So Fast *Daddy Don't You Walk So Fast* (4)	Chelsea 1001
			NEWTON-JOHN, Olivia	
			Born on 9/26/48 in Cambridge, England. To Australia in 1953. At age 16, won talent contest trip to England, sang with Pat Carroll as Pat & Olivia. With the group Toomorrow, in a British film of the same name. Consistent award winner in both pop and country. Granddaughter of Nobel Prize-winning German physicist Max Born. In films *Grease* (1978), *Xanadu* (1980) and *Two Of A Kind* (1983). Married actor Matt Lattanzi in 1984. Opened own chain of clothing boutiques (Koala Blue) in 1984.	
6/29/74	**1(1)**	20	● 1. If You Love Me, Let Me Know *If You Love Me (Let Me Know)* (5)/*I Honestly Love You* (1)	MCA 411
3/8/75	**1(1)**	17	● 2. Have You Never Been Mellow *Have You Never Been Mellow* (1)/*Please Mr. Please* (3)	MCA 2133
10/18/75	**12**	6	● 3. Clearly Love	MCA 2148
3/27/76	**13**	10	● 4. Come On Over	MCA 2186
11/27/76	**30**	4	● 5. Don't Stop Believin'	MCA 2223
8/27/77	**34**	4	6. Making A Good Thing Better	MCA 2280
11/12/77	**13**	13	▲ 7. Olivia Newton-John's Greatest Hits [G]	MCA 3028
5/27/78	**1(12)**	39	▲ 8. Grease [S] five songs by Olivia/others by various artists *You're The One That I Want* (1)/ *Hopelessly Devoted To You* (3)/*Summer Nights* (5)	RSO 4002 [2]
1/13/79	**7**	16	▲ 9. Totally Hot *A Little More Love* (3)	MCA 3067
8/9/80	**4**	15	▲ 10. Xanadu [S] side 1: Olivia; side 2: ELO *Magic* (1)/*Xanadu* (8)	MCA 6100
11/7/81	**6**	27	▲ 11. Physical *Physical* (1)/*Make A Move On Me* (5)	MCA 5229
10/16/82	**16**	21	▲ 12. Olivia's Greatest Hits, Vol. 2 [G] *Heart Attack* (3)	MCA 5347
12/24/83	**26**	8	▲ 13. Two Of A Kind [S] four songs by Olivia/others by various artists *Twist Of Fate* (5)	MCA 6127
11/16/85	**29**	5	14. Soul Kiss	MCA 6151
			NEW VAUDEVILLE BAND, The	
			Creation of British composer/record producer Geoff Stephens (b: 10/1/34, London).	
12/17/66	**5**	17	● 1. Winchester Cathedral *Winchester Cathedral* (1)	Fontana 27560
			NEW WORLD THEATRE ORCHESTRA	
			Also shown as the Cinema Sound Stage Orchestra.	
10/21/57	**8**	4	1. Around The World In 80 Days [I]	Stereo-Fid. 2800
			NEW YORK PHILHARMONIC — see BERNSTEIN, Leonard	

DATE	POS	WKS	ARTIST—RECORD TITLE	LABEL & NO.
			NICHOLS, Mike, & Elaine May	
			Improvisational comedy team. Nichols (born Michael Peschkowsky on 11/6/31 in Berlin) is a premier Broadway/film director. Films: *The Graduate*, *Catch-22*, *Silkwood* and others. Married to network newscaster Diane Sawyer. Elaine (b: 4/21/32, Pennsylvania) is a film writer/director/actress. Wrote screenplay for *California Suite* and *Heaven Can Wait*.	
7/13/59	**39**	1	1. Improvisations To Music　　　　　　　　　　[C] with Marty Rubenstein at the piano	Mercury 20376
1/23/61	**10**	8	2. An evening with Mike Nichols and Elaine May opened on Broadway on 10/8/60	[OC-C] Mercury 2200
3/24/62	**17**	9	3. Mike Nichols & Elaine May Examine Doctors　[C]	Mercury 20680
			NICKS, Stevie	
			Born Stephanie Nicks on 5/26/48 in Phoenix; raised in California. Became vocalist of Bay-area group Fritz and subsequently met guitarist Lindsey Buckingham. Teamed up and recorded album *Buckingham-Nicks* in 1973. Vocalist with Fleetwood Mac since January of 1975. Quit touring with band after 1990.	
8/15/81	**1(1)**	45	▲ 1. Bella Donna *Stop Draggin' My Heart Around* (3) with Tom Petty/ *Leather And Lace* (6) with Don Henley	Modern 139
7/9/83	**5**	22	▲ 2. The Wild Heart *Stand Back* (5)	Modern 90048
12/21/85	**12**	17	▲ 3. Rock A Little *Talk To Me* (4)	Modern 90479
6/17/89	**10**	11	● 4. The Other Side Of The Mirror	Modern 91245
			NIGHT RANGER	
			Rock group from California: lead singers Kelly Keagy (drums) and Jack Blades (bass), with guitarists Jeff Watson and Brad Gillis, and keyboardist Alan "Fitz" Gerald. Blades and Gillis were members of Rubicon. Gerald left in 1988; band split up in early 1989.	
3/5/83	**38**	8	1. Dawn Patrol	Boardwalk 33259
5/5/84	**15**	29	▲ 2. Midnight Madness *Sister Christian* (5)	MCA 5456
6/15/85	**10**	25	▲ 3. 7 Wishes *Sentimental Street* (8)	MCA/Camel 5593
5/2/87	**28**	3	● 4. Big Life	MCA 5839
			NILSSON	
			Born Harry Edward Nelson III on 6/15/41 in Brooklyn. Wrote Three Dog Night's hit "One"; scored the film *Skidoo* and TV's "The Courtship Of Eddie's Father." Close friend of John Lennon and Ringo Starr.	
4/10/71	**25**	8	1. The Point!　　　　　　　　　　　　　　　[TV] songs and narration from his animated TV special	RCA 1003
2/5/72	**3**	19	● 2. Nilsson Schmilsson *Without You* (1)/*Coconut* (8)	RCA 4515
8/5/72	**12**	13	● 3. Son Of Schmilsson	RCA 4717
			NITTY GRITTY DIRT BAND	
			Country-folk-rock group from Long Beach, California. Led by Jeff Hanna (vocals, guitar) and John McEuen (banjo, mandolin). Changed name to Dirt Band in 1976 when Hanna left the group. Resumed using Nitty Gritty Dirt Band name in 1982. Various members included ex-Eagle Bernie Leadon who replaced McEuen briefly in early 1987. Revamped quartet since late 1987: Hanna, Jimmy Ibbotson, Bob Carpenter and Jimmie Fadden.	
9/14/74	**28**	6	1. Stars & Stripes Forever　　　　　　　　　[L]	United Art. 184 [2]

DATE	POS	WKS	ARTIST—RECORD TITLE	LABEL & NO.
			NOVA, Aldo	
			Born Aldo Scarporuscio in Montreal. Rock singer/songwriter/guitarist/keyboardist.	
4/3/82	8	16	▲ 1. Aldo Nova	Portrait 37498
			NUGENT, Ted	
			Born on 12/13/48 in Detroit. Heavy-metal rock guitarist; leader of The Amboy Dukes.	
3/13/76	28	6	▲ 1. Ted Nugent	Epic 33692
10/16/76	24	8	▲ 2. Free-For-All	Epic 34121
			featuring vocals by Meat Loaf	
7/2/77	17	19	▲ 3. Cat Scratch Fever	Epic 34700
2/25/78	13	8	▲ 4. Double Live Gonzo! [L]	Epic 35069 [2]
11/18/78	24	10	▲ 5. Weekend Warriors	Epic 35551
6/9/79	18	6	● 6. State Of Shock	Epic 36000
6/7/80	13	9	● 7. Scream Dream	Epic 36404
			NUMAN, Gary	
			Synthesized techno-rock artist. Born Gary Webb on 3/8/58 in Hammersmith, England.	
3/29/80	16	14	1. The Pleasure Principle	Atco 120
			Cars (9)	
			NU SHOOZ	
			Portland, Oregon group centered around husband-and-wife team of guitarist/songwriter John Smith and lead singer Valerie Day.	
6/21/86	27	8	● 1. Poolside	Atlantic 81647
			I Can't Wait (3)	
			N.W.A.	
			Los Angeles-based rap outfit: Eric "Eazy-E" Wright, Lorenzo "M.C. Ren" Patterson, Andre "Dr. Dre" Young, Oshea "Ice Cube" Jackson and DJ Antoine "Yella" Carraby. N.W.A. stands for Niggas With Attitude. Wright records solo as "Eazy-E." Dr. Dre and Yella are also members of World Class Wreckin Cru and produce others.	
4/8/89	37	9	▲ 1. Straight Outta Compton	Ruthless 57102
			NYRO, Laura	
			Born Laura Nigro on 10/18/47 in the Bronx, New York. White soul-gospel singer/ songwriter. Wrote "Stoned Soul Picnic," "Wedding Bell Blues," "And When I Die" and "Stoney End."	
11/22/69	32	3	1. New York Tendaberry	Columbia 9737
			# O	
			OAK RIDGE BOYS, The	
			Country-pop vocal group formed as a gospel quartet in 1940 in Oak Ridge, Tennessee. Disbanded after World War II; re-formed in 1957. Many personnel changes. Lineup since early 1970s: Duane Allen (lead), Joe Bonsall (tenor), Richard Sterban (bass) and Bill Golden (baritone; left for a solo career in 1987, replaced by the group's guitarist, Steve Sanders).	
7/4/81	14	10	▲ 1. Fancy Free	MCA 5209
			Elvira (5)	
3/6/82	20	9	● 2. Bobbie Sue	MCA 5294

DATE	POS	WKS	ARTIST—RECORD TITLE	LABEL & NO.
			OCASEK, Ric	
			Born Richard Otcasek in Baltimore. Lead singer/guitarist of The Cars. Appeared in the 1987 film *Made In Heaven*. Married supermodel/actress Paulina Porizkova in 1989. His son Christopher Otcasek is leader of Glamour Camp.	
2/5/83	**28**	9	1. Beatitude	Geffen 2022
11/1/86	**31**	5	2. This Side Of Paradise	Geffen 24098
			OCEAN, Billy	
			Born Leslie Sebastian Charles on 1/21/50 in Trinidad. Raised in England, worked as a tailor. Did session work in London. Moved to the U.S. in the late 70s.	
9/22/84	**9**	57	▲ 1. Suddenly *Caribbean Queen (No More Love On The Run) (1)/Loverboy (2)/Suddenly (4)*	Jive 8213
5/24/86	**6**	30	▲ 2. Love Zone *There'll Be Sad Songs (To Make You Cry) (1)/Love Zone (10)*	Jive 8409
4/2/88	**18**	11	▲ 3. Tear Down These Walls *Get Outta My Dreams Get Into My Car (1)*	Jive 8495
			O'CONNOR, Sinead	
			Pronounced: Shin-NAYD. Female singer/songwriter raised in Dublin, Ireland. Born in 1967.	
4/9/88	**36**	5	● 1. The Lion And The Cobra	Chrysalis 41612
4/7/90	**1**(6)	27	▲ 2. I Do Not Want What I Haven't Got *Nothing Compares 2 U (1)*	Ensign 21759
			ODYSSEY	
			New York soul-disco trio: Manila-born Tony Reynolds, and sisters Lillian and Louise Lopez, originally from the Virgin Islands.	
12/3/77	**36**	5	1. Odyssey	RCA 2204
			OHIO PLAYERS	
			Originally an R&B instrumental group called the Ohio Untouchables, formed in Dayton in 1959. Backup on The Falcons' records. First recorded for Lupine in 1962. Members during prime (1974-79): Marshall Jones, Clarence "Satch" Satchell, Jimmy "Diamond" Williams, Marvin "Merv" Pierce, Billy Beck, Ralph "Pee Wee" Middlebrook and Leroy "Sugarfoot" Bonner.	
6/8/74	**11**	22	● 1. Skin Tight	Mercury 705
11/30/74	**1**(1)	19	● 2. Fire *Fire (1)*	Mercury 1013
8/23/75	**2**(1)	24	● 3. Honey *Love Rollercoaster (1)*	Mercury 1038
6/19/76	**12**	9	● 4. Contradiction	Mercury 1088
11/27/76	**31**	4	● 5. Ohio Players Gold [G]	Mercury 1122
			O'JAYS, The	
			R&B group from Canton, Ohio formed in 1958 as the Triumphs. Consisted of Eddie Levert, Walter Williams, William Powell, Bobby Massey and Bill Isles. Recorded as the Mascots for the King label in 1961. Renamed by Cleveland DJ, Eddie O'Jay. Isles left in 1965. Massey left to become a record producer in 1971. Levert, Williams and Powell continued as a trio. Powell retired from touring due to illness in late 1975 (d: 5/26/77); replaced by Sammy Strain, formerly with Little Anthony & The Imperials. Levert's sons, Gerald and Sean, are members of the trio Levert.	
10/7/72	**10**	11	● 1. Back Stabbers *Back Stabbers (3)/Love Train (1)*	Phil. Int. 31712
1/12/74	**11**	19	● 2. Ship Ahoy *Put Your Hands Together (10)/For The Love Of Money (9)*	Phil. Int. 32408

DATE	POS	WKS	ARTIST—RECORD TITLE	LABEL & NO.
8/10/74	17	7	● 3. The O'Jays Live In London [L]	Phil. Int. 32953
5/17/75	11	14	● 4. Survival	Phil. Int. 33150
12/6/75	7	17	▲ 5. Family Reunion	Phil. Int. 33807
			I Love Music (5)	
10/16/76	20	6	● 6. Message In The Music	Phil. Int. 34245
6/11/77	27	5	● 7. Travelin' At The Speed Of Thought	Phil. Int. 34684
5/13/78	6	8	▲ 8. So Full Of Love	Phil. Int. 35355
			Use Ta Be My Girl (4)	
9/22/79	16	8	▲ 9. Identify Yourself	Phil. Int. 36027
9/27/80	36	3	10. The Year 2000	TSOP 36416
			OLDFIELD, Mike	
			Born on 5/15/53 in Reading, England. Classical rock multi-instrumentalist/composer.	
1/26/74	3	23	● 1. Tubular Bells [I]	Virgin 105
			Tubular Bells (7) - one 49-minute recording (excerpts used in film *The Exorcist*)	
			OLIVER	
			Born William Oliver Swofford on 2/22/45 in North Wilkesboro, North Carolina.	
9/6/69	19	10	1. Good Morning Starshine	Crewe 1333
			Good Morning Starshine (3)/*Jean* (2)	
			O'NEAL, Alexander	
			Minneapolis-based black vocalist, born on 1/23/55 in Mississippi. Co-producer of Janet Jackson's hit "Control."	
9/5/87	29	8	● 1. Hearsay	Tabu 40320
			101 STRINGS	
			European orchestra under the direction of D.L. Miller.	
5/25/59	9	32	1. The Soul of Spain [I]	Somerset 6600
			this album was #1 for 46 of the 47 weeks that *Billboard* published a special "Best Selling Low Price LP's" chart (2/19/60/61)	
1/9/61	21	4	2. The Soul of Spain, Volume II [I]	Somerset 9900
			ONO, Yoko — see LENNON, John	
			ORBISON, Roy	
			Born on 4/23/36 in Vernon, Texas. Had own band, the Wink Westerners in 1952. Attended North Texas University with Pat Boone. First recorded for Je-Wel in early 1956. Toured with Sun Records shows to 1958. Toured with The Beatles in 1963. Wife Claudette killed in a motorcycle accident on 6/7/66; two sons died in a fire in 1968. Resurgence in career beginning in 1985. Inducted into the Rock and Roll Hall of Fame in 1987. Member of the 1988 supergroup Traveling Wilburys. Died of a heart attack on 12/6/88 in Madison, Tennessee.	
6/9/62	21	7	1. Crying	Monument 4007
			Running Scared (1)/*Crying* (2)	
9/15/62	13	48	● 2. Roy Orbison's Greatest Hits [G]	Monument 4009
			Only The Lonely (2)/*Blue Angel* (9)/*Dream Baby* (4)	
10/26/63	35	2	● 3. In Dreams	Monument 18003
			In Dreams (7)	
10/3/64	19	16	4. More Of Roy Orbison's Greatest Hits [G]	Monument 18024
			It's Over (9)/*Mean Woman Blues* (5)	
2/25/89	5	16	▲ 5. Mystery Girl	Virgin 91058
			You Got It (9)	

DATE	POS	WKS	ARTIST—RECORD TITLE	LABEL & NO.
			ORCHESTRAL MANOEUVRES IN THE DARK	
			English electro-pop quartet: keyboardists/vocalists Paul Humphreys and Andrew McCluskey with drummer Malcolm Holmes and multi-instrumentalist Martin Cooper.	
11/2/85	**38**	5	1. Crush	A&M 5077
			ORLANDO, Tony — see DAWN	
			ORLEANS	
			Rock group founded in New York City by John Hall with the Hoppen brothers (Lawrence and Lance), Wells Kelly and Jerry Marotta. Hall and Marotta left in 1977, replaced by Bob Leinbach and R.A. Martin.	
10/11/75	**33**	5	1. Let There Be Music *Dance With Me* (6)	Asylum 1029
10/2/76	**30**	5	2. Waking And Dreaming *Still The One* (5)	Asylum 1070
			ORMANDY, Eugene — see PHILADELPHIA ORCHESTRA	
			OSBORNE, Jeffrey	
			Born on 3/9/48 in Providence, Rhode Island. Soul singer/songwriter/drummer. Lead singer of L.T.D. until 1980.	
9/3/83	**25**	23	● 1. Stay With Me Tonight	A&M 4940
11/24/84	**39**	4	● 2. Don't Stop	A&M 5017
7/12/86	**26**	11	● 3. Emotional	A&M 5103
			OSBOURNE, Ozzy	
			Born John Osbourne on 12/3/48 in Birmingham, England. Heavy-metal artist; former lead singer of Black Sabbath. Appeared in the 1986 film *Trick Or Treat*.	
5/23/81	**21**	16	▲ 1. Blizzard Of Ozz	Jet 36812
11/28/81	**16**	23	▲ 2. Diary Of A Madman	Jet 37492
12/18/82	**14**	10	● 3. Speak Of The Devil [L] recorded at The Ritz, New York	Jet 38350 [2]
12/17/83	**19**	11	▲ 4. Bark At The Moon	CBS Assoc. 38987
2/22/86	**6**	17	▲ 5. The Ultimate Sin	CBS Assoc. 40026
5/16/87	**6**	14	● 6. Tribute [L] **OZZY OSBOURNE/RANDY RHOADS** live recordings from 1981 featuring Ozzy's guitarist, Randy Rhoads, who was killed in an airplane crash on 3/19/82 (age 25)	CBS As. 40714 [2]
10/29/88	**13**	13	▲ 7. No Rest For The Wicked	CBS Assoc. 44245
			OSKAR, Lee	
			Born on 3/24/48 in Copenhagen, Denmark. Harmonica player. Studio musician in Los Angeles. Original member of War.	
6/19/76	**29**	4	1. Lee Oskar	United Art. 594
			OSMOND, Donny	
			Born on 12/9/57 in Ogden, Utah. Seventh son of George and Olive Osmond, Donny became a member of The Osmonds in 1963. Owner of production company Night Star. Burst back on to the pop charts in March of 1989.	
7/24/71	**13**	18	● 1. The Donny Osmond Album *Sweet And Innocent* (7)	MGM 4782
11/13/71	**12**	14	● 2. To You With Love, Donny *Go Away Little Girl* (1)	MGM 4797
6/10/72	**6**	10	● 3. Portrait Of Donny *Hey Girl* (9)/*Puppy Love* (3)	MGM 4820
8/5/72	**11**	14	● 4. Too Young	MGM 4854

DATE	POS	WKS	ARTIST—RECORD TITLE	LABEL & NO.
1/6/73	29	6	● 5. My Best To You [G]	MGM 4872
4/14/73	26	7	6. Alone Together *The Twelfth Of Never* (8)	MGM 4886
			OSMOND, Donny & Marie Brother and sister co-hosts of own musical/variety TV series from 1976-78. Marie was born on 10/13/59 in Ogden, Utah.	
11/2/74	35	4	● 1. I'm Leaving It All Up To You *I'm Leaving It (All) Up To You* (4)/ *Morning Side Of The Mountain* (8)	MGM 4968
			OSMONDS, The Family group from Ogden, Utah. Alan (b: 6/22/49), Wayne (b: 8/28/51), Merrill (b: 4/30/53), Jay (b: 3/2/55) and Donny (b: 12/9/57). Began as a quartet in 1959, singing religious and barbershop-quartet songs. Regulars on Andy Williams' TV show from 1962-67.	
2/6/71	14	10	● 1. Osmonds *One Bad Apple* (1)	MGM 4724
7/3/71	22	10	● 2. Homemade	MGM 4770
2/5/72	10	13	● 3. Phase-III *Yo-Yo* (3)/*Down By The Lazy River* (4)	MGM 4796
7/1/72	13	15	● 4. The Osmonds "Live" [L]	MGM 4826 [2]
11/4/72	14	11	● 5. Crazy Horses	MGM 4851
			O'SULLIVAN, Gilbert Born Raymond O'Sullivan on 12/1/46 in Waterford, Ireland.	
8/19/72	9	14	1. Gilbert O'Sullivan-Himself *Alone Again (Naturally)* (1)	MAM 4
			OUTFIELD, The British pop-rock trio: Tony Lewis (lead singer), John Spinks (guitar) and Alan Jackman (drums).	
3/29/86	9	29	▲ 1. Play Deep	Columbia 40027
7/18/87	18	11	● 2. Bangin'	Columbia 40619
			OUTLAWS Southern-rock band formed in Tampa in 1974. Consisted of guitarists Hughie Thomasson, Billy Jones and Henry Paul, with drummer Monte Yoho and bassist Frank O'Keefe (replaced by Harvey Arnold in 1977). Paul, Yoho and Arnold left by 1980.	
9/20/75	13	7	● 1. Outlaws	Arista 4042
5/15/76	36	2	2. Lady In Waiting	Arista 4070
4/15/78	29	4	● 3. Bring It Back Alive [L]	Arista 8300 [2]
2/7/81	25	7	● 4. Ghost Riders	Arista 9542
			OUTSIDERS, The Cleveland rock quintet: Sonny Geraci (lead singer), Tom King (guitar), Bill Bruno (lead guitar), Mert Madsen (bass) and Rick Baker (drums). Geraci later led band Climax.	
7/16/66	37	3	1. Time Won't Let Me *Time Won't Let Me* (5)	Capitol 2501
			OZARK MOUNTAIN DAREDEVILS, The Country-rock group from Springfield, Missouri. Nucleus: Larry Lee (keyboards, guitar), Steve Cash (harp), John Dillon (guitar) and Michael Granda (bass).	
6/22/74	26	5	● 1. The Ozark Mountain Daredevils	A&M 4411

Willie Nelson's prolific career perhaps reached its zenith with 1982's *Always On My Mind*, which hit the No. 2 slot for 4 weeks, and stayed in the top 40 for 28 weeks.

Peter Nero's career as a popular pianist was capped by two career highs: 1963's *Hail The Conquering Nero* on RCA, which peaked at No. 5; and 1971's *Summer Of '42* on Columbia, which, though reaching only the No. 23 slot, stands as Nero's sole gold album.

New Edition begat some of the most-heard R&B acts of the early 90s, thanks to solo spinoff projects by group members Bobby Brown, Bell Biv DeVoe and the already-established Johnny Gill. 1988's *Heart Break* was produced by superstar team Jimmy Jam and Terry Lewis.

Stevie Nicks initially came to prominence via 1973's *Buckingham Nicks*, made with Lindsey Buckingham prior to joining Fleetwood Mac. Two of her biggest solo singles also involved male partners: 1981's "Stop Draggin' My Heart Around," featuring Tom Petty & the Heartbreakers; and "Leather And Lace," recorded with Don Henley. 1985's *Rock A Little* featured the hits "I Can't Wait" and "Some Become Strangers."

Night Ranger, who had a top 5 hit with 1983's "Sister Christian," was a hard-rocking California band featuring Jack Blades. *7 Wishes* was the group's sole top 10 album. In 1990 Blades joined forces with fellow rockers Ted Nugent and Styx's Tommy Shaw to form the "super trio" Damn Yankees.

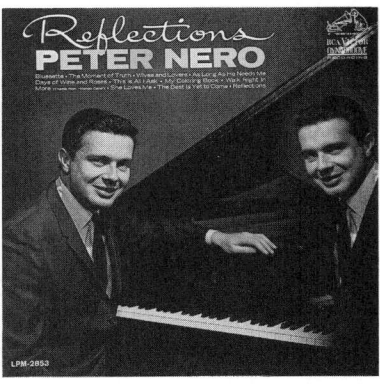

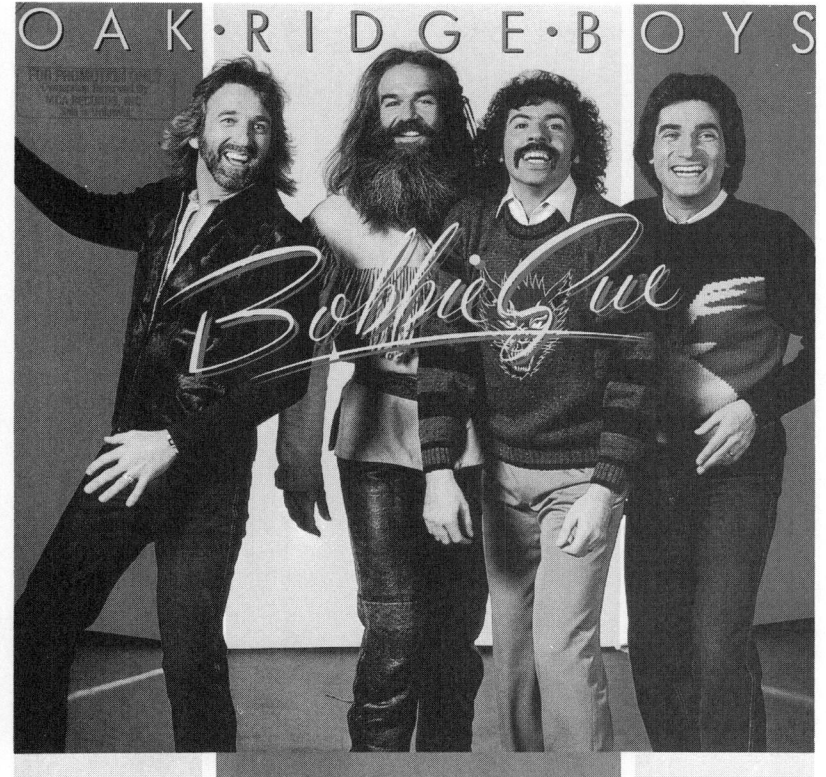

The **Oak Ridge Boys** may forever be remembered for their 1981 hit single "Elvira," from their *Fancy Free* LP. Their next album following that single's success, 1982's *Bobbie Sue*, only reached No. 20.

Billy Ocean's 1986 LP *Love Zone* contained two of his most popular hits: "When The Going Gets Tough, The Tough Get Going" and "There'll Be Sad Songs To Make You Cry."

Orchestral Manoeuvres In The Dark— a British group wisely dubbed "OMD" by time-conscious disk jockeys—met their greatest success with the 1986 single "If You Leave," taken from John Hughes' film *Pretty In Pink*. *Crush* remains the group's only top 40 album, charting in 1985.

Ozzy Osbourne's career as a lead singer began with the 1970 LP *Black Sabbath* and hasn't slowed since: The colorful singer, with seven top 40 albums under his belt, has remained a major concert attraction into the 90s.

Donny Osmond's series of hits began with the 1971 No.1 single "One Bad Apple," cut with his brothers, and continued through 1978, when he and his sister Marie released *Goin' Coconuts*. 1971's *The Donny Osmond Album* was his first solo effort; 1989's surprising comeback effort, *Donny Osmond* on Capitol, was his most recent.

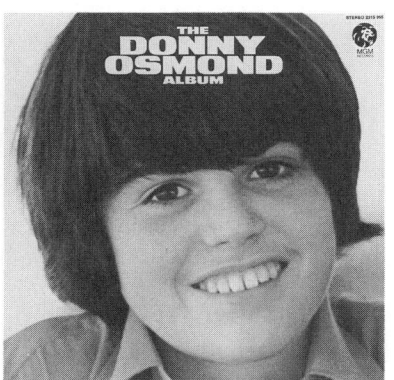

DATE	POS	WKS	ARTIST—RECORD TITLE	LABEL & NO.
2/8/75	**19**	7	2. It'll Shine When It Shines *Jackie Blue* (3)	A&M 3654

P

DATE	POS	WKS	ARTIST—RECORD TITLE	LABEL & NO.
			PABLO CRUISE	
			San Francisco pop-rock quartet formed in 1973. Consisted of Dave Jenkins (vocals, guitar), Bud Cockrell (member of It's A Beautiful Day; vocals, bass), Cory Lerios (keyboards) and Stephen Price (drums). Cockrell replaced by Bruce Day in 1977. John Pierce replaced Day, and guitarist Angelo Rossi joined group in 1980.	
7/2/77	**19**	17	▲ 1. A Place In The Sun *Whatcha Gonna Do?* (6)	A&M 4625
7/15/78	**6**	14	▲ 2. Worlds Away *Love Will Find A Way* (6)	A&M 4697
12/8/79	**39**	2	3. Part Of The Game	A&M 3712
8/22/81	**34**	5	4. Reflector	A&M 3726
			PAGE, Jimmy	
			Prolific English guitarist. Member of The Yardbirds, 1966 to July of 1968. In October of 1968 formed The New Yardbirds, which evolved into rock supergroup Led Zepplin. Page produced all of their music. Group disbanded with the 9/25/80 death of drummer John Bonham. Jimmy composed the score for the film *Death Wish II*. In 1984, formed The Firm with vocalist Paul Rodgers (formerly of Free and Bad Company); disbanded in 1986.	
7/16/88	**26**	6	● 1. Outrider vocals: Chris Farlow, Robert Plant and John Miles	Geffen 24188
			PAGE, Patti	
			Born Clara Ann Fowler on 11/8/27 in Muskogee, Oklahoma. One of 11 children. Raised in Tulsa. On radio KTUL with Al Klauser & His Oklahomans, as "Ann Fowler," late 40s. Another singer was billed as "Patti Page" for the Page Milk Company show on KTUL. When she left, Fowler took her place and name. With the Jimmy Joy band in 1947. On "Breakfast Club," Chicago radio, 1947; signed by Mercury Records. Used multi-voice effect on records from 1947. Own TV series "The Patti Page Show," 1955-58 and "The Big Record," 1957-58. In the 1960 film *Elmer Gantry*.	
11/24/56	**18**	2	1. Manhattan Tower a version of Gordon Jenkins' musical narrative	Mercury 20226
6/26/65	**27**	7	2. Hush, Hush, Sweet Charlotte *Hush, Hush, Sweet Charlotte* (8)	Columbia 9153
			PAGE, Tommy	
			Eighteen-year-old native of West Caldwell, New Jersey.	
4/28/90	**38**	2	1. Paintings In My Mind *I'll Be Your Everything* (1)	Sire 26148
			PALMER, Robert	
			Born on 1/19/49 in Batley, England; raised on the island of Malta. Lead singer of supergroup The Power Station.	
8/25/79	**19**	8	1. Secrets	Island 9544
3/22/86	**8**	35	▲ 2. Riptide *Addicted To Love* (1)/*I Didn't Mean To Turn You On* (2)	Island 90471
7/30/88	**13**	20	▲ 3. Heavy Nova *Simply Irresistible* (2)	EMI-Man. 48057

DATE	POS	WKS	ARTIST—RECORD TITLE	LABEL & NO.
			PARAMOR, Norrie	
			Born in England in 1914. Conductor/composer/arranger. A&R man for EMI Columbia; guided the careers of Cliff Richard, Frank Ifield and many others. **NORRIE PARAMOR HIS STRINGS AND ORCHESTRA:**	
9/8/56	**18**	3	1. In London, In Love... [I]	Capitol Int. 10025
			PARKER, Graham	
			Pub-rock vocalist/guitarist/songwriter, born in East London in 1950. Backing band The Rumour led by guitarist Brinsley Schwarz. **GRAHAM PARKER AND THE RUMOUR:**	
5/26/79	**40**	2	1. Squeezing Out Sparks	Arista 4223
7/5/80	**40**	1	2. The Up Escalator	Arista 9517
			Bruce Springsteen sings on one track	
			PARKER, Ray, Jr.	
			Born on 5/1/54 in Detroit. Prominent session guitarist in California; worked with Stevie Wonder, Barry White and others. Formed band Raydio in 1977 with Arnell Carmichael, Jerry Knight, Larry Tolbert, Darren Carmichael and Charles Fearing. Parker went solo in 1982. In 1984, Knight recorded in the duo Ollie & Jerry. **RAYDIO:**	
3/18/78	**27**	9	● 1. Raydio	Arista 4163
			Jack And Jill (8)	
			RAY PARKER JR. AND RAYDIO:	
5/10/80	**33**	5	● 2. Two Places At The Same Time	Arista 9515
5/2/81	**13**	16	● 3. A Woman Needs Love	Arista 9543
			A Woman Needs Love (Just Like You Do) (4)	
			RAY PARKER JR.:	
5/8/82	**11**	12	● 4. The Other Woman	Arista 9590
			The Other Woman (4)	
			PARKS, Michael	
			Born on 4/4/38 in Corona, California. Portrayed Jim Bronson on TV's "Then Came Bronson."	
2/28/70	**35**	5	1. Closing The Gap	MGM 4646
5/30/70	**24**	6	2. Long Lonesome Highway	MGM 4662
			PARLIAMENT	
			Funk aggregation which evolved from The Parliaments. Spearheaded by George Clinton, part of "A Parliafunkadelicament Thang" corporation. The group's nearly 40 members also recorded under the names Funkadelic, P. Funk All Stars and Parlet among others.	
4/10/76	**13**	17	▲ 1. Mothership Connection	Casablanca 7022
10/23/76	**20**	8	● 2. The Clones Of Dr. Funkenstein	Casablanca 7034
6/4/77	**29**	5	● 3. Parliament Live/P. Funk Earth Tour [L]	Casablanca 7053 [2]
1/21/78	**13**	19	▲ 4. Funkentelechy Vs. The Placebo Syndrome	Casablanca 7084
12/23/78	**23**	10	● 5. Motor-Booty Affair	Casablanca 7125
			PARSONS, Alan/Project	
			Duo formed in London in 1975. Consisted of producer Alan Parsons (guitar, keyboards) and lyricist Eric Woolfson (vocals, keyboards). Both had worked at the Abbey Road Studios; Parsons was an engineer, Woolfson a songwriter. Parsons engineered Pink Floyd's *Dark Side Of The Moon* and The Beatles *Abbey Road* albums. Project features varying musicians and vocalists. **THE ALAN PARSONS PROJECT:**	
7/4/76	**38**	4	1. Tales Of Mystery And Imagination - Edgar Allan Poe	20th Century 508
			musical interpretation of Poe's most notable works	
8/6/77	**9**	19	▲ 2. I Robot	Arista 7002
7/22/78	**26**	9	● 3. Pyramid	Arista 4180

DATE	POS	WKS	ARTIST—RECORD TITLE	LABEL & NO.
9/22/79	**13**	12	● 4. Eve	Arista 9504
11/29/80	**13**	21	▲ 5. The Turn Of A Friendly Card	Arista 9518
7/10/82	**7**	21	▲ 6. Eye In The Sky	Arista 9599
			Eye In The Sky (3)	
3/24/84	**15**	13	● 7. Ammonia Avenue	Arista 8204
			PARTON, Dolly	
			Born on 1/19/46 in Sevier County, Tennessee. Worked on Knoxville radio show at age 11. First recorded for Gold Band in 1957. To Nashville in 1964. Replaced Norma Jean on the Porter Wagoner TV show, 1967-74. Joined the Grand Ole Opry in 1969. Starred in the films *9 To 5*, *The Best Little Whorehouse In Texas* and *Steel Magnolias*. Hosted own TV variety show in 1987.	
12/3/77	**20**	13	▲ 1. Here You Come Again	RCA 2544
			Here You Come Again (3)	
9/16/78	**27**	8	● 2. Heartbreaker	RCA 2797
7/21/79	**40**	1	● 3. Great Balls Of Fire	RCA 3361
1/17/81	**11**	15	● 4. 9 to 5 and Odd Jobs	RCA 3852
			9 to 5 (1)	
			KENNY ROGERS & DOLLY PARTON:	
12/22/84	**31**	4	▲ 5. Once Upon A Christmas [X]	RCA 5307
			DOLLY PARTON, LINDA RONSTADT, EMMYLOU HARRIS:	
3/28/87	**6**	14	▲ 6. Trio	Warner 25491
			PARTRIDGE FAMILY, The	
			Popularized through "The Partridge Family" TV series, broadcast from 1970-74. Recordings by series stars David Cassidy (lead singer) and real-life stepmother Shirley Jones (backing vocals). David, son of actor Jack Cassidy, was born on 4/12/50 in New York City; raised in California. Shirley, born on 3/31/34 in Smithton, Pennsylvania, starred in the film musicals *Oklahoma* and *The Music Man*; married David's father in 1956.	
11/7/70	**4**	36	● 1. The Partridge Family Album	Bell 6050
			I Think I Love You (1)	
4/3/71	**3**	23	● 2. Up To Date	Bell 6059
			Doesn't Somebody Want To Be Wanted (6)/	
			I'll Meet You Halfway (9)	
9/4/71	**9**	22	● 3. The Partridge Family Sound Magazine	Bell 6064
4/1/72	**18**	7	● 4. The Partridge Family Shopping Bag	Bell 6072
10/7/72	**21**	10	● 5. The Partridge Family at home with their Greatest Hits [G]	Bell 1107
			PAUL, Billy	
			Born Paul Williams on 12/1/34 in Philadelphia. Sang on Philadelphia radio broadcasts at age 11. First recorded for Jubilee in 1952.	
1/6/73	**17**	9	● 1. 360 Degrees Of Billy Paul	Phil. Int. 31793
			Me And Mrs. Jones (1)	
			PAUL, Les, and Mary Ford	
			Les was born Lester Polfus on 6/9/16 in Waukesha, Wisconsin. Mary was born Colleen Summer on 7/7/28 in Pasadena; died on 9/30/77. Paul is a self-taught guitarist. Worked local radio stations, then to Chicago, 1932-37. Own trio in 1936. With Fred Waring from 1938-41. Innovator in electric guitar and multi-track recordings. Married vocalist Mary Ford on 12/29/49; divorced in 1963. Les was inducted into the Rock And Roll Hall Of Fame in 1988.	
5/14/55	**15**	6	1. Les and Mary	Capitol 577
			ten songs feature Mary's vocals; six are instrumentals by Les	

DATE	POS	WKS	ARTIST—RECORD TITLE	LABEL & NO.
			PAUL & PAULA	
			Real names: Ray Hildebrand (b: 12/21/40, Joshua, Texas) and Jill Jackson (b: 5/20/42, McCaney, Texas). Formed duo at Howard Payne College, Brownwood, Texas.	
3/16/63	9	8	1. Paul & Paula Sing For Young Lovers *Hey Paula* (1)/*Young Lovers* (6)	Philips 078
			PEACHES & HERB	
			Soul duo from Washington, D.C.: Herb Fame (born Herbert Feemster, 1942) and Francine Barker (born Francine Hurd, 1947). Fame had been recording solo, Francine sang in vocal group Sweet Things. Marlene Mack filled in for Francine from 1968-69. Re-formed with Fame and Linda Green in 1977.	
6/24/67	30	6	1. Let's Fall In Love *Close Your Eyes* (8)	Date 4004
2/17/79	2(6)	23	▲ 2. 2 Hot! *Shake Your Groove Thing* (5)/*Reunited* (1)	Polydor 6172
12/1/79	31	5	● 3. Twice The Fire	Polydor 6239
			PEBBLES	
			Her real name is Perri McKissack. Native of Oakland. Worked with Con Funk Shun in the early 80s while still a teenager. Her cousin is vocalist Cherrelle. Married to singer/songwriter/producer L.A. Reid of The Deele.	
4/2/88	14	19	▲ 1. Pebbles *Girlfriend* (5)/*Mercedes Boy* (2)	MCA 42094
			PENDERGRASS, Teddy	
			Born on 3/26/50 in Philadelphia. Worked local clubs, became drummer for Harold Melvin's Blue Notes in 1969; vocalist with same group in 1970. Went solo in 1976. Auto accident on 3/18/82 left him partially paralyzed.	
4/9/77	17	11	▲ 1. Teddy Pendergrass	Phil. Int. 34390
7/8/78	11	15	▲ 2. Life Is A Song Worth Singing	Phil. Int. 35095
6/30/79	5	14	▲ 3. Teddy	Phil. Int. 36003
1/26/80	33	4	● 4. Teddy Live! Coast To Coast [L] side 4: interviews and new studio recordings	Phil. Int. 36294 [2]
8/23/80	14	16	▲ 5. TP	Phil. Int. 36745
10/10/81	19	7	● 6. It's Time For Love	Phil. Int. 37491
7/21/84	38	5	● 7. Love Language	Asylum 60317
			PENN, Michael	
			L.A.-based singer/songwriter. Older brother of actors Sean and Christopher Penn. Son of actor/director Leo Penn and actress Eileen Ryan.	
3/10/90	31	8	1. March	RCA 9692
			PENNARIO, Leonard	
			Classical pianist. Born on 7/9/24 in Buffalo, New York. To Los Angeles at age 10 and appeared on Bing Crosby's "Kraft Music Hall." Debuted at age 12 with the Dallas Symphony. Has performed with nearly every prestigious international orchestra.	
6/8/59	29	1	1. Concertos under the Stars [I] with The Hollywood Bowl Symphony Orchestra, conducted by Carmen Dragon	Capitol 8326
			PERRY, Steve	
			Born on 1/22/49 in Hanford, California. Lead singer of Journey since 1978.	
5/5/84	12	18	▲ 1. Street Talk *Oh Sherrie* (3)	Columbia 39334

DATE	POS	WKS	ARTIST—RECORD TITLE	LABEL & NO.
			PETER & GORDON	
			Pop duo formed in London in 1963: Peter Asher (b: 6/22/44) and Gordon Waller (b: 6/4/45). Toured the U.S. in 1964, appeared on "Shindig," "Hullabaloo," Ed Sullivan TV shows. Disbanded in 1967. Asher went into production and management, including work with Linda Ronstadt and James Taylor.	
7/25/64	**21**	5	1. A World Without Love *A World Without Love* (1)	Capitol 2115
			PETER, PAUL AND MARY	
			Folk group formed in New York City in 1961. Consisted of Mary Travers (b: 11/7/37, Louisville); Peter Yarrow (b: 5/31/38, New York City); and Paul Stookey (b: 11/30/37, Baltimore). Yarrow had worked the Newport Folk Festival in 1960, Stookey had done TV work and Travers had been in the Broadway musical *The Next President*. Disbanded in 1971, reunited in 1978.	
6/2/62	**1**(7)	112	▲ 1. Peter, Paul And Mary *If I Had A Hammer* (10)	Warner 1449
1/26/63	**2**(9)	71	● 2. (Moving) *Puff The Magic Dragon* (2)	Warner 1473
10/26/63	**1**(5)	58	● 3. In The Wind *Blowin' In The Wind* (2)/ *Don't Think Twice, It's All Right* (9)	Warner 1507
8/29/64	**4**	25	● 4. Peter, Paul and Mary In Concert　　　　[L]	Warner 1555 [2]
5/1/65	**8**	26	● 5. A Song Will Rise	Warner 1589
11/27/65	**11**	8	● 6. See What Tomorrow Brings	Warner 1615
9/17/66	**22**	9	7. Peter, Paul and Mary Album	Warner 1648
9/9/67	**15**	25	● 8. Album 1700 *I Dig Rock And Roll Music* (9)/*Leaving On A Jet Plane* (1)	Warner 1700
10/12/68	**14**	12	9. Late Again	Warner 1751
6/21/69	**12**	9	10. Peter, Paul and Mommy	Warner 1785
6/27/70	**15**	11	▲ 11. 10 Years Together/The Best Of Peter, Paul and Mary [G]	Warner 2552
			PET SHOP BOYS	
			British duo: Neil Tennant (vocals) and Chris Lowe (keyboards). Tennant was a writer for the British fan magazine *Smash Hits*. In 1989, Tennant was also with the group Electronic.	
4/19/86	**7**	21	▲ 1. Please *West End Girls* (1)/*Opportunities* (10)	EMI America 17193
10/17/87	**25**	22	● 2. Pet Shop Boys, actually. *It's A Sin* (9)/ *What Have I Done To Deserve This?* (2) with Dusty Springfield	EMI-Man. 46972
11/26/88	**34**	3	● 3. Introspective *Always On My Mind* (4)	EMI-Man. 90868
			PETTY, Tom	
			Leader of rock group The Heartbreakers, formed in Los Angeles in 1975. Consisted of Petty (b: 10/20/53, Gainesville, Florida; guitar, vocals), Mike Campbell (guitar), Benmont Tench (keyboards), Ron Blair (bass) and Stan Lynch (drums). Petty, Campbell and Tench had been in Florida group Mudcrutch, early 70s. Backed Stevie Nicks on solo LP *Bella Donna*. Blair left in 1982, replaced by Howard Epstein. Petty appeared in the 1987 film *Made In Heaven*. Member of the 1988 supergroup Traveling Wilburys. **TOM PETTY AND THE HEARTBREAKERS:**	
7/1/78	**23**	8	● 1. You're Gonna Get It!	Shelter 52029
11/17/79	**2**(7)	29	▲ 2. Damn The Torpedoes *Don't Do Me Like That* (10)	Backstreet 5105
5/23/81	**5**	17	▲ 3. Hard Promises	Backstreet 5160
11/27/82	**9**	22	● 4. Long After Dark	Backstreet 5360

DATE	POS	WKS	ARTIST—RECORD TITLE	LABEL & NO.
4/13/85	**7**	18	▲ 5. Southern Accents	MCA 5486
1/18/86	**22**	9	6. Pack Up The Plantation - Live! [L]	MCA 8021 [2]
5/23/87	**20**	13	● 7. Let Me Up (I've Had Enough)	MCA 5836
			TOM PETTY:	
5/20/89	**3**	51	▲ 8. Full Moon Fever Petty solo with backing by all of The Heartbreakers except drummer Stan Lynch *Free Fallin'* (7)	MCA 6253
5/26/62	**17**	11	**PHILADELPHIA ORCHESTRA, The** Conducted by Eugene Ormandy (b: 11/18/1899, Budapest, Hungary; d: 3/12/85). Came to the U.S. in 1921. Conducted orchestra from 1938-1980. Also see Mormon Tabernacle Choir. 1. The Magnificent Sound Of The Philadelphia Orchestra compiled from 16 of their albums	[K-I] Columbia 1 [2]
9/20/75	**32**	6	**PHILLIPS, Esther** Born Esther Mae Jones on 12/23/35 in Galveston, Texas. One of the first female superstars of R&B. Recorded and toured with The Johnny Otis Orchestra as "Little Esther," 1948-54; scored seven top 10 hits on the R&B charts in 1950. Bouts with drug addiction interrupted her career and led to her death on 8/7/84. 1. What A Diff'rence A Day Makes with jazz guitarist Joe Beck	Kudu 23
12/15/62	**19**	3	**PICKETT, Bobby "Boris"** Born on 2/11/40 in Somerville, Massachusetts. Began recording career in Hollywood while aspiring to be an actor. Rickie Page of The Bermudas was member of his group. **BOBBY "BORIS" PICKETT AND THE CRYPT-KICKERS:** 1. The Original Monster Mash [N] *Monster Mash* (1)	Garpax 57001
10/15/66	**21**	7	**PICKETT, Wilson** Soul singer/songwriter. Born on 3/18/41 in Prattville, Alabama. Sang in local gospel groups. To Detroit in 1955. With The Falcons, 1961-63. Career took off after recording in Memphis with guitarist/producer Steve Cropper. 1. The Exciting Wilson Pickett *Land Of 1000 Dances* (6)	Atlantic 8129
1/27/68	**35**	8	2. The Best Of Wilson Pickett [G]	Atlantic 8151
3/31/73	**1(1)**	63	**PINK FLOYD** English progressive rock band formed in 1965: David Gilmour (b: 3/6/46; guitar; replaced Syd Barrett in 1968), Roger Waters (b: 9/6/44; bass), Nick Mason (b: 1/27/45; drums) and Rick Wright (b: 7/28/45; keyboards). Wright left in early 1982; Waters went solo in 1984. Band inactive, 1984-86. Gilmour, Mason and Wright re-grouped in 1987. ▲ 1. The Dark Side Of The Moon although the LP has sold over 11 million copies, it was not certified platinum until 1990 because, until recently, RIAA had ruled an album could not be considered for platinum if released prior to 1/1/76; charted a record 741 weeks on the "Top 200 Albums" chart	Harvest 11163
1/26/74	**36**	4	2. A Nice Pair [R] reissue of their first two British albums *The Piper At The Gates Of Dawn* and *A Saucerful Of Secrets*	Harvest 11257 [2]
9/27/75	**1(2)**	15	▲ 3. Wish You Were Here	Columbia 33453
2/19/77	**3**	9	▲ 4. Animals	Columbia 34474
12/22/79	**1(15)**	35	▲ 5. The Wall *Another Brick In The Wall (Part II)* (1)	Colum. 36183 [2]

DATE	POS	WKS	ARTIST—RECORD TITLE		LABEL & NO.
12/19/81	**31**	7	▲ 6. A Collection Of Great Dance Songs	[G]	Columbia 37680
4/9/83	**6**	12	▲ 7. The Final Cut		Columbia 38243
			group now a trio (minus Rick Wright)		
10/3/87	**3**	26	▲ 8. A Momentary Lapse of Reason		Columbia 40599
12/17/88	**11**	10	▲ 9. Delicate Sound Of Thunder	[L]	Colum. 44484 [2]
			recorded in August of 1988		
			PLANT, Robert		
			Born on 8/20/48 in Bromwich, England. Lead singer of Led Zeppelin and The Honeydrippers.		
7/24/82	**5**	14	● 1. Pictures At Eleven		Swan Song 8512
8/6/83	**8**	18	▲ 2. The Principle Of Moments		Es Paranza 90101
6/22/85	**20**	8	● 3. Shaken 'N' Stirred		Es Paranza 90265
3/19/88	**6**	25	▲ 4. Now And Zen		Es Paranza 90863
4/7/90	**13**	11	● 5. Manic Nirvana		Es Paranza 91336
			PLASTIC ONO BAND — see LENNON, John		
		˙	**PLATTERS, The**		
			R&B group formed in Los Angeles in 1953. Consisted of Tony Williams (lead), David Lynch (tenor), Paul Robi (baritone), Herb Reed (bass) and Zola Taylor. Group first recorded for Federal in 1954, with Alex Hodge instead of Robi, and without Zola Taylor. Hit "Only You" was written by manager Buck Ram and first recorded for Federal, who did not want to use it. To Mercury in 1955, re-recorded "Only You." Williams left to go solo, replaced by Sonny Turner in 1961. Taylor replaced by Sandra Dawn; Robi replaced by Nate Nelson (formerly in The Flamingos) in 1966. Lynch died of cancer on 1/2/81 (age 61). Robi died of cancer on 2/1/89. Group inducted into the Rock and Roll Hall of Fame in 1990. Several unrelated groups use The Platters' famous name today.		
7/14/56	**7**	26	1. The Platters		Mercury 20146
			My Prayer (1)		
1/19/57	**12**	8	2. The Platters, Volume Two		Mercury 20216
3/30/59	**15**	6	3. Remember When?		Mercury 20410
			Smoke Gets In Your Eyes (1)		
3/14/60	**6**	66	● 4. Encore Of Golden Hits	[G]	Mercury 20472
			Only You (And You Alone) (5)/*The Great Pretender* (1)/ *(You've Got) The Magic Touch* (4)/*Twilight Time* (1)		
11/14/60	**20**	7	● 5. More Encore Of Golden Hits	[G]	Mercury 20591
			Harbor Lights (8)		
			PLAYER		
			Pop-rock group formed in Los Angeles: Peter Beckett (vocals, guitar), John Crowley (vocals, guitar), Ronn Moss (bass), John Friesen (drums) and Wayne Cooke (keyboards). Moss joined cast of TV soap "The Bold & The Beautiful." Crowley began solo country career in 1988.		
1/28/78	**26**	6	● 1. Player		RSO 3026
			Baby Come Back (1)/*This Time I'm In It For Love* (10)		
11/4/78	**37**	2	● 2. Danger Zone		RSO 3036

DATE	POS	WKS	ARTIST—RECORD TITLE	LABEL & NO.
			POCO	
			Los Angeles country-rock band formed by Rusty Young (pedal steel guitar) and Buffalo Springfield members Richie Furay (rhythm guitar) and Jim Messina (lead guitar). Randy Meisner (The Eagles) was an early member. As of first single, group consisted of Furay, Messina, Young, George Grantham (drums) and Timothy B. Schmit (bass). Messina left in 1970, replaced by Paul Cotton, and Furay left in 1973. Grantham and Schmit (joins Eagles) left in 1977; replacements: Charlie Harrison, Kim Bullard and Steve Chapman. Disbanded in late 1984. In 1989, Young, Furay, Messina, Grantham and Meisner reunited as Poco.	
2/13/71	**26**	6	1. Deliverin' [L]	Epic 30209
10/20/73	**38**	2	2. Crazy Eyes	Epic 32354
			Richie Furay's last album as a member	
3/3/79	**14**	10	● 3. Legend	ABC 1099
11/11/89	**40**	2	● 4. Legacy	RCA 9694
			first album by Poco's original members in 20 years	
			POINTER SISTERS	
			Soul group formed in Oakland in 1971, consisting of sisters Ruth, Anita, Bonnie and June Pointer. Parents were ministers. Group was originally a trio, joined by youngest sister June in the early 70s. First recorded for Atlantic in 1971. Backup work for Cold Blood, Elvin Bishop, Boz Scaggs, Grace Slick and many others. Sang in nostalgic 1940s style, 1973-77. In the 1976 film *Car Wash*. Bonnie went solo in 1978, group continued as trio in new musical style.	
8/25/73	**13**	13	● 1. The Pointer Sisters	Blue Thumb 48
8/9/75	**22**	7	2. Steppin	Blue Thumb 6021
			Bonnie's last album with her sisters	
2/3/79	**13**	10	● 3. Energy	Planet 1
			Fire (2)	
11/1/80	**34**	5	4. Special Things	Planet 9
			He's So Shy (3)	
7/18/81	**12**	14	● 5. Black & White	Planet 18
			Slow Hand (2)	
3/17/84	**8**	65	▲ 6. Break Out	Planet 4705
			Automatic (5)/Jump (For My Love) (3)/I'm So Excited (9)/ Neutron Dance (6)	
4/20/85	**24**	17	▲ 7. Contact	RCA 5487
			POISON	
			Hard-rock quartet formed in Harrisburg, Pennsylvania: Bret Michaels (vocals), Bobby Dall (bass), Rikki Rockett (drums) and CC Deville (guitar).	
3/7/87	**3**	47	▲ 1. Look What The Cat Dragged In	Capitol 12523
			Talk Dirty To Me (9)	
5/21/88	**2(1)**	52	▲ 2. Open Up and Say...Ahh!	Enigma 48493
			Nothin' But A Good Time (6)/Every Rose Has Its Thorn (1)/ Your Mama Don't Dance (10)	
			POLICE, The	
			Rock trio formed in England in 1977: Gordon "Sting" Sumner (b: 10/2/51; vocals, bass), Andy Summers (b: 12/31/42; guitar) and Stewart Copeland (b: 7/16/52; drums). First guitarist was Henri Padovani, replaced by Summers in 1977. Copeland had been with Curved Air. Inactive as a group since appearance at "Amnesty '86." Sting began recording solo in 1985. Copeland formed group Animal Logic in 1989.	
3/31/79	**23**	11	▲ 1. Outlandos d'Amour	A&M 4753
11/17/79	**25**	8	● 2. Reggatta de Blanc	A&M 4792
11/1/80	**5**	31	▲ 3. Zenyatta Mondatta	A&M 4831
			De Do Do Do, De Da Da Da (10)/ Don't Stand So Close To Me (10)	

DATE	POS	WKS	ARTIST—RECORD TITLE	LABEL & NO.
10/24/81	**2**(6)	30	▲ 4. Ghost In The Machine *Every Little Thing She Does Is Magic* (3)/	A&M 3730
7/2/83	**1**(17)	50	▲ 5. Synchronicity *Every Breath You Take* (1)/*King Of Pain* (3)/ *Wrapped Around Your Finger* (8)	A&M 3735
11/29/86	**7**	13	▲ 6. Every Breath You Take - The Singles [G]	A&M 3902
			PONTY, Jean-Luc	
			Classically-trained, jazz-rock violinist born on 9/29/42 in Normandy, France. First American appearance at the 1967 Monterey Jazz Festival. Worked with Frank Zappa and Elton John. Emigrated to the U.S. in 1973. Member of Mahavishnu Orchestra, 1973-75.	
10/29/77	**35**	3	1. Enigmatic Ocean [I]	Atlantic 19110
10/28/78	**36**	3	2. Cosmic Messenger [I]	Atlantic 19189
			POWER STATION, The	
			Superstar quartet: Robert Palmer (lead singer), Chic's Tony Thompson (drums) and Duran Duran's John Taylor (bass) and Andy Taylor (guitar).	
4/20/85	**6**	25	▲ 1. The Power Station *Some Like It Hot* (6)/*Get It On* (9)	Capitol 12380
			PRADO, Perez	
			Born Damaso Perez Prado on 11/13/18 in Mantanzas, Cuba. Band leader/organist. Moved to Mexico City in 1948 and formed a big band. Toured and worked in the U.S. beginning in 1954. In the film *Underwater!* "The King Of Mambo" died on 9/14/89 after suffering a stroke in Colonia del Valle, Mexico.	
5/25/59	**22**	3	1. "Prez" [I]	RCA 1556
			PRESLEY, Elvis	
			"The King of Rock & Roll." Born on 1/8/35 in Tupelo, Mississippi. Died in Memphis on 8/16/77 (age 42) of heart failure caused by prescription drug abuse. Won talent contest at age eight, singing "Old Shep." First played guitar at age 11. Moved to Memphis in 1948. Sang in high school shows. Worked as an usher and truck driver after graduation. First recorded for Sun in 1954. Signed to RCA Records on 11/22/55. First film: *Love Me Tender* in 1956. In U.S. Army from 3/24/58 to 3/5/60. In many films thereafter. NBC-TV special in 1968. Married Priscilla Beaulieu on 5/1/67; divorced on 10/11/73. Priscilla pursued acting in the 1980s beginning with a role in TV's "Dallas." Their only child Lisa Marie was born on 2/1/68. Presley's last live performance was in Indianapolis on 6/26/77. Inducted into the Rock and Roll Hall of Fame in 1986.	
3/31/56	**1**(10)	48	● 1. Elvis Presley includes five Sun studio recordings	RCA LPM-1254
11/10/56	**1**(5)	32	● 2. Elvis *Love Me* (2)	RCA LPM-1382
5/13/57	**3**	9	3. Peace In The Valley [M] 7" EP of sacred songs	RCA EPA-4054
7/22/57	**1**(10)	29	● 4. Loving You [S] only side 1 has the soundtrack recordings *(Let Me Be Your) Teddy Bear* (1)	RCA LPM-1515
9/2/57	**18**	1	5. Loving You, Vol. II [M-S] 7" EP; four songs from the soundtrack of previous album	RCA EPA 2-1515
9/2/57	**22**	1	6. Love Me Tender [M-S] 7" EP of songs from his first film *Love Me Tender* (1)	RCA EPA-4006
9/30/57	**16**	1	7. Just For You [M] 7" EP; three of four songs from side two of *Loving You*	RCA EPA-4041
12/2/57	**1**(4)	7	● 8. Elvis' Christmas Album [X] with 10 pages of bound-in color photos of Elvis; includes all four songs from *Peace In The Valley* EP	RCA LOC-1035

DATE	POS	WKS	ARTIST—RECORD TITLE	LABEL & NO.
4/21/58	**3**	36	▲ 9. Elvis' Golden Records [G] *Heartbreak Hotel* (1)/ *I Want You, I Need You, I Love You* (1)/ *Don't Be Cruel* (1)/*Hound Dog* (1)/*Too Much* (1)/ *All Shook Up* (1)/*Jailhouse Rock* (1)	RCA LPM-1707
9/15/58	**2**(1)	15	10. King Creole [S] *Hard Headed Woman* (1)	RCA LPM-1884
3/23/59	**19**	7	11. For LP Fans Only [E] includes four Sun studio recordings - others from 1956	RCA LPM-1990
9/21/59	**32**	6	12. A Date With Elvis [E] includes five Sun studio recordings - others from 1956-57	RCA LPM-2011
2/15/60	**31**	6	● 13. 50,000,000 Elvis Fans Can't Be Wrong - Elvis' Gold Records-Volume 2 [G] *Don't* (1)/*I Beg Of You* (8)/ *Wear My Ring Around Your Neck* (2)/*One Night* (4)/ *I Got Stung* (8)/*A Fool Such As I* (2)/ *I Need Your Love Tonight* (4)/*A Big Hunk O' Love* (1)	RCA LPM-2075
5/9/60	**2**(3)	32	14. Elvis Is Back! recorded shortly after his March 5th release from the Army	RCA LSP-2231
10/31/60	**1**(10)	46	● 15. G.I. Blues [S]	RCA LSP-2256
12/31/60	**33**	1	16. Elvis' Christmas Album [X-R] repackage of LOC-1035 album (no photos)	RCA LPM-1951
1/9/61	**13**	9	● 17. His Hand in Mine Presley's first full album of sacred songs	RCA LSP-2328
7/24/61	**1**(3)	17	18. Something for Everybody	RCA LSP-2370
10/30/61	**1**(20)	53	● 19. Blue Hawaii [S] *Can't Help Falling In Love* (2)	RCA LSP-2426
7/14/62	**4**	18	20. Pot Luck	RCA LSP-2523
12/8/62	**3**	21	● 21. Girls! Girls! Girls! [S] *Return To Sender* (2)	RCA LSP-2621
4/27/63	**4**	18	22. It Happened At The World's Fair [S]	RCA LSP-2697
9/28/63	**3**	20	● 23. Elvis' Golden Records, Volume 3 [G] *Stuck On You* (1)/*It's Now Or Never* (1)/ *Are You Lonesome To-night* (1)/*Surrender* (1)/ *I Feel So Bad* (5)/*Little Sister* (5)/ *(Marie's the Name) His Latest Flame* (4)/ *Good Luck Charm* (1)/*She's Not You* (5)	RCA LSP-2765
4/4/64	**3**	16	24. Fun in Acapulco [S] includes two bonus songs not in the film *Bossa Nova Baby* (8)	RCA LSP-2756
4/18/64	**6**	15	25. Kissin' Cousins [S] includes two bonus songs not in the film	RCA LSP-2894
11/28/64	**1**(1)	20	● 26. Roustabout [S]	RCA LSP-2999
5/8/65	**8**	17	27. Girl Happy [S] includes one bonus song not in the film	RCA LSP-3338
9/18/65	**10**	11	28. Elvis For Everyone! [K] recordings from 2/57 to 1/64 (plus one Sun studio recording)	RCA LSP-3450
11/27/65	**8**	11	29. Harum Scarum [S] includes two bonus songs not in the film	RCA LSP-3468
5/14/66	**20**	9	30. Frankie And Johnny [S]	RCA LSP-3553
8/6/66	**15**	9	31. Paradise, Hawaiian Style [S] includes one bonus song not in the film	RCA LSP-3643
12/3/66	**18**	10	32. Spinout [S] includes three bonus songs not in the film	RCA LSP-3702
4/29/67	**18**	9	● 33. How Great Thou Art Presley's second full album of sacred songs *Crying In The Chapel* (3)	RCA LSP-3758

DATE	POS	WKS	ARTIST—RECORD TITLE	LABEL & NO.
2/10/68	**40**	1	34. Clambake [S] includes five bonus songs not in the film	RCA LSP-3893
5/11/68	**33**	4	35. Elvis' Gold Records, Volume 4 [G] *(You're the) Devil In Disguise* (3)	RCA LSP-3921
1/25/69	**8**	14	● 36. Elvis [TV-L] NBC-TV special; Presley's first live album	RCA LPM-4088

6/14/69	**13**	15	● 37. From Elvis In Memphis
			    first Memphis sessions since his 1955 Sun recordings
			    In The Ghetto (3)
				RCA LSP-4155

11/29/69	**12**	12	● 38. From Memphis To Vegas/From Vegas To Memphis [L]
			    record 1: Elvis in Person at the International Hotel,
			    Las Vegas, Nevada; record 2: Elvis Back In Memphis (studio)
				RCA LSP-6020 [2]

6/20/70	**13**	11	● 39. On Stage-February, 1970 [L]
			    recorded at the International Hotel, Las Vegas
			    The Wonder Of You (9)
				RCA LSP-4362

12/19/70	**21**	6	● 40. Elvis-That's The Way It Is [S-L] five of 12 songs are live (Las Vegas)	RCA LSP-4445
1/30/71	**12**	10	● 41. Elvis Country ("I'm 10,000 Years Old")	RCA LSP-4460
6/26/71	**33**	5	42. Love Letters from Elvis all songs recorded in Nashville during June, 1970	RCA LSP-4530
7/15/72	**11**	18	▲ 43. Elvis As Recorded At Madison Square Garden [L] the entire show of 6/10/72	RCA LSP-4776

11/25/72	**22**	11	44. Burning Love and hits from his movies, volume 2 [K]
			    featuring songs from eight of his films (1960-67)
			    Burning Love (2)
				RCA Camden 2595

3/10/73	**1(1)**	19	▲ 45. Aloha from Hawaii via Satellite [TV-L] RCA's first QuadraDisc - recorded on 1/14/73	RCA VPSX-6089 [2]
8/10/74	**33**	4	46. Elvis Recorded Live On Stage In Memphis [L]	RCA CPL-0606
7/30/77	**3**	17	▲ 47. Moody Blue [K-L] recordings from 1974-77 (four live; six recorded at Graceland)	RCA AFL-2428

10/29/77	**5**	7	▲ 48. Elvis In Concert [TV-L]
			    record 1: from the CBS-TV Special
			    record 2: from Elvis' final tour, June, 1977
				RCA APL-2587 [2]

8/30/80	**27**	5	49. Elvis Aron Presley [K]
			    eight album boxed set: side 1: An Early Live
			    Performance/Monolog 2: An Early Benefit Performance; 3:
			    Collectors' Gold From The Movie Years; 4: The TV Specials; 5:
			    The Las Vegas Years; 6: Lost Singles; 7: Elvis At The Piano/The
			    Concert Years- Part 1; 8: The Concert Years-Concluded
				RCA CPL-3699 [8]

			PRESTON, Billy	
			Born on 9/9/46 in Houston. R&B vocalist/keyboardist. To Los Angeles at an early age. With Mahalia Jackson in 1956. Played piano in film *St. Louis Blues*, 1958. Regular on "Shindig" TV show. Recorded with The Beatles on "Get Back" and "Let It Be"; worked Concert For Bangladesh in 1969. Prominent session man, played on Sly & The Family Stone hits. With The Rolling Stones U.S. tour in 1975.	
7/1/72	**32**	8	1. I Wrote A Simple Song *Outa-Space* (2)	A&M 3507
6/30/73	**32**	6	2. Music Is My Life *Will It Go Round In Circles* (1)	A&M 3516
10/12/74	**17**	6	3. The Kids & Me *Nothing From Nothing* (1)	A&M 3645

DATE	POS	WKS	ARTIST—RECORD TITLE	LABEL & NO.
			PRETENDERS, The	
			Rock quartet featuring lead singer/songwriter/guitarist Chrissie Hynde (b: 9/7/51, Akron, Ohio). Formed in 1978, early British lineup included guitarist James Honeyman- Scott (d: 6/16/82; replaced by Robbie MacIntosh), bassist Pete Farndon (d: 4/14/83; replaced in 1982 by Malcolm Foster) and drummer Martin Chambers. Hynde married Jim Kerr of Simple Minds in 1984. With the exception of Hynde, numerous personnel changes since 1985.	
3/15/80	9	17	▲ 1. Pretenders	Sire 6083
5/2/81	27	4	2. Extended Play [M]	Sire 3563
8/29/81	10	9	3. Pretenders II	Sire 3572
2/4/84	5	22	▲ 4. Learning To Crawl *Back On The Chain Gang* (5)	Sire 23980
11/15/86	25	14	● 5. Get Close *Don't Get Me Wrong* (10)	Sire 25488
			PREVIN, Andre	
			Classical-jazz pianist/conductor/arranger/composer born on 4/6/29 in Germany. Became musical director for MGM movies by the age of 21. Composed and arranged background music for *Gigi* and many other films. In the 1970s Previn served as resident conductor of the London Symphony Orchestra.	
6/29/59	16	13	1. Secret Songs For Young Lovers [I] with David Rose & His Orchestra	MGM 3716
7/4/60	25	6	2. Like Love [I]	Columbia 1437
			PRICE, Leontyne	
			Born on 2/10/27 in Laurel, Mississippi. One of the great sopranos of opera.	
5/18/63	29	9	1. Giacomo Puccini: Madama Butterfly [F] with Richard Tucker (tenor), Rosalind Elias (mezzo-soprano), Philip Maero (baritone) and Erich Leinsdorf (conductor)	RCA 6160 [3]
			PRICE, Ray	
			Country singer, born on 1/12/26 in Perryville, Texas. Ray charted over 80 top 40 hits on *Billboard*'s country charts. Known as "The Cherokee Cowboy."	
12/19/70	28	16	● 1. For The Good Times	Columbia 30106
			PRIDE, Charley	
			Born on 3/18/38 in Sledge, Mississippi. Discovered by Red Sovine in 1963. The most successful black country performer. Charted 29 #1 singles on the country charts.	
11/22/69	24	16	● 1. The Best Of Charley Pride [G]	RCA 4223
2/14/70	22	7	● 2. Just Plain Charley	RCA 4290
9/12/70	30	2	● 3. Charley Pride's 10th Album	RCA 4367
1/15/72	38	2	● 4. Charley Pride Sings Heart Songs	RCA 4617
			PRIMA, Louis	
			Born on 12/7/11 in New Orleans. Vocalist/trumpeter/composer/leader. Worked with Red Nichols in 1932. First recorded for Bluebird in 1933. Own band in 1934. Film work in Los Angeles from 1936-39. Wrote "Sing Sing Sing" in 1936. Married to jazz-styled vocalist Dorothy "Keely" Smith (b: 3/9/32 in Norfolk, Virginia) from 1952-61. The popular Las Vegas duo was backed by Sam Butera & The Witnesses. Louis was the voice for the cartoon character King Louis in Disney's *Jungle Book*, in 1969. Surgery for a brain tumor in 1975 left him in a coma until his death on 8/24/78.	
			LOUIS PRIMA & KEELY SMITH:	
6/23/58	12	4	1. Las Vegas Prima Style [L]	Capitol 1010
5/25/59	37	1	2. Hey Boy! Hey Girl! [S] Louis and Keely portray Las Vegas entertainers in the film	Capitol 1160
			LOUIS PRIMA:	
1/16/61	9	9	3. Wonderland By Night [I]	Dot 25352

DATE	POS	WKS	ARTIST—RECORD TITLE	LABEL & NO.
			PRINCE	
			Born Prince Roger Nelson on 6/7/58 in Minneapolis. R&B vocalist/multi-instrumentalist/composer/producer/actor. Named for the Prince Roger Trio, led by his father. Self-taught musician; own band, Grand Central, in junior high school. Self-produced first album in 1978. Starred in the films *Purple Rain* (1984), *Under The Cherry Moon* (1986) and *Sign 'O' The Times* (1987). Founded own label, Paisley Park. Prince's backing band The Revolution featured Lisa Coleman (keyboards), Wendy Melvoin (guitar; twin sister of The Family's vocalist, Susannah), Bobby Z (percussion), Matt "Dr." Fink (keyboards), Eric Leeds (saxophone) and Andre Cymone (bass, replaced by Brownmark in 1981. In 1986, Brownmark founded the band Mazarati (who also backed Prince); recorded solo in 1988. Leeds formed Madhouse in 1987. Coleman and Melvoin recorded as the duo Wendy & Lisa in 1988. Percussionist Sheila E. joined Prince's band in 1986. Prince's sister Tyka Nelson began recording career in 1988.	
12/15/79	**22**	10	▲ 1. Prince	Warner 3366
11/14/81	**21**	5	▲ 2. Controversy	Warner 3601
11/27/82	**9**	57	▲ 3. Prince **1999** *Little Red Corvette* (6)/*Delirious* (8)	Warner 23720 [2]
			PRINCE & THE REVOLUTION:	
7/14/84	**1(24)**	42	▲ 4. Purple Rain [S] film is a semi-autobiographical story about Prince's career *When Doves Cry* (1)/*Let's Go Crazy* (1)/*Purple Rain* (2)/ *I Would Die 4 U* (8)/*Take Me With U*	Warner 25110
5/11/85	**1(3)**	27	▲ 5. Around the World in a Day *Raspberry Beret* (2)/*Pop Life* (7)	Paisley P. 25286
4/19/86	**3**	17	▲ 6. Parade [S] music from the film *Under The Cherry Moon* *Kiss* (1)	Paisley P. 25395
			PRINCE:	
4/18/87	**6**	12	▲ 7. Sign "O" The Times *Sign 'O' The Times* (3)/*U Got The Look* (2)/ *I Could Never Take The Place Of Your Man* (10)	Paisley P. 25577 [2]
6/4/88	**11**	9	8. Lovesexy *Alphabet Street* (8)	Paisley P. 25720
7/8/89	**1(6)**	17	▲ 9. Batman [S] all tracks written by Prince *Batdance* (1)	Warner 25936
			PROCOL HARUM	
			British rock group led by Gary Brooker (vocals, piano) and Robin Trower (guitar, 1968-71). Translation of Latin group name: "beyond these things."	
12/7/68	**24**	7	1. Shine On Brightly	A&M 4151
5/31/69	**32**	5	2. A Salty Dog	A&M 4179
8/1/70	**34**	6	3. Home	A&M 4261
5/22/71	**32**	5	4. Broken Barricades	A&M 4294
5/20/72	**5**	19	● 5. Procol Harum Live In Concert with the Edmonton Symphony Orchestra	[L] A&M 4335
4/21/73	**21**	7	6. Grand Hotel	Chrysalis 1037
			PROVINE, Dorothy	
			Born on 1/20/37 in Deadwood, South Dakota. Portrayed songstress Pinky Pinkham in the TV series "The Roaring Twenties" (1960-62).	
9/25/61	**34**	3	1. The Roaring 20's medleys of 30 songs from the 1920s	Warner 1394

DATE	POS	WKS	ARTIST—RECORD TITLE	LABEL & NO.
			PRYOR, Richard	
			Born on 12/1/40 in Peoria, Illinois. Ribald comedian/actor. In films *Stir Crazy*, *Silver Streak*, *Superman III* and many others.	
10/19/74	29	8	● 1. That Nigger's Crazy [C]	Partee 2404
9/6/75	12	8	▲ 2. Is It Something I Said? [C]	Reprise 2227
10/23/76	22	7	● 3. Bicentennial Nigger [C]	Warner 2960
2/10/79	32	3	● 4. Wanted [C]	Warner 3364 [2]
5/1/82	21	7	5. Richard Pryor Live On The Sunset Strip [C-S] filmed live at the Hollywood Palladium	Warner 3660
			PSYCHEDELIC FURS	
			U.S.-based, British techno-rock group formed in 1979. Consists of brothers Richard (vocals) and Tim Butler (bass), with John Ashton (guitar) and Vince Ely (drums).	
3/28/87	29	11	1. Midnight To Midnight	Columbia 40466
			PUBLIC ENEMY	
			Rap group led by Chuck D. Includes MC Flavor-Flave (William Drayton), deejay Terminator X (Norman Rogers) and Professor Griff (Richard Griffin). Disbanded briefly in June of 1989 due to controversy over anti-Semitic remarks made by Griffin.	
4/28/90	10	15	▲ 1. Fear Of A Black Planet	Def Jam 45413
			PUCKETT, Gary	
			Singer/guitarist Puckett (b: 10/17/42, Hibbing, Minnesota) formed The Union Gap in San Diego in 1967; named after the town of Union Gap, Washington. Included Kerry Chater (bass), Paul Whitebread (drums), Dwight Bement (sax) and Gary Withem (keyboards).	
			THE UNION GAP FEATURING GARY PUCKETT:	
3/30/68	22	8	1. Woman, Woman *Woman, Woman* (4)	Columbia 9612
			GARY PUCKETT AND THE UNION GAP:	
6/29/68	21	11	● 2. Young Girl *Young Girl* (2)	Columbia 9664
11/23/68	20	10	3. Incredible *Lady Willpower* (2)/*Over You* (7)	Columbia 9715
			PURE PRAIRIE LEAGUE	
			Country-rock group formed in Cincinnati in 1971. Numerous personnel changes. Country singer Vince Gill was lead singer from 1980-83.	
6/21/75	24	6	1. Two Lane Highway	RCA 0933
6/21/75	34	6	● 2. Bustin' Out	RCA 4769
3/20/76	33	3	3. If The Shoe Fits	RCA 1247
7/12/80	37	3	4. Firin' Up *Let Me Love You Tonight* (10)	Casablanca 7212
			PURSELL, Bill	
			Pianist from Tulare, California. Appeared with the Nashville Symphony Orchestra. Taught musical composition at Vanderbilt University.	
4/13/63	28	6	1. Our Winter Love [I] arrangements by Bill Justis; orchestra directed by Grady Martin *Our Winter Love* (9)	Columbia 1992

The **Alan Parsons Project** had a continual series of hit albums since 1976's *Tales Of Mystery And Imagination*, including 1979's *Eve*, most of which have featured a revolving cast of session musicians playing works created by producer Parsons and partner Eric Woolfson. Parsons has used such intriguing vocalists as former Zombies singer Colin Blunstone, Procol Harum's Gary Brooker and Arthur Brown of "Fire" fame.

Dolly Parton's first appearance on the Top Pop Albums chart came in 1969 with *Just The Two Of Us*, recorded with famed partner Porter Wagoner. Her crossover into the pop market started with the 1977 album *Here You Come Again*, and peaked with two later No. 1 singles: 1980's "9 to 5," from the film of the same name, and "Islands In The Stream," a 1983 duet with Kenny Rogers.

The **Partridge Family**, teen idols of the early 70s, featured heart-throb David Cassidy and produced three consecutive albums that reached the top 10, the second of which was *Up To Date*. Interest in Cassidy as a pop culture figure apparently never died: In early 1990 Enigma Records proudly announced that the singer had been signed to an exclusive recording contract.

Peter, Paul and Mary followed up their eponymous 1962 album with *(Moving)*, which featured the well-known hit "Puff The Magic Dragon." The song was later deemed drug-related by former Vice President Spiro Agnew.

Tom Petty and The Heartbreakers' long track record together—the high point perhaps 1979's multi-platinum *Damn The Torpedoes*—made some wonder whether 1989's solo Petty project *Full Moon Fever* would fly. It did—right to the top of charts.

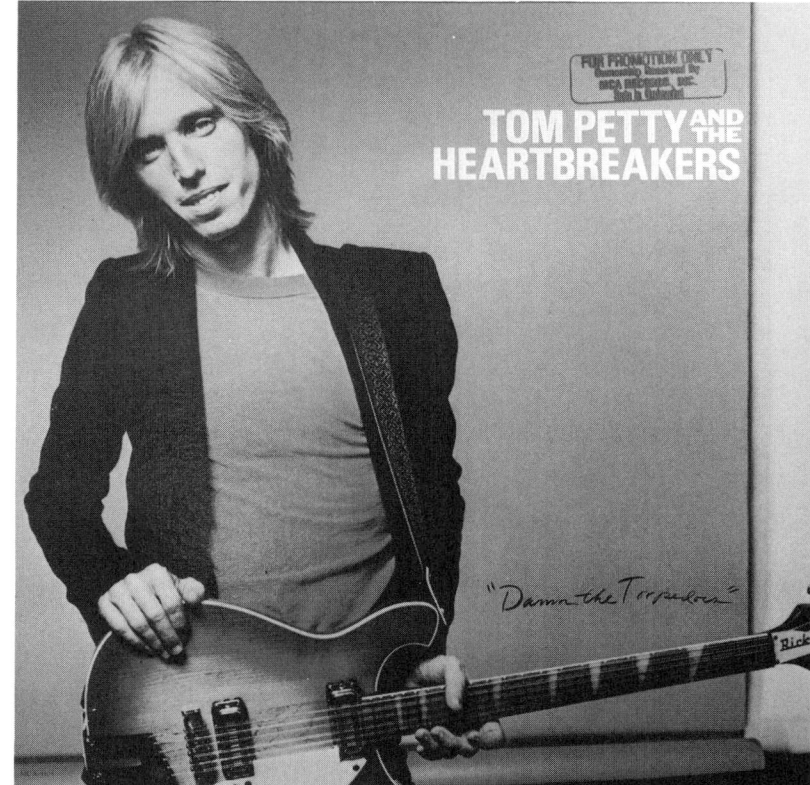

The **Platters** set the musical mood of the 50s for many with a string of hits that included "Only You (And You Alone)," "The Great Pretender," "My Prayer" and "Smoke Gets In Your Eyes." The Platters' name was so popular that years later, several unrelated groups performed across the U.S. using the same moniker—a point of considerable legal turmoil.

Poison, a hard-rocking quartet, moved to Los Angeles from their hometown of Harrisburg, Pennysylvania and had a No. 1 single with 1988's "Every Rose Has Its Thorn." The group was introduced to the public via 1987's *Look What The Cat Dragged In*.

The **Police**'s third album, 1980's *Zenyatta Mondatta*, peaked at No. 5 and bore two top 10 hits: "De Do Do Do, De Da Da Da" and "Don't Stand So Close To Me." The group later re-recorded the latter track for an A&M greatest hits collection.

Elvis Presley's *Roustabout* soundtrack of 1964 was the artist's sole No. 1 album between 1961's *Blue Hawaii* and 1973's *Aloha From Hawaii Via Satellite*. In 1990, longtime label RCA issued Presley's first-ever recording—a 1953 version of "My Happiness" that Presley cut as a gift for his mother Gladys.

Charley Pride, the first hugely successful black country singer, reached his highest slot on the Top Pop Albums chart with 1970's *Just Plain Charley*, which hit No. 22. It had just followed a best-selling hits collection issued the previous year. *Charley Pride Sings Heart Songs* was his last top 40 album, reaching No. 38 in 1972.

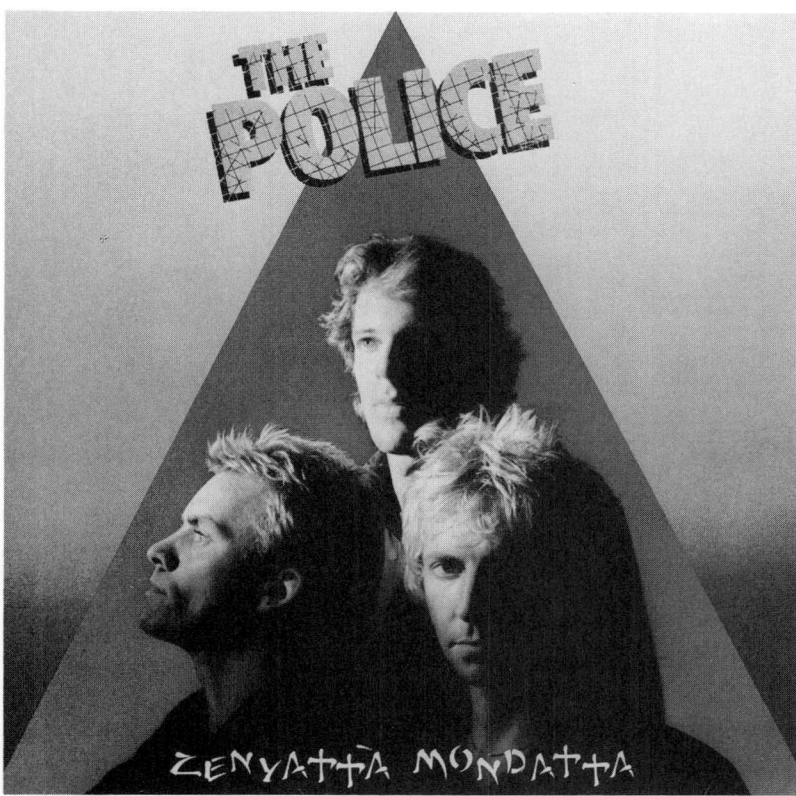

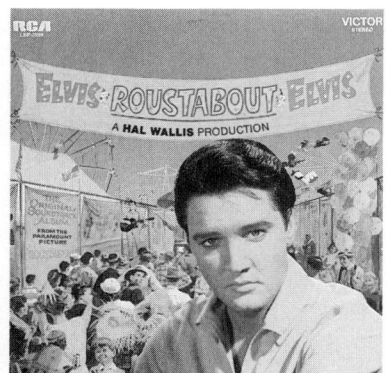

DATE	POS	WKS	ARTIST—RECORD TITLE	LABEL & NO.

Q

QUARTERFLASH

Rock group from Portland, led by the husband-and-wife team of Marv (guitar) and and Rindy (vocals, saxophone) Ross. Originally known as Seafood Mama.

DATE	POS	WKS	ARTIST—RECORD TITLE	LABEL & NO.
12/12/81	8	21	▲ 1. Quarterflash *Harden My Heart* (3)	Geffen 2003
8/6/83	34	4	2. Take Another Picture	Geffen 4011

QUATRO, Suzi

Rock singer born on 6/3/50 in Detroit. Portrayed Leather Tuscadero on TV's "Happy Days" in 1977.

DATE	POS	WKS	ARTIST—RECORD TITLE	LABEL & NO.
5/12/79	37	5	1. If You Knew Suzi... *Stumblin' In* (4) with Chris Norman	RSO 3044

QUEEN

Rock group formed in England in 1972. Consists of Freddie Mercury (born Fred Bulsara on 9/5/46 in Zanzibar; vocals), Brian May (guitar), John Deacon (bass) and Roger Taylor (drums). May and Taylor had been in the group Smile. Mercury had recorded as Larry Lurex. Wrote soundtrack for the film *Flash Gordon* in 1980.

DATE	POS	WKS	ARTIST—RECORD TITLE	LABEL & NO.
4/5/75	12	10	● 1. Sheer Heart Attack	Elektra 1026
1/24/76	4	28	● 2. A Night At The Opera *Bohemian Rhapsody* (9)	Elektra 1053
1/15/77	5	8	● 3. A Day At The Races	Elektra 101
12/3/77	3	21	▲ 4. News Of The World *We Are The Champions* (4)	Elektra 112
12/9/78	6	11	▲ 5. Jazz	Elektra 166
7/14/79	16	7	● 6. Queen Live Killers [L]	Elektra 702 [2]
7/19/80	1(5)	31	▲ 7. The Game *Crazy Little Thing Called Love* (1)/ *Another One Bites The Dust* (1)	Elektra 513
1/10/81	23	7	8. Flash Gordon [S]	Elektra 518
11/14/81	14	13	▲ 9. Greatest Hits [G]	Elektra 564
6/5/82	22	5	● 10. Hot Space	Elektra 60128
3/24/84	23	9	● 11. The Works	Capitol 12322
7/1/89	24	4	12. The Miracle	Capitol 92357

QUICKSILVER MESSENGER SERVICE

San Francisco acid-rock group featuring guitarist John Cipollina (brother of Huey Lewis & The News bassist Mario Cipollina; d: 5/29/89 [age 45] of emphysema) and bassist David Freiberg (joined Jefferson Starship in 1973). Many personnel changes.

DATE	POS	WKS	ARTIST—RECORD TITLE	LABEL & NO.
4/26/69	27	6	1. Happy Trails [L] includes several studio tracks	Capitol 120
2/7/70	25	5	2. Shady Grove	Capitol 391
9/5/70	27	8	3. Just For Love	Capitol 498
1/30/71	26	4	4. What About Me Nicky Hopkins (piano) featured on above three	Capitol 630

DATE	POS	WKS	ARTIST—RECORD TITLE	LABEL & NO.
			QUIET RIOT	
			Heavy-metal rock quartet from Los Angeles: Kevin DuBrow (lead singer), Carlos Cavazo (guitar), Frankie Banali (drums) and Rudy Sarzo (bass; replaced by Chuck Wright in 1985. Dubrow and Wright left group in 1987; replaced by Paul Shortino (vocals) and Sean McNabb (bass).	
7/16/83	1(1)	36	▲ 1. Metal Health *Cum On Feel The Noize* (5)	Pasha 38443
8/11/84	15	10	▲ 2. Condition Critical	Pasha 39516
9/6/86	31	9	3. QR III	Pasha 40321
			QUINN, Carmel	
			Quinn sings favorites from her native country, Ireland.	
4/2/55	4	10	1. Arthur Godfrey presents Carmel Quinn	Columbia 629

R

DATE	POS	WKS	ARTIST—RECORD TITLE	LABEL & NO.
			RABBITT, Eddie	
			Born Edward Thomas Rabbitt on 11/27/44 in Brooklyn; raised in East Orange, New Jersey. Country singer/songwriter/guitarist. First recorded for 20th Century in 1964. Moved to Nashville in 1968. Became established after Elvis Presley recorded his song "Kentucky Rain."	
9/27/80	19	15	▲ 1. Horizon *Drivin' My Life Away* (5)/*I Love A Rainy Night* (1)	Elektra 276
9/12/81	23	8	● 2. Step By Step *Step By Step* (5)	Elektra 532
1/22/83	31	7	3. Radio Romance *You And I* (7) with Crystal Gayle	Elektra 60160
			RAFFERTY, Gerry	
			Born on 4/16/47 in Paisley, Scotland. Singer/songwriter/guitarist. Co-leader of Stealers Wheel.	
6/3/78	1(1)	23	▲ 1. City to City *Baker Street* (2)	United Art. 840
6/23/79	29	6	● 2. Night Owl	United Art. 958
			RAIDERS, The — see REVERE, Paul	
			RAINBOW	
			Hard-rock band led by British guitarist Ritchie Blackmore and bassist Roger Glover, both members of Deep Purple. Fluctuating lineup included vocalists Ronnie James Dio and Joe Lynn Turner, keyboardist Toney Carey and drummer Cozy Powell. Group split up upon re-formation of Deep Purple in 1984. Turner joined Deep Purple in 1990.	
10/4/75	30	4	1. Ritchie Blackmore's R-A-I-N-B-O-W	Oyster 6049
5/29/82	30	5	2. Straight Between The Eyes	Mercury 4041
10/29/83	34	4	3. Bent Out Of Shape	Mercury 815305
			RAITT, Bonnie	
			Born on 11/8/49 in Burbank, California. Veteran blues-rock singer/guitarist. Daughter of Broadway actor/singer John Raitt. Winner of four Grammys for her 1989 album *Nick Of Time*.	
5/14/77	25	4	● 1. Sweet Forgiveness	Warner 2990
11/10/79	30	5	2. The Glow	Warner 3369
4/3/82	38	3	3. Green Light	Warner 3630

DATE	POS	WKS	ARTIST—RECORD TITLE	LABEL & NO.
5/13/89	**1**(3)	40	▲ 4. Nick Of Time 1989 Grammy winner: Album of the Year	Capitol 91268
			RAMIN, Sid Born on 1/22/24 in Boston. Conductor/composer/arranger. Won Oscar in 1961 for collaboration on *West Side Story* soundtrack. Music director for TV's "Patty Duke Show," "Milton Berle Show" and "Candid Camera." **SID RAMIN AND ORCHESTRA:**	
5/25/63	**34**	4	1. New Thresholds in Sound [I]	RCA 2658
			RAM JAM East Coast rock quartet led by Bill Bartlett (lead guitarist of The Lemon Pipers). Member Howie Blauvelt played bass in Billy Joel's group The Hassles.	
10/15/77	**34**	4	1. Ram Jam	Epic 34885
			RANDOLPH, Boots Born Homer Louis Randolph, III in Paducah, Kentucky. Premier Nashville session saxophonist.	
4/22/67	**36**	4	● 1. Boots with Strings [I]	Monument 18066
			RARE EARTH Nucleus of Detroit rock group: Gil Bridges (saxophone, flute), John Persh (trombone, bass) and Pete Rivera (drums). Worked as the Sunliners in the 60s. In 1970, added Ed Guzman (percussion) and Ray Monette (replaced guitarist Rob Richards). Mark Olson replaced Kenneth James (keyboards) in 1971. Many changes thereafter.	
3/14/70	**12**	28	1. Get Ready *Get Ready* (4) side 2 is a 21 minute version of the title song	Rare Earth 507
7/18/70	**15**	18	2. Ecology *(I Know) I'm Losing You* (7)	Rare Earth 514
8/14/71	**28**	11	3. One World *I Just Want To Celebrate* (7)	Rare Earth 520
1/29/72	**29**	4	4. Rare Earth In Concert [L]	Rare Earth 534 [2]
			RASCALS, The Blue-eyed, soul-pop quartet formed in New York City in 1964. Consisted of Felix Cavaliere, Dino Danelli, Eddie Brigati and Gene Cornish. All except Danelli had been in Joey Dee's Starliters. Brigati and Cornish left in 1971, replaced by Robert Popwell, Buzzy Feiten and Ann Sutton. Group disbanded in 1972. Cavaliere, Cornish and Danelli reunited in June of 1988. **THE YOUNG RASCALS:**	
6/11/66	**15**	14	● 1. The Young Rascals *Good Lovin'* (1)	Atlantic 8123
3/18/67	**14**	24	● 2. Collections	Atlantic 8134
8/19/67	**5**	21	● 3. Groovin' *Groovin'* (1)/*A Girl Like You* (10)/*How Can I Be Sure* (4)	Atlantic 8148
			RASCALS:	
3/9/68	**9**	12	4. Once Upon A Dream	Atlantic 8169
7/27/68	**1**(1)	32	● 5. Time Peace/The Rascals' Greatest Hits [G] *A Beautiful Morning* (3)	Atlantic 8190
4/5/69	**17**	6	● 6. Freedom Suite record 2 entitled *Music Music* is all instrumental *People Got To Be Free* (1)	Atlantic 901 [2]

DATE	POS	WKS	ARTIST—RECORD TITLE	LABEL & NO.
			RASPBERRIES	
			Cleveland pop-rock quartet: Eric Carmen (lead singer, guitar), Wally Bryson (lead guitar), David Smalley (bass) and Jim Bonfanti (drums). Smalley and Bonfanti replaced by Scott McCarl and Michael McBride in 1974. Carmen went solo in 1975.	
1/20/73	36	4	1. Fresh	Capitol 11123
			RATT	
			Hard-rock quintet from Los Angeles: Stephen Pearcy (lead singer), Warren DeMartini (guitar), Robbin Crosby (guitar), Juan Croucier (bass) and Bobby Blotzer (drums).	
6/16/84	7	26	▲ 1. Out Of The Cellar	Atlantic 80143
6/29/85	7	18	▲ 2. Invasion Of Your Privacy	Atlantic 81257
11/1/86	26	7	▲ 3. Dancin' Undercover	Atlantic 81683
11/26/88	17	13	▲ 4. Reach For The Sky	Atlantic 81929
			RAWLS, Lou	
			Born on 12/1/35 in Chicago. With the Pilgrim Travelers gospel group, 1957-59. Summer replacement TV show "Lou Rawls & The Golddiggers" in 1969. In films *Angel Angel, Down We Go* and *Believe In Me*. Voice of many Budweiser beer ads and featured singer in the "Garfield" TV specials.	
5/27/57	18	14	1. Too Much!	Capitol 2713
6/18/66	4	38	● 2. Lou Rawls Live! [L]	Capitol 2459
10/8/66	7	22	● 3. Lou Rawls Soulin'	Capitol 2566
3/4/67	20	10	4. Lou Rawls Carryin' On!	Capitol 2632
9/9/67	29	2	5. That's Lou	Capitol 2756
7/31/76	7	12	▲ 6. All Things In Time *You'll Never Find Another Love Like Mine* (2)	Phil. Int. 33957
			RAY, Johnnie	
			Born on 1/10/27 in Dallas, Oregon. Has worn hearing aid since age 14. First recorded for Okeh in 1951. Famous for emotion-packed delivery, with R&B influences. Appeared in three films. Active into the 1980s. Died on 2/25/90 of liver failure.	
3/2/57	19	2	1. The Big Beat	Columbia 961
			RAYDIO — see PARKER, Ray, Jr.	
			RAY, GOODMAN & BROWN	
			Soul group consisting of Harry Ray (tenor), Al Goodman (bass) and Billy Brown (falsetto). Formerly known as The Moments.	
3/1/80	17	11	● 1. Ray, Goodman & Brown *Special Lady* (5)	Polydor 6240
			READY FOR THE WORLD	
			Black sextet from Flint, Michigan, formed in 1982: Melvin Riley, Jr. (lead singer), Gordon Strozier, Gregory Potts, Willie Triplett, John Eaton and Gerald Valentine.	
8/31/85	17	30	▲ 1. Ready For The World *Oh Sheila* (1)	MCA 5594
2/14/87	32	5	● 2. Long Time Coming *Love You Down* (9)	MCA 5829
			REDBONE, Leon	
			Mysterious performer of 1920s and 1930s blues and ragtime. Rose to fame in the mid-70s with appearances on TV's "Saturday Night Live." Baritone voice of several TV commercials.	
2/26/77	38	4	1. Double Time	Warner 2971

DATE	POS	WKS	ARTIST—RECORD TITLE	LABEL & NO.
			REDDING, Otis	
			Born on 9/9/41 in Dawson, Georgia. Killed in a plane crash in Lake Monona in Madison, Wisconsin on 12/10/67. Soul singer/songwriter/producer/pianist. First recorded with Johnny Jenkins & The Pinetoppers on Confederate in 1960. Own label, Jotis. Plane crash also killed four members of the Bar-Kays. Otis was inducted into the Rock and Roll Hall of Fame in 1989.	
7/22/67	36	3	1. King & Queen **OTIS REDDING/CARLA THOMAS**	Stax 716
9/9/67	32	4	2. Otis Redding Live In Europe　　　　　　[L]	Volt 416
1/27/68	9	19	3. History Of Otis Redding　　　　　　　[G]	Volt 418
3/30/68	4	20	4. The Dock Of The Bay *(Sittin' On) The Dock Of The Bay (1)*	Volt 419
			OTIS REDDING/THE JIMI HENDRIX EXPERIENCE:	
9/26/70	16	8	● 5. Monterey International Pop Festival　　[S-L] recorded June, 1967 & featured in film *Monterey Pop*	Reprise 2029
			REDDY, Helen	
			Born on 10/25/42 in Melbourne, Australia. Family was in show business, Helen made stage debut at age four. Own TV series in the early 60s. Migrated to New York in 1966. To Los Angeles in 1968. Acted in the films *Airport 1975* (1974), *Pete's Dragon* (1977) and *Sgt. Pepper's Lonely Hearts Club Band* (1978).	
1/6/73	14	17	● 1. I Am Woman *I Am Woman (1)*	Capitol 11068
8/25/73	8	15	● 2. Long Hard Climb *Delta Dawn (1)/Leave Me Alone (Ruby Red Dress) (3)*	Capitol 11213
5/4/74	11	14	● 3. Love Song For Jeffrey *You And Me Against The World (9)*	Capitol 11284
11/23/74	8	16	● 4. Free And Easy *Angie Baby (1)*	Capitol 11348
8/9/75	11	10	● 5. No Way To Treat A Lady *Ain't No Way To Treat A Lady (8)*	Capitol 11418
12/20/75	5	11	● 6. Helen Reddy's Greatest Hits　　　　[G]	Capitol 11467
8/14/76	16	8	● 7. Music, Music	Capitol 11547
			REED, Lou	
			Born Louis Firbank on 3/2/42 in Freeport, Long Island, New York. Lead singer/ songwriter of the New York seminal rock band the Velvet Underground. Appeared in the film *One Trick Pony*.	
3/24/73	29	9	1. Transformer produced by David Bowie	RCA 4807
10/19/74	10	7	2. Sally Can't Dance	RCA 0611
4/8/89	40	1	3. New York	Sire 25829
			REESE, Della	
			Born Delloreese Patricia Early on 7/6/31 in Detroit. With Mahalia Jackson gospel troupe from 1945-49, and Erskine Hawkins in the early 50s. Solo since 1957. Actress/singer on many TV shows. Appeared in the 1958 film *Let's Rock* and the 1989 film *Harlem Nights*. Own series "Della" in 1970. Played "Della Rogers" on the TV series "Chico & The Man" from 1976-78.	
3/7/60	35	2	1. Della	RCA 2157

DATE	POS	WKS	ARTIST—RECORD TITLE	LABEL & NO.
			REEVES, Jim	
			Born James Travis Reeves on 8/20/24 in Panola County, Texas. Killed in a plane crash on 7/31/64 in Nashville. Aspirations of a professional baseball career cut short by an ankle injury. DJ at KWKH-Shreveport, Louisiana, home of the "Louisiana Hayride," early 50s. First recorded for Macy's in 1950. Joined "Hayride" cast following first country hit "Mexican Joe" in 1953. Joined the Grand Ole Opry in 1955. Own ABC-TV series in 1957. In the 1963 film *Kimberley Jim*. Posthumously, he continued to have many country hits into the 80s.	
5/23/60	**18**	13	1. He'll Have To Go	RCA 2223
			He'll Have To Go (2)	
9/5/64	**30**	2	2. Moonlight and Roses	RCA 2854
9/19/64	**9**	18	● 3. The Best Of Jim Reeves [G]	RCA 2890
7/16/66	**21**	10	● 4. Distant Drums [K]	RCA 3542
			R.E.M.	
			Athens, Georgia rock quartet formed in 1980: Michael Stipe (vocals), Peter Buck, Mike Mills and Bill Berry.	
7/30/83	**36**	3	1. Murmur	I.R.S. 70604
5/26/84	**27**	6	2. Reckoning	I.R.S. 70044
7/6/85	**28**	14	3. Fables Of The Reconstruction	I.R.S. 5592
9/6/86	**21**	12	● 4. Lifes Rich Pageant	I.R.S. 5783
10/3/87	**10**	20	▲ 5. R.E.M. No. 5: Document	I.R.S. 42059
			The One I Love (9)	
11/26/88	**12**	27	▲ 6. Green	Warner 25795
			Stand (6)	
			REO SPEEDWAGON	
			Rock quintet from Champaign, Illinois: Kevin Cronin (lead vocals, rhythm guitar), Gary Richrath (lead guitar), Neal Doughty (keyboards), Bruce Hall (bass) and Alan Gratzer (drums). Gratzer left in 1988, replaced by former Santana drummer Graham Lear. 1990 lineup: Cronin, Doughty and Hall joined by new members Bryan Hitt, Jesse Harms and Dave Amato. Group named after a 1911 fire truck.	
6/3/78	**29**	5	▲ 1. You can Tune a piano, but you can't Tuna fish	Epic 35082
9/8/79	**33**	5	● 2. Nine Lives	Epic 35988
12/27/80	**1**(15)	50	▲ 3. Hi Infidelity	Epic 36844
			Keep On Loving You (1)/*Take It On The Run* (5)	
7/10/82	**7**	16	▲ 4. Good Trouble	Epic 38100
			Keep The Fire Burnin' (7)	
2/2/85	**7**	21	5. Wheels are turnin'	Epic 39593
			Can't Fight This Feeling (1)	
3/14/87	**28**	7	● 6. Life As We Know It	Epic 40444
			RETURN TO FOREVER	
			Jazz-rock band: Chick Corea (keyboards), Stanley Clarke (bass), Lenny White (drums), Al DiMeola (guitar).	
11/23/74	**32**	4	1. Where Have I Known You Before [I]	Polydor 6509
4/5/75	**39**	2	2. No Mystery [I]	Polydor 6512
5/22/76	**35**	3	● 3. Romantic Warrior [I]	Columbia 34076
5/14/77	**38**	2	4. Musicmagic	Columbia 34682

DATE	POS	WKS	ARTIST—RECORD TITLE	LABEL & NO.
			REVERE, Paul	
			Leader of pop-rock group The Raiders, formed in Portland, Oregon in 1960. Group featured Paul (b: 1/7/42, Boise, Idaho; keyboards) and Mark Lindsay (lead singer). To Los Angeles in 1965. On daily ABC-TV show "Where The Action Is" in 1965. Own TV show "Happening" in 1968. Group had many personnel changes.	
			PAUL REVERE & THE RAIDERS:	
3/12/66	**5**	19	● 1. Just Like Us!	Columbia 9251
7/2/66	**9**	15	● 2. Midnight Ride	Columbia 9308
			Kicks (4)	
1/14/67	**9**	17	● 3. The Spirit Of '67	Columbia 9395
			Hungry (6)/*Good Thing* (4)	
5/27/67	**9**	19	● 4. Greatest Hits [G]	Columbia 9462
9/23/67	**25**	7	5. Revolution!	Columbia 9521
			Freddy Weller joins group as lead guitarist	
			Him or Me-What's It Gonna Be? (5)	
			RAIDERS:	
7/3/71	**19**	11	6. Indian Reservation	Columbia 30768
			Indian Reservation (1)	
			REYNOLDS, Debbie	
			Born Mary Reynolds on 4/1/32 in El Paso, Texas. Leading lady of 50s musicals and later in comedies. Married Eddie Fisher on 9/26/55; divorced by 1959. Mother of actress Carrie Fisher.	
6/11/66	**23**	4	1. The Singing Nun [S]	MGM 7
			film is a fictionalized story about Soeur Sourire	
			RHEIMS, Robert	
1/5/59	**25**	1	1. Merry Christmas in Carols [X-I]	Rheims 6006
			The ROBERT RHEIMS CHORALIERS:	
1/4/60	**39**	1	2. We Wish You A Merry Christmas [X]	Rheims 6008
			RHODES, Emitt	
			Lead singer of Merry-Go-Round.	
1/9/71	**29**	7	1. Emitt Rhodes	Dunhill 50089
			RHYTHM HERITAGE	
			Los Angeles studio group assembled by producers Steve Barri and Michael Omartian (keyboards). Vocals by Oren and Luther Waters.	
4/24/76	**40**	2	1. Disco-Fied [I]	ABC 934
			Theme From S.W.A.T. (1)	
			RICH, Charlie	
			Born on 12/14/32 in Colt, Arkansas. Rockabilly-country singer/pianist/songwriter. First played jazz and blues. Own jazz group, the Velvetones, mid-50s, while in U.S. Air Force. Session work with Sun Records in 1958. Known as the "Silver Fox."	
12/8/73	**8**	32	▲ 1. Behind Closed Doors	Epic 32247
			The Most Beautiful Girl (1)	
3/30/74	**36**	2	● 2. There Won't Be Anymore [E]	RCA 0433
4/6/74	**24**	11	● 3. Very Special Love Songs	Epic 32531
12/28/74	**25**	9	4. The Silver Fox	Epic 33250
			RICHARDS, Keith	
			Born on 12/18/43 in Dartford, England. Lead guitarist of The Rolling Stones. Dropped the "s" from his last name in the 60s and 70s. Married to model Patti Hansen.	
10/29/88	**24**	7	● 1. Talk Is Cheap	Virgin 90973

DATE	POS	WKS	ARTIST—RECORD TITLE	LABEL & NO.
			RICHIE, Lionel	
			Born on 6/20/49 in Tuskegee, Alabama. Grew up on the campus of Tuskegee Institute where his grandfather worked. Former lead singer of the Commodores. Appeared in the film *Thank God It's Friday* (1978).	
10/30/82	**3**	39	▲ 1. Lionel Richie *Truly* (1)/*You Are* (4)/*My Love* (5)	Motown 6007
11/12/83	**1**(3)	78	▲ 2. Can't Slow Down 1984 Grammy winner: Album of the Year *All Night Long (All Night)* (1)/*Running With The Night* (7)/ *Hello* (1)/*Stuck On You* (3)/*Penny Lover* (8)	Motown 6059
8/30/86	**1**(2)	38	▲ 3. Dancing On The Ceiling *Dancing On The Ceiling* (2)/*Love Will Conquer All* (9)/ *Ballerina Girl* (7)	Motown 6158
			RICHTER, Sviatoslav	
			Classical pianist from Russia.	
12/12/60	**5**	20	1. Brahms: Piano Concerto No. 2 [I] with the Chicago Symphony Orchestra conducted by Erich Leinsdorf	RCA 2466
			RIDDLE, Nelson	
			Born on 6/1/21 in Oradell, New Jersey; died on 10/6/85. Trombonist/arranger with Charlie Spivak and Tommy Dorsey in the 40s. One of the most in-demand of all arranger-conductors for many top artists, including Frank Sinatra (several classic 50s albums), Nat King Cole, Ella Mae Morse, and more recently, Linda Ronstadt; also arranger/musical director for many films. **NELSON RIDDLE AND HIS ORCHESTRA:**	
5/27/57	**20**	1	1. Hey...Let Yourself Go! [I]	Capitol 814
2/17/58	**20**	1	2. C'mon...Get Happy! [I]	Capitol 893
			RIGHTEOUS BROTHERS, The	
			Blue-eyed soul duo: Bill Medley (b: 9/19/40, Santa Ana, California; baritone) and Bobby Hatfield (b: 8/10/40, Beaver Dam, Wisconsin; tenor). Formed duo in 1962. First recorded as the Paramours for Smash in 1962. On "Hullabaloo" and "Shindig" TV shows. Split up from 1968-74. Medley went solo, replaced by Billy Walker; rejoined Hatfield in 1974.	
2/6/65	**4**	19	1. You've Lost That Lovin' Feelin' *You've Lost That Lovin' Feelin'* (1)	Philles 4007
2/6/65	**11**	9	2. Right Now! [E]	Moonglow 1001
2/6/65	**14**	10	3. Some Blue-Eyed Soul [E]	Moonglow 1002
7/17/65	**9**	18	4. Just Once In My Life... *Just Once In My Life* (9)/*Unchained Melody* (4)	Philles 4008
8/7/65	**39**	1	5. This Is New! [E]	Moonglow 1003
2/5/66	**16**	11	6. Back To Back *Ebb Tide* (5)	Philles 4009
5/7/66	**7**	19	● 7. Soul & Inspiration *(You're My) Soul And Inspiration* (1)	Verve 5001
10/15/66	**32**	6	8. Go Ahead And Cry	Verve 5004
11/11/67	**21**	5	● 9. Greatest Hits [G] Philles and Moonglow label hits; a CD reissue of album, with 10 additional cuts on Verve 823119, re-entered Top 40 on 9/22/90	Verve 5020
9/28/74	**27**	8	10. Give It To The People *Rock And Roll Heaven* (3)	Haven 9201
			RILEY, Jeannie C.	
			Born Jeanne Carolyn Stephenson on 10/19/45 in Anson, Texas. Country singer.	
11/2/68	**12**	12	● 1. Harper Valley P.T.A. all songs about characters mentioned in the title song *Harper Valley P.T.A.* (1)	Plantation 1

DATE	POS	WKS	ARTIST—RECORD TITLE	LABEL & NO.
			RIPERTON, Minnie	
			Born on 11/8/47 in Chicago; died of cancer on 7/12/79 in Los Angeles. Recorded as "Andrea Davis" on Chess in 1966. Lead singer of the rock-R&B sextet Rotary Connection from 1967-70. In Stevie Wonder's backup group Wonderlove in 1973.	
10/26/74	4	18	● 1. Perfect Angel *Lovin' You (1)*	Epic 32561
6/14/75	18	8	2. Adventures In Paradise	Epic 33454
8/25/79	29	4	3. Minnie	Capitol 11936
9/27/80	35	4	4. Love Lives Forever recordings from 1978 with new accompaniment	Capitol 12097
			RITCHARD, Cyril	
			British actor.	
1/9/61	19	3	1. Alice In Wonderland: The Mad Tea Party/The Lobster Quadrille Cyril reads (and sings) selections from the classic story	[T] Riverside 1406
			RITCHIE FAMILY, The	
			Philadelphia disco group named for arranger/producer Ritchie Rome. Group featured various session singers and musicians.	
10/2/76	30	7	1. Arabian Nights	Marlin 2201
			RITENOUR, Lee	
			Born on 1/11/52 in Los Angeles. Guitarist/composer/arranger. Top session guitarist, has appeared on more than 200 albums. Nicknamed "Captain Fingers."	
6/13/81	26	7	1. "Rit"	Elektra 331
			RIVERS, Joan	
			Born on 6/8/33 in New York City. Popular comedienne. Guest host for Johnny Carson, 1983-86; host of "The Late Show," 1986-87. Currently hosting own daytime TV talk show. In films *The Swimmer, Rabbit Test* and *The Muppets Take Manhattan.*	
5/14/83	22	6	1. What Becomes A Semi-Legend Most? [C]	Geffen 4007
			RIVERS, Johnny	
			Born John Ramistella on 11/7/42 in New York City; raised in Baton Rouge. Rock and roll singer/guitarist/songwriter/producer. Recorded with the Spades for Suede in 1956. Named Johnny Rivers by DJ Alan Freed in 1958. To Los Angeles in 1961. Began own Soul City label in 1966.	
7/11/64	12	20	1. Johnny Rivers At The Whisky a Go Go [L] *Memphis (2)*	Imperial 12264
12/12/64	38	1	2. Here We a Go Go Again! [L]	Imperial 12274
7/31/65	21	6	3. Meanwhile Back At The Whisky a Go Go [L] *Seventh Son (7)*	Imperial 12284
2/4/66	33	5	4. Changes *Poor Side Of Town (1)*	Imperial 12334
11/5/66	29	9	● 5. Johnny Rivers' Golden Hits [G]	Imperial 12324
7/8/67	14	8	6. Rewind *Baby I Need Your Lovin' (3)/The Tracks Of My Tears (10)*	Imperial 12341
7/27/68	5	16	● 7. Realization	Imperial 12372
7/12/69	26	10	● 8. A Touch Of Gold [G]	Imperial 12427
			ROB BASE & D.J. E-Z ROCK	
			Harlem rap duo: Robert Ginyard with DJ Rodney "Skip" Bryce.	
11/12/88	31	8	▲ 1. It Takes Two	Profile 1267

DATE	POS	WKS	ARTIST—RECORD TITLE	LABEL & NO.
			ROBBINS, Marty	
			Born Martin David Robinson on 9/26/25 in Glendale, Arizona; died of a heart attack on 12/8/82. Country singer/guitarist/songwriter. Own radio show with K-Bar Cowboys, late 1940s. Own TV show, "Western Caravan," KPHO-Phoenix, 1951. First recorded for Columbia in 1952. Regular on the Grand Ole Opry since 1953. Own Robbins label in 1958. Stock car racer. Films *Road To Nashville* and *Guns Of A Stranger*.	
12/28/59	6	36	▲ 1. Gunfighter Ballads and Trail Songs *El Paso* (1)	Columbia 1349
1/9/61	21	2	2. More Gunfighter Ballads and Trail Songs	Columbia 1481
1/12/63	35	1	3. Devil Woman	Columbia 1918
			ROBERTSON, Robbie	
			Jaime Robbie Robertson was born on 7/5/44 in Toronto, Canada. Vocalist/bassist/ composer/producer. Joined Ronnie Hawkins' Hawks in 1960 which evolved into The Band in 1967. Group disbanded Thanksgiving Day, 1976. Produced film soundtracks. Acted in the film *Carney*. Wrote Joan Baez's 1971 hit "The Night They Drove Old Dixie Down."	
12/19/87	38	3	● 1. Robbie Robertson guest musicians: BoDeans, Peter Gabriel, Maria McKee (Lone Justice) and U2	Geffen 24160
			ROBINSON, Smokey	
			Born William Robinson on 2/19/40 in Detroit. Formed The Miracles (then called the Matadors) at Northern High School in 1955. First recorded for End in 1958. Married Miracles' member Claudette Rogers in 1963. Left The Miracles on 1/29/72. Wrote dozens of hit songs for Motown artists. Vice President of Motown Records until 1988. Inducted into the Rock and Roll Hall of Fame in 1987.	
6/14/75	36	3	1. A Quiet Storm	Tamla 337
1/5/80	17	11	2. Where There's Smoke.. *Cruisin'* (4)	Tamla 366
4/5/80	14	12	3. Warm Thoughts	Tamla 367
4/4/81	10	17	● 4. Being With You *Being With You* (2)	Tamla 375
3/13/82	33	4	5. Yes It's You Lady	Tamla 6001
5/23/87	26	17	● 6. One Heartbeat *Just To See Her* (8)/*One Heartbeat* (10)	Motown 6226
			ROCKPILE	
			British pop-rock quartet: Dave Edmunds, Nick Lowe, Billy Bremner, Terry Williams.	
11/29/80	27	10	1. Seconds Of Pleasure includes a 7" EP of Edmunds and Lowe singing four Everly Brothers' tunes	Columbia 36886
			ROCKWELL	
			Born Kennedy Gordy on 3/15/64 in Detroit. Son of Motown chairman, Berry Gordy, Jr.	
3/3/84	15	12	● 1. Somebody's Watching Me *Somebody's Watching Me* (2)	Motown 6052
			RODGERS, Jimmie	
			Born on 9/18/33 in Camas, Washington. Vocalist/guitarist/pianist. Formed first group while in the Air Force. Own NBC-TV variety series in 1959. Career hampered following mysterious assault in Los Angeles on 12/1/67, which left him with a fractured skull. Returned to performing on 1/28/69.	
12/16/57	15	3	1. Jimmie Rodgers *Honeycomb* (1)/*Kisses Sweeter Than Wine* (3)	Roulette 25020

DATE	POS	WKS	ARTIST—RECORD TITLE	LABEL & NO.
			ROE, Tommy	
			Pop-rock singer/guitarist/composer. Born on 5/9/42 in Atlanta. Formed band The Satins at Brown High School, worked local dances in the late 50s. Group recorded for Judd in 1960. Moved to Britain in the mid-60s, returned in 1969.	
4/26/69	25	8	1. Dizzy	ABC 683
			Dizzy (1)	
1/17/70	21	13	2. 12 In A Roe/A Collection of Tommy Roe's Greatest Hits [G]	ABC 700
			Jam Up Jelly Tight (8)	
			ROGER	
			Born Roger Troutman from Hamilton, Ohio. Leader of the family group Zapp. Worked with Sly Stone and George Clinton. Father of male singer, Lynch.	
10/24/81	26	6	● 1. The Many Facets Of Roger	Warner 3594
1/23/88	35	5	● 2. Unlimited!	Reprise 25496
			I Want To Be Your Man (3)	
			ROGERS, Eric	
			ERIC ROGERS AND HIS ORCHESTRA:	
12/4/61	37	3	1. The Percussive Twenties [I]	London P. 4 44006
			ROGERS, Kenny	
			Born Kenneth Donald Rogers on 8/21/38 in Houston. With high school band the Scholars in 1958. Bass player of jazz group the Bobby Doyle Trio, recorded for Columbia. In Kirby Stone Four and The New Christy Minstrels, mid-1960s. Formed and fronted The First Edition in 1967. Original lineup included Thelma Camacho, Mike Settle, Terry Williams and Mickey Jones. All but Jones were members of The New Christy Minstrels. Group hosted own syndicated TV variety show "Rollin" in 1972. Rogers split from group in 1973. Starred in films *The Gambler*, *Coward Of The County* and *Six Pack*.	
			KENNY ROGERS AND THE FIRST EDITION:	
5/2/70	26	6	1. Something's Burning	Reprise 6385
			KENNY ROGERS:	
6/11/77	30	4	● 2. Kenny Rogers	United Art. 689
			Lucille (5)	
9/24/77	39	2	● 3. Daytime Friends	United Art. 754
3/18/78	33	4	▲ 4. Ten Years Of Gold [G]	United Art. 835
			side 1: new versions of his First Edition hits	
2/24/79	12	21	▲ 5. The Gambler	United Art. 934
			She Believes In Me (5)	
10/6/79	5	26	▲ 6. Kenny	United Art. 979
			You Decorated My Life (7)/*Coward Of The County* (3)	
4/26/80	12	11	▲ 7. Gideon	United Art. 1035
			Don't Fall In Love With A Dreamer (4) with Kim Carnes	
10/18/80	1(2)	36	▲ 8. Kenny Rogers' Greatest Hits [G]	Liberty 1072
			Lady (1)	
7/11/81	6	13	▲ 9. Share Your Love	Liberty 1108
			album produced by Lionel Richie	
			I Don't Need You (3)	
12/26/81	34	3	▲ 10. Christmas [X]	Liberty 51115
8/14/82	34	7	● 11. Love Will Turn You Around	Liberty 51124
3/12/83	18	12	● 12. We've Got Tonight	Liberty 51143
			We've Got Tonight (6) with Sheena Easton	
10/1/83	6	24	▲ 13. Eyes That See In The Dark	RCA 4697
			album produced by Barry Gibb	
			Islands In The Stream (1) with Dolly Parton	
11/26/83	22	11	▲ 14. Twenty Greatest Hits [G]	Liberty 51152

DATE	POS	WKS	ARTIST—RECORD TITLE		LABEL & NO.
10/13/84	**31**	8	▲ 15. What About Me?		RCA 5043
12/22/84	**31**	4	**KENNY ROGERS & DOLLY PARTON:** ▲ 16. Once Upon A Christmas	[X]	RCA 5307

ROLLING STONES, The

British R&B-influenced rock group formed in London in January, 1963. Consisted of Mick Jagger (b: 7/26/43; vocals), Keith Richards (b: 12/18/43; lead guitar), Brian Jones (b: 2/28/42; guitar), Bill Wyman (b: 10/24/36; bass) and Charlie Watts (b: 6/2/41; drums). Jagger was the lead singer of Blues, Inc. Group took name from a Muddy Waters song. Promoted as the bad boys in contrast to The Beatles. First UK tour, with Ronettes in 1964. Jones left group shortly before drowning on 7/3/69. Replaced by Mick Taylor (b: 1/17/48). In 1975, Ron Wood (ex-Jeff Beck Group, ex-Faces) replaced Taylor. Film *Gimme Shelter* is a documentary of their controversial Altamont concert on 12/6/69 at which a concertgoer was murdered by a member of the Hell's Angels. Inducted into the Rock and Roll Hall of Fame in 1989. Considered by many as the world's all-time greatest rock band.

DATE	POS	WKS	ARTIST—RECORD TITLE		LABEL & NO.
7/25/64	**11**	12	● 1. England's Newest Hit Makers/The Rolling Stones		London 375
11/28/64	**3**	20	● 2. 12 x 5 *Time Is On My Side* (6)		London 402
4/10/65	**5**	29	● 3. The Rolling Stones, Now!		London 420
8/14/65	**1**(3)	35	▲ 4. Out Of Our Heads *The Last Time* (9)/*(I Can't Get No) Satisfaction* (1)		London 429
12/18/65	**4**	22	● 5. December's Children (and everybody's) *Get Off Of My Cloud* (1)/*As Tears Go By* (6)		London 451
4/23/66	**3**	35	▲ 6. Big Hits (High Tide And Green Grass) *19th Nervous Breakdown* (2)	[G]	London 1
7/16/66	**2**(2)	26	▲ 7. Aftermath *Paint It, Black* (1)		London 476
12/31/66	**6**	11	● 8. got Live if you want it! recorded at the Royal Albert Hall, London	[L]	London 493
2/25/67	**2**(4)	19	● 9. Between The Buttons *Ruby Tuesday* (1)		London 499
7/29/67	**3**	18	● 10. Flowers *Mothers Little Helper* (8)/ *Have You Seen Your Mother, Baby, Standing In The Shadow?* (9)	[G]	London 509
12/23/67	**2**(6)	13	● 11. Their Satanic Majesties Request		London 2
12/21/68	**5**	13	▲ 12. Beggars Banquet		London 539
9/20/69	**2**(2)	16	▲ 13. Through The Past, Darkly (Big Hits Vol. 2) *Jumpin' Jack Flash* (3)/*Honky Tonk Women* (1)	[G]	London 3
12/13/69	**3**	19	▲ 14. Let It Bleed Brian Jones' last appearance/Mick Taylor's first with band		London 4
10/17/70	**6**	10	▲ 15. 'Get Yer Ya-Ya's Out!' recorded at New York's Madison Square Garden, November, 1969	[L]	London 5
5/15/71	**1**(4)	26	● 16. Sticky Fingers *Brown Sugar* (1)		Rolling S. 59100
1/8/72	**4**	30	▲ 17. Hot Rocks 1964-1971 reissued on CD on Abkco 6667 during its chart run in 1989	[G]	London 606/7 [2]
6/10/72	**1**(4)	17	● 18. Exile On Main St. *Tumbling Dice* (7)		Rolling S. 2900 [2]
1/20/73	**9**	12	● 19. More Hot Rocks (big hits & fazed cookies)	[G]	London 626/7 [2]
9/29/73	**1**(4)	19	● 20. Goats Head Soup *Angie* (1)		Rolling S. 59101
11/9/74	**1**(1)	11	● 21. It's Only Rock 'N Roll		Rolling S. 79101
6/21/75	**8**	8	22. Metamorphosis	[K]	Abkco 1
6/28/75	**6**	9	● 23. Made In The Shade	[G]	Rolling S. 79102

DATE	POS	WKS	ARTIST—RECORD TITLE	LABEL & NO.
5/8/76	1(4)	14	▲ 24. Black And Blue Ron Wood's first appearance with band *Fool To Cry* (10)	Rolling S. 79104
10/15/77	5	7	● 25. Love You Live　　　　　　　　　　　[L]	Rolling S. 9001 [2]
6/24/78	1(2)	32	▲ 26. Some Girls *Miss You* (1)/*Beast Of Burden* (8)	Rolling S. 39108
7/19/80	1(7)	20	▲ 27. Emotional Rescue *Emotional Rescue* (3)	Rolling S. 16015
4/4/81	15	6	● 28. Sucking In The Seventies　　　　　[G]	Rolling S. 16028
9/12/81	1(9)	30	▲ 29. Tattoo You *Start Me Up* (2)	Rolling S. 16052
7/3/82	5	10	● 30. "Still Life" (American Concert 1981)　[L]	Rolling S. 39113
11/26/83	4	12	▲ 31. Undercover *Undercover Of The Night* (9)	Rolling S. 90120
4/12/86	4	15	▲ 32. Dirty Work *Harlem Shuffle* (5)	Rolling S. 40250
9/23/89	3	27	▲ 33. Steel Wheels *Mixed Emotion* (5)	Rolling S. 45333
			ROMANTICS, The Rock quartet from Detroit formed in 1977. Original lineup: Wally Palmar (lead singer, guitar), Mike Skill (lead guitar), Richard Cole (bass) and Jimmy Marinos (drums).	
12/17/83	14	15	● 1. In Heat *Talking In Your Sleep* (3)	Nemperor 38880
			RONSTADT, Linda Born on 7/15/46 in Tucson, Arizona. While in high school formed folk trio The Three Ronstadts (with sister and brother). To Los Angeles in 1964. Formed the Stone Poneys with Bobby Kimmel (guitar) and Ken Edwards (keyboards); recorded for Sidewalk in 1965. Went solo in 1968. In 1971 formed backing band with Glenn Frey, Don Henley, Randy Meisner and Bernie Leadon (later became the Eagles). In *Pirates Of Penzance* operetta in New York City in 1980, also in film of same name in 1983.	
12/14/74	1(1)	19	● 1. Heart Like A Wheel *You're No Good* (1)/*When Will I Be Loved* (2)	Capitol 11358
10/11/75	4	10	▲ 2. Prisoner In Disguise *Heat Wave* (5)	Asylum 1045
9/4/76	3	15	▲ 3. Hasten Down The Wind	Asylum 1072
12/18/76	6	15	▲ 4. Greatest Hits　　　　　　　　　　[G] includes her hits on Capitol	Asylum 1092
10/1/77	1(5)	23	▲ 5. Simple Dreams *Blue Bayou* (3)/*It's So Easy* (5)	Asylum 104
10/7/78	1(1)	17	▲ 6. Living In The USA *Ooh Baby Baby* (7)	Asylum 155
3/15/80	3	17	▲ 7. Mad Love *How Do I Make You* (10)/*Hurt So Bad* (8)	Asylum 510
11/15/80	26	10	▲ 8. Greatest Hits, Volume Two　　　　[G]	Asylum 516
10/30/82	31	6	● 9. Get Closer	Asylum 60185
10/8/83	3	25	▲ 10. What's New	Asylum 60260
12/15/84	13	11	▲ 11. Lush Life above two arranged and conducted by Nelson Riddle	Asylum 60387
			DOLLY PARTON, LINDA RONSTADT, EMMYLOU HARRIS:	
3/28/87	6	14	▲ 12. Trio	Warner 25491

DATE	POS	WKS	ARTIST—RECORD TITLE	LABEL & NO.
10/28/89	7	37	**LINDA RONSTADT FEATURING AARON NEVILLE:** ▲ 13. Cry Like A Rainstorm - Howl Like The Wind includes four duets with Neville; *Don't Know Much* (2) with Aaron Neville	Elektra 60872
			## ROOFTOP SINGERS, The	
			Folk trio from New York City: Erik Darling, Willard Svanoe and Lynne Taylor (d: 1982). Disbanded in 1967. Darling was a member of The Tarriers in 1956 and The Weavers, 1958-62. Taylor was a vocalist with Benny Goodman and Buddy Rich.	
3/2/63	15	7	1. Walk Right In! *Walk Right In* (1)	Vanguard 9123
			## ROS, Edmundo	
			Born on 12/7/10 in Venezuela. London-based bandleader/drummer. **EDMUNDO ROS AND HIS ORCHESTRA:**	
5/25/59	28	2	1. Hollywood Cha Cha Cha [I]	London 152
9/22/62	31	5	2. Dance Again [I]	London P. 4 44015
			## ROSE, David	
			Born on 6/15/10 in London; moved to Chicago at an early age. Conductor/composer/ arranger for numerous films. Scored many TV series, such as "The Red Skelton Show," "Bonanza" and "Little House On The Prairie." Married to Martha Raye (1938-41) and Judy Garland (1941-43). Died on 8/23/90 of heart disease. **DAVID ROSE AND HIS ORCHESTRA:**	
7/7/62	3	28	● 1. The Stripper and other fun Songs for the family [I] *The Stripper* (1)	MGM 4062
			## ROSE ROYCE	
			Eight-member backing band formed in Los Angeles in early 70s. Backed Edwin Starr as Total Concept Unlimited in 1973. Backed The Temptations, became regular band for Undisputed Truth. Lead vocalist Gwen Dickey added, name changed to Rose Royce in 1976. Did soundtrack for the film *Car Wash*.	
12/18/76	14	13	● 1. Car Wash [S] *Car Wash* (1)/*I Wanna Get Next To You* (10)	MCA 6000 [2]
9/17/77	9	14	▲ 2. Rose Royce II/In Full Bloom	Whitfield 3074
9/23/78	28	6	● 3. Rose Royce III/Strikes Again!	Whitfield 3227
			## ROSS, Diana	
			Born Diane Earle on 3/26/44 in Detroit. In vocal group The Primettes, first recorded for LuPine in 1960. Lead singer of The Supremes from 1961-69. Went solo in late 1969. Oscar nominee for the 1972 film *Lady Sings The Blues*. Appeared in the films *Mahogany* and *The Wiz*. Own Broadway show *An Evening With Diana Ross*, 1976.	
7/18/70	19	18	1. Diana Ross *Ain't No Mountain High Enough* (1)	Motown 711
12/23/72	1(2)	24	2. Lady Sings The Blues [S] Diana portrayed Billie Holiday in the film	Motown 758 [2]
7/28/73	5	15	3. Touch Me In The Morning *Touch Me In The Morning* (1)	Motown 772
12/8/73	26	5	4. Diana & Marvin **DIANA ROSS & MARVIN GAYE**	Motown 803
12/13/75	19	10	5. Mahogany [S-I] Diana sings only the title song; instrumentals conducted by Lee Holdridge *Theme From Mahogany (Do You Know Where You're Going To)* (1)	Motown 858
3/27/76	5	18	6. Diana Ross *Love Hangover* (1)	Motown 861
8/14/76	13	14	7. Diana Ross' Greatest Hits [G]	Motown 869

DATE	POS	WKS	ARTIST—RECORD TITLE	LABEL & NO.
10/22/77	**18**	13	8. Baby It's Me	Motown 890
10/22/77	**29**	12	9. An Evening With Diana Ross [L]	Motown 877 [2]
			recorded at the Ahmanson Theatre, Los Angeles	
7/7/79	**14**	17	● 10. The Boss	Motown 923
6/21/80	**2(2)**	34	▲ 11. Diana	Motown 936
			Upside Down (1)/*I'm Coming Out* (5)	
3/28/81	**32**	4	12. To Love Again [K]	Motown 951
			It's My Turn (9)	
11/14/81	**15**	20	▲ 13. Why Do Fools Fall In Love	RCA 4153
			Why Do Fools Fall In Love (7)/*Mirror, Mirror* (8)	
11/21/81	**37**	3	● 14. All The Great Hits [G]	Motown 960 [2]
			includes medleys with The Supremes	
			Endless Love (1) with Lionel Richie	
10/30/82	**27**	7	● 15. Silk Electric	RCA 4384
			Muscles (10)	
8/6/83	**32**	4	16. Ross	RCA 4677
10/6/84	**26**	18	● 17. Swept Away	RCA 5009
			Missing You (10)	
			ROSSINGTON COLLINS BAND	
			Band formed by four surviving members of Lynyrd Skynyrd, featuring Gary Rossington and Allen Collins (paralyzed in a 1986 car crash). Disbanded in 1982. Gary and wife Dale Krantz-Rossington (vocals), Jay Johnson, Tim Lindsey, Ronnie Eades, Tim Sharpton and Mitch Rigel recorded as The Rossington Band in 1988. Collins died of pneumonia on 1/23/90 (age 37).	
7/19/80	**13**	13	● 1. Anytime, Anyplace, Anywhere	MCA 5130
10/17/81	**24**	5	2. This Is The Way	MCA 5207
			ROTARY CONNECTION	
			Canadian rock-R&B sextet - Minnie Riperton, lead singer.	
5/4/68	**37**	4	1. Rotary Connection	Cadet Concept 312
			ROTH, David Lee	
			Born on 10/10/55 in Bloomington, Indiana. Former lead singer of Van Halen.	
2/23/85	**15**	20	▲ 1. Crazy From The Heat [M]	Warner 25222
			California Girls (3)	
7/26/86	**4**	21	▲ 2. Eat 'Em And Smile	Warner 25470
2/13/88	**6**	16	▲ 3. Skyscraper	Warner 25671
			Just Like Paradise (6)	
			ROXETTE	
			Male/female Swedish duo: Marie Fredriksson (vocals) and Per Gessle (songwriter).	
4/29/89	**23**	21	▲ 1. Look Sharp!	EMI 91098
			The Look (1)/*Listen To Your Heart* (1)/*Dangerous* (2)	
			ROXY MUSIC	
			English art-rock band. Nucleus consisted of Bryan Ferry (vocals, keyboards), Phil Manzanera (guitar) and Andy Mackay (horns).	
3/8/75	**37**	3	1. Country Life	Atco 106
4/14/79	**23**	8	2. Manifesto	Atco 114
8/9/80	**35**	3	3. Flesh + Blood	Atco 102
			ROYAL PHILHARMONIC ORCHESTRA, The	
			British - Louis Clark, conductor (born in Birmingham, England; arranger for ELO).	
12/12/81	**4**	22	▲ 1. Hooked On Classics [I]	RCA 4194
			Hooked On Classics (10)	

DATE	POS	WKS	ARTIST—RECORD TITLE	LABEL & NO.
9/18/82	33	7	● 2. Hooked On Classics II (Can't Stop the Classics) [I]	RCA 4373
			ROYAL SCOTS DRAGOON GUARDS, The	
7/22/72	34	5	The Pipes and Drums and The Military Band of Scotland's armored regiment. 1. Amazing Grace [I]	RCA 4744
			RUBINSTEIN, Arthur	
2/13/61	30	1	Classical pianist. Born in Lodz, Poland; died on 12/20/82 (age 95). 1. Heart of the Piano Concerto [I] favorite movements from six piano concertos	RCA 2495
			RUDY, Ed — see BEATLES, The	
			RUFFIN, David	
			Born on 1/18/41 in Meridian, Mississippi. Brother of Jimmy Ruffin. With the Dixie Nightingales gospel group. Recorded for Anna in 1960. Co-lead singer of The Temptations from 1963-68.	
6/28/69	31	7	1. My Whole World Ended *My Whole World Ended (The Moment You Left Me)* (9)	Motown 685
1/17/76	31	6	2. Who I Am *Walk Away From Love* (9)	Motown 849
			RUFUS FEATURING CHAKA KHAN	
			Soul group from Chicago. Band was first known as Smoke, then Ask Rufus. Varying membership included Chaka Khan (vocals), Tony Maiden (guitar), Nate Morgan, Kevin Murphy (keyboards), Bobby Watson (bass), Andre Fischer (drums; later married Natalie Cole) and Moon Calhoun. Khan has been recording solo and with Rufus since 1978. After 1978, Maiden and David Wolinski also sang lead.	
8/3/74	4	11	● 1. Rags To Rufus *Tell Me Something Good* (3)	ABC 809
1/25/75	7	12	● 2. Rufusized *Once You Get Started* (10)	ABC 837
12/6/75	7	24	● 3. Rufus featuring Chaka Khan *Sweet Thing* (5)	ABC 909
2/12/77	12	10	▲ 4. Ask Rufus	ABC 975
2/25/78	14	14	● 5. Street Player	ABC 1049
11/24/79	14	16	● 6. Masterjam	MCA 5103
			RUNDGREN, Todd	
			Born on 6/22/48 in Upper Darby, Pennsylvania. Virtuoso musician/songwriter/producer/ engineer. Leader of groups Nazz and Utopia. Produced Meat Loaf's *Bat Out Of Hell* album and produced albums for Badfinger, Grand Funk Railroad, The Tubes, XTC, Patti Smith and many others.	
12/15/73	29	18	● 1. Something/Anything? *Hello It's Me* (5)	Bearsville 2066 [2]
6/17/78	36	2	2. Hermit Of Mink Hollow	Bearsville 6981
			RUN-D.M.C.	
			Rap trio from Queens, New York: rappers Joseph Simmons (Run), Darryl McDaniels (DMC) with DJ Jason Mizell (Jam Master Jay). In films *Krush Groove* and *Tougher Than Leather*.	
6/21/86	3	49	▲ 1. Raising Hell *Walk This Way* (4)	Profile 1217
6/4/88	9	14	▲ 2. Tougher Than Leather	Profile 1265

Prince's *Purple Rain* soundtrack of 1984 held the No. 1 slot for an astounding 24 weeks and generated four top 10 singles, including dual chart-toppers "When Doves Cry" and "Let's Go Crazy."

The **Psychedelic Furs**, a longstanding British group that emerged from the U.K. punk scene in 1980, will likely be remembered for their "Pretty In Pink" track, a song from their 1981 album *Talk Talk Talk* that inspired the later John Hughes film of the same name. 1987's *Midnight To Midnight* remains the group's only top 40 album to date.

The **Rascals** stopped being "Young" with their 1968 single, "Beautiful Morning." One of the most influential blue-eyed soul bands in rock history, the group experienced a resurgence of interest in the late 80s when oldies label Rhino reissued the bulk of their classic Atlantic albums, including 1967's *Groovin'.*

The **Raspberries** had a top 10 hit with 1972's "Go All The Way," but the group's obvious worship of mid-60s pop seemed directly at odds with the hippie, art-rock stylings of the time. The band's second LP, *Fresh*, was their only top 40 album. Group leader Eric Carmen later went solo and played an important role in the multi-platinum *Dirty Dancing* film soundtrack.

Jim Reeves, a Country Music Hall Of Fame member, had his biggest hit in 1960 with "He'll Have To Go," which appeared on his first top 40 LP of the same name. After his tragic death in a 1964 plane crash, Reeves continued to see chart action with several posthumous releases—but only 1966's *Distant Drums* cracked the top 40.

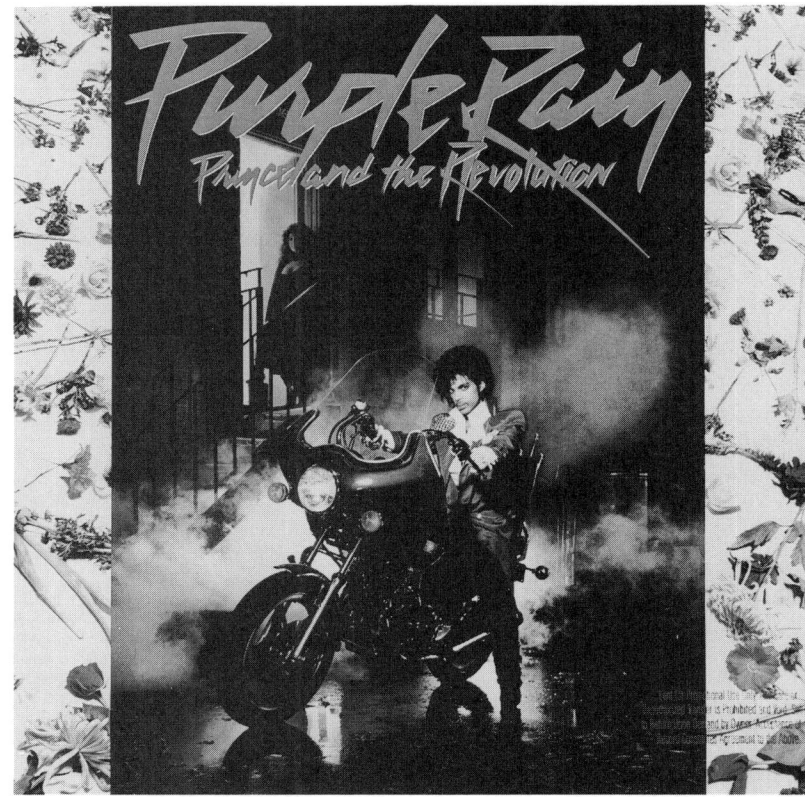

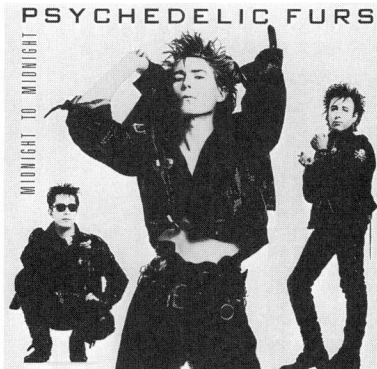

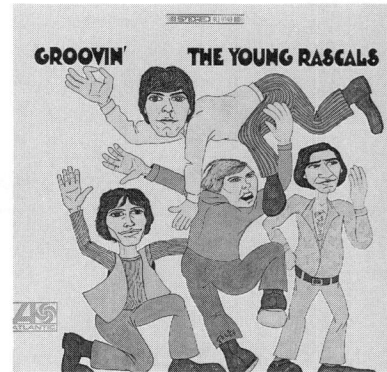

REO Speedwagon, from Champaign, Illinois, joke that they've outlasted just about everybody that has worked at their recording company, Epic Records. They may be right: The group's first album was released in 1971; they hit the top 40 for the first time in '78 with *You Can Tune A Piano But You Can't Tune A Fish*; and new LPs are still coming regularly. Despite numerous personnel changes, Gary Richrath and Alan Gratzer had always been two constants until the band's 1990 album, *The Earth, A Small Man, His Dog And A Chicken*, on which neither were to be found.

Lionel Richie, former lead singer with Motown's Commodores, found multi-platinum success with a string of solo albums in the early 80s, including 1982's *Lionel Richie*, 1983's *Can't Slow Down* and 1986's *Dancing On The Ceiling*.

Kenny Rogers has been making hit records since 1968, when as a member of the First Edition he "Just Dropped In (To See What Condition My Condition Was In)." From the 80s onward, Rogers continued to score with a series of duet hits. Partners included Kim Carnes, Sheena Easton, Dolly Parton and—for 1984's "What About Me?"—both Carnes and James Ingram.

The **Rolling Stones**, whose first LP hit U.S. shores in 1964, have released more greatest hits collections—seven—than most bands have albums. Their 1967 album, *Flowers*, a special collection of songs put together in the U.S. by London Records, never saw release in Great Britain.

Linda Ronstadt's diversity as an artist over the years is evidenced by her collaborations with such diverse artists as Nelson Riddle, Dolly Parton and Emmylou Harris, and the record *Canciones De Mi Padre*, a 1987 album of Mexican songs dedicated to her father. *Get Closer*, released in 1982, was her lowest ranking top 40 album, peaking at No. 31.

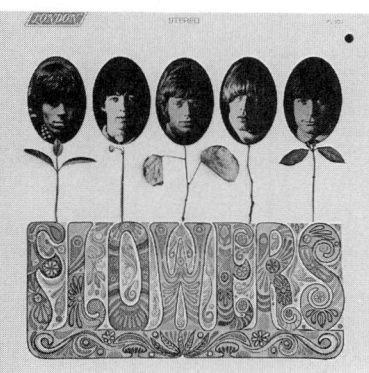

DATE	POS	WKS	ARTIST—RECORD TITLE	LABEL & NO.
			RUSH	
			Canadian power-rock trio: Geddy Lee (b: 7/29/53; vocals, bass), Alex Lifeson (b: 8/27/53; guitar) and Neil Peart (b: 9/12/52; drums).	
11/20/76	40	2	▲ 1. All The World's A Stage [L]	Mercury 7508 [2]
10/8/77	33	5	● 2. A Farewell To Kings	Mercury 1184
2/9/80	4	15	▲ 3. Permanent Waves	Mercury 4001
3/7/81	3	29	▲ 4. Moving Pictures	Mercury 4013
11/14/81	10	14	▲ 5. Exit...Stage Left [L]	Mercury 7001 [2]
10/2/82	10	11	▲ 6. Signals	Mercury 4063
5/5/84	10	12	▲ 7. Grace Under Pressure	Mercury 818476
11/2/85	10	14	▲ 8. Power Windows	Mercury 826098
10/3/87	13	14	● 9. Hold Your Fire	Mercury 832464
2/4/89	21	5	● 10. A Show Of Hands [L] recorded during their 1986 and 1988 world tours	Merc. 836346 [2]
12/9/89	16	11	● 11. Presto	Atlantic 82040
			RUSHEN, Patrice	
			Born on 9/30/54 in Los Angeles. Jazz-soul vocalist/pianist/songwriter. Much session work with Jean Luc-Ponty, Lee Ritenour and Stanley Turrentine.	
3/1/80	39	2	1. Pizzazz	Elektra 243
5/15/82	14	8	2. Straight From The Heart	Elektra 60015
7/28/84	40	3	3. Now	Elektra 60360
			RUSSELL, Leon	
			Born on 4/2/41 in Lawton, Oklahoma. Vocalist/songwriter/top multi-instrumentalist sessionman. Early in session career known as Russell Bridges. Regular with Phil Spector's "Wall of Sound" session group. Formed Shelter Records with British producer Denny Cordell in 1970. Recorded as Hank Wilson in 1973. Married Mary McCreary (vocalist with Little Sister, part of Sly Stone's "family") in 1976. Formed Paradise label in 1976. Wrote "Superstar" and "This Masquerade." Also see Joe Cocker.	
6/12/71	17	10	● 1. Leon Russell & The Shelter People	Shelter 8903
7/29/72	2(4)	20	● 2. Carney	Shelter 8911
7/14/73	9	12	● 3. Leon Live [L] recorded at the Long Beach Arena, Long Beach, California	Shelter 8917 [3]
9/29/73	28	5	4. Hank Wilson's Back, Vol. I an album of Country & Western songs	Shelter 8923
7/13/74	34	3	5. Stop All That Jazz	Shelter 2108
5/31/75	30	7	● 6. Will O' The Wisp	Shelter 2138
6/12/76	34	4	7. Wedding Album **LEON & MARY RUSSELL (wife Mary McCreary)**	Paradise 2943
12/4/76	40	1	● 8. Best Of Leon [G]	Shelter 52004
7/7/79	25	5	**WILLIE NELSON AND LEON RUSSELL:** ● 9. One For The Road	Columbia 36064 [2]
			RYDELL, Bobby	
			Born Robert Ridarelli on 4/26/42 in Philadelphia. Regular on Paul Whiteman's amateur TV show, 1951-54. Drummer with Rocco & The Saints, which included Frankie Avalon on trumpet in 1956. First recorded for Veko in 1957. Films Bye Bye Birdie and That Lady From Peking.	
2/27/61	12	8	1. Bobby's Biggest Hits [G] We Got Love (6)/Wild One (2)/Swingin' School (5)/ Volare (4)	Cameo 1009
12/25/61	7	11	2. Bobby Rydell/Chubby Checker	Cameo 1013

DATE	POS	WKS	ARTIST—RECORD TITLE	LABEL & NO.
			RYDER, Mitch	
			Born William Levise, Jr. on 2/26/45 in Detroit. Leader of white soul-rock group The Detroit Wheels. Group was originally known as Billy Lee & The Rivieras. Renamed by their producer Bob Crewe. Ryder went solo in 1967. Formed new rock group, Detroit, in 1971.	
			MITCH RYDER AND THE DETROIT WHEELS:	
2/25/67	23	7	1. Breakout…!!!	New Voice 2002
			Devil With A Blue Dress On & Good Golly Miss Molly (4)	
5/6/67	34	3	2. Sock It To Me!	New Voice 2003
			Sock It To Me-Baby! (6)	
1/20/68	37	4	3. All Mitch Ryder Hits! [G]	New Voice 2004

S

DATE	POS	WKS	ARTIST—RECORD TITLE	LABEL & NO.
			SADE	
			Born Helen Folasade Adu on 1/16/59 in Ibadan, Nigeria; moved to London at age four. Name pronounced Shaw-Day. Appeared in the 1986 film *Absolute Beginners*. Former designer of menswear. Won the 1985 Best New Artist Grammy Award.	
3/9/85	5	27	▲ 1. Diamond Life	Portrait 39581
			Smooth Operator (5)	
12/21/85	1(2)	27	▲ 2. Promise	Portrait 40263
			The Sweetest Taboo (5)	
6/11/88	7	21	▲ 3. Stronger Than Pride	Epic 44210
			SADLER, SSgt Barry	
			Born in New Mexico in 1940. Staff Sergeant of U.S. Army Special Forces (aka Green Berets). Served in Vietnam until injuring leg in booby trap. Shot in the head during a 1988 robbery attempt at his Guatemala home; suffered brain damage. Died of heart failure on 11/5/89 (age 49) in Murfreesboro, Tennessee.	
3/12/66	1(5)	20	● 1. Ballads of the Green Berets	RCA 3547
			The Ballad Of The Green Berets (1)	
			SAGA	
			Canadian rock quintet: Michael Sadler (lead singer), brothers Jim and Ian Crichton, Jim Gilmour and Steve Negus.	
1/8/83	29	13	● 1. Worlds Apart	Portrait 38246
			SAHL, Mort	
			Born in Montreal in 1927. Topical satirist/actor. Own one-man Broadway show *Mort Sahl On Broadway!*	
10/24/60	22	4	1. Mort Sahl At The Hungry i [C]	Verve 15012
			SAILCAT	
			Country-rock duo: Court Pickett and John Wyker.	
10/7/72	38	2	1. Motorcycle Mama	Elektra 75029
			SAKAMOTO, Kyu	
			Native of Kawasaki, Japan. One of 520 people killed in the crash of the Japan Airlines 747 near Tokyo on 8/12/85 (age 43).	
7/6/63	14	8	1. Sukiyaki and other Japanese hits [F]	Capitol 10349
			Sukiyaki (1)	

DATE	POS	WKS	ARTIST—RECORD TITLE	LABEL & NO.
			SALSOUL ORCHESTRA, The	
			Disco orchestra conducted by Philadelphia producer/arranger Vincent Montana, Jr. Vocalists included Phyllis Rhodes, Ronni Tyson, Carl Helm and Philip Hurt.	
2/7/76	**14**	14	1. The Salsoul Orchestra [I]	Salsoul 5501
			SALT-N-PEPA	
			Queens-based female rap trio: Cheryl "Salt" James, Sandy "Pepa" Denton (from Kingston, Jamaica) and Dee Dee "DJ Spinderella LaToya" Roper. James and Denton recorded earlier as Super Nature. Took a line from their Super Nature recording "Showstopper" and changed name to Salt-N-Pepa.	
2/6/88	**26**	14	▲ 1. Hot, Cool & Vicious	Next Plateau 1007
9/3/88	**38**	4	● 2. A Salt With A Deadly Pepa	Next Plat. 1011
4/28/90	**38**	2	● 3. Black's Magic	Next P. 1019
			SAM THE SHAM AND THE PHAROAHS	
			Dallas rock & roll group formed in the early 60s, featuring lead singer Domingo "Sam" Samudio (b: 1940, Dallas). First recorded for Dingo in 1965. Samudio went solo in 1970. Formed new band in 1974. On the 1982 film soundtrack *The Border*. Sam is currently a street preacher in Memphis.	
8/14/65	**26**	5	1. Wooly Bully *Wooly Bully* (2)	MGM 4297
			SANDPIPERS, The	
			Los Angeles-based trio: Jim Brady (b: 8/24/44), Michael Piano (b: 10/26/44) and Richard Shoff (b: 4/30/44); met while in the Mitchell Boys Choir.	
11/26/66	**13**	10	● 1. Guantanamera *Guantanamera* (9)	A&M 4117
			SANDS, Tommy	
			Born on 8/27/37 in Chicago. Pop singer/actor. Mother was a vocalist with Art Kassel's band. Married Nancy Sinatra in 1960; divorced in 1965. In the films *Sing Boy Sing*, *Mardi Gras*, *Babes In Toyland* and *The Longest Day*.	
5/6/57	**4**	18	1. Steady Date with Tommy Sands	Capitol 848
2/24/58	**17**	4	2. Sing Boy Sing [S] Tommy portrays fictional singer Virgil Walker in the film	Capitol 929
			SANG, Samantha	
			Born Cheryl Gray on 8/5/53 in Melbourne, Australia. Began career on Melbourne radio at age eight.	
4/8/78	**29**	3	● 1. Emotion *Emotion* (3)	Private S. 7009
			SAN SEBASTIAN STRINGS, The	
			Music composed by Anita Kerr (with sound effects), featuring narration of the poetry of Rod McKuen.	
2/1/69	**20**	4	1. Home To The Sea [I-T]	Warner 1764
			SANTA ESMERALDA	
			Spanish-flavored disco studio project produced by Nicolas Skorsky and Jean-Manuel De Scarano.	
1/14/78	**25**	8	● 1. Don't Let Me Be Misunderstood	Casablanca 7080

DATE	POS	WKS	ARTIST—RECORD TITLE	LABEL & NO.
			SANTANA	
			Latin-rock group formed in San Francisco in 1966. Consisted of Carlos Santana (b: 7/20/47, Autlan de Navarro, Mexico; vocals, guitar), Gregg Rolie (keyboards) and David Brown (bass). Added percussionists Michael Carabello, Jose Chepitos Areas and Michael Shrieve in 1969. Worked Fillmore West and Woodstock in 1969. Neal Schon (guitar) added in 1971. Santana began solo work in 1972. Schon and Rolie formed Journey in 1973. Shrieve left in 1975 to form Automatic Man.	
9/27/69	**4**	42	▲ 1. Santana *Evil Ways* (9)	Columbia 9781
10/10/70	**1**(6)	40	▲ 2. Abraxas *Black Magic Woman* (4)	Columbia 30130
10/16/71	**1**(5)	22	● 3. Santana III	Columbia 30595
11/11/72	**8**	17	▲ 4. Caravanserai	Columbia 31610
12/15/73	**25**	9	● 5. Welcome	Columbia 32445
8/24/74	**17**	11	▲ 6. Santana's Greatest Hits [G]	Columbia 33050
11/23/74	**20**	5	● 7. Borboletta	Columbia 33135
4/17/76	**10**	11	● 8. Amigos	Columbia 33576
1/29/77	**27**	4	● 9. Festival	Columbia 34423
11/12/77	**10**	9	▲ 10. Moonflower [L] set also features some new studio recordings	Columbia 34914 [2]
11/11/78	**27**	5	● 11. Inner Secrets	Columbia 35600
11/3/79	**25**	6	12. Marathon	Columbia 36154
5/2/81	**9**	21	● 13. Zebop!	Columbia 37158
9/11/82	**22**	10	14. Shango	Columbia 38122
			SANTANA, Carlos	
			Mexican-born rock and jazz-fusion guitarist. Leader of Santana. Added 'Devadip' to his name after becoming a disciple of guru Sri Chimmoy.	
7/29/72	**8**	14	▲ 1. Carlos Santana & Buddy Miles! Live! [L] recorded in Hawaii's Diamond Head volcano crater	Columbia 31308
7/21/73	**14**	7	● 2. Love Devotion Surrender [I] **CARLOS SANTANA/MAHAVISHNU JOHN McLAUGHLIN**	Columbia 32034
5/14/83	**31**	4	3. Havana Moon with guests: Willie Nelson, Booker T. Jones and The Fabulous Thunderbirds	Columbia 38642
			SANTO & JOHNNY	
			Brooklyn-born guitar duo: Santo Farina (b: 10/24/37; steel guitar) and his brother Johnny (b: 4/30/41; rhythm guitar).	
1/18/60	**20**	24	1. Santo & Johnny [I] *Sleep Walk* (1)	Canadian-Am. 1001
9/26/60	**11**	9	2. Encore [I]	Canadian-Am. 1002
			SATRIANI, Joe	
			Berkeley-based rock guitarist raised in Carle Place, Long Island. Former guitar teacher of Steve Vai (with David Lee Roth and Whitesnake) and Kirk Hammett (Metallica).	
4/9/88	**29**	9	● 1. Surfing With The Alien [I]	Relativity 8193
11/25/89	**23**	14	● 2. Flying In A Blue Dream six of 18 cuts feature Joe's vocals	Relativity 1015
			SAVOY BROWN	
			British blues-rock band led by guitarist Kim Simmonds. Many personnel changes.	
11/21/70	**39**	1	1. Looking In	Parrot 71042

DATE	POS	WKS	ARTIST—RECORD TITLE	LABEL & NO.
4/15/72	34	7	2. Hellbound Train	Parrot 71052

SAYER, Leo

Born Gerard Sayer on 5/21/48 in Shoreham, England. With Patches in the early 70s. Songwriting team with David Courtney, 1972-75. Own British TV show in 1978 and again in 1983.

DATE	POS	WKS	ARTIST—RECORD TITLE	LABEL & NO.
4/19/75	16	7	1. Just A Boy *Long Tall Glasses (I Can Dance)* (9)	Warner 2836
1/22/77	10	14	▲ 2. Endless Flight *You Make Me Feel Like Dancing* (1)/*When I Need You* (1)	Warner 2962
11/5/77	37	2	3. Thunder In My Heart	Warner 3089
12/27/80	36	6	4. Living In A Fantasy *More Than I Can Say* (2)	Warner 3483

SCAGGS, Boz

Born William Royce Scaggs on 6/8/44 in Ohio; raised in Texas. Joined Steve Miller's band The Marksmen in 1959. Joined R&B band The Wigs in 1963. To Europe in 1964, toured as a folk singer. Re-joined Miller in 1967, solo since 1969. Retired from music and opened a restaurant in San Francisco, 1983-87. Made comeback in 1988.

DATE	POS	WKS	ARTIST—RECORD TITLE	LABEL & NO.
5/1/76	2(5)	53	▲ 1. Silk Degrees *Lowdown* (3)	Columbia 33920
12/10/77	11	14	▲ 2. Down Two Then Left	Columbia 34729
4/19/80	8	21	▲ 3. Middle Man	Columbia 36106
12/6/80	24	14	● 4. Hits! [G]	Columbia 36841

SCANDAL

New York-based rock band led by Patty Smyth and Zack Smith.

DATE	POS	WKS	ARTIST—RECORD TITLE	LABEL & NO.
5/28/83	39	3	1. Scandal [M]	Columbia 38194
8/18/84	17	14	▲ 2. Warrior *The Warrior* (7)	Columbia 39173

SCHAFER, Kermit

Collection of 'bloopers' by radio and TV producer Schafer. Died on 3/8/79.

DATE	POS	WKS	ARTIST—RECORD TITLE	LABEL & NO.
1/27/58	17	1	1. Pardon My Blooper! Volume 6 [C] narrator: George de Holczer	Jubilee 6

SCHIFRIN, Lalo

Born Boris Schifrin on 6/21/32 in Buenos Aires, Argentina. Pianist/conductor/composer. Scored films *Bullitt*, *Dirty Harry*, *Brubaker* and many others.
LALO SCHIFRIN AND ORCHESTRA:

DATE	POS	WKS	ARTIST—RECORD TITLE	LABEL & NO.
12/29/62	35	2	1. Bossa Nova - New Brazilian Jazz [I]	Audio Fidel. 1981

SCHNEIDER, John

Born on 4/8/54 in Mount Kisco, New York. Country singer/actor. Played "Bo Duke" on TV's "The Dukes Of Hazzard." Appeared in many TV films. Scriptwriter and director.

DATE	POS	WKS	ARTIST—RECORD TITLE	LABEL & NO.
8/8/81	37	3	1. Now Or Never	Scotti Br. 37400

SCHORY, Dick

Born on 12/13/31 in Chicago; raised in Ames, Iowa. Percussionist. Vice president of Ludwig drum company, 1957-70. Owner of Ovation Records, 1970-82. Currently runs a Chicago marketing firm.
DICK SCHORY'S NEW PERCUSSION ENSEMBLE:

DATE	POS	WKS	ARTIST—RECORD TITLE	LABEL & NO.
6/29/59	11	26	1. Music For Bang, Baa room and Harp [I]	RCA 1866

DICK SCHORY'S PERCUSSION POPS ORCHESTRA:

DATE	POS	WKS	ARTIST—RECORD TITLE	LABEL & NO.
5/11/63	13	9	2. Supercussion [I]	RCA 2613

DATE	POS	WKS	ARTIST—RECORD TITLE	LABEL & NO.
			SCORPIONS	
			German heavy-metal rock quintet: Rudolf Schenker (Michael's brother; lead guitar), Klaus Meine (lead singer), Matthias Jabs (guitar), Francis Buchholz (bass) and Herman Rarebell (drums).	
4/10/82	10	18	▲ 1. Blackout	Mercury 4039
3/24/84	6	27	▲ 2. Love At First Sting	Mercury 814981
7/20/85	14	16	▲ 3. World Wide Live [L]	Mercury 824344 [2]
5/7/88	5	22	▲ 4. Savage Amusement	Mercury 832963
			SCOTT, Tom	
			Born on 5/19/48 in Los Angeles. Pop-jazz-fusion saxophonist. Session work for Joni Mitchell, Steely Dan, Carole King and others. Composer of films and TV scores. Led the house band for TV's "Pat Sajak Show." Son of Nathan Scott, a composer of TV scores for "Dragnet," "Wagon Train," "My Three Sons" and others.	
			TOM SCOTT & THE L.A. EXPRESS:	
5/3/75	18	8	1. Tom Cat [I]	Ode 77029
			SCOTT-HERON, Gil, And Brian Jackson	
			Keyboard duo: Gil (b: 4/1/49, Chicago) is the lyricist; Brian composes the music.	
3/22/75	30	3	1. The First Minute Of A New Day featuring backup group The Midnight Band	Arista 4030
			SEA LEVEL	
			Seven-man, jazzy blues-rock band formed by three members of The Allman Brothers Band (Jai Johnny Johanson, Chuck Leavell and Lamar Williams).	
3/4/78	31	3	1. Cats On The Coast	Capricorn 0198
			SEALS & CROFTS	
			Pop duo: Jim Seals (b: 10/17/41, Sidney, Texas; guitar, fiddle, saxophone) and Dash Crofts (b: 8/14/40, Cisco, Texas; drums, mandolin, keyboards, guitar). With Dean Beard, recorded for Edmoral and Atlantic in 1957. To Los Angeles in 1958. With the Champs from 1958-65. Own group the Dawnbreakers, late 60s; entire band converted to Baha'i faith in 1969.	
10/14/72	7	33	● 1. Summer Breeze *Summer Breeze* (6)	Warner 2629
5/5/73	4	31	● 2. Diamond Girl *Diamond Girl* (6)	Warner 2699
3/23/74	14	16	● 3. Unborn Child	Warner 2761
5/3/75	30	5	● 4. I'll Play For You	Warner 2848
11/22/75	11	11	▲ 5. Greatest Hits [G]	Warner 2886
5/29/76	37	10	● 6. Get Closer *Get Closer* (6)	Warner 2907
			SEARCHERS, The	
			Liverpool, England rock quartet formed in 1960: Mike Pender and John McNally (vocals, guitars), Tony Jackson (vocals, bass) and Chris Curtis (drums). Worked as backup band for Johnny Sandon; toured England and worked Star Club in Hamburg, Germany. Left Sandon in 1962. Jackson replaced by Frank Allen in 1965. Curtis replaced by Billy Adamson in 1969. Active into the 80s.	
6/13/64	22	8	1. Meet The Searchers/Needles & Pins	Kapp 3363
			SEBASTIAN, John	
			Born on 3/17/44 in New York City. Played with the Even Dozen Jug Band as "John Benson" in 1964. Did session work for Elektra Records and toured with Mississippi John Hurt. Formed Lovin' Spoonful in 1965. Went solo in 1968.	
4/18/70	20	7	1. John B. Sebastian album also released on Reprise 6379	MGM 4654

DATE	POS	WKS	ARTIST—RECORD TITLE	LABEL & NO.
			SEDAKA, Neil	
			Born on 3/13/39 in Brooklyn. Pop singer/songwriter/pianist. Studied piano since elementary school. Formed songwriting team with lyricist Howard Greenfield while attending Lincoln High School (partnership lasted over 20 years). Recorded with The Tokens on Melba in 1956. Attended Juilliard School for classical piano. Prolific hit songwriter. Career revived in 1974 after singing with Elton John's new Rocket label.	
2/8/75	**23**	8	● 1. Sedaka's Back compilation of cuts from three albums made in Britain *Laughter In The Rain* (1)	Rocket 463
11/8/75	**16**	10	● 2. The Hungry Years *Bad Blood* (1)/*Breaking Up Is Hard To Do* (8)	Rocket 2157
5/15/76	**26**	5	3. Steppin' Out	Rocket 2195
			SEDUCTION	
			Female vocal trio from New York: Idalis Leon, April Harris and Michelle Visage. Leon left in 1990, replaced by Sinoa Loren.	
2/17/90	**36**	7	● 1. Nothing Matters Without Love *Two To Make It Right* (2)	A&M 5280
			SEEKERS, The	
			Pop-folk, Australian-born quartet: Judith Durham (b: 7/3/43; lead singer), Keith Potger (guitar), Bruce Woodley (Spanish guitar) and Athol Guy (standup bass). Potger formed the New Seekers in 1970.	
3/25/67	**10**	12	1. Georgy Girl *Georgy Girl* (2)	Capitol 2431
			SEGER, Bob	
			Born on 5/6/45 in Dearborn, Michigan; raised in Detroit. Rock singer/songwriter/ guitarist. First recorded in 1966, formed the System in 1968. Left music to attend college in 1969, returned in 1970. Formed own backing group The Silver Bullet Band in 1976: Alto Reed (horns), Robyn Robbins (keyboards), Drew Abbott (guitar), Chris Campbell (bass) and Charlie Allen Martin (drums). Various personnel changes since then; Campbell is the only remaining original member. **BOB SEGER & THE SILVER BULLET BAND:**	
6/12/76	**34**	2	▲ 1. 'Live' Bullet [L] recorded at Cobo Hall, Detroit, Michigan	Capitol 11523 [2]
1/8/77	**8**	23	▲ 2. Night Moves *Night Moves* (4)	Capitol 11557
6/3/78	**4**	33	▲ 3. Stranger in Town *Still The Same* (4)	Capitol 11698
3/15/80	**1**(6)	43	▲ 4. Against The Wind *Fire Lake* (6)/*Against The Wind* (5)	Capitol 12041
9/26/81	**3**	21	▲ 5. Nine Tonight [L] *Tryin' To Live My Life Without You* (5)	Capitol 12182 [2]
1/15/83	**5**	23	▲ 6. The Distance *Shame On The Moon* (2)	Capitol 12254
4/26/86	**3**	28	▲ 7. Like A Rock	Capitol 12398
			SERENDIPITY SINGERS, The	
			Pop-folk group organized at the University of Colorado.	
4/11/64	**11**	18	1. The Serendipity Singers *Don't Let The Rain Come Down (Crooked Little Man)* (6)	Philips 115
			SESAME STREET — see CHILDRENS section	
			SEXTON, Charlie	
			Austin, Texas rock singer/guitarist. Lead guitarist for Joe Ely's band at age 13 in 1982.	
2/15/86	**15**	13	1. Pictures For Pleasure	MCA 5629

DATE	POS	WKS	ARTIST—RECORD TITLE	LABEL & NO.
			SHALAMAR	
			Black vocal trio formed in 1977 by Don Cornelius, the producer/host of TV's "Soul Train." Consisted of vocalists/dancers Jody Watley and Jeffrey Daniels with Gerald Brown. Howard Hewett replaced Brown in early 1978. Watley and Daniels (former husband of Stephanie Mills) pursued solo careers in 1984; replaced by Delisa Davis and Micki Free. Hewett left in 1985, replaced by Sydney Justin.	
2/9/80	23	11	● 1. Big Fun	Solar 3479
			The Second Time Around (8)	
3/28/81	40	2	● 2. Three For Love	Solar 3577
5/8/82	35	3	● 3. Friends	Solar 28
9/17/83	38	2	4. The Look	Solar 60239
			SHA NA NA	
			Fifties rock & roll specialists led by John "Bowzer" Baumann (b: 9/14/47, Queens, New York). Formed at Columbia University in 1969. Own syndicated variety TV show, 1977-81. Henry Gross was a member, left in 1970. Many personnel changes.	
6/9/73	38	2	● 1. The Golden Age Of Rock 'N' Roll [L]	Kama Sutra 2073 [2]
			SHANNON	
			Brenda Shannon Greene from Washington, D.C. Began singing career at York University.	
3/10/84	32	4	● 1. Let The Music Play	Mirage 90134
			Let The Music Play (8)	
			SHANNON, Del	
			Born Charles Westover on 12/30/39 in Coopersville, Michigan. With U.S. Army "Get Up And Go" radio show in Germany. Discovered by Ann Arbor DJ/producer Ollie McLaughlin. Formed own Berlee label in 1963. Wrote "I Go To Pieces" for Peter & Gordon. To Los Angeles in 1966, production work. Died on 2/8/90 of a self-inflicted gunshot wound.	
7/6/63	12	9	1. Little Town Flirt	Big Top 1308
			Runaway (1)/*Hats Off To Larry* (5)	
			SHARPLES, Bob	
			Bandleader from Bury, Lancashire, England.	
10/16/61	11	20	1. Pass In Review [I]	London P. 4 44001
			featuring patriotic songs	
			SHAW, Robert	
			Born in Red Bluff, California in 1916. Conductor/music director. Led the Fred Waring Glee Clubs, 1938-45; organized own singing group in 1948. Music director of Atlanta Symphony Orchestra and Chorus, 1967-87.	
			THE ROBERT SHAW CHORALE:	
12/23/57	5	4	● 1. Christmas Hymns And Carols [X]	RCA 1711
12/22/58	13	3	2. Christmas Hymns And Carols [X-R]	RCA 1711
5/25/59	21	1	3. Deep River and Other Spirituals	RCA 2247
6/8/63	27	7	4. This Is My Country	RCA 2662
			with the RCA Victor Symphony Orchestra	
			SHAW, Roland	
			English bandleader.	
			THE ROLAND SHAW ORCHESTRA:	
6/19/65	38	1	1. Themes From The James Bond Thrillers [I]	London 412
			SHEARING, George	
			Born on 8/13/19 in London. Piano stylist; blind since birth. Moved to the U.S. in 1947.	
			THE GEORGE SHEARING QUINTET:	
10/6/56	20	1	1. Velvet Carpet [I]	Capitol 720

DATE	POS	WKS	ARTIST—RECORD TITLE	LABEL & NO.
10/7/57	**13**	3	2. Black Satin [I]	Capitol 858
8/25/58	**17**	2	3. Burnished Brass [I]	Capitol 1038
7/25/60	**11**	23	4. White Satin	Capitol 1334
5/12/62	**27**	9	5. Nat King Cole Sings/George Shearing Plays	Capitol 1675

SHEILA E.

Born Sheila Escovedo on 12/12/59 in San Francisco. Singer/percussionist. With father Pete Escovedo in the band Azteca in the mid-70s. Toured with Lionel Richie, recorded with Prince. Brother Peto was in Con Funk Shun.

DATE	POS	WKS	ARTIST—RECORD TITLE	LABEL & NO.
9/1/84	**28**	9	● 1. Sheila E. in The Glamorous Life *The Glamorous Life* (7)	Warner 25107

SHERMAN, Allan

Born on 11/30/24 in Chicago; died on 11/21/73. Began as a professional comedy writer for Jackie Gleason, Joe E. Lewis and others. Creator/producer of TV's "I've Got A Secret."

DATE	POS	WKS	ARTIST—RECORD TITLE	LABEL & NO.
11/10/62	**1**(2)	29	● 1. My Son, The Folk Singer [C]	Warner 1475
1/26/63	**1**(1)	19	2. My Son, The Celebrity [C]	Warner 1487
8/24/63	**1**(8)	24	3. My Son, The Nut [C] *Hello Mudduh, Hello Fudduh!* (2)	Warner 1501
5/16/64	**25**	6	4. Allan In Wonderland [C]	Warner 1539
1/2/65	**32**	5	5. For Swingin' Livers Only!	Warner 1569

SHERMAN, Bobby

Born on 7/22/44 in Santa Monica, California. Regular on TV's "Shindig"; played Jeremy Bolt on TV's "Here Come The Brides." Currently involved in TV production.

DATE	POS	WKS	ARTIST—RECORD TITLE	LABEL & NO.
11/22/69	**11**	15	● 1. Bobby Sherman *Little Woman* (3)	Metromedia 1014
4/18/70	**10**	12	● 2. Here Comes Bobby *La La La (If I Had You)* (9)/*Easy Come, Easy Go* (9)	Metromedia 1028
10/24/70	**20**	8	● 3. With Love, Bobby *Julie, Do Ya Love Me* (5)	Metromedia 1032

SHIRELLES, The

R&B "girl group" from Passaic, New Jersey. Consisted of Shirley Owens Alston (b: 6/10/41), Beverly Lee (b: 8/3/41), Doris Kenner (b: 8/2/41) and Addie "Micki" Harris (b: 1/22/40; d: 6/10/82). Formed in junior high school as the Poquellos. First recorded for Tiara in 1958. Kenner left group in 1968; returned in 1975. Alston left for solo career in 1975, recorded as "Lady Rose."

DATE	POS	WKS	ARTIST—RECORD TITLE	LABEL & NO.
2/9/63	**19**	18	1. The Shirelles Greatest Hits [G] *Will You Love Me Tomorrow* (1)/ *Dedicated To The One I Love* (3)/*Mama Said* (4)	Scepter 507

SHIRLEY, Donald

Pianist/organist. Born in Kingston, Jamaica on 1/27/27.

DATE	POS	WKS	ARTIST—RECORD TITLE	LABEL & NO.
4/2/55	**14**	4	1. Tonal Expressions [I]	Cadence 1001

SHOCKING BLUE, The

Dutch rock quartet: Mariska Veres (lead singer), Robbie van Leeuwen (guitar), Cor van Beek (drums) and Klaasje van der Wal (bass). Disbanded in 1974.

DATE	POS	WKS	ARTIST—RECORD TITLE	LABEL & NO.
3/7/70	**31**	3	1. The Shocking Blue *Venus* (1)	Colossus 1000

DATE	POS	WKS	ARTIST—RECORD TITLE	LABEL & NO.
			SILVER CONVENTION	
			German studio disco act assembled by producer Michael Kunze and writer/arranger Silvester Levay. Female vocal trio formed in 1976 consisting of Penny McLean, Ramona Wolf and Linda Thompson.	
10/25/75	**10**	10	● 1. Save Me	Midland Int. 1129
			Fly, Robin, Fly (1)	
5/1/76	**13**	10	2. Silver Convention	Midland Int. 1369
			Get Up And Boogie (That's Right) (2)	
			SIMMONS, Gene	
			Born Gene Klein on 8/25/49 in Haifa, Israel. Bass guitarist of Kiss. Appeared in films *Runaway* (1984) and *Trick Or Treat* (1986).	
11/11/78	**22**	12	▲ 1. Gene Simmons	Casablanca 7120
			SIMON, Carly	
			Born on 6/25/45 in New York City. Pop vocalist/songwriter. Father is co-founder of Simon & Schuster publishing. Won the 1971 Best New Artist Grammy Award. Married James Taylor on 11/3/72; separated in 1982 and divorced a few years later.	
7/3/71	**30**	7	1. Carly Simon	Elektra 74082
			That's The Way I've Always Heard It Should Be (10)	
2/12/72	**30**	5	● 2. Anticipation	Elektra 75016
12/23/72	**1**(5)	23	● 3. No Secrets	Elektra 75049
			You're So Vain (1)	
2/9/74	**3**	16	● 4. Hotcakes	Elektra 1002
			Mockingbird (5) with James Taylor	
5/10/75	**10**	9	5. Playing Possum	Elektra 1033
12/20/75	**17**	9	● 6. The Best Of Carly Simon [G]	Elektra 1048
7/4/76	**29**	4	7. Another Passenger	Elektra 1064
5/13/78	**10**	17	▲ 8. Boys In The Trees	Elektra 128
			You Belong To Me (6)	
11/1/80	**36**	4	9. Come Upstairs	Warner 3443
8/29/87	**25**	10	▲ 10. Coming Around Again	Arista 8443
			SIMON, Paul	
			Born on 11/5/41 in Newark, New Jersey; raised in Queens, New York. Vocalist/composer/guitarist. Met Art Garfunkel in high school, recorded together as Tom & Jerry in 1957. Worked as Jerry Landis, Paul Kane, Harrison Gregory and True Taylor in the early 60s. To England from 1963-64. Returned to the U.S. and recorded first album with Garfunkel in 1965. Went solo in 1971. Married to actress Carrie Fisher from 1983-85. In the films *Annie Hall* and *One-Trick Pony*.	
2/19/72	**4**	18	▲ 1. Paul Simon	Columbia 30750
			Mother And Child Reunion (4)	
6/9/73	**2**(2)	24	▲ 2. There Goes Rhymin' Simon	Columbia 32280
			Kodachrome (2)/*Loves Me Like A Rock* (2)	
4/13/74	**33**	3	● 3. Paul Simon In Concert/Live Rhymin' [L]	Columbia 32855
11/1/75	**1**(1)	29	● 4. Still Crazy After All These Years	Columbia 33540
			1975 Grammy winner: Album of the Year	
			My Little Town (9) Simon & Garfunkel/	
			50 Ways To Leave Your Lover (1)	
12/17/77	**18**	9	▲ 5. Greatest Hits, Etc. [G]	Columbia 35032
			Slip Slidin' Away (5)	
9/6/80	**12**	13	● 6. One-Trick Pony [S]	Warner 3472
			Paul starred in the film	
			Late In The Evening (6)	
12/3/83	**35**	8	7. Hearts And Bones	Warner 23942

DATE	POS	WKS	ARTIST—RECORD TITLE	LABEL & NO.
9/27/86	3	53	▲ 8. Graceland 1986 Grammy winner: Album of the Year; South African-flavored tunes written by Simon, backed by a South African ensemble	Warner 25447
			SIMON AND GARFUNKEL Folk-rock duo from New York City: Paul Simon and Art Garfunkel. Recorded as Tom & Jerry in 1957. Duo split in 1964; Simon was working solo in England, Garfunkel was in graduate school. They re-formed in 1965 and stayed together until 1971. Reunited briefly in 1981 for national tour. Inducted into the Rock and Roll Hall of Fame in 1990.	
2/12/66	30	3	● 1. Wednesday Morning, 3 AM contains original unmixed version of *The Sounds Of Silence*	Columbia 9049
4/9/66	21	33	● 2. Sounds of Silence *The Sounds Of Silence* (1)/*I Am A Rock* (3)	Columbia 9269
11/19/66	4	60	▲ 3. Parsley, Sage, Rosemary and Thyme *Homeward Bound* (5)	Columbia 9363
3/23/68	1(9)	47	● 4. The Graduate [S] includes four previously released Simon & Garfunkel songs; the two *Mrs. Robinson* cuts are not the hit versions	Columbia 3180
5/25/68	1(7)	40	▲ 5. Bookends side 2: hit singles previously unavailable on an album *Mrs. Robinson* (1)	Columbia 9529
2/28/70	1(10)	24	▲ 6. Bridge Over Troubled Water 1970 Grammy winner: Album of the Year *The Boxer* (7)/*Bridge Over Troubled Water* (1)/ *Cecilia* (4)	Columbia 9914
7/8/72	5	22	▲ 7. Simon And Garfunkel's Greatest Hits [G]	Columbia 31350
3/13/82	6	11	▲ 8. The Concert In Central Park [L] recorded in New York City's Central Park on 9/19/81	Warner 3654 [2]
			SIMONE, Nina Born Eunice Waymon on 2/21/33 in Tryon, South Carolina. Jazz-influenced vocalist/ pianist/composer. Attended Juilliard School of Music in New York City. Devoted more time to political activism in the 70s, infrequent recording.	
3/6/61	23	1	1. Nina At Newport [L]	Colpix 412
			SIMPLE MINDS Scottish rock group; nucleus of band: Jim Kerr (lead singer; married to Chrissie Hynde of The Pretenders), Michael MacNeil (keyboards), Charles Burchill (guitar), Mel Gaynor (drums) and John Giblin (bass).	
11/16/85	10	27	● 1. Once Upon A Time *Alive & Kicking* (3)	A&M 5092
			SIMPLY RED British pop sextet led by vocalist Mick "Red" Hucknall. Includes Tony Bowers, Chris Joyce, Fritz McIntyre, Sylvan Richardson and Tim Kellett. Richardson left in 1988.	
5/31/86	16	28	▲ 1. Picture Book *Holding Back The Years* (1)	Elektra 60452
4/18/87	31	5	2. Men And Women	Elektra 60727
6/17/89	22	14	● 3. A New Flame *If You Don't Know Me By Now* (1)	Elektra 60828

DATE	POS	WKS	ARTIST—RECORD TITLE	LABEL & NO.
			SINATRA, Frank	
			Born Francis Albert Sinatra on 12/12/15 in Hoboken, New Jersey. With Harry James from 1939-40, first recorded for Brunswick in 1939; with Tommy Dorsey, 1940-42. Went solo in late 1942 and charted 40 top 10 hits through 1954. Appeared in many films from 1941 on. Won an Oscar for the film *From Here To Eternity* in 1953. Own TV show in 1957. Own Reprise record company, 1961, sold to Warner Bros. in 1963. Announced his retirement in 1970, but made comeback in 1973. Regarded by many as the greatest popular singer of the 20th century.	
5/28/55	**2**(18)	33	1. in the Wee Small Hours	Capitol 581
3/31/56	**2**(1)	50	● 2. songs for Swingin' Lovers!	Capitol 653
12/22/56	**8**	17	● 3. This is Sinatra! [G]	Capitol 768
			Young At Heart (2) 1954/*Three Coins In The Fountain* (7) 1954/ *Learnin' The Blues* (1)/*Love And Marriage* (5)/ *(Love Is) The Tender Trap* (7)	
3/2/57	**5**	14	4. Close To You	Capitol 789
			featuring The Hollywood String Quartet	
5/27/57	**2**(1)	36	5. a Swingin' Affair!	Capitol 803
9/23/57	**3**	21	6. Where are you?	Capitol 855
11/11/57	**2**(1)	27	7. Pal Joey [S]	Capitol 912
			Frank plays Joey Evans and sings on six of the tracks, including "The Lady Is A Tramp"	
12/30/57	**18**	2	● 8. a Jolly Christmas from Frank Sinatra [X]	Capitol 894
2/3/58	**1**(5)	50	9. Come fly with me	Capitol 920
4/28/58	**8**	7	10. This Is Sinatra, Volume Two [G]	Capitol 982
			Hey! Jealous Lover (3)	
6/2/58	**12**	1	11. The Frank Sinatra Story [K]	Columbia 6 [2]
9/29/58	**1**(5)	55	● 12. Frank Sinatra sings for Only The Lonely	Capitol 1053
2/9/59	**2**(5)	52	● 13. Come Dance With Me!	Capitol 1069
			1959 Grammy winner: Album of the Year	
6/1/59	**8**	11	14. Look to Your Heart [K]	Capitol 1164
8/31/59	**2**(2)	34	15. No One Cares	Capitol 1221
8/22/60	**1**(9)	35	● 16. Nice 'n' Easy	Capitol 1417
2/13/61	**3**	22	17. Sinatra's Swingin' Session!!!	Capitol 1491
2/13/61	**18**	36	18. Sinatra and Swingin' Brass	Reprise 1005
4/10/61	**4**	27	19. All The Way [G]	Capitol 1538
			All The Way (2)/*Witchcraft* (6)	
5/8/61	**4**	20	20. Ring-A-Ding Ding!	Reprise 1001
			the first album for Sinatra's own record company	
8/21/61	**8**	12	21. Come Swing With Me!	Capitol 1594
8/28/61	**6**	18	22. Sinatra Swings	Reprise 1002
11/20/61	**3**	23	23. I Remember Tommy...	Reprise 1003
			songs popularized by Tommy Dorsey	
3/17/62	**8**	20	24. Sinatra & Strings	Reprise 1004
5/5/62	**19**	23	25. Point Of No Return	Capitol 1676
8/25/62	**15**	9	26. Sinatra Sings...of love and things [K]	Capitol 1729
11/24/62	**25**	8	27. All Alone	Reprise 1007
2/9/63	**5**	22	28. Sinatra-Basie	Reprise 1008
			FRANK SINATRA/COUNT BASIE	
7/6/63	**6**	11	29. The Concert Sinatra	Reprise 1009
10/19/63	**8**	17	● 30. Sinatra's Sinatra	Reprise 1010
			newly recorded Sinatra favorites	

DATE	POS	WKS	ARTIST—RECORD TITLE	LABEL & NO.
4/25/64	**10**	16	31. Days Of Wine And Roses, Moon River, and other academy award winners	Reprise 1011
9/12/64	**13**	15	32. It Might As Well Be Swing **FRANK SINATRA/COUNT BASIE**	Reprise 1012
2/6/65	**19**	12	33. Softly, As I Leave You	Reprise 1013
7/17/65	**9**	32	34. Sinatra '65	Reprise 6167
9/25/65	**5**	46	● 35. September Of My Years *1965 Grammy winner: Album of the Year*	Reprise 1014
1/15/66	**9**	20	● 36. A Man And His Music [K] *1966 Grammy winner: Album of the Year;* *an anthology of Sinatra's career, narrated and sung by him*	Reprise 1016 [2]
2/19/66	**30**	3	37. My Kind Of Broadway	Reprise 1015
6/18/66	**34**	2	38. Moonlight Sinatra	Reprise 1018
7/2/66	**1**(1)	43	▲ 39. Strangers In The Night *Strangers In The Night (1)*	Reprise 1017
9/10/66	**9**	15	● 40. Sinatra At The Sands [L] *with Count Basie & The Orchestra*	Reprise 1019 [2]
1/21/67	**6**	22	● 41. That's Life *That's Life (4)*	Reprise 1020
5/13/67	**19**	6	42. Francis Albert Sinatra & Antonio Carlos Jobim *Jobim is a Brazilian songwriter/guitarist/vocalist*	Reprise 1021
9/30/67	**24**	9	43. Frank Sinatra *Somethin' Stupid (1) with Nancy Sinatra*	Reprise 1022
1/18/69	**18**	7	● 44. Cycles	Reprise 1027
5/17/69	**11**	8	● 45. My Way	Reprise 1029
9/27/69	**30**	5	46. A Man Alone & Other Songs of Rod McKuen	Reprise 1030
11/17/73	**13**	10	● 47. Ol' Blue Eyes Is Back	Reprise 2155
1/4/75	**37**	2	48. Sinatra - The Main Event Live [L] *recorded at New York's Madison Square Garden;* *with Woody Herman & The Young Thundering Herd*	Reprise 2207
5/3/80	**17**	12	● 49. Trilogy: Past, Present, Future	Reprise 2300 [3]
			SINATRA, Nancy	
			Born on 6/8/40 in Jersey City, New Jersey. First child of Frank and Nancy Sinatra. Moved to Los Angeles while a child. Made national TV debut with father and Elvis Presley in 1959. Married to Tommy Sands, 1960-65. Appeared on "Hullabaloo," "American Bandstand," and own specials, mid-60s. In films *For Those Who Think Young*, *Get Yourself A College Girl*, *The Oscar* and *Speedway*.	
3/26/66	**5**	24	● 1. Boots *These Boots Are Made For Walkin' (1)*	Reprise 6202
3/18/67	**18**	6	2. Sugar *Sugar Town (5)*	Reprise 6239
3/16/68	**37**	4	3. Movin' With Nancy [TV] *guests: Frank Sinatra, Dean Martin and Lee Hazlewood*	Reprise 6277
			NANCY SINATRA & LEE HAZLEWOOD:	
5/25/68	**13**	18	● 4. Nancy & Lee	Reprise 6273
			SINGING NUN, The	
			Sister Luc-Gabrielle (real name: Jeanine Deckers) from the Fichermont, Belgium convent. Recorded under the name Soeur Sourire ("Sister Smile"). Committed suicide on 3/31/85 (age 52).	
11/23/63	**1**(10)	22	● 1. The Singing Nun [F] *Dominique (1)*	Philips 203

DATE	POS	WKS	ARTIST—RECORD TITLE	LABEL & NO.
			SISTER SLEDGE	
			Sisters Debra, Joan, Kim and Kathie Sledge from North Philadelphia. First recorded as Sisters Sledge for Money Back label in 1971. Worked as backup vocalists. Began producing their own albums in 1981.	
3/24/79	**3**	19	▲ 1. We Are Family	Cotillion 5209
			He's The Greatest Dancer (9)/*We Are Family* (2)	
3/29/80	**31**	5	2. Love Somebody Today	Cotillion 16012
			SKID ROW	
			New York hard-rock quintet: Toronto native Sebastian "Bach" Bierk (vocals), Rachel Bolan (bass), Dave Sabo (guitar), Scott Hill (guitar) and Rob Affuso (drums).	
3/18/89	**6**	57	▲ 1. Skid Row	Atlantic 81936
			18 And Life (4)/*I Remember You* (6)	
			SKYY	
			Brooklyn R&B-pop-funk octet. Vocals by sisters Denise, Delores and Bonnie Dunning. Organized by Randy Muller, former leader of Brass Construction.	
2/6/82	**18**	11	● 1. Skyy Line	Salsoul 8548
			SLADE	
			English hard-rock quartet: Noddy Holder (b: 6/15/50; lead singer), David Hill (guitar), Jim Lea (bass, keyboards) and Don Powell (drums).	
6/16/84	**33**	4	1. Keep Your Hands Off My Power Supply	CBS Assoc. 39336
			SLATKIN, Felix	
			St. Louis native. Virtuoso violinist/conductor/composer/arranger. Worked with many film and record companies. Died on 2/9/63 (age 47).	
5/11/63	**20**	7	1. Our Winter Love [I]	Liberty 7287
			SLAUGHTER	
			Hard-rock quartet led by vocalist Mark Slaughter who, with bandmate Dana Strum (bass), was a member of the Vinnie Vincent Invasion.	
4/14/90	**18**	28+	● 1. Stick It To Ya	Chrysalis 21702
			SLAVE	
			Funk band from Dayton, Ohio formed by Steve Washington (trumpet) in 1975. Studio vocalist Steve Arrington was a member from 1978-82. Numerous personnel changes.	
6/18/77	**22**	12	● 1. Slave	Cotillion 9914
			SLEDGE, Percy	
			Born in 1941 in Leighton, Alabama. Worked local clubs with Esquires Combo until going solo.	
8/6/66	**37**	2	1. When A Man Loves A Woman	Atlantic 8125
			When A Man Loves A Woman (1)	
			SLICK, Grace	
			Born Grace Wing on 10/30/39 in Chicago. Female lead singer of Jefferson Airplane, Jefferson Starship and Starship.	
4/26/80	**32**	4	1. Dreams	RCA 3544
			SLICK RICK	
			Ricky Walters, born to Jamaican parents in South Wimbledon, London. Moved to the U.S. at age 14. Attended New York's High School of Music & Art. Teamed with Doug E. Fresh, 1984-85; known as "MC Ricky D."	
5/27/89	**31**	5	▲ 1. The Great Adventures Of Slick Rick	Def Jam 40513

DATE	POS	WKS	ARTIST—RECORD TITLE	LABEL & NO.
			SLY & THE FAMILY STONE	
			San Francisco interracial "psychedelic soul" group formed by Sylvester "Sly Stone" Stewart (b: 3/15/44, Dallas; lead singer, keyboards), Sly's brother Freddie Stone (guitar), Cynthia Robinson (trumpet), Jerry Martini (saxophone), Sly's sister Rosie Stone (piano, vocals), Larry Graham (bass) and Gregg Errico (drums). Sly recorded gospel at age four. Producer and writer for Bobby Freeman, the Mojo Men, the Beau Brummels. Formed own groups, The Stoners in 1966 and the Family Stone in 1967. Worked Woodstock Festival in 1969. Career waned in the mid-70s. Worked with George Clinton in 1982. Graham formed Graham Central Station in 1973.	
5/3/69	**13**	24	▲ 1. Stand! *Everyday People* (1)	Epic 26456
11/14/70	**2**(1)	27	▲ 2. Greatest Hits [G] *Hot Fun In The Summertime* (2)/ *Thank You (Falettinme Be Mice Elf Agin)* (1)	Epic 30325
11/13/71	**1**(2)	18	● 3. There's A Riot Goin' On *Family Affair* (1)	Epic 30986
7/7/73	**7**	16	● 4. Fresh	Epic 32134
8/17/74	**15**	7	● 5. Small Talk	Epic 32930
			SLY FOX	
			Black-and-white duo: Gary "Mudbone" Cooper (P-Funk) and Michael Camacho.	
4/26/86	**31**	4	1. Let's Go All The Way *Let's Go All The Way* (7)	Capitol 12367
			SMITH	
			Los Angeles-based rock quintet fronted by St. Louis blues rocker Gayle McCormick.	
11/1/69	**17**	11	1. a group called Smith *Baby It's You* (5)	Dunhill 50056
			SMITH, Jimmy	
			Born on 12/8/25 in Norristown, Pennsylvania. Pioneer jazz organist. Won Major Bowes Amateur Show in 1934. With father (James, Sr.) in song-and-dance team, 1942. With Don Gardner & The Sonotones, recorded for Bruce in 1953. Smith first recorded with own trio for Blue Note in 1956. Began doing vocals in 1966.	
4/21/62	**28**	5	1. Midnight Special [I] with Stanley Turrentine (sax) and Kenny Burrell (guitar)	Blue Note 84078
7/21/62	**10**	20	2. Bashin' [I]	Verve 8474
3/23/63	**14**	8	3. Back At The Chicken Shack [I] with Stanley Turrentine and Kenny Burrell	Blue Note 84117
5/25/63	**11**	15	4. Hobo Flats [I]	Verve 8544
11/30/63	**25**	7	5. Any Number Can Win [I]	Verve 8552
5/23/64	**16**	15	6. Who's Afraid Of Virginia Woolf? [I]	Verve 8583
10/31/64	**12**	13	7. The Cat [I]	Verve 8587
7/10/65	**35**	4	8. Monster [I]	Verve 8618
10/30/65	**15**	10	9. Organ Grinder Swing [I] featuring Kenny Burrell (guitar) and Grady Tate (drums)	Verve 8628
5/28/66	**28**	10	10. Get My Mojo Workin' [I]	Verve 8641
			SMITH, Kate	
			Born on 5/1/07 in Greenville, Alabama; died on 6/17/86. Tremendously popular soprano who was for years one of the most-listened-to of all radio singers. Later hosted own TV variety series, 1951-52, 1960. Kate introduced the classic Irving Berlin hit "God Bless America."	
4/16/66	**36**	5	1. How Great Thou Art	RCA 3445

DATE	POS	WKS	ARTIST—RECORD TITLE	LABEL & NO.
			SMITH, Keely	
			Born Dorothy Smith on 3/9/32 in Norfolk, Virginia. Jazz-styled vocalist. Married to singer/trumpeter/bandleader Louis Prima, 1952-61.	
6/23/58	12	4	1. Las Vegas Prima Style * [L]	Capitol 1010
10/20/58	14	8	2. Politely!	Capitol 1073
5/25/59	23	4	3. Swingin' Pretty	Capitol 1145
5/25/59	37	1	4. Hey Boy! Hey Girl! * [S]	Capitol 1160
			*LOUIS PRIMA & KEELY SMITH	
			Louis and Keely portray Las Vegas entertainers in the film	
1/4/60	40	1	5. Be My Love	Dot 3241
			SMITH, O.C.	
			Born Ocie Lee Smith on 6/21/36 in Mansfield, Louisiana. To Los Angeles in 1939. Sang while in U.S. Air Force from 1953-57. First recorded for Cadence in 1956. With Count Basie from 1961-63.	
11/23/68	19	10	1. Hickory Holler Revisited	Columbia 9680
			Little Green Apples (2)	
			SMITH, Patti	
			Born on 12/31/46 in Chicago; raised in New Jersey. Poet-turned-punk rocker. Married Fred "Sonic" Smith of the MC5.	
			PATTI SMITH GROUP:	
5/27/78	20	8	1. Easter	Arista 4171
5/26/79	18	7	2. Wave	Arista 4221
			produced by Todd Rundgren	
			SMITH, Rex	
			Born in Jacksonville, Florida. Vocalist/actor. Starred in several Broadway musicals and in TV film *Sooner Or Later*. Appeared in the films *Pirates Of Penzance* and *Streethawk*.	
5/12/79	19	8	● 1. Sooner Or Later	Columbia 35813
			You Take My Breath Away (10)	
			SMITH, Sammi	
			Born on 8/5/43 in Orange, California; raised in Oklahoma. Country singer.	
3/27/71	33	4	1. Help Me Make It Through The Night	Mega 1000
			Help Me Make It Through The Night (8)	
			SMOTHERS BROTHERS, The	
			Comedians Tom (b: 2/2/37; guitar) and Dick Smothers (b: 11/20/39; standup bass), both born in New York City. Hosts of their own TV comedy variety series from 1967-69. Own summer variety series, 1970; 1988-89.	
11/24/62	26	11	● 1. The Two Sides Of The Smothers Brothers [C]	Mercury 20675
			side 1: comedy; side 2: serious singing	
5/4/63	27	22	● 2. (Think Ethnic!) [C]	Mercury 20777
1/4/64	13	10	3. Curb Your Tongue, Knave! [C]	Mercury 20862
6/20/64	23	7	4. It Must Have Been Something I Said! [C]	Mercury 20904
1/29/66	39	2	5. Mom Always Liked You Best! [C]	Mercury 21051
			SNIFF 'N' THE TEARS	
			British rock group led by Paul Roberts (vocals) and Loz Netto (guitar).	
10/6/79	35	3	1. Fickle Heart	Atlantic 19242

DATE	POS	WKS	ARTIST—RECORD TITLE	LABEL & NO.
			SNOW, Phoebe	
			Born Phoebe Laub on 7/17/52 in New York City; raised in New Jersey. Vocalist/ guitarist/songwriter. Began performing in Greenwich Village in the early 70s.	
11/16/74	**4**	22	● 1. Phoebe Snow *Poetry Man* (5)	Shelter 2109
2/21/76	**13**	10	● 2. Second Childhood	Columbia 33952
11/27/76	**29**	7	3. It Looks Like Snow	Columbia 34387
			SNYDER, Terry — see LIGHT, Enoch	
			SOFT CELL	
			British electro-rock duo: Marc Almond (vocals) and David Ball (synthesizer). Almond began solo career in late 1988.	
3/20/82	**22**	18	1. Non-Stop Erotic Cabaret *Tainted Love* (8)	Sire 3647
			SONNY & CHER	
			Husband-and-wife duo: Sonny and Cher Bono. Session singers for Phil Spector. First recorded as Caesar & Cleo for Vault in 1963. Married in 1963; divorced in 1974. In the films *Good Times* (1966) and *Chastity* (1968). Own CBS-TV variety series from 1971-74. Brief TV reunion in 1975. Each recorded solo.	
9/4/65	**2**(8)	25	● 1. Look At Us *I Got You Babe* (1)	Atco 177
6/4/66	**34**	6	2. The Wondrous World Of Sonny & Cher	Atco 183
9/2/67	**23**	10	3. The Best of Sonny & Cher [G]	Atco 219
12/4/71	**35**	2	● 4. Sonny & Cher Live [L]	Kapp 3654
3/11/72	**14**	15	● 5. All I Ever Need Is You *All I Ever Need Is You* (7)/*A Cowboys Work Is Never Done* (8)	Kapp 3660
			S.O.S. BAND, The	
			Funk-R&B band originally known as Santa Monica while it was the house band at Atlanta's Regal Room. Lead singer/keyboardist Mary Davis went solo in 1986, various personnel changes since. Name means "Sounds Of Success."	
7/12/80	**12**	11	● 1. S.O.S. *Take Your Time (Do It Right)* (3)	Tabu 36332
			SOUL, David	
			Born David Solberg on 8/28/43 in Chicago. Ken Hutchinson of TV's "Starsky & Hutch" (1975-79). Began career as a folk singer and appeared several times on "The Merv Griffin Show" as "The Covered Man" (wore a ski mask).	
4/23/77	**40**	1	1. David Soul *Don't Give Up On Us* (1)	Private S. 2019
			SOUL II SOUL	
			South London soul outfit led by the duo of Beresford "Jazzie B." Romeo and Nellee Hooper. Features female vocalists Caron Wheeler, Do'Reen and Rose Windross and musical backing by the Reggae Philharmonic Orchestra. Wheeler left in 1990.	
7/29/89	**14**	36	▲ 1. Keep On Movin' *Back To Life* (4)	Virgin 91267
6/23/90	**21**	8	● 2. Vol II - 1990 - A New Decade	Virgin 91367
			SOUNDS ORCHESTRAL	
			English; Johnny Pearson on piano.	
6/19/65	**11**	9	1. Cast Your Fate To The Wind [I] *Cast Your Fate To The Wind* (10)	Parkway 7046

DATE	POS	WKS	ARTIST—RECORD TITLE	LABEL & NO.
			SOUTHER, HILLMAN, FURAY BAND, The	
			Country-rock sextet formed as a supergroup featuring veterans J.D. Souther, Chris Hillman and Richie Furay.	
8/3/74	**11**	11	● 1. The Souther, Hillman, Furay Band	Asylum 1006
7/26/75	**39**	1	2. Trouble In Paradise	Asylum 1036
			SPANDAU BALLET	
			English quintet: Tony Hadley (lead singer), Steve Norman (sax), John Keeble (drums) and brothers Gary (guitar) and Martin (bass) Kemp. The Kemps starred in the 1990 film *The Krays*.	
10/8/83	**19**	8	1. True *True* (4)	Chrysalis 41403
			SPINNERS	
			R&B vocal group from Ferndale High School near Detroit, originally known as the Domingoes. Discovered by producer/lead singer of The Moonglows, Harvey Fuqua, and became the Spinners in 1961. First recorded on Fuqua's Tri-Phi label. Many personnel changes. G.C. Cameron was lead singer from 1968-72. 1972 hit lineup included Phillippe Wynne (tenor; d: 7/14/84), Bobby Smith (tenor), Billy Henderson (tenor), Henry Fambrough (baritone) and Pervis Jackson (bass). Wynne left group in 1977 and toured with Parliament/Funkadelic; replaced by John Edwards.	
5/12/73	**14**	11	● 1. Spinners *I'll Be Around* (3)/*Could It Be I'm Falling In Love* (4)	Atlantic 7256
4/6/74	**16**	14	● 2. Mighty Love	Atlantic 7296
12/28/74	**9**	14	● 3. New And Improved *Then Came You* (1) with Dionne Warwick	Atlantic 18118
8/16/75	**8**	16	● 4. Pick Of The Litter *They Just Can't Stop It (The Games People Play)* (5)	Atlantic 18141
1/17/76	**20**	9	5. Spinners Live! [L]	Atlantic 910 [2]
8/14/76	**25**	9	● 6. Happiness Is Being With The Detroit Spinners *The Rubberband Man* (2)	Atlantic 18181
4/9/77	**26**	4	7. Yesterday, Today & Tomorrow	Atlantic 19100
3/22/80	**32**	4	8. Dancin' And Lovin' *Working My Way Back To You/Forgive Me, Girl* (2)	Atlantic 19256
			SPIRIT	
			Los Angeles eclectic rock group: Jay Ferguson (lead singer), Mark Andes (bass), Ed Cassidy (drums), Randy California (guitar) and John Locke (keyboards). Ferguson and Andes left to form Jo Jo Gunne in mid-1971. Andes became an original member of Firefall in 1975 and later joined Heart in 1983.	
8/31/68	**31**	16	1. Spirit	Ode 44004
2/8/69	**22**	12	2. The Family That Plays Together	Ode 44014
			SPLIT ENZ	
			Sextet from New Zealand, led by brothers Tim and Neil Finn. Neil was later a member of Crowded House.	
11/15/80	**40**	2	1. True Colours record pressed in laser-etched vinyl	A&M 4822
			SPRINGFIELD, Rick	
			Born on 8/23/49 in Sydney, Australia. Singer/actor/songwriter. With top Australian teen-idol band Zoot before going solo in 1972. Turned to acting in the late 70s, played Noah Drake on the TV soap opera "General Hospital" in the early 80s. Starred in the film *Hard To Hold* in 1984.	
9/30/72	**35**	4	1. Beginnings	Capitol 11047
6/27/81	**7**	38	▲ 2. Working Class Dog *Jessie's Girl* (1)/*I've Done Everything For You* (8)	RCA 3697

DATE	POS	WKS	ARTIST—RECORD TITLE		LABEL & NO.
4/3/82	**2**(3)	15	▲ 3. Success Hasn't Spoiled Me Yet *Don't Talk To Strangers* (2)		RCA 4125
5/7/83	**12**	24	▲ 4. Living in Oz *Affair Of The Heart* (9)		RCA 4660
4/21/84	**16**	9	▲ 5. Hard To Hold Rick starred in the film *Love Somebody* (5)	[S]	RCA 4935
5/11/85	**21**	11	● 6. Tao		RCA 5370
			SPRINGSTEEN, Bruce		
			Born on 9/23/49 in Freehold, New Jersey. Rock singer/songwriter/guitarist. Worked local clubs in New Jersey and Greenwich Village, mid-60s. Own E-Street Band in 1973, consisted of Clarence Clemons (saxophone), David Sancious and Danny Federici (keyboards), Gary Tallent (bass) and Vini Lopez (drums). Sancious and Lopez replaced by Roy Bittan and Max Weinberg. Miami Steve Van Zandt (guitar) joined group in 1975. Wrote Earth Band's "Blinded By The Light" and the Pointer Sisters' "Fire." After *Born To Run*, a court injunction prevented the release of any new albums until 1978. Married to model/actress Julianne Phillips from 1985-89. Appeared in the 1987 film *Hail! Hail! Rock 'N' Roll*. Split from the E-Street Band in November of 1989. "The Boss" is one of America's top rock stars of the 80s.		
9/20/75	**3**	12	▲ 1. Born To Run		Columbia 33795
6/17/78	**5**	17	▲ 2. Darkness on the Edge of Town		Columbia 35318
11/1/80	**1**(4)	22	▲ 3. The River *Hungry Heart* (5)		Columbia 36854 [2]
10/9/82	**3**	11	▲ 4. Nebraska recorded on a four-track cassette recorder at home		Columbia 38358
6/23/84	**1**(7)	96	▲ 5. Born In The U.S.A. *Dancing In The Dark* (2)/*Cover Me* (7)/ *Born In The U.S.A.* (9)/*I'm On Fire* (6)/*Glory Days* (5)/ *I'm Goin' Down* (9)/*My Hometown* (6)		Columbia 38653
11/29/86	**1**(7)	15	▲ 6. Bruce Springsteen & The E Street Band Live/1975-85 [L] contains 40 songs and a 36-page color booklet with lyrics *War* (8)		Columbia 40558 [5]
10/24/87	**1**(1)	33	▲ 7. Tunnel of Love *Brilliant Disguise* (5)/*Tunnel Of Love* (9)		Columbia 40999
			SPYRO GYRA		
			Jazz-pop band formed in 1975 in Buffalo, New York. Led by saxophonist Jay Beckenstein (b: 5/14/51).		
6/9/79	**27**	11	▲ 1. Morning Dance	[I]	Infinity 9004
4/5/80	**19**	8	● 2. Catching The Sun	[I]	MCA 5108
			SQUEEZE		
			English pop-rock group led by Chris Difford and Glenn Tilbrook. Originally known as UK Squeeze due to confusion with American band Tight Squeeze. Paul Carrack (Ace, Mike + The Mechanics) was lead singer of fluctuating lineup in 1981.		
6/26/82	**32**	4	1. Sweets From A Stranger		A&M 4899
11/21/87	**36**	7	2. Babylon And On		A&M 5161
			SQUIER, Billy		
			Born on 5/12/50 in Wellesley Hills, Massachusetts. Hard-rock singer/songwriter/ guitarist.		
6/20/81	**5**	38	▲ 1. Don't Say No		Capitol 12146
8/21/82	**5**	29	▲ 2. Emotions in Motion		Capitol 12217
8/11/84	**11**	14	▲ 3. Signs of Life		Capitol 12361

DATE	POS	WKS	ARTIST—RECORD TITLE	LABEL & NO.
			STAFFORD, Jo	
			Born on 11/12/20 in Coalinga, California. Member of Tommy Dorsey's vocal group the Pied Pipers, 1940-42. Married to orchestra leader Paul Weston.	
12/29/56	13	8	1. Ski Trails with husband Paul Weston (conductor) and the Norman Luboff Choir	Columbia 910
			STANLEY, Paul	
			Born Paul Stanley Eisen on 1/20/52 in Queens, New York. Rhythm guitarist of Kiss.	
12/16/78	40	3	▲ 1. Paul Stanley	Casablanca 7123
			STANSFIELD, Lisa	
			Lead singer of Blue Zone from Roachdale, England. Featured vocalist on Coldcut's 1989 club hit "People Hold On."	
3/17/90	9	25	▲ 1. Affection *All Around The World* (3)	Arista 8554
			STAPLE SINGERS, The	
			Family soul group consisting of Roebuck "Pop" Staples (b: 12/28/15, Winoma, Mississippi), with his son Pervis (who left in 1971) and daughters Cleotha, Yvonne and lead singer Mavis Staples. Roebuck was a blues guitarist in his teens, later with the Golden Trumpets gospel group. Moved to Chicago in 1935. Formed own gospel group in the early 50s. First recorded for United in 1953. Mavis recorded solo, early 70s.	
4/15/72	19	12	1. Bealtitude: Respect Yourself *I'll Take You There* (1)	Stax 3002
11/29/75	20	8	2. Let's Do It Again　　　　　　[S] *Let's Do It Again* (1)	Curtom 5005
			STARGARD	
			Disco trio: Rochelle Runnells, Debra Anderson and Janice Williams. Appeared as The Diamonds in film *Sgt. Pepper's Lonely Hearts Club Band*.	
3/18/78	26	6	1. Stargard	MCA 2321
			STARLAND VOCAL BAND	
			Washington, D.C.-based pop quartet: Bill and wife Taffy Danoff, John Carroll and Margot Chapman. Bill and Taffy had fronted Fat City folk quintet. Bill co-wrote "Take Me Home, Country Roads" with friend John Denver. Denver owned Windsong record label. Won the 1976 Best New Artist Grammy Award.	
7/10/76	20	10	1. Starland Vocal Band *Afternoon Delight* (1)	Windsong 1351
			STARR, Ringo	
			Born Richard Starkey on 7/7/40 in Liverpool, England. Ringo joined The Beatles following ousting of drummer Pete Best in 1962. First solo album in 1970. Acted in many films including: *The Magic Christian*, *200 Motels* and *Cave Man*.	
5/23/70	22	6	1. Sentimental Journey	Apple 3365
11/17/73	2(2)	19	● 2. Ringo featuring backing by the other three Beatles *Photograph* (1)/*You're Sixteen* (1)/*Oh My My* (5)	Apple 3413
12/7/74	8	12	● 3. Goodnight Vienna guests: John Lennon and Elton John *Only You* (6)/*No No Song* (3)	Apple 3417
12/27/75	30	5	4. Blast From Your Past　　　　[G] *It Don't Come Easy* (4)/*Back Off Boogaloo* (9)	Apple 3422
10/23/76	28	6	5. Ringo's Rotogravure guests: McCartney & Lennon, Eric Clapton, Peter Frampton	Atlantic 18193

Diana Ross had three No. 1 albums as a member of the Supremes—but since her first album as a solo artist, 1970's *Diana Ross*, her only effort to reach the top position has been her *Lady Sings The Blues* LP of 1972. *The Boss* didn't do badly—it reached No. 14 in 1979.

David Lee Roth, the former lead vocalist of Van Halen, created a stir with the unique approach he took on his 1986 solo album *Eat 'Em And Smile.* The high-energy set also came out under the name *Sonrisa Salvaje,* with Roth belting his same lyrics again entirely in Spanish. 1985's *Crazy From The Heat,* a four-song EP containing the hit "California Girls," brought Roth his first solo success.

Rush remain one of the most consistent three-piece bands in rock 'n' roll: Since drummer Neil Peart joined the Canadian group for its second album, 1975's *Fly By Night,* the trio of Peart, bassist Geddy Lee, and guitarist Alex Lifeson have stayed together. *Signals,* issued in 1982, was the group's fourth LP to crack the top 10.

Bobby Rydell's all-time greatest hit single was 1960's "Wild One," but the Philadelphia artist—born Robert Ridarelli—met his greatest album success with a 1961 LP recorded with Chubby Checker that peaked at No. 7.

Santana's long and distinguished career was recognized respectfully by Columbia's 1988 *Viva Santana!* compilation. Despite a seeming constant shift of band personnel, the San Francisco group's focus has remained around namesake guitarist Carlos Santana. 1978's *Inner Secrets* was the group's 10th gold album.

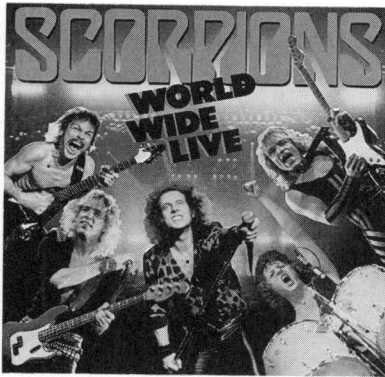

The **Scorpions**, long credited as a groundbreaking German heavy metal band, were first introduced to the U.S. through one-time indie label Billingsgate Records, who issued their *Lonesome Crow* debut in 1973. Albums such as *World Wide Live* continued to garner international attention for the group in the 80s.

Seals & Crofts, a Texas pair that originally recorded for the independent TA label, recorded a series of singles in the 70s that for many epitomized the atmosphere of the decade. However, none of their three biggest hits—"Summer Breeze," "Diamond Girl" or " Get Closer"—ever charted higher than No. 6 on the Hot 100, though their LP *Diamond Girl* made it to the No. 4 slot.

Simon and Garfunkel's groundbreaking Columbia albums, all of which reached the top 40 between 1966 and 1970—were collected in a CD-boxed set issued by the label in 1990. The set's only exclusion: the soundtrack from *The Graduate*, which was No. 1 for nine weeks in 1968. *Parsley, Sage, Rosemary and Thyme* includes the hits "Homeward Bound" and "Scarborough Fair/Canticle."

Frank Sinatra's recordings have now spanned half a century. He has had four No. 1 albums in his career: 1958's *Come Fly With Me* and *Frank Sinatra Sings For Only The Lonely*, 1960's *Nice 'N' Easy* and 1966's *Strangers In The Night*.

Jimmy Smith's organ placed the sounds of jazz high on the pop charts in the 60s, with a total of 10 albums recorded for either Verve or Blue Note reaching the top 40. His highest-charting effort ever, 1962's *Bashin'*, featured his memorable version of "Walk On The Wild Side."

DATE	POS	WKS	ARTIST—RECORD TITLE	LABEL & NO.
			STARS ON	
			Session musicians from Holland, performing hit song medleys.	Radio 16044
6/20/81	9	8	● 1. Stars On Long Play	
			side 1: medley of Beatles songs	
			STATON, Dakota	
			Born Aliyah Rabia on 6/3/31 in Pittsburgh. Jazz stylist.	
2/24/58	4	41	1. The Late, Late Show	Capitol 876
10/27/58	22	1	2. Dynamic!	Capitol 1054
6/8/59	23	6	3. Crazy He Calls Me	Capitol 1170
			STEELY DAN	
			Los Angeles-based, pop/jazz-styled group formed by Donald Fagen (b: 1/10/48, Passaic, New Jersey; keyboards, vocals) and Walter Becker (b: 2/20/50, New York City; bass, vocals). Group, primarily known as a studio unit, featured Fagen and Becker with various studio musicians. Duo went their separate ways in 1981. Drummer Jimmy Hodder drowned on 6/5/90 (age 42).	
2/10/73	17	17	● 1. Can't Buy A Thrill	ABC 758
			Do It Again (6)	
9/15/73	35	3	● 2. Countdown To Ecstasy	ABC 779
5/4/74	8	19	● 3. Pretzel Logic	ABC 808
			Rikki Don't Lose That Number (4)	
4/19/75	13	9	● 4. Katy Lied	ABC 846
5/29/76	15	9	● 5. The Royal Scam	ABC 931
10/15/77	3	52	▲ 6. Aja	ABC 1006
12/9/78	30	9	▲ 7. Greatest Hits [G]	ABC 1107 [2]
12/13/80	9	19	▲ 8. Gaucho	MCA 6102
			Hey Nineteen (10)	
			STEPPENWOLF	
			Hard-rock quintet formed in Los Angeles in 1967. Original lineup: John Kay (born Joachim Krauledat on 4/12/44 in Tilsit, East Germany; vocals, guitar) Michael Monarch (guitar), Goldy McJohn (keyboards), Nick St. Nicholas (bass), Mars Bonfire (born Dennis Edmonton; guitar) and brother Jerry Edmonton (drums). All but Monarch were members of the Canadian group Sparrow. Many personnel changes except for Kay.	
7/27/68	6	25	● 1. Steppenwolf	Dunhill 50029
			Born To Be Wild (2)	
10/19/68	3	24	● 2. The Second	Dunhill 50037
			Magic Carpet Ride (3)	
3/29/69	7	11	3. At Your Birthday Party	Dunhill 50053
			Rock Me (10)	
8/2/69	29	6	4. Early Steppenwolf [E-L]	Dunhill 50060
			recorded in 1967 when band was known as Sparrow; side 2 is a 21 1/2-minute version of "The Pusher"	
12/6/69	17	16	● 5. Monster	Dunhill 50066
4/25/70	7	15	● 6. Steppenwolf 'Live' [L]	Dunhill 50075 [2]
11/21/70	19	7	● 7. Steppenwolf 7	Dunhill 50090
3/13/71	24	9	● 8. Steppenwolf Gold/Their Great Hits [G]	Dunhill 50099

DATE	POS	WKS	ARTIST—RECORD TITLE	LABEL & NO.
			STEVENS, Cat	
			Born Steven Georgiou on 7/21/47 in London. Began career playing folk music at Hammersmith College in 1966. Contracted tuberculosis in 1968 and spent over a year recuperating. Adopted new style when he re-emerged. Lived in Brazil in the mid-70s. Converted to Muslim religion in late 1979, took name Yusef Islam.	
2/13/71	8	44	● 1. Tea for the Tillerman	A&M 4280
10/16/71	2(1)	37	● 2. Teaser And The Firecat	A&M 4313
			Peace Train (7)/*Morning Has Broken* (6)	
10/28/72	1(3)	26	● 3. Catch Bull At Four	A&M 4365
8/4/73	3	15	● 4. Foreigner	A&M 4391
4/20/74	2(3)	25	● 5. Buddha And The Chocolate Box	A&M 3623
			Oh Very Young (10)	
7/26/75	6	12	● 6. Greatest Hits [G]	A&M 4519
			Another Saturday Night (6)	
12/13/75	13	13	● 7. Numbers	A&M 4555
5/28/77	7	12	● 8. Izitso	A&M 4702
1/20/79	33	4	9. Back To Earth	A&M 4735
			STEVENS, Ray	
			Born Ray Ragsdale on 1/24/39 in Clarkdale, Georgia. Attended Georgia State University, studied music theory and composition. Production work in the mid-60s. Numerous appearances on Andy Williams' TV show in the late 60s. Own TV show in summer of 1970. Featured on "Music Country" TV show, 1973-74.	
7/4/70	35	3	1. Everything Is Beautiful	Barnaby 35005
			Everything Is Beautiful (1)	
			STEWART, Al	
			Born on 9/5/45 in Glasgow, Scotland. Pop-rock singer/composer/guitarist.	
4/12/75	30	3	1. Modern Times	Janus 7012
11/20/76	5	21	▲ 2. Year Of The Cat	Janus 7022
			Year Of The Cat (8)	
10/14/78	10	14	▲ 3. Time Passages	Arista 4190
			above three produced by Alan Parsons	
			Time Passages (7)	
10/4/80	37	4	4. 24 Carrots	Arista 9520
			STEWART, Amii	
			Born in Washington, D.C. in 1956. Disco singer/dancer/actress. In the Broadway musical *Bubbling Brown Sugar*. Her niece is singer Sinitta.	
3/31/79	19	9	● 1. Knock On Wood	Ariola 50054
			Knock On Wood (1)	
			STEWART, Jermaine	
			Chicago-bred singer. Former dancer on TV's "Soul Train." Worked as backup vocalist for Shalamar and Boy George.	
8/16/86	32	5	1. Frantic Romantic	Arista 8395
			We Don't Have To Take Our Clothes Off (5)	
			STEWART, John	
			Born on 9/5/39 in San Diego. Member of the Kingston Trio from 1961-67. Wrote "Daydream Believer."	
6/16/79	10	14	1. Bombs Away Dream Babies	RSO 3051
			Gold (5) with Stevie Nicks	

DATE	POS	WKS	ARTIST—RECORD TITLE	LABEL & NO.
			STEWART, Rod	
			Born Roderick Stewart on 1/10/45 in London. Worked as a folk singer in Europe in the early 60s. Recorded for English Decca in 1964. With the Hoochie Coochie Men, Steampacket and Shotgun Express. Joined Jeff Beck Group, 1967-69. With Faces from 1969-75, also recorded solo during this time. Left Faces in December, 1975.	
7/11/70	27	7	1. Gasoline Alley	Mercury 61264
6/26/71	1(4)	35	● 2. Every Picture Tells A Story *Maggie May* (1)	Mercury 609
8/12/72	2(3)	21	● 3. Never A Dull Moment	Mercury 646
8/11/73	31	3	● 4. Sing It Again Rod [G]	Mercury 680
11/9/74	13	5	5. Smiler *all Mercury albums feature members of Faces*	Mercury 1017
9/20/75	9	10	● 6. Atlantic Crossing	Warner 2875
7/31/76	2(5)	30	▲ 7. A Night On The Town *Tonight's The Night (Gonna Be Alright)* (1)	Warner 2938
11/26/77	2(6)	27	▲ 8. Foot Loose & Fancy Free *You're In My Heart (The Final Acclaim)* (4)	Warner 3092
1/6/79	1(3)	24	▲ 9. Blondes Have More Fun *Da Ya Think I'm Sexy?* (1)	Warner 3261
12/1/79	22	7	▲ 10. Rod Stewart Greatest Hits [G]	Warner 3373
12/6/80	12	15	▲ 11. Foolish Behaviour *Passion* (5)	Warner 3485
11/28/81	11	20	▲ 12. Tonight I'm Yours *Young Turks* (5)	Warner 3602
7/9/83	30	4	13. Body Wishes	Warner 23877
7/7/84	18	19	● 14. Camouflage *Infatuation* (6)/*Some Guys Have All The Luck* (10)	Warner 25095
7/26/86	28	7	15. Rod Stewart *Love Touch* (6)	Warner 25446
6/18/88	20	46	▲ 16. Out Of Order *My Heart Can't Tell You No* (4)	Warner 25684
4/7/90	20	12	● 17. Downtown Train: Selections From The Storyteller Anthology [G] *most of these 12 tracks are Rod's hits of the last 15 years* *Downtown Train* (3)/*This Old Heart Of Mine* (10)	Warner 26158
			STILLS, Stephen	
			Born on 1/3/45 in Dallas. Member of Buffalo Springfield and Crosby, Stills & Nash.	
10/5/68	12	10	● 1. Super Session **MIKE BLOOMFIELD/AL KOOPER/STEVE STILLS**	Columbia 9701
12/5/70	3	16	● 2. Stephen Stills *guests: Jimi Hendrix, Eric Clapton, David Crosby,* *Graham Nash*	Atlantic 7202
7/24/71	8	9	● 3. Stephen Stills 2	Atlantic 7206
5/6/72	4	15	● 4. Manassas	Atlantic 903 [2]
6/2/73	26	6	5. Down The Road *above two albums feature Stills' band, Manassas*	Atlantic 7250
7/12/75	19	6	6. Stills	Columbia 33575
6/19/76	31	3	7. Illegal Stills	Columbia 34148
			STILLS-YOUNG BAND (Neil Young):	
10/30/76	26	6	● 8. Long May You Run	Reprise 2253

DATE	POS	WKS	ARTIST—RECORD TITLE	LABEL & NO.
			STING	
			Born Gordon Sumner on 10/2/51 in Wallsend, England. Lead singer/bass guitarist of The Police. In the films *Quadrophenia*, *Dune*, *The Bride*, *Plenty* and others. Nicknamed Sting because of a yellow and black jersey he liked to wear.	
7/20/85	**2**(6)	37	▲ 1. The Dream Of The Blue Turtles *If You Love Somebody Set Them Free* (3)/ *Fortress Around Your Heart* (8)	A&M 3750
11/7/87	**9**	26	● 2. ...Nothing Like The Sun *We'll Be Together* (7)	A&M 6402 [2]
			STONE, Kirby	
			Born on 4/27/18 in New York City. Leader of own quartet, group includes: Eddie Hall, Larry Foster and Mike Gardner. Kirby was musical director for various TV shows. **THE KIRBY STONE FOUR:**	
8/25/58	**13**	9	1. Baubles, Bangles And Beads	Columbia 1211
			STORIES	
			New York rock quartet: Ian Lloyd (lead singer, bass), Michael Brown (founding member of Left Banke; keyboards), Steve Love (guitar) and Bryan Madey (drums). Brown left group in 1973, replaced by Ken Aaronson (bass) and Ken Bichel (keyboards).	
9/1/73	**29**	6	1. About Us *Brother Louie* (1)	Kama Sutra 2068
			STRAIT, George	
			Country singer from Pearsall, Texas. Graduated from Southwest Texas State with a degree in agriculture.	
6/16/90	**35**	3	● 1. Livin' It Up	MCA 6415
			STRAWBERRY ALARM CLOCK, The	
			West Coast psychedelic rock sextet: Ed King (lead guitar), Mark Weitz (keyboards), Lee Freeman (guitar), Gary Lovetro (bass), George Bunnel (bass) and Randy Seol (drums). King joined Lynyrd Skynyrd, 1973-75. Originally known as the Sixpence.	
12/2/67	**11**	13	1. Incense And Peppermints *Incense And Peppermints* (1)	Uni 73014
			STRAY CATS	
			Long Island, New York rockabilly trio: Brian Setzer (b: 4/10/60; lead singer, guitar), Lee Rocker (born Leon Drucher; string bass) and Slim Jim Phantom (born Jim McDonell; drums). Group disbanded in 1984; reunited in 1988. Phantom and Rocker formed trio Phantom, Rocker & Slim in 1985, also the year Phantom marries actress Britt Ekland. Setzer portrayed Eddie Cochran in the film *La Bamba*. Phantom portrayed Charlie Parker's drummer in the film *Bird*.	
9/4/82	**2**(15)	37	▲ 1. Built For Speed *Rock This Town* (9)/*Stray Cat Strut* (3)	EMI America 17070
9/17/83	**14**	10	● 2. Rant n' Rave with the Stray Cats *(She's) Sexy + 17* (5)	EMI America 17102
			STREISAND, Barbra	
			Born Barbara Joan Streisand on 4/24/42 in Brooklyn. Made Broadway debut in *I Can Get It For You Wholesale*, 1962. Lead role in Broadway's *Funny Girl*, 1964. Film debut in *Funny Girl* in 1968 (tied with Katharine Hepburn for Best Actress Oscar), also starred in *A Star Is Born*, *Hello Dolly*, *Funny Lady*, *The Way We Were* and many others. Produced, directed, starred in and co-wrote the 1983 film *Yentl*. Married for a time to actor Elliot Gould.	
5/4/63	**8**	78	● 1. The Barbra Streisand Album *1963 Grammy winner: Album of the Year*	Columbia 8807
9/28/63	**2**(3)	47	● 2. The Second Barbara Streisand Album	Columbia 8854

DATE	POS	WKS	ARTIST—RECORD TITLE		LABEL & NO.
3/14/64	5	8	● 3. The Third Album		Columbia 8954
5/2/64	2(3)	40	● 4. Funny Girl based on the early life of Fanny Brice	[OC]	Capitol 2059
10/10/64	1(5)	48	● 5. People *People* (5)		Columbia 9015
5/29/65	2(3)	46	● 6. My Name Is Barbra		Columbia 9136
11/13/65	2(3)	31	▲ 7. My Name Is Barbra, Two…		Columbia 9209
4/23/66	3	22	● 8. Color Me Barbra		Columbia 9278
12/3/66	5	13	9. Je m'appelle Barbra		Columbia 9347
12/2/67	12	12	10. Simply Streisand		Columbia 9482
11/9/68	12	31	▲ 11. Funny Girl screen version of the above Broadway musical	[S]	Columbia 3220
11/9/68	30	13	● 12. A Happening In Central Park	[L]	Columbia 9710
9/20/69	31	4	13. What About Today?		Columbia 9816
3/21/70	32	2	▲ 14. Barbra Streisand's Greatest Hits	[G]	Columbia 9968
2/27/71	10	11	▲ 15. Stoney End *Stoney End* (6)		Columbia 30378
9/25/71	11	15	● 16. Barbra Joan Streisand		Columbia 30792
12/16/72	19	8	▲ 17. Live Concert At The Forum	[L]	Columbia 31760
2/23/74	1(2)	12	▲ 18. The Way We Were not the soundtrack album (see Soundtracks) *The Way We Were* (1)		Columbia 32801
11/30/74	13	11	● 19. ButterFly		Columbia 33095
4/12/75	6	9	● 20. Funny Lady film is the sequel to *Funny Girl*	[S]	Arista 9004
11/15/75	12	10	● 21. Lazy Afternoon		Columbia 33815
12/25/76	1(6)	28	▲ 22. A Star Is Born Kris Kristofferson sings on five of the 12 tracks (all but four tracks are live); third version of the 1937 film classic *Evergreen* (1)	[S-L]	Columbia 34403
7/2/77	3	14	▲ 23. Streisand Superman *My Heart Belongs To Me* (4)		Columbia 34830
6/24/78	12	13	▲ 24. Songbird		Columbia 35375
12/2/78	1(3)	17	▲ 25. Barbra Streisand's Greatest Hits, Volume 2 *You Don't Bring Me Flowers* (1) with Neil Diamond	[G]	Columbia 35679
7/21/79	20	9	● 26. The Main Event three versions of title song - others by various artists *The Main Event/Fight* (3)	[S]	Columbia 36115
11/10/79	7	14	▲ 27. Wet *No More Tears (Enough Is Enough)* (1) with Donna Summer		Columbia 36258
10/11/80	1(3)	33	▲ 28. Guilty *Woman In Love* (1)/*Guilty* (3) with Barry Gibb/ *What Kind Of Fool* (10) with Barry Gibb		Columbia 36750
12/12/81	10	15	▲ 29. Memories	[K]	Columbia 37678
12/3/83	9	13	▲ 30. Yentl Barbra is the first woman to produce, direct, write and perform a film's title role	[S]	Columbia 39152
11/3/84	19	11	▲ 31. Emotion		Columbia 39480
11/30/85	1(3)	24	▲ 32. The Broadway Album Barbra sings 14 of her favorite Broadway tunes		Columbia 40092
5/16/87	9	13	▲ 33. One Voice recorded at her Malibu ranch for an audience of 500 invited guests	[L]	Columbia 40788
11/19/88	10	14	▲ 34. Till I Loved You		Columbia 40880

DATE	POS	WKS	ARTIST—RECORD TITLE	LABEL & NO.
10/28/89	**26**	12	▲ 35. A Collection Greatest Hits...And More [G]	Columbia 45369
			STRYPER	
			Christian heavy-metal band from Orange County, California: Michael Sweet (vocals), Robert Sweet (drums), Oz Fox (guitar) and Tim Gaines (bass).	
11/29/86	**32**	12	▲ 1. To Hell With The Devil	Enigma 73237
7/23/88	**32**	5	● 2. In God We Trust	Enigma 73317
			STYLISTICS, The	
			Soul group from Philadelphia formed in 1968. Consisted of Russell Thompkins, Jr. (b: 3/21/51; lead), Airron Love, James Smith, James Dunn and Herbie Murrell. Thompkins, Love and Smith sang with the Percussions; Murrell and Dunn with the Monarchs from 1965-68. First recorded for Sebring in 1969.	
1/15/72	**23**	18	● 1. The Stylistics *You Are Everything* (9)/*Betcha By Golly, Wow* (3)	Avco 33023
1/27/73	**32**	9	● 2. Round 2: The Stylistics *I'm Stone In Love With You* (10)/*Break Up To Make Up* (5)	Avco 11006
6/22/74	**14**	8	● 3. Let's Put It All Together	Avco 69001
			STYX	
			Chicago-based rock quintet: Dennis DeYoung (vocals, keyboards), Tommy Shaw (lead guitar), James Young (guitar), and twin brothers John (drums) and Chuck Panozzo (bass). Shaw replaced John Curulewski in 1976. Most songs written by Dennis DeYoung and/or Tommy Shaw. DeYoung and Shaw went solo in 1984. Band reunited in 1990 with guitarist Glen Burtnik replacing Shaw.	
2/22/75	**20**	6	● 1. Styx II originally released in 1973 (*Styx I* did not chart) *Lady* (6)	Wooden N. 1012
9/3/77	**6**	37	▲ 2. The Grand Illusion *Come Sail Away* (8)	A&M 4637
10/7/78	**6**	28	▲ 3. Pieces of Eight	A&M 4724
10/13/79	**2(1)**	26	▲ 4. Cornerstone *Babe* (1)	A&M 3711
1/31/81	**1(3)**	35	▲ 5. Paradise Theater *The Best Of Times* (3)/*Too Much Time On My Hands* (9)	A&M 3719
3/19/83	**3**	22	▲ 6. Kilroy Was Here *Mr. Roboto* (3)/*Don't Let It End* (6)	A&M 3734
5/5/84	**31**	6	7. Caught In The Act - Live [L]	A&M 6514 [2]
			SUGARLOAF	
			Rock quartet from Denver: Jerry Corbetta (lead singer, keyboards), Bob Webber (guitar), Bob Raymond (bass) and Bob MacVittie (drums). Robert Yeazel (guitar, vocals) joined in 1971. By 1974, Myron Pollock replaced MacVittie, and Yeazel had left.	
10/3/70	**24**	10	1. Sugarloaf *Green-Eyed Lady* (3)	Liberty 7640
			SUMMER, Donna	
			Born Adrian Donna Gaines on 12/31/48 in Boston. With group Crow, played local clubs. In German production of *Hair*, European productions of *Godspell*, *The Me Nobody Knows* and *Porgy And Bess*. Settled in Germany, where she recorded "Love To Love You Baby." In the film *Thank God It's Friday* in 1979. Married Bruce Sudano (Alive & Kicking and Brooklyn Dreams) in 1980. Dubbed "The Queen of Disco."	
12/13/75	**11**	13	● 1. Love To Love You Baby *Love To Love You Baby* (2)	Oasis 5003
5/1/76	**21**	9	● 2. A Love Trilogy	Oasis 5004

DATE	POS	WKS	ARTIST—RECORD TITLE	LABEL & NO.
11/20/76	**29**	5	● 3. Four Seasons Of Love	Casablanca 7038
6/18/77	**18**	18	● 4. I Remember Yesterday *I Feel Love* (6)	Casablanca 7056
12/3/77	**26**	10	● 5. Once Upon A Time…	Casablanca 7078 [2]
9/16/78	**1**(1)	32	▲ 6. Live And More [L] one of four sides is a studio recording *MacArthur Park* (1)/*Heaven Knows* (4)	Casablanca 7119 [2]
5/12/79	**1**(6)	26	▲ 7. Bad Girls *Hot Stuff* (1)/*Bad Girls* (1)/*Dim All The Lights* (2)	Casablanca 7150 [2]
11/10/79	**1**(1)	23	▲ 8. On The Radio-Greatest Hits-Volumes I & II [G] *Last Dance* (3)/*No More Tears (Enough Is Enough)* (1) with Barbra Streisand/*On The Radio* (5)	Casablanca 7191 [2]
11/8/80	**13**	9	● 9. The Wanderer *The Wanderer* (3)	Geffen 2000
8/21/82	**20**	9	● 10. Donna Summer *Love Is In Control (Finger On The Trigger)* (10)	Geffen 2005
7/23/83	**9**	15	● 11. She Works Hard For The Money *She Works Hard For The Money* (3)	Mercury 812265
10/13/84	**40**	2	12. Cats Without Claws	Geffen 24040
			SUPERTRAMP British rock quintet: Roger Hodgson (vocals, guitar), Rick Davies (vocals, keyboards), John Helliwell (sax), Dougie Thomson (bass) and Bob Siebenberg (drums). Hodgson went solo in 1983.	
5/17/75	**38**	3	● 1. Crime Of The Century	A&M 3647
5/14/77	**16**	17	● 2. Even In The Quietest Moments…	A&M 4634
4/7/79	**1**(6)	48	▲ 3. Breakfast In America *The Logical Song* (6)/*Take The Long Way Home* (10)	A&M 3708
10/11/80	**8**	11	● 4. Paris [L] recorded at the Paris Pavillon on 11/29/79	A&M 6702 [2]
11/13/82	**5**	17	● 5. …famous last words…	A&M 3732
6/15/85	**21**	10	6. Brother Where You Bound first album without Roger Hodgson	A&M 5014
			SUPREMES, The R&B vocal group from Detroit, formed as the Primettes in 1959. Consisted of lead singer Diana Ross (b: 3/26/44), Mary Wilson (b: 3/6/44), Florence Ballard (b: 6/30/43; d: 2/22/76 of cardiac arrest) and Barbara Martin. Recorded for LuPine in 1960. Signed to Motown's Tamla label in 1960. Changed name to The Supremes in 1961; Martin left shortly thereafter. Worked as backing vocalists for Motown until 1964. Backed Marvin Gaye on "Can I Get A Witness." Ballard discharged from group in 1967, replaced by Cindy Birdsong, formerly with Patti LaBelle's Blue Belles. Ross left in 1969 for solo career, replaced by Jean Terrell. Birdsong left in 1972, replaced by Lynda Lawrence. Terrell and Lawrence left in 1973. Mary Wilson re-formed group with Scherrie Payne (sister of Freda Payne) and Cindy Birdsong. Birdsong left again in 1976, replaced by Susaye Greene. In 1978, Wilson toured England with Karen Ragland and Karen Jackson, but lost rights to the name "Supremes" thereafter. Inducted into the Rock and Roll Hall of Fame in 1988.	
10/31/64	**2**(4)	48	1. Where Did Our Love Go *Where Did Our Love Go* (1)/*Baby Love* (1)/ *Come See About Me* (1)	Motown 621
1/23/65	**21**	8	2. A Bit Of Liverpool	Motown 623
9/11/65	**6**	17	3. More Hits By The Supremes *Stop! In The Name Of Love* (1)/*Back In My Arms Again* (1)	Motown 627
12/4/65	**11**	24	4. The Supremes at the Copa [L]	Motown 636
4/2/66	**8**	14	5. I Hear A Symphony *I Hear A Symphony* (1)/*My World Is Empty Without You* (5)	Motown 643

DATE	POS	WKS	ARTIST—RECORD TITLE	LABEL & NO.
10/8/66	**1**(2)	31	6. The Supremes A' Go-Go *Love Is Like An Itching In My Heart* (9)/ *You Can't Hurry Love* (1)	Motown 649
2/25/67	**6**	17	7. The Supremes sing Holland-Dozier-Holland songs written by Brian Holland, Lamont Dozier, Eddie Holland *You Keep Me Hangin' On* (1)/ *Love Is Here And Now You're Gone* (1)	Motown 650
7/1/67	**20**	7	8. The Supremes Sing Rodgers & Hart songwriting team: Richard Rodgers and Lorenz Hart	Motown 659
			DIANA ROSS & THE SUPREMES:	
10/7/67	**1**(5)	49	9. Diana Ross and the Supremes Greatest Hits [G] *The Happening* (1)	Motown 663 [2]
5/11/68	**18**	9	10. Reflections *Reflections* (2)/*In And Out Of Love* (9)	Motown 665
12/21/68	**2**(1)	14	11. Diana Ross & the Supremes Join the Temptations *I'm Gonna Make You Love Me* (2)	Motown 679
12/28/68	**14**	7	12. Love Child *Love Child* (1)	Motown 670
1/11/69	**1**(1)	19	13. TCB * [TV]	Motown 682
7/5/69	**24**	6	14. Let The Sunshine In *I'm Livin' In Shame* (10)	Motown 689
11/15/69	**28**	3	15. Together *	Motown 692
12/20/69	**33**	7	16. Cream Of The Crop *Someday We'll Be Together* (1)	Motown 694
12/20/69	**38**	2	17. On Broadway * [TV] ***DIANA ROSS & THE SUPREMES WITH THE TEMPTATIONS**	Motown 699
1/31/70	**31**	6	18. Diana Ross & the Supremes Greatest Hits, Volume 3 [G]	Motown 702
			THE SUPREMES:	
6/6/70	**25**	6	19. Right On *Up The Ladder To The Roof* (10)	Motown 705
			SURFARIS, The	
			Teenage surf band from Glendora, California. Consisted of Ron Wilson (drummer), Jim Fuller (lead guitar), Bob Berryhill (rhythm guitar), Pat Connolly (bass) and Jim Pash (sax, clarinet).	
9/7/63	**15**	16	1. Wipe Out [I] *Wipe Out* (2)	Dot 25535
			SURVIVOR	
			Midwest rock qroup: Dave Bickler (lead singer), Jim Peterik (keyboards; former lead singer of Ides Of March), Frankie Sullivan (guitar), Gary Smith (drums) and Dennis Johnson (bass). Smith and Johnson replaced by Marc Doubray and Stephan Ellis in 1981. Bickler replaced by Jimi Jamison in 1984. Droubay and Ellis left in 1988.	
7/3/82	**2**(4)	19	▲ 1. Eye Of The Tiger *Eye Of The Tiger* (1)	Scotti Br. 38062
3/9/85	**16**	27	2. Vital Signs *High On You* (8)/*The Search Is Over* (4)	Scotti Br. 39578
			SWAN, Billy	
			Born on 5/12/42 in Cape Girardeau, Missouri. Singer/songwriter/keyboardist/guitarist. Produced Tony Joe White's first three albums. Toured with Kris Kristofferson from the early 70s. Formed band Black Tie with Randy Meisner in 1986.	
1/4/75	**21**	7	1. I Can Help *I Can Help* (1)	Monument 33279

DATE	POS	WKS	ARTIST—RECORD TITLE	LABEL & NO.
			SWEAT, Keith	
			Soul singer/songwriter born and raised in Harlem.	
2/20/88	15	27	▲ 1. Make It Last Forever *I Want Her* (5)	Vintertn. 60763
6/30/90	6	17+	▲ 2. I'll Give All My Love To You *Make You Sweat* (14)	Elektra 60861
			SWEET	
			English rock band: Brian Connolly (lead singer), Steve Priest (bass, vocals), Andy Scott (guitar, keyboards) and Mick Tucker (drums).	
9/27/75	25	6	● 1. Desolation Boulevard *Ballroom Blitz* (5)/*Fox On The Run* (5)	Capitol 11395
3/20/76	27	7	2. Give Us A Wink	Capitol 11496
			SWINGLE SINGERS, The	
			Ward Swingle (b: 9/21/27, Mobile, Alabama; piano, sax) and his scat-singing French singers. Ward moved to Paris in 1956.	
11/23/63	15	24	1. Bach's Greatest Hits　　　　　　　　　　　[I]	Philips 097
			SWING OUT SISTER	
			British jazz-pop trio: Corinne Drewery (vocals), Andy Connell and Martin Jackson. Drewery was a fashion designer. Reduced to a duo in 1989 with departure of Jackson.	
2/27/88	40	1	● 1. It's Better To Travel *Breakout* (6)	Mercury 832213
			SWITCH	
			Soul-funk sextet from Mansfield, Ohio. Discovered by Jermaine Jackson. Consisted of Bobby DeBarge, Phillip Ingram (lead vocals), Greg Williams, Tommy DeBarge, Eddie Fluellen and Jody Sims. Williams, Sims and Bobby DeBarge were in White Heat. Brothers Bobby and Tommy DeBarge were later in family group DeBarge.	
11/18/78	37	4	1. Switch	Gordy 980
8/11/79	37	4	2. Switch II	Gordy 988
			SYLVESTER	
			Born Sylvester James in Los Angeles. Moved to San Francisco in 1967. With vocal group the Cockettes. In film *The Rose*. Backing vocals by Martha Wash, Izora Rhodes (later known as Two Tons O' Fun and The Weather Girls) and Jeanie Tracy. Died on 12/16/88 (age 40) of AIDS-related complications.	
9/30/78	28	6	● 1. Step II	Fantasy 9556
			# T	
			TACO	
			Born Taco Ockerse in 1955 to Dutch parents in Jaharta, Indonesia. German-based singer.	
8/6/83	23	11	1. After Eight *Puttin' On The Ritz* (4)	RCA 4818

DATE	POS	WKS	ARTIST—RECORD TITLE	LABEL & NO.
			TALKING HEADS	
			New York City-based new wave quartet: David Byrne (lead singer, guitar), Jerry Harrison (keyboards, guitar), Tina Weymouth (bass) and husband Chris Frantz (drums). Formed as a trio of Byrne, Weymouth and Frantz at the Rhode Island School of Design. Harrison was a member of The Modern Lovers. Also see Tom Tom Club.	
10/28/78	**29**	5	● 1. More Songs About Buildings And Food	Sire 6058
9/15/79	**21**	10	● 2. Fear Of Music	Sire 6076
11/15/80	**19**	9	● 3. Remain In Light	Sire 6095
			above three produced by Brian Eno	
5/8/82	**31**	4	4. The Name Of This Band Is Talking Heads [L]	Sire 3590 [2]
7/2/83	**15**	25	● 5. Speaking In Tongues	Sire 23883
			Burning Down The House (9)	
7/6/85	**20**	24	▲ 6. Little Creatures	Sire 25305
10/18/86	**17**	16	● 7. True Stories	Sire 25512
			contains Talking Heads' versions of songs featured in the film *True Stories*	
4/9/88	**19**	10	● 8. Naked	Sire 25654
			TASTE OF HONEY, A	
			Soul-disco quartet, formed in Los Angeles in 1972. Consisted of Janice Marie Johnson (vocals, guitar), Hazel Payne (vocals, bass), Perry Kimble (keyboards) and Donald Johnson (drums). Re-formed in 1980 with Janice Johnson and Hazel Payne. Won the 1978 Best New Artist Grammy Award.	
7/29/78	**6**	14	▲ 1. A Taste of Honey	Capitol 11754
			Boogie Oogie Oogie (1)	
5/23/81	**36**	4	2. Twice As Sweet	Capitol 12089
			Sukiyaki (3)	
			TAVARES	
			Family R&B group from New Bedford, Massachusetts. Consisted of brothers Ralph, Antone "Chubby," Feliciano "Butch," Arthur "Pooch" and Perry Lee "Tiny" Tavares. Worked as Chubby & The Turnpikes from 1964-69. Butch was married to Lola Falana.	
9/27/75	**26**	5	1. In The City	Capitol 11396
			It Only Takes A Minute (10)	
7/24/76	**24**	11	2. Sky High!	Capitol 11533
			TAYLOR, James	
			Born on 3/12/48 in Boston. Singer/songwriter/guitarist. With older brother Alex in the Fabulous Corsairs in 1964. In New York group The Flying Machine in 1967, with friend Danny Kortchmar. Moved to England in 1968, recorded for Peter Asher. Married Carly Simon on 11/3/72; filed for divorce in 1982. In film *Two Lane Blacktop* with Dennis Wilson in 1973. Sister Kate and brothers Alex and Livingston also recorded.	
4/18/70	**3**	54	▲ 1. Sweet Baby James	Warner 1843
			Fire And Rain (3)	
5/8/71	**2(4)**	31	▲ 2. Mud Slide Slim And The Blue Horizon	Warner 2561
			You've Got A Friend (1)	
12/16/72	**4**	12	● 3. One Man Dog	Warner 2660
7/27/74	**13**	10	4. Walking Man	Warner 2794
6/14/75	**6**	15	● 5. Gorilla	Warner 2866
			How Sweet It Is (To Be Loved By You) (5)	
7/10/76	**16**	14	● 6. In The Pocket	Warner 2912
12/18/76	**23**	7	▲ 7. Greatest Hits [G]	Warner 2979
7/16/77	**4**	24	▲ 8. JT	Columbia 34811
			Handy Man (4)	

DATE	POS	WKS	ARTIST—RECORD TITLE	LABEL & NO.
5/19/79	**10**	10	● 9. Flag	Columbia 36058
3/21/81	**10**	12	● 10. Dad Loves His Work	Columbia 37009
12/7/85	**34**	8	11. That's Why I'm Here	Columbia 40052
2/27/88	**25**	11	● 12. Never Die Young	Columbia 40851
			TAYLOR, Johnnie	
			Born on 5/5/38 in Crawfordsville, Arkansas. With gospel group the Highway QC's in Chicago, early 50s. In vocal group the Five Echoes, recorded for Sabre in 1954. In The Soul Stirrers gospel group before going solo. First solo recording for Sar in 1961.	
3/27/76	**5**	11	● 1. Eargasm *Disco Lady* (1)	Columbia 33951
			TEARS FOR FEARS	
			British duo: Roland Orzabal (vocals, guitar, keyboards) and Curt Smith (vocals, bass). Adopted name from Arthur Janev's book "Prisoners Of Pain." Assisted by Manny Elias (drums) and Ian Stanley (keyboards).	
4/20/85	**1**(5)	55	▲ 1. Songs From The Big Chair *Everybody Wants To Rule The World* (1)/*Shout* (1)/ *Head Over Heels* (3)	Mercury 824300
10/14/89	**8**	17	▲ 2. The Seeds Of Love *Sowing The Seeds Of Love* (2)	Fontana 838730
			TECHNOTRONIC	
			Dance outfit created by Belgian DJ/producer Jo "Thomas DeQuincy" Bogaert and 17-year-old rapper Manuella "Ya Kid K" Komosi. Includes London rapper MC Eric and backing vocalist/video model Felly as rapper. Komosi and Felly are from Zaire.	
1/20/90	**10**	22	▲ 1. Pump Up The Jam - The Album *Pump Up The Jam* (2)/*Get Up! (Before The Night Over)* (7)	SBK 93422
			TEENAGERS featuring Frankie Lymon	
			R&B group formed as the Premiers in the Bronx, New York in 1955. Lead singer Lymon (b: 9/30/42, New York City) died of a drug overdose on 2/28/68. Other members included Herman Santiago, Jimmy Merchant (tenors); Joe Negroni (d: 9/5/78; baritone); and Sherman Garnes (d: 2/26/77; bass). Group in films *Rock, Rock, Rock* and *Mister Rock 'n' Roll*.	
1/19/57	**19**	1	1. The Teenagers featuring Frankie Lymon *Why Do Fools Fall In Love* (6)	Gee 701
			TEMPTATIONS, The	
			Soul group formed in Detroit in 1960. Consisted of Eddie Kendricks, Paul Williams (d: 8/17/73), Melvin Franklin, Otis Williams and Elbridge Bryant, who was replaced by David Ruffin in 1964. Originally called the Primes and Elgins, first recorded for Miracle in 1961. Ruffin (cousin of Billy Stewart) replaced by Dennis Edwards (ex-Contours) in 1968. Kendricks and Paul Williams left in 1971, replaced by Ricky Owens (ex-Vibrations) and Richard Street. Owens was replaced by Damon Harris. Harris left in 1975, replaced by Glenn Leonard. Edwards left group, 1977-79, replaced by Louis Price. Ali Ollie Woodson replaced Edwards from 1984-87. 1988 lineup: Williams, Franklin, Street, Edwards and Ron Tyson. Recognized as America's all-time favorite soul group. Inducted into the Rock and Roll Hall of Fame in 1989.	
5/29/65	**35**	3	1. The Temptations Sing Smokey tribute to songwriter/producer Smokey Robinson *My Girl* (1)	Gordy 912
1/1/66	**11**	19	2. Temptin' Temptations	Gordy 914
8/13/66	**12**	18	3. Gettin' Ready	Gordy 918
1/14/67	**5**	65	4. The Temptations Greatest Hits [G] *Beauty Is Only Skin Deep* (3)	Gordy 919
4/15/67	**10**	18	5. Temptations Live! [L]	Gordy 921

DATE	POS	WKS	ARTIST—RECORD TITLE	LABEL & NO.
8/19/67	7	18	6. With A Lot O' Soul *(I Know) I'm Losing You* (8)/*All I Need* (8)/ *You're My Everything* (6)	Gordy 922
1/27/68	13	14	7. The Temptations in a Mellow Mood	Gordy 924
6/22/68	13	14	8. Wish It Would Rain *I Wish It Would Rain* (4)	Gordy 927
12/21/68	2(1)	13	9. Diana Ross & the Supremes Join the Temptations * *I'm Gonna Make You Love Me* (2)	Motown 679
1/11/69	1(1)	19	10. TCB * [TV]	Motown 682
2/1/69	15	9	11. Live At The Copa [L] Dennis Edwards replaces David Ruffin	Gordy 938
3/22/69	4	26	12. Cloud Nine *Cloud Nine* (6)/*Run Away Child, Running Wild* (6)	Gordy 939
8/16/69	24	10	13. The Temptations Show [TV] with guests Kaye Stevens and George Kirby	Gordy 933
10/25/69	5	19	14. Puzzle People *I Can't Get Next To You* (1)	Gordy 949
11/15/69	28	3	15. Together *	Motown 692
12/27/69	38	1	16. On Broadway * [TV] ***DIANA ROSS & THE SUPREMES WITH THE TEMPTATIONS**	Motown 699
4/11/70	9	18	17. Psychedelic Shack *Psychedelic Shack* (7)	Gordy 947
9/5/70	21	6	18. Live at London's Talk of The Town [L]	Gordy 953
10/10/70	15	12	19. Temptations Greatest Hits II [G] *Ball Of Confusion (That's What The World Is Today)* (3)	Gordy 954
5/22/71	16	15	20. Sky's The Limit *Just My Imagination (Running Away With Me)* (1)	Gordy 957
2/19/72	24	8	21. Solid Rock Damon Harris replaces Eddie Kendricks	Gordy 961
9/16/72	2(2)	25	22. All Directions *Papa Was A Rollin' Stone* (1)	Gordy 962
3/24/73	7	14	23. Masterpiece *Masterpiece* (7)	Gordy 965
1/26/74	19	8	24. 1990	Gordy 966
3/22/75	13	16	25. A Song For You	Gordy 969
12/20/75	40	2	26. House Party	Gordy 973
5/15/76	29	6	27. Wings Of Love	Gordy 971
6/5/82	37	2	28. Reunion Ruffin and Kendricks return for this album	Gordy 6008
			10cc English art-rock group which evolved from Hotlegs. Consisted of Eric Stewart (guitar), Graham Gouldman (bass), Lol Creme (guitar, keyboards) and Kevin Godley (drums). Stewart and Gouldman were members of The Mindbenders. Godley and Creme left in 1976, replaced by drummer Paul Burgess. Added members Rick Fenn, Stuart Tosh and Duncan MacKay in 1978. Gouldman later in duo, Wax. Also see Godley & Creme.	
6/28/75	15	10	1. The Original Soundtrack *I'm Not In Love* (2)	Mercury 1029
5/28/77	31	5	2. Deceptive Bends *The Things We Do For Love* (5)	Mercury 3702
			10,000 MANIACS Jamestown, New York fivesome: Natalie Merchant (vocals), Robert Buck, Dennis Drew, Steven Gustafson and Jerome Augustyniak.	
5/14/88	37	2	▲ 1. In My Tribe	Elektra 60738

DATE	POS	WKS	ARTIST—RECORD TITLE	LABEL & NO.
6/10/89	**13**	19	● 2. Blind Man's Zoo *above two produced by Peter Asher (Peter & Gordon)*	Elektra 60815
			TEN YEARS AFTER	
			British blues-rock quartet formed in 1967: Alvin Lee (vocals, guitar), Leo Lyons (bass), Chick Churchill (keyboards) and Ric Lee (drums). Inactive as band from 1975-1987.	
9/13/69	**20**	7	1. SSSH	Deram 18029
4/25/70	**14**	8	2. Cricklewood Green	Deram 18038
12/19/70	**21**	8	3. Watt	Deram 18050
9/11/71	**17**	10	▲ 4. A Space In Time	Columbia 30801
7/28/73	**39**	2	5. Recorded Live [L]	Columbia 32290 [2]
			TESLA	
			Sacramento hard-rock quintet: Jeff Keith (vocals), Frank Hannon, Tommy Skeoch, Brian Wheat and Troy Luccketta. Band named after inventor Nikola Tesla.	
3/14/87	**32**	8	▲ 1. Mechanical Resonance	Geffen 24120
2/25/89	**18**	17	▲ 2. The Great Radio Controversy *Love Song* (10)	Geffen 24224
			TEX, Joe	
			Born Joseph Arrington, Jr. on 8/8/33 in Rogers, Texas; died of a heart attack on 8/13/82. Sang with local gospel groups. Won recording contract at Apollo Theater talent contest in 1954. First recorded for King in 1955. Became a convert to Muslim faith, changed name to "Joseph Hazziez" in July, 1972.	
5/6/72	**17**	11	1. I Gotcha *I Gotcha* (2)	Dial 6002
			THIN LIZZY	
			Dublin, Ireland rock quartet led by Phil Lynott (d: 1/4/86 [age 35]).	
6/5/76	**18**	10	● 1. Jailbreak	Mercury 1081
10/29/77	**39**	2	2. Bad Reputation	Mercury 1186
			38 SPECIAL	
			Florida Southern-rock sextet: Donnie Van Zant (younger brother of Lynyrd Skynyrd's Ronnie Van Zant; lead singer), Don Barnes, Jeff Carlisi, Steve Brookins, Jack Grondin and Larry Jungstrom (replaced Ken Lyons in 1979). By 1988, Barnes and Brookins replaced by Danny Chauncey and Max Carl.	
3/14/81	**18**	18	▲ 1. Wild-Eyed Southern Boys	A&M 4835
6/5/82	**10**	11	▲ 2. Special Forces *Caught Up In You* (10)	A&M 4888
12/10/83	**22**	20	▲ 3. Tour De Force	A&M 4971
5/24/86	**17**	20	● 4. Strength In Numbers	A&M 5115
9/19/87	**35**	3	● 5. Flashback [G] *includes a bonus four-song live EP*	A&M 3910
			THOMAS, B.J.	
			Born Billy Joe Thomas on 8/7/42 in Hugo, Oklahoma; raised in Rosenberg, Texas. Sang in church choir as a teenager. Own band, the Triumphs; first recorded for Scepter in 1965. B.J. has featured gospel music since 1976.	
1/31/70	**12**	23	● 1. Raindrops Keep Fallin' On My Head *Raindrops Keep Fallin' On My Head* (1)	Scepter 580
			THOMAS, Carla	
			Born on 12/21/42 in Memphis. Daughter of Rufus Thomas. Sang with the Teentown Singers at age 10. First recorded with Rufus for Satellite in 1960. **OTIS REDDING & CARLA THOMAS:**	
7/22/67	**36**	3	1. King & Queen	Stax 716

DATE	POS	WKS	ARTIST—RECORD TITLE	LABEL & NO.
			THOMPSON TWINS	
			British trio: Tom Bailey (b: 1/18/56, England; lead singer, synthesizer), Alannah Currie (b: 9/28/57, New Zealand; xylophone, percussion) and Joe Leeway (b: England; conga, synthesizer). Leeway left in 1986.	
3/26/83	**34**	4	1. Side Kicks	Arista 6607
3/31/84	**10**	24	▲ 2. Into The Gap	Arista 8200
			Hold Me Now (3)	
10/26/85	**20**	24	● 3. Here's To Future Days	Arista 8276
			Lay Your Hands On Me (6)/*King For A Day* (8)	
			THOROGOOD, George	
			Leader of Delaware rock & blues band The Destroyers. Lineup since 1980: Thorogood (vocals, guitar), Billy Blough (bass), Jeff Simon (drums) and Hank Carter (sax). Added guitarist Steve Chrismar in 1986.	
			GEORGE THOROGOOD AND THE DESTROYERS:	
3/31/79	**33**	7	● 1. Move It On Over	Rounder 3024
4/6/85	**32**	15	● 2. Maverick	EMI America 17145
9/20/86	**33**	4	● 3. Live [L]	EMI America 17214
2/20/88	**32**	10	● 4. Born To Be Bad	EMI Man. 46973
			THORPE, Billy	
			English-born singer/guitarist; raised in Australia. Superstar artist in Australia.	
9/29/79	**39**	1	1. Children Of The Sun	Polydor 6228
			originally released on Capricom 0221	
			THREE DEGREES, The	
			Philadelphia R&B trio discovered by Richard Barrett. Originally consisted of Fayette Pinkney, Linda Turner and Shirley Porter. Turner and Porter replaced by Sheila Ferguson and Valerie Holiday in 1966.	
1/18/75	**28**	5	1. The Three Degrees	Phil. Int. 32406
			When Will I See You Again (2)	
			THREE DOG NIGHT	
			Los Angeles pop-rock group formed in 1968 featuring lead singers Danny Hutton (b: 9/10/42), Cory Wells (b: 2/5/42) and Chuck Negron (b: 6/8/42). Disbanded in the mid-70s. Re-formed in the mid-80s to tour.	
4/5/69	**11**	26	● 1. Three Dog Night	Dunhill 50048
			One (5)	
7/26/69	**16**	27	● 2. Suitable for Framing	Dunhill 50058
			Easy To Be Hard (4)/*Eli's Coming* (10)	
12/6/69	**6**	24	● 3. Captured Live At The Forum [L]	Dunhill 50068
5/9/70	**8**	20	● 4. It Ain't Easy	Dunhill 50078
			Mama Told Me (Not To Come) (1)	
12/19/70	**14**	22	● 5. Naturally	Dunhill 50088
			Joy To The World (1)/*Liar* (7)	
3/6/71	**5**	30	● 6. Golden Bisquits [G]	Dunhill 50098
10/23/71	**8**	21	● 7. Harmony	Dunhill 50108
			An Old Fashioned Love Song (4)/*Never Been To Spain* (5)	
8/12/72	**6**	19	● 8. Seven Separate Fools	Dunhill 50118
			Black & White (1)	
3/31/73	**18**	9	● 9. Around The World With Three Dog Night [L]	Dunhill 50138 [2]
11/10/73	**26**	6	● 10. Cyan	Dunhill 50158
			Shambala (3)	
4/27/74	**20**	8	● 11. Hard Labor	Dunhill 50168
			The Show Must Go On (4)	
1/11/75	**15**	8	● 12. Joy To The World-Their Greatest Hits [G]	Dunhill 50178

DATE	POS	WKS	ARTIST—RECORD TITLE	LABEL & NO.
			THREE SUNS, The	
			Instrumental trio: brothers Al (guitar; d: 1965) and Morty Nevins (accordion; d: 7/20/90 of cancer) with Artie Dunn (organ; D: 1989). Al Nevins founded, with Don Kirshner, Aldon Music, the famed publishing company largely responsible for the "Brill Building" rock and roll sound.	
5/28/55	**13**	9	1. Soft and Sweet [I]	RCA 1041
8/18/56	**19**	1	2. High Fi and Wide [I]	RCA 1249
1/26/57	**16**	6	3. Midnight For Two [I]	RCA 1333
			TIERRA	
			East Los Angeles group led by brothers Steve (trombone, timbales) and Rudy (guitar) Salas. Both formerly with El Chicano.	
3/7/81	**38**	4	1. City Nights	Boardwalk 36995
			TIFFANY	
			Tiffany Darwisch, born on 10/2/71. California pop singer, originally from Oklahoma.	
11/7/87	**1**(2)	35	▲ 1. Tiffany *I Think We're Alone Now* (1)/*Could've Been* (1)/ *I Saw Him Standing There* (7)	MCA 5793
12/17/88	**17**	19	▲ 2. Hold An Old Friend's Hand *All This Time* (6)	MCA 6267
			TILLOTSON, Johnny	
			Born on 4/20/39 in Jacksonville, Florida; raised in Palatka, Florida. On local radio "Young Folks Revue" from age nine. DJ on WWPF. Appeared on the "Toby Dowdy" TV show in Jacksonville, then own show. Signed by Cadence Records in 1958. In the film *Just For Fun*.	
8/25/62	**8**	10	1. It Keeps Right On A-Hurtin' *It Keeps Right On A-Hurtin'* (3)	Cadence 3058
			'TIL TUESDAY	
			Boston pop quartet: Aimee Mann (lead singer, bass), Michael Hausmann (drums), Robert Holmes (guitar) and Joey Pesce (keyboards; replaced by Michael Montes in 1988).	
6/1/85	**19**	12	● 1. Voices Carry *Voices Carry* (8)	Epic 39458
			TIME, The	
			Funk group formed in Minneapolis by Prince and Morris Day in 1981. Original lineup: Morris Day (lead singer), Terry Lewis, Jimmy "Jam" Harris, Monte Moir, Jesse Johnson and Jellybean Johnson. Lewis, Harris and Moir left prior to band's featured role in film *Purple Rain*. Paul "St. Paul" Peterson and Lewis' brother Jerome Benton joined in 1984; group disbanded later that year. Day and Jesse Johnson went solo; Lewis and Harris became a highly successful songwriting/producing team. Original lineup plus Benton re-grouped in 1990.	
10/2/82	**26**	8	● 1. What Time Is It?	Warner 23701
8/25/84	**24**	34	▲ 2. Ice Cream Castle	Warner 25109
			TIN MACHINE	
			Quartet of David Bowie (vocals), Reeves Gabrels (guitar), Hunt (drums) and Tony Sales (bass). The Sales brothers are the sons of television comedian Soupy Sales.	
6/17/89	**28**	5	1. Tin Machine	EMI 91990

DATE	POS	WKS	ARTIST—RECORD TITLE	LABEL & NO.
			TINY TIM	
			Born Herbert Khaury on 4/12/30 in New York City. Novelty singer/ukulele player. National phenomenon when he married "Miss Vicki" on "The Tonight Show" on 12/18/69.	
6/8/68	7	10	1. God Bless Tiny Tim [N]	Reprise 6292
			TOBY BEAU	
			Texas pop quintet: Danny McKenna, Rob Young, Balde Silva, Steve Zipper and Ron Rose.	
9/2/78	40	1	1. Toby Beau	RCA 2771
			TOMLIN, Lily	
			Born on 9/1/39 in Detroit. TV and film actress/comedienne. Member of TV's "Laugh-In" series (1970-73). In films *9 To 5*, *All of Me* and *Big Business*. In Broadway's *The Search For Signs Of Intelligent Life In The Universe*.	
4/10/71	15	11	1. This is a Recording [C]	Polydor 4055
			TOMMY TUTONE	
			San Francisco rock band led by Tommy Heath (lead singer) & Jim Keller (lead guitar).	
4/17/82	20	8	1. Tommy Tutone-2 *867-5309/Jenny* (4)	Columbia 37401
			TOM TOM CLUB	
			Studio project formed by Talking Heads members Chris Frantz and wife Tina Weymouth. Much production work for Ziggy Marley & The Melody Makers.	
2/20/82	23	10	● 1. Tom Tom Club	Sire 3628
			TONE LOC	
			L.A.-based rapper, Anthony Smith. Stage name derived from his Spanish nickname "Antonio Loco."	
2/25/89	1(1)	23	▲ 1. Loc-Ed After Dark *Wild Thing* (2)/*Funky Cold Medina* (3)	Delicious 3000
			TONY! TONI! TONE!	
			R&B-funk band from Oakland, California. Nucleus of group: brothers Dwayne & Raphael Wiggins, with cousin Timothy Christian.	
6/23/90	34	5	● 1. The Revival	Polygram 841902
			TOO SHORT	
			Born Todd Shaw on 4/28/66 in Los Angeles. 5pi1727″ Oakland-based rapper.	
4/29/89	37	8	▲ 1. Life Is…Too $hort	Dangerous 1149
			TOTO	
			Pop-rock group formed in Los Angeles in 1978. Consisted of Bobby Kimball (born Robert Toteaux; vocals), Steve Lukather (guitar), David Paich and Steve Porcaro (keyboards), David Hungate (bass) and Jeff Porcaro (drums). Prominent session musicians, most notably behind Boz Scaggs in the late 70s. Hungate was replaced by Mike Porcaro in 1983. (The Porcaros are brothers.) Kimball replaced by Fergie Frederiksen in 1984; Frederiksen replaced by Joseph Williams (conductor John's son) in 1986. Steve Porcaro left in 1988. South African native Jean-Michel Byron replaced Frederiksen in 1990. Paich and his father Marty Won an Emmy for writing the theme to the TV series "Ironside."	
12/9/78	9	20	▲ 1. Toto *Hold The Line* (5)	Columbia 35317
12/15/79	37	3	● 2. Hydra	Columbia 36229
5/8/82	4	42	▲ 3. Toto IV 1982 Grammy winner: Album of the Year *Rosanna* (2)/*Africa* (1)/*I Won't Hold You Back* (10)	Columbia 37728

DATE	POS	WKS	ARTIST—RECORD TITLE		LABEL & NO.
11/29/86	**40**	2	4. Fahrenheit		Columbia 40273
			TOWER OF POWER		
			Interracial Oakland-based, R&B-funk band formed by sax player Emilio "Mimi" Castillo in the late 60s. Lenny Williams sang lead from 1972-75. Originally known as the Motowns.		
7/28/73	**15**	8	● 1. Tower Of Power		Warner 2681
4/6/74	**26**	5	2. Back to Oakland		Warner 2749
2/22/75	**22**	5	3. Urban Renewal		Warner 2834
			TOWNSHEND, Pete		
			Born on 5/19/45 in London. Lead guitarist/songwriter of The Who.		
5/24/80	**5**	19	● 1. Empty Glass		Atco 100
			Let My Love Open The Door (9)		
7/24/82	**26**	9	2. All The Best Cowboys Have Chinese Eyes		Atco 149
4/9/83	**35**	4	3. Scoop	[K]	Atco 90063 [2]
			primarily a collection of Townshend's demo recordings		
12/28/85	**26**	11	● 4. White City - A Novel		Atco 90473
			T'PAU		
			Group from Shrewsbury, England; Carol Decker, lead singer. Band named after a Vulcan Princess in an episode of the TV series "Star Trek."		
8/22/87	**31**	3	1. T'Pau		Virgin 90595
			Heart And Soul (4)		
			TRAFFIC		
			British rock band - original lineup: Steve Winwood (keyboards, guitar), Dave Mason (guitar), Jim Capaldi (drums) and Chris Wood (flute, sax; d: 7/12/83). Many personnel changes during the group's seven-year existence.		
12/21/68	**17**	8	1. Traffic		United Art. 6676
5/24/69	**19**	7	2. Last Exit		United Art. 6702
7/25/70	**5**	16	● 3. John Barleycorn Must Die		United Art. 5504
10/16/71	**26**	7	4. Welcome To The Canteen	[L]	United Art. 5550
12/18/71	**7**	20	● 5. The Low Spark Of High Heeled Boys		Island 9306
2/17/73	**6**	12	● 6. Shoot Out At The Fantasy Factory		Island 9323
11/24/73	**29**	5	7. Traffic-On The Road	[L]	Island 9336 [2]
10/5/74	**9**	10	● 8. When The Eagle Flies		Asylum 1020
			TRAVELING WILBURYS		
			Supergroup masquerading as a band of brothers. Spearheaded by Nelson (George Harrison) with Lucky (Bob Dylan), Otis (Jeff Lynne of ELO), Lefty (Roy Orbison) and Charlie T. Junior (Tom Petty) Wilbury.		
11/19/88	**3**	32	▲ 1. Volume One		Wilbury 25796
			TRAVERS, Pat		
			Canadian blues-rock guitarist/vocalist.		
9/1/79	**29**	4	1. Pat Travers Band Live! Go For What You Know *	[L]	Polydor 6202
4/12/80	**20**	12	2. Crash And Burn *		Polydor 6262
			*PAT TRAVERS BAND		
4/25/81	**37**	2	3. Radio Active		Polydor 6313
			TRAVIS, Randy		
			Country singer/guitarist, born Randy Bruce Traywick in Marshville, North Carolina on 5/4/59. To Nashville in 1981. The youngest male member inducted into the Grand Ole Opry.		
6/6/87	**19**	21	▲ 1. Always & Forever		Warner 25568

DATE	POS	WKS	ARTIST—RECORD TITLE	LABEL & NO.
8/13/88	**35**	6	▲ 2. Old 8x10	Warner 25738
10/28/89	**33**	3	▲ 3. No Holdin' Back	Warner 25988
			TRAVOLTA, John	
			Born on 2/18/54 in Englewood, New Jersey. Vinnie Barbarino on the TV series "Welcome Back Kotter." Starred in the films *Saturday Night Fever*, *Grease*, *Urban Cowboy*, *Blow Out*, *Look Who's Talking* and others.	
7/17/76	**39**	4	1. John Travolta *Let Her In* (10)	Midland Int. 1563
			T. REX	
			British rock group led by Marc Bolan (born Marc Feld on 9/30/48 in London; killed in an auto accident on 9/16/77).	
3/18/72	**32**	5	1. Electric Warrior *Bang A Gong (Get It On)* (10)	Reprise 6466
10/7/72	**17**	11	2. The Slider	Reprise 2095
			TRIUMPH	
			Canadian hard-rock trio formed in Toronto in 1975. Consisted of Gil Moore (drums, vocals), Rik Emmett (guitar, vocals) and Mike Levine (keyboards, bass).	
4/19/80	**32**	6	1. Progessions Of Power	RCA 3524
10/17/81	**23**	9	● 2. Allied Forces	RCA 3902
2/12/83	**26**	12	● 3. Never Surrender	RCA 4382
2/2/85	**35**	7	4. Thunder Seven	MCA 5537
10/25/86	**33**	5	5. The Sport Of Kings	MCA 5786
			TRIUMVIRAT	
			German synthesized rock group: Helmut Kollen (guitar, vocals), Hans Bathelt (drums) and Jurgen Fritz (keyboards). Kollen replaced by Barry Palmer (vocals) and Dick Frangenberg (bass) in 1976.	
7/26/75	**27**	5	1. Spartacus	Capitol 11392
			TROWER, Robin	
			Rock guitarist born on 3/9/45 in London. Member of Procol Harum. James Dewar, vocalist (except on *B.L.T.* album).	
5/11/74	**7**	21	● 1. Bridge Of Sighs	Chrysalis 1057
3/8/75	**5**	9	● 2. For Earth Below	Chrysalis 1073
4/3/76	**10**	8	3. Robin Trower Live! [L]	Chrysalis 1089
10/16/76	**24**	6	● 4. Long Misty Days	Chrysalis 1107
10/22/77	**25**	6	● 5. In City Dreams	Chrysalis 1148
10/7/78	**37**	4	6. Caravan To Midnight	Chrysalis 1189
4/5/80	**34**	3	7. Victims Of The Fury	Chrysalis 1215
4/25/81	**37**	3	8. B.L.T. B.L.T.: Jack Bruce, Bill Lordan, Robin Trower	Chrysalis 1324
			TUBES, The	
			San Francisco theatre rock troupe led by vocalist Fee Waybill (born John Waldo on 9/17/50 in Omaha, Nebraska). Group appeared in musical *Xanadu* with Olivia Newton-John in 1980.	
7/18/81	**36**	4	1. The Completion Backward Principle	Capitol 12151
4/30/83	**18**	14	2. Outside Inside *She's A Beauty* (10)	Capitol 12260

DATE	POS	WKS	ARTIST—RECORD TITLE	LABEL & NO.
			TURNER, Ike & Tina	
			Husband-and-wife duo: guitarist Ike Turner (b: 11/5/31 in Clarksdale, Mississippi) and vocalist Tina (born Anna Mae Bullock on 11/26/38 in Brownsville, Tennessee). Married from 1958-76. At age 11, Ike was backing pianist for bluesmen Sonny Boy Williamson (Aleck Ford) and Robert Nighthawk (of the Nighthawks). Formed own band, the Kings of Rhythm, while in high school; backed Jackie Brenston's hit "Rocket '88'." Prolific session, production and guitar work during the 1950s. In 1960, developed a dynamic stage show around Tina; "The Ike & Tina Turner Revue" featured her backing vocalists, The Ikettes, and Ike's Kings Of Rhythm. Disbanded in 1974. In the mid-80s, Tina emerged as a successful solo artist.	
3/13/71	**25**	8	1. Workin' Together *Proud Mary* (4)	Liberty 7650
7/31/71	**25**	11	● 2. Live At Carnegie Hall/What You Hear Is What You Get [L]	United Art. 9953 [2]
			TURNER, Tina	
			Born Anna Mae Bullock on 11/26/38 in Brownsville, Tennessee. R&B-rock vocalist/ actress. Half of Ike & Tina Turner duo. In films *Tommy* and *Mad Max Beyond Thunderdome*.	
6/30/84	**3**	71	▲ 1. Private Dancer *What's Love Got To Do With It* (1)/*Better Be Good To Me* (5)/ *Private Dancer* (7)	Capitol 12330
10/4/86	**4**	17	▲ 2. Break Every Rule *Typical Male* (2)	Capitol 12530
10/14/89	**31**	5	● 3. Foreign Affair	Capitol 91873
			TURTLES, The	
			Pop-folk-rock group formed at Westchester High School in Los Angeles in 1961. Led by Mark Volman (b: 4/19/47, Los Angeles) and Howard Kaylan (born Howard Kaplan on 6/22/47, New York City). First called the Nightriders; then the Crossfires. Recorded for Capco in 1963. Name changed to The Turtles in 1965. Many personnel changes except for Volman and Kaylan. Group disbanded in 1970. Volman and Kaylan joined the Mothers Of Invention. Went out as a duo in 1972 and recorded as Phlorescent Leech & Eddie and later as Flo & Eddie. Did soundtrack for the film *Strawberry Shortcake*. Toured again as The Turtles in 1985.	
5/20/67	**25**	7	1. Happy Together *Happy Together* (1)/*She'd Rather Be With Me* (3)	White Whale 7114
12/16/67	**7**	16	● 2. The Turtles! Golden Hits [G]	White Whale 7115
			TWILLEY, Dwight	
			Born on 6/6/51 in Tulsa, Oklahoma. Rock singer/songwriter/pianist. Formed the Dwight Twilley Band with Phil Seymour (bass, drums) in 1974.	
4/14/84	**39**	3	1. Jungle	EMI America 17107
			TWISTED SISTER	
			Long Island, New York heavy-metal quintet led by Dee Snider (b: 3/15/55, Massapequa, Long Island, New York). Included Jay French (guitar), Eddie Ojeda (guitar), Mark Mendosa (bass) and A.J. Pero (drums). Pero replaced by Joey Franco in 1987. Disbanded in late 1987.	
8/4/84	**15**	26	▲ 1. Stay Hungry	Atlantic 80156
			2 LIVE CREW, The	
			Miami-based rap quartet: David "Mr. Mix" Hobbs, Chris "Fresh Kid-Ice" Won Wong, "Brother Marquis" Ross and Luther "Luke Skyywalker" Campbell (owner of Luke Skyywalker Records). Group's obscenity arrests sparked national censorship controversy in 1990.	
9/2/89	**29**	31	▲ 1. As Nasty As They Wanna Be	Luke Sky. 107 [2]

DATE	POS	WKS	ARTIST—RECORD TITLE	LABEL & NO.
			TYLER, Bonnie	
			Born Gaynor Hopkins on 6/8/53 in Swansea, Wales. Distinctive raspy vocals caused by operation to remove throat nodules in 1976.	
6/10/78	**16**	8	● 1. It's A Heartache *It's A Heartache* (3)	RCA 2821
9/10/83	**4**	18	▲ 2. Faster Than The Speed Of Night *Total Eclipse Of The Heart* (1)	Columbia 38710
			TYMES, The	
			Soul group formed in Philadelphia in 1956. Consisted of George Williams (lead), George Hilliard, Donald Banks, Albert Berry and Norman Burnett. First called the Latineers.	
8/24/63	**15**	9	1. So Much In Love *So Much In Love* (1)/*Wonderful! Wonderful!* (7)	Parkway 7032
			# U	
			UB40	
			British interracial reggae octet - Ali Campbell, lead singer. Took name from a British unemployment benefit form.	
4/14/84	**14**	15	▲ 1. Labour of Love originally peaked at POS 39 in 1984; re-entered and reached new peak in 1988 *Red Red Wine* (1)	A&M 4980
10/5/85	**40**	3	2. Little Baggariddim [M]	A&M 5090
			UFO	
			British hard-rock group led by Phil Mogg (vocals) and Michael Schenker (guitar).	
7/23/77	**23**	12	1. Lights Out	Chrysalis 1127
			ULLMAN, Tracy	
			Born on 12/30/59 in England. Actress/singer/comedienne. Own variety-style TV show on new Fox Broadcasting Co. network, 1987-90.	
4/28/84	**34**	5	1. You Broke My Heart In 17 Places *They Don't Know* (8)	MCA 5471
			ULTIMATE SPINACH	
			Psychedelic rock quintet from Boston: Ian Bruce-Douglas, Barbara Hudson, Keith Lahteinen, Richard Nese and Geoffrey Winthrop.	
4/20/68	**34**	4	1. Ultimate Spinach	MGM 4518
			UNION GAP — see PUCKETT, Gary	
			UNITED STATES MARINE BAND	
6/22/63	**22**	6	1. The United States Marine Band [I] directed by Lieutenant Colonel Albert F. Schoepper; proceeds from this album and the Navy album below donated to fund-raising project for The National Cultural Center in Washington, D.C.	RCA 2687
			UNITED STATES NAVY BAND	
6/22/63	**38**	1	1. The United States Navy Band with The Sea Chanters on two tracks; directed by Lieutenant Commander Anthony A. Mitchell	RCA 2688

Sonny & Cher's 1965 No. 1 hit, "I Got You, Babe," generally evokes 60s nostalgia. Yet the rankings of their first solo efforts while together—Cher's *All I Really Want To Do!* for Imperial reached No. 16; Sonny's *Inner Views* for Atco flopped—foreshadowed each artist's future recording success after they split up in 1974.

Bruce Springsteen's *Darkness On The Edge Of Town* was the artist's first platinum album ever. *Born To Run*, its best-selling predecessor, was released in 1975—one year prior to the creation of the RIAA's platinum certification award.

Barbra Streisand's nonstop ride to the top as America's premier female vocalist began in 1963, when her first album, *The Barbra Streisand Album* on Columbia, hit the No. 8 spot and stayed on the Top Pop Albums chart for a total of 101 weeks. 1978's *Songbird*, just one of her 35 top 40 LPs, made it to No. 12.

Donna Summer's popularity peaked during what has come to be regarded as the "Disco Era." Between 1978-1979, she had three consecutive No. 1 albums: *Live And More, Bad Girls* and *On The Radio—Greatest Hits—Volumes I & II*.

The **Supremes** placed a total of 42 albums on the Top Pop Albums chart, beginning with 1964's *Where Did Our Love Go*, followed by *A Bit Of Liverpool*, and extending through 1976's *High Energy*. Even after lead singer Diana Ross left in 1970, the group produced 10 albums that notably charted.

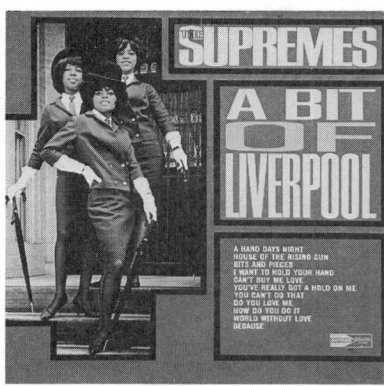

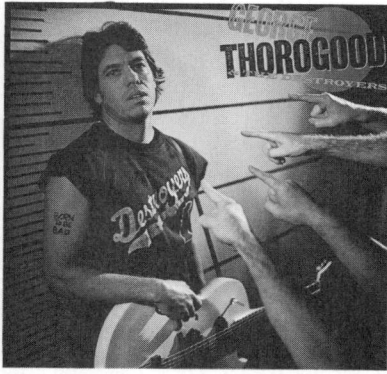

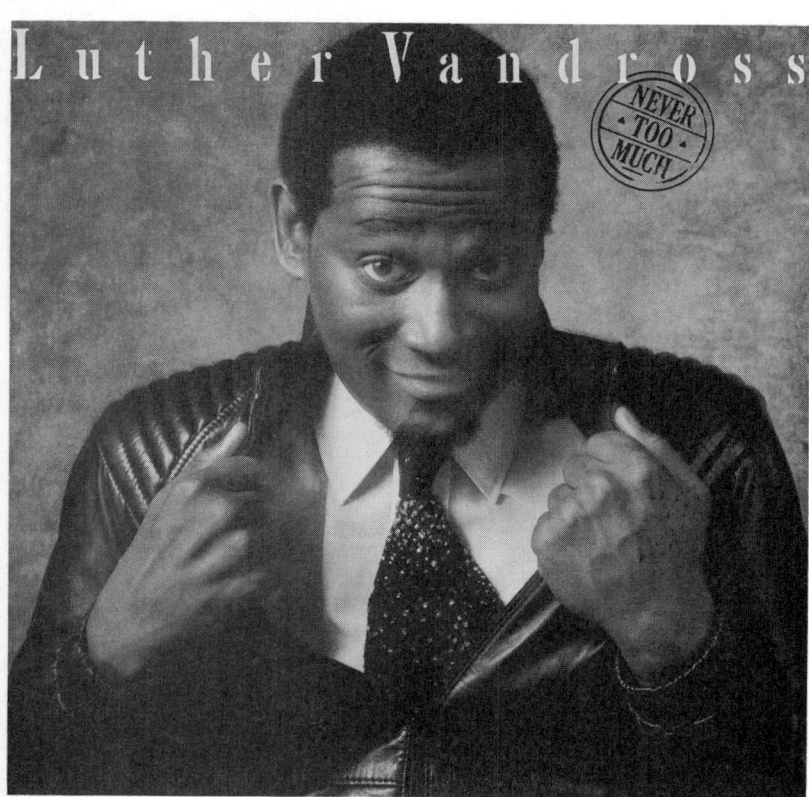

Tears For Fears, a Bath, England-based duo featuring Roland Orzabal and Curt Smith, were acclaimed world-wide for their 1985 album *Songs From The Big Chair*—so much so that it took a full four years for the group to come up with a follow-up, *The Seeds Of Love*.

The **Thompson Twins**, comprised of neither twins nor anyone named Thompson, reached the top 10 in 1984 with their platinum-certified *Into the Gap*. Group mainstays Tom Bailey and Alannah Currie would later bid goodbye to member Joe Leeway in 1986.

George Thorogood & The Destroyers surprised many in 1978 when their independently-distributed Rounder LP *Move It On Over* hit No. 33 on the album charts. The highly respected guitarist then shifted over to EMI distribution in 1982 and had success with such albums as *Bad To The Bone* and 1988's *Born To Be Bad*.

Van Halen's *1984* was a noteworthy album for the hard-rocking quartet for two reasons: It contained "Jump," their only No. 1 single, and it was their last LP to feature colorful lead singer David Lee Roth, who departed thereafter to begin a healthy solo career.

Luther Vandross' *Never Too Much* was his first album to reach the top 40, peaking at No. 19. Throughout the 80s, Vandross's silky-smooth soul sounds fared well on the Top Pop Albums chart, but not as well as on the black charts—illustrating the crossover problems some of the most highly-respected black artists faced during that decade.

DATE	POS	WKS	ARTIST—RECORD TITLE	LABEL & NO.
			URIAH HEEP	
			British hard-rock band. Key members: David Byron (lead singer), Mick Box (lead guitar) and Ken Hensley (keyboards; later with Blackfoot).	
8/26/72	**23**	13	● 1. Demons And Wizards	Mercury 630
1/6/73	**31**	8	● 2. The Magician's Birthday	Mercury 652
6/9/73	**37**	5	● 3. Uriah Heep Live [L]	Mercury 7503 [2]
11/3/73	**33**	3	● 4. Sweet Freedom	Warner 2724
8/24/74	**38**	2	5. Wonderworld	Warner 2800
			USA FOR AFRICA	
			USA: United Support of Artists - a collection of 46 major artists formed to help the suffering people of Africa and the U.S.	
4/20/85	**1**(3)	11	▲ 1. We Are The World tracks contributed by Northern Lights (Canada's superstar artists), Bruce Springsteen, Prince, Huey Lewis, Chicago, Tina Turner, Pointer Sisters, Kenny Rogers, Steve Perry *We Are The World* (1)	Columbia 40043
			UTOPIA	
			Veteran pop-rock group with own recording studio near Woodstock, New York. Consists of Todd Rundgren (guitar), Kasim Sulton (bass), Roger Powell (keyboards) and Willie Wilcox (drums).	
12/14/74	**34**	2	1. Todd Rundgren's Utopia	Bearsville 6954
2/16/80	**32**	5	2. Adventures In Utopia	Bearsville 6991
			U2	
			Rock band formed in Dublin, Ireland in 1976. Consists of Paul "Bono" Hewson (vocals), Dave "The Edge" Evans (guitar), Adam Clayton (bass) and Larry Mullen, Jr. (drums). Emerged as 1987's leading rock act. *Rattle And Hum* is U2's concert documentary film.	
4/2/83	**12**	16	▲ 1. War	Island 90067
1/7/84	**28**	13	▲ 2. Under A Blood Red Sky [M-L]	Island 90127
10/27/84	**12**	22	▲ 3. The Unforgettable Fire	Island 90231
6/29/85	**37**	1	4. Wide Awake In America [M-L] side A: live; side B: out takes from *The Unforgettable Fire* LP; album dropped by *Billboard* after charting for one week because it was only a four-cut album that listed for less than $5.98	Island 90279
4/4/87	**1**(9)	58	▲ 5. The Joshua Tree 1987 Grammy winner: Album of the Year *With Or Without You* (1)/ *I Still Haven't Found What I'm Looking For* (1)	Island 90581
10/29/88	**1**(6)	23	▲ 6. Rattle And Hum [S] music from their 1988 concert/documentary film *Desire* (3)	Island 91003 [2]
			# V	
			VAI, Steve	
			Rock guitarist from Carle Place, Long Island, New York. Joined Frank Zappa's band at age 18 in 1979. Former guitar student of Joe Satriani. With David Lee Roth's band, 1986-88. Briefly a member of Alcatrazz (1985) and Whitesnake (1989).	
6/16/90	**18**	13	● 1. Passion and Warfare [I] includes spoken introductions to songs	Relativity 1037

DATE	POS	WKS	ARTIST—RECORD TITLE	LABEL & NO.
			VALE, Jerry	
			Born Genero Vitaliano on 7/8/32 in the Bronx. Pop ballad singer.	
4/13/63	**34**	4	1. Arrivederci, Roma	Columbia 8755
10/26/63	**22**	6	2. The Language Of Love	Columbia 8843
3/21/64	**28**	6	3. Till The End Of Time	Columbia 8916
10/17/64	**26**	6	4. Be My Love	Columbia 8981
4/24/65	**30**	5	5. Have You Looked Into Your Heart	Columbia 9113
4/30/66	**38**	1	6. It's Magic	Columbia 9244
			VALENS, Ritchie	
			Born Richard Valenzuela on 5/13/41 in Pacoima, California. Latin rock and roll singer/songwriter/guitarist. Killed in the plane crash that also took the lives of Buddy Holly and the Big Bopper on 2/3/59. In the film *Go Johnny Go*. The 1987 film *La Bamba* was based on his life.	
4/6/59	**23**	5	1. Ritchie Valens *Donna* (2)	Del-Fi 1201
			VALLI, Frankie	
			Born Francis Castellucio on 5/3/37 in Newark, New Jersey. Recorded his first solo single in 1953 as Frank Valley on the Corona label. Formed own group the Variatones in 1955, and changed their name to the Four Lovers in 1956, which evolved into The 4 Seasons by 1961. Began solo work in 1965.	
8/26/67	**34**	2	1. Frankie Valli-Solo *Can't Take My Eyes Off You* (2)	Philips 247
			VANDROSS, Luther	
			Born on 4/20/51 in New York City. Soul singer/producer/songwriter. Commercial jingle singer, then a top session vocalist/arranger.	
10/10/81	**19**	10	● 1. Never Too Much	Epic 37451
10/30/82	**20**	12	▲ 2. Forever, For Always, For Love	Epic 38235
1/28/84	**32**	9	▲ 3. Busy Body	Epic 39196
4/20/85	**19**	15	▲ 4. The Night I Fell In Love	Epic 39882
11/8/86	**14**	32	▲ 5. Give Me The Reason	Epic 40415
10/29/88	**9**	16	▲ 6. Any Love	Epic 44308
11/25/89	**26**	22	▲ 7. The Best Of Luther Vandross...The Best Of Love [G] *Here And Now* (6)	Epic 45320 [2]
			VANGELIS	
			Born Evangelos Papathanassiou on 3/29/43 in Valos, Greece. Keyboardist/composer. Moved to Paris during the late 60s, then to London in the mid-70s. Formed rock band Aphrodite's Child in France with Demis Roussos, 1968-early 70s.	
2/20/82	**1**(4)	20	▲ 1. Chariots Of Fire [S-I] film is based on the true story of two members of Britain's 1924 Olympic team *Chariots Of Fire-Titles* (1)	Polydor 6335
			VAN HALEN	
			Hard-rock band formed in Pasadena, California in 1974. Consisted of David Lee Roth (b: 10/10/55; vocals), Eddie Van Halen (b: 1/26/57; guitar), Michael Anthony (b: 6/20/55; bass) and Alex Van Halen (b: 5/8/55; drums). The Van Halen brothers were born in Nijmegen, The Netherlands, and moved to Pasadena in 1968. Sammy Hagar replaced Roth as lead singer in 1985.	
4/15/78	**19**	12	▲ 1. Van Halen	Warner 3075
4/21/79	**6**	18	▲ 2. Van Halen II	Warner 3312
4/19/80	**6**	13	▲ 3. Women and Children First	Warner 3415
5/30/81	**5**	12	▲ 4. Fair Warning	Warner 3540

DATE	POS	WKS	ARTIST—RECORD TITLE	LABEL & NO.
5/8/82	**3**	16	▲ 5. Diver Down	Warner 3677
1/28/84	**2(5)**	52	▲ 6. 1984 (MCMLXXXIV)	Warner 23985
			Jump (1)	
4/12/86	**1(3)**	32	▲ 7. 5150	Warner 25394
			Sammy Hagar replaces David Lee Roth as lead singer; 5150: New York Police code for the criminally insane; also the name of Eddie Van Halen's recording studio	
			Why Can't This Be Love (3)	
6/18/88	**1(4)**	35	▲ 8. OU812	Warner 25732
			When It's Love (5)	

VANILLA FUDGE

Psychedelic rock quartet formed in New York in 1966. Consisted of Mark Stein (lead singer, keyboards), Vinnie Martell (guitar), Tim Bogert (bass) and Carmine Appice (drummer with Cactus, Rod Stewart and Blue Murder).

DATE	POS	WKS	ARTIST—RECORD TITLE	LABEL & NO.
9/23/67	**6**	39	● 1. Vanilla Fudge	Atco 224
			You Keep Me Hangin' On (6)	
3/9/68	**17**	9	2. The Beat Goes On	Atco 237
8/10/68	**20**	9	3. Renaissance	Atco 244
3/15/69	**16**	9	4. Near the Beginning [L]	Atco 278
			side 2 recorded live	
11/1/69	**34**	4	5. Rock & Roll	Atco 303

VANNELLI, Gino

Born on 6/16/52 in Montreal, Canada. Pop/soul-styled singer/songwriter.

DATE	POS	WKS	ARTIST—RECORD TITLE	LABEL & NO.
9/11/76	**32**	5	1. The Gist of The Gemini	A&M 4596
1/7/78	**33**	4	2. A Pauper In Paradise	A&M 4664
			side 2 with the Royal Philharmonic Orchestra	
11/4/78	**13**	11	▲ 3. Brother To Brother	A&M 4722
			I Just Wanna Stop (4)	
4/25/81	**15**	15	4. Nightwalker	Arista 9539
			Living Inside Myself (6)	

VAUGHAN, Sarah

Born on 3/27/24 in Newark, New Jersey. Jazz singer. Dubbed "The Divine One." Studied piano from 1931-39. Won amateur contest at the Apollo Theater in 1942, which led to her joining Earl Hines' band as vocalist/second pianist. First recorded solo for Continental in 1944. With Billy Eckstine from 1944-45. Married manager/trumpeter George Treadwell in 1947. Later husbands included pro football player Clyde Atkins and trumpeter Waymon Reed. Performed into the 80s. Died of lung cancer on 4/3/90.

DATE	POS	WKS	ARTIST—RECORD TITLE	LABEL & NO.
11/24/56	**20**	2	1. Linger Awhile	Columbia 914
12/1/56	**21**	1	2. Sassy	EmArcy 36089
4/13/57	**14**	9	3. Great Songs From Hit Shows	Mercury 100 [2]
8/19/57	**14**	9	4. Sarah Vaughan sings George Gershwin	Mercury 101 [2]

VAUGHAN, Stevie Ray

Dallas-bred, blues-rock guitarist. Leader of the Austin-based band Double Trouble. His brother is Jimmy Vaughan (The Fabulous Thunderbirds). Stevie was the lead guitarist on David Bowie's *Let's Dance* album. Died in a helicopter crash on 8/27/90 (age 35).

STEVIE RAY VAUGHAN AND DOUBLE TROUBLE:

DATE	POS	WKS	ARTIST—RECORD TITLE	LABEL & NO.
9/3/83	**38**	3	● 1. Texas Flood	Epic 38734
7/7/84	**31**	8	2. Couldn't Stand The Weather	Epic 39304
10/26/85	**34**	6	● 3. Soul To Soul	Epic 40036
8/12/89	**33**	6	● 4. In Step	Epic 45024

DATE	POS	WKS	ARTIST—RECORD TITLE		LABEL & NO.
			VAUGHN, Billy		
			Born Richard Vaughn on 4/12/19 in Glasgow, Kentucky. Organized the Hilltoppers vocal group in 1952. Music director for Dot Records. Arranger/conductor for Pat Boone, Gale Storm, The Fontane Sisters and many other Dot artists. Billy had more pop hits than any other orchestra leader during the rock era.		
			BILLY VAUGHN AND HIS ORCHESTRA:		
4/21/58	**5**	44	● 1. Sail Along Silv'ry Moon	[I]	Dot 3100
			Sail Along Silvery Moon (5)/*Raunchy* (10)		
10/13/58	**15**	41	2. Billy Vaughn Plays The Million Sellers	[I]	Dot 3119
5/4/59	**20**	3	3. Billy Vaughn Plays	[I]	Dot 3156
5/25/59	**7**	48	● 4. Blue Hawaii	[I]	Dot 3165
1/18/60	**36**	1	5. Golden Saxophones	[I]	Dot 3205
3/21/60	**1(2)**	38	● 6. Theme from A Summer Place	[I]	Dot 3276
8/15/60	**5**	21	7. Look For A Star	[I]	Dot 3322
12/19/60	**5**	13	8. Theme from The Sundowners	[I]	Dot 3349
5/8/61	**11**	20	9. Orange Blossom Special and Wheels	[I]	Dot 3366
10/9/61	**17**	9	10. Golden Waltzes	[I]	Dot 3280
12/4/61	**20**	15	11. Berlin Melody	[I]	Dot 3396
3/24/62	**18**	11	12. Greatest String Band Hits		Dot 3409
6/9/62	**14**	13	13. Chapel By The Sea	[I]	Dot 3424
10/6/62	**10**	10	14. A Swingin' Safari	[I]	Dot 3458
2/16/63	**17**	12	15. 1962's Greatest Hits	[I]	Dot 25497
7/6/63	**15**	6	16. Sukiyaki and 11 Hawaiian Hits	[I]	Dot 25523
3/6/65	**18**	9	17. Pearly Shells	[I]	Dot 25605
11/13/65	**31**	6	18. Moon Over Naples	[I]	Dot 25654
			VEE, Bobby		
			Born Robert Velline on 4/30/43 in Fargo, North Dakota. Formed The Shadows with his brother and a friend in 1959. After Buddy Holly's death in a plane crash, The Shadows filled in on Buddy's next scheduled show in Fargo. First recorded for Soma in 1959. In the films *Swingin' Along*, *It's Trad, Dad*, *Play It Cool*, *C'mon Let's Live A Little* and *Just For Fun*. Still performing on oldies tours.		
3/20/61	**18**	2	1. Bobby Vee		Liberty 7181
			Devil Or Angel (6)/*Rubber Ball* (6)		
12/1/62	**24**	9	2. Bobby Vee's Golden Greats	[G]	Liberty 7245
			VEGA, Suzanne		
			New York vocalist/acoustic guitarist/songwriter.		
7/4/87	**11**	17	● 1. Solitude Standing		A&M 5136
			Luka (3)		
			VENTURES, The		
			Guitar-based instrumental rock and roll band formed in the Seattle/Tacoma, Washington area. Consisted of lead guitarist Nokie Edwards (b: 5/9/39; bass) and lead guitarist Bob Bogle (b: 1/16/37), rhythm guitarist Don Wilson (b: 2/10/37), and drummer Howie Johnson. First recorded for own Blue Horizon label in 1959. Johnson was injured in an auto accident and was replaced by Mel Taylor in 1963. Taylor went solo in 1967, returned in 1978. Edwards left in 1968, replaced by Gerry McGee, returned in 1972. Added keyboardist John Durrill in 1969. Latest recordings featured Edwards, Bogle, Wilson and Taylor. McGee again replaced Edwards.		
12/5/60	**11**	9	1. Walk Don't Run	[I]	Dolton 8003
			Walk-Don't Run (2)		
7/31/61	**39**	2	2. Another Smash!!!	[I]	Dolton 8006

DATE	POS	WKS	ARTIST—RECORD TITLE		LABEL & NO.
2/3/62	24	12	3. Twist With The Ventures	[I]	Dolton 8010
1/19/63	8	11	● 4. The Ventures play Telstar, The Lonely Bull	[I]	Dolton 8019
6/1/63	30	5	5. "Surfing"	[I]	Dolton 8022
10/12/63	30	2	6. Let's Go!	[I]	Dolton 8024
2/15/64	27	7	7. (The) Ventures In Space	[I]	Dolton 8027
8/22/64	32	4	8. The Fabulous Ventures	[I]	Dolton 8029
11/7/64	17	10	9. Walk, Don't Run, Vol. 2 *Walk-Don't Run '64* (8)	[I]	Dolton 8031
4/10/65	31	5	10. The Ventures Knock Me Out!	[I]	Dolton 8033
8/28/65	27	9	11. The Ventures On Stage	[I-L]	Dolton 8035
10/23/65	16	20	12. The Ventures a go-go	[I]	Dolton 8037
4/23/66	33	3	13. Where The Action Is	[I]	Dolton 8040
8/20/66	39	2	14. Go With The Ventures!	[I]	Dolton 8045
11/5/66	33	6	15. Wild Things!	[I]	Dolton 8047
5/10/69	11	14	● 16. Hawaii Five-O *Hawaii Five-O* (4)	[I]	Liberty 8061

VERA, Billy

Born William McCord, Jr. on 5/28/44 in Riverside, California. Raised in Westchester County, New York. Wrote hit songs for many pop, R&B and country artists. Formed The Beaters in Los Angeles in 1979, an R&B-based, 10-piece band.

BILLY VERA & THE BEATERS:

DATE	POS	WKS	ARTIST—RECORD TITLE		LABEL & NO.
1/17/87	15	10	● 1. By Request (The Best Of Billy Vera & The Beaters) seven of nine tracks recorded at The Roxy in Hollywood in 1981 *At This Moment* (1)	[E-L]	Rhino 70858

VILLAGE PEOPLE

Campy New York disco group formed by French producer Jacques Morali. Consisted of Victor Willis (lead singer), Randy Jones, David Hodo, Felipe Rose, Glenn Hughes and Alexander Briley. Willis replaced by Ray Simpson (brother of Valerie Simpson of Ashford & Simpson) in late 1979. Group appeared in the film *Can't Stop The Music* (1980).

DATE	POS	WKS	ARTIST—RECORD TITLE		LABEL & NO.
7/29/78	24	8	▲ 1. Macho Man		Casablanca 7096
11/11/78	3	26	▲ 2. Cruisin' *Y.M.C.A.* (2)		Casablanca 7118
4/14/79	8	13	▲ 3. Go West *In The Navy* (3)		Casablanca 7144
11/17/79	32	5	● 4. Live and Sleazy record 1: live; record 2: studio	[L]	Casablanca 7183 [2]

VILLAGE STOMPERS, The

Greenwich Village, New York Dixieland-styled band.

DATE	POS	WKS	ARTIST—RECORD TITLE		LABEL & NO.
11/23/63	5	14	1. Washington Square *Washington Square* (2)	[I]	Epic 26078

VINCENT, Gene

Born Vincent Eugene Craddock on 2/11/35 in Norfolk, Virginia; died from an ulcer hemorrhage on 10/12/71. Innovative rock and roll singer/songwriter/guitarist. Injured left leg in motorcycle accident in 1953, had to wear steel brace thereafter. Formed The Bluecaps in Norfolk in 1956. Appeared in films *The Girl Can't Help It* and *Hot Rod Gang*. To England from 1960-67. Injured in car crash that killed Eddie Cochran in England in 1960.

GENE VINCENT AND HIS BLUE CAPS:

DATE	POS	WKS	ARTIST—RECORD TITLE		LABEL & NO.
9/29/56	16	2	1. Bluejean Bop!		Capitol 764

DATE	POS	WKS	ARTIST—RECORD TITLE	LABEL & NO.
			VINTON, Bobby	
			Born Stanley Robert Vinton on 4/16/35 in Canonsburg, Pennsylvania. Father was a bandleader. Formed own band while in high school; toured as backing band for Dick Clark's "Caravan of Stars" in 1960. Left band for a singing career in 1962. Own musical variety TV series from 1975-78.	
8/18/62	**5**	14	1. Roses Are Red *Roses Are Red (My Love)* (1)/*Mr. Lonely* (1) 1964	Epic 26020
9/7/63	**10**	18	2. Blue Velvet *Blue On Blue* (3)/*Blue Velvet* (1)	Epic 26068
2/22/64	**8**	12	3. There! I've Said It Again *There! I've Said It Again* (1)/ *My Heart Belongs To Only You* (9)	Epic 26081
8/22/64	**31**	4	4. Tell Me Why	Epic 26113
12/5/64	**12**	14	● 5. Bobby Vinton's Greatest Hits [G]	Epic 26098
1/30/65	**18**	7	6. Mr. Lonely album #1 above also contains the hit version of title song	Epic 26136
2/1/69	**21**	6	7. I Love How You Love Me *I Love How You Love Me* (9)	Epic 26437
12/21/74	**16**	7	● 8. Melodies Of Love *My Melody Of Love* (3)	ABC 851
			VOGUES, The	
			Vocal group formed in Turtle Creek, Pennsylvania in 1960. Consisted of Bill Burkette (lead), Hugh Geyer and Chuck Blasko (tenors) and Don Miller (baritone). Met in high school.	
12/7/68	**29**	4	1. Turn Around, Look At Me *Turn Around, Look At Me* (7)/*My Special Angel* (7)	Reprise 6314
4/5/69	**30**	6	2. Till	Reprise 6326
			VOYAGE	
			European disco group - Sylvia Mason, lead singer.	
7/1/78	**40**	2	1. Voyage	Marlin 2213

W

DATE	POS	WKS	ARTIST—RECORD TITLE	LABEL & NO.
			WAITE, John	
			Born on 7/4/55 in England. Lead singer of The Babys and Bad English.	
8/4/84	**10**	17	● 1. No Brakes *Missing You* (1)	EMI America 17124
10/5/85	**36**	3	2. Mask Of Smiles	EMI America 17164
			WAKEMAN, Rick	
			Born on 5/18/49 in London. Former keyboardist of Strawbs and Yes. In 1989, joined group Anderson, Bruford, Wakeman, Howe - all formerly with Yes.	
5/19/73	**30**	13	● 1. The Six Wives of Henry VIII [I]	A&M 4361
6/22/74	**3**	16	● 2. Journey To The Centre Of The Earth [L] with the London Symphony Orchestra	A&M 3621
5/3/75	**21**	6	3. The Myths and Legends of King Arthur and the Knights of the Round Table with the English Chamber Choir and orchestra	A&M 4515

DATE	POS	WKS	ARTIST—RECORD TITLE	LABEL & NO.
			WALSH, Joe	
			Born on 11/20/47 in Wichita, Kansas. Rock singer/songwriter/guitarist. Member of The James Gang (1969-71) and the Eagles (1975-82).	
8/18/73	6	20	● 1. The Smoker You Drink, The Player You Get	Dunhill 50140
2/1/75	11	10	● 2. So What	Dunhill 50171
4/17/76	20	9	3. You Can't Argue With A Sick Mind　　　　[L]	ABC 932
6/17/78	8	14	▲ 4. But Seriously, Folks…	Asylum 141
6/13/81	20	9	5. There Goes The Neighborhood	Asylum 523
			WANDERLEY, Walter	
			Brazilian organist/pianist/composer. Died of cancer on 9/4/86 (age 55).	
11/19/66	22	9	1. Rain Forest　　　　[I]	Verve 8658
			WANG CHUNG	
			British pop-rock group: Jack Hues (lead singer, guitar, keyboards), Nick Feldman (bass, keyboards) and Darren Costin (drums). Costin left in 1985.	
6/23/84	30	6	1. Points On The Curve	Geffen 4004
			WAR	
			Band formed in Long Beach, California in 1969. Consisted of Leroy "Lonnie" Jordan (keyboards), Howard Scott (guitar), Charles Miller (saxophone; murdered in 1980), Morris "B.B." Dickerson (bass), Harold Brown and Thomas "Papa Dee" Allen (percussion) and Lee Oskar (harmonica). Eric Burdon's backup band until 1971. Dickerson was replaced by Luther Rabb. Lee Oskar recorded solo, beginning in 1976. Alice Tweed Smyth (vocals) added in 1978. Pat Rizzo (horns) and Ron Hammond (former member of Aalon; percussion) added in 1979. Smyth left group in 1982.	
			ERIC BURDON & WAR:	
7/11/70	18	13	1. Eric Burdon Declares "War"	MGM 4663
			Spill The Wine (3)	
			WAR:	
3/4/72	16	20	● 2. All Day Music	United Art. 5546
12/16/72	1(2)	25	● 3. The World Is A Ghetto	United Art. 5652
			The World Is A Ghetto (7)/The Cisco Kid (2)	
9/8/73	6	14	● 4. Deliver The Word	United Art. 128
			Gypsy Man (8)	
4/6/74	13	11	● 5. War Live!　　　　[L]	United Art. 193 [2]
7/12/75	8	19	● 6. Why Can't We Be Friends?	United Art. 441
			Why Can't We Be Friends? (6)/Low Rider (7)	
9/4/76	6	13	▲ 7. Greatest Hits　　　　[G]	United Art. 648
			Summer (7)	
8/6/77	23	7	● 8. Platinum Jazz　　　　[K]	Blue Note 690 [2]
12/17/77	15	12	● 9. Galaxy	MCA 3030
			WARD, Anita	
			Born on 12/20/57 in Memphis. R&B-disco vocalist.	
6/9/79	8	10	1. Songs Of Love	Juana 200,004
			Ring My Bell (1)	
			WARING, Fred	
			Born on 6/9/1900 in Tyrone, Pennsylvania; died on 7/29/84. Glee club/bandleader from early 20s.	
			FRED WARING AND THE PENNSYLVANIANS:	
9/9/57	25	1	1. Fred Waring And The Pennsylvanians In Hi-Fi	Capitol 845
12/23/57	6	3	2. Now Is The Caroling Season　　　　[X]	Capitol 896
12/22/58	19	3	3. Now Is The Caroling Season　　　　[X-R]	Capitol 896

DATE	POS	WKS	ARTIST—RECORD TITLE	LABEL & NO.
			WARRANT	
			Los Angeles, male hard-rock band: Jani Lane (vocals), Erik Turner, Joey Allen, Jerry Dixon and Steven Sweet.	
4/15/89	10	33	▲ 1. Dirty Rotten Filthy Stinking Rich *Heaven* (2)	Columbia 44383
			WARREN, Rusty	
			Born Ilene Goldman in 1931 in New York; raised in Milton, Massachusetts. Singer/story teller of adult comedy.	
11/7/60	8	98	1. Knockers Up! [C]	Jubilee 2029
5/29/61	21	12	2. Sin-Sational [C]	Jubilee 2034
2/10/62	31	5	3. Rusty Warren Bounces Back [C]	Jubilee 2039
12/1/62	22	11	4. Rusty Warren In Orbit [C]	Jubilee 2044
			WARWICK, Dionne	
			Born Marie Dionne Warwick on 12/12/40 in East Orange, New Jersey. In church choir from age six. With the Drinkard Singers gospel group. Formed trio the Gospelaires, with sister Dee Dee and their aunt Cissy Houston. Attended Hartt College Of Music, Hartford, Connecticut. Much backup studio work in New York during the late 50s. Added an "e" to her last name for a time in the early 70s. She was Burt Bacharach and Hal David's main "voice" for the songs they composed. Co-hosted TV's "Solid Gold" (1980-81; 1985-86).	
7/1/67	18	15	● 1. Here Where There is Love	Scepter 555
11/11/67	22	6	2. The Windows of The World *I Say A Little Prayer* (4)	Scepter 563
12/2/67	10	23	3. Dionne Warwick's Golden Hits, Part One [G] *Anyone Who Had A Heart* (8) 1964	Scepter 565
3/16/68	6	18	● 4. Valley of the Dolls *(Theme From) Valley Of The Dolls* (2)/ *Do You Know The Way To San Jose* (10)	Scepter 568
1/18/69	18	11	5. Promises, Promises *This Girl's In Love With You* (7)	Scepter 571
4/19/69	11	9	6. Soulful	Scepter 573
9/20/69	31	5	● 7. Dionne Warwick's Greatest Motion Picture Hits [K]	Scepter 575
11/22/69	28	4	8. Dionne Warwick's Golden Hits, Part 2 [G] *Message To Michael* (8) 1966	Scepter 577
5/9/70	23	14	9. I'll Never Fall In Love Again *I'll Never Fall In Love Again* (6)	Scepter 581
1/9/71	37	4	10. Very Dionne	Scepter 587
8/18/79	12	13	▲ 11. Dionne produced by Barry Manilow *I'll Never Love This Way Again* (5)	Arista 4230
8/30/80	23	6	12. No Night So Long	Arista 9526
11/27/82	25	10	13. Heartbreaker produced by Barry Gibb *Heartbreaker* (10)	Arista 9609
1/11/86	12	13	● 14. Friends *That's What Friends Are For* (1) with Elton John, Stevie Wonder and Gladys Knight	Arista 8398

DATE	POS	WKS	ARTIST—RECORD TITLE	LABEL & NO.
			WASHINGTON, Dinah	
			Born Ruth Lee Jones on 8/29/24 in Tuscaloosa, Alabama; died on 12/14/63 (overdose of alcohol and pills). Jazz-blues vocalist/pianist. Moved to Chicago in 1927. With Sallie Martin Gospel Singers, 1940-41; local club work in Chicago, 1941-43. With Lionel Hampton, 1943-46. First recorded for Keynote in 1943. Solo touring from 1946. Married seven times, once to singer Eddie Chamblee.	
2/1/60	34	10	1. What a diff'rence a day makes! *What A Diff'rence A Day Makes* (8)	Mercury 20479
1/23/61	10	6	2. Unforgettable	Mercury 20572
7/28/62	33	4	3. Dinah '62	Roulette 25170
			WASHINGTON, Grover, Jr.	
			Born on 12/12/43 in Buffalo. Jazz-R&B saxophonist. Own band, the Four Clefs, at age 16. Much session work in Philadelphia, where he now resides.	
4/5/75	10	17	1. Mister Magic [I]	Kudu 20
11/22/75	10	7	2. Feels So Good [I]	Kudu 24
2/12/77	31	6	3. A Secret Place [I]	Kudu 32
2/4/78	11	9	4. Live At The Bijou [I-L]	Kudu 3637 [2]
11/18/78	35	5	5. Reed Seed [I] backed by the jazz ensemble, Locksmith	Motown 910
5/19/79	24	6	6. Paradise [I]	Elektra 182
3/29/80	24	6	7. Skylarkin' [I]	Motown 933
1/24/81	5	27	▲ 8. Winelight [I] *Just The Two Of Us* (2) with Bill Withers	Elektra 305
1/23/82	28	5	9. Come Morning [I]	Elektra 562
			WATERS, Roger	
			Born on 9/6/44 in Great Bookham, Cambridge, England. Former leader/bassist of Pink Floyd. Went solo in 1983.	
6/2/84	31	7	1. The Pros and Cons of Hitch Hiking	Columbia 39290
			WATLEY, Jody	
			Born on 1/30/59 in Chicago. Female vocalist of Shalamar (1977-84) and former dancer on TV's "Soul Train." Her godfather was Jackie Wilson. Won the 1987 Best New Artist Grammy Award.	
4/4/87	10	44	▲ 1. Jody Watley *Looking For A New Love* (2)/*Don't You Want Me* (6)/ *Some Kind Of Lover* (10)	MCA 5898
4/22/89	16	17	● 2. Larger Than Life *Real Love* (2)/*Friends* (9)/*Everything* (4)	MCA 6276
			WATSON, Johnny "Guitar"	
			Born on 2/3/35 in Houston. Funk-R&B vocalist/guitarist/pianist. First recorded (as Young John Watson) for Federal in 1952.	
5/21/77	20	13	● 1. A Real Mother For Ya	DJM 7
			WAYLON & WILLIE — see JENNINGS, Waylon, or NELSON, Willie	
			WEATHER REPORT	
			Jazz-fusion quintet formed in 1969 by Austrian-born Josef Zawinul (keyboards) and Wayne Shorter (sax). Zawinul was a member of Cannonball Adderley's combo for nine years; formed the Zawinul Syndicate in 1988.	
6/28/75	31	4	1. Tale Spinnin' [I]	Columbia 33417
4/30/77	30	5	● 2. Heavy Weather [I]	Columbia 34418

DATE	POS	WKS	ARTIST—RECORD TITLE	LABEL & NO.
			WEAVERS, The	
			Legendary folk quartet: Pete Seeger, Lee Hays (d: 8/26/81), Fred Hellerman and Ronnie Gilbert. Revived and popularized folk music in the early 50s. Political blacklisting cut short their recording career, but the group's 1955 Carnegie Hall concert helped trigger a new folk boom and such Seeger-Hays songs as "If I Had A Hammer" kept it alive.	
3/13/61	**24**	1	1. The Weavers at Carnegie Hall [E-L] recorded on Christmas Eve in 1955	Vanguard 9010
			WEBB, Jack	
			Born on 4/2/20 in Santa Monica, California; died on 12/23/82. Actor/TV producer. Creator, director and star (Joe Friday) of "Dragnet" TV series (1952-59; 1967-70). Married to singer/actress Julie London (1945-53).	
9/3/55	**2**(2)	15	1. Pete Kelly's Blues [T-I] Jack narrates the introduction to songs played by a seven-man jazz combo led by clarinetist Matty Matlock (same band that did scoring for the film - also see Ray Heindorf)	RCA 1126
			WEBBER, Andrew Lloyd — see VARIOUS ARTISTS	
			WE FIVE	
			California pop quintet: Beverly Bivens (lead singer), Mike Stewart (brother of John Stewart), Pete Fullerton, Bob Jones and Jerry Burgan.	
12/11/65	**32**	6	1. You Were On My Mind *You Were On My Mind* (3)	A&M 4111
			WEISBERG, Tim	
			Born in 1943 in Hollywood. Flautist; studied classical music as an adolescent. Performs pop-oriented music with a jazz appeal. **DAN FOGELBERG & TIM WEISBERG:**	
9/23/78	**8**	13	1. Twin Sons Of Different Mothers	Full Moon 35339
			WEISSBERG, Eric	
			Bluegrass multi-instrumentalist. Worked with The Greenbriar Boys and The Tarriers folk groups. Prolific session man.	
2/17/73	**1**(3)	14	● 1. Dueling Banjos [I] except for the title song, all tunes performed by Weissberg and Marshall Brickman (previously released on LP *New Dimensions in Banjo & Bluegrass*) *Dueling Banjos* (2) by Weissberg & Steve Mandell	Warner 2683
			WELCH, Bob	
			Born on 7/31/46 in Los Angeles. Guitarist/vocalist with Fleetwood Mac (1971-74). Formed the British rock group Paris in 1976.	
11/12/77	**12**	29	▲ 1. French Kiss *Sentimental Lady* (8)	Capitol 11663
3/17/79	**20**	5	● 2. Three Hearts	Capitol 11907
			WELK, Lawrence	
			Born on 3/11/03 in Strasburg, North Dakota. Accordionist and polka/sweet bandleader since the mid-20s. Band's style labeled "champagne music." Own national TV musical variety show began on 7/2/55 and ran on ABC until 9/4/71. New episodes in syndication from 1971 to 1982.	
1/28/56	**5**	11	1. Lawrence Welk and His Sparkling Strings [I]	Coral 57011
3/31/56	**13**	2	2. TV Favorites	Coral 57025
3/31/56	**18**	2	3. Shamrocks and Champagne	Coral 57036
5/12/56	**6**	17	4. Bubbles In The Wine title song is Lawrence's theme song	Coral 57038
8/18/56	**10**	30	5. Say It With Music [I] medleys of 36 dance favorites	Coral 57041

DATE	POS	WKS	ARTIST—RECORD TITLE	LABEL & NO.
8/25/56	17	4	6. Champagne Pops Parade	Coral 57078
10/20/56	18	1	7. Moments To Remember [I]	Coral 57068
12/22/56	8	3	8. Merry Christmas [X]	Coral 57093
3/16/57	20	1	9. Pick-a-Polka! [I]	Coral 57067
5/20/57	17	5	10. Waltz with Lawrence Welk [I] *medleys of 24 favorite waltzes*	Coral 57119
10/21/57	19	2	11. Lawrence Welk plays Dixieland [I] *featuring Pete Fountain on clarinet*	Coral 57146
12/23/57	18	3	12. Jingle Bells [X]	Coral 57186
12/19/60	4	17	13. Last Date [I]	Dot 3350
1/30/61	1(11)	50	● 14. Calcutta! [I] *Calcutta (1)*	Dot 3359
8/7/61	2(1)	41	15. Yellow Bird [I] *above two feature Frank Scott on harpsichord*	Dot 3389
1/13/62	4	43	16. Moon River [I]	Dot 3412
6/9/62	6	12	17. Young World [I]	Dot 3428
9/29/62	9	10	18. Baby Elephant Walk and Theme From The Brothers Grimm [I]	Dot 3457
4/13/63	20	12	19. 1963's Early Hits [I]	Dot 25510
4/20/63	34	5	20. Waltz Time [I]	Dot 25499
9/7/63	33	6	21. Scarlett O'Hara [I]	Dot 25528
2/15/64	29	3	22. Wonderful! Wonderful! [I]	Dot 25552
5/16/64	37	3	23. Early Hits Of 1964 [I]	Dot 25572
12/31/66	12	18	● 24. Winchester Cathedral [I]	Dot 25774
			WELLS, Mary	
			R&B vocalist born on 5/13/43 in Detroit. At age 17 presented "Bye Bye Love," a tune she had written for Jackie Wilson, to Wilson's songwriter, Berry Gordy, Jr. Gordy signed her to his new label and she became the first artist to record for Motown. Also was the first to have a top 10 and #1 single for that label. Married for a time to Cecil Womack (brother of Bobby Womack). Diagnosed with throat cancer in August of 1990.	
7/18/64	18	12	1. Greatest Hits [G] *The One Who Really Loves You (8)/ You Beat Me To The Punch (9)/My Guy (1)*	Motown 616
			WEST, BRUCE & LAING	
			Power-rock trio comprised of former Mountain members Leslie West (guitar, vocals) and Corky Laing (drums), and Cream's Jack Bruce (bass).	
12/9/72	26	6	1. Why Dontcha	Windfall 31929
			WESTON, Paul	
			Born Paul Wetstein on 3/12/12 in Springfield, Massachusetts. Top arranger and conductor of mood music since 1934. Married to Jo Stafford.	
10/29/55	15	2	1. Mood For 12 [I]	Columbia 693
9/1/56	12	5	2. Solo Mood [I] *above two feature same group of 12 big band soloists*	Columbia 879
			WHAM!	
			Pop duo from Bushey, England: George Michael (b: Georgios Kyriacos Panayiotou on 6/26/63; lead singer) and Andrew Ridgeley (b: 1/26/63; guitarist). Disbanded in 1986. Michael recorded solo. Ridgely pursued race car driving, then recorded solo in 1990.	
11/17/84	1(3)	56	▲ 1. Make It Big *Wake Me Up Before You Go-Go (1)/Careless Whisper (1)/ Everything She Wants (1)/Freedom (3)*	Columbia 39595

DATE	POS	WKS	ARTIST—RECORD TITLE	LABEL & NO.
7/26/86	**10**	11	▲ 2. Music From The Edge Of Heaven *I'm Your Man* (3)/*A Different Corner* (7) George Michael/ *The Edge Of Heaven* (10)	Columbia 40285

WHISPERS, The

Los Angeles soul group formed in 1964. Consisted of Gordy Harmon, twin brothers Walter and Wallace "Scotty" Scott, Marcus Hutson and Nicholas Caldwell. First recorded for Dore in 1964. Harmon replaced in 1973 by Leaveil Degree who was briefly a member of Friends Of Distinction.

DATE	POS	WKS	ARTIST—RECORD TITLE	LABEL & NO.
2/9/80	**6**	17	▲ 1. The Whispers	Solar 3521
2/14/81	**23**	11	● 2. Imagination	Solar 3578
4/3/82	**35**	4	● 3. Love Is Where You Find It	Solar 27
5/7/83	**37**	3	4. Love For Love	Solar 60216
7/25/87	**22**	12	▲ 5. Just Gets Better With Time *Rock Steady* (7)	Solar 72554

WHITE, Barry

Born on 9/12/44 in Galveston, Texas; raised in Los Angeles. Soul singer/songwriter/ keyboardist/producer/arranger. With Upfronts vocal group, recorded for Lummtone in 1960. A&R man for Mustang/Bronco, 1966-67. Formed Love Unlimited in 1969, which included future wife Glodean James. Leader of 40-piece Love Unlimited Orchestra.

DATE	POS	WKS	ARTIST—RECORD TITLE	LABEL & NO.
6/2/73	**16**	10	● 1. I've Got So Much To Give *I'm Gonna Love You Just A Little More Baby* (3)	20th Century 407
12/8/73	**20**	16	● 2. Stone Gon' *Never, Never Gonna Give Ya Up* (7)	20th Century 423
9/14/74	**1(1)**	13	● 3. Can't Get Enough *Can't Get Enough Of Your Love, Babe* (1)/ *You're The First, The Last, My Everything* (2)	20th Century 444
4/26/75	**17**	8	● 4. Just Another Way To Say I Love You *What Am I Gonna Do With You* (8)	20th Century 466
11/29/75	**23**	5	● 5. Barry White's Greatest Hits [G]	20th Century 493
9/24/77	**8**	13	▲ 6. Barry White Sings For Someone You Love *It's Ecstasy When You Lay Down Next To Me* (4)	20th Century 543
12/16/78	**36**	2	▲ 7. Barry White The Man	20th Century 571

WHITE, Karyn

Prominent session singer from Los Angeles. Touring vocalist with O'Bryan in 1984. Recorded with jazz-fusion keyboardist Jeff Lorber in 1986.

DATE	POS	WKS	ARTIST—RECORD TITLE	LABEL & NO.
1/28/89	**19**	17	▲ 1. Karyn White *The Way You Love Me* (7)/*Superwoman* (8)/*Secret Rendezvous* (6)	Warner 25637

WHITE LION

New York-based rock band: Mike Tramp (vocals), James Lomenzo, Vito Bratta and Greg D'Angelo (a founding member of Anthrax). Tramp is a native of Denmark.

DATE	POS	WKS	ARTIST—RECORD TITLE	LABEL & NO.
3/5/88	**11**	56	▲ 1. Pride *Wait* (8)/*When The Children Cry* (3)	Atlantic 81768
7/15/89	**19**	13	● 2. Big Game	Atlantic 81969

WHITEMAN, Paul

Born on 3/28/1890 in Denver; died on 12/29/67. The most popular bandleader of the pre-swing era. Formed own band in 1919. Band featured jazz greats Henry Busse (trumpet), Ferde Grofe (piano, arranger) and Bix Beiderbecke (cornet). Vocalist Bing Crosby made his professional debut with Whiteman's band in 1926.

DATE	POS	WKS	ARTIST—RECORD TITLE	LABEL & NO.
1/19/57	**20**	1	1. Paul Whiteman/50th Anniversary reunion with many of the great alumni of the Whiteman Orchestra: Tommy & Jimmy Dorsey, Bing Crosby, Hoagy Carmichael, Jack Teagarden and others	Grand Award 901 [2]

DATE	POS	WKS	ARTIST—RECORD TITLE	LABEL & NO.
			WHITESNAKE	
			British heavy-metal band. Lead singer David Coverdale recorded solo under the name Whitesnake in the late 1970s. Recruited band members after first two Whitesnake albums. Coverdale and early Whitesnake members Jon Lord and Ian Paice were members of Deep Purple. 1987 lineup: Coverdale, John Sykes (guitar), Neil Murray (bass) and Aynsley Dunbar (drums). Sykes left in 1988 to form Blue Murder. Coverdale fronted new lineup in 1989: Steve Vai (David Lee Roth's former guitarist), Adrian Vandenburg (former guitarist of Vandenberg), Rudy Sarzo (bass) and Tommy Aldridge (drums).	
8/25/84	**40**	2	▲ 1. Slide it in	Geffen 4018
4/25/87	**2**(3)	54	▲ 2. Whitesnake	Geffen 24099
			Here I Go Again (1)/*Is This Love* (2)	
11/25/89	**10**	20	▲ 3. Slip Of The Tongue	Geffen 24249
			WHITTAKER, Roger	
			Born on 3/22/36 in Nairobi, Kenya. British adult contemporary singer.	
6/7/75	**31**	5	● 1. "The Last Farewell" and other hits	RCA 0855
			WHO, The	
			Rock group formed in London in 1964. Consisted of Roger Daltrey (b: 3/1/44, lead singer), Pete Townshend (b: 5/19/45; guitar, vocals), John Entwistle (b: 10/9/44; bass) and Keith Moon (b: 8/23/47; drums). Originally known as the High Numbers in 1964. All but Moon had been in The Detours. Developed stage antics of destroying their instruments. 1969 rock opera album *Tommy* became a film in 1975. Solo work by members began in 1972. Moon died of a drug overdose on 9/7/78, replaced by Kenney Jones (formerly with Small Faces). 1973 rock opera album *Quadrophenia* became a film in 1979. The Who's biographical film *The Kids Are Alright* was released in 1979. Eleven fans trampled to death at their concert in Cincinnati on 12/3/79. Disbanded in 1982. Regrouped at "Live Aid" in 1986. Daltry, Townshend and Entwistle reunited with an ensemble of 15 for a U.S. tour in 1989. Inducted into the Rock and Roll Hall of Fame in 1990.	
11/30/68	**39**	2	1. Magic Bus-The Who On Tour [K]	Decca 75064
6/14/69	**4**	47	● 2. Tommy	Decca 7205 [2]
			also see Various-Rock Operas and Soundtrack versions	
6/6/70	**4**	24	● 3. Live At Leeds [L]	Decca 79175
8/21/71	**4**	20	● 4. Who's next	Decca 79182
11/20/71	**11**	8	● 5. Meaty Beaty Big And Bouncy [G]	Decca 79184
11/10/73	**2**(1)	18	● 6. Quadrophenia	MCA 10004
			Townshend's second rock opera; film version released in 1979	
11/2/74	**15**	8	● 7. Odds & Sods [K]	Track 2126
			previously unreleased recordings from 1964-72	
11/1/75	**8**	14	● 8. The Who By Numbers	MCA 2161
9/9/78	**2**(2)	13	▲ 9. Who Are You	MCA 3050
7/7/79	**8**	11	▲ 10. The Kids Are Alright [S-L]	MCA 11005 [2]
			film features interviews and performances from the groups past 15 years	
4/4/81	**4**	14	▲ 11. Face Dances	Warner 3516
9/25/82	**8**	10	● 12. It's Hard	Warner 23731
			WHODINI	
			New York rap group. Began as a duo of Jalil "Whodini" Hutchins and John Fletcher. Grandmaster Dee joined in 1986.	
1/26/85	**35**	5	▲ 1. Escape	Jive 8251
6/28/86	**35**	4	● 2. Back In Black	Jive 8407
10/31/87	**30**	6	● 3. Open Sesame	Jive 8494

DATE	POS	WKS	ARTIST—RECORD TITLE	LABEL & NO.
			WILD CHERRY	
			White funk band formed in Steubenville, Ohio in the early 70s. Consisted of Bob Parissi (lead vocals, guitar), Bryan Bassett (guitar), Mark Avsec (keyboards), Allen Wentz (bass) and Ron Beitle (drums).	
8/7/76	5	15	▲ 1. Wild Cherry *Play That Funky Music* (1)	Sweet City 34195
			WILDE, Kim	
			Born Kim Smith on 11/18/60 in Chiswick, England. Pop-rock singer. Daughter of singer Marty Wilde.	
6/13/87	40	2	1. Another Step *You Keep Me Hangin' On* (1)	MCA 5903
			WILLIAMS, Andy	
			Born Howard Andrew Williams on 12/3/28 in Wall Lake, Iowa. Formed quartet with his brothers and eventually moved to Los Angeles. With Bing Crosby on hit "Swingin' On A Star," 1944. With comedienne Kay Thompson in the mid-40s. Went solo in 1952. On Steve Allen's "Tonight Show" from 1952-55. Own NBC-TV variety series from 1962-67; 1969-71. Appeared in the film *I'd Rather Be Rich* in 1964. One of America's greatest pop-MOR singers. Formerly married to singer/actress Claudine Longet.	
1/25/60	38	1	1. Lonely Street *Lonely Street* (5)	Cadence 3030
3/24/62	19	8	2. "Danny Boy" and other songs I love to sing	Columbia 8551
6/2/62	3	106	● 3. Moon River & Other Great Movie Themes	Columbia 8609
11/10/62	16	22	4. Warm And Willing	Columbia 8679
4/20/63	1(16)	61	● 5. Days of Wine and Roses *Can't Get Used To Losing You* (2)	Columbia 8815
2/1/64	9	16	● 6. The Wonderful World Of Andy Williams with members of Andy's family	Columbia 8937
5/23/64	5	27	● 7. The Academy Award Winning "Call Me Irresponsible"	Columbia 8971
10/10/64	5	20	● 8. The Great Songs From "My Fair Lady" and other Broadway hits	Columbia 9005
4/24/65	4	45	● 9. Dear Heart	Columbia 9138
3/12/66	23	8	10. Andy Williams' Newest Hits [K]	Columbia 9183
6/11/66	6	18	● 11. The Shadow of Your Smile	Columbia 9299
3/4/67	21	11	12. In The Arms Of Love	Columbia 9333
5/27/67	5	35	● 13. Born Free	Columbia 9480
12/9/67	8	11	● 14. Love, Andy	Columbia 9566
6/29/68	9	24	● 15. Honey	Columbia 9662
5/31/69	9	10	● 16. Happy Heart	Columbia 9844
11/22/69	27	6	● 17. Get Together With Andy Williams with The Osmonds on three tracks	Columbia 9922
2/27/71	3	16	▲ 18. Love Story *(Where Do I Begin) Love Story* (9)	Columbia 30497
5/20/72	29	8	19. Love Theme From "The Godfather"	Columbia 31303
			WILLIAMS, Deniece	
			Born Deniece Chandler on 6/3/51 in Gary, Indiana. Soul vocalist/songwriter. Recorded for Toddlin' Town, early 60s. Member of Wonderlove, Stevie Wonder's backup group, from 1972-75.	
3/5/77	33	6	● 1. This is Niecy	Columbia 34242
7/29/78	19	8	● 2. That's What Friends Are For **JOHNNY MATHIS & DENIECE WILLIAMS**	Columbia 35435

DATE	POS	WKS	ARTIST—RECORD TITLE	LABEL & NO.
5/15/82	**20**	7	3. Niecy *It's Gonna Take A Miracle* (10)	ARC 37952
6/16/84	**26**	6	4. Let's Hear It For The Boy *Let's Hear It For The Boy* (1)	Columbia 39366
			WILLIAMS, Hank, Jr.	
			Born Randall Hank Williams on 5/26/49 in Shreveport, Louisiana; raised in Nashville. Country singer/songwriter/guitarist. Son of country music's first superstar, Hank Williams. Hank, Jr. has charted over 40 top 10 country singles.	
3/13/65	**16**	13	● 1. Your Cheatin' Heart [S] film is Hank Williams' life story (Hank is played by George Hamilton; songs sung by Hank, Jr.)	MGM 4260
9/12/87	**28**	3	▲ 2. Born To Boogie	Warner 25593
			WILLIAMS, Mason	
			Born on 8/24/38 in Abilene, Texas. Folk guitarist/songwriter/author/photographer/ TV comedy writer ("The Smothers Brothers Comedy Hour," 1967-69; "Saturday Night Live," 1980).	
8/17/68	**14**	8	1. The Mason Williams Phonograph Record *Classical Gas* (2)	Warner 1729
			WILLIAMS, Robin	
			Born on 7/21/52 in Chicago. Actor/comedian. Mork of TV series "Mork & Mindy," 1978- 82. Films include *Popeye, The World According To Garp, Good Morning, Vietnam, Dead Poets Society* and *Cadillac Man*.	
7/28/79	**10**	12	● 1. Reality…What A Concept [C]	Casablanca 7162
			WILLIAMS, Roger	
			Born Louis Weertz in 1925 in Omaha. Learned to play the piano by age three. Educated at Drake University, Idaho State University, and Juilliard School of Music. Took lessons from Lenny Tristano and Teddy Wilson. Win on the TV show "Arthur Godfrey's Talent Scouts" led to recording contract.	
3/31/56	**19**	2	1. Roger Williams [I] *Autumn Leaves* (1)	Kapp 1012
8/25/56	**19**	3	2. Daydreams [I]	Kapp 1031
10/27/56	**16**	2	3. Roger Williams plays the wonderful Music of the Masters [I] classical melodies	Kapp 1040
3/23/57	**6**	57	● 4. Songs Of The Fabulous Fifties [I]	Kapp 5000 [2]
10/7/57	**20**	5	5. Almost Paradise [I]	Kapp 1063
11/4/57	**19**	4	6. Songs Of The Fabulous Forties [I]	Kapp 5003 [2]
3/31/58	**4**	61	● 7. Till [I]	Kapp 1081
2/23/59	**10**	49	8. Near You [I] *Near You* (10)	Kapp 1112
6/15/59	**11**	14	● 9. More Songs Of The Fabulous Fifties [I]	Kapp 1130
10/26/59	**8**	29	10. With These Hands [I]	Kapp 1147
12/28/59	**12**	2	11. Christmas Time [X-I]	Kapp 1164
4/4/60	**25**	10	12. Always [I]	Kapp 1172
12/19/60	**5**	12	13. Temptation [I]	Kapp 1217
10/23/61	**35**	2	14. Songs Of The Soaring '60s [I]	Kapp 1251
3/31/62	**9**	19	15. Maria [I]	Kapp 3266
11/17/62	**27**	4	16. Mr. Piano [I]	Kapp 3290
3/7/64	**27**	4	17. The Solid Gold Steinway [I]	Kapp 3354
7/30/66	**24**	11	18. I'll Remember You [I]	Kapp 3470
12/17/66	**7**	23	● 19. Born Free [I] *Born Free* (7)	Kapp 3501

DATE	POS	WKS	ARTIST—RECORD TITLE	LABEL & NO.
			WILLIAMS, Vanessa	
			Singer/actress, born in Tarrytown, New York. In 1983, became the first black woman to win Miss America pageant; relinquished crown after *Penthouse* magazine scandal.	
4/1/89	38	4	● 1. The Right Stuff *Dreamin'* (8)	Wing 835694
			WILLIS, Bruce	
			Born on 3/19/55 in Penns Grove, New Jersey. Played David Addison on the TV series "Moonlighting." Married actress Demi Moore on 11/21/87. Appeared in the films *Blind Date* (1987), *Die Hard* (1988) and *Die Hard II* (1990).	
2/21/87	14	11	● 1. The Return Of Bruno *Respect Yourself* (5)	Motown 6222
			WILSON, Flip	
			Born Clerow Wilson on 12/8/33 in Jersey City, New Jersey. Black comedian. Host of own TV variety show, 1970-74.	
2/17/68	34	5	1. Cowboys & Colored People [C]	Atlantic 8149
5/23/70	17	9	● 2. "The Devil made me buy this dress" [C]	Little David 1000
			WILSON, Hank — see RUSSELL, Leon	
			WILSON, Jackie	
			Born on 6/9/34 in Detroit; died on 1/21/84. Sang with local gospel groups; became an amateur boxer. Worked as solo singer until 1953, then joined Billy Ward's Dominoes as Clyde McPhatter's replacement. Solo since 1957. His goddaughter is Jody Watley. Jackie collapsed from a stroke, on stage, at the Latin Casino in Camden, New Jersey on 9/25/75; spent rest of his life in hospitals. Inducted into the Rock and Roll Hall of Fame in 1987.	
7/20/63	36	2	1. Baby Workout *Baby Workout* (5)	Brunswick 754110
			WILSON, Nancy	
			Born on 2/20/37 in Chillicothe, Ohio. Jazz stylist with Rusty Bryant's Carolyn Club Band in Columbus. First recorded for Dot in 1956.	
7/7/62	30	5	1. Nancy Wilson/Cannonball Adderley	Capitol 1657
4/20/63	18	21	2. Broadway-My Way	Capitol 1828
8/31/63	11	20	3. Hollywod-My Way	Capitol 1934
2/1/64	4	26	4. Yesterday's Love Songs/Today's Blues	Capitol 2012
6/13/64	10	24	5. Today, Tomorrow, Forever	Capitol 2082
9/19/64	4	19	6. How Glad I Am	Capitol 2155
2/27/65	24	18	7. The Nancy Wilson Show! [L] recorded at the Cocoanut Grove in Los Angeles	Capitol 2136
7/31/65	7	11	8. Today-My Way	Capitol 2321
10/16/65	17	8	9. Gentle Is My Love	Capitol 2351
6/25/66	15	12	10. A Touch Of Today	Capitol 2495
10/29/66	35	3	11. Tender Loving Care	Capitol 2555
4/1/67	35	3	12. Nancy-Naturally	Capitol 2634
8/5/67	40	1	13. Just For Now	Capitol 2712
			WILSON PHILLIPS	
			Vocal/songwriting trio of sisters Carnie and Wendy Wilson with Chynna Phillips. Carnie and Wendy's father is Brian Wilson (The Beach Boys). Chynna is the daughter of John and Michelle Phillips (The Mamas & The Papas). The Wilsons sang backup on "I Saw Mommy Kissing Santa Claus" on The Beach Boys' 1978 album *M.I.U.*	
5/12/90	2(10)	24+	▲ 1. Wilson Phillips *Hold On* (1)/*Release Me* (1)	SBK 93745

DATE	POS	WKS	ARTIST—RECORD TITLE	LABEL & NO.
			WINGER	
			Hard-rock quartet formed in New York City in 1986: Kip Winger (vocals, bass), Reb Beach (guitar), Rod Morgenstein (drums) and Paul Taylor (keyboards). Golden, Colorado native Kip was a member of Alice Cooper's band.	
12/3/88	**21**	35	▲ 1. Winger	Atlantic 81867
			WINGS — see McCARTNEY, Paul	
			WINTER, Edgar	
			Born on 12/28/46 in Beaumont, Texas. Albino rock singer/keyboardist/saxophonist. Younger brother of Johnny Winter. His group included Rick Derringer and Dan Hartman, 1972-75.	
			EDGAR WINTER'S WHITE TRASH:	
4/15/72	**23**	9	● 1. Roadwork [L]	Epic 31249 [2]
			THE EDGAR WINTER GROUP:	
3/3/73	**3**	25	▲ 2. They Only Come Out At Night	Epic 31584
			album introduces Ronnie Montrose and Dan Hartman in group *Frankenstein* (1)	
6/15/74	**13**	13	● 3. Shock Treatment	Epic 32461
			Rick Derringer replaces Montrose as lead guitarist (Rick also appears on previous two albums)	
			WINTER, Johnny	
			Born on 2/23/44 in Leland, Mississippi. Blues-rock guitarist/vocalist. Both Johnny and brother Edgar are albinos.	
5/17/69	**40**	1	1. The Progressive Blues Experiment	Imperial 12431
5/17/69	**24**	8	1. Johnny Winter	Columbia 9826
5/29/71	**40**	2	● 2. Live/Johnny Winter And [L]	Columbia 30475
			features Rick Derringer on guitar	
5/5/73	**22**	11	3. Still Alive And Well	Columbia 32188
			WINTERS, Jonathan	
			Born on 11/11/25 in Dayton, Ohio. Comedian; master of improvisation. Own TV variety series, 1956-57; 1967-69; 1972-74. Played Mearth on TV's "Mork & Mindy," 1981-82.	
2/1/60	**18**	28	1. The Wonderful World Of Jonathan Winters [C]	Verve 15009
9/19/60	**25**	11	2. Down To Earth [C]	Verve 15011
7/3/61	**19**	6	3. Here's Jonathan [C]	Verve 15025
			WINWOOD, Steve	
			Born on 5/12/48 in Birmingham, England. Rock singer/keyboardist/guitarist. Lead singer of rock bands The Spencer Davis Group, Blind Faith and Traffic.	
7/30/77	**22**	10	1. Steve Winwood	Island 9494
2/14/81	**3**	26	● 2. Arc Of A Diver	Island 9576
			While You See A Chance (7)	
9/4/82	**28**	6	3. Talking Back To The Night	Island 9777
7/26/86	**3**	60	▲ 4. Back in the High Life	Island 25448
			Higher Love (1)/*The Finer Things* (8)	
12/5/87	**26**	10	▲ 5. Chronicles [K]	Island 25660
			contains 10 cuts from his four Island albums *Valerie* (9)	
7/9/88	**1(1)**	31	▲ 6. Roll With It	Virgin 90946
			Roll With It (1)/*Don't You Know What The Night Can Do?* (6)	

DATE	POS	WKS	ARTIST—RECORD TITLE	LABEL & NO.
			WITHERS, Bill	
			Born on 7/4/38 in Slab Fork, West Virginia. Black vocalist/guitarist/composer. Moved to California in 1967 and made demo records of his songs. First recorded for Sussex in 1970, produced by Booker T. Jones. Made professional singing debut in 1971. Married to actress Denise Nicholas.	
9/25/71	**39**	1	1. Just As I Am *Ain't No Sunshine (3)*	Sussex 7006
6/17/72	**4**	25	● 2. Still Bill *Lean On Me (1)/Use Me (2)*	Sussex 7014
2/4/78	**39**	3	● 3. Menagerie	Columbia 34903
			WOLF, Peter	
			Born Peter Blankfield on 3/7/46 in the Bronx. Lead singer of The J. Geils Band until 1983. Produced hits for Lou Gramm, Kenny Loggins and Go West. Married actress Faye Dunaway on 8/7/74, divorced in 1979.	
8/25/84	**24**	8	1. Lights Out	EMI America 17121
			WOMACK, Bobby	
			Born on 3/4/44 in Cleveland. Soul vocalist/guitarist/songwriter. Sang in family gospel group the Womack Brothers. Group recorded for Sar as The Valentinos and The Lovers, 1962-64. Toured as guitarist with Sam Cooke. Solo recording for Him label in 1965. Backup guitarist on many sessions, including Wilson Pickett, The Box Tops, Joe Tex, Aretha Franklin and Janis Joplin. Married for a time to Sam Cooke's widow.	
8/25/73	**37**	1	1. Facts Of Life	United Art. 043
2/20/82	**29**	6	2. The Poet	Beverly G. 10000
			WONDER, Stevie	
			Born Steveland Morris on 5/13/50 in Saginaw, Michigan. Singer/songwriter/multi-instrumentalist/producer. Blind since birth. Signed to Motown in 1960, did backup work. First recorded in 1962, renamed "Little Stevie Wonder" by Berry Gordy, Jr. Married to Syreeta Wright from 1970-72. Near-fatal auto accident on 8/16/73. Winner of 17 Grammy Awards. In the films *Bikini Beach* and *Muscle Beach Party*. Inducted into the Rock and Roll Hall of Fame in 1989.	
7/27/63	**1(1)**	13	1. Little Stevie Wonder/The 12 Year Old Genius [L] *Fingertips (1)*	Tamla 240
9/24/66	**33**	3	2. Up-Tight Everything's Alright *Uptight (Everything's Alright) (3)/Blowin' In The Wind (9)*	Tamla 268
7/6/68	**37**	4	3. Greatest Hits [G]	Tamla 282
11/1/69	**34**	4	4. My Cherie Amour *My Cherie Amour (4)/Yester-Me, Yester-You, Yesterday (7)*	Tamla 296
9/12/70	**25**	5	5. Signed Sealed & Delivered *Signed, Sealed, Delivered I'm Yours (3)/* *Heaven Help Us All (9)*	Tamla 304
6/10/72	**21**	11	6. Music Of My Mind	Tamla 314
12/30/72	**3**	30	7. Talking Book *Superstition (1)/You Are The Sunshine Of My Life (1)*	Tamla 319
8/25/73	**4**	58	8. Innervisions 1973 Grammy winner: Album of the Year *Higher Ground (4)/Living For The City (8)*	Tamla 326
8/17/74	**1(2)**	11	9. Fulfillingness' First Finale 1974 Grammy winner: Album of the Year *You Haven't Done Nothin (1)/Boogie On Reggae Woman (3)*	Tamla 332
10/16/76	**1(14)**	44	10. Songs In The Key Of Life 1976 Grammy winner: Album of the Year; double LP also includes a bonus four-song, 7" EP *I Wish (1)/Sir Duke (1)*	Tamla 340 [2]
2/4/78	**34**	3	11. Looking Back [K] compilation of recordings from 1962-1971	Motown 804 [3]

DATE	POS	WKS	ARTIST—RECORD TITLE		LABEL & NO.
11/24/79	4	15	12. Journey Through The Secret Life of Plants *Send One Your Love* (4)		Tamla 371 [2]
11/15/80	3	25	▲ 13. Hotter Than July *Master Blaster (Jammin')* (5)		Tamla 373
5/29/82	4	8	● 14. Stevie Wonder's Original Musiquarium I	[G]	Tamla 6002 [2]
			compilation of hits from 1972-1982 *That Girl* (4)		
9/29/84	4	21	▲ 15. The Woman in Red	[S]	Motown 6108
			featuring Dionne Warwick on three songs *I Just Called To Say I Love You* (1)		
10/19/85	5	29	▲ 16. In Square Circle *Part-Time Lover* (1)/*Go Home* (10)		Tamla 6134
12/12/87	17	13	▲ 17. Characters		Motown 6248
			WOODBURY, Woody		
			Adult comedy storyteller.		
3/7/60	10	39	1. Woody Woodbury Looks at love and life	[C]	Stereoddities 1
6/13/60	16	26	2. Woody Woodbury's Laughing Room	[C]	Stereoddities 2
			WORLD PARTY		
			London-based group featuring keyboardist/vocalist/producer/engineer Karl Wallinger from North Wales (formerly of The Waterboys).		
3/28/87	39	3	1. Private Revolution		Chrysalis 41552
			WRIGHT, Betty		
			Born on 12/21/53 in Miami. Soul singer. In family gospel group Echoes Of Joy, from 1956. First recorded for Deep City in 1966. Hostess of TV talk shows in Miami.		
9/9/78	26	7	1. Betty Wright Live	[L]	Alston 4408
			WRIGHT, Gary		
			Born on 4/26/43 in Creskill, New Jersey. Pop-rock singer/songwriter/keyboardist. Appeared in "Captain Video" TV series at age seven. In the Broadway play *Fanny*. Co-leader of the rock group Spooky Tooth.		
2/14/76	7	35	▲ 1. The Dream Weaver *Dream Weaver* (2)/*Love Is Alive* (2)		Warner 2868
1/29/77	23	9	2. The Light of Smiles		Warner 2951
			WYNETTE, Tammy		
			Born Virginia Wynette Pugh on 5/5/42 in Stawamba County, Mississippi. With over 15 #1 country hits, dubbed "The First Lady Of Country Music." Discovered by producer Billy Sherrill. Married to country star George Jones from 1969-75.		
11/8/69	37	2	▲ 1. Tammy's Greatest Hits	[G]	Epic 26486
			Y		
			YANKOVIC, "Weird Al"		
			Los Angeles novelty singer/accordionist. Specializes in song parodies. Wrote and starred in the 1989 film *UHF*.		
3/31/84	17	11	● 1. "Weird Al" Yankovic In 3-D	[N]	Rock 'n' R. 39221
5/28/88	27	9	● 2. Even Worse	[N]	Rock 'n' R. 44149

DATE	POS	WKS	ARTIST—RECORD TITLE	LABEL & NO.
			YARBROUGH, Glenn	
			Born on 1/12/30 in Milwaukee. Lead singer of The Limeliters (1959-63).	
7/10/65	35	3	1. Baby The Rain Must Fall	RCA 3422
			YARBROUGH & PEOPLES	
			Dallas soul duo: Cavin Yarbrough and Alisa Peoples. Discovered by The Gap Band.	
2/14/81	16	11	● 1. The Two Of Us	Mercury 3834
			YARDBIRDS, The	
			Legendary rock group formed in Surrey, England in 1963. Consisted of Keith Relf (d: 5/14/76; vocals, harmonica), Anthony "Top" Topham and Chris Dreja (guitars), Paul "Sam" Samwell-Smith (bass, keyboards) and Jim McCarty (drums). Formed as the Metropolitan Blues Quartet at Kingston Art School. Topham replaced by Eric Clapton in 1963. Clapton replaced by Jeff Beck in 1965. Samwell-Smith left in 1966, Dreja switched to bass and Jimmy Page (guitar) was added. Beck left in December of 1966. Group disbanded in July, 1968. Page formed the New Yardbirds in October of 1968, which evolved into Led Zeppelin. Relf and McCarty formed Renaissance in 1969. Keith Relf later in Armageddon, 1975. McCarty later in Illusion, 1977.	
5/27/67	28	8	1. The Yardbirds' Greatest Hits [G]	Epic 26246
			YES	
			Progressive rock group formed in London in 1968. Consisted of Jon Anderson (vocals), Peter Banks (guitar), Tony Kaye (keyboards), Chris Squire (bass) and Bill Bruford (drums). Banks replaced by Steve Howe in 1971. Kaye (joined Badfinger in 1978) replaced by Rick Wakeman in 1971. Bruford left to join King Crimson, replaced by Alan White, late 1972. Wakeman replaced by Patrick Moraz in 1974, rejoined in 1976 when Moraz left. Wakeman and Anderson left in 1980, replaced by The Buggles' Trevor Horne (guitar) and Geoff Downes (keyboards). Group disbanded in 1980. Howe and Downes went with Asia. Re-formed in 1983 with Anderson, Kaye, Squire, White and South African guitarist Trevor Rabin. Anderson left group in 1988. Anderson, Bruford, Wakeman and Howe formed self-named group in early 1989.	
1/22/72	40	1	● 1. The Yes Album	Atlantic 8243
2/5/72	4	21	● 2. Fragile	Atlantic 7211
			Rick Wakeman replaces Tony Kaye on keyboards	
10/21/72	3	15	● 3. Close To The Edge	Atlantic 7244
6/2/73	12	10	● 4. Yessongs [L]	Atlantic 100 [3]
			Alan White replaces Bill Bruford on drums	
2/9/74	6	11	● 5. Tales From Topographic Oceans	Atlantic 908
1/4/75	5	9	● 6. Relayer	Atlantic 18122
			Patrick Moraz replaces Rick Wakeman on keyboards	
3/29/75	17	5	7. Yesterdays [K]	Atlantic 19134
			featuring cuts from their first two albums (uncharted) *Yes* and *Time and a Word*	
8/6/77	8	11	● 8. Going For The One	Atlantic 19106
			Rick Wakeman returns as a replacement for Patrick Moraz	
10/21/78	10	7	▲ 9. Tormato	Atlantic 19202
9/13/80	18	7	10. Drama	Atlantic 16019
			Geoff Downes and Trevor Horn replace Wakeman & Anderson	
12/3/83	5	28	▲ 11. 90125	Atco 90125
			Owner Of A Lonely Heart (1)	
10/24/87	15	18	▲ 12. Big Generator	Atco 90522
			YOUNG, Jesse Colin	
			Born Perry Miller on 11/11/44 in New York City. Leader of The Youngbloods.	
7/20/74	37	3	1. Light Shine	Warner 2790

DATE	POS	WKS	ARTIST—RECORD TITLE	LABEL & NO.
4/19/75	26	4	2. Songbird	Warner 2845
5/8/76	34	3	3. On The Road [L]	Warner 2913

YOUNG, Neil

Born on 11/12/45 in Toronto. Rock singer/songwriter/guitarist. Formed rock band the Mynah Birds featuring lead singer Rick James, early 60s. Moved to Los Angeles in 1966 and formed Buffalo Springfield. Went solo in 1969 with backing band Crazy Horse. Joined with Crosby, Stills & Nash in 1970. Appeared in the 1987 film *Made In Heaven*.

DATE	POS	WKS	ARTIST—RECORD TITLE	LABEL & NO.
8/8/70	34	5	▲ 1. Everbody Knows This Is Nowhere *	Reprise 6349
9/19/70	8	21	▲ 2. After The Gold Rush	Reprise 6383
3/4/72	1(2)	25	▲ 3. Harvest *Heart Of Gold* (1)	Reprise 2032
11/3/73	22	6	● 4. Time Fades Away [L] guests: David Crosby and Graham Nash	Reprise 2151
8/10/74	16	9	● 5. On The Beach	Reprise 2180
7/26/75	25	5	6. Tonight's The Night	Reprise 2221
12/20/75	25	7	7. Zuma *	Reprise 2242
10/30/76	26	6	● 8. Long May You Run **STILLS-YOUNG BAND (Stephen Stills)**	Reprise 2253
7/16/77	21	9	● 9. American Stars 'N Bars * guests: Linda Ronstadt and Emmylou Harris	Reprise 2261
10/28/78	7	11	● 10. Comes A Time	Reprise 2266
7/28/79	8	17	▲ 11. Rust Never Sleeps *	Reprise 2295
12/15/79	15	13	▲ 12. Live Rust * [L]	Reprise 2296 [2]
12/6/80	30	6	13. Hawks & Doves	Reprise 2297
11/28/81	27	9	14. Re-ac-tor * ***NEIL YOUNG & CRAZY HORSE**	Reprise 2304
1/29/83	19	7	15. Trans	Geffen 2018
11/11/89	35	4	● 16. Freedom	Reprise 25899

YOUNG, Paul

Born on 1/17/56 in Bedfordshire, England. Pop-rock vocalist/guitarist.

DATE	POS	WKS	ARTIST—RECORD TITLE	LABEL & NO.
6/29/85	19	24	● 1. The Secret Of Association *Everytime You Go Away* (1)	Columbia 39957

YOUNG-HOLT UNLIMITED

Chicago instrumental soul group: Eldee Young (bass), Isaac "Red" Holt (drums; both of the Ramsey Lewis Trio) and Don Walker (piano). Walker left by 1968.

DATE	POS	WKS	ARTIST—RECORD TITLE	LABEL & NO.
2/1/69	9	14	1. Soulful Strut [I] *Soulful Strut* (3)	Brunswick 754144

YOUNG M.C.

Rapper Marvin Young. Born in England and raised in Queens, New York. Co-writer of Tone Loc's "Wild Thing" and "Funky Cold Medina." Graduated with economics degree from University of Southern California.

DATE	POS	WKS	ARTIST—RECORD TITLE	LABEL & NO.
10/7/89	9	30	▲ 1. Stone Cold Rhymin' *Bust A Move* (7)	Delicious 91309

DATE	POS	WKS	ARTIST—RECORD TITLE	LABEL & NO.

Z

DATE	POS	WKS	ARTIST—RECORD TITLE	LABEL & NO.
			ZAGER & EVANS	
			Lincoln, Nebraska duo: Denny Zager and Rick Evans. Disbanded in 1969.	
8/16/69	30	5	1. 2525 (Exordium & Terminus)	RCA 4214
			In The Year 2525 (1)	
			ZAPP	
			Dayton, Ohio funk band formed by the Troutman brothers: Roger ("Zapp") Lester, Tony and Larry. "Bootsy" Collins produced and played on first session. Shirley Murdock was backup singer. Roger recorded solo as "Roger."	
10/4/80	19	7	● 1. Zapp	Warner 3463
			with "Bootsy" Collins (guitars)	
8/28/82	25	6	● 2. Zapp II	Warner 23583
9/24/83	39	2	3. Zapp III	Warner 23875
			ZAPPA, Frank	
			Born on 12/21/40 in Baltimore, Maryland. Singer/songwriter/guitarist. Rock music's leading satirist. Formed The Mothers Of Invention in 1965. In the films *200 Motels* and *Baby Snakes*. Father of Dweezil and Moon Unit.	
4/13/68	30	4	1. We're Only In It For The Money *	Verve 5045
			album art work is a parody of the Beatles' *Sgt. Pepper's...* LP	
9/4/71	38	3	2. The Mothers/Fillmore East-June 1971 * [L]	Bizarre 2042
11/17/73	32	4	● 3. Over-nite Sensation *	DiscReet 2149
5/11/74	10	15	● 4. Apostrophe (')	DiscReet 2175
11/9/74	27	3	5. Roxy & Elsewhere * [L]	DiscReet 2202 [2]
8/2/75	26	5	6. One Size Fits All *	DiscReet 2216
			*THE MOTHERS OF INVENTION	
4/28/79	21	8	7. Sheik Yerbouti	Zappa 1501 [2]
9/29/79	27	5	8. Joe's Garage, Act I	Zappa 1603
7/17/82	23	6	9. Ship arriving too late to save a drowning witch	Barking P. 38066
			ZEBRA	
			Rock trio founded in New Orleans. Consisted of Randy Jackson (lead singer), Felix Hanemann (bass) and Guy Gelso (drums).	
7/23/83	29	7	● 1. Zebra	Atlantic 80054
			ZEVON, Warren	
			Born on 1/24/47 in Canada. Parents were Russian immigrants. Singer/songwriter/ pianist. Wrote Linda Ronstadt's "Poor Poor Pitiful Me." Worked as the keyboardist/ bandleader for The Everly Brothers.	
3/25/78	8	13	● 1. Excitable Boy	Asylum 118
			produced by Jackson Browne	
3/15/80	20	8	2. Bad Luck Streak In Dancing School	Asylum 509
			ZOMBIES, The	
			British rock quintet: Rod Argent (keyboards), Colin Blunstone (vocals), Paul Atkinson (guitar), Chris White (bass) and Hugh Grundy (drums). Group disbanded in late 1967. Rod formed Argent in 1969.	
5/1/65	39	1	1. The Zombies	Parrot 71001
			She's Not There (2)/*Tell Her No* (6)	

Bobby Vinton's all-time highest charting album was 1962's *Roses Are Red* on Epic—the same label for which he recorded follow-up hits ''Blue Velvet'' and ''There! I've Said It Again.'' His 1974 *Melodies Of Love*, released on ABC, went gold and peaked at No. 16 in 1974.

Walter Wanderley's *Rain Forest*, which reached No. 22 in 1966, depicted how the cool sounds of Brazilian bossa nova were permeating American music tastes. Wanderley had performed with fellow Brazilian Astrud Gilberto, who with Stan Getz two years earlier had released the hit ''The Girl From Ipanema.''

Whodini's 1983 debut album featured two tracks—''Magic's Wand'' and ''It's All In Mr. Magic's Wand''—produced by popular U.K. rocker Thomas Dolby. The New York rap duo's follow-ups included the high-charting *Escape* and *Open Sesame*.

The Whispers, who began recording in Los Angeles in 1964, continued their career well through the 80s with a series of hit albums for the Solar label. Despite some personnel changes, the group has always been based around twin brothers Walter and Wallace Scott. Their first top 40 LP, *The Whispers*, still ranks as their most sucessful, peaking at No. 6 in 1980.

Dinah Washington's *Unforgettable* was her only top 10 album, released on Mercury in 1961. Her three biggest hits were 1959's ''What A Difference A Day Makes'' and two 1960 duets with singer Brook Benton—''Baby (You've Got What It Takes)'' and ''A Rockin' Good Way (To Mess Around And Fall In Love).''

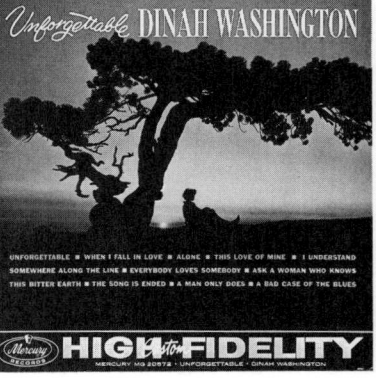

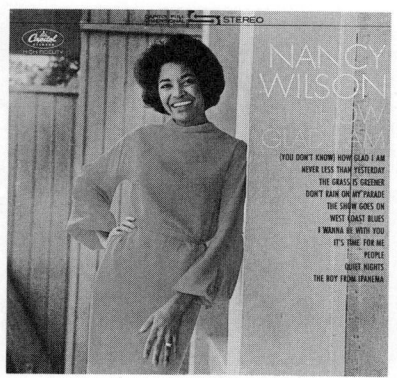

Nancy Wilson's career since the early 60s has included several collaborations with jazz artists, including Cannonball Adderley, Ramsey Lewis, Chick Corea, Stanley Clarke and Joe Henderson. Her two highest-charting albums were *How Glad I Am* and *Yesterday's Love Songs/Today's Blues*, both released in 1964.

Steve Winwood's first brush with chart fame came in 1967, when as the very young lead singer with the Spencer Davis Group, his "Gimme Some Lovin'" reached No. 7. Since then, the vocalist/multi-instrumentalist has continued the hit tradition with Traffic, Blind Faith and as a solo artist.

Stevie Wonder's first No. 1 album was his very debut LP—*Little Stevie Wonder/The 12-Year-Old Genius*, issued on Tamla in 1963. Beginning with 1972's *Talking Book*, the distinguished singer/multi-instrumentalist has ridden a hot streak that includes 1980's platinum-certified *Hotter Than July*.

Neil Young's all-time highest-charting album *Harvest*, issued on Reprise in 1972, demonstrated the former Buffalo Springfield member's folk-rock talents. His harder-rocking side has been amply displayed via several collaborations with backing band Crazy Horse, including 1979's *Live Rust*.

Frank Zappa started to gather a fervent following after his group, the Mothers Of Invention, released their first album, *Freak Out* in 1966. His only brush with the top 10, however, came via his 1974 solo effort *Apostrophe [']*, featuring the noteworthy track "Don't Eat The Yellow Snow."

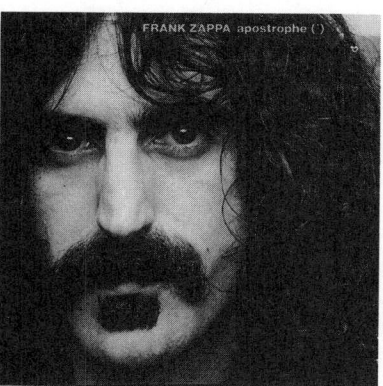

DATE	POS	WKS	ARTIST—RECORD TITLE	LABEL & NO.
			ZZ TOP	
			Boogie-rock trio formed in Houston in 1969. Consisted of Billy Gibbons (vocals, guitar), Dusty Hill (vocals, bass) and Frank Beard (drums). All were born in 1949 in Texas. Gibbons had been lead guitarist in Moving Sidewalks, a Houston psychedelic rock band. Hill and Beard had played in American Blues, based in Dallas. Inactive from 1977-79.	
9/29/73	8	24	● 1. Tres Hombres	London 631
5/31/75	10	21	● 2. Fandango! [L] side 1: live; side 2: studio	London 656
1/29/77	17	8	● 3. Tejas	London 680
12/22/79	24	14	▲ 4. Deguello	Warner 3361
8/15/81	17	12	● 5. El Loco	Warner 3593
4/23/83	9	82	▲ 6. Eliminator Legs (8)	Warner 23774
11/16/85	4	36	▲ 7. Afterburner Sleeping Bag (8)1	Warner 25342

DATE	POS	WKS	ARTIST—RECORD TITLE	LABEL & NO.

SOUNDTRACKS

Each film's stars are listed below the title. Also shown are the Composer (cp), Conductor (cd), Lyricist (ly), Music Writer (mu), Performer (pf) and Songwriter [music & lyrics] (sw). The following symbols are also used in this section: [I] Instrumental, [M] Musical, [O] Oldies, [R] Reissue and [V] Various Artists.

DATE	POS	WKS	ARTIST—RECORD TITLE	LABEL & NO.
			Advance To The Rear — see NEW CHRISTY MINSTRELS Glenn Ford/Stella Stevens/Melvyn Douglas	
4/7/84	**12**	12	● 1. Against All Odds　　　　　　　　　　　　[V] Rachel Ward/Jeff Bridges/James Woods side 2: instrumentals — cp/pf: Larry Carlton/Michel Colombier *Against All Odds (Take A Look At Me Now)* (1) Phil Collins	Atlantic 80152
12/5/60	**7**	15	2. Alamo, The　　　　　　　　　　　　　[I + V] John Wayne/Richard Widmark/Laurence Harvey cp/cd: Dimitri Tiomkin	Columbia 8358
4/12/80	**36**	3	3. All That Jazz　　　　　　　　　　　　　[M] Roy Scheider/Jessica Lange/Ann Reinking — cd: Ralph Burns	Casablanca 7198
3/15/80	**7**	15	● 4. American Gigolo　　　　　　　　　　[I + V] Richard Gere/Lauren Hutton/Hector Elizondo side 2: instrumentals — cp/pf: Giorgio Moroder *Call Me* (1) Blondie	Polydor 6259
10/6/73	**10**	41	● 5. American Graffiti　　　　　　　　　　[V-O] Ronny Howard/Richard Dreyfuss/Cindy Williams/Harrison Ford director George Lucas's first major film	MCA 8001 [2]
5/6/78	**31**	4	6. American Hot Wax　　　　　　　　　　[V-O] Tim McIntire/Fran Drescher/Laraine Newman/Chuck Berry based on the life of disc jockey Alan Freed — record 1: live; record 2: original 1950s recordings	A&M 6500 [2]
7/10/82	**35**	7	▲ 7. Annie　　　　　　　　　　　　　　　[M] Aileen Quinn (Annie)/Carol Burnett/Albert Finney mu: Charles Strouse/ly: Martin Charnin; cd: Ralph Burns — also see Original Cast (1977)	Columbia 38000
1/9/61	**18**	5	8. Apartment, The　　　　　　　　　　　[I] Jack Lemmon/Shirley MacLaine/Fred MacMurray cp: Adolph Deutsch; cd: Mitchell Powell	United Art. 3105
			April Love — see BOONE, Pat Pat Boone/Shirley Jones	
4/13/57	**1(10)**	88	9. Around The World In 80 Days　　　　　[I] David Niven/Cantinflas/Robert Newton/Shirley MacLaine cp/cd: Victor Young (also see New World Theatre Orchestra)	Decca 79046
10/10/81	**32**	7	10. Arthur (The Album)　　　　　　　　[I + V] Dudley Moore/Liza Minnelli/John Gielgud side 2: instrumentals — cp: Burt Bacharach *Arthur's Theme* (1) Christopher Cross	Warner 3582
8/10/85	**12**	14	● 11. Back To The Future　　　　　　　　[V] Michael J. Fox/Christopher Lloyd/Lea Thompson/Crispin Glover *The Power Of Love* (1) Huey Lewis & The News	MCA 6144
			Batman — also see ELFMAN, Danny, and PRINCE Jack Nicholson/Michael Keaton/Kim Basinger/Robert Wuhl	
			Beach Party — see ANNETTE Annette/Frankie Avalon/Robert Cummings	
			Beaches — see MIDLER, Bette Bette Midler/Barbara Hershey/John Heard	
6/23/84	**14**	9	● 12. Beat Street, Volume 1　　　　　　　[V] Rae Dawn Chong/Guy Davis/John Chardiet	Atlantic 80154
4/25/60	**6**	48	13. Ben-Hur　　　　　　　　　　　　　　[I] Charlton Heston — cp: Miklos Rozsa; cd: Carlo Savina — includes a full-color book about the movie	MGM 1
			Benny Goodman Story, The — see GOODMAN, Benny Steve Allen/Donna Reed	

DATE	POS	WKS	ARTIST—RECORD TITLE		LABEL & NO.
1/26/85	1(2)	36	▲ 14. Beverly Hills Cop Eddie Murphy/Judge Reingold/Lisa Eilbacher/John Ashton *Neutron Dance* (6) Pointer Sisters/*The Heat Is On* (2) Glenn Frey/*Axel F* (3) Harold Faltermeyer	[V]	MCA 5547
6/20/87	8	17	▲ 15. Beverly Hills Cop II Eddie Murphy/Judge Reinhold/Brigitte Nielsen *Shakedown* (1) Bob Seger	[V]	MCA 6207
11/12/83	17	19	▲ 16. Big Chill, The William Hurt/Glenn Close/Jobeth Williams/Kevin Kline	[V-O]	Motown 6062
2/2/63	33	6	17. Billy Rose's Jumbo Doris Day/Stephen Boyd/Jimmy Durante/Martha Raye mu: Richard Rodgers; ly: Lorenz Hart; cd: George Stoll	[M]	Columbia 2260
			Black Caesar — see BROWN, James Fred Williamson/Art Lund/Julius W. Harris/Gloria Hendry		
			Blue Hawaii — see PRESLEY, Elvis Elvis Presley (Chad Gates)/Joan Blackman/Angela Lansbury		
			Blues Brothers, The — see BLUES BROTHERS John Belushi/Dan Aykroyd/Carrie Fisher/Cab Calloway		
4/13/68	12	13	18. Bonnie And Clyde Warren Beatty/Faye Dunaway — cp: Charles Strouse includes excerpts of the original dialog	[I]	Warner 1742
2/24/90	32	4	19. Born On The Fourth Of July Tom Cruise/Kyra Sedgwick/Raymond J. Barry — side A: various artists; side B: instrumental (cp/cd: John Williams)	[V]	MCA 6340
			Breakfast At Tiffany's — see MANCINI, Henry Audrey Hepburn/George Peppard/Patricia Neal		
3/30/85	17	13	● 20. Breakfast Club, The Molly Ringwald/Anthony Michael Hall/Emilio Estevez/ Paul Gleason/Judd Nelson/Ally Sheedy *Don't You (Forget About Me)* (1) Simple Minds	[V]	A&M 5045
6/16/84	8	14	▲ 21. Breakin' Lucinda Dickey/Adolfo Quinones/Michael Chambers *Breakin'...There's No Stopping Us* (9) Ollie & Jerry	[V]	Polydor 821919
1/10/70	16	26	● 22. Butch Cassidy And The Sundance Kid Paul Newman/Robert Redford — cp/cd: Burt Bacharach *Raindrops Keep Fallin' On My Head* (1) B.J. Thomas	[I + V]	A&M 4227
5/11/63	2(2)	41	23. Bye Bye Birdie Ann-Margret/Jesse Pearson/Janet Leigh/Dick Van Dyke mu: Charles Strouse; ly: Lee Adams; cd: Johnny Green — also see Original Cast (1960)	[M]	RCA 1081
5/12/73	25	9	● 24. Cabaret Liza Minnelli/Michael York/Joel Grey mu: John Kander; ly: Fred Ebb — also see Original Cast (1967)	[M]	ABC 752
12/23/67	11	23	▲ 25. Camelot Richard Harris/Vanessa Redgrave — mu: Frederick Loewe; ly: Alan Jay Lerner; cd: Alfred Newman - also see Original Cast (1961)/Living Strings/Percy Faith	[M]	Warner 1712
5/2/60	3	36	26. Can-Can Frank Sinatra/Shirley MacLaine/Maurice Chevalier/Louis Jourdan sw: Cole Porter; cd: Nelson Riddle	[M]	Capitol 1301
			Car Wash — see ROSE ROYCE George Carlin/Richard Pryor/Ivan Dixon		
2/25/56	2(1)	46	● 27. Carousel Gordon MacRae/Shirley Jones — mu: Richard Rodgers; ly: Oscar Hammerstein II; cd: Alfred Newman — also see Original Cast (special version 1962)	[M]	Capitol 694
6/10/67	22	9	28. Casino Royale Peter Sellers/David Niven — cp/cd: Burt Bacharach	[I]	Colgems 5005

DATE	POS	WKS	ARTIST—RECORD TITLE	LABEL & NO.
			Charade — see MANCINI, Henry Cary Grant/Audrey Hepburn/Walter Matthau/James Coburn	
			Chariots Of Fire — see VANGELIS Ian Charleson/Ben Cross/Nigel Havers/Nick Farrell	
			Children of Sanchez — see MANGIONE, Chuck Anthony Quinn/Dolores Del Rio/Katy Jurado	
			Clambake — see PRESLEY, Elvis Elvis Presley (Scott Heywood)/Shelley Fabares/Will Hutchins	
			Claudine — see KNIGHT, Gladys/Pips James Earl Jones/Diahann Carroll/Lawrence Hinton-Jacobs	
6/29/63	**2**(3)	14	29. Cleopatra [I] Elizabeth Taylor/Richard Burton/Rex Harrison cp/cd: Alex North	20th Century 5008
4/8/72	**34**	5	30. Clockwork Orange [I] Malcolm McDowell/Patrick Magee — features classical pieces and the electronic synthesizer compositions of Walter Carlos	Warner 2573
1/21/78	**17**	8	● 31. Close Encounters Of The Third Kind [I] Richard Dreyfuss/Teri Garr — cp/cd: John Williams	Arista 9500
5/17/80	**40**	1	● 32. Coal Miner's Daughter Sissy Spacek/Tommy Lee Jones/Beverly D'Angelo/Levon Helm based on Loretta Lynn's life — Spacek plays Loretta and performs the vocals	MCA 5107
9/3/88	**2**(1)	28	▲ 33. Cocktail [V] Tom Cruise/Bryan Brown/Elisabeth Shue *Don't Worry Be Happy* (1) Bobby McFerrin)/*Kokomo* (1) Beach Boys	Elektra 60806
6/4/88	**31**	5	● 34. Colors [V] Sean Penn/Robert Duvall/Maria Conchita Alonso	Warner 25713
12/1/58	**21**	1	35. Damn Yankees [M] Tab Hunter/Gwen Verdon — sw: Richard Adler/Jerry Ross — also see Original Cast (1955)	RCA 1047
1/22/55	**4**	16	36. Deep In My Heart [M] Jose Ferrer/Merle Oberon/Walter Pidgeon based on the life and the melodies of composer Sigmund Romberg — cd: Adolph Deutsch	MGM 3153
			Dick Tracy — also see ELFMAN, Danny & MADONNA ("I'm Breathless") Warren Beatty/Al Pacino/Madonna/Glenne Headly	
9/26/87	**1**(18)	68	▲ 37. Dirty Dancing [V] Patrick Swayze/Jennifer Grey/Cynthia Rhodes/Jerry Orbach *(I've Had) The Time Of My Life* (1) Bill Medley & Jennifer Warnes/ *Hungry Eyes* (4) Eric Carmen/*She's Like The Wind* (3) Patrick Swayze with Wendy Fraser	RCA 6408
3/26/88	**3**	27	▲ 38. Dirty Dancing, More [V-O] 2nd volume released from the film of the same title	RCA 6965
			Divine Madness — see MIDLER, Bette	
5/28/66	**1**(1)	115	● 39. Doctor Zhivago [I] Omar Sharif/Julie Christie — cp/cd: Maurice Jarre	MGM 6
			Don't Knock The Twist — see CHECKER, Chubby Chubby Checker/Linda Scott	
8/7/82	**37**	5	● 40. E.T. — The Extra-Terrestrial [I] Henry Thomas/Peter Coyote/Dee Wallace — cp/cd: John Williams	MCA 6109
10/18/69	**6**	41	● 41. Easy Rider [V] Peter Fonda/Dennis Hopper/Jack Nicholson featuring songs by Jimi Hendrix, Steppenwolf and The Byrds	Dunhill 50063

DATE	POS	WKS	ARTIST—RECORD TITLE	LABEL & NO.
			Eddie And The Cruisers — see CAFFERTY, John Michael Pare/Tom Berenger/Ellen Barkin	
			Eddy Duchin Story, The — see CAVALLARO, Carmen Tyrone Power/Kim Novak/Victoria Shaw/James Whitmore	
9/8/62	**35**	3	42. El Cid [I] Charlton Heston/Sophia Loren — cp/cd: Miklos Rozsa	MGM 3977
			Elvis-That's The Way It Is — see PRESLEY, Elvis	
5/17/80	**4**	17	● 43. Empire Strikes Back, The [I] Mark Hamill/Harrison Ford/Carrie Fisher/Billy Dee Williams cp/cd: John Williams; pf: London Symphony Orchestra	RSO 4201 [2]
8/15/81	**9**	14	● 44. Endless Love [I + V] Brooke Shields/Martin Hewitt/Shirley Knight/Don Murray *Endless Love* (1) Diana Ross & Lionel Richie	Mercury 2001
1/16/61	**1(14)**	55	● 45. Exodus [I] Paul Newman/Eva Marie Saint — cp/cd: Ernest Gold — also see Hollywood Studio Orchestra	RCA 1058
			Experiment In Terror — see MANCINI, Henry Glenn Ford/Lee Remick/Stefanie Powers	
5/13/78	**5**	12	▲ 46. FM [V] Michael Brandon/Eileen Brennan/Alex Karras/Martin Mull featuring songs by 17 top rock artists	MCA 12000 [2]
7/26/80	**7**	16	▲ 47. Fame [M] Irene Cara/Eddie Barth/Maureen Teefy/Lee Curreri inspired by the students of New York's High School of The Performing Arts *Fame* (4) Irene Cara	RSO 3080
			Ferry Cross The Mersey — see GERRY AND THE PACEMAKERS	
1/1/72	**30**	4	● 48. Fiddler on the Roof [M] Topol — mu: Jerry Bock; ly: Sheldon Harnick; cd: John Williams — also see Original Cast (1964)	United Art. 10900 [2]
10/12/59	**22**	9	49. Five Pennies, The [M] Danny Kaye/Louis Armstrong/Barbara Bel Geddes based on the life of bandleader Loring *Red* Nichols	Dot 29500
			Flash Gordon — see QUEEN Sam Jones/Max von Sydow/Melody Anderson/Topol	
5/7/83	**1(2)**	54	▲ 50. Flashdance [V] Jennifer Beals/Michael Nouri/Marine Jahan/Lilia Skala *Flashdance...What A Feeling* (1) Irene Cara/ *Maniac* (1) Michael Sembello	Casablanca 811492
2/3/62	**15**	24	51. Flower Drum Song [M] Nancy Kwan/James Shigeta/Miyoshi Umeki mu: Richard Rodgers; ly: Oscar Hammerstein II; cd: Alfred Newman — also see Original Cast (1959)	Decca 79098
3/10/84	**1(10)**	27	▲ 52. Footloose [V] Kevin Bacon/Lori Singer — *Footloose* (1) Kenny Loggins/ *Let's Here It For The Boy* (1) Deniece Williams/ *Almost Paradise* (7) Mike Reno & Ann Wilson	Columbia 39242
			For The First Time — see LANZA, Mario Mario Lanza/Zsa Zsa Gabor	
			Frankie And Johnny — see PRESLEY, Elvis Elvis Presley (Johnny)/Donna Douglas (Frankie)/Nancy Kovack	
			Friends — see JOHN, Elton Sean Bury/Anicee Alvina	
7/25/64	**27**	6	53. From Russia with Love [I] Sean Connery/Daniela Bianchi — cp/cd: John Barry	United Art. 5114
			Fun in Acapulco — see PRESLEY, Elvis Elvis Presley (Mike Windgren)/Ursula Andress/Elsa Cardenas	

DATE	POS	WKS	ARTIST—RECORD TITLE	LABEL & NO.
			Funny Girl — see STREISAND, Barbra (both Soundtrack & Original Cast) Barbra Streisand/Omar Sharif	
			Funny Lady — see STREISAND, Barbra Barbra Streisand/James Caan/Omar Sharif	
			G.I. Blues — see PRESLEY, Elvis Elvis Presley (Tulsa McCauley)/Juliet Prowse/James Douglas	
7/14/84	**6**	17	▲ 54. Ghostbusters [V] Bill Murray/Dan Aykroyd/Sigourney Weaver/Harold Ramis *Ghostbusters* (1) Ray Parker, Jr.	Arista 8246
7/8/89	**14**	10	● 55. Ghostbusters II [V] Bill Murray/Dan Aykroyd/Sigourney Weaver/Harold Ramis *On Our Own* (2) Bobby Brown	MCA 6306
12/29/56	**16**	7	56. Giant [I] Elizabeth Taylor/Rock Hudson/James Dean cp/cd: Dimitri Tiomkin	Capitol 773
6/23/58	**1**(10)	78	● 57. Gigi [M] Leslie Caron/Maurice Chevalier/Louis Jordan ly: Alan Jay Lerner/mu: Frederick Loewe; cd: Andre Previn	MGM 3641
			Girl Happy — see PRESLEY, Elvis Elvis Presley (Rusty Wells)/Shelley Fabares/Gary Crosby	
			Girls! Girls! Girls! — see PRESLEY, Elvis Elvis Presley (Ross Carpenter)/Stella Stevens/Laurel Goodwin	
			Give my regards to Broad Street — see McCARTNEY, Paul Paul McCartney/Bryan Brown/Ringo Starr	
4/29/72	**21**	14	58. Godfather, The [I] Marlon Brando/Al Pacino/James Caan/Robert Duvall cp: Nino Rota; cd: Carlo Savina	Paramount 1003
2/6/65	**1**(3)	36	59. Goldfinger [I] Sean Connery/Gert Frobe (Goldfinger) — cp/cd: John Barry *Goldfinger* (8) Shirley Bassey	United Art. 5117
12/23/67	**24**	9	60. Gone With The Wind [I] Clark Gable/Vivien Leigh/Leslie Howard/Olivia de Havilland first album taken directly from the film soundtrack (premiered in 1939) — cp/cd: Max Steiner	MGM 10
2/20/88	**10**	14	▲ 61. Good Morning, Vietnam [V-O] Robin Williams/Forest Whitaker/Tung Thanh Tran/Bruno Kirby	A&M 3913
3/16/68	**4**	21	● 62. Good, The Bad and The Ugly, The [I] Clint Eastwood/Lee Van Cleef — cp/cd: Ennio Morricone — also see Hugo Montenegro	United Art. 5172
			Graduate, The — see SIMON AND GARFUNKEL Dustin Hoffman/Anne Bancroft/Katharine Ross	
5/27/78	**1**(12)	39	▲ 63. Grease [M] Olivia Newton-John/John Travolta/Stockard Channing/Jeff Conaway *You're The One That I Want* (1)/*Summer Nights* (5)/ *Hopelessly Devoted To You* (3) Olivia Newton-John/ *Grease* (1) Frankie Valli	RSO 4002 [2]
1/26/63	**10**	13	64. Gypsy [M] Rosalind Russell/Natalie Wood/Karl Malden — mu: Jule Styne; ly: Stephen Sondheim — also see Original Cast (1959)	Warner 1480
			Hard Day's Night, A — see BEATLES, The The Beatles	
			Hard To Hold — see SPRINGFIELD, Rick Rick Springfield/Janet Eilber/Patti Hansen/Bill Mumy	
			Harum Scarum — see PRESLEY, Elvis Elvis Presley (Johnny Tyronne)/Mary Ann Mobley/Fran Jeffries	
			Hatari! — see MANCINI, Henry John Wayne/Red Buttons/Hardy Kruger	

DATE	POS	WKS	ARTIST—RECORD TITLE	LABEL & NO.
			Having A Wild Weekend — see CLARK, Dave The Dave Clark Five	
8/29/81	**12**	13	● 65. Heavy Metal [V] animated film; features songs by 13 rock artists	Asylum 90004 [2]
2/3/58	**25**	1	66. Helen Morgan Story, The Ann Blyth (portrays Helen)/Paul Newman vocals performed by Gogi Grant; cd: Ray Heindorf	RCA 1030
			Help! — see BEATLES The Beatles/Leo McKern/Eleanor Bron	
			Hey Boy! Hey Girl! — see PRIMA, Louis, & SMITH, Keely	
			Hey, Let's Twist! — see DEE, Joey Joey Dee & The Starliters/Teddy Randazzo	
8/25/56	**5**	28	67. High Society [M] Bing Crosby/Grace Kelly/Frank Sinatra adapted from the play *Philadelphia Story* — sw: Cole Porter *True Love* (3) Bing Crosby & Grace Kelly	Capitol 750
			Hold On! — see HERMAN'S HERMITS Peter Noone/Shelley Fabares/Sue Ane Langdon	
			Honeysuckle Rose — see NELSON, Willie Willie Nelson/Dyan Cannon/Amy Irving/Slim Pickens	
4/20/63	**4**	34	● 68. How The West Was Won Gregory Peck/Henry Fonda/James Stewart/Debbie Reynolds cd: Alfred Newman	MGM 5
			I Want To Live! — see MULLIGAN, Gerry Susan Hayward	
			Imagine: John Lennon — see LENNON, John	
			It Happened At The World's Fair — see PRESLEY, Elvis Elvis Presley (Mike Edwards)/Joan O'Brien/Gary Lockwood	
8/30/75	**30**	4	69. Jaws [I] Roy Scheider/Richard Dreyfuss/Robert Shaw cp/cd: John Williams	MCA 2087
			Jazz Singer, The — see DIAMOND, Neil Neil Diamond/Laurence Olivier/Lucie Arnaz	
8/11/73	**21**	8	● 70. Jesus Christ Superstar [M] Ted Neely/Yvonne Elliman/Carl Anderson/Barry Dennen mu: Andrew Lloyd Webber; ly: Tim Rice — also see Various-Rock Operas (1970)/Original Cast (1972)	MCA 11000 [2]
			Jonathan Livingston Seagull — see DIAMOND, Neil James Franciscus/Juliet Mills — also see Richard Harris	
3/9/68	**19**	11	71. Jungle Book, The Disney cartoon based on Rudyard Kipling's "Mowgli" stories sw: Richard M. Sherman/Robert B. Sherman	Disneyland 3948
8/2/86	**30**	9	72. Karate Kid Part II, The [V] Ralph Macchio/Noriyuki "Pat" Morita/Martin Kove *Glory Of Love* (1) Peter Cetera	United Art. 40414
			Kids Are Alright, The — see WHO, The	
7/21/56	**1(1)**	178	● 73. King And I, The [M] Yul Brynner/Deborah Kerr — mu: Richard Rodgers; ly: Oscar Hammerstein II; cd: Alfred Newman	Capitol 740
			King Creole — see PRESLEY, Elvis Elvis Presley (Danny Fisher)/Carolyn Jones/Walter Matthau	
11/6/61	**10**	24	74. King of Kings [I] Jeffrey Hunter (Jesus Christ) — cp/cd: Miklos Rozsa includes a full-color book about the movie	MGM 2
			Kissin' Cousins — see PRESLEY, Elvis Elvis Presley (Josh Morgan/Jodie Tatum)/Arthur O'Connell	
			La Bamba — see LOS LOBOS Lou Diamond Phillips/Esai Morales/Rosana DeSoto/Elizabeth Pena	

DATE	POS	WKS	ARTIST—RECORD TITLE	LABEL & NO.
			Lady Sings The Blues — see ROSS, Diana Diana Ross/Billy Dee Williams/Richard Pryor	
			Last Waltz, The — see BAND, The	
3/23/63	**2**(2)	40	75. Lawrence Of Arabia [I] Peter O'Toole/Alec Guinness/Anthony Quinn cp/cd: Maurice Jarre; pf: London Philharmonic Orchestra	Colpix 514
1/9/88	**31**	5	● 76. Less Than Zero [V] Robert Downey, Jr./Andrew McCarthy/Jami Gertz *Hazy Shade Of Winter* (2) Bangles	Columbia 44042
			Let It Be — see BEATLES, The The Beatles	
			Let's Do It Again — see STAPLE SINGERS Sidney Poitier/Bill Cosby/Jimmie Walker/John Amos	
2/3/90	**32**	6	▲ 77. Little Mermaid, The animated film; not available on vinyl mu: Alan Menken/ly: Howard Ashman; orchestration: Thomas Pasatieri	Walt Dis. 018
8/11/73	**17**	7	78. Live And Let Die [I] Roger Moore/Jane Seymour — cp/cd: George Martin *Live And Let Die* (2) Paul McCartney & Wings	United Art. 100
2/3/79	**39**	2	79. Lord Of The Rings, The [I] animated film based on the novels of J.R.R. Tolkien cp/cd: Leonard Rosenman	Fantasy 1 [2]
8/29/87	**15**	9	● 80. Lost Boys, The [V] Kiefer Sutherland/Dianne Wiest/Jami Gertz/Jason Patric	Atlantic 81767
			Love Me Or Leave Me — see DAY, Doris Doris Day/James Cagney/Cameron Mitchell	
			Love Me Tender — see PRESLEY, Elvis Elvis Presley (Clint)/Richard Egan/Debra Paget	
1/23/71	**2**(6)	22	● 81. Love Story [I] Ali MacGraw/Ryan O'Neal — cp/cd: Francis Lai	Paramount 6002
			Loving You — see PRESLEY, Elvis Elvis Presley (Deke Rivers)/Lizabeth Scott/Dolores Hart	
			Mad Dogs & Englishmen — see COCKER, Joe	
9/21/85	**39**	2	82. Mad Max Beyond Thunderdome Mel Gibson/Tina Turner — cp/cd: Maurice Jarre *We Don't Need Another Hero (Thunderdome)*(2-Tina Turner)	Capitol 12429
			Magical Mystery Tour — see BEATLES, The The Beatles	
			Mahogany — see ROSS, Diana Diana Ross/Billy Dee Williams/Anthony Perkins	
			Main Event, The — see STREISAND, Barbra Barbra Streisand/Ryan O'Neal	
1/28/67	**10**	44	● 83. Man And A Woman, A [F] Jean-Louis Trintignant/Anouk Aimee — cp: Francis Lai grand prize-winner of the 1966 Cannes Film Festival	United Art. 5147
3/24/56	**2**(4)	17	84. Man With The Golden Arm, The [I] Frank Sinatra/Eleanor Parker/Kim Novak cp/cd: Elmer Bernstein jazz sequences played by Shorty Rogers & His Giants	Decca 78257
12/5/64	**1**(14)	78	● 85. Mary Poppins [M] Julie Andrews/Dick Van Dyke/David Tomlinson/Glynis Johns sw: Richard M. Sherman/Robert B. Sherman; cd: Irwin Kostal	Buena Vista 4026
			Maximum Overdrive — see AC/DC Emilio Estevez/Pat Hingle/Laura Harrington/Christopher Murney	

DATE	POS	WKS	ARTIST—RECORD TITLE		LABEL & NO.
			McVicar — see DALTREY, Roger		
			Roger Daltrey/Adam Faith/Cheryl Campbell		
9/20/69	**19**	19	● 86. Midnight Cowboy	[I+V]	United Art. 5198
			Dustin Hoffman/Jon Voight/Sylvia Miles		
			Everybody's Talkin' (6) Nilsson		
7/27/63	**15**	13	87. Mondo Cane	[I]	United Art. 5105
			documentary depicting various cultures around the world —		
			cp: Riz Ortolani and Nino Oliviero		
			Monterey Pop — see REDDING, Otis/HENDRIX, Jimi		
			Muppet Movie, The — see CHILDRENS Albums		
8/11/62	**2(6)**	35	● 88. Music Man, The	[M]	Warner 1459
			Robert Preston/Shirley Jones — cp: Meredith Willson;		
			cd: Ray Heindorf — also see Original Cast (1958)		
1/5/63	**14**	11	89. Mutiny On The Bounty	[I]	MGM 4
			Marlon Brando/Trevor Howard/Richard Harris		
			cp: Bronislau Kaper; cd: Robert Armbruster		
			includes a full-color souvenir book		
10/31/64	**4**	77	● 90. My Fair Lady	[M]	Columbia 2600
			Audrey Hepburn/Rex Harrison/Stanley Holloway		
			mu: Frederick Loewe; ly: Alan Jay Lerner; cd: Andre Previn		
			also see Percy Faith/Sammy Kaye/Andy Williams/		
			Original Cast (1956)		
1/30/61	**2(5)**	53	91. Never On Sunday	[I]	United Art. 5070
			Melina Mercouri/Jules Dassin — cp/cd: Manos Hadjidakis		
			Nighthawks — see EMERSON, Keith		
			Sylvester Stallone/Rutger Hauer/Billy Dee Williams		
12/4/82	**38**	3	92. Officer And A Gentleman, An	[V]	Island 90017
			Richard Gere/Debra Winger/David Keith/Louis Gossett, Jr.		
			Up Where We Belong (1) Joe Cocker & Jennifer Warnes		
			includes songs by ZZ Top, Pat Benatar and Dire Straits		
9/17/55	**1(4)**	229	● 93. Oklahoma!	[M]	Capitol 595
			Gordon MacRae/Shirley Jones — mu: Richard Rodgers;		
			ly: Oscar Hammerstein II; cd: Jay Blackton		
5/10/69	**20**	8	● 94. Oliver!	[M]	Colgems 5501
			Mark Lester (Oliver)/Ron Moody/Jack Wild/Oliver Reed		
			sw: Lionel Bart; cd: John Green — also see Original Cast (1962)		
			One-Trick Pony — see SIMON, Paul		
			Paul Simon/Blair Brown/Rip Torn		
4/26/86	**38**	2	95. Out Of Africa	[I]	MCA 6158
			Meryl Streep/Robert Redford — cp/cd: John Barry		
12/6/69	**28**	4	● 96. Paint Your Wagon	[M]	Paramount 1001
			Lee Marvin/Clint Eastwood/Jean Seberg		
			mu: Frederick Loewe; ly: Alan Jay Lerner		
9/23/57	**9**	14	97. Pajama Game, The	[M]	Columbia 5210
			Doris Day/John Raitt — sw: Richard Adler/Jerry Ross;		
			cd: Ray Heindorf		
			Pal Joey — see SINATRA, Frank		
			Frank Sinatra/Rita Hayworth/Kim Novak		
			Paradise, Hawaiian Style — see PRESLEY, Elvis		
			Elvis Presley (Rick Richards)/Suzanne Leigh/James Shigeta		
			Pat Garrett & Billy The Kid — see DYLAN, Bob		
			James Coburn/Kris Kristofferson/Jason Robards		
5/5/56	**6**	18	98. Picnic	[I]	Decca 78320
			William Holden/Kim Novak/Rosalind Russell		
			cp: George Duning; cd: Morris Stoloff		
			Moonglow and Theme From Picnic (1) Morris Stoloff		
			Pink Panther, The — see MANCINI, Henry		
			Peter Sellers/David Niven/Robert Wagner/Capucine		

DATE	POS	WKS	ARTIST—RECORD TITLE	LABEL & NO.
8/3/59	**8**	47	● 99. Porgy and Bess [M] Sidney Poitier/Dorothy Dandridge — mu: George Gershwin; ly: DuBose Heyward/Ira Gershwin; cd: Andre Previn also see Harry Belafonte/Percy Faith	Columbia 2016
3/22/86	**5**	17	▲ 100. Pretty In Pink [V] Molly Ringwald/Jon Cryer/Andrew McCarthy/Harry Dean Stanton *If You Leave* (4) Orchestral Manoeuvres In The Dark	A&M 3901
4/21/90	**4**	27+	● 101. Pretty Woman [V] Richard Gere/Julia Roberts *It Must Have Been Love* (1) Roxette/*King Of Wishful Thinking* (8) Go West	[V] EMI 93492
			Purple Rain — see PRINCE Prince/Apollonia Kotero/Morris Day	
4/15/89	**31**	5	102. Rain Man [V] Dustin Hoffman/Tom Cruise/Valeria Golino	Capitol 91866
			Rainbow Bridge — see HENDRIX, Jimi	
			Rattle And Hum — see U2	
6/18/83	**20**	6	103. Return Of The Jedi [I] Mark Hamill/Harrison Ford/Carrie Fisher/Billy Dee Williams cp/cd: John Williams; pf: London Symphony Orchestra	RSO 811767
			Richard Pryor Live On The Sunset Strip -- see PRYOR, Richard	
3/9/57	**16**	9	104. Rock, Pretty Baby Sal Mineo/John Saxon/Luana Patten cp: Henry Mancini; pf: Jimmy Daley & The Ding-A-Lings	Decca 8429
4/23/77	**4**	14	● 105. Rocky Sylvester Stallone/Talia Shire — cp/cd: Bill Conti *Gonna Fly Now* (1) Bill Conti	United Art. 693
7/24/82	**15**	10	▲ 106. Rocky III Sylvester Stallone/Talia Shire/Mr. T — cp/cd: Bill Conti *Eye Of The Tiger* (1) Survivor	Liberty 51130
12/28/85	**10**	16	● 107. Rocky IV [V] Sylvester Stallone/Talia Shire/Burt Young/Carl Weathers *Burning Heart* (2) Survivor/*Living In America* (4) James Brown/	Scotti Br. 40203
6/30/62	**5**	20	108. Rome Adventure [I] Troy Donahue/Suzanne Pleshette/Angie Dickinson cp: Max Steiner — side 2: *Neapolitan Favorites* by The Cafe Milano Orchestra *Al Di La* (6) Emilio Pericoli	Warner 1458
5/3/69	**2(2)**	31	▲ 109. Romeo & Juliet Leonard Whiting/Olivia Hussey — cp/cd: Nino Rota includes dialogue highlights	Capitol 2993
			Rose, The — see MIDLER, Bette Bette Midler/Alan Bates/Frederic Forrest	
			Roustabout — see PRESLEY, Elvis Elvis Presley (Charlie Rogers)/Barbara Stanwyck/Joan Freeman	
7/19/86	**20**	9	▲ 110. Ruthless People [V] Danny DeVito/Bette Midler/Judge Reinhold/Helen Slater *Modern Woman* (10) Billy Joel	Epic 40398
12/10/77	**1(24)**	54	● 111. Saturday Night Fever [V] John Travolta — biggest selling soundtrack album of all-time *If I Can't Have You* (1) Yvonne Elliman — also see Bee Gees	RSO 4001 [2]
			Serenade — see LANZA, Mario Mario Lanza/Joan Fontaine/Vincent Price/Vincent Edwards	
			Seven Hills Of Rome — see LANZA, Mario Mario Lanza/Renato Roscel/Marisa Allasio	

DATE	POS	WKS	ARTIST—RECORD TITLE	LABEL & NO.
8/12/78	**5**	12	● 112. Sgt. Pepper's Lonely Hearts Club Band [M] Peter Frampton/Bee Gees — sw: John Lennon/Paul McCartney film inspired by The Beatles *Sgt. Pepper's...* album *Got To Get You Into My Life* (9) Earth, Wind & Fire	RSO 4100 [2]
			Shaft — see HAYES, Isaac Richard Roundtree/Moses Gunn/Gwenn Mitchell	
			Sing Boy Sing — see SANDS, Tommy Tommy Sands/Lili Gentle/Edmond O'Brien	
			Singing Nun, The — see REYNOLDS, Debbie Debbie Reynolds/Ricardo Montalban/Greer Garson	
			Song Remains The Same, The — see LED ZEPPELIN	
4/10/65	**1**(2)	161	▲ 113. Sound Of Music, The [M] Julie Andrews/Christopher Plummer — story of Maria von Trapp's family — mu: Richard Rodgers; ly: Oscar Hammerstein II; cd: Irwin Kostal — also see Original Cast (1959)	RCA 2005
3/31/58	**1**(31)	161	▲ 114. South Pacific [M] Rossano Brazzi/Mitzi Gaynor/John Kerr — mu: Richard Rodgers; ly: Oscar Hammerstein II; cd: Alfred Newman	RCA 1032
			Sparkle — see FRANKLIN, Aretha Irene Cara/Philip Thomas/Lonette McKee	
			Spinout — see PRESLEY, Elvis Elvis Presley (Mike McCoy)/Shelley Fabares/Diane McBain	
11/5/77	**40**	2	115. Spy Who Loved Me, The [I] Roger Moore/Barbara Bach — cp/cd: Marvin Hamlisch *Nobody Does It Better* (2) Carly Simon	United Art. 774
8/10/85	**21**	11	▲ 116. St. Elmo's Fire [V] Emilio Estevez/Rob Lowe/Andrew McCarthy/Demi Moore/Judd Nelson/Ally Sheedy/Mare Winningham *St. Elmo's Fire (Man In Motion)* (1) John Parr	Atlantic 81261
			St. Louis Blues — see COLE, Nat King Nat King Cole/Eartha Kitt/Pearl Bailey/Cab Calloway	
11/22/86	**31**	11	▲ 117. Stand By Me [V-O] Wil Wheaton/River Phoenix/Corey Feldman/Jerry O'Connell *Stand By Me* (9) Ben E. King	Atlantic 81677
			Star Is Born, A — see STREISAND, Barbra Barbra Streisand/Kris Kristofferson	
7/2/77	**2**(3)	22	● 118. Star Wars [I] Mark Hamill/Harrison Ford/Carrie Fisher/Alec Guinness cp/cd: John Williams; pf: London Symphony Orchestra *Star Wars (Main Title)* (1) — also see Meco	20th Century 541 [2]
1/21/78	**36**	2	▲ 119. Star Wars, The Story Of storyline excerpts from the film — narrator: Roscoe Lee Browne	20th Century 550
5/19/62	**12**	15	120. State Fair [M] Pat Boone/Ann-Margret/Bobby Darin — mu: Richard Rodgers; ly: Oscar Hammerstein II; cd: Alfred Newman	Dot 29011
7/30/83	**6**	14	● 121. Staying Alive [V] John Travolta — side 1: Bee Gees; side 2: Various Artists *Far From Over* (10) Frank Stallone	RSO 813269
3/2/74	**1**(5)	23	▲ 122. Sting, The [I] Paul Newman/Robert Redford/Robert Shaw — cp: Scott Joplin; cd/pianist: Marvin Hamlisch *The Entertainer* (3) Marvin Hamlisch	MCA 390
7/14/84	**32**	6	123. Streets Of Fire [V] Michael Pare/Diane Lane/Rick Moranis/Amy Madigan *I Can Dream About You* (6) Dan Hartman	MCA 5492
			Superfly — see MAYFIELD, Curtis Ron O'Neal/Carl Lee/Julius Harris	

DATE	POS	WKS	ARTIST—RECORD TITLE	LABEL & NO.
12/7/85	**29**	5	▲ 124. Sweet Dreams — The Life And Times Of Patsy Cline Jessica Lange/Ed Harris — featuring Patsy's original vocals	MCA 6149
11/24/84	**34**	4	▲ 125. Teachers [V] Nick Nolte/Jobeth Williams/Judd Hirsch/Ralph Macchio features songs by 38 Special, Joe Cocker and eight others	Capitol 12371
5/5/90	**13**	11	● 126. Teenage Mutant Ninja Turtles [V] Judith Hoag/Elias Koteas; based on the live action/animatronics characters created by Kevin Eastman & Peter Laird	SBK 91066
5/20/78	**10**	15	● 127. Thank God It's Friday [V] Jeff Goldblum/Valerie Landsburg — includes bonus 12" single Last Dance (3) Donna Summer	Casablanca 7099 [2]
			That's The Way Of The World — see EARTH, WIND & FIRE Harvey Keitel/Ed Nelson/Cynthia Bostwick/Bert Parks	
1/22/55	**6**	8	128. There's No Business Like Show Business [M] Ethel Merman/Donald O'Connor/Dan Dailey — sw: Irving Berlin	Decca 8091
5/13/67	**16**	12	▲ 129. Thoroughly Modern Millie [M] Julie Andrews/Mary Tyler Moore/Carol Channing cd: Andre Previn	Decca 71500
1/22/66	**10**	13	130. Thunderball [I] Sean Connery/Claudine Auger — cp/cd: John Barry	United Art. 5132
11/15/80	**37**	4	131. Times Square [V] Tim Curry/Trini Alvarado/Robin Johnson featuring recordings by 20 rock artists	RSO 4203 [2]
11/11/67	**16**	11	132. To Sir, With Love [I + V] Sidney Poitier/Judy Geeson To Sir With Love (1) Lulu	Fontana 67569
5/30/64	**38**	31	133. Tom Jones [I] Albert Finney/Susannah York — cp/cd: John Addison	United Art. 5113
4/12/75	**2**(1)	19	▲ 134. Tommy [M] Roger Daltrey/Ann-Margret/Oliver Reed/Elton John rock opera — all but four songs written by Pete Townshend also see The Who/Various "Rock Operas"	Polydor 9502 [2]
6/14/86	**1**(5)	33	● 135. Top Gun [V] Tom Cruise/Kelly McGillis/Val Kilmer/Anthony Edwards Danger Zone (2) Kenny Loggins/Take My Breath Away (1) Berlin	Columbia 40323
			Trouble Man — see GAYE, Marvin Robert Hooks/Paul Winfield/Ralph Waite/Paula Kelly	
12/24/83	**26**	8	● 136. Two Of A Kind [V] John Travolta/Olivia Newton-John Twist Of Fate (5) Olivia Newton-John	MCA 6127
10/5/68	**24**	11	▲ 137. 2001: A Space Odyssey [I] Gary Lockwood/Keir Dullea features classical music by various orchestras	MGM 13
			Under The Cherry Moon — see PRINCE Prince/Jerome Benton/Kristin Scott Thomas/Steven Berkoff	
8/15/64	**11**	16	138. Unsinkable Molly Brown, The [M] Debbie Reynolds/Harve Presnell — sw: Meredith Willson; cd: Robert Armbruster — also see Original Cast ('60)	MGM 4232
6/7/80	**3**	23	● 139. Urban Cowboy [V] John Travolta/Debra Winger Lookin' For Love (5) Johnny Lee	Asylum 90002 [2]
2/24/68	**11**	9	140. Valley Of The Dolls Barbara Parkins/Patty Duke/Sharon Tate/Susan Hayward sw: Dory & Andre Previn; cd: Johnny Williams	20th Century 4196
7/13/85	**38**	4	141. View To A Kill, A [I] Roger Moore/Tanya Roberts/Christopher Walken/Grace Jones cp/cd: John Barry — A View To A Kill (1) Duran Duran	Capitol 12413

DATE	POS	WKS	ARTIST—RECORD TITLE	LABEL & NO.
3/23/85	**11**	12	● 142. Vision Quest [V] Matthew Modine/Linda Fiorentino/Michael Schoeffling *Only The Young* (9) Journey/*Crazy For You* (1) Madonna	Geffen 24063
9/8/62	**33**	2	143. Walk On The Wild Side [I] Laurence Harvey/Jane Fonda — cp/cd: Elmer Bernstein	Ava 4
3/2/74	**20**	5	▲ 144. Way We Were, The [I] Barbra Streisand/Robert Redford — cp: Marvin Hamlisch	Columbia 32830
11/20/61	**1**(54)	144	● 145. West Side Story [M] Natalie Wood/Richard Beymer/Rita Moreno/George Chakiris mu: Leonard Bernstein; ly: Stephen Sondheim; cd: Johnny Green also see Ferrante & Teicher/Stan Kenton/Original Cast (1958)	Columbia 2070
8/21/65	**14**	10	146. What's New Pussycat? [I + V] Peter Sellers/Peter O'Toole — mu: Burt Bacharach; ly: Hal David — *What's New Pussycat?* (3) Tom Jones	United Art. 5117
12/7/85	**17**	12	▲ 147. White Nights [V] Mikhail Baryshnikov/Gregory Hines/Geraldine Page/Helen Mirren *Separate Lives* (1) Phil Collins & Marilyn Martin	Atlantic 81273
			Who's That Girl — see MADONNA Madonna/Griffin Dunne/Haviland Morris/John McMartin/Sir John Mills *Who's That Girl* (1) Madonna	
			Wild Angels, The — see ALLAN, Davie Peter Fonda/Nancy Sinatra — cp/cd: Mike Curb	
9/21/68	**12**	12	148. Wild In The Streets Christopher Jones/Diana Varsi/Shelley Winters sw: Barry Mann/Cynthia Weil; cd: Mike Curb	Tower 5099
11/25/78	**40**	1	▲ 149. Wiz, The [M] a soul musical version of *The Wizard Of Oz* Diana Ross/Michael Jackson — sw: Charlie Smalls; cd: Quincy Jones	MCA 14000 [2]
			Woman in Red, The — see WONDER, Stevie Gene Wilder/Charles Grodin/Judith Ivey/Gilda Radner	
			Woodstock — see VARIOUS — Concerts/Festivals	
			Xanadu — see NEWTON-JOHN, Olivia/ ELECTRIC LIGHT ORCHESTRA Olivia Newton-John/Michael Beck/Gene Kelly	
			Yellow Submarine — see BEATLES, The The Beatles	
			Yentl — see STREISAND, Barbra Barbra Streisand/Mandy Patinkin/Amy Irving	
11/5/77	**17**	5	▲ 150. You Light Up My Life Didi Conn/Joe Silver — cp/cd: Joseph Brooks	Arista 4159
8/19/67	**27**	6	151. You Only Live Twice [I] Sean Connery — cp/cd: John Barry	United Art. 5155
			Young At Heart — see DAY, Doris Doris Day/Frank Sinatra/Gig Young	
			Your Cheatin' Heart — see WILLIAMS, Hank, Jr. George Hamilton/Susan Oliver/Red Buttons/Arthur O'Connell	
7/17/65	**26**	23	152. Zorba The Greek [I] Anthony Quinn/Irene Papas — cp/cd: Mikis Theodorakis	20th Century 4167
			# SOUNDTRACK COMPILATIONS	
1/23/61	**2**(3)	63	1. Great Motion Picture Themes [I] *Exodus* (Ferrante & Teicher)/*Never On Sunday* (Don Costa)	United Art. 3122

DATE	POS	WKS	ARTIST—RECORD TITLE	LABEL & NO.
6/23/62	**31**	3	2. Original Motion Picture Hit Themes *Town Without Pity* (Gene Pitney)/*Tonight* (Ferrante & Teicher)	United Art. 3197

ORIGINAL CASTS

The original cast stars are listed below the title. Also shown are the Lyricist (ly), Music Writer (mu) and Songwriter (sw).

DATE	POS	WKS	ARTIST—RECORD TITLE	LABEL & NO.
4/21/62	**21**	6	1. All American Ray Bolger/Eileen Herlie/Ron Husmann mu: Charles Strouse; ly: Lee Adams	Columbia 2160
12/30/57	**12**	5	2. Annie Get Your Gun Mary Martin/John Raitt — sw: Irving Berlin — San Francisco/ Los Angeles production selected by NBC for a TV spectacular (introduced on Broadway in 1946 — starring Ethel Merman)	Capitol 913
2/9/57	**20**	1	3. Bells are Ringing Judy Holliday/Sydney Chaplin — mu: Jule Styne; ly: Betty Comden/Adolph Green	Columbia 5170
7/18/60	**12**	21	4. Bye Bye Birdie Chita Rivera/Dick Van Dyke/Kay Medford/Dick Gautier (Conrad Birdie) — mu: Charles Strouse; ly: Lee Adams also see Soundtrack (1963)	Columbia 5510
3/25/67	**37**	3	5. Cabaret Jill Haworth/Jack Gilford/Bert Convy/Lotte Lenya mu: John Kander; ly: Fred Ebb — also see Soundtrack (1972)	Columbia 3040
1/23/61	**1(6)**	151	● 6. Camelot Richard Burton/Julie Andrews/Robert Goulet mu: Frederick Loewe; ly: Alan Jay Lerner also see Percy Faith/Soundtrack (1967)	Columbia 2031
6/12/61	**1(1)**	29	7. Carnival Anna Maria Alberghetti/James Mitchell — sw: Bob Merrill	MGM 3946
11/17/62	**12**	12	8. Carousel version of the Rodgers & Hammerstein musical — produced by Enoch Light and featuring vocalists Alfred Drake & Roberta Peters — also see Soundtrack (1956)	Command 843
4/29/57	**15**	1	9. Cinderella Julie Andrews — mu: Richard Rodgers; ly: Oscar Hammerstein II a special CBS-TV production (3/31/57)	Columbia 5190
6/11/55	**6**	12	10. Damn Yankees Gwen Verdon/Stephen Douglass/Ray Walston sw: Richard Adler/Jerry Ross — also see Soundtrack (1958)	RCA 1021
3/6/61	**12**	11	11. Do Re Mi Phil Silvers/Nancy Walker — mu: Jule Styne; ly: Betty Comden/Adolph Green	RCA 2002
6/12/82	**11**	15	12. Dreamgirls Jennifer Holliday/Loretta Devine/Cleavant Derricks mu: Henry Krieger; ly: Tom Eyen	Geffen 2007
			Evening With Mike Nichols And Elaine May, An — see NICHOLS, Mike, &	Elaine May
1/22/55	**7**	2	13. Fanny Ezio Pinza/Walter Slezak/Florence Henderson — sw: Harold Rome	RCA 1015
12/26/64	**7**	60	▲ 14. Fiddler On The Roof Zero Mostel/Maria Karnilova/Beatrice Arthur mu: Jerry Bock; ly: Sheldon Harnick also see Soundtrack (1971)	RCA 1093
1/11/60	**7**	32	15. Fiorello! Tom Bosley/Patricia Wilson/Ellen Hanley/Howard Da Silva mu: Jerry Bock; ly: Sheldon Harnick	Capitol 1321

DATE	POS	WKS	ARTIST—RECORD TITLE	LABEL & NO.
1/12/59	**1**(3)	67	● 16. Flower Drum Song Miyoshi Umeki/Larry Blyden/Pat Suzuki — mu: Richard Rodgers; ly: Oscar Hammerstein II — also see Sountrack (1961)	Columbia 2009
			Funny Girl — see STREISAND, Barbra (both Original Cast and Soundtrack)	
2/15/64	**33**	3	17. Girl Who Came To Supper, The Jose Ferrer/Florence Henderson — sw: Noel Coward	Columbia 2420
7/8/72	**34**	12	● 18. Godspell Stephen Nathan/David Haskell — sw: Stephen Schwartz based upon the gospel according to St. Matthew	Bell 1102
2/13/65	**36**	3	19. Golden Boy Sammy Davis, Jr./Billy Daniels — mu: Charles Strouse; ly: Lee Adams	Capitol 2124
7/20/59	**13**	41	20. Gypsy Ethel Merman/Jack Klugman/Sandra Church — mu: Jule Styne; ly: Stephen Sondheim — based on memoirs of Gypsy Rose Lee also see Soundtrack (1962)	Columbia 2017
11/23/68	**1**(13)	59	● 21. Hair Gerome Ragni/James Rado/Lynn Kellogg — mu: Galt MacDermot; ly: Gerome Ragni/James Rado	RCA 1150
2/29/64	**1**(1)	58	● 22. Hello, Dolly! Carol Channing/David Burns/Eileen Brennan — sw: Jerry Herman	RCA 1087
1/18/64	**38**	1	23. Here's Love Janis Paige/Craig Stevens — sw: Meredith Willson based on *Miracle On 34th Street*	Columbia 2400
12/18/61	**19**	19	24. How To Succeed In Business Without Really Trying Robert Morse/Rudy Vallee — sw: Frank Loesser	RCA 1066
12/5/60	**9**	9	25. Irma La Douce Elizabeth Seal/Keith Michell/Clive Revill mu: Marguerite Monnot; original lyrics: Alexandre Breffort	Columbia 2029
1/8/72	**31**	12	26. Jesus Christ Superstar Ben Vereen/Jeff Fenbolt/Yvonne Elliman/Bob Bingham mu: Andrew Lloyd Webber; ly: Tim Rice also see Various-Rock Operas (1970)/Soundtrack (1973)	Decca 1503
12/29/56	**19**	3	27. Li'l Abner Edith Adams/Peter Palmer/Howard St. John/Stubby Kaye mu: Gene de Paul; ly: Johnny Mercer	Columbia 5150
8/20/66	**23**	14	● 28. Mame Angela Lansbury/Beatrice Arthur — sw: Jerry Herman based on the movie *Auntie Mame*	Columbia 3000
2/18/67	**31**	13	● 29. Man of La Mancha Richard Kiley/Irving Jacobson/Joan Diener — mu: Mitch Leigh; ly: Joe Darion — an adaptation of *Don Quixote* — featuring the song *The Impossible Dream*	Kapp 4505
11/20/61	**10**	27	30. Milk and Honey Robert Weede/Mimi Benzell/Molly Picon — sw: Jerry Herman	RCA 1065
12/1/62	**14**	13	31. Mr. President Robert Ryan/Nanette Fabray — sw: Irving Berlin	Columbia 2270
8/4/56	**11**	4	32. Most Happy Fella, The Robert Weede/Jo Sullivan — sw: Frank Loesser	Columbia 2330
2/24/58	**1**(12)	123	● 33. Music Man, The Robert Preston/Barbara Cook — sw: Meredith Willson also see Soundtrack (1962)	Capitol 990
4/28/56	**1**(15)	292	▲ 34. My Fair Lady Rex Harrison/Julie Andrews — mu: Frederick Loewe; ly: Alan Jay Lerner — adapted from Bernard Shaw's *Pygmalion* — also see Soundtrack ('64)	Columbia 5090

DATE	POS	WKS	ARTIST—RECORD TITLE	LABEL & NO.
8/5/57	**17**	3	35. New Girl in Town Gwen Verdon/Thelma Ritter/George Wallace — sw: Bob Merrill	RCA 1027
4/28/62	**5**	27	36. No Strings Richard Kiley/Diahann Carroll — sw: Richard Rodgers	Capitol 1695
11/3/62	**4**	53	● 37. Oliver! Clive Revill/Georgia Brown/Bruce Prochnik (Oliver) sw: Lionel Bart — also see Soundtrack (1968)	RCA 2004
2/15/64	**37**	2	38. 110 In The Shade Robert Horton/Inga Swenson/Stephen Douglass mu: Harvey Schmidt; ly: Tom Jones	RCA 1085
4/2/55	**4**	8	39. Peter Pan Mary Martin/Cyril Ritchard — mu: Mark Charlap/Jule Styne; ly: Carolyn Leigh/Betty Comden/Adolph Green	RCA 1019
3/5/88	**33**	4	▲ 40. Phantom of the Opera, The original London cast — Michael Crawford/Sarah Brightman/ Steve Barton — mu: Andrew Lloyd Webber; ly: Charles Hart	Polydor 831273 [2]
1/6/62	**36**	2	41. Sail Away Elaine Stritch/James Hurst — sw: Noel Coward	Capitol 1643
6/22/63	**15**	8	42. She Loves Me Barbara Cook/Daniel Massey/Barbara Baxley/Jack Cassidy mu: Jerry Bock; ly: Sheldon Harnick	MGM 4118 [2]
4/16/55	**9**	6	43. Silk Stockings Hildegarde Neff/Don Ameche/Gretchen Wyler — sw: Cole Porter	RCA 1016
12/21/59	**1**(16)	168	● 44. Sound Of Music, The Mary Martin/Theodore Bikel — mu: Richard Rodgers; ly: Oscar Hammerstein II — also see Soundtrack (1965)	Columbia 2020
11/24/62	**3**	22	45. Stop The World-I Want To Get Off Anthony Newley/Anna Quayle — sw: Leslie Bricusse/ Anthony Newley	London 88001
1/9/61	**15**	8	46. Tenderloin Maurice Evans/Ron Husmann/Wayne Miller/Eileen Rodgers mu: Jerry Bock; ly: Sheldon Harnick	Capitol 1492
12/26/60	**6**	35	47. Unsinkable Molly Brown, The Tammy Grimes/Harve Presnell — sw: Meredith Willson also see Soundtrack (1964)	Capitol 1509
3/17/58	**5**	120	● 48. West Side Story Carol Lawrence/Larry Kert/Chita Rivera/Art Smith mu: Leonard Bernstein; ly: Stephen Sondheim also see Soundtrack (1961)	Columbia 5230
5/9/64	**28**	3	49. What Makes Sammy Run? Steve Lawrence/Sally Ann Howes/Robert Alda — sw: Ervin Drake	Columbia 2440
1/23/61	**6**	31	50. Wildcat Lucille Ball/Keith Andes — mu: Cy Coleman; ly: Carolyn Leigh	RCA 1060

TELEVISION SHOWS

The stars of the show are listed directly below the title.

DATE	POS	WKS	ARTIST—RECORD TITLE	LABEL & NO.
11/27/71	**8**	12	● 1. All In The Family [C] Carroll O'Connor/Jean Stapleton/Rob Reiner/Sally Struthers comedy excerpts from the show	Atlantic 7210
8/23/69	**18**	8	2. Dark Shadows [I] Jonathan Frid/David Selby — cp/cd: Robert Cobert	Philips 314
10/12/85	**1**(11)	22	▲ 3. Miami Vice [V] Don Johnson/Philip Michael Thomas — includes five instrumentals composed & performed by Jan Hammer *Miami Vice* (1) Jan Hammer/*You Belong To The City* (2) Glenn Frey	MCA 6150
			Mr. Lucky — see MANCINI, Henry	

DATE	POS	WKS	ARTIST—RECORD TITLE	LABEL & NO.

5/9/60	**30**	2	4. One Step Beyond (Music From) [I]
			   from the *Alcoa Presents* TV series — Harry Lubin conducts
			   the Berliner Symphoniker orchestra
				Decca 8970

			Peter Gunn — see MANCINI, Henry	
			Roaring 20's, The — see PROVINE, Dorothy	
			Roots — see JONES, Quincy	
2/5/77	**38**	3	5. Saturday Night Live! [C] John Belushi/Dan Aykroyd/Chevy Chase/Jane Curtin & cast	Arista 4107

4/20/59	**3**	27	6. 77 Sunset Strip [I]
			   Efrem Zimbalist, Jr./Roger Smith/Ed "Kookie" Byrnes
			   musical director: Warren Barker
				Warner 1289

1/12/74	**34**	7	7. Sunshine
			   TV film starring Christina Raines and Cliff DeYoung
			   music composed by John Denver; vocals by Cliff DeYoung
				MCA 387

1/18/75	**30**	3	● 8. Tonight Show/Here's Johnny [C]
			   actual musical and comedy excerpts from the TV show hosted
			   by Johnny Carson since 10/1/62
				Casablanca 1296 [2]

11/10/58	**2(4)**	50	9. Victory At Sea, Vol 2 [I]	RCA 2226

9/25/61	**7**	19	10. Victory At Sea, Vol. 3 [I]
			   above two are orchestral suites from the NBC-TV series
			   which featured actual film of World War II naval battles
			   cp: Richard Rodgers; cd: Robert Russell Bennett
				RCA 2523

			TELEVISION SPECIALS:	
			Aloha From Hawaii via Satellite — see PRESLEY, Elvis	
			Cinderella — see ORIGINAL CASTS	
			Elvis — see PRESLEY, Elvis	
			Elvis In Concert — see PRESLEY, Elvis	
			Goin' Back To Indiana — see JACKSON 5	
			Liza With A "Z" — see MINNELLI, Liza	
			Movin' With Nancy — see SINATRA, Nancy	
			On Broadway — see SUPREMES & TEMPTATIONS	
			Point!, The — see NILSSON	
			Really Rosie — see KING, Carole	
			TCB — see SUPREMES/TEMPTATIONS	
			Temptations Show, The — see TEMPTATIONS	
			# VARIOUS ARTISTS — Label Compilations A sampling of artists and songs are listed below each title.	
			ATLANTIC	
11/24/56	**20**	2	1. Rock & Roll Forever fourteen selections by Atlantic's top R&B artists	Atlantic 1239
9/2/67	**12**	14	2. The Super Hits *Respect* Aretha Franklin/*Good Lovin'* Young Rascals	Atlantic 501
			CAPITOL	
6/1/59	**5**	3	3. What's New? on Capitol Stereo, vol. 1 preview of 12 new Capitol stereo albums	Capitol SN-1

DATE	POS	WKS	ARTIST—RECORD TITLE	LABEL & NO.
			COLUMBIA	
6/12/61	**1**(9)	39	4. Stars For A Summer Night twenty-five perfomances by 22 pop and classical artists	Columbia 1 [2]
			END	
2/27/61	**19**	2	5. 12 + 3 = 15 Hits Flamingos/Chantels/Little Anthony & The Imperials/Dubs	End 310
			ORIGINAL SOUND	
9/28/59	**12**	61	6. Oldies But Goodies *Earth Angel* Penguins/*In The Still Of The Night* 5 Satins	Original Snd. 5001
9/11/61	**12**	20	7. Oldies But Goodies, Vol. 3 *Come Go With Me* Dell-Vikings/*Sea Cruise* Frankie Ford	Original Snd. 5004
9/11/61	**15**	20	8. Oldies But Goodies, Vol. 4 *Silhouettes* Rays/*Blue Suede Shoes* Carl Perkins	Original Snd. 5005
8/4/62	**16**	11	9. Oldies But Goodies, Vol. 5 *Alley-Oop* Hollywood Argyles/*Little Star* Elegants	Original Snd. 5007
7/6/63	**31**	14	10. Oldies But Goodies, Vol. 6 *Raindrops* Dee Clark/*Quarter To Three* Gary U.S. Bonds	Original Snd. 5011
			RCA	
10/15/55	**9**	9	11. Pop Shopper twelve selections from RCA Victor's album releases	RCA 13
11/30/59	**2**(7)	39	● 12. 60 Years Of Music America Loves Best performances by RCA Victor artists, from Caruso to Belafonte	RCA 6074 [2]
10/31/60	**6**	12	13. 60 Years Of Music America Loves Best, Volume II thirty performances by RCA artists, from Sousa to Eddie Fisher	RCA 6088 [2]
9/25/61	**5**	12	14. 60 Years Of Music America Loves Best, Volume III (Popular) *Frenesi* Artie Shaw/*Night And Day* Frank Sinatra	RCA 1509
			VARIOUS ARTISTS — **Radio/TV Celebrity** **Compilations**	
			Collections of hits gathered together by famous radio and TV names.	
8/11/73	**27**	7	● 1. Dick Clark/20 Years Of Rock N' Roll original hits from 1953-1972	Buddah 5133 [2]
1/27/62	**26**	7	2. Murray the K's Blasts From The Past *Sweet Little 16* Chuck Berry/*Bo Diddley* Bo Diddley	Chess 1461
			VARIOUS ARTISTS — **Concerts/Festivals**	
			Concert For Bangla Desh, The — see HARRISON, George	
5/2/81	**36**	3	1. Concerts For The People Of Kampuchea December, 1979 four day benefit concert in London, EnglandThe Who/Paul McCartney/Pretenders/Rockestra and six others	Atlantic 7005 [2]

DATE	POS	WKS	ARTIST—RECORD TITLE	LABEL & NO.
8/26/72	**40**	2	2. Fillmore: The Last Days Bill Graham's Fillmore-San Francisco rock shows ran from 11/6/65-7/4/71 — album includes a booklet and 7" interview record	Fillmore 31390 [3]
			Last Waltz, The — see BAND, The	
			Monterey International Pop Festival — see REDDING, Otis/HENDRIX, Jimi	
1/5/80	**19**	9	● 3. No Nukes/The MUSE Concerts For A Non-Nuclear Future benefit concerts at New York's Madison Square Garden Jackson Browne/Bruce Springsteen/Tom Petty/Doobie Bros.	Asylum 801 [3]
4/17/82	**29**	5	4. Secret Policeman's Other Ball/The Music Sting/Jeff Beck & Eric Clapton/Phil Collins/Donovan benefit concert recorded in London for Amnesty International	Island 9698
3/24/73	**28**	6	● 5. Wattstax: The Living Word [S] Isaac Hayes/Staple Singers/Rufus & Carla Thomas/Eddie Floyd	Stax 3010 [2]
6/6/70	**1(4)**	36	● 6. Woodstock [S] film of historic rock festival in upstate New York on August 15-17, 1969 — Jimi Hendrix/Crosby, Stills, Nash & Young/Santana/The Who/Ten Years After/Joe Cocker/Sha-Na-Na	Cotillion 500 [3]
4/10/71	**7**	9	● 7. Woodstock Two [S] more songs from the festival — Jefferson Airplane/Joan Baez/ Melanie/Mountain/Canned Heat/Butterfield Blues Band	Cotillion 400 [2]

VARIOUS ARTISTS — Rock Operas

DATE	POS	WKS	ARTIST—RECORD TITLE	LABEL & NO.
			Godspell — see ORIGINAL CASTS	
			Hair — see ORIGINAL CASTS	
11/21/70	**1(3)**	65	● 1. Jesus Christ Superstar a rock opera featuring Ian Gillan (Jesus), Murray Head and Yvonne Elliman — mu: Andrew Lloyd Webber; ly: Tim Rice also see Soundtrack and Original Cast versions	Decca 7206 [2]
12/23/72	**5**	13	● 2. Tommy featuring the London Symphony Orchestra and English Chamber Choir with guests Pete Townshend, Roger Daltrey, Rod Stewart, Ringo Starr and others — also see The Who/Soundtrack versions	Ode 99001 [2]

VARIOUS ARTISTS — Jazz

DATE	POS	WKS	ARTIST—RECORD TITLE	LABEL & NO.
7/9/55	**5**	10	1. I Like Jazz! [K] a sampling of the development of jazz (ragtime, swing, etc.)	Columbia 1

VARIOUS ARTISTS — Dance/Disco

DATE	POS	WKS	ARTIST—RECORD TITLE	LABEL & NO.
8/18/79	**21**	6	● 1. Night At Studio 54, A specially sequenced disco favorites at the New York club	Casablanca 7161 [2]

DATE	POS	WKS	ARTIST—RECORD TITLE	LABEL & NO.
			# AEROBICS	
			Albums for aerobic exercising — with music, narration, instructions and and illustrations.	
			FONDA, Jane	
7/17/82	**15**	27	▲ 1. Jane Fonda's Workout Record music: Jacksons/REO Speedwagon/Brothers Johnson/Boz Scaggs	Columbia 38054 [2]
			# CHILDRENS	
			Children oriented albums.	
			MICKEY MOUSE	
5/24/80	**35**	4	z 1. Mickey Mouse Disco disco songs performed by session musicians	Disneyland 2504
			SESAME STREET/MUPPETS	
8/29/70	**23**	9	● 2. The Sesame Street Book & Record [TV] Loretta Long/Bob McGrath/Jim Henson's Muppets & cast	Columbia 1069
10/27/79	**32**	5	● 3. The Muppet Movie [S] *Rainbow Connection* Kermit	Atlantic 16001
12/22/79	**26**	4	**JOHN DENVER & THE MUPPETS:** ▲ 4. A Christmas Together [X]	RCA 3451
			# CHRISTMAS (Top Pop Albums Chart)	
			The following various artist Christmas albums made *Billboard*'s Top Pop Albums charts:	
12/30/57	**19**	3	1. Merry Christmas [EP] 7" EP (originally released as a 10" LP in 1952) Ames Brothers/Don Cornell/Johnny Desmond/Eileen Barton	Coral 82003
12/5/87	**20**	7	▲ 2. Very Special Christmas, A Christmas songs contributed by 15 rock superstars; proceeds donated to the Special Olympics	A&M 3911
			# CHRISTMAS (Special Christmas Charts)	
			For the years 1963 through 1973, *Billboard* did not chart Christmas albums on their Top Pop Albums charts. Instead, they issued special Christmas charts for 3-4 weeks during each Christmas season. These special charts were discontinued from 1974 thru 1982 when *Billboard* again charted Christmas albums on their regular album charts. Since 1983, *Billboard* again issued special Christmas charts, however, they also listed the best selling Christmas albums on their Top Pop Albums charts. The following list includes only those albums which made the top 10 of *Billboard*'s special Christmas Albums chart, and never made *Billboard*'s Top Pop Albums charts. The number in brackets after title indicates total years (Christmas seasons) album made *Billboard*'s Christmas charts.	
			AIR SUPPLY	
12/10/88	**10**	1	1. Air Supply's Christmas	Arista 8528

DATE	POS	WKS	ARTIST—RECORD TITLE	LABEL & NO.
12/7/68	**1**(2)	8	**ALPERT, Herb & The Tijuana Brass** ● 2. Herb Alpert & The Tijuana Brass Christmas Album [2 yrs.]	[I] A&M 4166
12/2/67	9	1	**ANDREWS, Julie** 3. A Christmas Treasure <small>with the orchestra, harpsichord and arrangements of Andre Previn</small>	RCA 3829
12/3/66	6	5	**BAEZ, Joan** 4. Noel [2 yrs.]	Vanguard 79230
12/5/64	6	3	**BEACH BOYS, The** ● 5. The Beach Boys' Christmas Album [2 yrs.]	Capitol 2164
12/14/68	10	1	**BENNETT, Tony** 6. Snowfall/The Tony Bennett Christmas Album	Columbia 9739
12/19/70	9	1	**BOSTON POPS ORCHESTRA/ARTHUR FIEDLER** 7. A Christmas Festival [I]	Polydor 5004
12/25/71	6	1	**BRADY BUNCH** 8. Merry Christmas from the Brady Bunch	Paramount 5026
12/13/69	10	1	**BROWN, James** 9. A Soulful Christmas	King 1040
12/7/68	**1**(2)	6	**CAMPBELL, Glen** ● 10. That Christmas Feeling [2 yrs.]	Capitol 2978
12/13/69	7	1	**CASH, Johnny** 11. The Christmas Spirit	Columbia 8917
12/21/63	9	1	**CHIPMUNKS, The** 12. Christmas with the Chipmunks, Vol. 2 [N]	Liberty 7334
12/21/63	**1**(2)	37	**COLE, Nat King** ● 13. The Christmas Song [16 yrs.]	Capitol 1967
12/5/70	5	2	**COMO, Perry** ● 14. The Perry Como Christmas Album	RCA 4016

DATE	POS	WKS	ARTIST—RECORD TITLE	LABEL & NO.
			CONNIFF, Ray	
12/12/70	**10**	1	15. Here We Come A-Caroling	Columbia GP 3
			CROSBY, Bing/Frank Sinatra/Fred Waring	
12/19/64	**9**	2	16. 12 Songs of Christmas	Reprise 2022
			DOMINGO, Placido	
12/15/84	**9**	1	17. Christmas with Placido Domingo with the Vienna Symphony Orchestra	CBS 37245
			ELMO & PATSY	
12/19/87	**8**	1	18. Grandma Got Run Over By A Reindeer	Epic 39931
			FELICIANO, Jose	
12/1/73	**3**	3	19. Jose Feliciano	RCA 4421
			GARY, John	
12/5/64	**3**	4	20. The John Gary Christmas Album	RCA 2940
			GORME, Eydie, and The Trio Los Panchos	
12/17/66	**9**	2	21. Navidad means Christmas [F]	Columbia 9357
			GOULET, Robert	
12/7/63	**4**	6	22. This Christmas I Spend With You [2 yrs.]	Columbia 8876
			GRANT, Amy	
12/21/85	**9**	2	23. A Christmas Album	A&M 5057
			GUARALDI, Vince, Trio	
12/24/88	**9**	3	24. A Charlie Brown Christmas [2 yrs.]	Fantasy 8431
			HAGGARD, Merle	
12/8/73	**4**	2	25. Merle Haggard's Christmas Present (Something Old, Something New)	Capitol 11230
			JACKSON, Mahalia	
12/13/69	**2**(1)	2	26. Christmas with Mahalia	Columbia 9727
			JACKSON 5	
12/5/70	**1**(6)	16	27. Christmas Album [4 yrs.]	Motown 713
			JUDDS, The	
12/19/87	**9**	2	28. Christmas Time with The Judds [2 yrs.]	RCA 6422

DATE	POS	WKS	ARTIST—RECORD TITLE	LABEL & NO.
			KAEMPFERT, Bert, and his orchestra	
12/7/63	10	2	29. Christmas Wonderland [I]	Decca 74441
			KING FAMILY, The	
12/18/65	8	2	30. Christmas With The King Family	Warner 1627
			LEE, Brenda	
12/16/72	7	1	31. Merry Christmas from Brenda Lee	Decca 74583
			LEWIS, Ramsey, Trio	
12/19/64	8	2	32. More Sounds of Christmas [I]	Argo 745
			MANDRELL, Barbara	
12/15/84	8	2	33. Christmas At Our Home	MCA 5519
			MANTOVANI And His Orchestra	
12/14/63	7	3	34. Christmas Greetings From Mantovani [2 yrs.] [I]	London 338
			MARTIN, Dean	
12/3/66	1(1)	14	● 35. The Dean Martin Christmas Album [4 yrs.]	Reprise 6222
			MARTINO, Al	
12/12/64	8	2	36. A Merry Christmas	Capitol 2165
			MATHIS, Johnny	
11/30/63	2(2)	7	37. Sounds Of Christmas [2 yrs.]	Mercury 60837
12/6/69	1(1)	15	● 38. Give Me Your Love For Christmas [4 yrs.]	Columbia 9923
			MORMON TABERNACLE CHOIR, The	
12/11/65	8	1	● 39. The Joy Of Christmas with Leonard Bernstein conducting the New York Philharmonic	Columbia 6499
12/20/69	3	4	40. Handel: Messiah [3 yrs.] with Eugene Ormandy conducting The Philadelphia Orchestra featured vocalists: Eileen Farrell (soprano) and William Warfield (baritone)	Columbia 607 [2]
			NABORS, Jim	
12/9/67	1(1)	17	● 41. Jim Nabors' Christmas Album [6 yrs.]	Columbia 9531
			NEW CHRISTY MINSTRELS, The	
12/28/63	5	1	42. Merry Christmas!	Columbia 8896
			NEW EDITION	
12/21/85	9	2	43. It's Christmas All Over The World	MCA 39040

DATE	POS	WKS	ARTIST—RECORD TITLE	LABEL & NO.
			NEWTON, Wayne	
12/3/66	**10**	3	44. Songs For A Merry Christmas	Capitol 2588
			PARTRIDGE FAMILY	
12/4/71	**1**(4)	6	● 45. A Partridge Family Christmas Card [2 yrs.]	Bell 6066
			PAVAROTTI, Luciano	
12/17/83	**6**	4	● 46. O Holy Night [2 yrs.] with Kurt Adler conducting the National Philharmonic; recorded in 1976	London 26473
			PRESLEY, Elvis	
12/5/70	**2**(3)	5	47. Elvis' Christmas Album [2 yrs.] eight of 10 songs are from his 1957 Christmas album	RCA Camden 2428
12/4/71	**1**(3)	12	▲ 48. Elvis sings The Wonderful World of Christmas [3 yrs.] an all new Christmas LP (recorded May, 1971)	RCA 4579
			PRIDE, Charley	
12/12/70	**5**	6	49. Christmas in My Home [3 yrs.]	RCA 4406
			RAWLS, Lou	
12/2/67	**2**(1)	5	50. Merry Christmas Ho! Ho! Ho!	Capitol 2790
			REVERE, Paul, & The Raiders	
12/9/67	**10**	1	51. A Christmas Present…And Past	Columbia 9555
			SHAW, Robert, Chorale and Orchestra	
12/7/68	**8**	2	52. Handel: Messiah *Messiah* was composed by George Frideric Handel from 8/22 to 9/14, 1741	RCA 6175 [3]
			SHERMAN, Bobby	
12/12/70	**2**(1)	3	53. Bobby Sherman Christmas Album	Metromedia 1038
			SIMEONE, Harry, Chorale	
12/3/66	**5**	4	54. O Bambino/The Little Drummer Boy [3 yrs.] includes Simeone's new recording of "The Little Drummer Boy"	Kapp 3450
			SINATRA FAMILY	
12/13/69	**3**	2	55. The Sinatra Family Wish You A Merry Christmas Frank and daughters Nancy & Tina, and son Frank, Jr.	Reprise 1026
			SMITH, Jimmy	
12/5/64	**8**	1	56. Christmas '64 [I]	Verve 8604

DATE	POS	WKS	ARTIST—RECORD TITLE	LABEL & NO.
			SUPREMES, The	
12/11/65	6	3	57. Merry Christmas	Motown 638
			TEMPTATIONS, The	
12/19/70	4	5	58. The Temptations' Christmas Card [3 yrs.]	Gordy 951
12/17/83	6	2	59. Give Love At Christmas	Gordy 998
			VENTURES, The	
12/18/65	9	2	60. The Ventures' Christmas Album [I]	Dolton 8038
			WILLIAMS, Andy	
11/30/63	1(9)	26	● 61. The Andy Williams Christmas Album [8 yrs.]	Columbia 8887
12/18/65	1(3)	12	● 62. Merry Christmas [4 yrs.]	Columbia 9220
			VARIOUS ARTISTS	
12/9/72	7	3	63. Christmas Album, The [2 yrs.] features songs by Barbra Streisand, Mahalia Jackson, Johnny Mathis, Frank Sinatra, Tony Bennett, Johnny Cash & 14 others	Columbia 30763 [2]
12/1/73	7	1	64. Christmas Greetings from Nashville features Eddy Arnold, Chet Atkins, Jim Reeves & seven others	RCA 0262
12/8/73	1(1)	3	65. Motown Christmas, A Temptations/Stevie Wonder/Jackson Five/Miracles/Supremes	Motown 795 [2]
12/5/70	7	1	66. Peace On Earth Beach Boys/Glen Campbell/Nat King Cole/Lettermen + 13 others	Capitol 585 [2]
12/23/72	6	3	67. Phil Spector's Christmas Album [2 yrs.] Crystals/Ronettes/Darlene Love/Bob B. Soxx & Blue Jeans — reissue of *A Christmas Gift For You* (Philles/1963)	Apple 3400
12/6/69	8	2	68. Soul Christmas [2 yrs.] Otis Redding/Clarence Carter/Joe Tex plus five others	Atco 269

CLASSICAL

Various artist compilations.

DATE	POS	WKS	ARTIST—RECORD TITLE	LABEL & NO.
9/25/61	6	9	1. 60 Years Of Music America Loves Best, Volume III (Red Seal) Caruso/Fiedler/Toscanini plus nine more classical greats	RCA 2574
5/25/63	39	3	2. Sound of Genius, The nineteen favorites by 18 of Columbia's greatest classical artists	Columbia SGS 1 [2]
6/16/62	24	9	3. Summer Festival nineteen favorites by 20 of RCA's greatest classical artists	RCA 6097 [2]

COMEDY

Comedy concept productions.

DATE	POS	WKS	ARTIST—RECORD TITLE	LABEL & NO.
1/26/63	27	4	1. Other Family, The starring Larry Foster, Marty Brill and Toby Deane	Laurie 5000
11/12/66	40	2	2. Our Wedding Album or The Great Society Affair spoof of President Johnson's family — with Kenny Solms, Gail Parent, Fannie Flagg, Robert Klein & Jo Ann Worley	Jamie 3028
1/26/63	35	4	3. President Strikes Back!, The an answer album to Vaughn Meader's *The First Family* starring Marc London and Sylvia Miles	Kapp 1322

DATE	POS	WKS	ARTIST—RECORD TITLE	LABEL & NO.
12/4/65	**3**	14	● 4. Welcome to the LBJ Ranch! featuring the actual recorded voices of political leaders	Capitol 2423
5/7/66	**22**	5	5. When You're In Love The Whole World Is Jewish starring Betty Walker, Lou Jacobi, Frank Gallop and four others	Kapp 4506
10/23/65	**9**	14	6. You Don't Have To Be Jewish starring Betty Walker, Lou Jacobi, Frank Gallop and five others	Kapp 4503

MISCELLANEOUS

The following albums, because of their unusual content, are listed in this section and are categorized with special headings.

CARS

DATE	POS	WKS	ARTIST—RECORD TITLE	LABEL & NO.
2/29/64	**27**	2	1. Big Sounds Of The Drags!, The actual sounds of drag racing at a quarter-mile track	Capitol 2001
7/27/63	**7**	31	2. Shut Down *Shut Down* Beach Boys/*Black Denim Trousers* Cheers, plus 10 other car songs	Capitol 1918

MINSTREL SHOW

DATE	POS	WKS	ARTIST—RECORD TITLE	LABEL & NO.
5/26/56	**9**	9	3. Gentlemen, Be Seated! recreation of a complete minstrel show (conducted by Allen Roth)	Epic 3238

OLYMPICS

DATE	POS	WKS	ARTIST—RECORD TITLE	LABEL & NO.
10/15/88	**31**	3	● 4. 1988 Summer Olympics Album/One Moment In Time features tracks by 11 artists especially written and recorded for the NBC-TV broadcast of the 1988 Summer Olympic Games *One Moment In Time* (5-Whitney Houston)	Arista 8551

RADIO

DATE	POS	WKS	ARTIST—RECORD TITLE	LABEL & NO.
3/29/69	**31**	7	5. Themes Like Old Times features 180 of the most famous original radio themes	Viva 36018 [2]

THE RECORD HOLDERS

TOP ARTIST AND ALBUM ACHIEVEMENTS

TOP 100 ARTISTS OF THE ROCK ERA

An artist's rank is determined by a point system wherein each top 40 album is assigned a value based on its chart performance. The point system that determines an artist's ranking has changed since the last edition of *Top 40 Albums*. A larger portion of points are awarded to albums appearing in the upper echelons of the chart. With this shift in emphasis, an artist with one major hit album may fare better than an artist with several lower-charting albums.

Each album's point total is tabulated using the following formula:

1. Points are awarded based on its highest charted position:

No. 1	=	50 points for its first week at No. 1, plus
		15 points for each additional week at No. 1
No. 2	=	40 points
No. 3	=	30
No. 4-5	=	25
No. 6-10	=	20
No. 11-20	=	15
No. 21-30	=	10
No. 31-40	=	5

2. Total weeks charted in the top 40 are added in to each album's score.

When two artists combine for a hit album (Electric Light Orchestra/Olivia Newton-John or Diana Ross/Marvin Gaye, for example) the full point value is given to each artist. Artists such as Simon and Garfunkel, Sonny & Cher and Loggins & Messina are considered regular recording teams and their points are not split or shared by either of the artists individually.

ARTISTS	POINTS	ARTISTS	POINTS
1. THE BEATLES	3267	24. PRINCE	901
2. ELVIS PRESLEY	2699	25. STEVIE WONDER	897
3. FRANK SINATRA	2383	26. RAY CONNIFF	891
4. THE ROLLING STONES	2128	27. THE TEMPTATIONS	891
5. BARBRA STREISAND	1836	28. LAWRENCE WELK	891
6. THE KINGSTON TRIO	1757	29. RAY CHARLES	852
7. ELTON JOHN	1516	30. THE BEACH BOYS	832
8. JOHNNY MATHIS	1422	31. SIMON AND GARFUNKEL	825
9. HERB ALPERT/THE TIJUANA BRASS	1387	32. BILLY JOEL	824
10. HARRY BELAFONTE	1320	33. EAGLES	805
11. MITCH MILLER	1316	34. PETER, PAUL AND MARY	786
12. CHICAGO	1136	35. THE SUPREMES	774
13. BOB DYLAN	1080	36. ROD STEWART	742
14. ANDY WILLIAMS	1063	37. BRUCE SPRINGSTEEN	716
15. PAUL McCARTNEY/WINGS	1051	38. JEFFERSON AIRPLANE/STARSHIP	698
16. MANTOVANI	1022	39. OLIVIA NEWTON-JOHN	680
17. HENRY MANCINI	1021	40. NEIL DIAMOND	679
18. MICHAEL JACKSON	1009	41. CAROLE KING	671
19. BEE GEES	1008	42. PINK FLOYD	661
20. FLEETWOOD MAC	1001	43. BILLY VAUGHN	660
21. LED ZEPPELIN	988	44. ARETHA FRANKLIN	651
22. ENOCH LIGHT	937	45. LINDA RONSTADT	634
23. THE MONKEES	926	46. SANTANA	632

TOP 100 ARTISTS OF THE ROCK ERA

ARTISTS	POINTS	ARTISTS	POINTS
47. MADONNA	622	74. QUEEN	449
48. NAT "KING" COLE	617	75. JOAN BAEZ	444
49. ERIC CLAPTON	614	76. JAMES TAYLOR	443
50. ROGER WILLIAMS	613	77. BOB NEWHART	437
51. THE MOODY BLUES	604	78. BARRY MANILOW	433
52. JETHRO TULL	584	79. BOB SEGER & THE SILVER BULLET BAND	433
53. JOHN DENVER	581	80. REO SPEEDWAGON	429
54. EARTH, WIND & FIRE	577	81. GRAND FUNK RAILROAD	428
55. WHITNEY HOUSTON	574	82. KENNY ROGERS	427
56. THE POLICE	538	83. THE JACKSON 5/JACKSONS	426
57. DIANA ROSS	536	84. THREE DOG NIGHT	425
58. GEORGE HARRISON	531	85. DAVID BOWIE	422
59. FOREIGNER	529	86. CROSBY, STILLS & NASH (& YOUNG)	422
60. CREEDENCE CLEARWATER REVIVAL	520	87. TENNESSEE ERNIE FORD	419
61. VAN HALEN	515	88. COMMODORES	418
62. DONNA SUMMER	511	89. NEIL YOUNG	410
63. JOHN LENNON	504	90. JOURNEY	409
64. GLEN CAMPBELL	498	91. PHIL COLLINS	393
65. THE DOOBIE BROTHERS	484	92. KISS	389
66. U2	473	93. BILL COSBY	384
67. THE DOORS	466	94. JUDY GARLAND	383
68. THE WHO	464	95. CARPENTERS	378
69. HEART	464	96. YES	373
70. JIMI HENDRIX	464	97. DAVE BRUBECK QUARTET	373
71. CAT STEVENS	458	98. DORIS DAY	373
72. JOHN COUGAR MELLENCAMP	455	99. BON JOVI	372
73. DARYL HALL & JOHN OATES	449	100. ROBERTA FLACK	370

THE TOP 100 ARTISTS (A-Z)

ARTIST	RANK	ARTIST	RANK
Alpert, Herb/The Tijuana Brass	9	Kiss	92
Baez, Joan	75	Led Zeppelin	21
Beach Boys, The	30	Lennon, John	63
Beatles, The	1	Light, Enoch	22
Bee Gees	19	Madonna	47
Belafonte, Harry	10	Mancini, Henry	17
Bon Jovi	99	Manilow, Barry	78
Bowie, David	85	Mantovani	16
Brubeck, Dave, Quartet	97	Mathis, Johnny	8
Campbell, Glen	64	McCartney, Paul/Wings	15
Carpenters	95	Mellencamp, John Cougar	72
Charles, Ray	29	Miller, Mitch	11
Chicago	12	Monkees, The	23
Clapton, Eric	49	Moody Blues, The	51
Cole, Nat "King"	48	Newhart, Bob	77
Collins, Phil	91	Newton-John, Olivia	39
Commodores	88	Peter, Paul and Mary	34
Conniff, Ray	26	Pink Floyd	42
Cosby, Bill	93	Police, The	56
Creedence Clearwater Revival	60	Presley, Elvis	2
Crosby, Stills & Nash (& Young)	86	Prince	24
Day, Doris	98	Queen	74
Denver, John	53	REO Speedwagon	80
Diamond, Neil	40	Rogers, Kenny	82
Doobie Brothers, The	65	Rolling Stones, The	4
Doors, The	67	Ronstadt, Linda	45
Dylan, Bob	13	Ross, Diana	57
Eagles	33	Santana	46
Earth, Wind & Fire	54	Seger, Bob	79
Flack, Robert	100	Simon and Garfunkel	31
Fleetwood Mac	20	Sinatra, Frank	3
Ford, Tennessee Ernie	87	Springsteen, Bruce	37
Foreigner	59	Stevens, Cat	71
Franklin, Aretha	44	Stewart, Rod	36
Garland, Judy	94	Streisand, Barbra	5
Grand Funk Railroad	81	Summer, Donna	62
Hall, Daryl, & John Oates	73	Supremes, The	35
Harrison, George	58	Taylor, James	76
Heart	69	Temptations, The	27
Hendrix, Jimi	70	Three Dog Night	84
Houston, Whitney	55	U2	66
Jackson, Michael	18	Van Halen	61
Jackson 5/Jacksons, The	83	Vaughn, Billy	43
Jefferson Airplane/Starship	38	Welk, Lawrence	28
Jethro Tull	52	Who, The	68
Joel, Billy	32	Williams, Andy	14
John, Elton	7	Williams, Roger	50
Journey	90	Wonder, Stevie	25
King, Carole	41	Yes	96
Kingston Trio, The	6	Young, Neil	89

THE TOP 25 ARTISTS BY DECADE

ARTIST	POINTS	ARTIST	POINTS
## THE FIFTIES (1955-59)		## THE SEVENTIES	
1. HARRY BELAFONTE	1103	1. ELTON JOHN	1329
2. FRANK SINATRA	1015	2. CHICAGO	944
3. ELVIS PRESLEY	927	3. PAUL McCARTNEY/WINGS	833
4. JOHNNY MATHIS	851	4. BEE GEES	831
5. THE KINGSTON TRIO	749	5. THE ROLLING STONES	820
6. MITCH MILLER	747	6. EAGLES	769
7. MANTOVANI	585	7. FLEETWOOD MAC	732
8. ROGER WILLIAMS	418	8. LED ZEPPELIN	720
9. TENNESSEE ERNIE FORD	384	9. CAROLE KING	671
10. DORIS DAY	356	10. BOB DYLAN	642
11. JACKIE GLEASON	341	11. BARBRA STREISAND	628
12. NAT "KING" COLE	338	12. STEVIE WONDER	592
13. PAT BOONE	327	13. JOHN DENVER	558
14. LAWRENCE WELK	286	14. PINK FLOYD	536
15. HENRY MANCINI	280	15. ROD STEWART	524
16. VAN CLIBURN	273	16. OLIVIA NEWTON-JOHN	524
17. RAY CONNIFF	262	17. JETHRO TULL	511
18. BILLY VAUGHN	211	18. SANTANA	504
19. PERRY COMO	207	19. NEIL DIAMOND	486
20. MARTIN DENNY	207	20. GEORGE HARRISON	466
21. RICKY NELSON	195	21. CAT STEVENS	458
22. SAMMY DAVIS, JR.	186	22. EARTH, WIND & FIRE	457
23. THE FOUR FRESHMEN	151	23. ERIC CLAPTON	426
24. CARMEN CAVALLARO	149	24. DONNA SUMMER	421
25. BING CROSBY	146	25. GRAND FUNK RAILROAD	410
## THE SIXTIES		## THE EIGHTIES	
1. THE BEATLES	2817	1. PRINCE	881
2. ELVIS PRESLEY	1469	2. MICHAEL JACKSON	860
3. FRANK SINATRA	1309	3. BRUCE SPRINGSTEEN	632
4. HERB ALPERT/THE TIJUANA BRASS	1302	4. WHITNEY HOUSTON	574
5. THE KINGSTON TRIO	1008	5. MADONNA	566
6. ANDY WILLIAMS	999	6. THE ROLLING STONES	550
7. ENOCH LIGHT	930	7. BILLY JOEL	501
8. THE MONKEES	904	8. THE POLICE	499
9. RAY CHARLES	852	9. U2	473
10. BARBRA STREISAND	808	10. JOHN COUGAR MELLENCAMP	455
11. PETER, PAUL AND MARY	760	11. VAN HALEN	450
12. THE ROLLING STONES	758	12. REO SPEEDWAGON	404
13. THE SUPREMES	747	13. BARBRA STREISAND	400
14. HENRY MANCINI	727	14. PHIL COLLINS	393
15. THE BEACH BOYS	643	15. BON JOVI	372
16. RAY CONNIFF	629	16. MEN AT WORK	361
17. LAWRENCE WELK	605	17. JOURNEY	349
18. THE TEMPTATIONS	579	18. FOREIGNER	347
19. MITCH MILLER	569	19. PAT BENATAR	340
20. SIMON AND GARFUNKEL	538	20. LIONEL RICHIE	330
21. JOHNNY MATHIS	510	21. DEF LEPPARD	327
22. BILLY VAUGHN	449	22. BOB SEGER & THE SILVER BULLET BAND	325
23. MANTOVANI	437	23. DARYL HALL & JOHN OATES	322
24. BOB NEWHART	437	24. RUSH	300
25. GLEN CAMPBELL	398	25. KENNY ROGERS	294

TOP ARTIST ACHIEVEMENTS*

ARTIST	TOTAL	ARTIST	TOTAL

THE MOST WEEKS AT NO. 1

1.	THE BEATLES	119
2.	ELVIS PRESLEY	64
3.	THE KINGSTON TRIO	46
4.	MICHAEL JACKSON	43
5.	ELTON JOHN	39
6.	THE ROLLING STONES	38
7.	HARRY BELAFONTE	37
8.	FLEETWOOD MAC	37
9.	THE MONKEES	37
10.	PRINCE	33
11.	BEE GEES	31
12.	LED ZEPPELIN	28
13.	EAGLES	27
14.	HERB ALPERT/THE TIJUANA BRASS	26
15.	SIMON AND GARFUNKEL	26
16.	WHITNEY HOUSTON	25
17.	BARBRA STREISAND	22
18.	CHICAGO	22
19.	PAUL McCARTNEY/WINGS	22
20.	HENRY MANCINI	22
21.	FRANK SINATRA	20
22.	ENOCH LIGHT	20
23.	BRUCE SPRINGSTEEN	19
24.	CAROLE KING	19
25.	M.C. HAMMER	19**
26.	PINK FLOYD	18
27.	STEVIE WONDER	17
28.	THE POLICE	17
29.	DORIS DAY	17

THE MOST NO. 1 ALBUMS

1.	THE BEATLES	15
2.	ELVIS PRESLEY	9
3.	THE ROLLING STONES	9
4.	ELTON JOHN	7
5.	PAUL McCARTNEY/WINGS	7
6.	BARBRA STREISAND	6
7.	LED ZEPPELIN	6
8.	THE KINGSTON TRIO	5
9.	HERB ALPERT/THE TIJUANA BRASS	5
10.	CHICAGO	5
11.	FRANK SINATRA	4
12.	THE MONKEES	4
13.	EAGLES	4
14.	BRUCE SPRINGSTEEN	4
15.	MITCH MILLER	3
16.	BOB DYLAN	3
17.	BEE GEES	3
18.	FLEETWOOD MAC	3
19.	PRINCE	3
20.	STEVIE WONDER	3
21.	SIMON AND GARFUNKEL	3
22.	BILLY JOEL	3
23.	THE SUPREMES	3
24.	OLIVIA NEWTON-JOHN	3
25.	CAROLE KING	3
26.	PINK FLOYD	3
27.	LINDA RONSTADT	3
28.	MADONNA	3
29.	JOHN DENVER	3
30.	DONNA SUMMER	3
31.	JOHN LENNON	3
32.	CROSBY, STILLS, NASH & YOUNG	3
33.	ALLAN SHERMAN	3

THE MOST TOP 10 ALBUMS

1.	FRANK SINATRA	31
2.	THE ROLLING STONES	31
3.	ELVIS PRESLEY	25
4.	THE BEATLES	23
5.	BARBRA STREISAND	22
6.	JOHNNY MATHIS	16
7.	THE KINGSTON TRIO	14
8.	MITCH MILLER	14
9.	BOB DYLAN	14
10.	ELTON JOHN	13
11.	THE BEACH BOYS	13
12.	CHICAGO	12
13.	ANDY WILLIAMS	12
14.	PAUL McCARTNEY/WINGS	12
15.	RAY CONNIFF	12
16.	NEIL DIAMOND	12
17.	MANTOVANI	11
18.	LED ZEPPELIN	10
19.	STEVIE WONDER	10
20.	THE TEMPTATIONS	10
21.	LAWRENCE WELK	10
22.	LINDA RONSTADT	10
23.	HERB ALPERT/THE TIJUANA BRASS	9
24.	HARRY BELAFONTE	9
25.	HENRY MANCINI	9
26.	BILLY JOEL	9
27.	THE WHO	9

THE MOST TOP 40 ALBUMS

1.	FRANK SINATRA	49
2.	ELVIS PRESLEY	48
3.	BARBRA STREISAND	35
4.	THE ROLLING STONES	33
5.	BOB DYLAN	29
6.	THE TEMPTATIONS	28
7.	THE BEATLES	27
8.	JOHNNY MATHIS	27
9.	ELTON JOHN	26
10.	MANTOVANI	26
11.	RAY CONNIFF	26
12.	LAWRENCE WELK	24
13.	NEIL DIAMOND	21
14.	ARETHA FRANKLIN	21
15.	THE BEACH BOYS	20
16.	JEFFERSON AIRPLANE/STARSHIP	20
17.	THE KINGSTON TRIO	19
18.	ANDY WILLIAMS	19
19.	THE SUPREMES	19
20.	ROGER WILLIAMS	19
21.	MITCH MILLER	18
22.	CHICAGO	18
23.	BILLY VAUGHN	18
24.	ERIC CLAPTON	18
25.	PAUL McCARTNEY/WINGS	17
26.	STEVIE WONDER	17
27.	ROD STEWART	17
28.	NAT "KING" COLE	17
29.	JETHRO TULL	17
30.	DIANA ROSS	17

*Ties are broken according to rank in the "Top 100 Artists of the Rock Era" section.

**Subject to change since album was still charted as of the 10/20/90 cut-off date

324

TOP 100 ALBUMS OF THE ROCK ERA

Following is a listing, in rank order, of the top No. 1 albums from January, 1955 through October 20, 1990. The ranking is based on this order: total weeks at No. 1, total weeks in the top 10, total weeks in the top 40, and lastly, total weeks charted.

Columnar headings show the following data:

PK YR:	Year album reached its peak position
WEEKS CH:	Total weeks charted
WEEKS 40:	Total weeks in the Top 40
WEEKS 10:	Total weeks in the Top 10
WEEKS #1:	Total weeks album held the No. 1 position

PK YR	CH	WEEKS 40	10	#1	ALBUM TITLE / Artist
62	198	144	106	54	1. WEST SIDE STORY Soundtrack
83	122	91	78	37	2. THRILLER Michael Jackson
58	262	161	90	31	3. SOUTH PACIFIC Soundtrack
56	99	72	58	31	4. CALYPSO Harry Belafonte
77	134	60	52	31	5. RUMOURS Fleetwood Mac
78	120	54	35	24	6. SATURDAY NIGHT FEVER Bee Gees/Soundtrack
84	72	42	32	24	7. PURPLE RAIN Prince & The Revolution/Soundtrack
61	79	53	39	20	8. BLUE HAWAII Elvis Presley/Soundtrack
90	33*	32*	28*	19*	9. PLEASE HAMMER DON'T HURT 'EM M.C. Hammer
87	96	68	48	18	10. DIRTY DANCING Soundtrack
67	96	45	25	18	11. MORE OF THE MONKEES The Monkees
83	75	50	40	17	12. SYNCHRONICITY The Police
55	28	28	25	17	13. LOVE ME OR LEAVE ME Doris Day/Soundtrack
60	276	168	105	16	14. THE SOUND OF MUSIC Original Cast
63	107	61	23	16	15. DAYS OF WINE AND ROSES Andy Williams
56	480	292	173	15	16. MY FAIR LADY Original Cast
71	302	68	46	15	17. TAPESTRY Carole King
67	175	63	33	15	18. SGT. PEPPER'S LONELY HEARTS CLUB BAND The Beatles
82	90	48	31	15	19. BUSINESS AS USUAL Men At Work
59	118	43	31	15	20. THE KINGSTON TRIO AT LARGE The Kingston Trio
81	101	50	30	15	21. HI INFIDELITY REO Speedwagon
80	123	35	27	15	22. THE WALL Pink Floyd
65	114	78	48	14	23. MARY POPPINS Soundtrack
86	162	78	46	14	24. WHITNEY HOUSTON Whitney Houston
60	108	67	44	14	25. THE BUTTON-DOWN MIND OF BOB NEWHART Bob Newhart
61	89	55	38	14	26. EXODUS Soundtrack
76	80	44	35	14	27. SONGS IN THE KEY OF LIFE Stevie Wonder
62	101	59	33	14	28. MODERN SOUNDS IN COUNTRY AND WESTERN MUSIC Ray Charles
64	51	40	28	14	29. A HARD DAY'S NIGHT The Beatles/Soundtrack
60	124	105	43	13	30. PERSUASIVE PERCUSSION Enoch Light/Terry Snyder And The All-Stars
61	95	73	37	13	31. JUDY AT CARNEGIE HALL Judy Garland
66	102	49	32	13	32. THE MONKEES The Monkees
69	151	59	28	13	33. HAIR Original Cast
58	245	123	63	12	34. THE MUSIC MAN Original Cast

TOP 100 ALBUMS OF THE ROCK ERA

PK YR	CH	WEEKS 40	10	#1	ALBUM TITLE / Artist
88	87	69	51	12	35. FAITH George Michael
62	96	69	46	12	36. BREAKFAST AT TIFFANY'S Henry Mancini/Soundtrack
60	73	42	29	12	37. SOLD OUT The Kingston Trio
78	77	39	29	12	38. GREASE Olivia Newton-John/Soundtrack
62	49	26	17	12	39. THE FIRST FAMILY Vaughn Meader
61	64	50	33	11	40. CALCUTTA! Lawrence Welk
87	85	51	31	11	41. WHITNEY Whitney Houston
69	129	32	27	11	42. ABBEY ROAD The Beatles
64	71	27	21	11	43. MEET THE BEATLES! The Beatles
85	34	22	18	11	44. MIAMI VICE TV Soundtrack
89	118*	78	64	10	45. FOREVER YOUR GIRL Paula Abdul
57	88	88	54	10	46. AROUND THE WORLD IN 80 DAYS Soundtrack
58	172	78	54	10	47. GIGI Soundtrack
76	97	55	52	10	48. FRAMPTON COMES ALIVE! Peter Frampton
56	48	48	43	10	49. ELVIS PRESLEY Elvis Presley
59	119	47	43	10	50. THE MUSIC FROM PETER GUNN Henry Mancini/TV Soundtrack
81	81	52	34	10	51. 4 Foreigner
60	111	46	29	10	52. G.I. BLUES Elvis Presley/Soundtrack
84	61	27	20	10	53. FOOTLOOSE Soundtrack
60	60	27	20	10	54. STRING ALONG The Kingston Trio
57	29	29	19	10	55. LOVING YOU Elvis Presley/Soundtrack
63	39	22	18	10	56. THE SINGING NUN The Singing Nun
70	85	24	17	10	57. BRIDGE OVER TROUBLED WATER Simon and Garfunkel
74	104	20	11	10	58. ELTON JOHN - GREATEST HITS Elton John
85	97	55	37	9	59. BROTHERS IN ARMS Dire Straits
87	103	58	36	9	60. THE JOSHUA TREE U2
66	129	59	32	9	61. WHAT NOW MY LOVE Herb Alpert & The Tijuana Brass
82	64	35	27	9	62. ASIA Asia
68	65	47	26	9	63. THE GRADUATE Simon and Garfunkel/Soundtrack
82	107	41	22	9	64. AMERICAN FOOL John Cougar
81	58	30	22	9	65. TATTOO YOU The Rolling Stones
61	40	39	21	9	66. STARS FOR A SUMMER NIGHT Various Artists
79	57	36	21	9	67. THE LONG RUN Eagles
60	86	35	19	9	68. NICE 'N' EASY Frank Sinatra
70	69	26	19	9	69. COSMO'S FACTORY Creedence Clearwater Revival
65	71	38	16	9	70. BEATLES '65 The Beatles
65	44	33	15	9	71. HELP! The Beatles/Soundtrack
68	155	25	15	9	72. THE BEATLES [WHITE ALBUM] The Beatles
71	42	23	15	9	73. PEARL Janis Joplin
72	51	20	13	9	74. CHICAGO V Chicago
65	185	141	61	8	75. WHIPPED CREAM & OTHER DELIGHTS Herb Alpert's Tijuana Brass
58	204	128	53	8	76. SING ALONG WITH MITCH Mitch Miller & The Gang
86	94	60	46	8	77. SLIPPERY WHEN WET Bon Jovi
89	78	61	41	8	78. GIRL YOU KNOW IT'S TRUE Milli Vanilli
73	103	43	36	8	79. GOODBYE YELLOW BRICK ROAD Elton John

TOP 100 ALBUMS OF THE ROCK ERA

PK YR	CH	WEEKS 40	WEEKS 10	#1	ALBUM TITLE / Artist
57	94	55	31	8	80. LOVE IS THE THING Nat "King" Cole
77	107	32	28	8	81. HOTEL CALIFORNIA Eagles
59	126	40	26	8	82. HERE WE GO AGAIN! The Kingston Trio
80	74	27	24	8	83. DOUBLE FANTASY John Lennon/Yoko Ono
78	76	34	22	8	84. 52ND STREET Billy Joel
68	66	29	19	8	85. CHEAP THRILLS Big Brother & The Holding Company
68	91	30	14	8	86. MAGICAL MYSTERY TOUR The Beatles/Soundtrack
63	32	24	12	8	87. MY SON, THE NUT Allan Sherman
62	185	112	85	7	88. PETER, PAUL AND MARY Peter, Paul and Mary
84	139	96	83	7	89. BORN IN THE U.S.A. Bruce Springsteen
69	109	66	50	7	90. BLOOD, SWEAT & TEARS Blood, Sweat & Tears
61	57	57	42	7	91. STEREO 35/MM Enoch Light And His Orchestra
58	125	76	39	7	92. TCHAIKOVSKY: PIANO CONCERTO NO. 1 Van Cliburn
85	123	70	31	7	93. NO JACKET REQUIRED Phil Collins
89	63	40	27	7	94. THE RAW & THE COOKED Fine Young Cannibals
69	98	29	24	7	95. LED ZEPPELIN II Led Zeppelin
76	51	27	21	7	96. WINGS AT THE SPEED OF SOUND Wings
68	66	40	20	7	97. BOOKENDS Simon and Garfunkel
87	68	37	19	7	98. LICENSED TO ILL Beastie Boys
79	41	28	18	7	99. IN THROUGH THE OUT DOOR Led Zeppelin
72	48	26	17	7	100. AMERICAN PIE Don McLean

* subject to change since album was still charted as of the October 20, 1990 cut-off date

THE TOP 100 ALBUMS (A-Z)

ALBUM TITLE	RANK	ALBUM TITLE	RANK
Abbey Road	42	Licensed To Ill	98
American Fool	64	Long Run, The	67
American Pie	100	Love Is The Thing	80
Around The World In 80 Days	46	Love Me Or Leave Me	13
Asia	62	Loving You	55
Beatles '65	70	Magical Mystery Tour	86
Beatles, The [White Album]	72	Mary Poppins	23
Blood, Sweat & Tears	90	Meet The Beatles!	43
Blue Hawaii	8	Miami Vice	44
Bookends	97	Modern Sounds In	
Born In The U.S.A.	89	Country And Western Music	28
Breakfast At Tiffany's	36	Monkees, The	32
Bridge Over Troubled Water	57	More Of The Monkees	11
Brothers In Arms	59	Music Man, The	34
Business As Usual	19	My Fair Lady	16
Button-Down Mind Of Bob Newhart, The	25	My Son, The Nut	87
Calcutta!	40	Nice 'N' Easy	68
Calypso	4	No Jacket Required	93
Cheap Thrills	85	Pearl	73
Chicago V	74	Persuasive Percussion	30
Cosmo's Factory	69	Peter Gunn, The Music From	50
Days Of Wine And Roses	15	Peter, Paul And Mary	88
Dirty Dancing	10	Please Hammer Don't Hurt 'Em	9
Double Fantasy	83	Purple Rain	7
Elton John - Greatest Hits	58	Raw & The Cooked, The	94
Elvis Presley	49	Rumours	5
Exodus	26	Saturday Night Fever	6
Faith	35	Sgt. Pepper's Lonely Hearts Club Band	18
52nd Street	84	Sing Along With Mitch	76
First Family, The	39	Singing Nun, The	56
Footloose	53	Slippery When Wet	77
Forever Your Girl	45	Sold Out	37
4	51	Songs In The Key Of Life	27
Frampton Comes Alive!	48	Sound Of Music, The	14
G.I. Blues	52	South Pacific	3
Gigi	47	Stars For A Summer Night	66
Girl You Know It's True	78	Stereo 35/MM	91
Goodbye Yellow Brick Road	79	String Along	54
Graduate, The	63	Synchronicity	12
Grease	38	Tapestry	17
Hair	33	Tattoo You	65
Hard Day's Night, A	29	Tchaikovsky: Piano Concerto No. 1	92
Help!	71	Thriller	2
Here We Go Again!	82	Wall, The	22
Hi Infidelity	21	West Side Story	1
Hotel California	81	What Now My Love	61
In Through The Out Door	99	Whipped Cream & Other Delights	75
Joshua Tree, The	60	Whitney	41
Judy At Carnegie Hall	31	Whitney Houston	24
Kingston Trio At Large, The	20	Wings At The Speed Of Sound	96
Led Zeppelin II	95		

TOP 35 ALBUMS OF THE FIFTIES

PK YR	CH	WEEKS 40	10	#1	TITLE/Artist
58	262	161	90	31	1. SOUTH PACIFIC Soundtrack
56	99	72	58	31	2. CALYPSO Harry Belafonte
55	28	28	25	17	3. LOVE ME OR LEAVE ME Doris Day/Soundtrack
56	480	292	173	15	4. MY FAIR LADY Original Cast
59	118	43	31	15	5. THE KINGSTON TRIO AT LARGE The Kingston Trio
58	245	123	63	12	6. THE MUSIC MAN Original Cast
57	88	88	54	10	7. AROUND THE WORLD IN 80. DAYS Soundtrack
58	172	78	54	10	8. GIGI Soundtrack
56	48	48	43	10	9. ELVIS PRESLEY Elvis Presley
59	119	47	43	10	10. THE MUSIC FROM PETER GUNN Henry Mancini/TV Soundtrack
57	29	29	19	10	11. LOVING YOU Elvis Presley/Soundtrack
58	204	128	53	8	12. SING ALONG WITH MITCH Mitch Miller & The Gang
57	94	55	31	8	13. LOVE IS THE THING Nat "King" Cole
59	126	40	26	8	14. HERE WE GO AGAIN! The Kingston Trio
58	125	76	39	7	15. TCHAIKOVSKY: PIANO CONCERTO NO. 1 Van Cliburn
56	62	62	54	6	16. BELAFONTE Harry Belafonte
55	27	27	24	6	17. STARRING SAMMY DAVIS, JR Sammy Davis, Jr.
59	295	40	38	5	18. HEAVENLY Johnny Mathis
56	32	32	24	5	19. ELVIS Elvis Presley
58	120	55	19	5	20. FRANK SINATRA SINGS FOR ONLY THE LONELY Frank Sinatra
59	63	46	19	5	21. EXOTICA Martin Denny
58	71	50	18	5	22. COME FLY WITH ME Frank Sinatra
56	305	229	116	4	23. OKLAHOMA! Soundtrack
57	7	7	6	4	24. ELVIS' CHRISTMAS ALBUM Elvis Presley
58	490	178	57	3	25. JOHNNY'S GREATEST HITS Johnny Mathis
59	151	67	17	3	26. FLOWER DRUM SONG Original Cast
55	23	23	22	2	27. LONESOME ECHO Jackie Gleason
58	33	33	18	2	28. RICKY Ricky Nelson
55	20	20	18	2	29. CRAZY OTTO Crazy Otto
58	5	5	3	2	30. CHRISTMAS SING-ALONG WITH MITCH Mitch Miller & The Gang
56	277	178	78	1	31. THE KING AND I Soundtrack
56	99	99	49	1	32. THE EDDY DUCHIN STORY Carmen Cavallaro/Soundtrack
59	231	113	43	1	33. FILM ENCORES Mantovani and His Orchestra
58	195	114	22	1	34. THE KINGSTON TRIO The Kingston Trio
57	7	7	6	1	35. MERRY CHRISTMAS Bing Crosby

TOP 40 ALBUMS OF THE SIXTIES

PK YR	CH	WEEKS 40	10	#1	TITLE/Artist
62	198	144	106	54	1. WEST SIDE STORY Soundtrack
61	79	53	39	20	2. BLUE HAWAII Elvis Presley/Soundtrack
67	96	45	25	18	3. MORE OF THE MONKEES The Monkees
60	276	168	105	16	4. THE SOUND OF MUSIC Original Cast
63	107	61	23	16	5. DAYS OF WINE AND ROSES Andy Williams
67	175	63	33	15	6. SGT. PEPPER'S LONELY HEARTS CLUB BAND The Beatles
65	114	78	48	14	7. MARY POPPINS Soundtrack
60	108	67	44	14	8. THE BUTTON-DOWN MIND OF BOB NEWHART Bob Newhart
61	89	55	38	14	9. EXODUS Soundtrack
62	101	59	33	14	10. MODERN SOUNDS IN COUNTRY AND WESTERN MUSIC Ray Charles
64	51	40	28	14	11. A HARD DAY'S NIGHT The Beatles/Soundtrack
60	124	105	43	13	12. PERSUASIVE PERCUSSION Enoch Light/Terry Snyder and The All-Stars
61	95	73	37	13	13. JUDY AT CARNEGIE HALL Judy Garland
66	102	49	32	13	14. THE MONKEES The Monkees
69	151	59	28	13	15. HAIR Original Cast
62	96	69	46	12	16. BREAKFAST AT TIFFANY'S Henry Mancini/Soundtrack
60	73	42	29	12	17. SOLD OUT The Kingston Trio
62	49	26	17	12	18. THE FIRST FAMILY Vaughn Meader
61	64	50	33	11	19. CALCUTTA Lawrence Welk
69	129	32	27	11	20. ABBEY ROAD The Beatles
64	71	27	21	11	21. MEET THE BEATLES The Beatles
60	111	46	29	10	22. G.I. BLUES Elvis Presley
60	60	27	20	10	23. STRING ALONG The Kingston Trio
63	39	22	18	10	24. THE SINGING NUN The Singing Nun
66	129	59	32	9	25. WHAT NOW MY LOVE Herb Alpert's Tijuana Brass
68	65	47	26	9	26. THE GRADUATE Simon & Garfunkel
61	40	39	21	9	27. STARS FOR A SUMMER NIGHT Various Artists
60	86	35	19	9	28. NICE 'N' EASY Frank Sinatra
65	71	38	16	9	29. BEATLES '65 The Beatles
65	44	33	15	9	30. HELP The Beatles
68	155	25	15	9	31. THE BEATLES [WHITE ALBUM] The Beatles
65	185	141	61	8	32. WHIPPED CREAM & OTHER DELIGHTS Herb Alpert & The Tijuana Brass
68	66	29	19	8	33. CHEAP THRILLS Big Brother & The Holding Company
68	91	30	14	8	34. MAGICAL MYSTERY TOUR The Beatles
63	32	24	12	8	35. MY SON, THE NUT Allan Sherman
62	185	112	85	7	36. PETER, PAUL AND MARY Peter, Paul and Mary
69	109	66	50	7	37. BLOOD, SWEAT & TEARS Blood, Sweat & Tears
61	57	57	42	7	38. STEREO 35/MM Enoch Light And His Orchestra
69	98	29	24	7	39. LED ZEPPELIN II Led Zeppelin
68	66	40	20	7	40. BOOKENDS Simon & Garfunkel

TOP 40 ALBUMS OF THE SEVENTIES

PK YR	CH	WEEKS 40	10	#1	TITLE/Artist
77	134	60	52	31	1. RUMOURS Fleetwood Mac
78	120	54	35	24	2. SATURDAY NIGHT FEVER Bee Gees
71	302	68	46	15	3. TAPESTRY Carole King
76	80	44	35	14	4. SONGS IN THE KEY OF LIFE Stevie Wonder
78	77	39	29	12	5. GREASE Soundtrack
76	97	55	52	10	6. FRAMPTON COMES ALIVE! Peter Frampton
70	85	24	17	10	7. BRIDGE OVER TROUBLED WATER Simon and Garfunkel
74	104	20	11	10	8. ELTON JOHN - GREATEST HITS Elton John
79	57	36	21	9	9. THE LONG RUN Eagles
70	69	26	19	9	10. COSMO'S FACTORY Creedence Clearwater Revival
71	42	23	15	9	11. PEARL Janis Joplin
72	51	20	13	9	12. CHICAGO V Chicago
73	103	43	36	8	13. GOODBYE YELLOW BRICK ROAD Elton John
77	107	32	28	8	14. HOTEL CALIFORNIA Eagles
78	76	34	22	8	15. 52ND STREET Billy Joel
76	51	27	21	7	16. WINGS AT THE SPEED OF SOUND Wings
79	41	28	18	7	17. IN THROUGH THE OUT DOOR Led Zeppelin
72	48	26	17	7	18. AMERICAN PIE Don McLean
75	43	24	17	7	19. CAPTAIN FANTASTIC AND THE BROWN DIRT COWBOY Elton John
71	38	22	14	7	20. ALL THINGS MUST PASS George Harrison
70	88	40	30	6	21. ABRAXAS Santana
79	88	48	26	6	22. BREAKFAST IN AMERICA Supertramp
77	51	28	18	6	23. A STAR IS BORN Barbra Streisand/Soundtrack
79	55	26	18	6	24. SPIRITS HAVING FLOWN Bee Gees
79	49	26	16	6	25. BAD GIRLS Donna Summer
75	41	15	12	6	26. PHYSICAL GRAFFITI Led Zeppelin
74	93	42	19	5	27. YOU DON'T MESS AROUND WITH JIM Jim Croce
75	56	43	18	5	28. ONE OF THESE NIGHTS Eagles
72	61	25	18	5	29. HONKY CHATEAU Elton John
79	87	30	16	5	30. MINUTE BY MINUTE The Doobie Brothers
77	47	23	16	5	31. SIMPLE DREAMS Linda Ronstadt
73	56	24	15	5	32. BROTHERS AND SISTERS The Allman Brothers Band
74	41	23	15	5	33. THE STING Soundtrack
79	40	22	15	5	34. GET THE KNACK The Knack
72	54	26	14	5	35. FIRST TAKE Roberta Flack
73	71	23	14	5	36. NO SECRETS Carly Simon
75	72	22	13	5	37. CHICAGO IX - CHICAGO'S GREATEST HITS Chicago
72	40	22	13	5	38. AMERICA America
76	35	17	13	5	39. DESIRE Bob Dylan
76	133	57	12	5	40. EAGLES/THEIR GREATEST HITS 1971-1975 Eagles

TOP 40 ALBUMS OF THE EIGHTIES

PK YR	CH	WEEKS 40	10	#1	TITLE/Artist
83	122	91	78	37	1. THRILLER Michael Jackson
84	72	42	32	24	2. PURPLE RAIN Prince And The Revolution/Soundtrack
87	96	68	48	18	3. DIRTY DANCING Soundtrack
83	75	50	40	17	4. SYNCHRONICITY The Police
82	90	48	31	15	5. BUSINESS AS USUAL Men At Work
81	101	50	30	15	6. HI INFIDELITY REO Speedwagon
80	123	35	27	15	7. THE WALL Pink Floyd
86	162	78	46	14	8. WHITNEY HOUSTON Whitney Houston
88	87	69	51	12	9. FAITH George Michael
87	85	51	31	11	10. WHITNEY Whitney Houston
85	34	22	18	11	11. MIAMI VICE TV Soundtrack
89	118*	78	64	10	12. FOREVER YOUR GIRL Paula Abdul
81	81	52	34	10	13. 4 Foreigner
84	61	27	20	10	14. FOOTLOOSE Soundtrack
85	97	55	37	9	15. BROTHERS IN ARMS Dire Straits
87	103	58	36	9	16. THE JOSHUA TREE U2
82	64	35	27	9	17. ASIA Asia
82	107	41	22	9	18. AMERICAN FOOL John Cougar
81	58	30	22	9	19. TATTOO YOU The Rolling Stones
86	94	60	46	8	20. SLIPPERY WHEN WET Bon Jovi
89	78	61	41	8	21. GIRL YOU KNOW IT'S TRUE Milli Vanilli
80	74	27	24	8	22. DOUBLE FANTASY John Lennon/Yoko Ono
84	139	96	83	7	23. BORN IN THE U.S.A. Bruce Springsteen
85	123	70	31	7	24. NO JACKET REQUIRED Phil Collins
89	63	40	27	7	25. THE RAW & THE COOKED Fine Young Cannibals
87	68	37	19	7	26. LICENSED TO ILL Beastie Boys
80	51	20	14	7	27. EMOTIONAL RESCUE The Rolling Stones
86	26	15	11	7	28. BRUCE SPRINGSTEEN & THE E STREET BAND LIVE/1975-85 Bruce Springsteen
88	133	96	78	6	29. HYSTERIA Def Leppard
89	97	69	46	6	30. DON'T BE CRUEL Bobby Brown
87	87	54	39	6	31. BAD Michael Jackson
80	73	35	25	6	32. GLASS HOUSES Billy Joel
80	110	43	22	6	33. AGAINST THE WIND Bob Seger & The Silver Bullet Band
89	77	31	16	6	34. LIKE A PRAYER Madonna
82	72	38	15	6	35. BEAUTY AND THE BEAT Go-Go's
88	38	23	14	6	36. RATTLE AND HUM U2/Soundtrack
89	34	17	10	6	37. BATMAN Prince/Soundtrack
88	147	78	52	5	38. APPETITE FOR DESTRUCTION Guns N' Roses
85	83	55	32	5	39. SONGS FROM THE BIG CHAIR Tears For Fears
86	82	52	25	5	40. TRUE BLUE Madonna

* subject to change since album was still charted as of the 10/20/90 cut-off date

NO. 1 ALBUMS LISTED CHRONOLOGICALLY

For the years 1958 through 1963, when separate stereo and mono charts were published each week, there are special columns on the right side of the page to show the weeks each album held the No. 1 spot on each of these pop charts. If an album peaked at No. 1 on both the mono and stereo charts in the same week, it is counted as only one week at No. 1. Therefore, the grand total of an album's weeks at No. 1 on all charts may equal more than the total shown on the left side of the page.

The date shown is the earliest date that an album hit No. 1 on any of the three pop charts. Some dates are duplicated because different albums peaked at No. 1 on the same date on different charts.

DATE: Date album first hit the No. 1 position.
WKS: Total weeks album held the No. 1 position.
*: Album appeared non-consecutively at the No. 1 position.

CHARTS COLUMN:
1 CH: One chart published
ST: Stereo chart
MO: Mono chart

The No. 1 album of each year is shown in **bold type** and is based on total weeks at the No. 1 spot. Ties are broken by total weeks charted. The album qualifies for the award only in the year that it first peaked at No. 1.

349 albums have hit the No. 1 position on *Billboard*'s pop charts from 1955 through October 20, 1990.

DATE	WKS	ALBUM TITLE	ARTIST
		1955	
5/28	2	1. CRAZY OTTO	Crazy Otto
6/11	6	2. STARRING SAMMY DAVIS, JR.	Sammy Davis, Jr.
7/23	2	3. LONESOME ECHO	Jackie Gleason
8/6	17	4. **LOVE ME OR LEAVE ME**	Doris Day/Soundtrack

Two albums from 1954 continued into 1955 at the No. 1 spot: *The Student Prince,* Mario Lanza (eighteen weeks), and *Music, Martinis And Memories,* Jackie Gleason (two weeks). For all of 1955 and up to 3/24/56, the album chart was published mainly on a biweekly basis. The chart was considered "frozen" for a nonpublished week and, therefore, each position on the published chart was counted twice. In addition to these biweekly "frozen" charts, there were five other weeks of unpublished charts that did not count toward weeks at the No. 1 spot.

DATE	WKS	ALBUM TITLE	ARTIST
		1956	
1/28	4	1. OKLAHOMA!	Soundtrack
3/24	6	2. BELAFONTE	Harry Belafonte
5/5	10	3. ELVIS PRESLEY	Elvis Presley
7/14	15*	4. MY FAIR LADY	Original Cast
		Peaked at No. 1 in four consecutive years: 1956 (eight wks.), 1957 (one wk.), 1958 (three wks.), & 1959 (three wks.-Stereo chart)	
9/8	31*	5. **CALYPSO**	Harry Belafonte
10/6	1	6. THE KING AND I	Soundtrack
10/13	1	7. THE EDDY DUCHIN STORY	Carmen Cavallaro/Soundtrack
12/8	5	8. ELVIS	Elvis Presley

Beginning with 3/24/56, *Billboard* published the album chart on a weekly basis. From the first of the year to that date, there were two published charts, two frozen charts, and seven weeks of unpublished charts.

DATE	WKS	ALBUM TITLE	ARTIST
		1957	
5/27	8	1. LOVE IS THE THING	Nat "King" Cole
7/22	10*	2. **AROUND THE WORLD IN 80 DAYS**	Soundtrack
7/29	10	3. LOVING YOU	Elvis Presley/Soundtrack
12/16	4*	4. ELVIS' CHRISTMAS ALBUM	Elvis Presley
12/30	1	5. MERRY CHRISTMAS	Bing Crosby

DATE	WKS	ALBUM TITLE	ARTIST	Multiple Charts		
				1 CH	ST	MO
		1958				
1/20	2	1. RICKY	Ricky Nelson	2	—	—
2/10	5	2. COME FLY WITH ME	Frank Sinatra	5	—	—
3/17	12*	3. THE MUSIC MAN	Original Cast	12	—	—
5/19	31*	4. **SOUTH PACIFIC**	Soundtrack	3	28	—
		Three wks. No. 1 in 1958; twenty-eight wks. No. 1 on Stereo charts beginning 5/25/59				
6/9	3*	5. JOHNNY'S GREATEST HITS	Johnny Mathis	3	—	—
7/21	10*	6. GIGI	Soundtrack	6	—	4
		Three wks. No. 1 in 1958; three wks. No. 1 on Stereo chart in 1959; and four wks. No. 1 on Mono charts beginning 5/29/59				
8/11	7*	7. TCHAIKOVSKY: PIANO CONCERTO NO. 1	Van Cliburn	7	—	—
10/6	8*	8. SING ALONG WITH MITCH	Mitch Miller & The Gang	8	—	—
10/13	5	9. FRANK SINATRA SINGS FOR ONLY THE LONELY	Frank Sinatra	5	—	—
11/24	1	10. THE KINGSTON TRIO	The Kingston Trio	1	—	—
12/29	2	11. CHRISTMAS SING-ALONG WITH MITCH	Mitch Miller & The Gang	2	—	—
		1959				
				1 CH	ST	MO
2/2	3	1. FLOWER DRUM SONG	Original Cast	3	—	—
2/23	10	2. THE MUSIC FROM PETER GUNN	Henry Mancini	10	—	—
		5/25/59: Separate Stereo and Mono charts begin				
6/22	5	3. EXOTICA	Martin Denny	—	—	5
7/13	1	4. FILM ENCORES	Mantovani And His Orchestra	—	1	—
7/27	15	5. **THE KINGSTON TRIO AT LARGE**	The Kingston Trio	—	—	15
11/9	5	6. HEAVENLY	Johnny Mathis	—	—	5
12/14	8	7. HERE WE GO AGAIN!	The Kingston Trio	—	2	8
		1960				
				1 CH	ST	MO
1/11	1	1. THE LORD'S PRAYER	The Mormon Tabernacle Choir	—	1	—
1/25	16	2. **THE SOUND OF MUSIC**	Original Cast	—	15	12
4/25	13*	3. PERSUASIVE PERCUSSION	Enoch Light/ Terry Snyder And The All-Stars	—	13	—
5/2	2*	4. THEME FROM A SUMMER PLACE	Billy Vaughn And His Orchestra	—	—	2
5/9	12*	5. SOLD OUT	The Kingston Trio	—	3	10
7/25	14*	6. THE BUTTON-DOWN MIND OF BOB NEWHART	Bob Newhart	—	—	14
8/29	10*	7. STRING ALONG	The Kingston Trio	—	10	5
10/24	9*	8. NICE 'N' EASY	Frank Sinatra	—	9	1
12/5	10	9. G.I. BLUES	Elvis Presley/Soundtrack	—	2	8

DATE	WKS	ALBUM TITLE	ARTIST	Multiple Charts		
				1 CH	ST	MO

1961

DATE	WKS	ALBUM TITLE	ARTIST	Multiple Charts		
				1 CH	ST	MO
1/9	1	1. THE BUTTON-DOWN MIND STRIKES BACK!	Bob Newhart	—	—	1
1/16	5*	2. WONDERLAND BY NIGHT	Bert Kaempfert And His Orchestra	—	—	5
1/23	14*	3. EXODUS	Soundtrack	—	14	3
3/13	11*	4. CALCUTTA!	Lawrence Welk	—	11	8
6/5	6	5. CAMELOT	Original Cast	—	—	6
7/17	9	6. STARS FOR A SUMMER NIGHT	Various Artists	—	9	4
7/17	1	7. CARNIVAL	Original Cast	—	—	1
8/21	3	8. SOMETHING FOR EVERYBODY	Elvis Presley	—	—	3
9/11	13	9. JUDY AT CARNEGIE HALL	Judy Garland	—	9	13
11/18	7	10. STEREO 35/MM	Enoch Light	—	7	—
12/11	20	11. **BLUE HAWAII**	Elvis Presley/Soundtrack	—	4	20

1962

DATE	WKS	ALBUM TITLE	ARTIST	Multiple Charts		
				1 CH	ST	MO
1/13	1	1. HOLIDAY SING ALONG WITH MITCH	Mitch Miller & The Gang	—	1	—
2/10	12*	2. BREAKFAST AT TIFFANY'S	Henry Mancini/Soundtrack	—	12	—
5/5	54*	3. **WEST SIDE STORY**	Soundtrack	—	53	12
		Most weeks at No. 1 for the 1955-90 era				
6/23	14	4. MODERN SOUNDS IN COUNTRY AND WESTERN MUSIC	Ray Charles	—	1	14
10/20	7*	5. PETER, PAUL AND MARY	Peter, Paul And Mary	1	—	6
		Returned to the No. 1 spot for one week on 10/26/63				
12/1	2	6. MY SON, THE FOLK SINGER	Allan Sherman	—	—	2
12/15	12	7. THE FIRST FAMILY	Vaughn Meader	—	—	12

1963

DATE	WKS	ALBUM TITLE	ARTIST	Multiple Charts		
				1 CH	ST	MO
3/9	1	1. MY SON, THE CELEBRITY	Allan Sherman	—	—	1
3/9	1	2. JAZZ SAMBA	Stan Getz/Charlie Byrd	—	1	—
3/16	5	3. SONGS I SING ON THE JACKIE GLEASON SHOW	Frank Fontaine	—	—	5
5/4	16	4. **DAYS OF WINE AND ROSES**	Andy Williams	1	11	15
		8/17/63: Stereo & Mono charts combined into one single chart				
8/24	1	5. LITTLE STEVIE WONDER/ THE 12 YEAR OLD GENIUS	Stevie Wonder	1	—	—
8/31	8	6. MY SON, THE NUT	Allan Sherman	8	—	—
11/2	5	7. IN THE WIND	Peter, Paul And Mary	5	—	—
12/7	10	8. THE SINGING NUN	The Singing Nun	10	—	—

1964

DATE	WKS	ALBUM TITLE	ARTIST
2/15	11	1. MEET THE BEATLES!	The Beatles
5/2	5	2. THE BEATLES' SECOND ALBUM	The Beatles
6/6	1	3. HELLO, DOLLY!	Original Cast
6/13	6	4. HELLO, DOLLY!	Louis Armstrong
7/25	14	5. **A HARD DAY'S NIGHT**	The Beatles/Soundtrack
10/31	5	6. PEOPLE	Barbra Streisand
12/5	4	7. BEACH BOYS CONCERT	The Beach Boys

DATE	WKS	ALBUM TITLE	ARTIST
		1965	
1/2	1	1. ROUSTABOUT	Elvis Presley/Soundtrack
1/9	9	2. BEATLES '65	The Beatles
3/13	14*	3. **MARY POPPINS**	Soundtrack
3/20	3	4. GOLDFINGER	Soundtrack
7/10	6	5. BEATLES VI	The Beatles
8/21	3	6. OUT OF OUR HEADS	The Rolling Stones
9/11	9	7. HELP!	The Beatles/Soundtrack
11/13	2	8. THE SOUND OF MUSIC	Soundtrack
11/27	8*	9. WHIPPED CREAM & OTHER DELIGHTS	Herb Alpert's Tijuana Brass
		1966	
1/8	6	1. RUBBER SOUL	The Beatles
3/5	6*	2. GOING PLACES	Herb Alpert And The Tijuana Brass
3/12	5	3. BALLADS OF THE GREEN BERETS	SSgt Barry Sadler
5/21	1	4. IF YOU CAN BELIEVE YOUR EYES AND EARS	The Mamas And The Papas
5/28	9*	5. WHAT NOW MY LOVE	Herb Alpert & The Tijuana Brass
7/23	1	6. STRANGERS IN THE NIGHT	Frank Sinatra
7/30	5	7. "YESTERDAY" . . . AND TODAY	The Beatles
9/10	6	8. REVOLVER	The Beatles
10/22	2	9. THE SUPREMES A' GO-GO	The Supremes
11/5	1	10. DOCTOR ZHIVAGO	Soundtrack
11/12	13	11. **THE MONKEES**	The Monkees
		1967	
2/11	18	1. **MORE OF THE MONKEES**	The Monkees
6/17	1	2. SOUNDS LIKE	Herb Alpert & The Tijuana Brass
6/24	1	3. HEADQUARTERS	The Monkees
7/1	15	4. SGT. PEPPER'S LONELY HEARTS CLUB BAND	The Beatles
10/14	2	5. ODE TO BILLIE JOE	Bobbie Gentry
10/28	5	6. DIANA ROSS AND THE SUPREMES GREATEST HITS	 The Supremes
12/2	5	7. PISCES, AQUARIUS, CAPRICORN & JONES LTD.	The Monkees
		1968	
1/6	8	1. MAGICAL MYSTERY TOUR	The Beatles
3/2	5	2. BLOOMING HITS	Paul Mauriat And His Orchestra
4/6	9*	3. THE GRADUATE	Simon and Garfunkel/Soundtrack
5/25	7*	4. BOOKENDS	Simon and Garfunkel
7/27	2	5. THE BEAT OF THE BRASS	Herb Alpert & The Tijuana Brass
8/10	4	6. WHEELS OF FIRE	Cream
9/7	4*	7. WAITING FOR THE SUN	The Doors
9/28	1	8. TIME PEACE/THE RASCALS' GREATEST HITS	The Rascals
10/12	8*	9. CHEAP THRILLS	Big Brother & The Holding Company
11/16	2	10. ELECTRIC LADYLAND	Jimi Hendrix Experience
12/21	5*	11. WICHITA LINEMAN	Glen Campbell
12/28	9*	12. **THE BEATLES [WHITE ALBUM]**	The Beatles

DATE	WKS	ALBUM TITLE	ARTIST
		1969	
2/8	1	1. TCB	The Supremes With The Temptations
3/29	7*	2. BLOOD, SWEAT & TEARS	Blood, Sweat & Tears
4/26	13	3. **HAIR**	Original Cast
8/23	4	4. JOHNNY CASH AT SAN QUENTIN	Johnny Cash
9/20	2	5. BLIND FAITH	Blind Faith
10/4	4	6. GREEN RIVER	Creedence Clearwater Revival
11/1	11*	7. ABBEY ROAD	The Beatles
12/27	7*	8. LED ZEPPELIN II	Led Zeppelin
		1970	
3/7	10	1. **BRIDGE OVER TROUBLED WATER**	Simon and Garfunkel
5/16	1	2. DEJA VU	Crosby, Stills, Nash & Young
5/23	3	3. McCARTNEY	Paul McCartney
6/13	4	4. LET IT BE	The Beatles/Soundtrack
7/11	4	5. WOODSTOCK	Various Artists/Soundtrack
8/8	2	6. BLOOD, SWEAT & TEARS 3	Blood, Sweat & Tears
8/22	9	7. COSMO'S FACTORY	Creedence Clearwater Revival
10/24	6*	8. ABRAXAS	Santana
10/31	4	9. LED ZEPPELIN III	Led Zeppelin
		1971	
1/2	7	1. ALL THINGS MUST PASS	George Harrison
2/20	3*	2. JESUS CHRIST SUPERSTAR	Various Artists
2/27	9	3. PEARL	Janis Joplin
5/15	1	4. 4 WAY STREET	Crosby, Stills, Nash & Young
5/22	4	5. STICKY FINGERS	The Rolling Stones
6/19	15	6. **TAPESTRY**	Carole King
10/2	4	7. EVERY PICTURE TELLS A STORY	Rod Stewart
10/30	1	8. IMAGINE	John Lennon
11/6	1	9. SHAFT	Isaac Hayes/Soundtrack
11/13	5	10. SANTANA III	Santana
12/18	2	11. THERE'S A RIOT GOIN' ON	Sly & The Family Stone
		1972	
1/1	3	1. MUSIC	Carole King
1/22	7	2. AMERICAN PIE	Don McLean
3/11	2	3. HARVEST	Neil Young
3/25	5	4. AMERICA	America
4/29	5	5. FIRST TAKE	Roberta Flack
6/3	2	6. THICK AS A BRICK	Jethro Tull
6/17	4	7. EXILE ON MAIN ST.	The Rolling Stones
7/15	5	8. HONKY CHATEAU	Elton John
8/19	9	9. **CHICAGO V**	Chicago
10/21	4	10. SUPERFLY	Curtis Mayfield/Soundtrack
11/18	3	11. CATCH BULL AT FOUR	Cat Stevens
12/9	5	12. SEVENTH SOJOURN	The Moody Blues

DATE	WKS	ALBUM TITLE	ARTIST
		1973	
1/13	5	1. NO SECRETS	Carly Simon
2/17	2	2. THE WORLD IS A GHETTO	War
3/3	2	3. DON'T SHOOT ME I'M ONLY THE PIANO PLAYER	Elton John
3/17	3	4. DUELING BANJOS	Eric Weissberg
4/7	2	5. LADY SINGS THE BLUES	Diana Ross/Soundtrack
4/21	1	6. BILLION DOLLAR BABIES	Alice Cooper
4/28	1	7. THE DARK SIDE OF THE MOON	Pink Floyd
5/5	1	8. ALOHA FROM HAWAII VIA SATELLITE	Elvis Presley
5/12	2	9. HOUSES OF THE HOLY	Led Zeppelin
5/26	1	10. THE BEATLES/1967-1970	The Beatles
6/2	3	11. RED ROSE SPEEDWAY	Paul McCartney & Wings
6/23	5	12. LIVING IN THE MATERIAL WORLD	George Harrison
7/28	5*	13. CHICAGO VI	Chicago
8/18	1	14. A PASSION PLAY	Jethro Tull
9/8	5	15. BROTHERS AND SISTERS	The Allman Brothers Band
10/13	4	16. GOATS HEAD SOUP	The Rolling Stones
11/10	8	17. **GOODBYE YELLOW BRICK ROAD**	Elton John
		1974	
1/5	1	1. THE SINGLES 1969-1973	Carpenters
1/12	5	2. YOU DON'T MESS AROUND WITH JIM	Jim Croce
2/16	4	3. PLANET WAVES	Bob Dylan
3/16	2	4. THE WAY WE WERE	Barbra Streisand
3/30	3*	5. JOHN DENVER'S GREATEST HITS	John Denver
4/13	4*	6. BAND ON THE RUN	Paul McCartney & Wings
4/27	1	7. CHICAGO VII	Chicago
5/4	5	8. THE STING	Soundtrack (Marvin Hamlisch)
6/22	2	9. SUNDOWN	Gordon Lightfoot
7/13	4	10. CARIBOU	Elton John
8/10	1	11. BACK HOME AGAIN	John Denver
8/17	4	12. 461 OCEAN BOULEVARD	Eric Clapton
9/14	2	13. FULFILLINGNESS' FIRST FINALE	Stevie Wonder
9/28	1	14. BAD COMPANY	Bad Company
10/5	1	15. ENDLESS SUMMER	The Beach Boys
10/12	1	16. IF YOU LOVE ME, LET ME KNOW	Olivia Newton-John
10/19	1	17. NOT FRAGILE	Bachman-Turner Overdrive
10/26	1	18. CAN'T GET ENOUGH	Barry White
11/2	1	19. SO FAR	Crosby, Stills, Nash & Young
11/9	1	20. WRAP AROUND JOY	Carole King
11/16	1	21. WALLS AND BRIDGES	John Lennon
11/23	1	22. IT'S ONLY ROCK 'N ROLL	The Rolling Stones
11/30	10	23. **ELTON JOHN - GREATEST HITS**	Elton John

DATE	WKS	ALBUM TITLE	ARTIST
		1975	
2/8	1	1. FIRE	Ohio Players
2/15	1	2. HEART LIKE A WHEEL	Linda Ronstadt
2/22	1	3. AWB	Average White Band
3/1	2	4. BLOOD ON THE TRACKS	Bob Dylan
3/15	1	5. HAVE YOU NEVER BEEN MELLOW	Olivia Newton-John
3/22	6	6. PHYSICAL GRAFFITI	Led Zeppelin
5/3	2	7. CHICAGO VIII	Chicago
5/17	3	8. THAT'S THE WAY OF THE WORLD	Earth, Wind & Fire/Soundtrack
6/7	7*	9. **CAPTAIN FANTASTIC** **AND THE BROWN DIRT COWBOY** *Album debuted at No. 1*	Elton John
7/19	1	10. VENUS AND MARS	Wings
7/26	5	11. ONE OF THESE NIGHTS	Eagles
9/6	4*	12. RED OCTOPUS	Jefferson Starship
9/13	1	13. THE HEAT IS ON	The Isley Brothers
9/20	1	14. BETWEEN THE LINES	Janis Ian
10/4	2	15. WISH YOU WERE HERE	Pink Floyd
10/18	2	16. WINDSONG	John Denver
11/8	3	17. ROCK OF THE WESTIES *Album debuted at No. 1*	Elton John
12/6	1	18. STILL CRAZY AFTER ALL THESE YEARS	Paul Simon
12/13	5	19. CHICAGO IX - CHICAGO'S GREATEST HITS	Chicago
		1976	
1/17	3	1. GRATITUDE	Earth, Wind & Fire
2/7	5	2. DESIRE	Bob Dylan
3/13	5*	3. EAGLES/THEIR GREATEST HITS 1971-1975	Eagles
4/10	10*	4. FRAMPTON COMES ALIVE!	Peter Frampton
4/24	7*	5. WINGS AT THE SPEED OF SOUND	Wings
5/1	2	6. PRESENCE	Led Zeppelin
5/15	4*	7. BLACK AND BLUE	The Rolling Stones
7/31	2	8. BREEZIN'	George Benson
9/4	1	9. FLEETWOOD MAC	Fleetwood Mac
10/16	14*	10. **SONGS IN THE KEY OF LIFE** *Album debuted at No. 1*	Stevie Wonder
		1977	
1/15	8*	1. HOTEL CALIFORNIA	Eagles
1/22	1	2. WINGS OVER AMERICA	Wings
2/12	6	3. A STAR IS BORN	Barbra Streisand/Soundtrack
4/2	31*	4. **RUMOURS**	Fleetwood Mac
7/16	1	5. BARRY MANILOW/LIVE	Barry Manilow
12/3	5	6. SIMPLE DREAMS	Linda Ronstadt

DATE	WKS	ALBUM TITLE	ARTIST
		1978	
1/21	24	1. **SATURDAY NIGHT FEVER**	Bee Gees/Soundtrack
7/8	1	2. CITY TO CITY	Gerry Rafferty
7/15	2	3. SOME GIRLS	The Rolling Stones
7/29	12*	4. GREASE	Olivia Newton-John/Soundtrack
9/16	2*	5. DON'T LOOK BACK	Boston
11/4	1	6. LIVING IN THE USA	Linda Ronstadt
11/11	1	7. LIVE AND MORE	Donna Summer
11/18	8*	8. 52ND STREET	Billy Joel
		1979	
1/6	3	1. BARBRA STREISAND'S GREATEST HITS, VOLUME 2	Barbra Streisand
2/3	1	2. BRIEFCASE FULL OF BLUES	Blues Brothers
2/10	3	3. BLONDES HAVE MORE FUN	Rod Stewart
3/3	6*	4. SPIRITS HAVING FLOWN	Bee Gees
4/7	5*	5. MINUTE BY MINUTE	The Doobie Brothers
5/19	6*	6. BREAKFAST IN AMERICA	Supertramp
6/16	6*	7. BAD GIRLS	Donna Summer
8/11	5	8. GET THE KNACK	The Knack
9/15	7	9. IN THROUGH THE OUT DOOR	Led Zeppelin
11/3	9	10. **THE LONG RUN**	Eagles
		1980	
1/5	1	1. ON THE RADIO-GREATEST HITS-VOLUMES I & II	Donna Summer
1/12	1	2. BEE GEES GREATEST	Bee Gees
1/19	15	3. **THE WALL**	Pink Floyd
5/3	6	4. AGAINST THE WIND	Bob Seger & The Silver Bullet Band
6/14	6	5. GLASS HOUSES	Billy Joel
7/26	7	6. EMOTIONAL RESCUE	The Rolling Stones
9/13	1	7. HOLD OUT	Jackson Browne
9/20	5	8. THE GAME	Queen
10/25	3*	9. GUILTY	Barbra Streisand
11/8	4	10. THE RIVER	Bruce Springsteen
12/13	2	11. KENNY ROGERS' GREATEST HITS	Kenny Rogers
12/27	8	12. DOUBLE FANTASY	John Lennon/Yoko Ono
		1981	
2/21	15*	1. **HI INFIDELITY**	REO Speedwagon
4/4	3*	2. PARADISE THEATER	Styx
6/27	4	3. MISTAKEN IDENTITY	Kim Carnes
7/25	3	4. LONG DISTANCE VOYAGER	The Moody Blues
8/15	1	5. PRECIOUS TIME	Pat Benatar
8/22	10*	6. 4	Foreigner
9/5	1	7. BELLA DONNA	Stevie Nicks
9/12	1	8. ESCAPE	Journey
9/19	9	9. TATTOO YOU	The Rolling Stones
12/26	3	10. FOR THOSE ABOUT TO ROCK WE SALUTE YOU	AC/DC

DATE	WKS	ALBUM TITLE	ARTIST
1982			
2/6	4	1. FREEZE-FRAME	J. Geils Band
3/6	6	2. BEAUTY AND THE BEAT	Go-Go's
4/17	4	3. CHARIOTS OF FIRE	Vangelis/Soundtrack
5/15	9*	4. ASIA	Asia
5/29	3	5. TUG OF WAR	Paul McCartney
8/7	5	6. MIRAGE	Fleetwood Mac
9/11	9	7. AMERICAN FOOL	John Cougar
11/13	15	8. **BUSINESS AS USUAL**	Men At Work
1983			
2/26	37*	1. **THRILLER**	Michael Jackson
6/25	2	2. FLASHDANCE	Soundtrack
7/23	17*	3. SYNCHRONICITY	The Police
11/26	1	4. METAL HEALTH	Quiet Riot
12/3	3	5. CAN'T SLOW DOWN	Lionel Richie
1984			
4/21	10	1. FOOTLOOSE	Soundtrack
6/30	1	2. SPORTS	Huey Lewis And The News
7/7	7*	3. BORN IN THE U.S.A.	Bruce Springsteen
8/4	24	4. **PURPLE RAIN**	Prince And The Revolution/Soundtrack
1985			
2/9	3	1. LIKE A VIRGIN	Madonna
3/2	3	2. MAKE IT BIG	Wham!
3/23	1	3. CENTERFIELD	John Fogerty
3/30	7*	4. NO JACKET REQUIRED	Phil Collins
4/27	3	5. WE ARE THE WORLD	USA for Africa
6/1	3	6. AROUND THE WORLD IN A DAY	Prince & The Revolution
6/22	2	7. BEVERLY HILLS COP	Soundtrack
7/13	5*	8. SONGS FROM THE BIG CHAIR	Tears For Fears
8/10	2	9. RECKLESS	Bryan Adams
8/31	9	10. BROTHERS IN ARMS	Dire Straits
11/2	11*	11. **MIAMI VICE**	TV Soundtrack
12/21	1	12. HEART	Heart

DATE	WKS	ALBUM TITLE	ARTIST
		1986	
1/25	3	1. THE BROADWAY ALBUM	Barbra Streisand
2/15	2	2. PROMISE	Sade
3/1	1	3. WELCOME TO THE REAL WORLD	Mr. Mister
3/8	14*	4. **WHITNEY HOUSTON**	Whitney Houston
4/26	3	5. 5150	Van Halen
7/5	2	6. CONTROL	Janet Jackson
7/19	1	7. WINNER IN YOU	Patti LaBelle
7/26	5*	8. TOP GUN	Soundtrack
8/16	5	9. TRUE BLUE	Madonna
9/27	2	10. DANCING ON THE CEILING	Lionel Richie
10/18	1	11. FORE!	Huey Lewis And The News
10/25	8*	12. SLIPPERY WHEN WET	Bon Jovi
11/1	4	13. THIRD STAGE	Boston
11/29	7	14. BRUCE SPRINGSTEEN & THE E STREET BAND LIVE/1975-85 *Album debuted at No. 1*	Bruce Springsteen
		1987	
3/7	7	1. LICENSED TO ILL	Beastie Boys
4/25	9	2. THE JOSHUA TREE	U2
6/27	11	3. WHITNEY *Album debuted at No. 1*	Whitney Houston
9/12	2	4. LA BAMBA	Los Lobos/Soundtrack
9/26	6	5. BAD *Album debuted at No. 1*	Michael Jackson
11/7	1	6. TUNNEL OF LOVE	Bruce Springsteen
11/14	18*	7. **DIRTY DANCING**	Soundtrack
		1988	
1/16	12*	1. **FAITH**	George Michael
1/23	2	2. TIFFANY	Tiffany
6/25	4	3. OU812	Van Halen
7/23	6*	4. HYSTERIA	Def Leppard
8/6	5*	5. APPETITE FOR DESTRUCTION	Guns N' Roses
8/20	1	6. ROLL WITH IT	Steve Winwood
8/27	1	7. TRACY CHAPMAN	Tracy Chapman
10/15	4	8. NEW JERSEY	Bon Jovi
11/12	6	9. RATTLE AND HUM	U2/Soundtrack
12/24	4	10. GIVING YOU THE BEST THAT I GOT	Anita Baker

DATE	WKS	ALBUM TITLE	ARTIST
		1989	
1/21	6*	1. DON'T BE CRUEL	Bobby Brown
3/11	5	2. ELECTRIC YOUTH	Debbie Gibson
4/15	1	3. LOC-ED AFTER DARK	Tone Loc
4/22	6	4. LIKE A PRAYER	Madonna
6/3	7	5. THE RAW & THE COOKED	Fine Young Cannibals
7/22	6	6. BATMAN	Prince/Soundtrack
9/2	1	7. REPEAT OFFENDER	Richard Marx
9/9	2	8. HANGIN' TOUGH	New Kids On The Block
9/23	8*	9. GIRL YOU KNOW IT'S TRUE	Milli Vanilli
10/7	10*	10. **FOREVER YOUR GIRL**	Paula Abdul
10/14	2	11. DR. FEELGOOD	Motley Crue
10/28	4	12. JANET JACKSON'S RHYTHM NATION 1814	Janet Jackson
12/16	1	13. STORM FRONT	Billy Joel
		1990	
1/6	1	1. . . . BUT SERIOUSLY	Phil Collins
4/7	3	2. NICK OF TIME	Bonnie Raitt
4/28	6	3. I DO NOT WANT WHAT I HAVEN'T GOT	Sinead O'Connor
6/9	19*	4. **PLEASE HAMMER DON'T HURT 'EM**	M.C. Hammer
		Still No. 1 as of the 10/20/90 cut-off date	
6/30	1	5. STEP BY STEP	New Kids On The Block

ALBUMS OF LONGEVITY

PK YR	PK POS	WKS T40	RANK TITLE/ARTIST
56	1	292	1. MY FAIR LADY Original Cast
56	1	229	2. OKLAHOMA! Soundtrack
58	1	178	3. JOHNNY'S GREATEST HITS Johnny Mathis
56	1	178	4. THE KING AND I Soundtrack
60	1	168	5. THE SOUND OF MUSIC Original Cast
58	1	161	6. SOUTH PACIFIC Soundtrack
65	1	161	7. THE SOUND OF MUSIC Soundtrack
61	1	151	8. CAMELOT Original Cast
62	1	144	9. WEST SIDE STORY Soundtrack
65	1	141	10. WHIPPED CREAM & OTHER DELIGHTS Herb Alpert's Tijuana Brass
57	2	138	11. HYMNS Tennessee Ernie Ford
58	1	128	12. SING ALONG WITH MITCH Mitch Miller & The Gang
58	1	123	13. THE MUSIC MAN Original Cast
62	5	119	14. WEST SIDE STORY Original Cast
59	4	117	15. MORE SING ALONG WITH MITCH Mitch Miller & The Gang
66	1	115	16. DOCTOR ZHIVAGO Soundtrack
58	1	114	17. THE KINGSTON TRIO The Kingston Trio
59	1	113	18. FILM ENCORES Mantovani and his orchestra
62	1	112	19. PETER, PAUL AND MARY Peter, Paul and Mary
66	1	107	20. GOING PLACES Herb Alpert And The Tijuana Brass
63	3	106	21. MOON RIVER & OTHER GREAT MOVIE THEMES Andy Williams
60	1	105	22. PERSUASIVE PERCUSSION Enoch Light/Terry Snyder And The All-Stars
56	1	99	23. THE EDDY DUCHIN STORY Carmen Cavallaro/Soundtrack
61	8	98	24. KNOCKERS UP! Rusty Warren
84	1	96	25. BORN IN THE U.S.A. Bruce Springsteen
88	1	96	26. HYSTERIA Def Leppard
83	1	91	27. THRILLER Michael Jackson
57	1	88	28. AROUND THE WORLD IN 80 DAYS Soundtrack
69	4	87	29. IN-A-GADDA-DA-VIDA Iron Butterfly
61	2	86	30. TIME OUT FEATURING "TAKE FIVE" The Dave Brubeck Quartet
60	3	86	31. BELAFONTE AT CARNEGIE HALL Harry Belafonte
62	5	83	32. I LEFT MY HEART IN SAN FRANCISCO Tony Bennett
83	9	82	33. ELIMINATOR ZZ Top
80	6	81	34. CHRISTOPHER CROSS Christopher Cross
86	1	78	35. WHITNEY HOUSTON Whitney Houston
65	1	78	36. MARY POPPINS Soundtrack
58	1	78	37. GIGI Soundtrack
88	1	78	38. APPETITE FOR DESTRUCTION Guns N' Roses
83	1	78	39. CAN'T SLOW DOWN Lionel Richie
63	8	78	40. THE BARBRA STREISAND ALBUM Barbra Streisand
86	1	77	41. CONTROL Janet Jackson
65	4	77	42. MY FAIR LADY Soundtrack
68	5	77	43. ARE YOU EXPERIENCED? Jimi Hendrix Experience
58	1	76	44. TCHAIKOVSKY: PIANO CONCERTO NO. 1 Van Cliburn

59	4	74	45. OPEN FIRE, TWO GUITARS Johnny Mathis
61	1	73	46. JUDY AT CARNEGIE HALL Judy Garland
56	1	72	47. CALYPSO Harry Belafonte
87	11	72	48. RAPTURE Anita Baker
84	1	71	49. SPORTS Huey Lewis And The News
63	2	71	50. (MOVING) Peter, Paul and Mary
84	3	71	51. PRIVATE DANCER Tina Turner
59	4	71	52. STILL MORE! SING ALONG WITH MITCH Mitch Miller & The Gang
85	1	70	53. NO JACKET REQUIRED Phil Collins
78	2	70	54. THE STRANGER Billy Joel
62	10	70	55. JOAN BAEZ IN CONCERT Joan Baez
62	13	70	56. JOAN BAEZ, VOL. 2 Joan Baez
62	1	69	57. BREAKFAST AT TIFFANY'S Henry Mancini/Soundtrack
88	1	69	58. FAITH George Michael
89	1	69	59. DON'T BE CRUEL Bobby Brown
87	1	68	60. DIRTY DANCING Soundtrack
71	1	68	61. TAPESTRY Carole King
76	1	68	62. FLEETWOOD MAC Fleetwood Mac
60	2	68	63. PROVOCATIVE PERCUSSION Enoch Light/The Command All-Stars
60	1	67	64. THE BUTTON-DOWN MIND OF BOB NEWHART Bob Newhart
59	1	67	65. FLOWER DRUM SONG Original Cast
69	1	66	66. BLOOD, SWEAT & TEARS Blood, Sweat & Tears
85	1	66	67. RECKLESS Bryan Adams
64	3	66	68. HONEY IN THE HORN Al Hirt
88	3	66	69. KICK INXS
60	6	66	70. ENCORE OF GOLDEN HITS The Platters
60	7	66	71. PARTY SING ALONG WITH MITCH Mitch Miller and The Gang
71	1	65	72. JESUS CHRIST SUPERSTAR Various Artists
67	5	65	73. THE TEMPTATIONS GREATEST HITS The Temptations
84	8	65	74. BREAK OUT Pointer Sisters
67	1	63	75. SGT. PEPPER'S LONELY HEARTS CLUB BAND The Beatles
73	1	63	76. THE DARK SIDE OF THE MOON Pink Floyd
61	2	63	77. GREAT MOTION PICTURE THEMES Soundtrack Compilations
88	8	63	78. RICHARD MARX Richard Marx
56	1	62	79. BELAFONTE Harry Belafonte
83	4	62	80. AN INNOCENT MAN Billy Joel
84	4	62	81. SHE'S SO UNUSUAL Cyndi Lauper
59	6	62	82. TABOO Arthur Lyman
63	1	61	83. DAYS OF WINE AND ROSES Andy Williams
89	1	61	84. GIRL YOU KNOW IT'S TRUE Milli Vanilli
86	3	61	85. INVISIBLE TOUCH Genesis
58	4	61	86. TILL Roger Williams
59	12	61	87. OLDIES BUT GOODIES Various Artists
77	1	60	88. RUMOURS Fleetwood Mac
86	1	60	89. SLIPPERY WHEN WET Bon Jovi
86	3	60	90. BACK IN THE HIGH LIFE Steve Winwood
66	4	60	91. PARSLEY, SAGE, ROSEMARY AND THYME Simon and Garfunkel
65	7	60	92. FIDDLER ON THE ROOF Original Cast
62	1	59	93. MODERN SOUNDS IN COUNTRY AND WESTERN MUSIC Ray Charles

69	1	59	94. HAIR Original Cast
66	1	59	95. WHAT NOW MY LOVE Herb Alpert & The Tijuana Brass
87	1	58	96. THE JOSHUA TREE U2
63	1	58	97. IN THE WIND Peter, Paul and Mary
81	1	58	98. ESCAPE Journey
85	1	58	99. HEART Heart
64	1	58	100. HELLO, DOLLY! Original Cast
83	2	58	101. PYROMANIA Def Leppard
73	4	58	102. INNERVISIONS Stevie Wonder

INDEX TO ALBUMS OF LONGEVITY (A-Z BY ARTIST)

THE BILLBOARD CHARTS
from Top to Bottom!

Only Joel Whitburn's Record Research Books
List Every Record To Ever Appear
On Every Major Billboard Chart.

When the talk turns to music, more people turn to Joel Whitburn's Record Research Collection than to any other reference source.

That's because these are the only books that get right to the bottom of *Billboard*'s major charts, with complete, fully accurate chart data on every record ever charted. So they're quoted with confidence by DJ's, music show hosts, program directors, collectors and other music enthusiasts worldwide.

Each book lists every record's significant chart data, such as peak position, debut date, peak date, weeks charted, label, record number and much more, all conveniently arranged for fast, easy reference. Most books also feature artist biographies, record notes, RIAA Platinum/Gold Record certifications, top artist and record achievements, all-time artist and record rankings, a chronological listing of all number one hits, and additional in-depth chart information.

And now, the new large-format Billboard Hot 100 Charts book series takes chart research one step further, by actually reproducing weekly "Hot 100" charts by decade.

Joel Whitburn's Record Research Collection. Number one on everyone's hit list.

THE BILLBOARD HOT 100 CHARTS:

THE SIXTIES
1960–1969

THE SEVENTIES
1970–1979

Two complete collections of all 520 actual "Hot 100" charts from each decade, reproduced in black-and-white at 70% of original size. Deluxe Hardcover. $90.00 each.

TOP POP ALBUMS
1955–1985

The 14,000 LPs that appeared on *Billboard*'s Pop albums charts, arranged by artist. Softcover. $50.00.

TOP POP SINGLES
1955–1986

18,000 Pop singles—every "Hot 100" hit—arranged by artist. $60.00 Hardcover/$50.00 Softcover.

POP MEMORIES
1890–1954

The only documented chart history of early American popular music, arranged by artist. $60.00 Hardcover/$50.00 Softcover.

TOP COUNTRY SINGLES
1944–1988

An artist-by-artist listing of every "Country" single ever charted. $60.00 Hardcover/$50.00 Softcover.

TOP R&B SINGLES
1942–1988
Every "Soul," "Black," "Urban Contemporary" and "Rhythm & Blues" charted single, listed by artist. $60.00 Hardcover/$50.00 Softcover.

BILLBOARD'S TOP 10 CHARTS
1958–1988
1,550 actual, weekly Top 10 Pop singles charts in the original "Hot 100" chart format. $60.00 Hardcover/$50.00 Softcover.

BUBBLING UNDER THE HOT 100
1959–1981
Over 4,000 big regional hits, one-shot efforts and other semi-popular singles from the "Bubbling Under" Pop charts, arranged by artist. Softcover. $35.00.

BILLBOARD'S TOP 3000+
1955–1990
Every single that ever appeared in the Top 10 of *Billboard*'s Pop charts, ranked by all-time popularity. Softcover. $40.00.

MUSIC YEARBOOKS
1983/1984/1985/1986
The complete story of each year in music, covering *Billboard*'s biggest singles and albums charts. Softcover. $35.00 each.

MUSIC & VIDEO YEARBOOKS
1987/1988/1989
Comprehensive, yearly updates on *Billboard*'s major singles, albums and videocassettes charts. Softcover. $35.00 each.

DAILY #1 HITS
1940–1989
A day-by-day listing of the #1 Pop records of the past 50 years. Spiral-bound softcover. $25.00.

For complete book descriptions and ordering information, call, write or fax today.

**The World's Leading Authority
On Recorded Entertainment**

RECORD RESEARCH INC.
P.O. Box 200
Menomonee Falls, WI 53052-0200
Phone 414-251-5408
Fax 414-251-9452